Look for this iPod icon throughout the text.

Icons connect textbook content to your iPod or other MP3/MP4 device.

Images courtesy of Apple.

What if I Don't Have an iPod?

Content can be downloaded and viewed on any computer, with or without an iPod.

Visit this text's Web site for directions or use the DVD available for purchase with this text.

iPod content includes:

- Lecture presentations
  Audio-based
  Video-based
  Slideshow only
- Demonstration problems⁺
- Interactive self quizzes
- Videos on various course topics

+Available with some textbooks

Want to see iPod in action?

Visit **www.mhhe.com/ipod** to view a demonstration of our iPod content.

iPod® Content Installer DVD for use with

Introduction to Managerial Accounting, 4e

BREWER | GARRISON | NOREEN

MEDIA INTEGRATED EDITION

This DVD-rom will autostart on most machines. OR, from the start menu, select run, and type: D:\ Autorun.exe where D represents the letter of your DVD-rom drive.

introduction to MANAGERIAL ACCOUNTING

BREWER GARRISON NOREEN

ISBN 978-0-07-723497-3
MHID 0-07-723497-9

McGraw-Hill Irwin

D1445258

McGraw-Hill's
HOMEWORK MANAGER PLUS™

THE COMPLETE SOLUTION

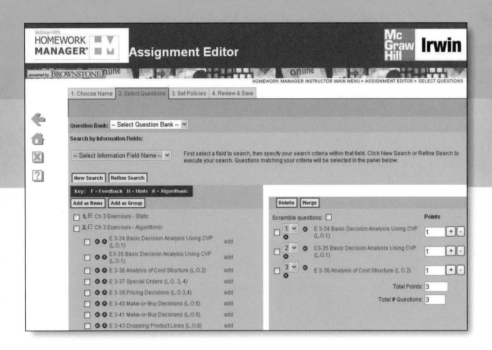

McGraw-Hill's
Homework Manager®

This online homework management solution contains the textbook's end-of-chapter material. Now you have the option to build assignments from static and algorithmic versions of the text problems and exercises or to build self-graded quizzes from the additional questions provided in the online test bank.

Features:

- Assigns book-specific problems/exercises to students

- Provides integrated test bank questions for quizzes and tests

- Automatically grades assignments and quizzes, storing results in one grade book

- Dispenses immediate feedback to students regarding their work

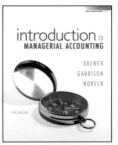

McGraw-Hill's
HOMEWORK MANAGER PLUS **HM**
THE COMPLETE SOLUTION

Brewer / Garrison / Noreen
**Introduction to
Managerial Accounting, 4e**
978-0-07-334481-2

1 TERM

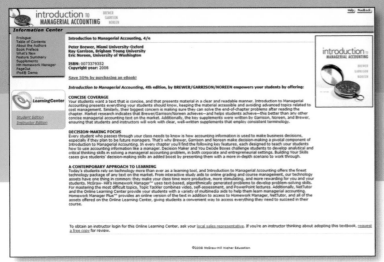

Interactive Online Version
of the Textbook

In addition to the textbook, students can rely on this online version of the text for a convenient way to study. The interactive content is fully integrated with McGraw-Hill's Homework Manager® to give students quick access to relevant content as they work through problems, exercises, and practice quizzes.

Features:

- Online version of the text integrated with McGraw-Hill's Homework Manager

- Students referred to appropriate sections of the online book as they complete an assignment or take a practice quiz

- Direct link to related material that corresponds with the learning objective within the text

McGraw-Hill's Homework Manager Plus™ combines the power of McGraw-Hill's Homework Manager® with the latest interactive learning technology to create a comprehensive, fully integrated online study package. Students working on assignments in McGraw-Hill's Homework Manager can click a simple hotlink and instantly review the appropriate material in the Interactive Online Textbook.

By including McGraw-Hill's Homework Manager Plus with your textbook adoption, you're giving your students a vital edge as they progress through the course and ensuring that the help they need is never more than a mouse click away. Contact your McGraw-Hill representative or visit the book's Web site to learn how to add McGraw-Hill's Homework Manager Plus to your adoption.

Imagine being able to create and access your test anywhere, at any time without installing the testing software. Now with **McGraw-Hill's EZ Test Online**, instructors can select questions from multiple McGraw-Hill test banks, author their own and then either print the test for paper distribution or give it online.

Use our EZ Test Online to help your students prepare to succeed with Apple® iPod® iQuiz.

Using our EZ Test Online you can make test and quiz content available for a student's Apple iPod.

Students must purchase the iQuiz game application from Apple for 99¢ in order to use the iQuiz content. It works on the iPod fifth generation iPods and better.

Instructors only need EZ Test Online to produce iQuiz ready content. Instructors take their existing tests and quizzes and export them to a file that can then be made available to the student to take as a self-quiz on their iPods. It's as simple as that.

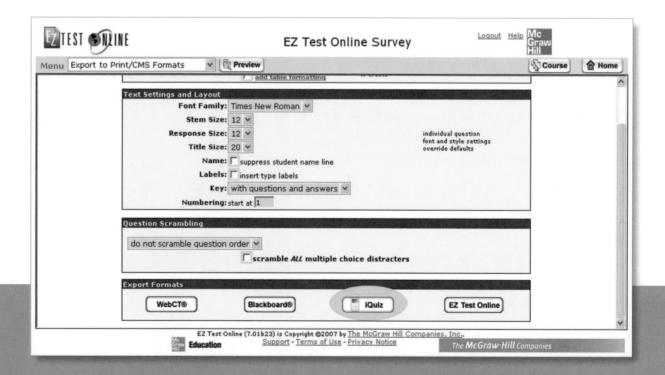

introduction TO
MANAGERIAL ACCOUNTING
4th edition

PETER C. BREWER
Professor, Miami University

RAY H. GARRISON
Professor Emeritus, Brigham Young University

ERIC W. NOREEN
Professor Emeritus, University of Washington

**McGraw-Hill
Irwin**

Boston   Burr Ridge, IL   Dubuque, IA   New York   San Francisco   St. Louis
Bangkok   Bogotá   Caracas   Kuala Lumpur   Lisbon   London   Madrid   Mexico City
Milan   Montreal   New Delhi   Santiago   Seoul   Singapore   Sydney   Taipei   Toronto

McGraw-Hill
Irwin

INTRODUCTION TO MANAGERIAL ACCOUNTING
Published by McGraw-Hill/Irwin, a business unit of The McGraw-Hill Companies, Inc., 1221
Avenue of the Americas, New York, NY, 10020. Copyright © 2008, 2007, 2005, 2002 by The McGraw-Hill
Companies, Inc. All rights reserved. No part of this publication may be reproduced or distributed in
any form or by any means, or stored in a database or retrieval system, without the prior written consent
of The McGraw-Hill Companies, Inc., including, but not limited to, in any network or other electronic
storage or transmission, or broadcast for distance learning.

Some ancillaries, including electronic and print components, may not be available to customers
outside the United States.

This book is printed on acid-free paper.

3 4 5 6 7 8 9 0 QWV/QWV 0 9 8

ISBN   978-0-07-337935-7
MHID   0-07-337935-2

Editorial director: *Stewart Mattson*
Executive editor: *Tim Vertovec*
Developmental editor: *Emily A. Hatteberg*
Executive marketing manager: *Krista Bettino*
Media producer: *Greg Bates*
Lead project manager: *Pat Frederickson*
Lead production supervisor: *Carol A. Bielski*
Design manager: *Kami Carter*
Senior photo research coordinator: *Jeremy Cheshareck*
Senior media project manager: *Susan Lombardi*
Cover design: *Kami Carter*
Interior design: © *Getty Images*
Typeface: *10.5/12 Times Roman*
Compositor: *Aptara, Inc.*
Printer: *Quebecor World Versailles Inc.*

Library of Congress Cataloging-in-Publication Data

Brewer, Peter C.
    Introduction to managerial accounting / Peter C. Brewer, Ray H. Garrison, Eric W.
Noreen.—4th ed.
      p. cm.
    Includes index.
    ISBN-13: 978-0-07-337935-7 (alk. paper)
    ISBN-10: 0-07-337935-2 (alk. paper)
    1. Managerial accounting. I. Garrison, Ray H. II. Noreen, Eric W. III. Title.
HF5657.4.B74 2008
658.15′11—dc22
                                                                          2007031238

www.mhhe.com

DEDICATION

To our families and to our colleagues who use this book.
—Peter C. Brewer, Ray H. Garrison, and Eric W. Noreen

Peter C. Brewer is a professor in the Department of Accountancy at Miami University, Oxford, Ohio. He holds a BS degree in accounting from Penn State University, an MS degree in accounting from the University of Virginia, and a PhD from the University of Tennessee. He has published 30 articles in a variety of journals including: *Management Accounting Research*, the *Journal of Information Systems*, *Cost Management*, *Strategic Finance*, the *Journal of Accountancy*, *Issues in Accounting Education*, and the *Journal of Business Logistics*.

Professor Brewer is a member of the editorial boards of *Issues in Accounting Education* and the *Journal of Accounting Education*. His article *"Putting Strategy into the Balanced Scorecard"* won the 2003 International Federation of Accountants' Articles of Merit competition and his articles *"Using Six Sigma to Improve the Finance Function"* and *"Lean Accounting: What's It All About?"* were awarded the Institute of Management Accountants' Lybrand Gold and Silver Medals in 2005 and 2006. He has received Miami University's Richard T. Farmer School of Business Teaching Excellence Award and has been recognized on two occasions by the Miami University Associated Student Government for "making a remarkable commitment to students and their educational development." He is a leading thinker in undergraduate management accounting curriculum innovation and is a frequent presenter at various professional and academic conferences.

Prior to joining the faculty at Miami University, Professor Brewer was employed as an auditor for Touche Ross in the firm's Philadelphia office. He also worked as an internal audit manager for the Board of Pensions of the Presbyterian Church (U.S.A.). He frequently collaborates with companies such as Harris Corporation, Ghent Manufacturing, Cintas, Ethicon Endo-Surgery, Schneider Electric, Lenscrafters, and Fidelity Investments in a consulting or case writing capacity.

Ray H. Garrison

is emeritus professor of accounting at Brigham Young University, Provo, Utah. He received his BS and MS degrees from Brigham Young University and his DBA degree from Indiana University.

As a certified public accountant, Professor Garrison has been involved in management consulting work with both national and regional accounting firms. He has published articles in *The Accounting Review, Management Accounting,* and other professional journals. Innovation in the classroom has earned Professor Garrison the Karl G. Maeser Distinguished Teaching Award from Brigham Young University.

Eric W. Noreen is a globe-

trotting academic who has held appointments at institutions in the United States, Europe, and Asia. He is emeritus professor of accounting at the University of Washington.

He received his BA degree from the University of Washington and MBA and PhD degrees from Stanford University. A Certified Management Accountant, he was awarded a Certificate of Distinguished Performance by the Institute of Certified Management Accountants.

Professor Noreen has served as associate editor of *The Accounting Review* and the *Journal of Accounting and Economics.* He has numerous articles in academic journals including: the *Journal of Accounting Research; The Accounting Review;* the *Journal of Accounting and Economics; Accounting Horizons; Accounting, Organizations and Society; Contemporary Accounting Research;* the *Journal of Management Accounting Research;* and the *Review of Accounting Studies.*

Professor Noreen has taught management accounting at the undergraduate and master's levels and has won a number of awards from students for his teaching.

Empowering Students to Rise to New Levels

"When will I ever use managerial accounting?"

Many students ask this and similar questions about the relevance of their managerial accounting course. *Introduction to Managerial Accounting*, 4th edition, by Brewer, Garrison, and Noreen not only teaches students managerial accounting skills, but also how they apply in the real world.

More important, students will learn the critical thinking skills crucial to success in business. This combination of conceptual understanding and the ability to apply this knowledge in the real world empowers students to make business decisions and ascend to new heights.

Here's how your colleagues have described *Introduction to Managerial Accounting*:

*"The Brewer text is an **engaging text** with a real-world focus that is presented in an easy to understand format. It gives students a clear understanding of how managerial accounting information is used in **planning, decision-making and day-to-day operations** of a business. It provides sufficient problems and exercises to facilitate the development skills related to problem solving, communicating and solving ethical dilemmas."*

—Natalie Allen, Texas A&M University

*"A well planned, well written text, building on **the authors' expertise and experience**, it makes the material both logical and understandable for your students and provides you with **significant resources** to manage the course."*

—Paul E. Dascher, Stetson University

*"BGN is a clear and concise textbook that does an **excellent job of covering the variety of topics** in managerial accounting. It gives students **enough information** to get a general understanding of the topics without giving them too much information which can sometimes confuse students more."*

—Dawn McKinley, William Rainey Harper College

*"An outstanding **easy to understand** book with currency on Ethics, Internal Controls, Risk Management. It also has a solid systems orientation."*

—Jai S. Kang, San Francisco State University

CONCISE COVERAGE

Your students want a text that is concise, and that presents material in a clear and readable manner. *Introduction to Managerial Accounting* presents everything your students should know, keeping the material accessible while avoiding advanced topics related to cost accounting topics. Their biggest concern is making sure they can solve the end-of-chapter problems after reading the chapter. Market research indicates that Brewer/Garrison/Noreen helps students achieve this better than any other concise managerial accounting text on the market. Additionally, the key supplements were written by Garrison, Noreen, and Brewer, ensuring that students and instructors will work with clear, well-written supplements that employ consistent terminology.

DECISION-MAKING FOCUS

All students who pass through your class need to know how accounting information is used to make business decisions, especially if they plan to be future managers. That's why Brewer, Garrison and Noreen make decision making a pivotal component of *Introduction to Managerial Accounting*. In every chapter you'll find the following key features that are designed to teach your students how to use accounting information. **Decision Maker** and **You Decide Boxes** help students to develop analytical, critical thinking, and problem-solving skills. **Building Your Skills** cases challenge students' decision-making skills.

A CONTEMPORARY APPROACH TO LEARNING

Today's students rely on technology more than ever as a learning tool, and Introduction to Managerial Accounting offers the finest technology package of any text on the market. From interactive study aids to online grading and course management, our technology assets have one thing in common: they make your class time more productive, more stimulating, and more rewarding for you and your students. McGraw-Hill's *Media Integration* allows students to maximize the technological package available to them with Brewer. Apple® iPod® icons throughout the text link content back to quizzes, audio and visual lecture presentations, review problems, and course-related videos—all of which can be downloaded to their iPod or other portable MP3/MP4 players so they can study and review on the go. McGraw-Hill's *Homework Manager®* uses text-based, algorithmically generated problems to develop problem-solving skills. For mastering the most difficult topics, *Topic Tackler* combines video, self-assessment, and PowerPoint lectures. Additionally, the Online Learning Center provides your students with a variety of multimedia aids to help them learn managerial accounting. *Homework Manager Plus™* provides an online version of the text in addition to access to Homework Manager and all of the assets offered on the Online Learning Center, giving students a convenient way to access everything they need to succeed in their course.

BREWER / GARRISON / NOREEN'S

Introduction to Managerial Accounting is full of pedagogy designed to make studying productive and hassle-free. On the following pages, you'll see the kind of engaging, helpful pedagogical features that have made Brewer one of the best-selling Managerial Accounting texts on the market.

OPENING VIGNETTE

Each chapter opens with a **Decision Feature** that provides a real-world example for students, allowing them to see how the chapter's information and insights apply to the world outside the classroom. **Learning Objectives** alert students to what they should expect as they progress through the chapter.

SERVICE EXAMPLES

To reflect our service-based economy, the text is replete with examples from service-based businesses. A helpful icon distinguishes service-related examples in the text.

INFOGRAPHICS

Infographics help students visualize key accounting concepts, such as Static versus Flexible Budgets, the Activity-Based Costing Model, and Management by Exception.

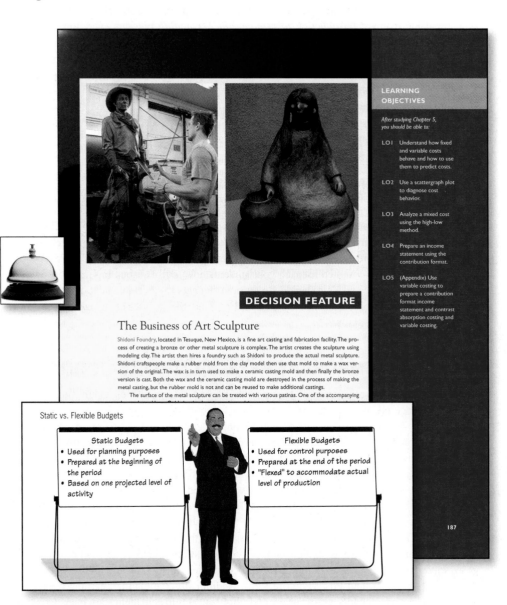

LEARNING OBJECTIVES

After studying Chapter 5, you should be able to:

LO1 Understand how fixed and variable costs behave and how to use them to predict costs.

LO2 Use a scattergraph plot to diagnose cost behavior.

LO3 Analyze a mixed cost using the high-low method.

LO4 Prepare an income statement using the contribution format.

LO5 (Appendix) Use variable costing to prepare a contribution format income statement and contrast absorption costing and variable costing.

DECISION FEATURE

The Business of Art Sculpture

Shidoni Foundry, located in Tesuque, New Mexico, is a fine art casting and fabrication facility. The process of creating a bronze or other metal sculpture is complex. The artist creates the sculpture using modeling clay. The artist then hires a foundry such as Shidoni to produce the actual metal sculpture. Shidoni craftspeople make a rubber mold from the clay model then use that mold to make a wax version of the original. The wax is in turn used to make a ceramic casting mold and then finally the bronze version is cast. Both the wax and the ceramic casting mold are destroyed in the process of making the metal casting, but the rubber mold is not and can be reused to make additional castings.

The surface of the metal sculpture can be treated with various patinas. One of the accompanying

Static vs. Flexible Budgets

Static Budgets
• Used for planning purposes
• Prepared at the beginning of the period
• Based on one projected level of activity

Flexible Budgets
• Used for control purposes
• Prepared at the end of the period
• "Flexed" to accommodate actual level of production

187

*"The **infographics** are **superb**!"*
—Angela H. Sandberg, Jacksonville State University

POWERFUL PEDAGOGY

> "The **In Business features** are a **great strength** of this text."
>
> —Jan Duffy, Iowa State University

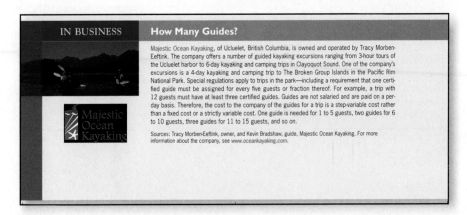

IN BUSINESS BOXES

These helpful boxed features offer a glimpse into how real companies use the managerial accounting concepts discussed within the chapter. Every chapter contains these current examples.

1. Which of the following statements is false? (You may select more than one answer.)
   a. Under some circumstances, a sunk cost may be a relevant cost.
   b. Future costs that do not differ between alternatives are irrelevant.
   c. The same cost may be relevant or irrelevant depending on the decision context.
   d. Only variable costs are relevant costs. Fixed costs cannot be relevant costs.

2. Assume that in October you bought a $450 nonrefundable airline ticket to Telluride, Colorado, for a 5-day/4-night winter ski vacation. You now have an opportunity to buy an airline ticket for a 5-day/4-night winter ski vacation in Stowe, Vermont, for $400 that includes a free ski lift ticket. The price of your lift ticket for the Telluride vacation would be $300. The price of a hotel room in Telluride is $180 per night. The price of a hotel room in Stowe is $150 per night. Which of the following costs is not relevant in a decision of whether to proceed with the planned trip to Telluride or to change to a trip to Stowe?
   a. The $450 airline ticket to Telluride.
   b. The $400 airline ticket to Stowe.
   c. The $300 lift ticket for the Telluride vacation.
   d. The $180 per night hotel room in Telluride.

3. Based on the facts in question 2 above, does a differential cost analysis favor Telluride or Stowe, and by how much?
   a. Stowe by $470.
   b. Stowe by $20.
   c. Telluride by $70.
   d. Telluride $20

CONCEPT CHECK

CONCEPT CHECK

Concept Checks allow students to test their comprehension of topics and concepts covered at various stages throughout each chapter.

The **DECISION MAKER** feature fosters critical thinking and decision-making skills by providing real-world business scenarios that require the resolution of a business issue. The suggested solution is located at the end of the chapter.

Job-Order Costing	Process Costing
1. Many different jobs are worked on during each period, with each job having different production requirements.	1. A single product is produced either on a continuous basis or for long periods of time. All units of product are identical.
2. Costs are accumulated by individual job.	2. Costs are accumulated by department.
3. Unit costs are computed *by job* on the job cost sheet.	3. Unit costs are computed *by department.*

Cost Analyst   DECISION MAKER

Your company is planning a new production facility that will process wood chips into standard rolls of newsprint for sale to printers. Would you recommend that the company use job-order costing or process costing to account for the costs of producing the rolls of newsprint?

COST FLOWS IN PROCESS COSTING

Before we go through a detailed example of process costing, it will be helpful to see how manufacturing costs flow through a process costing system.

Company had underapplied overhead of $5,000. The entry to close this underapplied overhead to Cost of Goods Sold would be:

                                (14)
| Cost of Goods Sold . . . . | 5,000 | |
| Manufacturing Overhead. . . . . | | 5,000 |

Note that because the Manufacturing Overhead account has a debit balance, Manufacturing Overhead must be credited to close out the account. This has the effect of increasing Cost of Goods Sold for April by $5,000 to $123,500:

Unadjusted cost of goods sold [from entry (13)]	$118,500
Add underapplied overhead [entry (14) above]	5,000
Adjusted cost of goods sold	$123,500

After this adjustment has been made, Rand Company's income statement for April will appear as shown earlier in Exhibit 2–12.

Remaining Balance in the Overhead Account   YOU DECIDE

The simplest method for disposing of any balance remaining in the Overhead account is to close it out to Cost of Goods Sold. If there is a debit balance (that is, overhead has been underapplied), the entry to dispose of the balance would include a debit to Cost of Goods Sold. That debit would increase the balance in the Cost of Goods Sold account. On the other hand, if there is a credit balance, the entry to dispose of the balance would include a credit to Cost of Goods Sold. That credit would decrease the balance in the Cost of Goods Sold account. If you were the company's controller, would you want a debit balance, a credit balance, or no balance in the Overhead account at the end of the period?

A General Model of Product Cost Flows

Exhibit 2–14 presents a T-account model of the flow of costs in a product costing system. This model applies as much to a process costing system as it does to a job-order costing system. Examination of this model can be very helpful in understanding how costs enter a system, flow through it, and finally end up as Cost of Goods Sold on the income statement.

Multiple Predetermined Overhead Rates

Our discussion in this chapter has assumed that there is a single predetermined overhead rate for an entire factory called a **plantwide overhead rate.** This is a fairly common practice—particularly in smaller companies. But in larger companies, *multiple predetermined overhead rates* are often used. In a **multiple predetermined overhead rate** system, each production department may have its own predetermined overhead rate. Such a system, while more complex, is more accurate, since it can reflect differences across departments in how overhead costs are incurred. For example, overhead might be allocated based on direct labor-hours in departments that are relatively labor intensive and based on machine-hours in departments that are relatively machine intensive. When multiple predetermined overhead rates are used, overhead is applied in each department according to its own overhead rate as a job proceeds through the department.

The **YOU DECIDE** feature challenges students to apply the tools of analysis and make decisions. The suggested solution is found at the end of the chapter.

"Excellent, relevant, worthwhile."
—Jane G. Wiese, Valencia Community College

END-OF-CHAPTER MATERIAL

Introduction to Managerial Acounting has earned a reputation for the best end-of-chapter review and discussion material of any text on the market. Our problem and case material continues to conform to AICPA and AACSB recommendations and makes a great starting point for class discussions and group projects. Other helpful features include:

- Spreadsheets have become an increasingly common budgeting tool for managerial accountants; therefore, to assist students in understanding how budgets look in a spreadsheet, all figures pertaining to budgeting will appear as Microsoft Excel® screen captures.

- Excel spreadsheet templates are available for use with select problems and cases.

- Ethics assignments serve as a reminder that good conduct is vital in business.

- Group projects can be assigned either as homework or as in-class discussion projects.

- Internet assignments teach students how to find information online and apply it to managerial accounting situations.

- The writing icon denotes problems that require students to use critical thinking as well as writing skills to explain their decision.

- Check figures provide key answers for select problems.

AUTHOR-WRITTEN SUPPLEMENTS

Unlike other managerial accounting texts, Brewer, Garrison, and Noreen write all of the text's major supplements, ensuring a perfect fit between text and supplements. For more information on *Introduction to Managerial Accounting*'s supplements package see pages xviii–xix.

Changes to the 4th edition

- **Full media integration with iPod icons** throughout the text linking content back to chapter-specific quizzes, audio and visual lecture presentations, review problems, and course-related videos. This gives students access to a portable, electronic learning option to support their classroom instruction.

- **Research and Application Cases using 10K data** from actual companies such as Dell, FedEx, and Target offer end-of-chapter learning opportunities for students to identify strategy and business risks and evaluate managerial accounting concepts within a real-world context.

- The authors have refreshed and **updated all end-of-chapter problems** and exercises.

- **New "In Business" boxes** contain relevant insights gleaned from the business press. As always, the authors fine-tuned the text with the objective of making it as user-friendly as possible.

- **More questions and worked out solutions to the test bank.** All testbank questions have been mapped to AACSB-AICPA standards.

Specific significant changes were made in the following chapters:

Prologue
- Updated globalization discussion, including new U.S. import and export graphic.
- The latest version of the IMA's Statement of Ethical Professional Practice has been incorporated into the text.
- Discussion of salaries in accounting has been updated.

Chapter 1
- Discussion of planning has been updated.
- Discussion of Period Costs has been updated.
- Added content on Prime Cost and Conversion Cost.
- More quantitative information has been added to the "Schedule of Cost of Goods Manufactured" content, tying it directly to the exhibit that illustrates the concept (Exhibit 1–6).

Chapter 4
- New learning objectives added:
  - Compute the cost per equivalent unit using the weighted-average method.
  - Assign costs to units using the weighted-average method.
- Coverage of both the weighted-average and FIFO methods has been revised, eliminating the production report and simplifying the procedure for assigning costs to units.
- New Decision Maker box added relating to job-order versus process costing discussion.

Chapter 5
- New Decision Feature vignette on chapter opener.
- Discussion of Step-Variable Costs, The Linearity Assumption and the Relevant Range, Fixed Costs, and Committed Fixed Costs has been updated.

Chapter 7
- Discussion of "Personal Budgets and Planning and Control" has been streamlined and incorporated into the overview of "The Basic Framework of Budgeting."
- Updated section on "The Self-Imposed Budget."
- Zero-based budgeting section has been removed.
- The master budget overview has been streamlined.
- In the cash budget, the nature of the loans taken out to maintain minimum ending cash balances has been simplified. This significantly reduces the complexity of determining loan repayments and interest accruals.

Chapter 9
- New Decision Feature vignette on chapter opener.
- The "Activity-Based Costing and the Flexible Budget" content has been streamlined and an example inserted to make the discussion more accessible to students.

Chapter 10
- The Monthaven Burger Grill example used to illustrate ROI has been revised for clarity.

Chapter 11
- Another example of *sunk cost* has been added to further illustrate the concept.
- The discussion of "Adding and Dropping Product Lines and Other Segments" has been streamlined.
- Quantitative updates have been made to the tables in the "Special Orders" section.

Chapter 12
- New Decision Feature vignette on chapter opener.
- The discussion of "The Net Present Value Method" has been updated to enhance clarity and understanding.
- Future value tables have been deleted from Appendix 12B.

Chapter 14
- Financial information for McDonald's has been updated to illustrate trend percentages.
- The procedures used to calculate ratios have been standardized.

A Market-Leading Book Deserves
Market-Leading Technology

 **PLUS**™

McGRAW-HILL'S HOMEWORK MANAGER PLUS™ combines the
power of McGraw-Hill's Homework Manager®
with the latest interactive learning technology
to create a comprehensive, fully integrated
online study package.

Students using McGraw-Hill's Homework
Manager Plus can access not only McGraw-
Hill's Homework Manager itself, but the
interactive Online Textbook as well. Far more
than a textbook on a screen, this resource is
completely integrated into McGraw-Hill's
Homework Manager, allowing students
working on assignments to click a hotlink and
instantly review the appropriate material in the
textbook.

By including McGraw-Hill's Homework
Manager Plus with your textbook adoption,
you're giving your students a vital edge as they
progress through the course and ensuring that
the help they need is never more than a mouse
click away.

Students receive full access to McGraw-Hill's
Homework Manager when they purchase
Homework Manager Plus.

McGRAW-HILL'S HOMEWORK MANAGER®

Homework Manager is a web-based supplement that duplicates
problems directly from the textbook end-of-chapter material, using
algorithms to provide a limitless supply of online self-graded practice
for students, or assignments and tests with unique versions of every
problem. Say goodbye to cheating in your classroom; say hello to the
power and flexibility you've been waiting for in creating assignments.

The enhanced version of McGraw-Hill's Homework Manager integrates
all of Managerial Accounting's online and multimedia assets to allow
your students to brush up on a topic before doing their homework.
You now have the option to give your students pre-populated hints and
feedback. The test bank has been added to Homework Manager so you
can create online quizzes and exams and have them autograded and
recorded in the same grade book as your homework assignments.
Lastly, the enhanced version provides you with the option of
incorporating the complete online version of the textbook, so your
students can easily reference the chapter material as they do their
homework assignment, even when their textbook is far away.

McGraw-Hill's Homework Manager is also a useful grading tool.
All assignments can be delivered over the Web and are graded
automatically, with the results stored in your private grade book.
Detailed results let you see at a glance how each student does on an
assignment or an individual problem—you can even see how many
tries it took them to solve it.

Students receive full access to McGraw-Hill's Homework Manager
when they purchase Homework Manager Plus or you can have
Homework Manager pass codes shrinkwrapped with the textbook.
Students can also purchase access to Homework Manager directly from
your class home page.

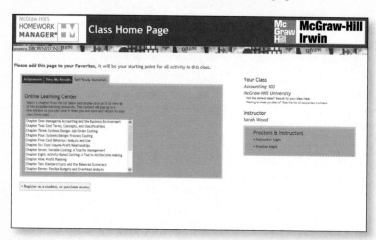

iPod® Content

Harness the power of one of the most popular technology tools today—the Apple® iPod®. Our innovative approach allows students to download audio and video presentations right into their iPod and take learning materials with them wherever they go.

Students can visit the Online Learning Center at **www.mhhe.com/brewer4e** to download our iPod content. For each chapter of the book they will be able to download narrated lecture presentations, managerial accounting videos, and even self-quizzes designed for use on various versions of iPods. It makes review and study time as easy as putting on earphones.

CPS Classroom Performance System by eInstruction

This is a revolutionary system that brings ultimate interactivity to the classroom. CPS is a wireless response system that gives you immediate feedback from every student in the class. CPS units include easy-to-use software for creating and delivering questions and assessments to your class. With CPS you can ask subjective and objective questions. Then every student simply responds with their individual, wireless response pad, providing instant results. CPS is the perfect tool for engaging students while gathering important assessment data.

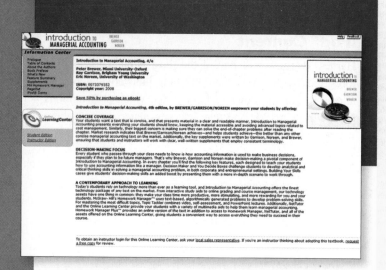

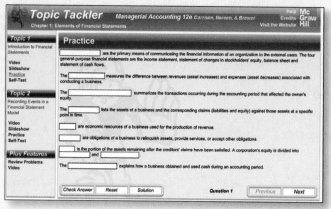

ONLINE LEARNING CENTER (OLC)
www.mhhe.com/brewer4e

More and more students are studying online. That's why we offer an Online Learning Center (OLC) that follows *Introduction to Managerial Accounting* chapter by chapter. It doesn't require any building or maintenance on your part. It's ready to go the moment you and your students type in the URL.

As your students study, they can refer to the OLC website for such benefits as:

- Internet-based activities
- Self-grading quizzes
- Alternate problems
- Excel spreadsheets
- Learning objectives
- Chapter overviews
- PowerPoint slides
- Topic Tackler Plus
- iPod® Content

A secured Instructor Resource Center stores your essential course materials to save you prep time before class. The Instructor's Resource Guide, Solutions Manual, and PowerPoint slides are now just a couple of clicks away. You will also find useful packaging information and transition notes.

The OLC website also serves as a doorway to other technology solutions like PageOut (see next page) which is free to *Introduction to Managerial Accounting* adopters.

TOPIC TACKLER PLUS

This program is a complete tutorial focusing on those areas in the managerial accounting course that give students the most trouble. Providing extensive help on two key topics for every single chapter, this program delves into the material via the following:

- Video Clips
- PowerPoint slide shows
- Interactive exercises
- Self-grading quizzes
- Website hotlinks

The highly engaging presentation will give your students command of the most fundamental aspects of managerial accounting. Students can access Topic Tackler Plus through the Online Learning Center.

> "Topic Tackler is **so useful** and provides students a **fantastic opportunity** to **enhance** their understanding of the text."
>
> —Denise English, Boise State University

Creating an Online Course Is Easy
WITH THE RIGHT GUIDE

For the instructor needing to educate students online, we offer *Introduction to Managerial Accounting* content for complete online courses. To make this possible, we have joined forces with the most popular delivery platforms currently available. These platforms are designed for instructors who want complete control over course content and how it is presented to students. You can customize the Managerial Accounting Online Learning Center content and author your own course materials. It's entirely up to you.

Products like WebCT, Blackboard, and eCollege all expand the reach of your course. Online discussion and message boards will now complement your office hours. Thanks to a sophisticated tracking system, you will know which students need more attention—even if they don't ask for help. That's because online testing scores are recorded and automatically placed in your grade book, and if a student is struggling with coursework, a special alert message lets you know.

Remember, *Introduction to Managerial Accounting*'s content is flexible enough to use with any platform currently available. If your department or school is already using a platform, we can help. For information on McGraw-Hill/Irwin's course management tool, visit **www.mhhe.com/solutions.**

PageOut®

PageOut—McGraw-Hill's Course Management System

PageOut is the easiest way to create a website for your accounting course.

There's no need for HTML coding, graphic design, or a thick how-to book. Just fill in a series of boxes with simple English and click on one of our professional designs. In no time, your course is online with a Web site that contains your syllabus!

Should you need assistance in preparing your website, we can help. Our team of product specialists is ready to take your course materials and build a custom website to your specifications; you simply need to call a McGraw-Hill/Irwin PageOut specialist (1-800-634-3963) to start the process. Best of all, PageOut is free when you adopt *Introduction to Managerial Accounting*! To learn more, please visit www.pageout.net.

Enhanced Cartridge

The Enhanced Cartridge is developed to help you get your course up and running with much less time and effort. The content, enhanced with more assignments and more study materials than a standard cartridge, is pre-populated into appropriate chapters and content categories. Now there's no need to cut and paste our content into your course—it's already there!

In addition to the standard instructor supplement content, this cartridge also includes:

- Pre-populated course syllabus
- iPod/MP3 content
- Chapter pre-and post-tests
- Mid-term and final tests
- Discussion boards
- Additional assignments
- Personalized graphics/banners/icons for your school
- Gradebook functionality

The Enhanced Cartridge allows students to access their course anytime, anywhere. For students the Enhanced Cartridge includes:

- Key term flashcards
- Excel templates
- Narrated review problems
- Topic Tackler Plus
- PowerPoint slides

A Great Learning System

Introduction to Managerial Accounting authors Brewer, Garrison, and Noreen know from their own years of teaching experience what separates a great textbook from a merely adequate one. Every component of the learning package must be imbued with the same style and approach, and that's why the *Introduction to Managerial Accounting* authors write every major ancillary themselves, whether printed or online. It's one more thing that sets *Introduction to Managerial Accounting* far above the competition.

INSTRUCTOR SUPPLEMENTS

Assurance of Learning Ready

Many educational institutions today are focused on the notion of assurance of learning, an important element of some accreditation standards. *Introduction to Managerial Accounting* is designed specifically to support your assurance of learning initiatives with a simple, yet powerful, solution.

Each test bank question for *Introduction to Managerial Accounting* maps to a specific chapter learning outcome/objective listed in the text. You can use our test bank software, EZ Test, to easily query for learning outcomes/objectives that directly relate to the learning objectives for your course. You can then use the reporting features of EZ Test to aggregate student results in similar fashion, making the collection and presentation of assurance of learning data simple and easy. You can also use our Algorithmic-Diploma Test Bank to do this.

AACSB Statement

McGraw-Hill Companies is a proud corporate member of AACSB International. Recognizing the importance and value of AACSB accreditation, we have sought to recognize the curricula guidelines detailed in AACSB standards for business accreditation by connecting selected test bank questions in *Introduction to Managerial Accounting* with the general knowledge and skill guidelines found in the AACSB standards.

The statements contained in *Introduction to Managerial Accounting,* Fourth Edition, are provided only as a guide for the users of this text. The AACSB leaves content coverage and assessment clearly within the realm and control of individual schools, the mission of the school, and the faculty. The AACSB also charges schools with the obligation of doing assessment against their own content and learning goals. While *Introduction to Managerial Accounting,* Fourth Edition, and its teaching package make no claim of any specific AACSB qualification or evaluation, we have labeled selected questions according to the six general knowledge and skills areas.

Instructor CD-ROM

MHID: 0-07-334479-6
ISBN: 978-0-07-334479-9

Allowing instructors to create a customized multimedia presentation, this all-in-one resource incorporates the Test Bank, PowerPoint® Slides, Instructor's Resource Guide, Solutions Manual, and Teaching Transparency Masters.

Instructor's Resource Guide

(Available on the password-protected Instructor OLC and Instructor's Resource CD)

This supplement contains the teaching transparency masters, PowerPoint slides, and extensive chapter-by-chapter lecture notes to help with classroom presentation. It contains useful suggestions for presenting key concepts and ideas.

Solutions Manual

(Available on the password-protected Instructor OLC and Instructor's Resource CD)

This supplement contains completely worked-out solutions to all assignment material and a general discussion of the use of group exercises. In addition, the manual contains suggested course outlines and a listing of exercises, problems, and cases scaled according to difficulty.

PowerPoint® Slides

(Available on the OLC and Instructor's Resource CD)

Prepared by Jon Booker and Charles Caldwell of Tennessee Technological University, and Susan Galbreath of Lipscomb University, these slides offer a great visual complement for your lectures. A complete set of slides covers each chapter.

Doesn't Stop with the Book.

Computerized Test Bank

(Available on the Instructor's Resource CD)

This test bank utilizes McGraw-Hill's EZ Test software to quickly create customized exams. This user-friendly program allows instructors to sort questions by format; edit existing questions or add new ones. It also can scramble questions for multiple versions of the same test.

Algorithmic-Diploma Test

MHID: 0-07-334476-1
ISBN: 978-0-07-3344768

This computerized test bank is an algorithmic problem generator enabling instructors to create similarly structured problems with different values, which allows every student to be assigned a unique quiz or test. The user-friendly interface gives faculty the ability to easily create different versions of the same test, change the answer order, edit or add questions, and even conduct online testing.

Excel Template Solutions

(Available on the password-protected Instructor OLC and Instructor's Resource CD)

Prepared by Jack Terry of ComSource Associates, Inc., these Excel templates offer solutions to the student version.

McGraw-Hill's Homework Manager Plus™

McGraw-Hill's Homework Manager Plus combines the power of McGraw-Hill's Homework Manager® with the latest interactive learning technology to create a comprehensive, fully integrated Online Study Package.

McGraw-Hill's Homework Manager®

This web-based software duplicates problem structures directly from the end-of-chapter material in the textbook. It uses algorithms to provide a limitless supply of self-graded practice.

Online Learning Center (OLC)

www.mhhe.com/brewer4e

See page xvi for details.

iPod® Content

See page xv for details.

STUDENT SUPPLEMENTS

Topic Tackler Plus

(Available on the OLC)

Free with the text, the Topic Tackler Plus helps students master difficult concepts in managerial accounting through a creative, interactive learning process. Designed for study outside the classroom, it delves into chapter concepts with graphical slides and diagrams, web links, video clips, and animations, all centered around engaging exercises designed to put students in control of their learning of managerial accounting topics.

Workbook/Study Guide

MHID: 0-07-334485-0
ISBN: 978-0-07-334485-0

This study aid provides suggestions for studying chapter material, summarizes essential points in each chapter, and tests students' knowledge using self-test questions and exercises.

Working Papers

MHID: 0-07-334487-7
ISBN: 978-0-07-334487-4

This study aid contains forms that help students organize their solutions to homework exercises and problems.

Excel Templates

(Available on the OLC)

Prepared by Jack Terry of ComSource Associates, Inc., this spreadsheet-based software uses Excel to solve selected problems and cases in the text. These selected problems and cases are identified in the margin of the text with an appropriate icon.

Practice Set

MHID: 0-07-339619-2
ISBN: 978-0-07-339619-4

Authored by Janice L. Cobb of Texas Christian University, *Doing the Job of the Managerial Accountant* is a real-world application for the Introductory Managerial Accounting student. The case is based on an actual growing, entrepreneurial, manufacturing company that is complex enough to demonstrate decisions management must make, yet simple enough that a sophomore student can easily understand the entire operations of the company. The case requires students to do tasks they would perform working as the managerial accountant for the company. The required tasks are directly related to the concepts learned in all managerial accounting classes. The practice set can be used by the professor as a teaching tool for class lectures, as additional homework assignments, or as a semester project.

We are grateful for the outstanding support from McGraw-Hill/Irwin. In particular, we would like to thank Stewart Mattson, Editorial Director; Tim Vertovec, Executive Editor; Emily Hatteberg, Developmental Editor; Pat Frederickson, Lead Project Manager; Carol Bielski, Lead Production Supervisor; Kami Carter, Design Manager; Gregory Bates, Senior Product Manager; Susan Lombardi, Senior Product Manager ; and Jeremy Cheshareck, Senior Photo Research Coordinator.

Finally, we would like to thank Beth Woods and Barbara Schnathorst, for working so hard to ensure an error-free fourth edition.

We are grateful to the Institute of Certified Management Accountants for permission to use questions and/or unofficial answers from past Certificate in Management Accounting (CMA) examinations. Likewise, we thank the American Institute of Certified Public Accountants, the Society of Management Accountants of Canada, and the Chartered Institute of Management Accountants (United Kingdom) for permission to use (or to adapt) selected problems from their examinations. These problems bear the notations CMA, CPA, SMA, and CIMA, respectively.

Peter C. Brewer
Ray H. Garrison
Eric W. Noreen

BRIEF CONTENTS

TABLE OF CONTENTS

CHAPTER FIVE
Cost Behavior: Analysis and Use 186

CHAPTER SIX
Cost-Volume-Profit Relationships 238

CHAPTER TEN
Decentralization   418

CHAPTER ELEVEN
Relevant Costs for Decision Making   450

CHAPTER TWELVE
Capital Budgeting Decisions   494

CHAPTER THIRTEEN
"How Well Am I Doing?" Statement of Cash Flows   536

CHAPTER FOURTEEN
"How Well Am I Doing?" Financial Statement Analysis   580

Managerial Accounting and the Business Environment

<< A LOOK AT THE PROLOGUE

Today's managers know that their world is constantly changing and becoming more complex. Before we get down to the basics, this Prologue will introduce you to a few of the revolutionary changes that today's managers face.

A LOOK AHEAD >>

Chapter 1 describes the work performed by managers, stresses the need for managerial accounting information, contrasts managerial and financial accounting, and defines many of the cost terms that will be used throughout the textbook. You will begin to build your base there.

PROLOGUE OUTLINE

Globalization

Strategy

Organizational Structure

- Decentralization
- The Functional View of Organizations

Process Management

- Lean Production
- The Theory of Constraints (TOC)
- Six Sigma

Technology in Business

- E-Commerce
- Enterprise Systems

The Importance of Ethics in Business

- Code of Conduct for Management Accountants
- Company Codes of Conduct
- Codes of Conduct on the International Level

Corporate Governance

- The Sarbanes-Oxley Act of 2002

Enterprise Risk Management

- Identifying and Controlling Business Risks

The Certified Management Accountant (CMA)

Throughout this book you will study how management accounting functions within organizations. However, before embarking on the study of management accounting, you need to develop an appreciation for the larger business environment within which it operates. The Prologue is divided into nine sections: (1) globalization, (2) strategy, (3) organizational structure, (4) process management, (5) technology in business, (6) the importance of ethics in business, (7) corporate governance, (8) enterprise risk management, and (9) the Certified Management Accountant (CMA). Other business classes provide greater detail on many of these topics. Nonetheless, a broad discussion of these topics is useful for placing management accounting in its proper context.

GLOBALIZATION

The world has become much more intertwined over the last 20 years. Reductions in tariffs, quotas, and other barriers to free trade; improvements in global transportation systems; explosive expansion in Internet usage; and increasing sophistication in international markets have created a truly global marketplace. Exhibit P–1 illustrates this tremendous

EXHIBIT P–1
United States Global Trade Activity
(in billions of U.S. dollars)

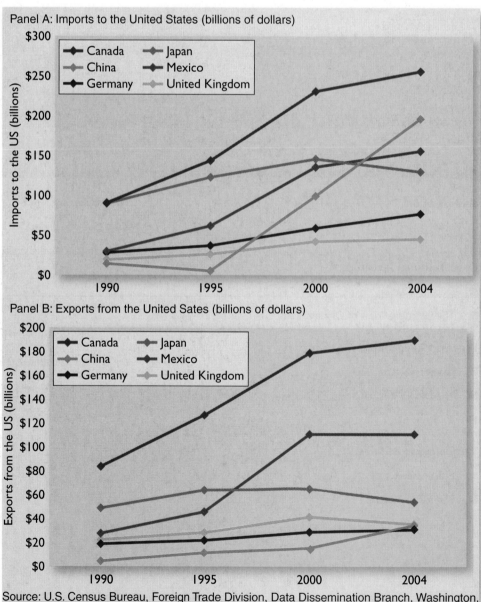

Source: U.S. Census Bureau, Foreign Trade Division, Data Dissemination Branch, Washington, D.C. 20233. www.census.gov/foreign-trade/balance.

growth in international trade from the standpoint of the United States and some of its key trading partners. Panel A of the exhibit shows the dollar value of imports (stated in billions of dollars) into the United States from six countries; Panel B shows the dollar value of exports from the United States to those same six countries. As you can see, the increase in import and export activity from 1990 to 2004 was huge. In particular, trade with China expanded enormously as did trade with Mexico and Canada, which are part of the North American Free Trade Agreement (NAFTA).

In a global marketplace, a company that has been very successful in its local market may suddenly find itself facing competition from halfway around the globe. For example, in the 1980s American automobile manufacturers began losing market share to Japanese competitors who offered American consumers higher-quality cars at lower prices. For consumers, this type of heightened international competition promises a greater variety of goods and services, at higher quality and lower prices. However, heightened international competition threatens companies that may have been quite profitable in their own local markets.

Although globalization leads to greater competition, it also means greater access to new markets, customers, and workers. For example, the emerging markets of China, India, Russia, and Brazil contain more than 2.5 billion potential customers and workers.[1] Many companies such as FedEx, McDonald's, and Nike are actively seeking to grow their sales by investing in emerging markets. In addition, the movement of jobs from the United States and Western Europe to other parts of the world has been notable in recent years. For example, one study estimates that by the end of the decade more than 825,000 financial services and high-tech jobs will transfer from Western Europe to less expensive labor markets such as India, China, Africa, Eastern Europe, and Latin America.[2]

The Internet fuels the globalization phenomenon by providing companies with greater access to geographically dispersed customers, employees, and suppliers. While the number of Internet users worldwide more than doubled during the first four years of the new millennium, as of 2004, more than 87% of the world's population was still not connected to the Internet. This suggests that the Internet's impact on global business has yet to fully develop.

---

[1] *The Economist: Pocket World in Figures 2004,* Profile Books Ltd., London, U.K.
[2] Job Exports: Europe's Turn, *Business Week*, April 19, 2004, p. 50.

The Implications of Globalization

IN BUSINESS

International competition goes hand-in-hand with globalization. China's entrance into the global marketplace has highlighted this stark reality for many U.S. companies. For example, from 2000 to 2003, China's wooden bedroom furniture exports to the United States climbed from $360 million to $1.2 billion. During this same time, the number of workers employed by U.S. furniture manufacturers dropped by 35,000, which is one of every three U.S. workers employed within that industry.

However, globalization means more than international competition. It brings opportunities for companies to enter new markets. FedEx has pushed hard to be an important player in the emerging Asian cargo market. FedEx makes 622 weekly flights to and from Asian markets, including service to 224 Chinese cities. FedEx currently has 39% of the U.S.–China express market and it plans to pursue continual growth in that region of the world.

Sources: Ted Fishman, "How China Will Change Your Business," *Inc.,* magazine March 2005, pp. 70–84; Matthew Boyle, "Why FedEx Is Flying High," *Fortune*, November 1, 2004, pp. 145–150.

STRATEGY

Even more than in the past, companies that now face global competition must have a viable *strategy* for succeeding in the marketplace. A **strategy** is a "game plan" that enables a company to attract customers by distinguishing itself from competitors. The focal point of a company's strategy should be its target customers. A company can only succeed if it creates a reason for customers to choose it over a competitor. These reasons, or what are more formally called *customer value propositions*, are the essence of strategy.

Customer value propositions tend to fall into three broad categories—*customer intimacy, operational excellence,* and *product leadership*. Companies that adopt a *customer intimacy* strategy are in essence saying to their target customers, "The reason that you should choose us is because we understand and respond to your individual needs better than our competitors." Ritz-Carlton, Nordstrom, and Starbucks rely primarily on a customer intimacy value proposition for their success. Companies that pursue the second customer value proposition, called *operational excellence,* are saying to their target customers, "The reason that you should choose us is because we can deliver products and services faster, more conveniently, and at a lower price than our competitors." Southwest Airlines, Wal-Mart, and The Vanguard Group are examples of companies that succeed first and foremost because of their operational excellence. Companies pursuing the third customer value proposition, called *product leadership,* are saying to their target customers, "The reason that you should choose us is because we offer higher-quality products than our competitors." BMW, Cisco Systems, and W.L. Gore (the creator of Gore-Tex fabrics) are examples of companies that succeed because of their product leadership. Although one company may offer its customers a combination of these three customer value propositions, one usually outweighs the others in terms of importance.[3]

Next, we turn our attention to how businesses create organizational structures to help accomplish their strategic goals.

---

[3]These three customer value propositions were defined by Michael Treacy and Fred Wiersema in "Customer Intimacy and Other Value Disciplines," *Harvard Business Review,* January/February 1993, 84–93.

IN BUSINESS

Operational Excellence Comes to the Diamond Business

An average engagement ring purchased from Blue Nile, an Internet diamond retailer, costs $5,200 compared to $9,500 if purchased from Tiffany & Co., a bricks-and-mortar retailer. Why is there such a difference? There are three reasons. First, Blue Nile allows wholesalers to sell directly to customers using its website. In the bricks-and-mortar scenario, diamonds change hands as many as seven times before being sold to a customer—passing through various cutters, wholesalers, brokers, and retailers, each of whom demands a profit. Second, Blue Nile carries very little inventory and incurs negligible overhead. Diamonds are shipped directly from wholesalers after they have been purchased by a customer—no retail outlets are necessary. Bricks-and-mortar retailers tie up large amounts of money paying for the inventory and employees on their showroom floors. Third, Blue Nile generates a high volume of transactions by selling to customers anywhere in the world; therefore, it can accept a lower profit margin per transaction than local retailers, who complete fewer transactions to customers within a limited geographic radius.

Perhaps you are wondering why customers are willing to trust an Internet retailer when buying an expensive item such as a diamond? The answer is that all of the diamonds sold through Blue Nile's website are independently certified by the Gemological Institute of America in four categories—carat count, type of cut, color, and clarity. In essence, Blue Nile has turned diamonds into a commodity and is using an operational excellence customer value proposition to generate annual sales of $154 million.

Source: Victoria Murphy, "Romance Killer," *Forbes,* November 29, 2004, pp. 97–101.

ORGANIZATIONAL STRUCTURE

Our discussion of organizational structure is divided into two parts. First, we highlight the fact that presidents of all but the smallest companies cannot execute their strategies alone. They must seek the help of their employees by empowering them to make decisions—they must *decentralize*. Next, we describe the most common formal decentralized organizational structure in use today—the functional structure.

Decentralization

Decentralization is the delegation of decision-making authority throughout an organization by giving managers the authority to make decisions relating to their area of responsibility. Some organizations are more decentralized than others. For example, consider Good Vibrations, an international retailer of music CDs with shops in major cities scattered across the Pacific Rim. Because of Good Vibrations' geographic dispersion and the peculiarities of local markets, the company is highly decentralized.

Good Vibrations' president (also often synonymous with the term *chief executive officer,* or *CEO*) sets the broad strategy for the company and makes major strategic decisions such as opening stores in new markets. However, much of the remaining decision-making authority is delegated to managers at various levels throughout the organization. Each of the company's numerous retail stores has a store manager as well as a separate manager for each music category such as international rock and classical/jazz. In addition, the company has support departments such as a central Purchasing Department and a Personnel Department.

The Functional View of Organizations

Exhibit P–2 shows Good Vibrations' organizational structure in the form of an **organization chart.** The purpose of an organization chart is to show how responsibility is divided among managers and to show formal lines of reporting and communication, or *chain of command*. Each box depicts an area of management responsibility, and the lines between the boxes show the lines of formal authority between managers. The chart tells us, for example, that the store managers are responsible to the operations vice president. In turn, the operations vice president is responsible to the company president, who in turn is responsible to the board of directors. Following the lines of authority and communication on the organization chart, we can see that the manager of the Hong Kong store would ordinarily report to the operations vice president rather than directly to the president of the company.

An organization chart also depicts *line* and *staff* positions in an organization. A person in a **line** position is *directly* involved in achieving the basic objectives of the organization. A person in a **staff** position, by contrast, is only *indirectly* involved in achieving those basic objectives. Staff positions provide assistance to line positions or other parts of the organization, but they do not have direct authority over line positions. Refer again to the organization chart in Exhibit P–2. Because the basic objective of Good Vibrations is to sell recorded music at a profit, those managers whose areas of responsibility are directly related to selling music occupy line positions. These positions, which are shown in a darker color in the exhibit, include the managers of the various music departments in each store, the store managers, the operations vice president, the president, and the board of directors.

By contrast, the managers of the central Purchasing Department and the Personnel Department occupy staff positions, because their departments support other departments rather than carry out the company's basic missions. The chief financial officer is a member of the top management team who also occupies a staff position. The **chief financial officer (CFO)** is responsible for providing timely and relevant data to support planning and control activities and for preparing financial statements for external users. In the United States, a manager known as the **controller** often runs the accounting department and reports directly to the CFO. More than ever, the accountants who work under the

EXHIBIT P-2   Organization Chart, Good Vibrations.

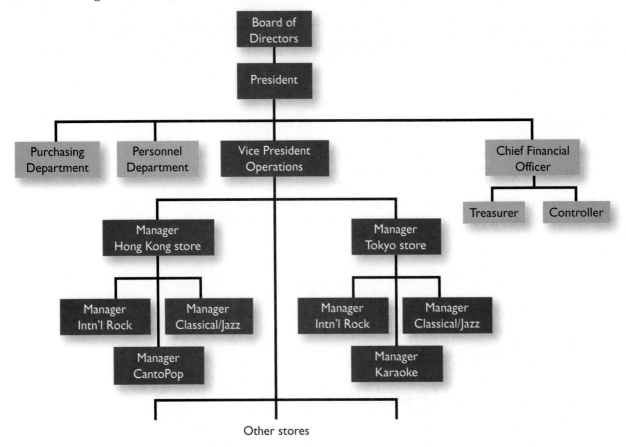

Other stores

CFO are focusing their efforts on supporting the needs of co-workers in line positions as one report concluded:

> Growing numbers of management accountants spend the bulk of their time as internal consultants or business analysts within their companies. Technological advances have liberated them from the mechanical aspects of accounting. They spend less time preparing standardized reports and more time analyzing and interpreting information. Many have moved from the isolation of accounting departments to be physically positioned in the [line] departments with which they work. Management accountants work on cross-functional teams, have extensive face-to-face communications with people throughout their organizations, and are actively involved in decision making . . . They are trusted advisors.[4]

The evolving role of management accountants as described in the quote above speaks to the importance of working cross-functionally to solve problems. This is the essence of the discussion in the next section.

PROCESS MANAGEMENT

A **business process** is a series of steps that are followed in order to carry out some task in a business. It is quite common for the linked set of steps constituting a business process to span departmental boundaries. The term *value chain* is often used when we

---

[4]Gary Siegel Organization, *Counting More, Counting Less: Transformations in the Management Accounting Profession, The 1999 Practice Analysis of Management Accounting,* Institute of Management Accountants, Montvale, NJ, August 1999, p. 3.

EXHIBIT P–3   Business Functions Making Up the Value Chain

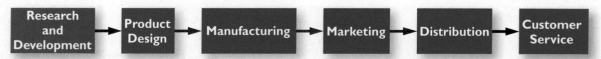

look at how the functional departments of an organization interact with one another to form business processes. A **value chain,** as shown in Exhibit P–3, consists of the major business functions that add value to a company's products and services. The customer's needs are most effectively met by coordinating the business processes that span these functions.

This section discusses three different approaches to managing and improving business processes—Lean Production, the Theory of Constraints (TOC), and Six Sigma. Although each is unique in certain respects, they all share the common theme of focusing on managing and improving business processes.

Lean Production

Traditionally, managers in manufacturing companies have sought to minimize the unit costs of products on the theory that in the long run only the lowest-cost producer will survive and prosper. This strategy led managers to maximize output to spread the fixed costs of investments in equipment and other assets over as many units as possible. In addition, managers have traditionally felt that an important part of their job was to keep everyone busy—idleness wastes money. These traditional views, often aided and abetted by traditional management accounting practices, resulted in a number of practices that have come under criticism in recent years.

For example, in a traditional manufacturing company, work is *pushed* through the system in order to produce as much as possible and to keep everyone busy—even if products cannot be immediately sold and pile up in warehouses. The push process starts by accumulating large amounts of raw material inventories from suppliers so that operations can proceed smoothly even if unanticipated disruptions occur. Next, enough materials are released to workstations to keep everyone busy. When a workstation completes its tasks, the partially completed goods are "pushed" forward to the next workstation regardless of whether that workstation is ready to receive them. The result is that partially completed goods stack up, waiting for the next workstation to become available. They may not be completed for days, weeks, or even months. Additionally, when the units are finally completed, customers may or may not want them. If finished goods are produced faster than the market will absorb, the result is bloated finished goods inventories.

Although some may argue that maintaining large amounts of inventory has its benefits, it clearly has its costs. According to experts, in addition to tying up money, maintaining inventories encourages inefficient and sloppy work, results in too many defects, and dramatically increases the amount of time required to complete a product. For example, when partially completed goods are stored for long periods of time before being processed by the next workstation, defects introduced by the preceding workstation go unnoticed. If a machine is out of calibration or incorrect procedures are being followed, many defective units will be produced before the problem is discovered. And when the defects are finally discovered, it may be very difficult to track down the source of the problem. In addition, units may be obsolete or out of fashion by the time they are finally completed.

Large inventories of partially completed goods create many other problems that are best discussed in more advanced courses. These problems are not obvious—if they were, companies would have long ago reduced their inventories. Managers at Toyota are credited with the insight that large inventories often create many more problems than they solve. Toyota pioneered what is known today as *Lean Production*.

EXHIBIT P–4   The Lean Thinking Model

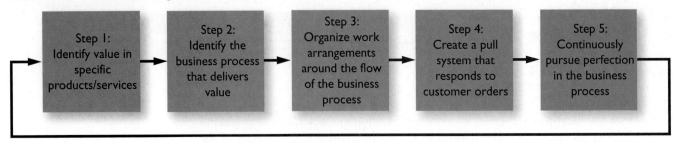

The Lean Thinking Model   The **lean thinking model** is a five-step management approach that organizes resources such as people and machines around the flow of business processes and that pulls units through these processes in response to customer orders. The result is lower inventories, fewer defects, less wasted effort, and quicker customer response times. Exhibit P–4 depicts the five stages of the lean thinking model.[5]

The first step is to identify the value to customers in specific products and services. The second step is to identify the business process that delivers this value to customers.[6] As discussed earlier, the linked set of steps constituting a business process typically spans the departmental boundaries that are specified in an organization chart. The third step is to organize work arrangements around the flow of the business process. This is often accomplished by creating what is known as a *manufacturing cell*. The cellular approach takes employees and equipment from departments that were previously separated from one another and places them side-by-side in a work space called a *cell*. The equipment within the cell is aligned in a sequential manner that follows the steps of the business process. Each employee is trained to perform all the steps within his or her cell.

The fourth step in the lean thinking model is to create a pull system where production is not initiated until a customer has ordered a product. Inventories are reduced to a minimum by purchasing raw materials and producing units only as needed to meet customer demand. Under ideal conditions, a company operating a pull system would purchase only enough materials each day to meet that day's needs. Moreover, the company would have no goods still in process at the end of the day, and all goods completed during the day would be shipped immediately to customers. As this sequence suggests, work takes place just-in-time, in the sense that raw materials are received by each manufacturing cell just in time to go into production, manufactured parts are completed just in time to be assembled into products, and products are completed just in time to be shipped to customers. Not surprisingly, this facet of the lean thinking model is often called **Just-In-Time** production, or **JIT** for short.

The change from *push* to *pull* production is more profound than it may appear. Among other things, producing only in response to a customer order means that workers will be idle whenever demand falls below the company's production capacity. This can be an extremely difficult cultural change for an organization. It challenges the core beliefs of many managers and raises anxieties in workers who have become accustomed to being kept busy all of the time.

The fifth step of the lean thinking model is to continuously pursue perfection. In a traditional company, parts and materials are inspected for defects when they are received from suppliers, and quality inspectors inspect units as they progress along the production line. In a Lean Production system, the company's suppliers are responsible for the quality of incoming parts and materials. And instead of using quality inspectors, the company's production workers are directly responsible for spotting defective units. A worker who discovers a defect immediately stops the flow of production. Supervisors and other workers go to the cell to

---

[5]This exhibit is adapted from James P. Womack and Daniel T. Jones, *Lean Thinking: Banish Waste and Create Wealth in Your Corporation, Revised and Updated,* 2003, Simon & Schuster, New York, NY.
[6]The Lean Production literature uses the term *value stream* rather than business process.

determine the cause of the problem and correct it before any further defective units are produced. This procedure ensures that problems are quickly identified and corrected.

The lean thinking model can also be used to improve the business processes that link companies together. The term **supply chain management** is commonly used to refer to the coordination of business processes across companies to better serve end consumers. For example, Procter & Gamble and Costco coordinate their business processes to ensure that Procter & Gamble's products, such as Bounty, Tide, and Crest, are on Costco's shelves when customers want them. Both Procter & Gamble and Costco realize that their mutual success depends on working together to ensure Procter & Gamble's products are available to Costco's customers.

The Power of Lean   IN BUSINESS

Lean thinking can benefit all types of businesses. For example, Dell Inc.'s Lean Production system can produce a customized personal computer within 36 hours. Even more impressive, Dell doesn't start ordering components and assembling computers until orders are booked. By ordering right before assembly, Dell's parts are on average 60 days newer than those of its competitors, which translates into a 6% profit advantage in components alone.

In the service arena, Jefferson Pilot Financial (JPF) realized that "[l]ike an automobile on the assembly line, an insurance policy goes through a series of processes, from initial application to underwriting, or risk assessment, to policy issuance. With each step, value is added to the work in progress—just as a car gets doors or a coat of paint." Given this realization, JPF organized its work arrangements into a cellular layout and synchronized the rate of output to the pace of customer demand. JPF's lean thinking enabled it to reduce attending physician statement turnaround times by 70%, decrease labor costs by 26%, and reduce reissue errors by 40%.

Sources: Gary McWilliams, "Whirlwind on the Web," *BusinessWeek,* April 7, 1997, p. 134; Stephen Pritchard, "Inside Dell's Lean Machine," *Works Management,* December 2002, pp. 14–16; and Cynthia Karen Swank, "The Lean Service Machine," *Harvard Business Review,* October 2003, pp. 123–129.

The Theory of Constraints (TOC)

A **constraint** is anything that prevents you from getting more of what you want. Every individual and every organization faces at least one constraint. You may not have enough time to study thoroughly for every subject and to go out with your friends on the weekend, so time is your constraint. United Airlines has only a limited number of loading gates available at its busy Chicago O'Hare hub, so its constraint is loading gates. Vail Resorts has only a limited amount of land to develop as home sites and commercial lots at its ski areas, so its constraint is land.

The **Theory of Constraints (TOC)** is based on the insight that effectively managing the constraint is the key to success. For example, long waiting periods for surgery are a chronic problem in the National Health Service (NHS), the government-funded provider of health care in the United Kingdom. The diagram in Exhibit P–5 illustrates a simplified version of the steps followed by a surgery patient. The number of patients who can be processed through each step in a day is indicated in the exhibit. For example, appointments for outpatient visits can be made for as many as 100 referrals from general practitioners in a day.

The constraint, or *bottleneck,* in a system is determined by the step that has the smallest capacity—in this case, surgery. The total number of patients processed through the entire system cannot exceed 15 per day—the maximum number of patients who can be treated in surgery. No matter how hard managers, doctors, and nurses try to improve the processing rate elsewhere in the system, they will never succeed in driving down wait

EXHIBIT P–5   Processing Surgery Patients at an NHS Facility (simplified)*

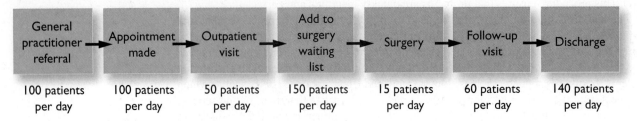

General practitioner referral	Appointment made	Outpatient visit	Add to surgery waiting list	Surgery	Follow-up visit	Discharge
100 patients per day	100 patients per day	50 patients per day	150 patients per day	15 patients per day	60 patients per day	140 patients per day

*This diagram originally appeared in the February 1999 issue of the U.K. magazine *Health Management*.

lists until the capacity of surgery is increased. In fact, improvements elsewhere in the system—particularly before the constraint—are likely to result in even longer waiting times and more frustrated patients and health care providers. Thus, to be effective, improvement efforts must be focused on the constraint. A business process, such as the process for serving surgery patients, is like a chain. If you want to increase the strength of a chain, what is the most effective way to do this? Should you concentrate your efforts strengthening the strongest link, all the links, or the weakest link? Clearly, focusing your efforts on the weakest link will bring the biggest benefit.

The procedure to follow to strengthen the chain is clear. First, identify the weakest link, which is the constraint. In the case of the NHS, the constraint is surgery. Second, do not place a greater strain on the system than the weakest link can handle—if you do, the chain will break. In the case of the NHS, more referrals than surgery can accommodate leads to unacceptably long waiting lists. Third, concentrate improvement efforts on strengthening the weakest link. In the case of the NHS, this means finding ways to increase the number of surgeries that can be performed in a day. Fourth, if the improvement efforts are successful, eventually the weakest link will improve to the point where it is no longer the weakest link. At that point, the new weakest link (i.e., the new constraint) must be identified, and improvement efforts must be shifted over to that link. This simple sequential process provides a powerful strategy for optimizing business processes.

IN BUSINESS   **Watch Where You Cut Costs**

At one hospital, the emergency room became so backlogged that its doors were closed to the public and patients were turned away for over 36 hours in the course of a single month. It turned out, after investigation, that the constraint was not the emergency room itself; it was the housekeeping staff. To cut costs, managers at the hospital had laid off housekeeping workers. This created a bottleneck in the emergency room because rooms were not being cleaned as quickly as the emergency room staff could process new patients. Thus, laying off some of the lowest paid workers at the hospital had the effect of forcing the hospital to idle some of its most highly paid staff and most expensive equipment!

Source: Tracey Burton-Houle, "AGI Continues to Steadily Make Advances with the Adaptation of TOC into Healthcare," www.goldratt.com/toctquarterly/august2002.htm.

Six Sigma

Six Sigma is a process improvement method that relies on customer feedback and fact-based data gathering and analysis techniques to drive process improvement. Motorola and General Electric are closely identified with the emergence of the Six Sigma movement. Technically, the term Six Sigma refers to a process that generates no more than 3.4 defects per million opportunities. Because this rate of defects is so low, Six Sigma is sometimes associated with the slogan *zero defects*.

The most common framework used to guide Six Sigma process improvement efforts is known as DMAIC (pronounced: du-may-ik), which stands for *D*efine, *M*easure, *A*nalyze, *I*mprove, and *C*ontrol. As summarized in Exhibit P–6, the Define stage of the process focuses on defining three things, namely, the scope and purpose of the project, the flow of the current process, and the customer's requirements for the process. The Measure stage is used to gather baseline performance data concerning the existing process and to narrow the scope of the project to the most important problems. The Analyze stage focuses on identifying the root causes of the problems that were identified during the Measure stage. The Analyze stage often reveals that the process includes many *activities that do not add value to the product or service*. Activities that customers are not willing to pay for because they add no value are known as **non-value-added activities** and such activities should be eliminated wherever possible. The Improve stage is where potential solutions are developed, evaluated, and implemented to eliminate non-value-added activities and any other problems uncovered in the Analyze stage. Finally, the objective in the Control stage is to ensure that the problems remain fixed and that the new methods are improved over time.[7]

Managers must be very careful when attempting to translate Six Sigma improvements into financial benefits. There are only two ways to increase profits—decrease costs or increase sales. Cutting costs may seem easy—lay off workers who are no longer needed because of improvements such as eliminating non-value-added activities. However, if this approach is taken, employees quickly get the message that process improvements lead to job losses and they will understandably resist further improvement efforts. If improvement is to continue, employees must be convinced that the end result of improvement will be more secure rather than less secure jobs. This can only happen if management uses tools such as Six Sigma to generate more sales rather than to cut the workforce.

---

[7]Peter C. Brewer, "Six Sigma Helps a Company Create a Culture of Accountability," *Journal of Organizational Excellence,* Summer 2004, pp. 45–59.

EXHIBIT P–6
The Six Sigma DMAIC Framework

Stage	Goals
Define	• Establish the scope and purpose of the project. • Diagram the flow of the current process. • Establish the customer's requirements for the process.
Measure	• Gather baseline performance data related to the existing process. • Narrow the scope of the project to the most important problems.
Analyze	• Identify the root cause(s) of the problems identified in the Measure stage.
Improve	• Develop, evaluate, and implement solutions to the problems.
Control	• Ensure that problems remain fixed. • Seek to improve the new methods over time.

Source: Peter C. Brewer and Nancy A. Bagranoff, "Near Zero-Defect Accounting with Six Sigma," *Journal of Corporate Accounting and Finance,* January–February 2004, pp. 67–72.

TECHNOLOGY IN BUSINESS

Technology is being harnessed in many ways by businesses. In this section we will discuss two of these ways—e-commerce and enterprise systems.

E-Commerce

E-commerce refers to business that is conducted using the Internet. At the start of the new millennium, e-commerce was riding high. The stock prices of dot.com companies (companies that focus on generating revenue exclusively through the Internet) were climbing by leaps and bounds. On January 30, 2000, more than 20 dot.com companies, such as Pets.com and Epidemic.com, paid as much as $3 million for 30-second commercials during the Super Bowl. However, by November of that same year, prospects for dot.com companies began to worsen as companies such as Pets.com, Garden.com, and Furniture.com all failed. By the spring of 2001, EToys had folded and monthly statistics for dot.com layoffs and closures had peaked at 17,554 and 64, respectively. In short, the dot.com collapse was under way.[8]

Since the collapse of the dot.com bubble in 2001, e-commerce has slowly been rebuilding momentum. Internet advertising is projected to exceed $12 billion per year before the end of the decade.[9] And while e-commerce has already had a major impact on the sale of books, music, and airline tickets, it appears that companies such as Blue Nile, eBay, Amazon.com, Lending Tree, and Expedia will continue to disrupt and redefine other markets such as the jewelry, real estate, and hotel industries.[10] In addition to dot.com companies, established bricks-and-mortar companies such as General Electric, Wells Fargo, and Target will undoubtedly continue to expand into cyberspace—both for business-to-business transactions and for retailing.

The growth in e-commerce is occurring because the Internet has important advantages over more conventional marketplaces for many kinds of transactions. For example, the Internet is an ideal technology for streamlining the mortgage lending process. Customers can complete loan applications over the Internet rather than tying up the time of a staffperson in an office. And data and funds can be sent back and forth electronically—no UPS or FedEx delivery truck needs to drop by the consumer's home to deliver a check.

In conclusion, building a successful dot.com business remains a tenuous and high-risk proposition. Nevertheless, e-commerce is here to stay. The stock prices of dot.com companies will rise and fall, but the benefits that the Internet provides to businesses and their customers will ensure that e-commerce grows over time.

---

[8]See the timeline published by BBC News in the United Kingdom. The web address for BBC news is http://news.bbc.co.uk

[9]Stephen Baker, "Where the Real Internet Money Is Made," *BusinessWeek,* December 27, 2004, p. 99.

[10]Timothy J. Mullaney, "E-Biz Strikes Again!" *BusinessWeek,* May 10, 2004, pp. 80–90.

IN BUSINESS   Internet Innovations

Companies continue to develop new ways of using the Internet to improve their performance. Below is a summary of intriguing Internet applications categorized into four descriptive groups.

1. Collaboration
    - Eli Lilly has a website where scientific problems are posed to its global workforce. The best solutions earn cash rewards.
    - Lockheed Martin used the Internet to help 80 of its suppliers from around the world to collaborate in designing and building a new stealth fighter plane.

(continued)

2. Customer Service
   - General Motors uses the Internet to auction off vehicles with expired leases.
   - IndyMac Bancorp uses the Internet to link its nationwide network of loan brokers to its central computers. Using these links, the brokers can electronically submit and then monitor their clients' loan applications.
3. Management
   - CareGroup's approximately 2,500 doctors are rated on 20 criteria related to the care they provide for insured patients. The results are summarized on digital report cards that have helped spot inefficiencies, saving the company $4 million annually.
   - Bristol-Myers Squibb uses the Internet to speed up drug research and development. The Web-based system has reduced by one-third the time needed to develop new medications.
4. Cutting Edge
   - Fresh Direct is an on-line grocer in New York City. Using the Internet to streamline order processing, the company is able to charge prices as much as 35% below its competitors.
   - eArmyU is a virtual Internet-based university that provides educational opportunities to 40,000 geographically dispersed U.S. soldiers.

Source: Heather Green, "The Web Smart 50," *BusinessWeek,* November 24, 2003, pp. 82–106.

Enterprise Systems[11]

Historically, most companies implemented specific software programs to support specific business functions. For example, the accounting department would select its own software applications to meet its needs, while the manufacturing department would select different software programs to support its needs. The separate systems were not integrated and could not easily pass data back and forth. The end result was data duplication and data inconsistencies coupled with lengthy customer response times and high costs.

An **enterprise system** is designed to overcome these problems by integrating data across an organization into a single software system that enables all employees to have simultaneous access to a common set of data. There are two keys to the data integration inherent in an enterprise system. First, all data are recorded only once in the company's centralized digital data repository known as a database. When data are added to the database or are changed, the new information is simultaneously available to everyone across the organization on a real-time basis. Second, the unique data elements contained within the database can be linked together. For example, one data element, such as a customer identification number, can be related to other data elements, such as that customer's address, billing history, shipping history, merchandise returns history, and so on. The ability to forge such relationships among data elements explains why this type of database is called a *relational database.*

Data integration helps employees communicate with one another and it also helps them communicate with their suppliers and customers. For example, consider how the *customer relationship management* process is improved when enterprise-wide information resides in one location. Whether meeting the customer's needs requires accessing information related to billing (an accounting function), delivery status (a distribution function), price quotes (a marketing function), or merchandise returns (a customer service function), the required information is readily available to the employee interacting with the customer. Though enterprise systems are expensive and risky to install, the benefits of data integration have led many companies to invest in them.

---

[11]"Enterprise systems" is a broad term that encompasses many enterprise-wide computer applications such as customer relationship management and supply chain management systems. Perhaps the most frequently mentioned type of enterprise system is an Enterprise Resource Planning (ERP) system.

THE IMPORTANCE OF ETHICS IN BUSINESS

A series of major financial scandals involving Enron, Tyco International, HealthSouth, Adelphia Communications, WorldCom, Global Crossing, Rite Aid, and other companies has raised deep concerns about ethics in business. The managers and companies involved in these scandals have suffered mightily—from huge fines to jail terms and financial collapse. And the recognition that ethical behavior is absolutely essential for the functioning of our economy has led to numerous regulatory changes, some of which we will discuss in a later section on corporate governance. But why is ethical behavior so important? This is not a matter of just being "nice." Ethical behavior is the lubricant that keeps the economy running. Without that lubricant, the economy would operate much less efficiently—less would be available to consumers, quality would be lower, and prices would be higher.

Take a very simple example. Suppose that dishonest farmers, distributors, and grocers knowingly tried to sell wormy apples as good apples and that grocers refused to take back wormy apples. What would you do as a consumer of apples? Go to another grocer? But what if all grocers acted this way? What would you do then? You would probably either stop buying apples or you would spend a lot of time inspecting apples before buying them. So would everyone else. Now notice what has happened. Because farmers, distributors, and grocers could not be trusted, sales of apples would plummet and those who did buy apples would waste a lot of time inspecting them minutely. Everyone loses. Farmers, distributors, and grocers make less money; consumers enjoy fewer apples; and consumers waste time looking for worms. In other words, without fundamental trust in the integrity of businesses, the economy would operate much less efficiently. James Surowiecki summed up this point as follows:

> [F]lourishing economies require a healthy level of trust in the reliability and fairness of everyday transactions. If you assumed every potential deal was a rip-off or that the products you were buying were probably going to be lemons, then very little business would get done. More important, the costs of the transactions that did take place would be exorbitant, since you'd have to do enormous work to investigate each deal and you'd have to rely on the threat of legal action to enforce every contract. For an economy to prosper, what's needed is not a Pollyannaish faith that everyone else has your best interests at heart—"caveat emptor" [buyer beware] remains an important truth—but a basic confidence in the promises and commitments that people make about their products and services.[12]

---

[12]James Surowiecki, "A Virtuous Cycle," *Forbes,* December 23, 2002, pp. 248–256.

Thus, for the good of everyone—including profit-making companies—it is vitally important that business be conducted within an ethical framework that builds and sustains trust.

No Trust—No Enron   IN BUSINESS

Jonathan Karpoff reports on a particularly important, but often overlooked, aspect of the Enron debacle:

> As we know, some of Enron's reported profits in the late 1990s were pure accounting fiction. But the firm also had legitimate businesses and actual assets. Enron's most important businesses involved buying and selling electricity and other forms of energy. [Using Enron as an intermediary, utilities that needed power bought energy from producers with surplus generating capacity.] Now when an electric utility contracts to buy electricity, the managers of the utility want to make darned sure that the seller will deliver the electrons exactly as agreed, at the contracted price. There is no room for fudging on this because the consequences of not having the electricity when consumers switch on their lights are dire. . . .
>
> This means that the firms with whom Enron was trading electricity . . . had to trust Enron. And trust Enron they did, to the tune of billions of dollars of trades every year. But in October 2001, when Enron announced that its previous financial statements overstated the firm's profits, it undermined such trust. As everyone recognizes, the announcement caused investors to lower their valuations of the firm. Less understood, however, was the more important impact of the announcement; by revealing some of its reported earnings to be a house of cards, Enron sabotaged its reputation. The effect was to undermine even its legitimate and (previously) profitable operations that relied on its trustworthiness.
>
> This is why Enron melted down so fast. Its core businesses relied on the firm's reputation. When that reputation was wounded, energy traders took their business elsewhere. . . .

Energy traders lost their faith in Enron, but what if no other company could be trusted to deliver on its commitments to provide electricity as contracted? In that case, energy traders would have nowhere to turn. As a direct result, energy producers with surplus generating capacity would be unable to sell their surplus power. As a consequence, their existing customers would have to pay higher prices. And utilities that did not have sufficient capacity to meet demand on their own would have to build more capacity, which would also mean higher prices for their consumers. So a general lack of trust in companies such as Enron would ultimately result in overinvestment in energy-generating capacity and higher energy prices for consumers.

Source: Jonathan M. Karpoff, "Regulation vs. Reputation in Preventing Corporate Fraud," *UW Business*, Spring 2002, pp. 28–30.

The Institute of Management Accountants (IMA) of the United States has adopted an ethical code called the Statement of Ethical Professional Practice that describes in some detail the ethical responsibilities of management accountants. Even though the standards were specifically developed for management accountants, they have much broader application.

Code of Conduct for Management Accountants

The IMA's Statement of Ethical Professional Practice is presented in full in Exhibit P–7. The statement has two parts. The first part provides general guidelines for ethical behavior. In a nutshell, a management accountant has ethical responsibilities in four broad areas: First, to maintain a high level of professional competence; second, to treat sensitive matters with confidentiality; third, to maintain personal integrity; and fourth, to maintain credibility. The second part of the standards specifies what should be done if an individual finds evidence of ethical misconduct. We recommend that you stop at this point and read the standards in Exhibit P–7.

EXHIBIT P–7
Statement of Ethical Professional Practice Established by the Institute of Management Accountants (IMA)

Members of IMA shall behave ethically. A commitment to ethical professional practice includes overarching principles that express our values, and standards that guide our conduct.

PRINCIPLES
IMA's overarching ethical principles include: Honesty, Fairness, Objectivity, and Responsibility. Members shall act in accordance with these principles and shall encourage others within their organizations to adhere to them.

STANDARDS
A member's failure to comply with the following standards may result in disciplinary action.

I. COMPETENCE
Each member has a responsibility to:

1. Maintain an appropriate level of professional expertise by continually developing knowledge and skills.
2. Perform professional duties in accordance with relevant laws, regulations, and technical standards.
3. Provide decision support information and recommendations that are accurate, clear, concise, and timely.
4. Recognize and communicate professional limitations or other constraints that would preclude responsible judgment or successful performance of an activity.

II. CONFIDENTIALITY
Each member has a responsibility to:

1. Keep information confidential except when disclosure is authorized or legally required.
2. Inform all relevant parties regarding appropriate use of confidential information. Monitor subordinates' activities to ensure compliance.
3. Refrain from using confidential information for unethical or illegal advantage.

III. INTEGRITY
Each member has a responsibility to:

1. Mitigate actual conflicts of interest, regularly communicate with business associates to avoid apparent conflicts of interest. Advise all parties of any potential conflicts.
2. Refrain from engaging in any conduct that would prejudice carrying out duties ethically.
3. Abstain from engaging in or supporting any activity that might discredit the profession.

IV. CREDIBILITY
Each member has a responsibility to:

1. Communicate information fairly and objectively.
2. Disclose all relevant information that could reasonably be expected to influence an intended user's understanding of the reports, analyses, or recommendations.
3. Disclose delays or deficiencies in information, timeliness, processing, or internal controls in conformance with organization policy and/or applicable law.

RESOLUTION OF ETHICAL CONFLICT
In applying the Standards of Ethical Professional Practice, you may encounter problems identifying unethical behavior or resolving an ethical conflict. When faced with ethical issues, you should follow your organization's established policies on the resolution of such conflict. If these policies do not resolve the ethical conflict, you should consider the following courses of action:

1. Discuss the issue with your immediate supervisor except when it appears that the supervisor is involved. In that case, present the issue to the next level. If you cannot achieve a satisfactory resolution, submit the issue to the next management level. If your

immediate superior is the chief executive officer or equivalent, the acceptable reviewing authority may be a group such as the audit committee, executive committee, board of directors, board of trustees, or owners. Contact with levels above the immediate superior should be initiated only with your superior's knowledge, assuming he or she is not involved. Communication of such problems to authorities or individuals not employed or engaged by the organization is not considered appropriate, unless you believe there is a clear violation of the law.

2. Clarify relevant ethical issues by initiating a confidential discussion with an IMA Ethics Counselor or other impartial advisor to obtain a better understanding of possible courses of action.

3. Consult your own attorney as to legal obligations and rights concerning the ethical conflict.

The ethical standards provide sound, practical advice for management accountants and managers. Most of the rules in the ethical standards are motivated by a very practical consideration—if these rules were not generally followed in business, then the economy and all of us would suffer. Consider the following specific examples of the consequences of not abiding by the standards:

- Suppose employees could not be trusted with confidential information. Then top managers would be reluctant to distribute such information within the company, and as a result, decisions would be based on incomplete information and operations would deteriorate.

- Suppose employees accepted bribes from suppliers. Then contracts would tend to go to suppliers who pay the highest bribes rather than to the most competent suppliers. Would you like to fly in aircraft whose wings were made by the subcontractor who paid the highest bribe? Would you fly as often? What would happen to the airline industry if its safety record deteriorated due to shoddy workmanship on contracted parts and assemblies?

- Suppose the presidents of companies routinely lied in their annual reports and financial statements. If investors could not rely on the basic integrity of a company's financial statements, they would have little basis for making informed decisions. Suspecting the worst, rational investors would pay less for securities issued by companies and may not be willing to invest at all. As a consequence, companies would have less money for productive investments—leading to slower economic growth, fewer goods and services, and higher prices.

As these examples suggest, if ethical standards were not generally adhered to, everyone would suffer—businesses as well as consumers. Essentially, abandoning ethical standards would lead to a lower standard of living with lower-quality goods and services, less to choose from, and higher prices. In short, following ethical rules such as those in the Statement of Ethical Professional Practice is absolutely essential for the smooth functioning of an advanced market economy.

Who Is to Blame?   IN BUSINESS

Don Keough, a retired Coca-Cola executive, recalls that, "In my time, CFOs [chief financial officers] were basically tough, smart, and mean. Bringing good news wasn't their function. They were the truth-tellers." But that had changed by the late 1990s in some companies. Instead of being truth-tellers, CFOs became corporate spokesmen, guiding stock analysts in their quarterly earnings estimates—and then making sure those earnings estimates were beaten using whatever means necessary, including accounting tricks and in some cases outright fraud. But does the buck stop there?

interests of stockholders, an effective corporate governance system also should protect the interests of the company's many other *stakeholders*—its customers, creditors, employees, suppliers, and the communities within which it operates. These parties are referred to as stakeholders because their welfare is tied to the company's performance.

Unfortunately, history has repeatedly shown that unscrupulous top managers, if unchecked, can exploit their power to defraud stakeholders. This unpleasant reality became all too clear in 2001 when the fall of Enron kicked off an unprecedented wave of corporate scandals. These scandals were characterized by financial reporting fraud and misuse of corporate funds at the very highest levels—including CEOs and CFOs. While this was disturbing in itself, it also indicated that the institutions intended to prevent such abuses weren't working, thus raising fundamental questions about the adequacy of the existing corporate governance system. In an attempt to respond to these concerns, the U.S. Congress passed the most important reform of corporate governance in many decades—the Sarbanes-Oxley Act of 2002.

IN BUSINESS   Spilled Milk at Parmalat

Corporate scandals have not been limited to the United States. In 2003, Parmalat, a publicly traded dairy company in Italy, went bankrupt. The CEO, Calisto Tanzi, admitted to manipulating the books for more than a decade so that he could skim off $640 million to cover losses at various of his family businesses. But the story doesn't stop there. Parmalat's balance sheet contained $13 billion in nonexistent assets, including a $5 billion Bank of America account that didn't exist. All in all, Parmalat was the biggest financial fraud in European history.

Source: Gail Edmondson, David Fairlamb, and Nanette Byrnes, "The Milk Just Keeps on Spilling," *BusinessWeek*, January 26, 2004, pp. 54–58.

The Sarbanes-Oxley Act of 2002

The **Sarbanes-Oxley Act of 2002** is intended to protect the interests of those who invest in publicly traded companies by improving the reliability and accuracy of corporate financial reports and disclosures. We would like to highlight six key aspects of the legislation.[17]

First, the act requires that both the CEO and CFO certify in writing that their company's financial statements and accompanying disclosures fairly represent the results of operations—with possible jail time if a CEO or CFO certifies results that they know are false. This creates very powerful incentives for the CEO and CFO to ensure that the financial statements contain no misrepresentations.

Second, the act established the Public Company Accounting Oversight Board to provide additional oversight over the audit profession. The act authorizes the board to conduct investigations, to take disciplinary actions against audit firms, and to enact various standards and rules concerning the preparation of audit reports.

Third, the act places the power to hire, compensate, and terminate the public accounting firm that audits a company's financial reports in the hands of the audit committee of the board of directors. Previously, management often had the power to hire and fire its auditors. Furthermore, the act specifies that all members of the audit committee must be independent, meaning that they do not have an affiliation with the company they are overseeing, nor do they receive any consulting or advisory compensation from the company.

Fourth, the act places important restrictions on audit firms. Historically, public accounting firms earned a large part of their profits by providing consulting services to the companies

---

[17]Further information concerning the Sarbanes-Oxley Act of 2002 can be obtained at the American Institute of Certified Public Accountants website http://thecaq.aicpa.org/Resources/Sarbanes+Oxley/.

that they audited. This provided the appearance of a lack of independence since a client that was dissatisfied with an auditor's stance on an accounting issue might threaten to stop using the auditor as a consultant. To avoid this possible conflict of interests, the act prohibits a public accounting firm from providing a wide variety of nonauditing services to an audit client.

Fifth, the act requires that a company's annual report contain an *internal control report*. Internal controls are put in place by management to provide assurance to investors that financial disclosures are reliable. The report must state that it is management's responsibility to establish and maintain adequate internal controls and it must contain an assessment by management of the effectiveness of its internal control structure. The internal control report is accompanied by an opinion from the company's audit firm as to whether management's assessment of its internal control over financial reporting is fairly stated.[18]

Sarbanes-Oxley: An Expensive Piece of Legislation

IN BUSINESS

You wouldn't think 169 words could be so expensive! But that is the case with what is known as Section 404 of the Sarbanes-Oxley Act of 2002, which requires that a publicly traded company's annual report contain an internal control report certified by its auditors. Although this may sound simple enough, estimates indicate that Sarbanes-Oxley compliance will cost the Fortune 1000 companies alone about $6 billion annually—much of which will go to public accounting firms in fees. With the increased demand for audit services, public accounting firms such as KPMG, PricewaterhouseCoopers, Ernst & Young, and Deloitte are returning to campuses to hire new auditors in large numbers and students are flocking to accounting classes.

Source: Holman W. Jenkins Jr., "Thinking Outside the Sarbox," *The Wall Street Journal,* November 24, 2004, p. A13.

Finally, the act establishes severe penalties of as many as 20 years in prison for altering or destroying any documents that may eventually be used in an official proceeding and as many as 10 years in prison for managers who retaliate against a so-called whistleblower who goes outside the chain of command to report misconduct. Collectively, these six aspects of the Sarbanes-Oxley Act of 2002 should help reduce the incidence of fraudulent financial reporting.

ENTERPRISE RISK MANAGEMENT

Businesses face risks every day. Most risks are foreseeable. For example, a company could reasonably be expected to foresee the possibility of a natural disaster or a fire destroying its centralized data storage facility. Companies respond to this type of risk by having off-site backup data storage facilities. On the other hand, some risks are unforeseeable. For example, in 1982 Johnson & Johnson never could have imagined that a deranged killer would insert poison into bottles of Tylenol and then place these tainted bottles on retail shelves, ultimately killing seven people.[19] Johnson & Johnson—guided by the first line of its Credo (see page 18)—responded to this crisis by acting to reduce the risks faced by its customers and itself. First, it immediately recalled and destroyed 31 million bottles of Tylenol with a

---

[18]The Public Company Accounting Oversight Board's Auditing Standard No. 2 requires the audit firm to issue a second opinion on whether its client maintained effective internal control over the financial reporting process. This opinion is in addition to the opinion regarding the fairness of management's assessment of the effectiveness of its own internal controls.

[19]Tamara Kaplan, "The Tylenol Crisis: How Effective Public Relations Saved Johnson & Johnson," in Glen Broom, Allen Center, and Scott Cutlip, *Effective Public Relations,* 1994, Prentice Hall, Upper Saddle River, NJ.

retail value of $100 million to reduce the risk of additional fatalities. Second, it developed the tamper-resistant packaging that we take for granted today to reduce the risk that the same type of crime could be repeated in the future.

Every business strategy or decision involves risks. **Enterprise risk management** is a process used by a company to proactively identify the business risks that it faces and to develop responses to those risks that enable the company to be reasonably assured of satisfying stakeholder expectations.

Identifying and Controlling Business Risks

Companies should identify foreseeable risks before they occur rather than react to unfortunate events that have already happened. The left-hand column of Exhibit P–9 provides 12 examples of business risks. This list is not meant to be exhaustive; rather, its purpose is to introduce you to the diverse nature of business risks that companies face. Whether the risks relate to the weather, computer hackers, complying with the law, employee theft, financial reporting, or strategic decision making, they all have one thing in common: if they are not managed effectively, they can infringe on a company's ability to meet its goals.

Once a company identifies its risks, it can respond to them in various ways such as accepting, avoiding, sharing, or reducing the risk. Perhaps the most common risk management tactic is to reduce risks by implementing specific controls. The right-hand column of Exhibit P–9 provides an example of a control that could be implemented to

EXHIBIT P–9
Identifying and Controlling Business Risks

Examples of Business Risks	Examples of Controls to Reduce Business Risks
• Intellectual assets being stolen from computer files	• Create firewalls that prohibit computer hackers from corrupting or stealing intellectual property.
• Products harming customers	• Develop a formal and rigorous new product-testing program.
• Losing market share due to the unforeseen actions of competitors	• Formalize an approach for legally gathering information about competitors' plans and practices.
• Poor weather conditions shutting down operations	• Develop contingency plans for overcoming any disruptions due to weather.
• A website malfunctioning	• Develop a pilot testing program before going "live" on the Internet.
• A supplier strike halting the flow of raw materials	• Establish a relationship with two companies capable of providing needed raw materials.
• An incentive compensation system causing employees to make poor decisions	• Create a balanced set of performance measures that motivates the desired behavior.
• Financial statements unfairly reporting the value of inventory	• Count the physical inventory on hand to make sure that it agrees with the accounting records.
• An employee stealing assets	• Segregate duties so that the same employee does not have physical custody of an asset and the ability to account for it.
• An employee accessing unauthorized information	• Create password-protected barriers that prohibit employees from obtaining information not needed to do their jobs.
• Inaccurate budget estimates causing excessive or insufficient production	• Implement a rigorous budget review process.
• Failing to comply with equal employment opportunity laws	• Create a report that tracks key metrics related to compliance with the laws.

help reduce each of the risks mentioned in the left-hand column of the exhibit. Again, the list of controls is far from exhaustive, rather it is meant to be illustrative.

In conclusion, a sophisticated enterprise risk management system cannot guarantee that a company will be able to satisfy the needs of its stakeholders. Nonetheless, many companies understand that managing risks is a superior alternative to reacting, perhaps too late, to unfortunate events.

Managing Weather Risk

IN BUSINESS

The National Oceanic and Atmospheric Administration claims that the weather influences one-third of the U.S. gross domestic product. In 2004, the word "unseasonable" was used by more than 120 publicly traded companies to explain unfavorable financial performance. Indeed, it would be easy to conclude that the weather poses an uncontrollable risk to businesses, right? Wrong! Weather risk management is a growing industry with roughly 80 companies offering weather risk management services to clients.

For example, Planalytics is a weather consulting firm that helps Wise Metal Group, an aluminum can sheeting manufacturer, manage its natural gas purchases. Wise's $3 million monthly gas bill fluctuates sharply depending on the weather. Planalytics' software helps Wise plan its gas purchases in advance of changing temperatures. Beyond influencing natural gas purchases, the weather can also delay the boats that deliver Wise's raw materials and it can affect Wise's sales to the extent that cooler weather conditions lead to a decline in canned beverage sales.

Source: Abraham Lustgarten, "Getting Ahead of the Weather," *Fortune*, February 7, 2005, pp. 87–94.

THE CERTIFIED MANAGEMENT ACCOUNTANT (CMA)

An individual who possesses the necessary qualifications and who passes a rigorous professional exam earns the right to be known as a *Certified Management Accountant (CMA)*. In addition to the prestige that accompanies a professional designation, CMAs are often given greater responsibilities and higher compensation than those who do not have such a designation. Information about becoming a CMA and the CMA program can be accessed on the Institute of Management Accountants' (IMA) website at www.imanet.org or by calling 1-800-638-4427.

To become a Certified Management Accountant, the following four steps must be completed:

1. File an Application for Admission and register for the CMA examination.
2. Pass all four parts of the CMA examination within a three-year period.
3. Satisfy the experience requirement of two continuous years of professional experience in management and/or financial accounting prior to or within seven years of passing the CMA examination.
4. Comply with the IMA Statement of Ethical Professional Practice.

How's the Pay?

IN BUSINESS

The Institute of Management Accountants has created the following table that allows an individual to estimate what his salary would be as a management accountant. (The table below applies specifically to men. A similar table exists for women.)

(continued)

			Your Calculation
Start with this base amount		$74,779	$74,779
If you are top-level management	ADD	$15,893	
OR, if you are senior-level management	ADD	$6,369	
OR, if you are entry-level management	SUBTRACT	$21,861	
Number of years in the field _____	TIMES	$355	
If you have an advanced degree	ADD	$13,861	
OR, if you have no degree	SUBTRACT	$19,289	
If you hold the CMA	ADD	$13,619	
If you hold the CPA	ADD	$6,832	
If you have had one or more career interruptions	SUBTRACT	$13,367	_____
Your estimated salary level			_____

For example, if you make it to top-level management in ten years, have an advanced degree and a CMA, and no career interruptions, your estimated salary would be $121,702 (= $74,779 + $15,893 + (10 × $355) + $13,861 + $13,619).

Source: David L. Schroeder and Karl E. Reichardt, "2004 Salary Survey," *Strategic Finance*, June 2005, pp. 28–43.

SUMMARY

Successful companies follow strategies that differentiate themselves from competitors. Strategies often focus on three customer value propositions—customer intimacy, operational excellence, and product leadership.

Most organizations rely on decentralization to some degree. Decentralization is formally depicted in an organization chart that shows who works for whom and which units perform line and staff functions.

Lean Production, the Theory of Constraints, and Six Sigma are three management approaches that focus on business processes. Lean Production organizes resources around business processes and pulls units through those processes in response to customer orders. The result is lower inventories, fewer defects, less wasted effort, and quicker customer response times. The Theory of Constraints emphasizes the importance of managing an organization's constraints. Since the constraint is whatever is holding back the organization, improvement efforts usually must be focused on the constraint to be effective. Six Sigma uses the DMAIC (Define, Measure, Analyze, Improve, and Control) framework to eliminate non-value-added activities and to improve processes.

E-commerce and enterprise systems are being used to reshape business practices. An enterprise system integrates data across the organization in a single software system that makes the same data available to all managers.

Ethical behavior is the foundation of a successful market economy. If we cannot trust others to act ethically in their business dealings with us, we will be inclined to invest less, scrutinize purchases more, and generally waste time and money trying to protect ourselves from the unscrupulous—resulting in fewer goods available to consumers at higher prices and lower quality.

Unfortunately, trust in our corporate governance system has been undermined in recent years by numerous high-profile financial reporting scandals. The Sarbanes-Oxley Act of 2002 was passed with the objective of improving the reliability of the financial disclosures provided by publicly traded companies.

GLOSSARY

At the end of each chapter, a list of key terms for review is given, along with the definition of each term. (These terms are printed in boldface where they are defined in the chapter.) Carefully study each term to be sure you understand its meaning. The list for the Prologue follows.

Business process A series of steps that are followed to carry out some task in a business. (p. 6)

Chief financial officer (CFO) The member of the top management team who is responsible for providing timely and relevant data to support planning and control activities and for preparing financial statements for external users. (p. 5)

Controller The member of the top management team who is responsible for providing relevant and timely data to managers and for preparing financial statements for external users. The controller reports to the CFO. (p. 5)

Constraint Anything that prevents an organization or individual from getting more of what it wants. (p. 9)

Corporate governance The system by which a company is directed and controlled. If properly implemented it should provide incentives for top management to pursue objectives that are in the interests of the company and it should effectively monitor performance. (p. 19)

Decentralization The delegation of decision-making authority throughout an organization by providing managers with the authority to make decisions relating to their area of responsibility. (p. 5)

Enterprise system A software system that integrates data from across an organization into a single centralized database that enables all employees to access a common set of data. (p. 13)

Enterprise risk management A process used by a company to help identify the risks that it faces and to develop responses to those risks that enable the company to be reasonably assured of meeting its goals. (p. 22)

Just-In-Time (JIT) A production and inventory control system in which materials are purchased and units are produced only as needed to meet actual customer demand. (p. 8)

Lean thinking model A five-step management approach that organizes resources around the flow of business processes and that pulls units through these processes in response to customer orders. (p. 8)

Line A position in an organization that is directly related to the achievement of the organization's basic objectives. (p. 5)

Non-value-added activity An activity that consumes resources but that does not add value for which customers are willing to pay. (p. 11)

Organization chart A diagram of a company's organizational structure that depicts formal lines of reporting, communication, and responsibility between managers. (p. 5)

Sarbanes-Oxley Act of 2002 Legislation enacted to protect the interests of stockholders who invest in publicly traded companies by improving the reliability and accuracy of the disclosures provided to them. (p. 20)

Six Sigma A method that relies on customer feedback and objective data gathering and analysis techniques to drive process improvement. (p. 10)

Staff A position in an organization that is only indirectly related to the achievement of the organization's basic objectives. Such positions provide service or assistance to line positions or to other staff positions. (p. 5)

Strategy A "game plan" that enables a company to attract customers by distinguishing itself from competitors. (p. 3)

Supply chain management A management approach that coordinates business processes across companies to better serve end consumers. (p. 9)

Theory of Constraints (TOC) A management approach that emphasizes the importance of managing constraints. (p. 9)

Value chain The major business functions that add value to a company's products and services such as research and development, product design, manufacturing, marketing, distribution, and customer service. (p. 7)

1

An Introduction to Managerial Accounting and Cost Concepts

<< **A LOOK BACK**

In the Prologue, we established the business context within which management accounting operates. We discussed topics such as strategy, Lean Production, and corporate governance that influence how managers perform their jobs. In addition, we introduced Good Vibrations, an international retailer of music CDs, and learned about its organizational structure.

A LOOK AT THIS CHAPTER

After describing the three major activities of managers in the context of Good Vibrations, this chapter compares and contrasts financial and managerial accounting. We define many of the terms that are used to classify costs in business. Because these terms will be used throughout the text, you should be sure that you are familiar with each of them.

A LOOK AHEAD >>

Chapters 2, 3, and 4 describe costing systems that are used to compute product costs. Chapter 2 describes job-order costing. Chapter 3 describes activity-based costing, an elaboration of job-order costing. Chapter 4 covers process costing.

CHAPTER OUTLINE

LEARNING OBJECTIVES

After studying Chapter 1, LP 1
you should be able to:

LO1 Identify and give examples of each of the three basic manufacturing cost categories.

LO2 Distinguish between product costs and period costs and give examples of each.

LO3 Prepare an income statement including calculation of the cost of goods sold.

LO4 Prepare a schedule of cost of goods manufactured.

LO5 Define and give examples of variable costs and fixed costs.

LO6 Define and give examples of direct and indirect costs.

LO7 Define and give examples of cost classifications used in making decisions: differential costs, opportunity costs, and sunk costs.

DECISION FEATURE

The Role of Management Accounting

It is estimated that 95% of all finance professionals work inside corporations, governments, and other organizations integrating accounting with operations and reporting to the outside world. While some of the effort expended by these people relates to financial accounting, the profession needs to further stress the role management accountants play within organizations supporting decision making, planning, and control. In short, the emphasis in business and the role of accounting should be more about *doing* business rather than tabulating and reporting historical financial results.

Management accounting is undergoing a renaissance in response to technological changes, globalization, and growing risk management concerns. In these challenging times, management accountants help "steady the ship" by acting as their organization's interpreters, sage advisors, and ethical "keepers of the numbers." Managers understand that good business results come from dynamic processes, procedures, and practices that are well designed and properly implemented and managed. Certified Management Accountants are qualified to help their fellow managers achieve good business results because they have earned an advanced certification that addresses all important aspects of accounting inside organizations.

Source: Conversation with Paul Sharman, CEO of the Institute of Management Accountants.

Managerial accounting is concerned with providing information to managers—that is, people *inside* an organization who direct and control its operations. In contrast, **financial accounting** is concerned with providing information to stockholders, creditors, and others who are *outside* an organization. Managerial accounting provides the essential data that are needed to run organizations. Financial accounting provides the essential data that are used by outsiders to judge a company's past financial performance.

Managerial accountants prepare a variety of reports. Some reports focus on how well managers or business units have performed—comparing actual results to plans and to benchmarks. Some reports provide timely, frequent updates on key indicators such as orders received, order backlog, capacity utilization, and sales. Other analytical reports are prepared as needed to investigate specific problems such as a decline in the profitability of a product line. And yet other reports analyze a developing business situation or opportunity. In contrast, financial accounting is oriented toward producing a limited set of specific prescribed annual and quarterly financial statements in accordance with generally accepted accounting principles (GAAP).

THE WORK OF MANAGEMENT AND THE NEED FOR MANAGERIAL ACCOUNTING INFORMATION

Every organization—large and small—has managers. Someone must be responsible for formulating strategy, making plans, organizing resources, directing personnel, and controlling operations. This is true of the Bank of America, the Peace Corps, the University of Illinois, the Red Cross, and the Coca-Cola Corporation, as well as the local 7-Eleven convenience store. We will use a particular organization—Good Vibrations—to illustrate the work of management. What we have to say about the management of Good Vibrations, however, is very general and can be applied to virtually any organization.

Good Vibrations runs a chain of retail outlets that sell a full range of music CDs. The chain's stores are concentrated in Pacific Rim cities such as Sydney, Singapore, Hong Kong, Beijing, Tokyo, and Vancouver. The company has found that the best way to generate sales, and profits, is to create an exciting shopping environment following a customer intimacy strategy. Consequently, the company puts a great deal of effort into planning the layout and decor of its stores—which are often quite large and extend over several floors in key downtown locations. Management knows that different types of clientele are attracted to different kinds of music. The international rock section is decorated with bold, brightly colored graphics, and the aisles are purposely narrow to create a crowded feeling much like one would experience at a popular nightclub on Friday night. In contrast, the classical music section is wood-paneled and fully sound insulated, with the rich, spacious feeling of a country club meeting room.

Managers at Good Vibrations, like managers everywhere, carry out three major activities—*planning, directing and motivating,* and *controlling.* **Planning** involves establishing a basic strategy, selecting a course of action, and specifying how the action will be implemented. **Directing and motivating** involves mobilizing people to carry out plans and run routine operations. **Controlling** involves ensuring that the plan is actually carried out and is appropriately modified as circumstances change. Management accounting information plays a vital role in these basic management activities—but most particularly in the planning and control functions.

Planning

An important part of planning is to identify alternatives and then to select from among the alternatives the one that best fits the organization's strategy and objectives. The basic objective of Good Vibrations is to earn profits for the owners of the company by providing superior service at competitive prices in as many markets as possible. To further this strategy, every year top management carefully considers a range of options, or alternatives, for expanding into new geographic markets. This year management is considering opening new stores in Shanghai, Los Angeles, and Auckland.

When making this choice, management must balance the potential benefits of opening a new store against the costs and demands on the company's resources. Management knows from bitter experience that opening a store in a major new market is a big step that cannot be taken lightly. It requires enormous amounts of time and energy from the company's most experienced, talented, and busy professionals. When the company attempted to open stores in both Beijing and Vancouver in the same year, resources were stretched too thinly. The result was that neither store opened on schedule, and operations in the rest of the company suffered. Therefore, Good Vibrations plans very carefully before entering a new market.

Among other data, top management looks at the sales volumes, profit margins, and costs of the company's established stores in similar markets. These data, supplied by the management accountant, are combined with projected sales volume data at the proposed new locations to estimate the profits that would be generated by the new stores. In general, virtually all important alternatives considered by management in the planning process impact revenues or costs, and management accounting data are essential in estimating those impacts.

After considering all of the alternatives, Good Vibrations' top management decided to open a store in the booming Shanghai market in the third quarter of the year, but to defer opening any other new stores to another year. As soon as this decision was made, detailed plans were drawn up for all parts of the company that would be involved in the Shanghai opening. For example, the Personnel Department's travel budget was increased, since it would be providing extensive on-site training to the new personnel hired in Shanghai.

As in the case of the Personnel Department, the plans of management are often expressed formally in **budgets,** and the term *budgeting* is generally used to describe this part of the planning process. Budgets are usually prepared under the direction of the *controller,* who is the manager in charge of the Accounting Department. Typically, budgets are prepared annually and represent management's plans in specific, quantitative terms. In addition to a travel budget, the Personnel Department will be given goals in terms of new hires, courses taught, and detailed breakdowns of expected expenses. Similarly, the store managers will be given targets for sales volume, profit, expenses, pilferage losses, and employee training. Good Vibrations' management accountants will collect, analyze, and summarize these data in the form of budgets.

Directing and Motivating

In addition to planning for the future, managers oversee day-to-day activities and try to keep the organization functioning smoothly. This requires motivating and directing people. Managers assign tasks to employees, arbitrate disputes, answer questions, solve on-the-spot problems, and make many small decisions that affect customers and employees. In effect, directing is that part of a manager's job that deals with the routine and the here and now. Managerial accounting data, such as daily sales reports, are often used in this type of day-to-day activity.

Controlling

In carrying out the **control** function, managers seek to ensure that the plan is being followed. **Feedback,** which signals whether operations are on track, is the key to effective control. In sophisticated organizations, this feedback is provided by various detailed reports. One of these reports, which compares budgeted to actual results, is called a **performance report.** Performance reports suggest where operations are not proceeding as planned and where some parts of the organization may require additional attention. For example, the manager of the new Shanghai store will be given sales volume, profit, and expense targets. As the year progresses, performance reports will be constructed that compare actual sales volume, profit, and expenses to the targets. If the actual results fall below the targets, top management will be alerted that the Shanghai store requires more attention. Experienced

EXHIBI 1-1 The Planning and Control Cycle

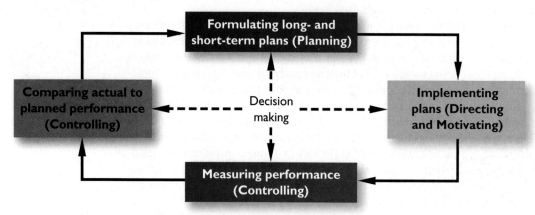

personnel can be flown in to help the new manager, or top management may conclude that its plans need to be revised. As we shall see in later chapters, one of the central purposes of managerial accounting is to provide this kind of feedback to managers.

The End Results of Managers' Activities

When a customer enters a Good Vibrations store, the results of management's planning, directing and motivating, and controlling activities are evident in the many details that make the difference between a pleasant and an irritating shopping experience. The store is clean, fashionably decorated, and logically laid out. Featured artists' videos are displayed on TV monitors throughout the store, and the background rock music is loud enough to send older patrons scurrying for the classical music section. Popular CDs are in stock, and the latest hits are available for private listening on earphones. Specific titles are easy to find. Regional music, such as CantoPop in Hong Kong, is prominently featured. Checkout clerks are alert, friendly, and efficient. In short, what the customer experiences doesn't simply happen; it is the result of the efforts of managers who visualize and then fit together the processes that are needed to get the job done.

The Planning and Control Cycle

Exhibit 1–1 depicts the work of management in the form of the *planning and control cycle*. The **planning and control cycle** involves the smooth flow of management activities from planning through directing and motivating, controlling, and then back to planning again. All of these activities involve decision making, which is the hub around which the other activities revolve.

COMPARISON OF FINANCIAL AND MANAGERIAL ACCOUNTING

Financial accounting reports are prepared for external parties such as shareholders and creditors, whereas managerial accounting reports are prepared for managers inside the organization. This contrast in orientation results in a number of major differences between financial and managerial accounting, even though they often rely on the same underlying financial data. Exhibit 1–2 summarizes these differences.

As shown in Exhibit 1–2, financial and managerial accounting differ not only in their orientation but also in their emphasis on the past and the future, in the type of data provided to users, and in several other ways. These differences are discussed in the following paragraphs.

Emphasis on the Future

Since *planning* is such an important part of the manager's job, managerial accounting has a strong future orientation. In contrast, financial accounting primarily summarizes past

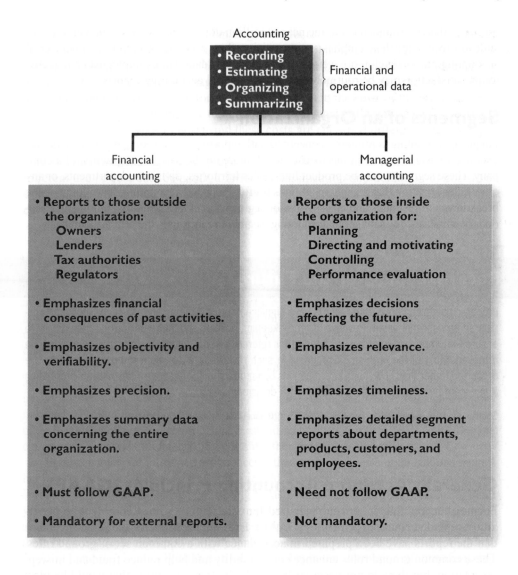

EXHIBIT 1–2
Comparison of Financial and
Managerial Accounting

financial transactions. These summaries may be useful in planning, but only to a point. The future is not simply a reflection of what has happened in the past. Changes constantly occur in economic conditions, customer needs and desires, competitive conditions, and so on. All of these changes demand that the manager's planning be based in large part on estimates of what will happen rather than on summaries of what has already happened.

Relevance of Data

Financial accounting data should be objective and verifiable. However, for internal uses, managers want information that is relevant even if it is not completely objective or verifiable. By relevant, we mean *appropriate for the problem at hand.* For example, it is difficult to verify estimated sales volumes for a proposed new store at Good Vibrations, but this is exactly the type of information that is most useful to managers. Managerial accounting should be flexible enough to provide whatever data are relevant for a particular decision.

Less Emphasis on Precision

Making sure that dollar amounts are accurate down to the last dollar or penny takes time and effort. While that kind of accuracy is required for external reports, most managers would rather have a good estimate immediately than wait for a more precise answer later. For this reason, managerial accountants often place less emphasis on precision than financial accountants do. For example, in a decision involving hundreds of millions of dollars,

Manufacturing Companies: Classifications of Inventory

Raw Materials

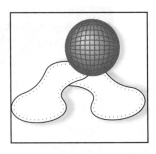

Work in Process

Finished Goods

COST CLASSIFICATIONS ON FINANCIAL STATEMENTS

In this section of the chapter, we compare the cost classifications used on the financial statements of manufacturing and merchandising companies. The financial statements prepared by a *manufacturing* company are more complex than the statements prepared by a merchandising company because a manufacturing company must produce its goods as well as market them. The production process involves many costs that do not exist in a merchandising company, and these costs must be properly accounted for on the manufacturing company's financial statements. In this section, we explain how these costs are recorded on the balance sheet. In the following section, we explain how they are recorded on the income statement.

The Balance Sheet

The balance sheet, or statement of financial position, of a manufacturing company is similar to that of a merchandising company. However, their inventory accounts differ. A merchandising company has only one class of inventory—goods purchased from suppliers for resale to customers. In contrast, manufacturing companies have three classes of inventories—*raw materials, work in process,* and *finished goods.* Raw materials, as we've noted, are the materials that are used to make a product. **Work in process** consists of units of product that are only partially complete and will require further work before they are ready for sale to a customer. **Finished goods** consist of completed units of product that have not yet been sold to customers. Ordinarily, the sum total of these three categories of inventories is the only amount shown on the balance sheet in external reports. However, the footnotes to the financial statements often provide more detail.

We will use two companies—Graham Manufacturing and Reston Bookstore—to illustrate the concepts discussed in this section. Graham Manufacturing is located in Portsmouth, New Hampshire, and makes precision brass fittings for yachts. Reston Bookstore is a small bookstore in Reston, Virginia, specializing in books about the Civil War.

The footnotes to Graham Manufacturing's Annual Report reveal the following information concerning its inventories:

Graham Manufacturing Corporation Inventory Accounts		
	Beginning Balance	Ending Balance
Raw materials	$ 60,000	$ 50,000
Work in process	90,000	60,000
Finished goods	125,000	175,000
Total inventory accounts	$275,000	$285,000

Graham Manufacturing's raw materials inventory consists largely of brass rods and brass blocks. The work in process inventory consists of partially completed brass fittings. The finished goods inventory consists of brass fittings that are ready to be sold to customers.

In contrast, the inventory account at Reston Bookstore consists entirely of the costs of books the company has purchased from publishers for resale to the public. In merchandising companies like Reston, these inventories may be called *merchandise inventory*. The beginning and ending balances in this account appear as follows:

Reston Bookstore Inventory Accounts	Beginning Balance	Ending Balance
Merchandise inventory	$100,000	$150,000

The Income Statement

Exhibit 1–4 compares the income statements of Reston Bookstore and Graham Manufacturing. For purposes of illustration, these statements contain more detail about cost of goods sold than you will generally find in published financial statements.

At first glance, the income statements of merchandising and manufacturing companies like Reston Bookstore and Graham Manufacturing are very similar. The only apparent difference is in the labels of some of the entries in the computation of the cost of goods sold. In the exhibit, the computation of cost of goods sold relies on the following basic

LEARNING OBJECTIVE 3

Prepare an income statement including calculation of the cost of goods sold.

EXHIBIT 1–4 Comparative Income Statements: Merchandising and Manufacturing Companies

Merchandising Company Reston Bookstore		
Sales		$1,000,000
Cost of goods sold:		
Beginning merchandise inventory	$100,000	
Add: Purchases	650,000	
Goods available for sale	750,000	
Deduct: Ending merchandise inventory	150,000	600,000
Gross margin..		400,000
Selling and administrative expenses:		
Selling expense	100,000	
Administrative expense...	200,000	300,000
Net operating income		$ 100,000

The cost of merchandise inventory purchased from outside suppliers during the period.

Manufacturing Company Graham Manufacturing		
Sales		$1,500,000
Cost of goods sold:		
Beginning finished goods inventory..........................	$125,000	
Add: Cost of goods manufactured	850,000	
Goods available for sale	975,000	
Deduct: Ending finished goods inventory	175,000	800,000
Gross margin..		700,000
Selling and administrative expenses:		
Selling expense	250,000	
Administrative expense...	300,000	550,000
Net operating income		$ 150,000

The manufacturing costs associated with the goods that were finished during the period. (See Exhibit 1–6 for details.)

Topic Tackler

PLUS

Concept 1-2

equation for inventory accounts:

BASIC EQUATION FOR INVENTORY ACCOUNTS

$$\begin{array}{c}\text{Beginning}\\\text{balance}\end{array} + \begin{array}{c}\text{Additions}\\\text{to inventory}\end{array} = \begin{array}{c}\text{Ending}\\\text{balance}\end{array} + \begin{array}{c}\text{Withdrawals}\\\text{from inventory}\end{array}$$

The logic underlying this equation, which applies to any inventory account, is illustrated in Exhibit 1–5. The beginning inventory consists of any units that are in the inventory at the beginning of the period. Additions are made to the inventory during the period. The sum of the beginning balance and the additions to the account is the total amount of inventory available. During the period, withdrawals are made from inventory. The ending balance is whatever is left at the end of the period after the withdrawals.

These concepts are used to determine the cost of goods sold for a merchandising company like Reston Bookstore as follows:

COST OF GOODS SOLD IN A MERCHANDISING COMPANY

$$\begin{array}{c}\text{Beginning}\\\text{merchandise}\\\text{inventory}\end{array} + \text{Purchases} = \begin{array}{c}\text{Ending}\\\text{merchandise}\\\text{inventory}\end{array} + \begin{array}{c}\text{Cost of}\\\text{goods sold}\end{array}$$

or

$$\begin{array}{c}\text{Cost of}\\\text{goods sold}\end{array} = \begin{array}{c}\text{Beginning}\\\text{merchandise}\\\text{inventory}\end{array} + \text{Purchases} - \begin{array}{c}\text{Ending}\\\text{merchandise}\\\text{inventory}\end{array}$$

To determine the cost of goods sold in a merchandising company, we only need to know the beginning and ending balances in the Merchandise Inventory account and the purchases. Total purchases can be easily determined in a merchandising company by simply adding together all purchases from suppliers.

The cost of goods sold for a manufacturing company like Graham Manufacturing is determined as follows:

COST OF GOODS SOLD IN A MANUFACTURING COMPANY

$$\begin{array}{c}\text{Beginning finished}\\\text{goods inventory}\end{array} + \begin{array}{c}\text{Cost of goods}\\\text{manufactured}\end{array} = \begin{array}{c}\text{Ending finished}\\\text{goods inventory}\end{array} + \begin{array}{c}\text{Cost of}\\\text{goods sold}\end{array}$$

or

$$\begin{array}{c}\text{Cost of}\\\text{goods sold}\end{array} = \begin{array}{c}\text{Beginning finished}\\\text{goods inventory}\end{array} + \begin{array}{c}\text{Cost of goods}\\\text{manufactured}\end{array} - \begin{array}{c}\text{Ending finished}\\\text{goods inventory}\end{array}$$

To determine the cost of goods sold in a manufacturing company, we need to know the *cost of goods manufactured* and the beginning and ending balances in the Finished Goods inventory account. The **cost of goods manufactured** consists of the manufacturing costs associated with goods that were *finished* during the period. The cost of goods manufactured for Graham Manufacturing is derived in the *schedule of cost of goods manufactured* shown in Exhibit 1–6.

EXHIBIT 1–5 Inventory Flows

Beginning balance   + Additions   = Total available   − Withdrawals   = Ending balance

Schedule of Cost of Goods Manufactured

At first glance, the **schedule of cost of goods manufactured** in Exhibit 1–6 appears complex and perhaps even intimidating. However, it is all quite logical. The schedule of cost of goods manufactured contains the three elements of product costs that we discussed earlier—direct materials, direct labor, and manufacturing overhead.

The direct materials cost of $410,000 is not the cost of raw materials purchased during the period—it is the cost of raw materials *used* during the period. The purchases of raw materials are added to the beginning balance to determine the cost of the materials available for use. The ending raw materials inventory is deducted from this amount to arrive at the cost of raw materials used in production. The sum of the three manufacturing cost elements—direct materials, direct labor, and manufacturing overhead—is the total manufacturing cost of $820,000. However, you'll notice that this is *not* the same thing as the cost of goods manufactured for the period of $850,000. The subtle distinction between the total manufacturing cost and the cost of goods manufactured is very easy to miss. Some of the direct materials, direct labor, and manufacturing overhead costs incurred during the period relate to goods that are not yet completed. As stated above, the cost of goods manufactured consists of the manufacturing costs associated with the goods that were finished during the period. Consequently, adjustments need to be made to the total manufacturing cost of the period for the partially completed goods that were in process at the beginning and at the end of the period. The costs that relate to goods that are not yet completed are shown in the work in process inventory figures at the bottom of the schedule. Note that the beginning work in process inventory must be added to the manufacturing costs of the period, and the ending work in process inventory must be deducted, to arrive at the cost of goods manufactured. Since the work in process account declined by $30,000 during the year ($90,000 – $60,000), this explains the $30,000 difference between the total manufacturing cost and the cost of goods manufactured.

EXHIBIT 1–6   Schedule of Cost of Goods Manufactured

Direct Materials	Direct materials:	
	Beginning raw materials inventory*.	$ 60,000
	Add: Purchases of raw materials	400,000
	Raw materials available for use	460,000
	Deduct: Ending raw materials inventory	50,000
	Raw materials used in production.	$410,000
Direct Labor	Direct labor.	60,000
Manufacturing Overhead	Manufacturing overhead:	
	Insurance, factory.	6,000
	Indirect labor.	100,000
	Machine rental	50,000
	Utilities, factory	75,000
	Supplies	21,000
	Depreciation, factory.	90,000
	Property taxes, factory	8,000
	Total manufacturing overhead cost.	350,000
Cost of Goods Manufactured	Total manufacturing cost.	820,000
	Add: Beginning work in process inventory	90,000
		910,000
	Deduct: Ending work in process inventory	60,000
	Cost of goods manufactured (taken to Exhibit 1–4)	$850,000

*We assume in this example that the Raw Materials inventory account contains only direct materials and that indirect materials are carried in a separate Supplies account. Using a Supplies account for indirect materials is a common practice. In Chapter 2, we discuss the procedure to be followed if both direct and indirect materials are carried in a single account.

PRODUCT COST FLOWS

Earlier in the chapter, we defined product costs as costs incurred to either purchase or manufacture goods. For manufactured goods, these costs consist of direct materials, direct labor, and manufacturing overhead. It will be helpful at this point to look briefly at the flow of costs in a manufacturing company. This will help us understand how product costs move through the various accounts and how they affect the balance sheet and the income statement.

Exhibit 1–7 illustrates the flow of costs in a manufacturing company. Raw materials purchases are recorded in the Raw Materials inventory account. When raw materials are used in production, their costs are transferred to the Work in Process inventory account as direct materials. Notice that direct labor cost and manufacturing overhead cost are added directly to Work in Process. Work in Process can be viewed most simply as products on an assembly line. The direct materials, direct labor, and manufacturing overhead costs added to Work in Process in Exhibit 1–7 are the costs needed to complete these products as they move along this assembly line.

Notice from the exhibit that as goods are completed, their costs are transferred from Work in Process to Finished Goods. Here the goods await sale to customers. As goods are sold, their costs are transferred from Finished Goods to Cost of Goods Sold. At this point the various costs required to make the product are finally recorded as an expense. Until that point, these costs are in inventory accounts on the balance sheet.

Inventoriable Costs

As stated earlier, product costs are often called inventoriable costs. The reason is that these costs go directly into inventory accounts as they are incurred (first into Work in Process and then into Finished Goods), rather than going into expense accounts. Thus, they are termed *inventoriable costs. This is a key concept because such costs can end up on the balance sheet as assets if goods are only partially completed or are unsold at the end of a period.* To illustrate this point, refer again to Exhibit 1–7. At the end of the period, the materials, labor, and overhead costs that are associated with the units in the Work in Process and Finished Goods inventory accounts will appear on the balance sheet as assets. As explained earlier, these costs will not become expenses until the goods are completed and sold.

EXHIBIT 1–7   Cost Flows and Classifications in a Manufacturing Company

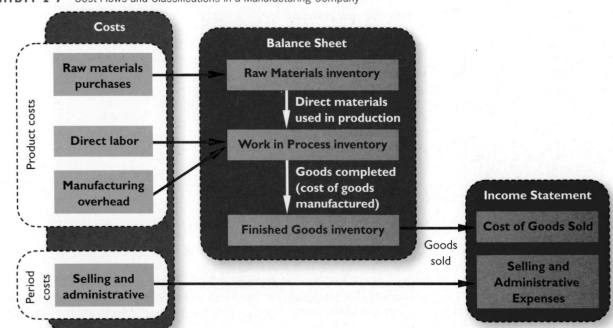

Selling and administrative expenses are not involved in making a product. For this reason, they are not treated as product costs but rather as period costs that are expensed as they are incurred as shown in Exhibit 1–7.

Benetton and the Value Chain

United Colors of Benetton, an Italian apparel company headquartered in Ponzano, is unusual in that it is involved in all activities in the "value chain" from clothing design through manufacturing, distribution, and ultimate sale to customers in Benetton retail outlets. Most companies are involved in only one or two of these activities. Looking at this company allows us to see how costs are distributed across the entire value chain. A recent income statement from the company contained the following data:

	Millions of Euros	Percent of Revenues
Revenues...	1,686	100.0%
Cost of sales..	929	55.1%
Selling and administrative expenses:		
Payroll and related cost......................................	125	7.4%
Distribution and transport...................................	30	1.8%
Sales commissions	74	4.4%
Advertising and promotion	54	3.2%
Depreciation and amortization.............................	78	4.6%
Other expenses..	179	10.6%
Total selling and administrative expenses	540	32.0%

Even though this company spends large sums on advertising and runs its own shops, the cost of sales is still quite high in relation to the net sales—55.1% of net sales. And despite the company's lavish advertising campaigns, advertising and promotion costs amounted to only 3.2% of net sales. (Note: One U.S. dollar was worth about 0.7331 euros at the time of this financial report.)

An Example of Cost Flows

To provide an example of cost flows in a manufacturing company, assume that a company's annual insurance cost is $2,000. Three-fourths of this amount ($1,500) applies to factory operations, and one-fourth ($500) applies to selling and administrative activities. Therefore, $1,500 of the $2,000 insurance cost would be a product (inventoriable) cost and would be added to the cost of the goods produced during the year. This concept is illustrated in Exhibit 1–8, where $1,500 of insurance cost is added to Work in Process. As shown in the exhibit, this portion of the year's insurance cost will not become an expense until the goods that are produced during the year are sold—which may not happen until the following year or even later. Until the goods are sold, the $1,500 will be part of inventories—either Work in Process or Finished Goods—along with the other costs of producing the goods.

By contrast, the $500 of insurance cost that applies to the company's selling and administrative activities will be expensed immediately.

Thus far, we have been mainly concerned with classifications of manufacturing costs for the purpose of determining inventory valuations on the balance sheet and cost of goods sold on the income statement in external financial reports. However, costs are used for many other purposes, and each purpose requires a different classification of costs. We will consider several different purposes for cost classifications in the remaining sections of this chapter. These purposes and the corresponding cost classifications are summarized in Exhibit 1–9. To help keep the big picture in mind, we suggest that you refer back to this exhibit frequently as you progress through the rest of this chapter.

EXHIBIT 1–8 An Example of Cost Flows in a Manufacturing Company

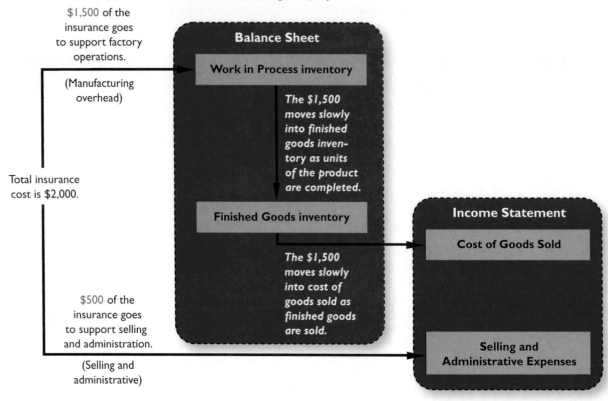

EXHIBIT 1–9
Summary of Cost Classifications

Purpose of Cost Classification	Cost Classifications

Preparing external financial statements	• Product costs (inventoriable)
	  • Direct materials
	  • Direct labor
	  • Manufacturing overhead
	• Period costs (expensed)
	  • Nonmanufacturing costs
	    • Selling costs
	    • Administrative costs

Predicting cost behavior in response to changes in activity	• Variable cost (proportional to activity) • Fixed cost (constant in total)
Assigning costs to cost objects such as departments or products	• Direct cost (can be easily traced) • Indirect cost (cannot be easily traced)
Making decisions	• Differential cost (differs between alternatives) • Sunk cost (past cost not affected by a decision) • Opportunity cost (forgone benefit)

COST CLASSIFICATIONS FOR PREDICTING COST BEHAVIOR

Quite frequently, it is necessary to predict how a certain cost will behave in response to a change in activity. For example, a manager at Qwest may want to estimate the impact a 5% increase in long-distance calls would have on the company's total electric bill. **Cost behavior** refers to how a cost reacts to changes in the level of activity. As the activity level rises and falls, a particular cost may rise and fall as well—or it may remain constant. For planning purposes, a manager must be able to anticipate which of these will happen; and if a cost can be expected to change, the manager must be able to estimate how much it will change. To help make such distinctions, costs are often categorized as variable or fixed.

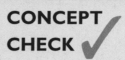

LEARNING OBJECTIVE 5

Define and give examples of variable costs and fixed costs.

Video 1–1

Variable Cost

A **variable cost** is a cost that varies, in total, in direct proportion to changes in the level of activity. The activity can be expressed in many ways, such as units produced, units sold, miles driven, beds occupied, lines of print, hours worked, and so forth. Direct materials is a good example of a variable cost. The cost of direct materials used during a period will vary, in total, in direct proportion to the number of units that are produced. As an example, consider the Saturn Division of General Motors. Each auto requires one battery. As the output of autos increases and decreases, the number of batteries used will increase and decrease proportionately. If auto production goes up 10%, then the number of batteries used will also go up 10%. The concept of a variable cost is shown graphically in Exhibit 1–10.

EXHIBIT 1–10   Variable and Fixed Cost Behavior

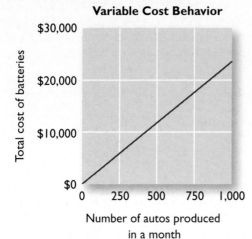

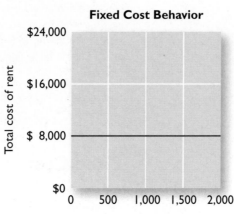

The graph on the left-hand side of Exhibit 1–10 illustrates that the *total* variable cost rises and falls as the activity level rises and falls. This idea is presented below, assuming that a Saturn's battery costs $24:

Number of Autos Produced	Cost per Battery	Total Variable Cost—Batteries
1	$24	$24
500	$24	$12,000
1,000	$24	$24,000

While total variable costs change as the activity level changes, it is important to note that a variable cost is constant if expressed on a *per unit* basis. For example, the per unit cost of batteries remains constant at $24 even though the total cost of the batteries increases and decreases with activity.

There are many examples of costs that are variable with respect to the products and services provided by a company. In a manufacturing company, variable costs include items such as direct materials, shipping costs, sales commissions, and some elements of manufacturing overhead such as lubricants. We will also usually assume that direct labor is a variable cost, although direct labor may act more like a fixed cost in some situations as we shall see in a later chapter. In a merchandising company, the variable costs of carrying and selling products include items such as cost of goods sold, sales commissions, and billing costs. In a hospital, the variable costs of providing health care services to patients would include the costs of supplies, drugs, meals, and perhaps nursing services.

When we say that a cost is variable, we ordinarily mean that it is variable with respect to the amount of goods or services the organization produces. However, costs can be variable with respect to other things. For example, the wages paid to employees at a Blockbuster Video outlet will depend on the number of hours the store is open and not strictly on the number of videos rented. In this case, we would say that wage costs are variable with respect to the hours of operation. Nevertheless, when we say that a cost is variable, we ordinarily mean it is variable with respect to the amount of goods and services produced. This could be how many Jeep Cherokees are produced, how many videos are rented, how many patients are treated, and so on.

IN BUSINESS

Brown Is Thinking Green

United Parcel Service (UPS) truck drivers travel more than 1.3 billion miles annually to deliver more than 4.5 billion packages. Therefore, it should come as no surprise that fuel is a huge variable cost for the company. Even if UPS can shave just a penny of cost from each mile driven, the savings can be enormous. This explains why UPS is so excited about swapping its old diesel powered trucks for diesel-electric hybrid vehicles, which have the potential to cut fuel costs by 50%. Beyond the savings for UPS, the environment would also benefit from the switch since hybrid vehicles cut emissions by 90%. As UPS television commercials ask, "What can Brown do for you?" Thanks to diesel-electric technology, the answer is that Brown can help make the air you breathe a little bit cleaner.

Source: Charles Haddad and Christine Tierney, "FedEx and Brown Are Going Green," *BusinessWeek*, August 4, 2003, pp. 60–62.

Fixed Cost

A **fixed cost** is a cost that remains constant, in total, regardless of changes in the level of activity. Unlike variable costs, fixed costs are not affected by changes in activity. Consequently, as the activity level rises and falls, total fixed costs remain constant unless influenced by some outside force, such as a price change. Rent is a good example of a fixed cost. Suppose the Mayo Clinic rents a machine for $8,000 per month that tests blood samples for the presence of leukemia cells. The $8,000 monthly rental cost will be incurred regardless of the number of tests that may be performed during the month. The concept of a fixed cost is shown graphically on the right-hand side of Exhibit 1–10.

Food Costs at a Luxury Hotel   IN BUSINESS

The Sporthotel Theresa (http://www.theresa.at/), owned and operated by the Egger family, is a four star hotel located in Zell im Zillertal, Austria. The hotel features access to hiking, skiing, biking, and other activities in the Ziller Alps as well as its own fitness facility and spa.

Three full meals a day are included in the hotel room charge. Breakfast and lunch are served buffet-style while dinner is a more formal affair with as many as six courses. A sample dinner menu appears below:

> Tyrolean cottage cheese with homemade bread
> ***
> Salad bar
> ***
> Broccoli-terrine with saddle of venison and smoked goose-breast
> Or
> Chicken liver pâté with gorgonzola cheese ravioli and port wine sauce
> ***
> Clear vegetable soup with fine vegetable strips
> Or
> Whey-yoghurt juice
> ***
> Roulade of pork with zucchini, ham, and cheese on pesto ribbon noodles and saffron sauce
> Or
> Roasted fillet of Irish salmon and prawn with spring vegetables and sesame mash
> Or
> Fresh white asparagus with scrambled egg, fresh herbs, and parmesan
> Or
> Steak of Tyrolean organic beef
> ***
> Strawberry terrine with homemade chocolate ice cream
> Or
> Iced Viennese coffee

The chef, Stefan Egger, believes that food costs are roughly proportional to the number of guests staying at the hotel; that is, they are a variable cost. He must order food two or three days in advance from suppliers, but he adjusts his purchases to the number of guests who are currently staying at the hotel and their consumption patterns. In addition, guests make their selections from the dinner menu early in the day, which helps Stefan plan which foodstuffs will be required for dinner. Consequently, he is able to prepare just enough food so that all guests are satisfied and yet waste is held to a minimum.

Source: Conversation with Stefan Egger, chef at the Sporthotel Theresa.

Very few costs are completely fixed. Most will change if activity changes enough. For example, suppose that the capacity of the leukemia diagnostic machine at the Mayo Clinic is 2,000 tests per month. If the clinic wishes to perform more than 2,000 tests in a month, it would be necessary to rent an additional machine, which would cause a jump in the fixed costs. When we say a cost is fixed, we mean it is fixed within some *relevant range*. The **relevant range** is the range of activity within which the assumptions about variable and fixed costs are valid. For example, the assumption that the rent for diagnostic machines is $8,000 per month is valid within the relevant range of 0 to 2,000 tests per month.

Fixed costs can create confusion if they are expressed on a per unit basis. This is because the average fixed cost per unit increases and decreases *inversely* with changes in activity. In the Mayo Clinic, for example, the average cost per test will fall as the number of tests performed increases because the $8,000 rental cost will be spread over more tests. Conversely, as the number of tests performed in the clinic declines, the average cost per test will rise as the $8,000 rental cost is spread over fewer tests. This concept is illustrated in the table below:

Monthly Rental Cost	Number of Tests Performed	Average Cost per Test
$8,000	10	$800
$8,000	500	$16
$8,000	2,000	$4

Note that if the Mayo Clinic performs only 10 tests each month, the rental cost of the equipment will average $800 per test. But if 2,000 tests are performed each month, the average cost will drop to only $4 per test. More will be said later about the misunderstandings created by this variation in average unit costs.

Examples of fixed costs include straight-line depreciation, insurance, property taxes, rent, supervisory salaries, administrative salaries, and advertising.

A summary of both variable and fixed cost behavior is presented in Exhibit 1–11.

IN BUSINESS

The Power of Shrinking Average Fixed Cost Per Unit

Intel has recently built five new computer chip manufacturing facilities that have put its competitors on the defensive. Each plant can produce chips using a 12-inch wafer that is imprinted with 90-nanometer circuit lines that are 0.1% of the width of a human hair. These plants can produce 1.25 million chips a day or about 375 million chips a year. Better yet, these new plants slash Intel's production costs in half since each plant's volume of output is 2.5 times greater than any of Intel's seven older plants. Building a computer chip manufacturing facility is a very expensive undertaking due to the required investment in fixed equipment costs. So why are Intel's competitors on the defensive? Because they are struggling to match Intel's exceptionally low average fixed cost per unit of output. Or, in an economist's terms they are struggling to match Intel's economies of scale.

Source: Cliff Edwards, Intel, *BusinessWeek*, March 8, 2004, pp. 56–64.

EXHIBIT 1–11
Summary of Variable and Fixed
Cost Behavior

	Behavior of the Cost (within the relevant range)	
Cost	In Total	Per Unit
Variable cost	Total variable cost increases and decreases in proportion to changes in the activity level.	Variable cost per unit remains constant.
Fixed cost	Total fixed cost is not affected by changes in the activity level within the relevant range.	Fixed cost per unit decreases as the activity level rises and increases as the activity level falls.

COST CLASSIFICATIONS FOR ASSIGNING COSTS TO COST OBJECTS

Costs are assigned to cost objects for a variety of purposes including pricing, preparing profitability studies, and controlling spending. A **cost object** is anything for which cost data are desired—including products, product lines, customers, jobs, and organizational subunits. For purposes of assigning costs to cost objects, costs are classified as either *direct* or *indirect*.

LEARNING OBJECTIVE 6

Define and give examples of direct and indirect costs.

Direct Cost

A **direct cost** is a cost that can be easily and conveniently traced to a specified cost object. The concept of direct cost extends beyond just direct materials and direct labor. For example, if Reebok is assigning costs to its various regional and national sales offices, then the salary of the sales manager in its Tokyo office would be a direct cost of that office.

Video 1–1

Indirect Cost

An **indirect cost** is a cost that cannot be easily and conveniently traced to a specified cost object. For example, a Campbell Soup factory may produce dozens of varieties of canned soups. The factory manager's salary would be an indirect cost of a particular variety such as chicken noodle soup. The reason is that the factory manager's salary is incurred as a consequence of running the entire factory—it is not incurred to produce any one soup variety. *To be traced to a cost object such as a particular product, the cost must be caused by the cost object.* The factory manager's salary is called a *common cost* of producing the various products of the factory. A **common cost** is a cost that is incurred to support a number of cost objects but that cannot be traced to them individually. A common cost is a type of indirect cost.

A particular cost may be direct or indirect, depending on the cost object. While the Campbell Soup factory manager's salary is an *indirect* cost of manufacturing chicken noodle soup, it is a *direct* cost of the manufacturing division. In the first case, the cost object is chicken noodle soup. In the second case, the cost object is the entire manufacturing division.

COST CLASSIFICATIONS FOR DECISION MAKING

Costs are an important feature of many business decisions. In making decisions, it is essential to have a firm grasp of the concepts *differential cost, opportunity cost,* and *sunk cost.*

LEARNING OBJECTIVE 7

Define and give examples of cost classifications used in making decisions: differential costs, opportunity costs, and sunk costs.

Differential Cost and Revenue

Decisions involve choosing between alternatives. In business decisions, each alternative will have costs and benefits that must be compared to the costs and benefits of the other available alternatives. A difference in costs between any two alternatives is known as a **differential cost.** A difference in revenues between any two alternatives is known as **differential revenue.**

A differential cost is also known as an **incremental cost,** although technically an incremental cost should refer only to an increase in cost from one alternative to another; decreases in cost should be referred to as *decremental costs.* Differential cost is a broader term, encompassing both cost increases (incremental costs) and cost decreases (decremental costs) between alternatives.

The accountant's differential cost concept can be compared to the economist's marginal cost concept. When speaking of changes in cost and revenue, the economist uses the terms *marginal cost* and *marginal revenue.* The revenue that can be obtained from selling one more unit of product is called marginal revenue, and the cost involved in producing one more unit of product is called marginal cost. The economist's marginal concept is basically the same as the accountant's differential concept applied to a single unit of output.

Video 1–1

The Cost of a Healthier Alternative

McDonald's is under pressure from critics to address the health implications of its menu. In response, McDonald's announced plans to switch from the partially hydrogenated vegetable oil that it had been using to fry foods to a new soybean oil that would cut trans-fat levels by 48%. After making the announcement, McDonald's came to the realization that the unhealthy oil is much cheaper than the soybean oil and it lasts twice as long. What were the cost implications of this change? A typical McDonald's restaurant uses 500 pounds of the relatively unhealthy oil per week at a cost of about $186. In contrast, the same restaurant would need to use 1,000 pounds of the new soybean oil per week at a cost of about $571. This is a differential cost of $385 per restaurant per week. This may seem like a small amount of money until the calculation is expanded to include 13,000 McDonald's restaurants operating 52 weeks a year. Now, the total tab rises to about $260 million per year.

Source: Matthew Boyle, "Can You Really Make Fast Food Healthy?" *Fortune,* August 9, 2004, pp. 134–139.

Differential costs can be either fixed or variable. To illustrate, assume that Nature Way Cosmetics, Inc., is thinking about changing its marketing method from distribution through retailers to distribution by a network of neighborhood sales representatives. Present costs and revenues are compared to projected costs and revenues in the following table:

	Retailer Distribution (present)	Sales Representatives (projected)	Differential Costs and Revenues
Revenues (Variable)	$700,000	$800,000	$100,000
Cost of goods sold (Variable)	350,000	400,000	50,000
Advertising (Fixed)	80,000	45,000	(35,000)
Commissions (Variable)	0	40,000	40,000
Warehouse depreciation (Fixed) . . .	50,000	80,000	30,000
Other expenses (Fixed).	60,000	60,000	0
Total expenses	540,000	625,000	85,000
Net operating income	$160,000	$175,000	$ 15,000

According to the above analysis, the differential revenue is $100,000 and the differential costs total $85,000, leaving a positive differential net operating income of $15,000 under the proposed marketing plan.

The decision of whether Nature Way Cosmetics should stay with the present retail distribution or switch to sales representatives could be made on the basis of the net operating incomes of the two alternatives. As we see in the above analysis, the net operating income under the present distribution method is $160,000, whereas the net operating income with sales representatives is estimated to be $175,000. Therefore, using sales representatives is preferred, since it would result in $15,000 higher net operating income. Note that we would have arrived at exactly the same conclusion by simply focusing on the differential revenues, differential costs, and differential net operating income, which also show a $15,000 advantage for the sales representatives.

In general, only the differences between alternatives are relevant in decisions. Those items that are the same under all alternatives are not affected by the decision and can be ignored. For example, in the Nature Way Cosmetics example above, the "Other expenses" category, which is $60,000 under both alternatives, can be ignored, since it is not affected by the decision. If it were removed from the calculations, the sales representatives would still be preferred by $15,000. This is an extremely important principle in management accounting that we will revisit in later chapters.

Opportunity Cost

Opportunity cost is the potential benefit that is given up when one alternative is selected over another. To illustrate this important concept, consider the following examples:

Example 1   Vicki has a part-time job that pays $200 per week while she attends college. She would like to spend a week at the beach during spring break, and her employer has agreed to give her the time off, but without pay. The $200 in lost wages would be an opportunity cost of taking the week off to be at the beach.

Example 2   Suppose that Neiman Marcus is considering investing a large sum of money in land that may be a site for a future store. Rather than invest the funds in land, the company could invest the funds in high-grade securities. If the land is acquired, the opportunity cost is the investment income that could have been realized by purchasing the securities instead.

Example 3   Steve is employed by a company that pays him a salary of $38,000 per year. He is thinking about leaving the company and returning to school. Since returning to school would require that he give up his $38,000 salary, the forgone salary would be an opportunity cost of seeking further education.

Opportunity costs are not usually found in the accounting records of an organization, but they are costs that must be explicitly considered in every decision a manager makes. Virtually every alternative involves an opportunity cost. In Example 3 above, for instance, the higher income that could be realized in future years as a result of returning to school is an opportunity cost of staying in his present job.

Using Those Empty Seats

Cancer patients who seek specialized or experimental treatments must often travel far from home. Flying on a commercial airline can be an expensive and grueling experience for these patients. Priscilla Blum noted that many corporate jets fly with empty seats and she wondered why these seats couldn't be used for cancer patients. Taking the initiative, she founded Corporate Angel Network (www.corpangelnetwork.org), an organization that arranges free flights on some 1,500 jets from over 500 companies. There are no tax breaks for putting cancer patients in empty corporate jet seats, but filling an empty seat with a cancer patient doesn't involve any significant incremental cost. Since its founding, Corporate Angel Network has provided over 16,000 free flights.

Sources: Scott McCormack, "Waste Not, Want Not," *Forbes*, July 26, 1999, p. 118; Roger McCaffrey, "A True Tale of Angels in the Sky," *The Wall Street Journal*, February 2002, p. A14; and Helen Gibbs, Communication Director, Corporate Angel Network, private communication.

Your Decision to Attend Class

When you make the decision to attend class on a particular day, what are the opportunity costs that are inherent in that decision?

Sunk Cost

A **sunk cost** is a cost *that has already been incurred* and that cannot be changed by any decision made now or in the future. Because sunk costs cannot be changed by any decision, they are not differential costs. And because only differential costs are relevant in a decision, sunk costs can and should be ignored.

To illustrate a sunk cost, assume that a company paid $50,000 several years ago for a special-purpose machine. The machine was used to make a product that is now obsolete and is no longer being sold. Even though in hindsight purchasing the machine may have been unwise, the $50,000 cost has already been incurred and cannot be undone. And it would be folly to continue making the obsolete product in a misguided attempt to "recover" the original cost of the machine. In short, the $50,000 originally paid for the machine is a sunk cost that should be ignored in current decisions.

CONCEPT CHECK

3. Which of the following cost behavior assumptions is true? (You may select more than one answer.)
   a. Variable costs are constant if expressed on a per unit basis.
   b. Total variable costs increase as the level of activity increases.
   c. The average fixed cost per unit increases as the level of activity increases.
   d. Total fixed costs decrease as the level of activity decreases.
4. Which of the following statements is true? (You may select more than one answer.)
   a. A common cost is one type of direct cost.
   b. A sunk cost is usually a differential cost.
   c. Opportunity costs are not usually recorded in the accounts of an organization.
   d. A particular cost may be direct or indirect depending on the cost object.

IN BUSINESS   **What Number Did You Have in Mind?**

Caterpillar has long been at the forefront of management accounting practice. When asked by a manager for the cost of something, accountants at Caterpillar have been trained to ask "What are you going to use the cost for?" One management accountant at Caterpillar explains: "We want to make sure the information is formatted and the right elements are included. Do you need a variable cost, do you need a fully burdened cost, do you need overhead applied, are you just talking about discretionary cost? The cost that they really need depends on the decision they are making."

Source: Gary Siegel, "Practice Analysis: Adding Value," *Strategic Finance*, November 2000, pp. 89–90.

SUMMARY

LO1 Identify and give examples of each of the three basic manufacturing cost categories.
Manufacturing costs consist of two categories of costs that can be conveniently and directly traced to units of product—direct materials and direct labor—and one category that cannot be conveniently traced to units of product—manufacturing overhead.

LO2 Distinguish between product costs and period costs and give examples of each.
For purposes of valuing inventories and determining expenses for the balance sheet and income statement, costs are classified as either product costs or period costs. Product costs are assigned to inventories and are considered assets until the products are sold. A product cost becomes an expense—cost of goods sold—only when the product is sold. In contrast, period costs are taken directly to the income statement as expenses in the period in which they are incurred.

In a merchandising company, product cost is whatever the company paid for its merchandise. For external financial reports in a manufacturing company, product costs consist of all manufacturing costs. In both kinds of companies, selling and administrative costs are considered to be period costs and are expensed as incurred.

LO3 Prepare an income statement including calculation of the cost of goods sold.
See Exhibit 1–4 for examples of income statements for both a merchandising and a manufacturing company. Net operating income is computed by deducting the cost of goods sold and selling and administrative expenses from sales. In a merchandising company, cost of goods sold is calculated by adding purchases to the beginning merchandise inventory and then deducting the ending merchandise inventory. In a manufacturing company, cost of goods sold is computed by adding the cost of goods manufactured to the beginning finished goods inventory and then deducting the ending finished goods inventory.

LO4   Prepare a schedule of cost of goods manufactured.

The cost of goods manufactured is the sum of direct materials, direct labor, and manufacturing overhead costs associated with the goods that were finished during the period. See Exhibit 1–6 for an example of a schedule of cost of goods manufactured.

LO5   Define and give examples of variable costs and fixed costs.

For purposes of predicting cost behavior—how costs will react to changes in activity—costs are commonly categorized as variable or fixed. Total variable costs are strictly proportional to activity. Thus, the variable cost per unit is constant. Total fixed costs remain the same when the level of activity fluctuates within the relevant range. Thus, the average fixed cost per unit decreases as the number of units increases.

LO6   Define and give examples of direct and indirect costs.

A direct cost such as direct materials is a cost that can be easily and conveniently traced to a cost object. An indirect cost is a cost that cannot be easily and conveniently traced to a cost object. For example, the salary of the administrator of a hospital is an indirect cost of serving a particular patient.

LO7   Define and give examples of cost classifications used in making decisions: differential costs, opportunity costs, and sunk costs.

The concepts of differential cost and revenue, opportunity cost, and sunk cost are vitally important for purposes of making decisions. Differential costs and revenues refer to the costs and revenues that differ between alternatives. Opportunity cost is the benefit that is forgone when one alternative is selected over another. Sunk cost is a cost that occurred in the past and cannot be altered. Differential costs and opportunity costs are relevant in decisions and should be carefully considered. Sunk costs are always irrelevant in decisions and should be ignored.

The various cost classifications discussed in this chapter are different ways of looking at costs. A particular cost, such as the cost of cheese in a taco served at Taco Bell, can be a manufacturing cost, a product cost, a variable cost, a direct cost, and a differential cost—all at the same time. Taco Bell essentially manufactures fast food. Therefore the cost of the cheese in a taco would be considered a manufacturing cost as well as a product cost. In addition, the cost of cheese would be considered variable with respect to the number of tacos served and would be a direct cost of serving tacos. Finally, the cost of the cheese in a taco would be considered a differential cost of the taco.

GUIDANCE ANSWER TO *YOU DECIDE*

Your Decision to Attend Class (p. 51)

Every alternative involves an opportunity cost. Think about what you could be doing instead of attending class.

- You could have been working at a part-time job; you could quantify that cost by multiplying your pay rate by the time you spend preparing for and attending class.
- You could have spent the time studying for another class; the opportunity cost could be measured by the improvement in the grade that would result from spending more time on the other class.
- You could have slept in or taken a nap; depending on your level of sleep deprivation, this opportunity cost might be priceless.

GUIDANCE ANSWERS TO CONCEPT CHECKS

1. **Choices b and d.** Conversion costs do not include direct materials. Prime costs include direct materials and direct labor, which are not part of manufacturing overhead.
2. **Choice c.** The cost of goods manufactured equals the cost of goods sold of $100,000 plus the increase in the inventory account of $30,000.
3. **Choices a and b.** The average fixed cost per unit decreases, rather than increases, as the level of activity increases. Total fixed costs do not change as the level of activity decreases (within the relevant range).
4. **Choices c and d.** A common cost is one type of indirect cost, rather than direct cost. A sunk cost is not a differential cost.

REVIEW PROBLEM 1: COST TERMS

Many new cost terms have been introduced in this chapter. It will take you some time to learn what each term means and how to properly classify costs in an organization. Consider the following example: Chippen Corporation manufactures furniture, including tables. Selected costs are given below:

2. The cost goods sold would be computed as follows:

Finished goods inventory, January 1	$ 260,000
Add: Cost of goods manufactured	1,650,000
Goods available for sale	1,910,000
Deduct: Finished goods inventory, December 31	210,000
Cost of goods sold	$1,700,000

3.

Klear-Seal Corporation
Income Statement
For the Year Ended December 31

Sales		$2,500,000
Cost of goods sold (above)		1,700,000
Gross margin		800,000
Selling and administrative expenses:		
Selling expenses	$140,000	
Administrative expenses	270,000	410,000
Net operating income		$ 390,000

GLOSSARY

Administrative costs   All executive, organizational, and clerical costs associated with the general management of an organization rather than with manufacturing or selling. (p. 35)

Budget   A detailed plan for the future, usually expressed in formal quantitative terms. (p. 29)

Common cost   A cost that is incurred to support a number of cost objects but that cannot be traced to them individually. For example, the wage cost of the pilot of a 747 airliner is a common cost of all of the passengers on the aircraft. Without the pilot, there would be no flight and no passengers. But no part of the pilot's wage is caused by any one passenger taking the flight. (p. 49)

Control   The process of instituting procedures and obtaining feedback to ensure that all parts of the organization are functioning effectively and moving toward overall company goals. (p. 29)

Controlling   Ensuring that the plan is actually carried out and is appropriately modified as circumstances change. (p. 28)

Conversion cost   Direct labor cost plus manufacturing overhead cost. (p. 36)

Cost behavior   The way in which a cost reacts to changes in the level of activity. (p. 45)

Cost object   Anything for which cost data are desired. Examples of cost objects are products, customers, jobs, and parts of the organization such as departments or divisions. (p. 49)

Cost of goods manufactured   The manufacturing costs associated with the goods that were finished during the period. (p. 40)

Differential cost   A difference in cost between any two alternatives. Also see *Incremental cost*. (p. 49)

Differential revenue   A difference in revenue between two alternatives. (p. 49)

Direct cost   A cost that can be easily and conveniently traced to a specified cost object. (p. 49)

Direct labor   Labor costs that can be easily traced to individual units of product. Also called *touch labor*. (p. 34)

Direct materials   Materials that become an integral part of a finished product and whose costs can be conveniently traced to it. (p. 33)

Directing and motivating   Mobilizing people to carry out plans and run routine operations. (p. 28)

Feedback   Accounting and other reports that help managers monitor performance and focus on problems and/or opportunities that might otherwise go unnoticed. (p. 29)

Financial accounting   The phase of accounting concerned with providing information to stockholders, creditors, and others outside the organization. (p. 28)

Finished goods   Units of product that have been completed but have not yet been sold to customers. (p. 38)

Fixed cost   A cost that remains constant, in total, regardless of changes in the level of activity within the relevant range. If a fixed cost is expressed on a per unit basis, it varies inversely with the level of activity. (p. 46)

Incremental cost   An increase in cost between two alternatives. Also see *Differential cost.* (p. 49)

Indirect cost   A cost that cannot be easily and conveniently traced to a specified cost object. (p. 49)

Indirect labor   The labor costs of janitors, supervisors, materials handlers, and other factory workers that cannot be conveniently traced to particular products. (p. 34)

Indirect materials   Small items of material such as glue and nails that may be an integral part of a finished product but whose costs cannot be easily or conveniently traced to it. (p. 34)

Inventoriable costs   Synonym for *product costs.* (p. 36)

Managerial accounting   The phase of accounting concerned with providing information to managers for use in planning and controlling operations and in decision making. (p. 28)

Manufacturing overhead   All manufacturing costs except direct materials and direct labor. (p. 34)

Opportunity cost   A potential benefit that is given up when one alternative is selected over another. (p. 51)

Performance report   A detailed report comparing budgeted data to actual data. (p. 29)

Period costs   Costs that are taken directly to the income statement as expenses in the period in which they are incurred or accrued. (p. 36)

Planning   Selecting a course of action and specifying how the action will be implemented. (p. 28)

Planning and control cycle   The flow of management activities through planning, directing and motivating, and controlling, and then back to planning again. (p. 30)

Prime cost   Direct materials cost plus direct labor cost. (p. 36)

Product costs   All costs that are involved in acquiring or making a product. In the case of manufactured goods, these costs consist of direct materials, direct labor, and manufacturing overhead. Also see *Inventoriable costs.* (p. 35)

Raw materials   Materials that are used to make a product. (p. 33)

Relevant range   The range of activity within which assumptions about variable and fixed cost behavior are valid. (p. 48)

Schedule of cost of goods manufactured   A schedule showing the direct materials, direct labor, and manufacturing overhead costs incurred during a period and the portion of those costs that are assigned to Work in Process and Finished Goods. (p. 41)

Segment   Any part of an organization that can be evaluated independently of other parts and about which the manager seeks financial data. Examples include a product line, a sales territory, a division, or a department. (p. 32)

Selling costs   All costs that are incurred to secure customer orders and get the finished product or service into the hands of the customer. (p. 35)

Sunk cost   A cost that has already been incurred and that cannot be changed by any decision made now or in the future. (p. 51)

Variable cost   A cost that varies, in total, in direct proportion to changes in the level of activity. (p. 45)

Work in process   Units of product that are only partially complete and will require further work before they are ready for sale to a customer. (p. 38)

Multiple-choice questions are provided on the text website at www.mhhe.com/brewer4e.

Quiz 1

QUESTIONS

1–1   What is the basic difference between the purposes of financial and managerial accounting?

1–2   What are the three major activities of a manager?

1–3   Describe the four steps in the planning and control cycle.

1–4   What are the major differences between financial and managerial accounting?

1–5   What are the three major elements of product costs in a manufacturing company?

1–6   Define the following: (a) direct materials, (b) indirect materials, (c) direct labor, (d) indirect labor, and (e) manufacturing overhead.

1–7   Explain the difference between a product cost and a period cost.

1–8   Describe how the income statement of a manufacturing company differs from the income statement of a merchandising company.

1–9   Describe the schedule of cost of goods manufactured? How does it tie into the income statement?

1–10   What inventory accounts are used by a manufacturing company? A merchandising company?

1–11   Why are product costs sometimes called inventoriable costs? Describe the flow of such costs in a manufacturing company from the point of incurrence until they finally become expenses on the income statement.

1–12   Is it possible for costs such as salaries or depreciation to end up as assets on the balance sheet? Explain.

1–13   What is meant by the term *cost behavior*?

B

from a restrictive angle. The new computer displays would not require any new wiring. The hotel's chef believes the funds would be better spent on a new bulk freezer for the kitchen.

Required:

For each of the items below, indicate by placing an X in the appropriate column whether it should be considered a differential cost, an opportunity cost, or a sunk cost in the decision to replace the old computer terminals with new flat-panel displays. If none of the categories apply for a particular item, leave all columns blank.

Item	Differential Cost	Opportunity Cost	Sunk Cost
Ex. Cost of electricity to run the terminals	X		
1. Cost of the new flat-panel displays			
2. Cost of the old computer terminals			
3. Rent on the space occupied by the registration desk			
4. Wages of registration desk personnel			
5. Benefits from a new freezer			
6. Costs of maintaining the old computer terminals			
7. Cost of removing the old computer terminals			
8. Cost of existing registration desk wiring			

EXERCISES

EXERCISE 1–8 Preparation of a Schedule of Cost of Goods Manufactured and Cost of Goods Sold (LO3, LO4)

The following cost and inventory data are taken from the accounting records of Eccles Company for the year just completed:

Costs incurred:

Advertising expense	$100,000
Direct labor cost	$90,000
Purchases of raw materials	$132,000
Rent, factory building	$80,000
Indirect labor	$56,300
Sales commissions	$35,000
Utilities, factory	$9,000
Maintenance, factory equipment	$24,000
Supplies, factory	$700
Depreciation, office equipment	$8,000
Depreciation, factory equipment	$40,000

	Beginning of Year	End of Year
Inventories:		
Raw materials	$8,000	$10,000
Work in process	$5,000	$20,000
Finished goods	$70,000	$25,000

Required:

1. Prepare a schedule of cost of goods manufactured.
2. Prepare the cost of goods sold section of Eccles Company's income statement for the year.

EXERCISE 1–9 Product Cost Flows; Product versus Period Costs (LO2, LO3)

Ryser Company was organized on May 1. On that date the company purchased 35,000 plastic emblems, each with a peel-off adhesive backing. The front of the emblems contained the company's name, accompanied by an attractive logo. Each emblem cost Ryser Company $2.

During May, 31,000 emblems were drawn from the Raw Materials inventory account. Of these, 1,000 were taken by the sales manager to an important sales meeting with prospective customers and handed out as an advertising gimmick. The remaining emblems drawn from inventory were affixed to units of the company's product that were being manufactured during May. Of the units of product having emblems affixed during May, 90% were completed and transferred from Work in Process to Finished Goods. Of the units completed during the month, 75% were sold and shipped to customers.

Required:
1. Determine the cost of emblems that would appear in each of the following accounts at May 31:
   a. Raw Materials.
   b. Work in Process.
   c. Finished Goods.
   d. Cost of Goods Sold.
   e. Advertising Expense.
2. Specify whether each of the above accounts would appear on the balance sheet or on the income statement at May 31.

EXERCISE I–10   Using Cost Terms (LO2, LO5, LO7)
Following are a number of cost terms introduced in the chapter:

period cost	fixed cost
variable cost	prime cost
opportunity cost	conversion cost
product cost	sunk cost

Choose the term or terms above that most appropriately describe the cost identified in each of the following situations. A cost term can be used more than once.

1. Crestline Books, Inc., prints a small book titled *The Pocket Speller.* The paper used to manufacture the book would be called direct materials and classified as a _____. In terms of cost behavior, the paper could also be described as a _____ with respect to the number of books printed.
2. Instead of compiling the words in the book, the author hired by the company could have earned considerable fees consulting with business organizations. The consulting fees forgone by the author would be called _____.
3. The paper and other materials used in the manufacture of the book, combined with the direct labor cost involved, would be called _____.
4. The salary of Crestline Books' president would be classified as a _____.
5. Depreciation on the equipment used to print the book would be classified by Crestline Books as a _____. However, depreciation on any equipment used by the company in selling and administrative activities would be classified as a _____. In terms of cost behavior, depreciation would probably be classified as a _____ with respect to the number of books printed.
6. A _____ is also known as an inventoriable cost, since such costs go into the Work in Process inventory account and then into the Finished Goods inventory account before appearing on the income statement as part of cost of goods sold.
7. Taken together, the direct labor cost and manufacturing overhead cost involved in producing books would be called _____.
8. Crestline Books sells the book through agents who are paid a commission on each book sold. The company would classify these commissions as a _____. In terms of cost behavior, commissions would be classified as a _____.
9. Several hundred copies of the book were left over from the previous edition and are stored in a warehouse. The amount invested in these books would be called a _____.
10. Costs are often classified in several ways. For example, Crestline Books pays $4,000 rent each month on the building that houses its printing press. The rent would be part of manufacturing overhead. In terms of cost behavior, it would be classified as a _____. The rent can also be classified as a _____ and as part of _____.

EXERCISE I–11   Cost Classification (LO5, LO6)
Various costs associated with manufacturing operations are given below:

1. Plastic washers used in assembling autos.
2. Production superintendent's salary.

3. Wages of workers who assemble a product.
4. Electricity to run production equipment.
5. Janitorial salaries.
6. Clay used to make bricks.
7. Rent on a factory building.
8. Wood used to make skis.
9. Screws used to make furniture.
10. A supervisor's salary.
11. Cloth used to make shirts.
12. Depreciation of cafeteria equipment.
13. Glue used to make textbooks.
14. Lubricants for production equipment.
15. Paper used to make textbooks.

Required:
Classify each cost as either variable or fixed with respect to the number of units produced and sold. Also indicate whether each cost would typically be treated as a direct cost or an indirect cost with respect to units of product. Prepare your answer sheet as shown below:

Cost Item	Cost Behavior		To Units of Product	
	Variable	Fixed	Direct	Indirect
Example: Factory insurance		X		X

EXERCISE 1–12   Classification of Costs as Variable or Fixed and as Selling and Administrative or Product (LO2, LO5)
Below are listed various costs that are found in organizations.

1. The costs of turn signal switches used at a General Motors plant. These are one of the parts installed in the steering columns assembled at the plant.
2. Interest expense on CBS's long-term debt.
3. Salespersons' commissions at Avon Products, a company that sells cosmetics door to door.
4. Insurance on one of Cincinnati Milacron's factory buildings.
5. The costs of shipping brass fittings from Graham Manufacturing's plant in New Hampshire to customers in California.
6. Depreciation on the bookshelves at Reston Bookstore.
7. The costs of X-ray film at the Mayo Clinic's radiology lab.
8. The cost of leasing an 800 telephone number at L. L. Bean. The monthly charge for the 800 number is independent of the number of calls taken.
9. The depreciation on the playground equipment at a McDonald's outlet.
10. The cost of mozzarella cheese used at a Pizza Hut outlet.

Required:
Classify each cost as either variable or fixed with respect to the number of units produced and sold. Also classify each cost as either a selling and administrative cost or a product cost. Prepare your answer sheet as shown below, placing X's in the appropriate columns.

Cost Item	Cost Behavior		Selling and Administrative Cost	Product Cost
	Variable	Fixed		

EXERCISE 1–13   Classification of Costs (LO1, LO2, LO5, LO7)
Several years ago Medex Company purchased a small building adjacent to its manufacturing plant in order to have room for expansion when needed. Since the company had no immediate need for the extra space, the building was rented out to another company for a rental revenue of $40,000 per year. The renter's lease

will expire next month, and rather than renew the lease, Medex Company has decided to use the building itself to manufacture a new product.

Direct materials cost for the new product will total $40 per unit. It will be necessary to hire a supervisor to oversee production. Her salary will be $2,500 per month. Workers will be hired to manufacture the new product, with direct labor cost amounting to $18 per unit. Manufacturing operations will occupy all of the building space, so it will be necessary to rent space in a warehouse nearby in order to store finished units of product. The rental cost will be $1,000 per month. In addition, the company will need to rent equipment for use in producing the new product; the rental cost will be $3,000 per month. The company will continue to depreciate the building on a straight-line basis, as in past years. Depreciation on the building is $10,000 per year.

Advertising costs for the new product will total $50,000 per year. Costs of shipping the new product to customers will be $10 per unit. Electrical costs of operating machines will be $2 per unit.

To provide funds to purchase materials, meet payrolls, and so forth, the company will have to liquidate some temporary investments. These investments are presently yielding a return of $6,000 per year.

Required:
Prepare an answer sheet with the following column headings:

Name of the Cost	Variable Cost	Fixed Cost	Product Cost			Period (Selling and Administrative) Cost	Opportunity Cost	Sunk Cost
			Direct Materials	Direct Labor	Manufacturing Overhead			

List the different costs associated with the new product decision down the extreme left column (under Name of the Cost). Then place an X under each heading that helps to describe the type of cost involved. There may be X's under several column headings for a single cost. (For example, a cost may be a fixed cost, a period cost, and a sunk cost; you would place an X under each of these column headings opposite the cost.)

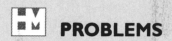

PROBLEMS

PROBLEM 1–14A   Classification of Salary Cost (LO2)

You have just been hired by Luxmor Corporation to fill a new position that was created in response to the upcoming launch of a newly developed product. It is your responsibility to design an advertising campaign for this product's debut in Mexico and Central America.

The company is unsure how to classify your annual salary in its cost records. The company's cost analyst says that your salary should be classified as a manufacturing (product) cost; the controller says that it should be classified as a selling expense; and the president says that it doesn't matter which way your salary cost is classified.

Required:
1. Which viewpoint is correct? Why?
2. From the point of view of the reported net operating income for the year, is the president correct in his statement that it doesn't matter which way your salary cost is classified? Explain.

PROBLEM 1–15A   Working with Incomplete Data from the Income Statement and Schedule of Cost of Goods Manufactured (LO3, LO4)

Data are provided below for four cases. Each case is independent of the others.

CHECK FIGURE
Case 1: Goods available for sale: $59,500

Required:
Supply the missing data in the following cases.

		Case		
	1	**2**	**3**	**4**
Schedule of Cost of Goods Manufactured				
Direct materials	$28,000	$12,000	$18,000	$22,000
Direct labor.	?	11,000	10,000	18,000
Manufacturing overhead.	6,000	8,000	?	5,000
Total manufacturing costs	46,000	?	35,000	?
Beginning work in process inventory	6,500	?	12,000	?
Ending work in process inventory	?	1,500	6,000	15,000
Cost of goods manufactured	$44,500	$34,000	$?	$?
Income Statement				
Sales	$57,000	$42,000	$62,000	$58,000
Beginning finished goods inventory	15,000	9,000	?	13,000
Cost of goods manufactured	?	?	?	41,000
Goods available for sale.	?	?	?	?
Ending finished goods inventory	?	10,000	17,000	16,000
Cost of goods sold	42,500	?	45,000	?
Gross margin	14,500	?	17,000	?
Selling and administrative expenses	?	6,000	?	?
Net operating income.	$ 2,500	$?	$ 2,000	$ 500

CHECK FIGURE
Seeds, earth, pots and
fertilizer: variable, direct
materials

PROBLEM 1–16A   Classification of Various Costs (LO1, LO2, LO5, LO7)

Yuko Makiyama began growing miniature bonsai trees several years ago as a hobby. Her work is quite creative, and it has been so popular with friends and others that she has decided to quit her job in the food industry and grow bonsai trees full time. The salary from Yuko's food industry job is $3,000 per month.

Yuko will rent an airy, brightly lit loft near her home to use as a place for growing the bonsai trees. The rent will be $400 per month. She estimates that the cost of seeds, earth, fertilizers, and pots will be $7 for each finished bonsai tree. She will hire an experienced gardener to plant and water the bonsai trees at a labor rate of $12 per hour. To sell her bonsai trees, Yuko feels that she must launch an advertising campaign that focuses on hard-core gardeners. An advertising agency states that it will handle all advertising for a fee of $550 per month.

Nurseries will sell the bonsai trees on consignment and will be paid a commission of $8 for each tree sold. Production equipment will be rented at a cost of $250 per month. Yuko has already paid the legal and filing fees associated with incorporating her business in the state. These fees amounted to $300. A small room has been located in the area that Yuko will use as a sales office. The rent will be $200 per month. A phone installed in the room for taking orders will cost $30 per month.

Yuko has some money in savings that is earning interest of $3,000 per year. These savings will be withdrawn and used to get the business going. For the time being, Yuko does not intend to draw any salary from the new company.

Required:

1. Prepare an answer sheet with the following column headings:

Name of the Cost	Variable Cost	Fixed Cost	Product Cost			Period (Selling and Administrative) Cost	Opportunity Cost	Sunk Cost
			Direct Materials	Direct Labor	Manufacturing Overhead			

List the different costs associated with the new company down the extreme left column (under Name of the Cost). Then place an X under each heading that helps to describe the type of cost involved. There may be X's under several column headings for a single cost. (That is, a cost may be a fixed cost, a period cost, and a sunk cost; thus you would place an X under each of these column headings opposite the cost.)

Under the Variable Cost column, list only those costs that would be variable with respect to the number of bonsai trees that are produced and sold.

2. All of the costs you have listed above, except one, would be differential costs between the alternatives of Yuko producing bonsai trees or staying with the food industry. Which cost is *not* differential? Explain.

PROBLEM 1–17A Cost Classification and Cost Behavior (LO2, LO5, LO6)

CHECK FIGURE
(1) Total variable cost:
$383,000

The Sloane Company specializes in producing a set of wood patio furniture consisting of a table and four chairs. The set enjoys great popularity, and the company has ample orders to keep production going at its full capacity of 3,000 patio sets per year. Annual cost data at full capacity follow:

Factory labor, direct	$150,000
Advertising	$35,000
Factory supervision	$29,000
Property taxes, factory building	$4,400
Sales commissions	$95,000
Insurance, factory.	$5,600
Depreciation, office equipment.	$5,500
Lease cost, factory equipment	$20,000
Indirect materials, factory	$8,000
Depreciation, factory building.	$23,000
General office supplies (billing)	$4,000
General office salaries	$72,000
Direct materials used (wood, bolts, etc.)	$111,000
Utilities, factory.	$15,000

Required:

1. Prepare an answer sheet with the column headings shown below. Enter each cost item on your answer sheet, placing the dollar amount under the appropriate headings. As examples, this has been done already for the first two items in the list above. Note that each cost item is classified in two ways: first, as variable or fixed with respect to the number of units produced and sold; and second, as a selling and administrative cost or a product cost. (If the item is a product cost, it should also be classified as either direct or indirect with respect to units of product.

	Cost Behavior		Selling or Administrative	Product Cost	
Cost Item	Variable	Fixed	Cost	Direct	Indirect
Factory labor, direct . . .	$150,000			$150,000	
Advertising		$35,000	$35,000		

2. Total the dollar amounts in each of the columns in (1) above. Compute the average product cost per patio set.
3. Assume that production drops to 2,800 sets annually. Would you expect the average product cost per patio set to increase, decrease, or remain unchanged? Explain. No computations are necessary.
4. Refer to the original data. The president's brother-in-law has considered making himself a patio set and has priced the necessary materials at a building supply store. The brother-in-law has asked the president if he could purchase a patio set from the Sloane Company "at cost," and the president agreed to let him do so.
   a. Would you expect any disagreement between the two men over the price the brother-in-law should pay? Explain. What price does the president probably have in mind? The brother-in-law?
   b. Since the company is operating at full capacity, what cost term used in the chapter might be justification for the president to charge the full, regular price to the brother-in-law and still be selling "at cost"?

PROBLEM 1–18A Cost Classification (LO2, LO5, LO6)

Listed below are a number of costs found in organizations.

1. Wood used in producing furniture.
2. Insurance, finished goods warehouses.
3. Ink used in book production.

CHECK FIGURE
Insurance, finished goods
warehouses: fixed, selling
cost

4. Advertising costs.
5. Property taxes, factory.
6. Thread in a garment factory.
7. Wage of receptionist, executive offices.
8. Salespersons' commissions.
9. Shipping costs on merchandise sold.
10. Depreciation, executive autos.
11. Magazine subscriptions, factory lunchroom.
12. Wages of workers assembling computers.
13. Executive life insurance.
14. Boxes used for packaging television sets.
15. Zippers used in jeans production.
16. Fringe benefits, assembly-line workers.
17. Supervisor's salary, factory.
18. Billing costs.
19. Packing supplies for international shipments.
20. Lubricants for production equipment.

Required:

Prepare an answer sheet with column headings as shown below. For each cost item, indicate whether it would be variable or fixed with respect to the number of units produced and sold; and then whether it would be a selling cost, an administrative cost, or a manufacturing cost. If it is a manufacturing cost, indicate whether it would typically be treated as a direct cost or an indirect cost with respect to units of product. Three sample answers are provided for illustration.

Cost Item	Variable or Fixed	Selling Cost	Administrative Cost	Manufacturing (Product) Cost Direct	Manufacturing (Product) Cost Indirect
Direct labor.	V			X	
Executive salaries	F		X		
Factory rent	F				X

CHECK FIGURE
(1) Cost of goods manufactured: $244,000

PROBLEM 1–19A   Schedule of Cost of Goods Manufactured; Income Statement; Cost Behavior (LO1, LO2, LO3, LO4, LO5)

Selected account balances for the year ended December 31 are provided below for Rolling Company:

Selling and administrative salaries.	$55,000
Insurance, factory.	$6,000
Utilities, factory.	$10,000
Purchases of raw materials	$76,000
Indirect labor	$3,000
Direct labor.	?
Advertising expense.	$26,000
Cleaning supplies, factory	$4,000
Sales commissions	$33,000
Rent, factory building	$49,000
Maintenance, factory	$15,000

Inventory balances at the beginning and end of the year were as follows:

	Beginning of of the Year	End of the Year
Raw materials	$3,000	$9,000
Work in process	?	$13,000
Finished goods.	$25,000	?

The total manufacturing costs for the year were $242,000; the goods available for sale totaled $269,000; and the cost of goods sold totaled $229,000.

Required:

1. Prepare a schedule of cost of goods manufactured and the cost of goods sold section of the company's income statement for the year.
2. The company produced the equivalent of 7,000 units during the year. Compute the average cost per unit for direct materials used and the average cost per unit for rent on the factory building.
3. In the following year the company expects to produce 5,000 units. What average cost per unit and total cost would you expect to be incurred for direct materials? For rent on the factory building? (Assume that direct materials is a variable cost and that rent is a fixed cost.)
4. Explain to the president the reason for any difference in the average cost per unit between (2) and (3) above.

PROBLEM 1–20A   Schedule of Cost of Goods Manufactured; Income Statement; Cost Behavior (LO3, LO4, LO5)

Various cost and sales data for Jaskot Company for the just completed year follow:

CHECK FIGURE
(1) Cost of goods manufactured: $233,000

Microsoft Excel		
	A	B
1	Finished goods inventory, beginning	$16,000
2	Finished goods inventory, ending	$14,000
3	Depreciation, factory	$21,000
4	Administrative expenses	$45,000
5	Utilities, factory	$12,000
6	Maintenance, factory	$26,000
7	Supplies, factory	$6,000
8	Insurance, factory	$7,000
9	Purchases of raw materials	$72,000
10	Raw materials inventory, beginning	$5,000
11	Raw materials inventory, ending	$8,000
12	Direct labor	$61,000
13	Indirect labor	$32,000
14	Work in process inventory, beginning	$13,000
15	Work in process inventory, ending	$14,000
16	Sales	$355,000
17	Selling expenses	$61,000

Required:

1. Prepare a schedule of cost of goods manufactured.
2. Prepare an income statement.
3. The company produced the equivalent of 12,000 units of product during the year just completed. What was the average cost per unit for direct materials? What was the average cost per unit for factory depreciation?
4. The company expects to produce 10,000 units of product during the coming year. What average cost per unit and what total cost would you expect the company to incur for direct materials at this level of activity? For factory depreciation? (In preparing your answer, assume that direct materials is a variable cost and that depreciation is a fixed cost that is computed on a straight-line basis.)
5. Explain to the president any difference in the average cost per unit between (3) and (4) above.

PROBLEM 1–21A   Schedule of Cost of Goods Manufactured; Income Statement (LO3, LO4)

Madlinx Company was organized on April 1 of the current year. After five months of start-up losses, management had expected to earn a profit during September. Management was disappointed, however, when the income statement for September also showed a loss. September's income

CHECK FIGURE
(1) Cost of goods manufactured: $185,765

statement follows:

Madlinx Company Income Statement For the Month Ended September 30		
Sales		$266,000
Less operating expenses:		
Indirect labor cost	$ 7,200	
Utilities	9,100	
Direct labor cost	47,000	
Depreciation, factory equipment	10,000	
Raw materials purchased	95,000	
Depreciation, sales equipment	10,400	
Insurance	2,500	
Rent on facilities	27,000	
Selling and administrative salaries	23,000	
Advertising	39,000	270,200
Net operating loss		$ (4,200)

After seeing the $4,200 loss for September, Madlinx's president stated, "I was sure we'd be profitable within six months, but our six months are up and this loss for September is even worse than August's. I think it's time to start looking for someone to buy out the company's assets—if we don't, within a few months there won't be any assets to sell. By the way, I don't see any reason to look for a new controller. We'll just limp along with Harry for the time being."

The company's controller resigned a month ago. Harry, a new inexperienced assistant in the controller's office, prepared the income statement above. Additional information about the company follows:

a. Some 65% of the utilities cost and 70% of the insurance apply to factory operations. The remaining amounts apply to selling and administrative activities.

b. Inventory balances at the beginning and end of September were:

	September 1	September 30
Raw materials	$4,600	$7,000
Work in process	$9,000	$12,000
Finished goods	$24,000	$30,000

c. Only 90% of the rent on facilities applies to factory operations; the remainder applies to selling and administrative activities.

The president has asked you to check over the income statement and make a recommendation as to whether the company should look for a buyer for its assets.

Required:

1. As one step in gathering data for a recommendation to the president, prepare a schedule of cost of goods manufactured for September.
2. As a second step, prepare a new income statement for September.
3. On the basis of your statements prepared in (1) and (2) above, would you recommend that the company look for a buyer?

BUILDING YOUR SKILLS

ETHICS CHALLENGE (LO2)

The top management of General Electronics, Inc., is well known for "managing by the numbers." With an eye on the company's desired growth in overall net profit, the company's CEO (chief executive officer) sets target profits at the beginning of the year for each of the company's divisions. The CEO has stated her policy as follows: "I won't interfere with operations in the divisions. I am available for advice, but the division vice presidents are free to do anything they want so long as they hit the target profits for the year."

In November, Stan Richart, the vice president in charge of the Cellular Telephone Technologies Division, saw that making the current year's target profit for his division was going to be very difficult. Among other actions, he directed that discretionary expenditures be delayed until the beginning of the new year. On December 30, he was angered to discover that a warehouse clerk had ordered $350,000 of cellular telephone parts earlier in December even though the parts weren't really needed by the assembly department until January or February. Contrary to common accounting practice, the General Electronics, Inc., Accounting Policy Manual states that such parts are to be recorded as an expense when delivered. To avoid recording the expense, Mr. Richart asked that the order be canceled, but the purchasing department reported that the parts had already been delivered and the supplier would not accept returns. Since the bill had not yet been paid, Mr. Richart asked the accounting department to correct the clerk's mistake by delaying recognition of the delivery until the bill is paid in January.

Required:
1. Are Mr. Richart's actions ethical? Explain why they are or are not ethical.
2. Do the general management philosophy and accounting policies at General Electronics encourage or discourage ethical behavior? Explain.

TEAMWORK IN ACTION   (LO5)

Understanding the natures of fixed and variable costs is extremely important to managers. This knowledge is used in planning, making strategic and tactical decisions, evaluating performance, and controlling operations.

Required:
Form a team consisting of four persons. Each team member will be responsible for one of the following businesses:

a.   Retail store that sells music CDs
b.   Dental clinic
c.   Fast-food restaurant
d.   Auto repair shop

1. In each business decide what single measure best reflects the overall level of activity in the business and give examples of costs that are fixed and variable with respect to small changes in the measure of activity you have chosen.
2. Explain the relationship between the level of activity in each business and each of the following: total fixed costs, fixed cost per unit of activity, total variable costs, variable cost per unit of activity, total costs, and average total cost per unit of activity.
3. Discuss and refine your answers to each of the above questions with your group. Which of the above businesses seems to have the highest ratio of variable to fixed costs? The lowest? Which of the businesses' profits would be most sensitive to changes in demand for its services? The least sensitive? Why?

CASE   (LO3, LO4)
While snoozing at the controls of his Pepper Six airplane, Dunse P. Sluggard leaned heavily against the door; suddenly, the door flew open and a startled Dunse tumbled out. As he parachuted to the ground, Dunse watched helplessly as the empty plane smashed into Operex Products' plant and administrative offices.

"The insurance company will never believe this," cried Mercedes Juliet, the company's controller, as she watched the ensuing fire burn the building to the ground. "The entire company is wiped out!"

"There's no reason to even contact the insurance agent," replied Ford Romero, the company's operations manager. "We can't file a claim without records, and all we have left is this copy of last year's annual report. It shows that raw materials at the beginning of this year (January 1) totaled $30,000, work in process totaled $50,000, and finished goods totaled $90,000. But what we need is a record of these inventories as of today, and our records are up in smoke."

"All except this summary page I was working on when the plane hit the building," said Mercedes. "It shows that our sales to date this year have totaled $1,350,000 and that manufacturing overhead cost has totaled $520,000."

"Hey! This annual report is more helpful than I thought," exclaimed Ford. "I can see that our gross margin was 40% of sales. I can also see that direct labor cost is one-quarter of the manufacturing overhead cost."

"We may have a chance after all," cried Mercedes. "My summary sheet lists the sum of direct labor and direct materials at $510,000 for the year, and it says that our goods available for sale to customers this year has totaled $960,000 at cost. Now if we just knew the amount of raw materials purchased so far this year."

"I know that figure," yelled Ford. "It's $420,000! The purchasing agent gave it to me in our planning meeting yesterday."

"Fantastic," shouted Mercedes. "We'll have our claim ready before the day is over!"

To file a claim with the insurance company, Operex Products must determine the amount of cost in its inventories as of the date of the accident. You may assume that all of the materials used in production during the year were direct materials.

Required:

Determine the amount of cost in the Raw Materials, Work in Process, and Finished Goods inventory accounts as of the date of the accident. (Hint: One way to proceed would be to reconstruct the various schedules and statements that would have been affected by the company's inventory accounts during the year.)

CHECK FIGURE
(1) Cost of goods
    manufactured:
    $450,000

ANALYTICAL THINKING   (LO1, LO2, LO3, LO4)

Hickey Corporation, a manufacturing company, produces a single product. The following information has been taken from the company's production, sales, and cost records for the just completed year:

Production in units	30,000
Sales in units	?
Ending finished goods inventory in units	?
Sales in dollars.	$650,000
Costs:	
Advertising	$50,000
Direct labor	$80,000
Indirect labor	$60,000
Raw materials purchased	$160,000
Building rent (production uses 80% of the space;	
administrative and sales offices use the rest)	$50,000
Utilities, factory	$35,000
Royalty paid for use of production patent,	
$1 per unit produced.	?
Maintenance, factory	$25,000
Rent for special production equipment,	
$6,000 per year plus $0.10 per unit produced	?
Selling and administrative salaries	$140,000
Other factory overhead costs	$11,000
Other selling and administrative expenses	$20,000

	Beginning of Year	End of Year
Inventories:		
Raw materials.	$20,000	$10,000
Work in process	$30,000	$40,000
Finished goods.	$0	?

The finished goods inventory is being carried at the average unit production cost for the year. The selling price of the product is $25 per unit.

Required:

1. Prepare a schedule of cost of goods manufactured for the year.
2. Compute the following:
   a.   The number of units in the finished goods inventory at the end of the year.
   b.   The cost of the units in the finished goods inventory at the end of the year.
3. Prepare an income statement for the year.

RESEARCH AND APPLICATION (LO1, LO2, LO5, LO6)

The questions in this exercise are based on Dell, Inc. To answer the questions, you will need to download Dell's Form 10-K for the fiscal year ended January 28, 2005 by going to www.sec.gov/edgar/searchedgar/companysearch.html. Input CIK code 826083 and hit enter. In the gray box on the right-hand side of your computer screen define the scope of your search by inputting 10-K and then pressing enter. Select the 10-K with a filing date of March 8, 2005. You do not need to print this document in order to answer the questions.

REQUIRED:

1. What is Dell's strategy for success in the marketplace? Does the company rely primarily on a customer intimacy, operational excellence, or product leadership customer value proposition? What evidence supports your conclusion?
2. What business risks does Dell face that may threaten its ability to satisfy stockholder expectations? What are some examples of control activities that the company could use to reduce these risks? (Hint: Focus on pages 7–10 of the 10-K.)
3. How has the Sarbanes-Oxley Act of 2002 explicitly affected the disclosures contained in Dell's 10-K report? (Hint: Focus on pages 34–35, 59, and 76–78.)
4. Is Dell a merchandiser or a manufacturer? What information contained in the 10-K supports your answer?
5. What are some examples of direct and indirect inventoriable costs for Dell? Why has Dell's gross margin (in dollars) steadily increased from 2003 to 2005, yet the gross margin as a percent of net revenue has only increased slightly?
6. What is the inventory balance on Dell's January 28, 2005, balance sheet? Why is the inventory balance so small compared to the other current asset balances? What competitive advantage does Dell derive from its low inventory levels? Page 27 of Dell's 10-K reports a figure called the *cash conversion cycle*. The cash conversion cycle for Dell has consistently been negative. Is this a good sign for Dell or a bad sign? Why?
7. Describe some of the various types of operating expenses incurred by Dell. Why are these expenses treated as period costs?
8. List four different cost objects for Dell. For each cost object, mention one example of a direct cost and an indirect cost.

Systems Design: Job-Order Costing

<< A LOOK BACK

Chapter 1 described the three major activities of managers and compared and contrasted financial and managerial accounting. It also defined many of the terms that are used to classify costs in business. We will use many of these terms in Chapter 2. Now would be a good time to check your understanding of those terms by referring to the glossary at the end of Chapter 1.

A LOOK AT THIS CHAPTER

Chapter 2 distinguishes between two costing systems, job-order and process costing, and then provides an in-depth look at a job-order costing system. We describe how direct material and direct labor costs are accumulated on jobs. Then we address manufacturing overhead, an indirect cost that must be allocated (or applied) to jobs. Finally, we take a more detailed look at the flow of costs through a company's accounting system using journal entries.

A LOOK AHEAD >>

Chapter 3 continues the discussion of the allocation of manufacturing overhead costs, showing how these costs can be more accurately assigned using activity-based costing. We cover process costing in Chapter 4.

CHAPTER OUTLINE

DECISION FEATURE

Two College Students Succeeding as Entrepreneurs

When the University of Dayton athletic department needed 2,000 customized T-shirts to give away as part of a promotion for its first home basketball game of the year, it chose University Tees to provide the shirts. Numerous larger competitors could have been chosen, but University Tees won the order because of its fast customer response time, low price, and high quality.

University Tees is a small business that was started in February 2003 by two Miami University seniors—Joe Haddad and Nick Dadas (see the company's website at www.universitytees.com). The company creates the artwork for customized T-shirts and then relies on carefully chosen suppliers to manufacture the product. University Tees must provide a specific price quote for each potential customer order since each order is unique and the customer is always looking for the best deal.

Calculating the cost of a particular customer order is critically important to University Tees because the company needs to be sure that each price quote exceeds the cost associated with satisfying the order. The costs that University Tees factors into its bidding process include the cost of the T-shirts themselves, printing costs (which vary depending on the quantity of shirts produced and the number of colors printed per shirt), silk screen costs (which also vary depending on the number of colors included in a design), shipping costs, and the artwork needed to create a design. In addition to using cost information, the company also relies on knowledge of its competitors' pricing strategies when establishing price quotes.

Source: Conversation with Joe Haddad, cofounder of University Tees.

LO1 Distinguish between process costing and job-order costing and identify companies that would use each costing method.

LO2 Identify the documents used in a job-order costing system.

LO3 Compute predetermined overhead rates and explain why estimated overhead costs (rather than actual overhead costs) are used in the costing process.

LO4 Prepare journal entries to record costs in a job-order costing system.

LO5 Apply overhead cost to Work in Process using a predetermined overhead rate.

LO6 Prepare schedules of cost of goods manufactured and cost of goods sold.

LO7 Use T-accounts to show the flow of costs in a job-order cost system.

LO8 Compute underapplied or overapplied overhead cost and prepare the journal entry to close the balance in Manufacturing Overhead to the appropriate accounts.

As discussed in the previous chapter, product costing is the process of assigning costs to the products and services provided by a company. An understanding of this costing process is vital to managers because the way in which a product or service is costed can have a substantial impact on reported profits, as well as on key management decisions.

The essential purpose of any managerial costing system should be to provide cost data to help managers plan, control, direct, and make decisions. Nevertheless, external financial reporting and tax reporting requirements often heavily influence how costs are accumulated and summarized on managerial reports. This is true of product costing.

In this chapter, we use *absorption costing* to determine product costs. This method was also used in the previous chapter. In **absorption costing,** *all* manufacturing costs, fixed and variable, are assigned to units of product—units are said to *fully absorb manufacturing costs.* The absorption costing approach is also known as the *full cost* approach. In a later chapter, we look at an alternative to absorption costing known as *variable costing.*

Most countries—including the United States—require some form of absorption costing for both external financial reporting and tax reporting. In addition, the vast majority of companies throughout the world also use absorption costing for managerial accounting purposes. Since absorption costing is the most common approach to product costing, we discuss it first and then deal with alternatives in subsequent chapters.

PROCESS AND JOB-ORDER COSTING

LEARNING OBJECTIVE 1

Distinguish between process costing and job-order costing and identify companies that would use each costing method.

Managers are faced with two complications when attempting to accurately compute the cost of a product or service. First, their companies often produce or provide a wide variety of products or services in a given period of time within the same factory or office. Second, many costs (such as rent) do not change from month to month despite fluctuations in the level of monthly output of products and services. Managers typically respond to these complications by averaging across time and outputs. The way in which this averaging is carried out depends heavily on the type of process involved. We will describe two different costing systems commonly used in manufacturing and service companies that rely on averaging in different ways—*process costing* and *job-order costing*. Our discussion of these costing systems focuses primarily on manufacturing applications; however, selected problems at the end of the chapter are used to help you understand how the concepts readily apply to service companies.

Process Costing

A **process costing system** is used in situations where the company produces many units of a single product for long periods. Examples include producing paper at Weyerhaeuser, refining aluminum ingots at Reynolds Aluminum, mixing and bottling beverages at Coca-Cola, and making wieners at Oscar Mayer. All of these industries are characterized by an essentially homogeneous product that flows through the production process on a continuous basis.

Process costing systems accumulate costs in a particular operation or department for an entire period (month, quarter, year) and then divide this total cost by the number of units produced during the period. The basic formula for process costing is:

$$\text{Unit product cost} = \frac{\text{Total manufacturing cost}}{\text{Total units produced}}$$

Since one unit of product is indistinguishable from any other unit of product, each unit produced during the period is assigned the same average cost. This costing technique results in a broad, average unit cost figure that applies to homogeneous units flowing in a continuous stream out of the production process.

Job-Order Costing

A **job-order costing system** is used in situations where many *different* products are produced each period. For example, a Levi Strauss clothing factory would typically make many different types of jeans for both men and women during a month. A particular order might consist of 1,000 stonewashed men's blue denim jeans, style number A312. This order of 1,000 jeans is called a *batch* or a *job*. In a job-order costing system, costs are traced and allocated to jobs and then the costs of the job are divided by the number of units in the job to arrive at an average cost per unit.

Other examples of situations where job-order costing would be used include large-scale construction projects managed by Bechtel International, commercial aircraft produced by Boeing, greeting cards designed and printed by Hallmark, and airline meals prepared by LSG Sky Chefs. All of these examples are characterized by diverse outputs. Each Bechtel project is unique and different from every other—the company may be simultaneously constructing a dam in Zaire and a bridge in Indonesia. Likewise, each airline orders a different type of meal from LSG Sky Chefs' catering service.

Job-order costing is also used extensively in service industries. Hospitals, law firms, movie studios, accounting firms, advertising agencies, and repair shops, for example, all use a variation of job-order costing to accumulate costs for accounting and billing purposes. Although the detailed example of job-order costing provided in the following section deals with a manufacturing company, the same basic concepts and procedures are used by many service organizations.

The record-keeping and cost assignment problems are more complex when a company sells many different products and services than when it has only a single product. Since the products are different, the costs are typically different. Consequently, cost records must be maintained for each distinct product or job. For example, an attorney in a large criminal law practice would ordinarily keep separate records of the costs of advising and defending clients. And the Levi Strauss factory mentioned above would keep separate

Continuous Process Manufacturing vs. Job-Order Manufacturing

Continuous Process:

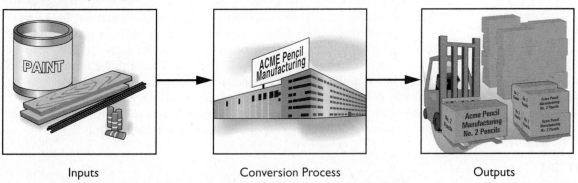

| Inputs | Conversion Process | Outputs |

Job-Order Process:

| Inputs | Conversion Process | Outputs |

track of the costs of filling orders for particular styles of jeans. Thus, a job-order costing system requires more effort than a process costing system. Nevertheless, job-order costing is used by over half of the manufacturers in the United States.

In this chapter, we focus on the design of a job-order costing system. In Chapter 4, we focus on process costing and also look more closely at the similarities and differences between the two costing methods.

JOB-ORDER COSTING—AN OVERVIEW

Video 2–1

Concept 2-1

To introduce job-order costing, we will follow a specific job as it progresses through the manufacturing process at Yost Precision Machining, a small company that specializes in fabricating precision metal parts that are used in a variety of applications ranging from deep-sea exploration vehicles to the inertial triggers in automobile air bags. Loops Unlimited, a designer and builder of roller coaster rides, has ordered two experimental couplings from Yost Precision Machining. The couplings would connect the cars on a new high-speed roller coaster that is currently under development. Loops Unlimited has ordered just two couplings to evaluate their performance and safety.

Before we begin our discussion of the costing of these two experimental couplings, recall from the previous chapter that companies generally classify manufacturing costs into three broad categories: (1) direct materials, (2) direct labor, and (3) manufacturing overhead. As we study job-order costing, we will see how each of these three types of costs is recorded and accumulated.

Measuring Direct Materials Cost

Yost Precision Machining will require four G7 Connectors and two M46 Housings to make the two experimental couplings for Loops Unlimited. If this were a standard product, it would be accompanied by a *bill of materials*. A **bill of materials** is a document that lists the type and quantity of each raw material needed to complete a unit of product. In this case, there is no established bill of materials, so Yost's production staff determined the materials requirements from the blueprints submitted by the customer. Each coupling requires two connectors and one housing, so to make two couplings, four connectors and two housings are required.

A *production order* is issued when an agreement has been reached with the customer concerning the quantities, prices, and shipment date for the order. The Production Department then prepares a *materials requisition form* similar to the form in Exhibit 2–1. The **materials requisition form** is a detailed source document that specifies the type and quantity of materials to be drawn from the storeroom and identifies the job that will be charged for the cost of the materials. The form is used to control the flow of materials into production and also for making entries in the accounting records.

EXHIBIT 2–1
Materials Requisition Form

Materials Requisition Number	14873	Date	March 2
Job Number to Be Charged	2B47		
Department	Milling		

Description	Quantity	Unit Cost	Total Cost
M46 Housing	2	$124	$248
G7 Connector	4	$103	412
			$660

Authorized Signature ___ *Bill White* ___

EXHIBIT 2–2
Job Cost Sheet

JOB COST SHEET

Job Number **2B47**   Date Initiated **March 2**

Date Completed _____

Department **Milling**   Units Completed _____

Item **Special order coupling**

For Stock _____

Direct Materials		Direct Labor			Manufacturing Overhead		
Req. No.	Amount	Ticket	Hours	Amount	Hours	Rate	Amount
14873	$660	843	5	$45			

Cost Summary		Units Shipped		
Direct Materials	$	Date	Number	Balance
Direct Labor	$			
Manufacturing Overhead	$			
Total Cost	$			
Unit Cost	$			

The Yost Precision Machining materials requisition form in Exhibit 2–1 shows that the company's Milling Department has requisitioned two M46 Housings and four G7 Connectors for the Loops Unlimited job, which has been designated as Job 2B47. A production worker presents the completed form to the storeroom clerk who then issues the specified materials to the worker. The storeroom clerk is not allowed to release materials without a completed and properly authorized materials requisition form.

Job Cost Sheet

After being notified that the production order has been issued, the Accounting Department prepares a *job cost sheet* like the one presented in Exhibit 2–2. A **job cost sheet** is a form that records the materials, labor, and overhead costs charged to the job.

After direct materials are issued, the Accounting Department records their costs directly on the job cost sheet. Note from Exhibit 2–2, for example, that the $660 cost for direct materials shown earlier on the materials requisition form has been charged to Job 2B47 on its job cost sheet. The requisition number 14873 from the materials requisition form is also recorded on the job cost sheet to make it easier to identify the source document for the direct materials charge. Job cost sheets serve as a subsidiary ledger to the Work in Process account because the detailed records that they provide for the jobs in process add up to the balance in Work in Process.

Measuring Direct Labor Cost

Direct labor cost is handled similarly to direct materials cost. Direct labor consists of labor charges that are easily traced to a particular job. Labor charges that cannot be easily traced directly to any job are treated as part of manufacturing overhead. As discussed in the previous chapter, this latter category of labor costs is called *indirect labor* and includes tasks such as maintenance, supervision, and cleanup.

EXHIBIT 2–3
Employee Time Ticket

Time Ticket No. 843			Date March 3		
Employee Mary Holden			Station 4		
Started	Ended	Time Completed	Rate	Amount	Job Number
7:00	12:00	5.0	$9	$45	2B47
12:30	2:30	2.0	$9	18	2B50
2:30	3:30	1.0	$9	9	Maintenance
Totals		8.0		$72	

Supervisor   *R.W. Pace*

Workers use *time tickets* to record the time they spend on each job and task. A completed **time ticket** is an hour-by-hour summary of the employee's activities throughout the day. An example of an employee time ticket is shown in Exhibit 2–3. When working on a specific job, the employee enters the job number on the time ticket and notes the amount of time spent on that job. When not assigned to a particular job, the employee records the nature of the indirect labor task (such as cleanup and maintenance) and the amount of time spent on the task.

At the end of the day, the time tickets are gathered and the Accounting Department enters the direct labor-hours and costs on individual job cost sheets. (See Exhibit 2–2 for an example of how direct labor costs are entered on the job cost sheet.) The daily time tickets are source documents that are used as the basis for labor cost entries into the accounting records.

The system we have just described is a manual method for recording and posting labor costs. Today many companies rely on computerized systems and no longer record labor time by hand on sheets of paper. One computerized approach uses bar codes to capture the basic data. Each employee and each job has a unique bar code. When beginning work on a job, the employee scans three bar codes using a handheld device much like the bar code readers at grocery store checkout stands. The first bar code indicates that a job is being started; the second is the unique bar code on the employee's identity badge; and the third is the unique bar code of the job itself. This information is fed automatically via an electronic network to a computer that notes the time and records all of the data. When the task is completed, the employee scans a bar code indicating the task is complete, the bar code on his or her identity badge, and the bar code attached to the job. This information is relayed to the computer that again notes the time, and a time ticket is automatically prepared. Since all of the source data are already in computer files, the labor costs can be automatically posted to job cost sheets (or their electronic equivalents). Computers, coupled with technology such as bar codes, can eliminate much of the drudgery involved in routine bookkeeping activities while at the same time increasing timeliness and accuracy.

Application of Manufacturing Overhead

LEARNING OBJECTIVE 3

Compute predetermined overhead rates and explain why estimated overhead costs (rather than actual overhead costs) are used in the costing process.

Recall that product costs include manufacturing overhead as well as direct materials and direct labor. Therefore, manufacturing overhead also needs to be recorded on the job cost sheet. However, assigning manufacturing overhead to a specific job involves some difficulties. There are three reasons for this:

1. Manufacturing overhead is an *indirect cost*. This means that it is either impossible or difficult to trace these costs to a particular product or job.
2. Manufacturing overhead consists of many different items ranging from the grease used in machines to the annual salary of the production manager.
3. Even though output may fluctuate due to seasonal or other factors, total manufacturing overhead costs tend to remain relatively constant due to the presence of fixed costs.

Given these problems, overhead costs are usually assigned to products using an allocation process. This allocation of overhead costs is accomplished by selecting an

Topic Tackler
PLUS

Concept 2-2

allocation base that is common to all of the company's products and services. An **allocation base** is a measure such as direct labor-hours (DLH) or machine-hours (MH) that is used to assign overhead costs to products and services.

The most widely used allocation bases are direct labor-hours and direct labor cost, with machine-hours and even units of product (where a company has only a single product) also used to some extent.

Manufacturing overhead is commonly applied to products using a *predetermined overhead rate*. The **predetermined overhead rate** is computed by dividing the total estimated manufacturing overhead cost for the period by the estimated total amount of the allocation base as follows:

$$\text{Predetermined overhead rate} = \frac{\text{Estimated total manufacturing overhead cost}}{\text{Estimated total amount of the allocation base}}$$

Note that the predetermined overhead rate is based on *estimates* rather than actual results.[1] This is because the *predetermined* overhead rate is computed *before* the period begins and is used to *apply* overhead cost to jobs throughout the period. The process of assigning overhead cost to jobs is called **overhead application.** The formula for determining the amount of overhead cost to apply to a particular job is:

$$\begin{array}{c}\text{Overhead applied to} \\ \text{a particular job}\end{array} = \begin{array}{c}\text{Predetermined} \\ \text{overhead rate}\end{array} \times \begin{array}{c}\text{Amount of the allocation} \\ \text{base incurred by the job}\end{array}$$

For example, if the predetermined overhead rate is $8 per direct labor-hour, then $8 of overhead cost is *applied* to a job for each direct labor-hour incurred by the job. When the allocation base is direct labor-hours, the formula becomes:

$$\begin{array}{c}\text{Overhead applied to} \\ \text{a particular job}\end{array} = \begin{array}{c}\text{Predetermined} \\ \text{overhead rate}\end{array} \times \begin{array}{c}\text{Actual direct labor-hours} \\ \text{incurred by the job}\end{array}$$

Using the Predetermined Overhead Rate

To illustrate the steps involved in computing and using a predetermined overhead rate, let's return to Yost Precision Machining. The company has estimated its total manufacturing overhead costs at $320,000 for the year and its total direct labor-hours at 40,000. Its predetermined overhead rate for the year would be $8 per direct labor-hour, as shown below:

$$\text{Predetermined overhead rate} = \frac{\text{Estimated total manufacturing overhead cost}}{\text{Estimated total amount of the allocation base}}$$

$$= \frac{\$320,000}{40,000 \text{ direct labor-hours}}$$

$$= \$8 \text{ per direct labor-hour}$$

The job cost sheet in Exhibit 2–4 indicates that 27 direct labor-hours (i.e., DLHs) were charged to Job 2B47. Therefore, a total of $216 of manufacturing overhead cost would be applied to the job:

$$\begin{array}{c}\text{Overhead applied to} \\ \text{Job 2B47}\end{array} = \begin{array}{c}\text{Predetermined} \\ \text{overhead rate}\end{array} \times \begin{array}{c}\text{Actual direct labor-hours} \\ \text{incurred by Job 2B47}\end{array}$$

$$= \$8 \text{ per direct labor-hour} \times 27 \text{ direct labor-hours}$$

$$= \$216 \text{ of overhead applied to Job 2B47}$$

This amount of overhead has been entered on the job cost sheet in Exhibit 2–4. Note that this is *not* the actual amount of overhead caused by the job. Actual overhead costs are *not* assigned to jobs—if that could be done, the costs would be direct costs, not overhead. The

---

[1]Some experts argue that the predetermined overhead rate should be based on activity at capacity rather than on estimated activity. See Appendix 3A of Ray Garrison, Eric Noreen, and Peter Brewer, *Managerial Accounting,* 12th edition, for details.

Understanding Cost Drivers Can Be Tricky Business

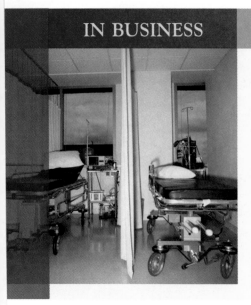

In recent years, hospitals have developed a keen interest in controlling their costs. Conventional wisdom in the health care industry was that costs could be reduced by reducing a patient's length of stay in a hospital. It seemed logical that reducing the number of days that a patient spends in the hospital should reduce the cost of treating that patient. However, researchers John Evans, Yuhchang Hwang, and Nandu Nagarajan provide evidence within one hospital that when doctors were motivated to reduce length of stay, it did not reduce costs. The researchers found that doctors compensated for a reduction in length of stay by increasing the number of procedures performed per patient per day. Thus, any potential savings from reducing one cost driver—length of stay—were offset by cost increases caused by increasing another cost driver—number of procedures performed per patient per day.

Source: John H. Evans, Yuhchang Hwang, and Nandu J. Nagarajan, "Management Control and Hospital Cost Reduction: Additional Evidence," *Journal of Accounting and Public Policy*, Spring 2001, pp. 73–88.

overhead. Indeed, most manufacturing companies in the United States continue to use direct labor as the primary or secondary allocation base for manufacturing overhead. The key point is that the allocation base used by the company should really drive, or cause, overhead costs, and direct labor is not always an appropriate allocation base.

Computation of Unit Costs

With the application of Yost Precision Machining's $216 of manufacturing overhead to the job cost sheet in Exhibit 2–4, the job cost sheet is complete except for two final steps. First, the totals for direct materials, direct labor, and manufacturing overhead are transferred to the Cost Summary section of the job cost sheet and added together to obtain the total cost for the job. Then the total product cost ($1,800) is divided by the number of units (2) to obtain the unit product cost ($900). As indicated earlier, *this unit product cost is an average cost and should not be interpreted as the cost that would actually be incurred if another unit were produced.* Much of the actual overhead costs would not change if another unit were produced, so the incremental cost of an additional unit is less than the average unit cost of $900.

The completed job cost sheet will serve as the basis for valuing unsold units in ending inventory and for determining cost of goods sold.

Treasurer, Class Reunion Committee

You've agreed to handle the financial arrangements for your high school reunion. You call the restaurant where the reunion will be held and jot down the most important information. The meal cost (including beverages) will be $30 per person plus a 15% gratuity. An additional $200 will be charged for a banquet room with a dance floor. A band has been hired for $500. One of the members of the reunion committee informs you that there is just enough money left in the class bank account to cover the printing and mailing costs. He mentions that at least one-half of the class of 400 will attend the reunion and wonders if he should add the 15% gratuity to the $30 per person meal cost when he drafts the invitation, which will indicate that a check must be returned with the reply card.

How should you respond? How much will you need to charge to cover the various costs? After making your decision, label your answer with the managerial accounting terms covered in this chapter. Finally, identify any issues that should be investigated further.

Summary of Document Flows

The sequence of events discussed in the prior pages is summarized in Exhibit 2–5. A careful study of the flow of documents in this exhibit provides a good overview of the overall operation of a job-order costing system.

EXHIBIT 2–5   The Flow of Documents in a Job-Order Costing System

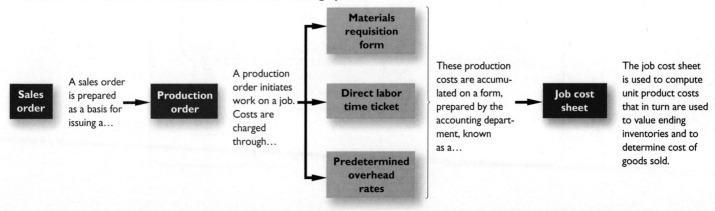

1. Which of the following statements is false? (You may select more than one answer.)
   a. Absorption costing assigns fixed and variable manufacturing overhead costs to products.
   b. Job-order costing systems are used when companies produce many different types of products.
   c. A normal costing system assigns costs to products by multiplying the actual overhead rate by the actual amount of the allocation base.
   d. A company such as Coca-Cola is more likely to use a process costing system than a job-order costing system.

CONCEPT CHECK ✓

JOB-ORDER COSTING—THE FLOW OF COSTS

We are now ready to take a more detailed look at the flow of costs through a company's general ledger. To illustrate, we shall consider a single month's activity for Rand Company, a producer of gold and silver commemorative medallions. Rand Company has two jobs in process during April, the first month of its fiscal year. Job A, a special minting of 1,000 gold medallions commemorating the invention of motion pictures, was started during March. By the end of March, $30,000 in manufacturing costs had been recorded for the job. Job B, an order for 10,000 silver medallions commemorating the fall of the Berlin Wall, was started in April.

> **LEARNING OBJECTIVE 4**
>
> Prepare journal entries to record costs in a job-order costing system.

The Purchase and Issue of Materials

On April 1, Rand Company had $7,000 in raw materials on hand. During the month, the company purchased on account an additional $60,000 in raw materials. The purchase is recorded in journal entry (1) below:

	(1)		
Raw Materials.		60,000	
Accounts Payable			60,000

As explained in the previous chapter, Raw Materials is an asset account. Thus, when raw materials are purchased, they are initially recorded as an asset—not as an expense.

EXHIBIT 2–6 Raw Materials Cost Flows

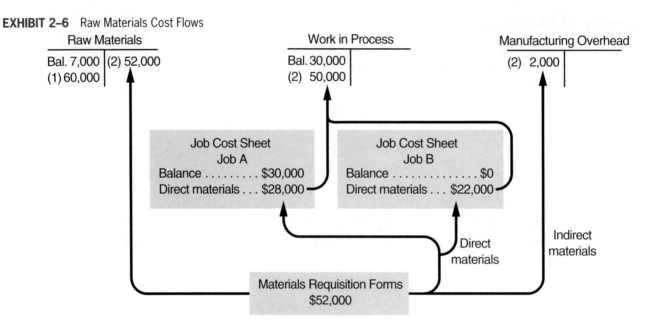

Issue of Direct and Indirect Materials   During April, $52,000 in raw materials were requisitioned from the storeroom for use in production. These raw materials included $50,000 of direct and $2,000 of indirect materials. Entry (2) records issuing the materials to the production departments.

(2)

Work in Process	50,000	
Manufacturing Overhead	2,000	
Raw Materials		52,000

The materials charged to Work in Process represent direct materials for specific jobs. These costs are also recorded on the appropriate job cost sheets. This point is illustrated in Exhibit 2–6, where $28,000 of the $50,000 in direct materials is charged to Job A's cost sheet and the remaining $22,000 is charged to Job B's cost sheet. (In this example, all data are presented in summary form and the job cost sheet is abbreviated.)

The $2,000 charged to Manufacturing Overhead in entry (2) represents indirect materials used in production during April. Observe that the Manufacturing Overhead account is separate from the Work in Process account. The purpose of the Manufacturing Overhead account is to accumulate all manufacturing overhead costs as they are incurred during a period.

Before leaving Exhibit 2–6 we need to point out one additional thing. Notice from the exhibit that the job cost sheet for Job A contains a beginning balance of $30,000. We stated earlier that this balance represents the cost of work done during March that has been carried forward to April. Also note that the Work in Process account contains the same $30,000 balance. *The reason the $30,000 appears in both places is that the Work in Process account is a control account and the job cost sheets form a subsidiary ledger. Thus, the Work in Process account contains a summarized total of all costs appearing on the individual job cost sheets for all jobs in process at any given point in time.* (Since Rand Company had only Job A in process at the beginning of April, Job A's $30,000 balance on that date is equal to the balance in the Work in Process account.)

Labor Cost

As work is performed each day, employee time tickets are filled out by workers, collected, and forwarded to the Accounting Department. In the Accounting Department, wages are computed and the resulting costs are classified as either direct or indirect

EXHIBIT 2–7 Labor Cost Flows

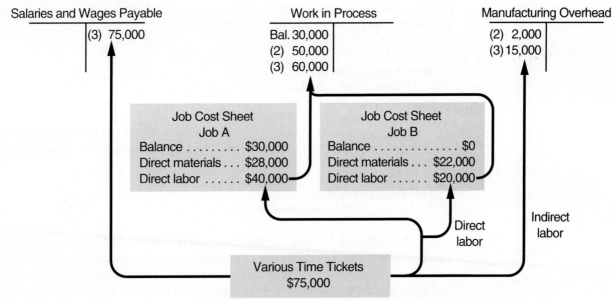

labor. In April, $60,000 was recorded for direct labor and $15,000 for indirect labor. The following entry summarizes these accruals:

(3)

Work in Process	60,000	
Manufacturing Overhead	15,000	
Salaries and Wages Payable.		75,000

Only the direct labor cost is added to the Work in Process account. For Rand Company, this amounted to $60,000 for April.

At the same time that direct labor costs are added to Work in Process, they are also added to the individual job cost sheets, as shown in Exhibit 2–7. During April, $40,000 of direct labor cost was charged to Job A and the remaining $20,000 was charged to Job B.

The labor costs charged to Manufacturing Overhead represent the indirect labor costs of the period, such as supervision, janitorial work, and maintenance.

Manufacturing Overhead Costs

Recall that all manufacturing costs other than direct materials and direct labor are classified as manufacturing overhead costs. These costs are entered directly into the Manufacturing Overhead account as they are incurred. To illustrate, assume that Rand Company incurred the following general factory costs during April:

Utilities (heat, water, and power)	$21,000
Rent on factory equipment	16,000
Miscellaneous factory overhead costs . .	3,000
Total	$40,000

The following entry records the incurrence of these costs:

(4)

Manufacturing Overhead	40,000	
Accounts Payable, Cash, etc.		40,000

In addition, assume that during April, Rand Company recognized $13,000 in accrued property taxes and that $7,000 in prepaid insurance expired on factory buildings and equipment. The following entry records these items:

(5)

Manufacturing Overhead	20,000	
Property Taxes Payable.		13,000
Prepaid Insurance.		7,000

Finally, assume that the company recognized $18,000 in depreciation on factory equipment during April. The following entry records the accrual of this depreciation:

(6)

| Manufacturing Overhead . . . . | 18,000 | |
| Accumulated Depreciation . . . . | | 18,000 |

In short, *all* manufacturing overhead costs are recorded directly into the Manufacturing Overhead account as they are incurred. It is important to understand that Manufacturing Overhead is a control account for many—perhaps thousands—of subsidiary accounts such as Indirect Materials, Indirect Labor, Factory Utilities, and so forth. As the Manufacturing Overhead account is debited for costs during a period, the various subsidiary accounts are also debited. In the example above and also in the assignment material for this chapter, for the sake of brevity we omit the entries to the subsidiary accounts.

Applying Manufacturing Overhead

Since actual manufacturing costs are charged to the Manufacturing Overhead control account rather than to Work in Process, how are manufacturing overhead costs assigned to Work in Process? The answer is, by means of the predetermined overhead rate. Recall from our discussion earlier in the chapter that a predetermined overhead rate is established at the beginning of each year. The rate is calculated by dividing the estimated total manufacturing overhead cost for the year by the estimated total amount of the allocation base (measured in machine-hours, direct labor-hours, or some other base). The predetermined overhead rate is then used to apply overhead costs to jobs. For example, if direct labor-hours is the allocation base, overhead cost is applied to each job by multiplying the predetermined overhead rate by the number of direct labor-hours charged to the job.

To illustrate, assume that Rand Company's predetermined overhead rate is $6 per machine-hour. Also assume that during April, 10,000 machine-hours were worked on Job A and 5,000 machine-hours were worked on Job B (a total of 15,000 machine-hours). Thus, $90,000 in overhead cost ($6 per machine-hour × 15,000 machine-hours = $90,000) would be applied to Work in Process. The following entry records the application of Manufacturing Overhead to Work in Process:

(7)

| Work in Process. . . . . | 90,000 | |
| Manufacturing Overhead. . . . . | | 90,000 |

The flow of costs through the Manufacturing Overhead account is shown in Exhibit 2–8.

The actual overhead costs in the Manufacturing Overhead account in Exhibit 2–8 are the costs that were added to the account in entries (2)–(6). Observe that the incurrence of these actual overhead costs [entries (2)–(6)] and the application of overhead to Work in Process [entry (7)] represent two separate and entirely distinct processes.

The Concept of a Clearing Account   The Manufacturing Overhead account operates as a clearing account. As we have noted, actual factory overhead costs are debited to the account as they are incurred throughout the year. At certain intervals during the year (usually when a job is completed) overhead cost is applied to the job using the

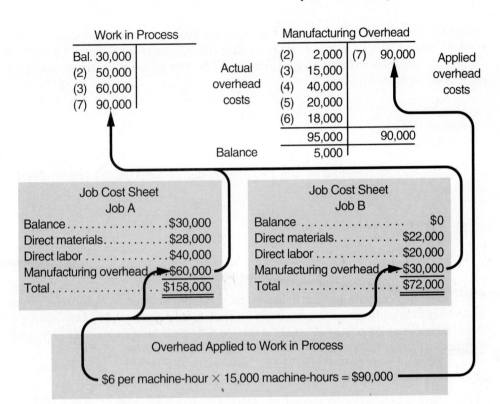

EXHIBIT 2–8
The Flow of Costs in Overhead
Application

predetermined overhead rate, and Work in Process is debited and Manufacturing Overhead is credited. This sequence of events is illustrated below:

Manufacturing Overhead (A Clearing Account)	
Actual overhead costs are charged to this account as they are incurred throughout the period.	Overhead is removed from this account and is applied to Work in Process using the predetermined overhead rate.

As we emphasized earlier, the predetermined overhead rate is based entirely on estimates of what overhead costs are *expected* to be, and it is established before the year begins. As a result, the overhead cost applied during a year will almost certainly turn out to be more or less than the actual overhead cost incurred. For example, notice from Exhibit 2–8 that Rand Company's actual overhead costs for the period are $5,000 greater than the overhead cost that has been applied to Work in Process, resulting in a $5,000 debit balance in the Manufacturing Overhead account. We will reserve discussion of what to do with this $5,000 balance until the next section, Problems of Overhead Application.

For the moment, we can conclude by noting from Exhibit 2–8 that the cost of a completed job consists of the actual direct materials cost of the job, the actual direct labor cost of the job, and the manufacturing overhead cost *applied* to the job. Pay particular attention to the following subtle but important point: *Actual overhead costs are not charged to jobs; actual overhead costs do not appear on the job cost sheet nor do they appear in the Work in Process account. Only the applied overhead cost, based on the predetermined overhead rate, appears on the job cost sheet and in the Work in Process account.*

Nonmanufacturing Costs

In addition to manufacturing costs, companies also incur selling and administrative costs. As explained in the previous chapter, these costs should be treated as period expenses and charged directly to the income statement. *Nonmanufacturing costs should not go into the Manufacturing Overhead account.* To illustrate the correct treatment of nonmanufacturing costs, assume that Rand Company incurred $30,000 in selling and administrative salary costs during April. The following entry summarizes the accrual of those salaries:

(8)

Salaries Expense.................................	30,000	
Salaries and Wages Payable, Cash, etc.		30,000

Assume that depreciation on office equipment during April was $7,000. The entry would be:

(9)

Depreciation Expense	7,000	
Accumulated Depreciation		7,000

Pay particular attention to the difference between this entry and entry (6) where we recorded depreciation on factory equipment. In journal entry (6), depreciation on factory equipment was debited to Manufacturing Overhead and is therefore a product cost. In journal entry (9) above, depreciation on office equipment is debited to Depreciation Expense. Depreciation on office equipment is considered to be a period expense rather than a product cost.

Finally, assume that advertising was $42,000 and that other selling and administrative expenses in April totaled $8,000. The following entry records these items:

(10)

Advertising Expense.............................	42,000	
Other Selling and Administrative Expense.............	8,000	
Accounts Payable, Cash, etc...................		50,000

The amounts in entries (8) through (10) all go directly into expense accounts—they have no effect on product costs. The same will be true of any other selling and administrative expenses incurred during April, including sales commissions, depreciation on sales equipment, rent on office facilities, insurance on office facilities, and related costs.

Cost of Goods Manufactured

When a job has been completed, the finished output is transferred from the production departments to the finished goods warehouse. By this time, the accounting department will have charged the job with direct materials and direct labor cost, and manufacturing overhead will have been applied using the predetermined overhead rate. A transfer of these costs is made within the costing system that *parallels* the physical transfer of goods to the finished goods warehouse. The costs of the completed job are transferred out of the Work in Process account and into the Finished Goods account. The sum of all amounts transferred between these two accounts represents the cost of goods manufactured for the period.

In the case of Rand Company, assume that Job A was completed during April. The following entry transfers the cost of Job A from Work in Process to Finished Goods:

(11)

Finished Goods	158,000	
Work in Process		158,000

The $158,000 represents the completed cost of Job A, as shown on the job cost sheet in Exhibit 2–8. Since Job A was the only job completed during April, the $158,000 also represents the cost of goods manufactured for the month.

   Job B was not completed by the end of the month, so its cost will remain in the Work in Process account and carry over to the next month. If a balance sheet is prepared at the end of April, the cost accumulated thus far on Job B will appear as an asset—"Work in process inventory." The $158,000 cost of goods manufactured for the month is added to the $10,000 beginning balance in the Finished Goods account that is carried over from the previous month.

Cost of Goods Sold

As finished goods are shipped to customers, their costs are transferred from the Finished Goods account into the Cost of Goods Sold account. If an entire job is shipped at one time, then the entire cost appearing on the job cost sheet is transferred into the Cost of Goods Sold account. In most cases, however, only a portion of the units involved in a particular job will be immediately sold. In these situations, the unit product cost must be used to determine how much product cost should be removed from Finished Goods and charged to Cost of Goods Sold.

   For Rand Company, we will assume 750 of the 1,000 gold medallions in Job A were shipped to customers on account by the end of the month for total sales revenue of $225,000. Since 1,000 units were produced and the total cost of the job from the job cost sheet was $158,000, the unit product cost was $158. The following journal entries would record the sale:

(12)		
Accounts Receivable	225,000	
Sales		225,000

(13)		
Cost of Goods Sold	118,500	
Finished Goods		118,500
(750 units × $158 per unit = $118,500)		

   Entry (13) completes the flow of costs through the job-order costing system.

Summary of Cost Flows

LEARNING OBJECTIVE 7

Use T-accounts to show the flow of costs in a job-order cost system.

To pull the entire Rand Company example together, journal entries (1) through (13) are summarized in Exhibit 2–9. The flow of costs through the accounts is presented in T-account form in Exhibit 2–10.

   Exhibit 2–11 presents a schedule of cost of goods manufactured and a schedule of cost of goods sold for Rand Company. Note particularly from Exhibit 2–11 that the manufacturing overhead cost on the schedule of cost of goods manufactured is the overhead applied to jobs during the month—not the actual manufacturing overhead costs incurred. The reason for this can be traced back to journal entry (7) and the T-account for Work in Process that appears in Exhibit 2–10. Under a normal costing system as illustrated in this chapter, applied—not actual—overhead costs are assigned to jobs and thus to Work in Process inventory. In contrast, in Chapter 1 actual overhead costs were assigned to Work in Process and included in the schedule of cost of goods manufactured. This is because we had not introduced the concept of a normal costing system in that chapter.

   Note also, as shown in Exhibit 2–11, that the cost of goods manufactured for the month ($158,000) agrees with the amount transferred from Work in Process to Finished Goods for the month as recorded earlier in entry (11). Also note that this $158,000 is used in computing the cost of goods sold for the month.

   An income statement for April is presented in Exhibit 2–12. Observe that the cost of goods sold on this statement ($123,500) is carried down from Exhibit 2–11.

EXHIBIT 2–11
Schedules of Cost of Goods
Manufactured and Cost of
Goods Sold

Cost of Goods Manufactured		
Direct materials:		
Raw materials inventory, beginning	$ 7,000	
Add: Purchases of raw materials	60,000	
Total raw materials available	67,000	
Deduct: Raw materials inventory, ending	15,000	
Raw materials used in production	52,000	
Less indirect materials included in manufacturing overhead	2,000	$ 50,000
Direct labor		60,000
Manufacturing overhead applied to work in process		90,000
Total manufacturing costs		200,000
Add: Beginning work in process inventory		30,000
		230,000
Deduct: Ending work in process inventory		72,000
Cost of goods manufactured		$158,000

Cost of Goods Sold	
Finished goods inventory, beginning	$ 10,000
Add: Cost of goods manufactured	158,000
Goods available for sale	168,000
Deduct: Finished goods inventory, ending	49,500
Unadjusted cost of goods sold	118,500
Add: Underapplied overhead	5,000
Adjusted cost of goods sold	$123,500

*Note that the underapplied overhead is added to cost of goods sold. If overhead were overapplied, it would be deducted from cost of goods sold.

EXHIBIT 2–12
Income Statement

Rand Company Income Statement For the Month Ending April 30		
Sales		$225,000
Less cost of goods sold ($118,500 + $5,000)		123,500
Gross margin		101,500
Less selling and administrative expenses:		
Salaries expense	$30,000	
Depreciation expense	7,000	
Advertising expense	42,000	
Other expense	8,000	87,000
Net operating income		$ 14,500

PROBLEMS OF OVERHEAD APPLICATION

Video 2–1

We need to consider two complications relating to overhead application: (1) the computation of underapplied and overapplied overhead; and (2) the disposition of any balance remaining in the Manufacturing Overhead account at the end of a period.

Underapplied and Overapplied Overhead

Since the predetermined overhead rate is established before the period begins and is based entirely on estimated data, the amount of overhead cost applied to Work in Process will generally differ from the amount of overhead cost actually incurred. In the case of Rand Company, for example, the predetermined overhead rate of $6 per hour was used to apply $90,000 of overhead cost to Work in Process, whereas actual overhead costs for April proved to be $95,000 (see Exhibit 2–8). The difference between the overhead cost applied to Work in Process and the actual overhead costs of a period is called either **underapplied** or **overapplied overhead.** For Rand Company, overhead was underapplied because the applied cost ($90,000) was $5,000 less than the actual cost ($95,000). If the situation had been reversed and the company had applied $95,000 in overhead cost to Work in Process while incurring actual overhead costs of only $90,000, then the overhead would have been overapplied.

> **LEARNING OBJECTIVE 8**
>
> Compute underapplied or overapplied overhead cost and prepare the journal entry to close the balance in Manufacturing Overhead to the appropriate accounts.

What is the cause of underapplied or overapplied overhead? The causes can be complex, and a full explanation will have to wait for later chapters. Nevertheless, the basic problem is that the method of applying overhead to jobs using a predetermined overhead rate assumes that actual overhead costs will be proportional to the actual amount of the allocation base incurred during the period. If, for example, the predetermined overhead rate is $6 per machine-hour, then it is assumed that actual overhead costs incurred will be $6 for every machine-hour that is actually worked. There are at least two reasons why this may not be true. First, much of the overhead often consists of fixed costs that do not change as the number of machine-hours incurred goes up or down. Second, spending on overhead items may or may not be under control. If individuals who are responsible for overhead costs do a good job, those costs should be less than were expected at the beginning of the period. If they do a poor job, those costs will be more than expected. As we indicated above, however, a fuller explanation of the causes of underapplied and overapplied overhead will have to wait for later chapters.

To illustrate what can happen, suppose that two companies—Turbo Crafters and Black & Howell—have prepared the following estimated data for the coming year:

	Turbo Crafters	Black & Howell
Allocation base	Machine-hours	Direct materials cost
Estimated manufacturing overhead cost (a).	$300,000	$120,000
Estimated total amount of the allocation base (b)	75,000 machine-hours	$80,000 direct materials cost
Predetermined overhead rate (a) ÷ (b)	$4 per machine-hour	150% of direct materials cost

Note that when the allocation base is dollars—such as direct materials cost in the case of Black & Howell—the predetermined overhead rate is expressed as a percentage of the allocation base. When dollars are divided by dollars, the result is a percentage.

Now assume that because of unexpected changes in overhead spending and changes in demand for the companies' products, the *actual* overhead cost and the actual activity recorded during the year in each company are as follows:

	Turbo Crafters	Black & Howell
Actual manufacturing overhead cost	$290,000	$130,000
Actual total amount of the allocation base	68,000 machine-hours	$90,000 direct materials cost

For each company, note that the actual data for both cost and the allocation base differ from the estimates used in computing the predetermined overhead rate. This results in underapplied and overapplied overhead as follows:

	Turbo Crafters	Black & Howell
Actual manufacturing overhead cost	$290,000	$130,000
Manufacturing overhead cost applied to Work in Process during the year:		
Predetermined overhead rate (a)	$4 per machine-hour	150% of direct materials cost
Actual total amount of the allocation base (b)......	68,000 machine-hours	$90,000 direct materials cost
Manufacturing overhead applied (a) × (b)	$272,000	$135,000
Underapplied (overapplied) manufacturing overhead....	$18,000	$(5,000)

For Turbo Crafters, notice that the amount of overhead cost applied to Work in Process ($272,000) is less than the actual overhead cost for the year ($290,000). Therefore, overhead is underapplied. Also, notice that the original estimate of overhead for Turbo Crafters ($300,000) is not directly involved in this computation. Its impact is felt only through the $4 predetermined overhead rate.

For Black & Howell, the amount of overhead cost applied to Work in Process ($135,000) is greater than the actual overhead cost for the year ($130,000), and so overhead is overapplied.

A summary of the concepts discussed above is presented in Exhibit 2–13.

Disposition of Underapplied or Overapplied Overhead Balances

What happens to any underapplied or overapplied balance remaining in the Manufacturing Overhead account at the end of a period? The simplest method is to close out the balance to Cost of Goods Sold. More complicated methods are sometimes used, but they are beyond the scope of this book. To illustrate the simplest method, recall that Rand

EXHIBIT 2–13
Summary of Overhead Concepts

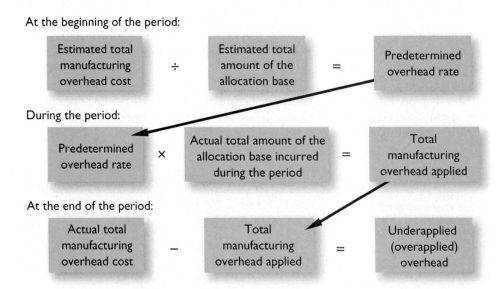

Company had underapplied overhead of $5,000. The entry to close this underapplied overhead to Cost of Goods Sold would be:

(14)

| Cost of Goods Sold .... | 5,000 | |
| Manufacturing Overhead. .... | | 5,000 |

Note that because the Manufacturing Overhead account has a debit balance, Manufacturing Overhead must be credited to close out the account. This has the effect of increasing Cost of Goods Sold for April by $5,000 to $123,500:

Unadjusted cost of goods sold [from entry (13)]..........................	$118,500
Add underapplied overhead [entry (14) above]	5,000
Adjusted cost of goods sold...	$123,500

After this adjustment has been made, Rand Company's income statement for April will appear as shown earlier in Exhibit 2–12.

Remaining Balance in the Overhead Account   YOU DECIDE

The simplest method for disposing of any balance remaining in the Overhead account is to close it out to Cost of Goods Sold. If there is a debit balance (that is, overhead has been underapplied), the entry to dispose of the balance would include a debit to Cost of Goods Sold. That debit would increase the balance in the Cost of Goods Sold account. On the other hand, if there is a credit balance, the entry to dispose of the balance would include a credit to Cost of Goods Sold. That credit would decrease the balance in the Cost of Goods Sold account. If you were the company's controller, would you want a debit balance, a credit balance, or no balance in the Overhead account at the end of the period?

A General Model of Product Cost Flows

Exhibit 2–14 presents a T-account model of the flow of costs in a product costing system. This model applies as much to a process costing system as it does to a job-order costing system. Examination of this model can be very helpful in understanding how costs enter a system, flow through it, and finally end up as Cost of Goods Sold on the income statement.

Multiple Predetermined Overhead Rates

Our discussion in this chapter has assumed that there is a single predetermined overhead rate for an entire factory called a **plantwide overhead rate.** This is a fairly common practice—particularly in smaller companies. But in larger companies, *multiple predetermined overhead rates* are often used. In a **multiple predetermined overhead rate** system, each production department may have its own predetermined overhead rate. Such a system, while more complex, is more accurate, since it can reflect differences across departments in how overhead costs are incurred. For example, overhead might be allocated based on direct labor-hours in departments that are relatively labor intensive and based on machine-hours in departments that are relatively machine intensive. When multiple predetermined overhead rates are used, overhead is applied in each department according to its own overhead rate as a job proceeds through the department.

EXHIBIT 2–14 A General Model of Cost Flows

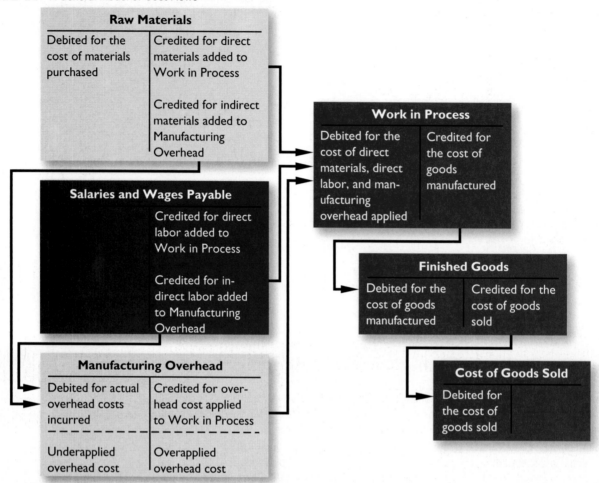

CONCEPT CHECK ✓

2. Which of the following statements is true? (You may select more than one answer.)
   a. The Manufacturing Overhead account is debited when manufacturing overhead is applied to Work in Process.
   b. Job cost sheets accumulate the actual overhead costs incurred to complete a job.
   c. When products are transferred from work in process to finished goods it results in a debit to Finished Goods and a credit to Work in Process.
   d. Selling expenses are applied to production using a predetermined overhead rate that is computed at the beginning of the period.

3. The predetermined overhead rate is $50 per machine hour, underapplied overhead is $5,000, and the actual amount of machine hours is 2,000. What is the actual amount of total manufacturing overhead incurred during the period?
   a. $105,000
   b. $95,000
   c. $150,000
   d. $110,000

JOB-ORDER COSTING IN SERVICE COMPANIES

Job-order costing is also used in service organizations such as law firms, movie studios, hospitals, and repair shops, as well as in manufacturing companies. In a law firm, for example, each client is considered to be a "job," and the costs of that job are accumulated day by day on a job cost sheet as the client's case is handled by the firm. Legal forms and similar inputs represent the direct materials for the job; the time expended by attorneys represents the direct labor; and the costs of secretaries, clerks, rent, depreciation, and so forth, represent the overhead.

In a movie studio such as Columbia Pictures, each film produced by the studio is a "job," and costs for direct materials (costumes, props, film, etc.) and direct labor (actors, directors, and extras) are charged to each film's job cost sheet. A share of the studio's overhead costs, such as utilities, depreciation of equipment, wages of maintenance workers, and so forth, is also charged to each film.

In sum, job-order costing is a versatile and widely used costing method that may be encountered in virtually any organization that provides diverse products or services.

Managing Job Costs in a Service Business

IN BUSINESS

IBM has created a software program called Professional Marketplace to match IBM employees with client needs. "Using Marketplace, IBM consultants working for customers can search through 100 job classifications and 10,000 skills, figuring out who inside IBM is available, where they are located and roughly how much it costs the company to use them." Thus far, the results have been encouraging. IBM has reduced its reliance on outside contractors by 5% to 7% and its consultants spend more of their time in billable work. Furthermore, IBM's senior consultants can search across the globe for available employees with particular niche skills with the click of a mouse instead of having to rely on numerous time-consuming phone calls and emails.

Source: Charles Forelle, "IBM Tool Deploys Employees Efficiently," *The Wall Street Journal*, July 14, 2005, p. B3.

SUMMARY

LO1 Distinguish between process costing and job-order costing and identify companies that would use each costing method.

Job-order costing and process costing are widely used to track costs. Job-order costing is used in situations where the organization offers many different products or services, such as in furniture manufacturing, hospitals, and law firms. Process costing is used where units of product are homogeneous, such as in flour milling or cement production.

LO2 Identify the documents used in a job-order costing system.

In a job-order costing system, each job has its own job cost sheet. Materials requisition forms and labor time tickets are used to record direct materials and direct labor costs. These costs, together with manufacturing overhead, are accumulated on job cost sheets.

LO3 Compute predetermined overhead rates and explain why estimated overhead costs (rather than actual overhead costs) are used in the costing process.

Manufacturing overhead costs are assigned to jobs using a predetermined overhead rate. The rate is determined at the beginning of the period so that jobs can be costed throughout the period rather than waiting until the end of the period. The predetermined overhead rate is determined by dividing the estimated total manufacturing overhead cost for the period by the estimated total amount of the allocation base for the period.

LO4   Prepare journal entries to record costs in a job-order costing system.
Direct materials costs are debited to Work in Process when they are released for use in production. Direct labor costs are debited to Work in Process as incurred. Actual manufacturing overhead costs are debited to the Manufacturing Overhead control account as incurred. Manufacturing overhead costs are applied to Work in Process using the predetermined overhead rate. The journal entry that accomplishes this is a debit to Work in Process and a credit to the Manufacturing Overhead control account.

LO5   Apply overhead cost to Work in Process using a predetermined overhead rate.
Overhead is applied to jobs by multiplying the predetermined overhead rate by the actual amount of the allocation base used by the job.

LO6   Prepare schedules of cost of goods manufactured and cost of goods sold.
See Exhibit 2–11 for an example of these schedules.

LO7   Use T-accounts to show the flow of costs in a job-order cost system.
See Exhibit 2–14 for a summary of the cost flows through the T-accounts.

LO8   Compute underapplied or overapplied overhead cost and prepare the journal entry to close the balance in Manufacturing Overhead to the appropriate accounts.
The difference between the actual overhead cost incurred during a period and the amount of overhead cost applied to production is referred to as underapplied or overapplied overhead. Underapplied or overapplied overhead is closed out to Cost of Goods Sold. When overhead is underapplied, the balance in the Manufacturing Overhead control account is debited to Cost of Goods Sold. This has the effect of increasing the Cost of Goods Sold and occurs because costs assigned to products have been understated. When overhead is overapplied, the balance in the Manufacturing Overhead control account is credited to Cost of Goods Sold. This has the effect of decreasing the Cost of Goods Sold and occurs because costs assigned to products have been overstated.

GUIDANCE ANSWERS TO *DECISION MAKER* AND *YOU DECIDE*

Treasurer, Class Reunion Committee (p. 82)
You should charge $38.00 per person to cover the costs calculated as follows:

Meal cost	$30.00	Direct material cost
Gratuity ($30 × 0.15)	4.50	Direct labor cost
Room charge ($200 ÷ 200 expected attendees)	1.00	Overhead cost
Band cost ($500 ÷ 200 expected attendees)	2.50	Overhead cost
Total cost	$38.00	

If exactly 200 classmates attend the reunion, the $7,600 of receipts (200 @ $38) will cover the expenditures of $7,600 [meal cost of $6,000 (or 200 @ $30) plus gratuity cost of $900 (or $6,000 × 0.15) plus the $200 room charge plus the $500 band cost]. Unfortunately, if less than 200 attend, the Reunion Committee will come up short in an amount equal to the difference between the 200 estimated attendees and the actual number of attendees times $3.50 (the total per person overhead charge). As such, you should talk to the members of the Reunion Committee to ensure that (1) the estimate is as reasonable as possible, and (2) there is a plan to deal with any shortage. On the other hand, if more than 200 attend, the Reunion Committee will collect more money than it needs to disburse. The amount would be equal to the difference between the actual number of attendees and the 200 estimated attendees times $3.50.

Remaining Balance in the Overhead Account (p. 95)
A quick response on your part might have been that you would prefer a credit balance in the Overhead account. The entry to dispose of the balance would decrease the balance in the Cost of Goods Sold account and would cause the company's gross margin and net operating income to be higher than might have otherwise been expected. However, the impact on decision making during the period should be carefully considered.

Ideally, a controller would want the balance in the Overhead account to be zero. If there is no remaining balance in the Overhead account at the end of the period, that means that the actual overhead costs for the period (which are debited to the Overhead account) exactly equaled the overhead costs that were applied (or allocated to the products made by being added to the Work in Process account) during the period. As a result, the products made during the period would have had the "correct" amount of overhead assigned as they moved from the factory floor to the finished goods area to the customer. Typically, this would not be the case because the predetermined overhead rate (used to apply or allocate overhead to the products made) is developed using two estimates (the total amount of overhead expected and the total amount of the allocation base expected during the period). It would be difficult, if not impossible, to accurately predict one or both estimates.

If there is a remaining balance in the Overhead account, then the products manufactured during the period either received too little overhead (if there is a debit or underapplied balance) or too much overhead (if there is a credit or overapplied balance).

GUIDANCE ANSWERS TO CONCEPT CHECKS

1. **Choice c.** A predetermined overhead rate rather than an actual overhead rate is used in a normal costing system.
2. **Choice c.** The Manufacturing Overhead account is credited when manufacturing overhead is applied to Work in Process. Job cost sheets do not accumulate actual overhead costs. They accumulate the amount of the overhead that has been applied to the job using the predetermined overhead rate. Selling expenses are period costs. They are not applied to production.
3. **Choice a.** The amount of overhead applied to production is 2,000 hours multiplied by the $50 predetermined rate, or $100,000. If overhead is underapplied by $5,000, the actual amount of overhead is $100,00 + $5,000, or $105,000.

REVIEW PROBLEM: JOB-ORDER COSTING

Hogle Corporation is a manufacturer that uses job-order costing. On January 1, the beginning of its fiscal year, the company's inventory balances were as follows:

Raw Materials	$20,000
Work in Process.	$15,000
Finished Goods	$30,000

The company applies overhead cost to jobs on the basis of machine-hours worked. For the current year, the company estimated that it would work 75,000 machine-hours and incur $450,000 in manufacturing overhead cost. The following transactions were recorded for the year:

a. Raw materials were purchased on account, $410,000.
b. Raw materials were requisitioned for use in production, $380,000 ($360,000 direct materials and $20,000 indirect materials).
c. The following costs were accrued for employee services: direct labor, $75,000; indirect labor, $110,000; sales commissions, $90,000; and administrative salaries, $200,000.
d. Sales travel costs were $17,000.
e. Utility costs in the factory were $43,000.
f. Advertising costs were $180,000.
g. Depreciation was recorded for the year, $350,000 (80% relates to factory operations, and 20% relates to selling and administrative activities).
h. Insurance expired during the year, $10,000 (70% relates to factory operations, and the remaining 30% relates to selling and administrative activities).

i. Manufacturing overhead was applied to production. Due to greater than expected demand for its products, the company worked 80,000 machine-hours during the year.

j. Goods costing $900,000 to manufacture according to their job cost sheets were completed during the year.

k. Goods were sold on account to customers during the year for a total of $1,500,000. The goods cost $870,000 to manufacture according to their job cost sheets.

Required:

1. Prepare journal entries to record the preceding transactions.
2. Post the entries in (1) above to T-accounts (don't forget to enter the beginning balances in the inventory accounts).
3. Is Manufacturing Overhead underapplied or overapplied for the year? Prepare a journal entry to close any balance in the Manufacturing Overhead account to Cost of Goods Sold.
4. Prepare an income statement for the year.

Solution to Review Problem

1.	a.	Raw Materials	410,000	
		Accounts Payable		410,000
	b.	Work in Process	360,000	
		Manufacturing Overhead	20,000	
		Raw Materials		380,000
	c.	Work in Process	75,000	
		Manufacturing Overhead	110,000	
		Sales Commissions Expense	90,000	
		Administrative Salaries Expense	200,000	
		Salaries and Wages Payable		475,000
	d.	Sales Travel Expense	17,000	
		Accounts Payable		17,000
	e.	Manufacturing Overhead	43,000	
		Accounts Payable		43,000
	f.	Advertising Expense	180,000	
		Accounts Payable		180,000
	g.	Manufacturing Overhead	280,000	
		Depreciation Expense	70,000	
		Accumulated Depreciation		350,000
	h.	Manufacturing Overhead	7,000	
		Insurance Expense	3,000	
		Prepaid Insurance		10,000
	i.	The predetermined overhead rate for the year would be computed as follows:		

$$\text{Predetermined overhead rate} = \frac{\text{Estimated total manufacturing overhead cost}}{\text{Estimated total amount of the allocation base}}$$

$$= \frac{\$450,000}{75,000 \text{ machine-hours}}$$

$$= \$6 \text{ per machine-hours}$$

On the basis of the 80,000 machine-hours actually worked during the year, the company would have applied $480,000 in overhead cost to production: $6 per machine-hour × 80,000 machine-hours = $480,000. The following entry records this application of overhead cost:

		Work in Process	480,000	
		Manufacturing Overhead		480,000
	j.	Finished Goods	900,000	
		Work in Process		900,000
	k.	Accounts Receivable	1,500,000	
		Sales		1,500,000
		Cost of Goods Sold	870,000	
		Finished Goods		870,000

2.

Accounts Receivable			Manufacturing Overhead				Sales		
(k)	1,500,000		(b)	20,000	(i)	480,000		(k)	1,500,000
			(c)	110,000					
Prepaid Insurance			(e)	43,000				**Cost of Goods Sold**	
		(h) 10,000	(g)	280,000			(k)	870,000	
			(h)	7,000					
Raw Materials				460,000		480,000		**Commissions Expense**	
Bal.	20,000	(b) 380,000			Bal.	20,000	(c)	90,000	
(a)	410,000		**Accumulated Depreciation**						
Bal.	50,000							**Administrative Salaries Expense**	
					(g)	350,000	(c)	200,000	
Work in Process			**Accounts Payable**						
Bal.	15,000	(j) 900,000			(a)	410,000		**Sales Travel Expense**	
(b)	360,000				(d)	17,000	(d)	17,000	
(c)	75,000				(e)	43,000			
(i)	480,000				(f)	180,000		**Advertising Expense**	
Bal.	30,000						(f)	180,000	
			Salaries and Wages Payable						
Finished Goods								**Depreciation Expense**	
					(c)	475,000	(g)	70,000	
Bal.	30,000	(k) 870,000							
(j)	900,000							**Insurance Expense**	
Bal.	60,000						(h)	3,000	

3. Manufacturing overhead is overapplied for the year. The entry to close it out to Cost of Goods Sold is as follows:

Manufacturing Overhead	20,000	
Cost of Goods Sold		20,000

4.

Hogle Corporation
Income Statement
For the Year Ended December 31

Sales		$1,500,000
Cost of goods sold ($870,000 − $20,000).....................		850,000
Gross margin...		650,000
Selling and administrative expenses:		
Sales commissions expense	$ 90,000	
Administrative salaries expense	200,000	
Sales travel expense	17,000	
Advertising expense	180,000	
Depreciation expense..	70,000	
Insurance expense	3,000	560,000
Net operating income		$ 90,000

GLOSSARY

Absorption costing   A costing method that includes all manufacturing costs—direct materials, direct labor, and both variable and fixed manufacturing overhead—in the cost of a product. (p. 74)

Allocation base   A measure of activity such as direct labor-hours or machine-hours that is used to assign costs to cost objects. (p. 79)

Bill of materials   A document that shows the quantity of each type of direct material required to make a product. (p. 76)

Cost driver   A factor, such as machine-hours, beds occupied, computer time, or flight-hours, that causes overhead costs. (p. 81)

Job cost sheet   A form prepared for a job that records the materials, labor, and manufacturing overhead costs charged to that job. (p. 77)

Job-order costing system   A costing system used in situations where many different products, jobs, or services are produced each period. (p. 75)

Materials requisition form   A detailed source document that specifies the type and quantity of materials to be drawn from the storeroom and that identifies the job that is charged for the cost of those materials. (p. 76)

Multiple predetermined overhead rates   A costing system with multiple overhead cost pools with a different predetermined overhead rate for each cost pool, rather than a single predetermined overhead rate for the entire company. Each production department is often treated as a separate overhead cost pool. (p. 95)

Normal cost system   A costing system in which overhead costs are applied to a job by multiplying a predetermined overhead rate by the actual amount of the allocation base incurred by the job. (p. 80)

Overapplied overhead   A credit balance in the Manufacturing Overhead account that occurs when the amount of overhead cost applied to Work in Process exceeds the amount of overhead cost actually incurred during a period. (p. 93)

Overhead application   The process of charging manufacturing overhead cost to job cost sheets and to the Work in Process account. (p. 79)

Plantwide overhead rate   A single predetermined overhead rate that is used throughout a plant. (p. 95)

Predetermined overhead rate   A rate used to charge overhead cost to jobs that is established in advance for each period. It is computed by dividing the estimated total manufacturing overhead cost by the estimated total amount of the allocation base for the period. (p. 79)

Process costing system   A costing system used in situations where a single, homogeneous product (such as cement or flour) is produced for long periods of time. (p. 74)

Time ticket   A detailed source document that is used to record the amount of time an employee spends on various activities during a day. (p. 78)

Underapplied overhead   A debit balance in the Manufacturing Overhead account that arises when the amount of overhead cost actually incurred exceeds the amount of overhead cost applied to Work in Process during a period. (p. 93)

Quiz 2

Multiple-choice questions are provided on the text website at www.mhhe.com/brewer4e.

QUESTIONS

2–1   Why aren't actual overhead costs traced to jobs just as direct materials and direct labor costs are traced to jobs?

2–2   When would job-order costing be used instead of process costing?

2–3   What is the purpose of the job cost sheet in a job-order costing system?

2–4   What is a predetermined overhead rate, and how is it computed?

2–5   Explain how a sales order, a production order, a materials requisition form, and a labor time ticket are involved in producing and costing products.

2–6   Explain why some production costs must be allocated rather than traced to products. Name several such costs. Would such costs be classified as *direct* or as *indirect* costs?

2–7   Why are predetermined overhead rates rather than actual manufacturing overhead costs used to apply manufacturing overhead to jobs?

2–8   What factors should be considered in selecting an allocation base?

2–9   If a company allocates all of its overhead costs to jobs, does this guarantee that the company will earn a profit?

2–10   What account is credited when overhead cost is applied to Work in Process? Would you expect the amount applied for a period to equal the actual overhead costs of the period? Why or why not?

2–11 What is underapplied overhead? Overapplied overhead? What disposition is made of these amounts at the end of the period?

2–12 Give two reasons why overhead might be underapplied in a given year.

2–13 What adjustment is made for underapplied overhead on the schedule of cost of goods sold? What adjustment is made for overapplied overhead?

2–14 What is a plantwide overhead rate? Why are multiple overhead rates, rather than a plantwide rate, used in some companies?

2–15 What happens to overhead rates based on direct labor when automated equipment replaces direct labor?

 BRIEF EXERCISES

BRIEF EXERCISE 2–1 Process versus Job-Order Costing (LO1)

Which would be more appropriate in each of the following situations—job-order costing or process costing?

a. A custom yacht builder.
b. A golf course designer.
c. A potato chip manufacturer.
d. A business consultant.
e. A plywood manufacturer.
f. A soft-drink bottler.
g. A film studio.
h. A company that supervises bridge construction projects.
i. A manufacturer of fine custom jewelry.
j. A made-to-order clothing factory.
k. A factory making one personal computer model.
l. A fertilizer factory.

BRIEF EXERCISE 2–2 Job-Order Costing Documents (LO2)

Mountain Gearing Company has incurred the following costs on Job ES34, an order for 40 gearing wheels to be delivered at the end of next month.

Direct materials:
   On March 5, requisition number 870 was issued for 40 titanium blanks to be used in the special order. The blanks cost $8.00 each.
   On March 8, requisition number 873 was issued for 960 hardened nibs also to be used in the special order. The nibs cost $0.60 each.
Direct labor:
   On March 9, Harry Kerst worked from 9:00 A.M. until 12:15 P.M. on Job ES34. He is paid $12.00 per hour.
   On March 21, Mary Rosas worked from 2:15 P.M. until 4:30 P.M. on Job ES34. She is paid $14.00 per hour.

Required:
1. On what documents would these costs be recorded?
2. How much cost should have been recorded on each of the documents for Job ES34?

BRIEF EXERCISE 2–3 Compute the Predetermined Overhead Rate (LO3)

Logan Products computes its predetermined overhead rate annually on the basis of direct labor-hours. At the beginning of the year it estimated that its total manufacturing overhead would be $586,000 and the total direct labor would be 40,000 hours. Its actual total manufacturing overhead for the year was $713,400 and its actual total direct labor was 41,000 hours.

Required:
Compute the company's predetermined overhead rate for the year.

BRIEF EXERCISE 2–4 Prepare Journal Entries (LO4)

Kirkaid Company recorded the following transactions for the just completed month.

a. $86,000 in raw materials were purchased on account.
b. $84,000 in raw materials were requisitioned for use in production. Of this amount, $72,000 was for direct materials and the remainder was for indirect materials.

c. Total labor wages of $108,000 were incurred. Of this amount, $105,000 was for direct labor and the remainder was for indirect labor.

d. Additional manufacturing overhead costs of $197,000 were incurred.

Required:

Record the above transactions in journal entries.

BRIEF EXERCISE 2–5   Apply Overhead (LO5)

Westan Corporation uses a predetermined overhead rate of $23.10 per direct labor-hour. This predetermined rate was based on 12,000 estimated direct labor-hours and $277,200 of estimated total manufacturing overhead.

The company incurred actual total manufacturing overhead costs of $266,000 and 12,600 total direct labor-hours during the period.

Required:

Determine the amount of manufacturing overhead that would have been applied to units of product during the period.

BRIEF EXERCISE 2–6   Prepare Schedules of Cost of Goods Manufactured and Cost of Goods Sold (LO6)

Parmitan Corporation has provided the following data concerning last month's manufacturing operations.

Purchases of raw materials		$53,000
Indirect materials included in manufacturing overhead		$8,000
Direct labor		$62,000
Manufacturing overhead applied to work in process		$41,000
Underapplied overhead		$8,000

	Beginning	**Ending**
Inventories:		
Raw materials	$24,000	$6,000
Work in process	$41,000	$38,000
Finished goods	$86,000	$93,000

Required:

1. Prepare a Schedule of Cost of Goods Manufactured.
2. Prepare a Schedule of Cost of Goods Sold.

BRIEF EXERCISE 2–7   Prepare T-Accounts (LO7, LO8)

Granger Products recorded the following transactions for the just completed month. The company had no beginning inventories.

a. $75,000 in raw materials were purchased for cash.

b. $73,000 in raw materials were requisitioned for use in production. Of this amount, $67,000 was for direct materials and the remainder was for indirect materials.

c. Total labor wages of $152,000 were incurred and paid. Of this amount, $134,000 was for direct labor and the remainder was for indirect labor.

d. Additional manufacturing overhead costs of $126,000 were incurred and paid.

e. Manufacturing overhead costs of $178,000 were applied to jobs using the company's predetermined overhead rate.

f. All of the jobs in progress at the end of the month were completed and shipped to customers.

g. The underapplied or overapplied overhead for the period was closed out to Cost of Goods Sold.

Required:

1. Post the above transactions to T-accounts.
2. Determine the cost of goods sold for the period.

BRIEF EXERCISE 2–8   Underapplied and Overapplied Overhead (LO8)

Cretin Enterprises uses a predetermined overhead rate of $21.40 per direct labor-hour. This predetermined rate was based on 8,000 estimated direct labor-hours and $171,200 of estimated total manufacturing overhead.

The company incurred actual total manufacturing overhead costs of $172,500 and 8,250 total direct labor-hours during the period.

Required:
1. Determine the amount of underapplied or overapplied manufacturing overhead for the period.
2. Assuming that the entire amount of the underapplied or overapplied overhead is closed out to Cost of Goods Sold, what would be the effect of the underapplied or overapplied overhead on the company's gross margin for the period?

 **EXERCISES**

EXERCISE 2–9 Journal Entries and T-Accounts (LO4, LO5, LO7)

Foley Company uses a job-order costing system. The following data relate to the month of October, the first month of the company's fiscal year:

a. Raw materials purchased on account, $210,000.
b. Raw materials issued to production, $190,000 (80% direct and 20% indirect).
c. Direct labor cost incurred, $49,000; and indirect labor cost incurred, $21,000.
d. Depreciation recorded on factory equipment, $105,000.
e. Other manufacturing overhead costs incurred during October, $130,000 (credit Accounts Payable).
f. The company applies manufacturing overhead cost to production on the basis of $4 per machine-hour. A total of 75,000 machine-hours were recorded for October.
g. Production orders costing $510,000 according to their job cost sheets were completed during October and transferred to Finished Goods.
h. Production orders that had cost $450,000 to complete according to their job cost sheets were shipped to customers during the month. These goods were sold on account at 50% above cost.

Required:
1. Prepare journal entries to record the information given above.
2. Prepare T-accounts for Manufacturing Overhead and Work in Process. Post the relevant information above to each account. Compute the ending balance in each account, assuming that Work in Process has a beginning balance of $35,000.

EXERCISE 2–10 Applying Overhead; Journal Entries; T-Accounts (LO3, LO4, LO5, LO7)

Custom Metal Works produces castings and other metal parts to customer specifications. The company uses a job-order costing system and applies overhead costs to jobs on the basis of machine-hours. At the beginning of the year, the company estimated that it would work 576,000 machine-hours and incur $4,320,000 in manufacturing overhead cost.

The company had no work in process at the beginning of the year. The company spent the entire month of January working on one large order—Job 382, which was an order for 8,000 machined parts. Cost data for January follow:

a. Raw materials purchased on account, $315,000.
b. Raw materials requisitioned for production, $270,000 (80% direct materials and 20% indirect materials).
c. Labor cost incurred in the factory, $190,000, of which $80,000 was direct labor and $110,000 was indirect labor.
d. Depreciation recorded on factory equipment, $63,000.
e. Other manufacturing overhead costs incurred, $85,000 (credit Accounts Payable).
f. Manufacturing overhead cost was applied to production on the basis of 40,000 machine-hours actually worked during January.
g. The completed job was moved into the finished goods warehouse on January 31 to await delivery to the customer. (In computing the dollar amount for this entry, remember that the cost of a completed job consists of direct materials, direct labor, and *applied* overhead.)

Required:
1. Prepare journal entries to record items (a) through (f) above. Ignore item (g) for the moment.
2. Prepare T-accounts for Manufacturing Overhead and Work in Process. Post the relevant items from your journal entries to these T-accounts.
3. Prepare a journal entry for item (g) above.
4. Compute the unit product cost that will appear on the job cost sheet for Job 382.

Sifting through ashes and interviewing selected employees has turned up the following additional information:

a. The controller remembers clearly that the predetermined overhead rate was based on an estimated 60,000 direct labor-hours to be worked over the year and an estimated $180,000 in manufacturing overhead costs.

b. The production superintendent's cost sheets showed only one job in process on April 30. Materials of $2,600 had been added to the job, and 300 direct labor-hours had been expended at $6 per hour.

c. The accounts payable are for raw material purchases only, according to the accounts payable clerk. He clearly remembers that the balance in the account was $6,000 on April 1. An analysis of canceled checks (kept in the treasurer's office) shows that payments of $40,000 were made to suppliers during April. (All materials used during April were direct materials.)

d. A charred piece of the payroll ledger shows that 5,200 direct labor-hours were recorded for the month. The personnel department has verified that there were no variations in pay rates among employees. (This infuriated Orville, who felt that his services were underpaid.)

e. Records maintained in the finished goods warehouse indicate that the finished goods inventory totaled $11,000 on April 1.

f. From another charred piece in the vault, you are able to discern that the cost of goods manufactured for April was $89,000.

Required:

1. Assign one of the following sets of accounts to each member of the team:
    a. Raw Materials and Accounts Payable.
    b. Work in Process and Manufacturing Overhead.
    c. Finished Goods and Cost of Goods Sold.
    Determine the types of transactions that would be posted to each account and present a summary to the other team members. When agreement is reached, the team should work together to complete steps 2 through 4.

2. Determine the company's predetermined overhead rate and the total manufacturing overhead applied for the month.

3. Determine the April 30 balance in the company's Work in Process account.

4. Prepare the company's T-accounts for the month. (It is easiest to complete the T-accounts in the following order: Accounts Payable, Work in Process, Raw Materials, Manufacturing Overhead, Finished Goods, Cost of Goods Sold.)

COMMUNICATING IN PRACTICE   (LO1, LO3, LO5)

Look in the yellow pages or contact your local chamber of commerce or local chapter of the Institute of Management Accountants to find the names of manufacturing companies in your area. Call or make an appointment to meet with the controller or chief financial officer of one of these companies.

Required:

Ask the following questions and write a brief memorandum to your instructor that addresses what you found out.

1. What are the company's main products?

2. Does the company use job-order costing, process costing, or some other method of determining product costs?

3. How is overhead assigned to products? What is the overhead rate? What is the basis of allocation? Is more than one overhead rate used?

4. Has the company recently changed its cost system or is it considering changing its cost system? If so, why? What changes were made or what changes are being considered?

RESEARCH AND APPLICATION   [LO1, LO2, LO3]

The questions in this exercise are based on Toll Brothers, Inc., one of the largest home builders in the United States. To answer the questions, you will need to download Toll Brothers' 2004 annual report (www.tollbrothers.com/homesearch/servlet/HomeSearch?app=IRannual) and its Form 10-K for the fiscal year ended October 31, 2004. To access the 10-K report, go to www.sec.gov/edgar/searchedgar/companysearch.html. Input CIK code 794170 and hit enter. In the gray box on the right-hand side of your computer screen define the scope of your search by inputting 10-K and then pressing enter. Select the 10-K with a filing date of January 13, 2005. You do not need to print these documents to answer the questions.

REQUIRED:

1. What is Toll Brothers' strategy for success in the marketplace? Does the company rely primarily on a customer intimacy, operational excellence, or product leadership customer value proposition? What evidence supports your conclusion?
2. What business risks does Toll Brothers face that may threaten the company's ability to satisfy stockholder expectations? What are some examples of control activities that the company could use to reduce these risks? (*Hint:* Focus on pages 10–11 of the 10-K.)
3. Would Toll Brothers be more likely to use process costing or job-order costing? Why?
4. What are some examples of Toll Brothers' direct material costs? Would you expect the bill of materials for each of Toll Brothers' homes to be the same or different? Why?
5. Describe the types of direct labor costs incurred by Toll Brothers. Would Toll Brothers use employee time tickets at their homesites under construction? Why or why not?
6. What are some examples of overhead costs that are incurred by Toll Brothers?
7. Some companies establish prices for their products by marking up their full manufacturing cost (i.e., the sum of direct materials, direct labor, and manufacturing overhead costs). For example, a company may set prices at 150% of each product's full manufacturing cost. Does Toll Brothers price its houses using this approach?
8. How does Toll Brothers assign manufacturing overhead costs to cost objects? From a financial reporting standpoint, why does the company need to assign manufacturing overhead costs to cost objects?

3

Systems Design: Activity-Based Costing

<< A LOOK BACK

Chapter 2 provided an overview of job-order costing. Direct materials and direct labor costs are traced directly to jobs. Manufacturing overhead is applied to jobs using a predetermined overhead rate.

A LOOK AT THIS CHAPTER

In Chapter 3, we continue the discussion of allocation of overhead. Activity-based costing is a technique that uses a number of allocation bases to assign overhead costs to products.

A LOOK AHEAD >>

After comparing job-order and process costing systems, we go into the details of a process costing system in Chapter 4.

CHAPTER OUTLINE

Assigning Overhead Costs to Products

- Plantwide Overhead Rate

- Departmental Overhead Rates

- Activity-Based Costing (ABC)

Designing an Activity-Based Costing System

- Hierarchy of Activities

- An Example of an Activity-Based Costing System Design

Using Activity-Based Costing

- Comtek Sound, Inc.'s Basic Data

- Direct Labor-Hours as a Base

- Computing Activity Rates

- Computing Product Costs

- Shifting of Overhead Cost

Targeting Process Improvements

Evaluation of Activity-Based Costing

- The Benefits of Activity-Based Costing

- Limitations of Activity-Based Costing

- Activity-Based Costing and Service Industries

Cost Flows in an Activity-Based Costing System

- An Example of Cost Flows

LEARNING OBJECTIVES

LP 3

*After studying Chapter 3,
you should be able to:*

LO1 Understand the basic approach in activity-based costing and how it differs from conventional costing.

LO2 Compute activity rates for an activity-based costing system.

LO3 Compute product costs using activity-based costing.

LO4 Contrast the product costs computed under activity-based costing and conventional costing methods.

LO5 Record the flow of costs in an activity-based costing system.

DECISION FEATURE

The Payoff from Activity-Based Costing

Implementing an activity-based costing system can be expensive. To be worthwhile, the data supplied by the system must actually be used to make decisions and improve profitability. Insteel Industries manufactures a range of products, such as concrete reinforcing steel, industrial wire, and bulk nails, for the construction, home furnishings, appliance, and tire manufacturing industries. The company implemented an activity-based costing system at its manufacturing plant in Andrews, South Carolina, and immediately began using activity-based data to make strategic and operating decisions.

In terms of strategic decisions, Insteel dropped some unprofitable products, raised prices on others, and in some cases even discontinued relationships with unprofitable customers. Of course, Insteel realized that simply discontinuing products and customers does not improve profits. The company needed to either deploy its freed-up capacity to increase sales, or it needed to eliminate its freed-up capacity to reduce costs. Insteel chose the former and used its activity-based costing system to identify which new business opportunities to pursue.

In terms of operational improvements, Insteel's activity-based costing system revealed that its 20 most expensive activities consumed 87% of the plant's $21.4 million in physical and human resource costs. Almost $4.9 million was being consumed by non-value-added activities. Teams were formed to reduce quality costs, material handling and freight costs, and maintenance costs. Within one year, quality costs had been cut by $1,800,000 and freight costs by $550,000. Overall, non-value-added activity costs dropped from 22% to 17% of total activity costs.

Source: V. G. Narayanan and R. Sarkar, "The Impact of Activity-Based Costing on Managerial Decisions at Insteel Industries—A Field Study," *Journal of Economics & Management Strategy*, Summer 2002, pp. 257–288.

As discussed in earlier chapters, direct materials and direct labor costs can be directly traced to products. Overhead costs, on the other hand, cannot be easily traced to products. Some other means must be found for assigning them to products for financial reporting and other purposes. In the previous chapter, overhead costs were assigned to products using a plantwide predetermined overhead rate. This method is simpler than the methods of assigning overhead costs to products described in this chapter, but this simplicity has a cost. A plantwide predetermined overhead rate spreads overhead costs uniformly over products in proportion to whatever allocation base is used—most commonly, direct labor-hours. This procedure results in high overhead costs for products with a high direct labor-hour content and low overhead costs for products with a low direct labor-hour content. However, the real causes of overhead may have little to do with direct labor-hours and as a consequence, product costs may be distorted. Activity-based costing attempts to correct these distortions by more accurately assigning overhead costs to products.

ASSIGNING OVERHEAD COSTS TO PRODUCTS

Video 3–1

Companies use three common approaches to assign overhead costs to products. The simplest method is to use a plantwide overhead rate. A slightly more refined approach is to use departmental overhead rates. The most complex method is activity-based costing, which is the most accurate of the three approaches to overhead cost assignment.

Plantwide Overhead Rate

The preceding chapter assumed that a single overhead rate, called a *plantwide overhead rate,* was used throughout an entire factory. This simple approach to overhead assignment can result in distorted unit product costs, as we shall see below.

When cost systems were developed in the 1800s, cost and activity data had to be collected by hand and all calculations were done with paper and pen. Consequently, the emphasis was on simplicity. Companies often established a single overhead cost pool for an entire facility or department as described in Chapter 2. Direct labor was the obvious choice as an allocation base for overhead costs. Direct labor-hours were already being recorded for purposes of determining wages. In the labor-intensive production processes of that time, direct labor was a large component of product costs—larger than it is today. Moreover, managers believed direct labor and overhead costs were highly correlated. (Two variables, such as direct labor and overhead costs, are highly correlated if they tend to move together.) And finally, most companies produced a very limited variety of similar products, so in fact there was probably little difference in the overhead costs attributable to different products. Under these conditions, it was not cost-effective to use a more elaborate costing system.

Conditions have changed. Many companies now sell a large variety of products that consume significantly different amounts of overhead resources. Consequently, a costing system that assigns essentially the same overhead cost to every product may no longer be adequate. Additionally, factors other than direct labor often drive overhead costs.

On an economywide basis, direct labor and overhead costs have been moving in opposite directions for a long time. As a percentage of total cost, direct labor has been declining, whereas overhead has been increasing. Many tasks previously done by hand are now done with largely automated equipment—a component of overhead. Furthermore, product diversity has increased. Companies are introducing new products and services at an ever-accelerating rate. Managing and sustaining this product diversity requires many more overhead resources such as production schedulers and product design engineers, and many of these overhead resources have no obvious connection with direct labor. Finally, computers, bar code readers, and other technology have dramatically reduced the costs of collecting and processing data—making more complex (and accurate) costing systems such as activity-based costing much less expensive to build and maintain.

Nevertheless, direct labor remains a viable base for applying overhead to products in some companies—particularly for external reports. Direct labor is an appropriate allocation base for overhead when overhead costs and direct labor are highly correlated. And indeed, most companies throughout the world continue to base overhead allocations on direct labor or machine-hours. However, if factorywide overhead costs do not move in tandem with factorywide direct labor or machine-hours, product costs will be distorted.

Departmental Overhead Rates

Rather than use a plantwide overhead rate, many companies use departmental overhead rates with a different predetermined overhead rate in each production department. The nature of the work performed in a department will determine the department's allocation base. For example, overhead costs in a machining department may be allocated on the basis of machine-hours. In contrast, the overhead costs in an assembly department may be allocated on the basis of direct labor-hours.

Unfortunately, even departmental overhead rates will not correctly assign overhead costs in situations where a company has a range of products and complex overhead costs. The reason is that the departmental approach usually relies on volume as the base for allocating overhead cost to products. For example, if the machining department's overhead is applied to products on the basis of machine-hours, it is assumed that the department's overhead costs are caused by, and are directly proportional to, machine-hours. However, the department's overhead costs are probably more complex than this and are caused by a variety of factors, including the range of products processed in the department, the number of batch setups that are required, the complexity of the products, and so on. A more sophisticated method like *activity-based costing* is required to adequately account for these diverse factors.

Activity-Based Costing (ABC)

Activity-based costing (ABC) is a technique that attempts to assign overhead costs more accurately to products than the simpler methods discussed thus far. The basic idea underlying the activity-based costing approach is illustrated in Exhibit 3–1. A customer order triggers a number of activities. For example, if Nordstrom orders a line of women's skirts from Calvin Klein, a production order is generated, patterns are created, materials are ordered, textiles are cut to pattern and then sewn, and the finished products are packed for shipping. These activities consume resources. For example, ordering the appropriate materials consumes clerical time—a resource the company must pay for. In activity-based costing, an attempt is made to trace these costs directly to the products that cause them.

Rather than a single allocation base such as direct labor-hours or machine-hours, in activity-based costing a company uses a number of allocation bases for assigning costs to products. Each allocation base in an activity-based costing system represents a major *activity* that causes overhead costs. An **activity** in activity-based costing is an event that causes the consumption of overhead resources. Examples of activities in various organizations include the following:

- Setting up machines.
- Admitting patients to a hospital.
- Scheduling production.
- Performing blood tests at a clinic.
- Billing customers.
- Maintaining equipment.
- Ordering materials or supplies.
- Stocking shelves at a store.
- Meeting with clients at a law firm.
- Preparing shipments.
- Inspecting materials for defects.
- Opening an account at a bank.

Activity-based costing focuses on these activities. Each major activity has its own overhead cost pool (also known as an *activity cost pool*), its own *activity measure*, and its

EXHIBIT 3–1
The Activity-Based Costing Model

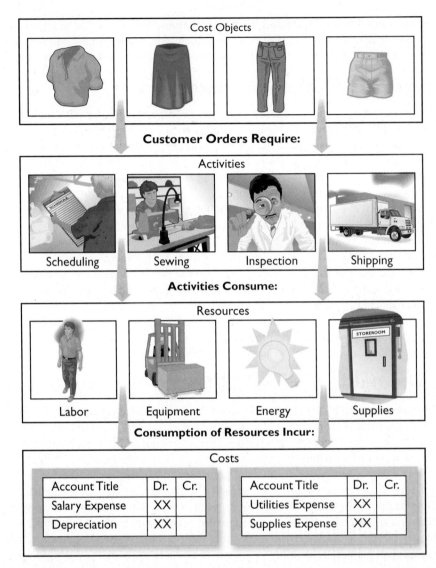

own predetermined overhead rate (also known as an *activity rate*). An **activity cost pool** is a "cost bucket" in which costs related to a particular activity measure are accumulated. The **activity measure** expresses how much of the activity is carried out and it is used as the allocation base for applying overhead costs to products and services. For example, *the number of patients admitted* is a natural choice of an activity measure for the activity *admitting patients to the hospital*. An **activity rate** is a predetermined overhead rate in an activity-based costing system. Each activity has its own activity rate that is used to apply overhead costs to cost objects.

IN BUSINESS   Shedding Light on Product Profitability

Reichhold, Inc., one of the world's leading suppliers of synthetic materials, has adopted activity-based costing. Reichhold's prior cost system used one allocation base, reactor hours, to assign overhead costs to products. The new ABC system uses four additional activity measures—preprocess preparation hours, thin-tank hours, filtration hours, and waste disposal costs per batch—to assign costs to products. Reichhold has rolled out ABC to all 19 of its North American plants because the management team believes that ABC helps improve the company's "capacity management, cycle times, value-added pricing decisions, and analysis of product profitability."

Source: Edward Blocher, Betty Wong, and Christopher McKittrick, "Making Bottom-Up ABC Work at Reichhold, Inc.," *Strategic Finance*, April 2002, pp. 51–55.

For example, the activity *setting up machines to process a batch* would have its own activity cost pool. Products are ordinarily processed in batches. And since each product has its own machine settings, machines must be set up when changing over from a batch of one product to another. If the total cost in this activity cost pool is $150,000 and the total expected activity is 1,000 machine setups, the predetermined overhead rate (i.e., activity rate) for this activity would be $150 per machine setup ($150,000 ÷ 1,000 machine setups = $150 per machine setup). Each product that requires a machine setup would be charged $150. Note that this charge does not depend on how many units are produced after the machine is set up. A small batch requiring a machine setup would be charged $150—just the same as a large batch.

Taking each activity in isolation, this system works exactly like the job-order costing system described in the last chapter. A predetermined overhead rate is computed for each activity and then applied to jobs and products based on the amount of activity consumed by the job or product.

Is E-Tailing Really Easier?

IN BUSINESS

The company art.com™ sells prints and framed prints over the web. An ABC study identified the following 12 activities carried out in the company:

1. Service customers
2. Website optimization
3. Merchandise inventory selection and management
4. Purchasing and receiving
5. Customer acquisition and retention—paid-for marketing
6. Customer acquisition and retention—revenue share marketing (affiliate group)
7. Sustain information system
8. Sustain business—administration
9. Sustain business—production
10. Maintain facility—administrative
11. Maintain facility—production
12. Sustain business—executive

For example, the activity "merchandise inventory selection and management" involves scanning, describing, classifying, and linking each inventory item to search options. "Staff must carefully manage each change to the database, which is similar to adding and removing inventory items from the shelf of a store. They annotate added inventory items and upload them into the system, as well as remove obsolete and discontinued items... The number of inventory items for an e-tailer is typically much greater than for a bricks-and-mortar [store], which is a competitive advantage, but experience shows managing a large inventory consumes substantial resources."

Source: Thomas L. Zeller, David R. Kublank, and Philip G. Makris, "How art.com™ Uses ABC to Succeed," *Strategic Finance*, March 2001, pp. 25–31. Reprinted with permission from the IMA, Montvale, NJ, USA, www.imanet.org.

DESIGNING AN ACTIVITY-BASED COSTING SYSTEM

The most important decisions in designing an activity-based costing system concern what activities will be included in the system and how the activities will be measured. In most companies, hundreds or even thousands of different activities cause overhead costs. These activities range from taking a telephone order to training new employees. Setting up and maintaining a complex costing system that includes all of these activities would be prohibitively expensive. The challenge in designing an activity-based costing system is to identify a reasonably small number of activities that explain the bulk of the variation in overhead costs. This is usually done by interviewing a broad range of managers in the

Topic Tackler
PLUS

Concept 3-1

Level	Activities	Activity Measures
Unit-level	Processing units on machines	Machine-hours
	Processing units by hand	Direct labor-hours
	Consuming factory supplies	Units produced
Batch-level	Processing purchase orders	Purchase orders processed
	Processing production orders	Production orders processed
	Setting up equipment	Number of setups; setup hours
	Handling material	Pounds of material handled; number of times material moved
Product-level	Testing new products	Hours of testing time
	Administering parts inventories	Number of part types
	Designing products	Hours of design time
Facility-level	General factory administration	Direct labor-hours*
	Plant building and grounds	Direct labor-hours*

*Facility-level costs cannot be traced on a cause-and-effect basis to individual products. Nevertheless, these costs are usually allocated to products for external reports using some arbitrary allocation basis such as direct labor-hours.

organization to find out what activities they think are important and that consume most of the resources they manage. This often results in a long list of potential activities that could be included in the activity-based costing system. This list is refined and pruned in consultation with top managers. Related activities are frequently combined to reduce the amount of detail and record-keeping cost. For example, several actions may be involved in handling and moving raw materials, but these may be combined into a single activity titled *material handling*. The end result of this stage of the design process is an *activity dictionary* that defines each of the activities that will be included in the activity-based costing system and how the activities will be measured.

Some of the activities commonly found in activity-based costing systems in manufacturing companies are listed in Exhibit 3–2. In the exhibit, activities have been grouped into a four-level hierarchy: *unit-level activities*, *batch-level activities, product-level activities*, and *facility-level activities*. This cost hierarchy is useful in understanding the difference between activity-based costing and conventional approaches. It also serves as a guide when simplifying an activity-based costing system. In general, activities and costs should be combined in the activity-based costing system only if they fall within the same level in the cost hierarchy.

Hierarchy of Activities

Unit-level activities are performed each time a unit is produced. The costs of unit-level activities should be proportional to the number of units produced. For example, providing power to run processing equipment would be a unit-level activity since power tends to be consumed in proportion to the number of units produced.

Batch-level activities consist of tasks that are performed each time a batch is processed, such as processing purchase orders, setting up equipment, packing shipments to customers, and handling material. Costs at the batch level depend on *the number of batches processed* rather than on the number of units produced. For example, the cost of processing a purchase order is the same no matter how many units of an item are ordered.

Product-level activities (sometimes called *product-sustaining activities*) relate to specific products and typically must be carried out regardless of how many batches or units of the product are manufactured. Product-level activities include maintaining inventories of parts for a product, issuing engineering change notices to modify a product to meet a customer's specifications, and developing special test routines when a product is first placed into production.

Facility-level activities (also called *organization-sustaining activities*) are activities that are carried out regardless of which products are produced, how many batches are run, or how many units are made. Facility-level costs include items such as factory management salaries, insurance, property taxes, and building depreciation. The costs of facility-level activities must be allocated to products for external financial reports. This is usually accomplished by combining all facility-level costs into a single cost pool and allocating those costs to products using an arbitrary allocation base such as direct labor-hours. However, as we will see later in the book, allocating such costs to products results in misleading data that can lead to bad decisions.

Dining in the Canyon

IN BUSINESS

Western River Expeditions (www.westernriver.com) runs river rafting trips on the Colorado, Green, and Salmon rivers. One of its most popular trips is a six-day trip down the Grand Canyon, which features famous rapids such as Crystal and Lava Falls as well as the awesome scenery accessible only from the bottom of the Grand Canyon. The company runs trips of one or two rafts, each of which carries two guides and up to 18 guests. The company provides all meals on the trip, which are prepared by the guides.

In terms of the hierarchy of activities, a guest can be considered as a unit and a raft as a batch. In that context, the wages paid to the guides are a batch-level cost since each raft requires two guides regardless of the number of guests in the raft. Each guest is given a mug to use during the trip and to take home at the end of the trip as a souvenir. The cost of the mug is a unit-level cost since the number of mugs given away is strictly proportional to the number of guests on a trip.

What about the costs of food served to guests and guides—is this a unit-level cost, a batch-level cost, a product-level cost, or an organization-sustaining cost? At first glance, it might be thought that food costs are a unit-level cost—the greater the number of guests, the higher the food costs. However, that is not quite correct. Standard menus have been created for each day of the trip. For example, the first night's menu might consist of shrimp cocktail, steak, cornbread, salad, and cheesecake. The day before a trip begins, all of the food needed for the trip is taken from the central warehouse and packed in modular containers. It isn't practical to finely adjust the amount of food for the actual number of guests planned to be on a trip—most of the food comes prepackaged in large lots. For example, the shrimp cocktail menu may call for two large bags of frozen shrimp per raft and that many bags will be packed regardless of how many guests are expected on the raft. Consequently, the costs of food are not a unit-level cost that varies with the number of guests actually on a trip. Instead, the costs of food are a batch-level cost.

Source: Conversations with Western River Expeditions personnel.

An Example of an Activity-Based Costing System Design

The complexity of an activity-based costing system will differ from company to company. In some companies, the activity-based costing system will be simple with only one or two activity cost pools at the unit, batch, and product levels. For other companies, the activity-based costing system will be much more complex.

Under activity-based costing, the manufacturing overhead costs at the top of Exhibit 3–3 are allocated to products via a two-stage process. In the first stage, overhead costs are assigned to the activity cost pools. In the second stage, the costs in the activity cost pools are allocated to products using activity rates and activity measures. For example, in the first-stage cost assignment, various manufacturing overhead costs are assigned to the production-order activity cost pool. These costs could include the salaries of

EXHIBIT 3–3   Graphic Example of Activity-Based Costing

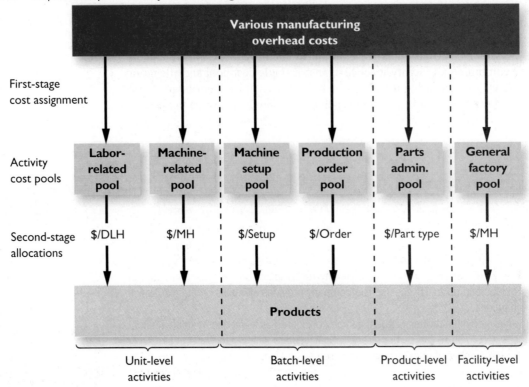

engineers who modify products for individual orders, the costs of scheduling and monitoring orders, and other costs that are incurred as a consequence of the number of different orders received and processed by the company. We will not go into the details of how these first-stage cost assignments are made. In all of the examples and assignments in this book, the first-stage cost assignments have already been completed. Once the amount of cost in the production-order activity cost pool is known, procedures from Chapter 2 can be followed. The activity rate for the production-order cost pool is computed by dividing the total cost in the production-order activity cost pool by the anticipated number of orders for the upcoming year. For example, the total cost in the production-order activity cost pool might be $450,000 and the company might expect to process a total of 1,200 orders. In that case, the activity rate would be $375 per order. Each order would be charged $375 for production-order costs. This is no different from the way overhead was applied to products in Chapter 2 except that the number of orders is the allocation base rather than direct labor-hours.

CONCEPT
CHECK ✓

1. Which of the following statements is false? (You may select more than one answer.)
   a.   In recent years, most companies have experienced increasing manufacturing overhead costs in relation to direct labor costs.
   b.   Activity-based costing systems may use direct labor-hours and/or machine-hours to assign unit-level costs to products.
   c.   Facility-level costs are not caused by particular products.
   d.   Product-level costs are larger for high-volume products than for low-volume products.

ABC Helps a Dairy Understand Its Costs

Kemps LLC, headquartered in Minneapolis, Minnesota, produces dairy products such as milk, yogurt, and ice cream. The company implemented an ABC system that helped managers understand the impact of product and customer diversity on profit margins. The ABC model "captured differences in how the company entered orders from customers (customer phone call, salesperson call, fax, truck-driver entry, EDI, or Internet), how it packaged orders (full stacks of six cases, individual cases, or partial break-pack cases for small orders), how it delivered orders (commercial carriers or its own fleet, including route miles), and time spent by the driver at each customer location."

Kemps' ABC system helped the company acquire a large national customer because it identified "the specific manufacturing, distribution, and order handling costs associated with serving this customer." The ability to provide the customer with accurate cost information built a trusting relationship that distinguished Kemps from other competitors. Kemps also used its ABC data to transform unprofitable customers into profitable ones. For example, one customer agreed to accept a 13% price increase, to eliminate two low-volume products, and to begin placing full truckload orders rather than requiring partial truckload shipments, thereby lowering Kemps' costs by $150,000 per year.

Source: Robert S. Kaplan, and Steven R. Anderson, "Time-Driven Activity-Based Costing," *Harvard Business Review,* November 2004, pp. 131–139.

USING ACTIVITY-BASED COSTING

Different products place different demands on resources. This is not recognized by conventional costing systems, which assume that overhead resources are consumed in direct proportion to direct labor-hours or machine-hours. The following example illustrates the distortions in product costs that can result from using a traditional costing system.

Comtek Sound, Inc., makes two products, a radio with a built-in CD player (called a CD unit) and a radio with a built-in DVD player (called a DVD unit). Both of these products are sold to automobile manufacturers for installation in new vehicles. Recently, the company has been losing bids to supply CD players because competitors have been bidding less than Comtek Sound has been willing to bid. At the same time, Comtek Sound has been winning every bid it has submitted for its DVD player, which management regards as a secondary product. The marketing manager has been complaining that at the prices Comtek Sound is willing to bid, competitors are taking the company's high-volume CD business and leaving Comtek Sound with just low-volume DVD business. However, the prices competitors quote on the CD players are below Comtek Sound's manufacturing cost for these units—at least according to Comtek Sound's conventional accounting system that applies manufacturing overhead to products based on direct labor-hours. Production managers suspected that the conventional costing system might be distorting the relative costs of the CD player and the DVD player—the DVD player takes more overhead resources to make than the CD player and yet their manufacturing overhead costs are identical under the conventional costing system. With the enthusiastic cooperation of the company's accounting department, a cross-functional team was formed to develop an activity-based costing system to more accurately assign overhead costs to the two products.

Comtek Sound, Inc.'s Basic Data

The ABC team gathered basic information relating to the company's two products. A summary of some of this information follows. For the current year, the company's budget provides for selling 50,000 DVD units and 200,000 CD units. Both products require two direct labor-hours to complete. Therefore, the company plans to work 500,000 direct labor-hours (DLHs) during the current year, computed as follows:

DVD units: 50,000 units × 2 DLHs per unit	100,000
CD units: 200,000 units × 2 DLHs per unit	400,000
Total direct labor-hours.	500,000

Costs for direct materials and direct labor for one unit of each product are given below:

	DVD Units	CD Units
Direct materials	$90	$50
Direct labor (at $10 per DLH).	$20	$20

The company's estimated manufacturing overhead costs for the current year total $10,000,000. The ABC team discovered that although the same amount of direct labor time is required for each product, the more complex DVD units require more machine time, more machine setups, and more testing than the CD units. Also, the team found that it is necessary to manufacture the DVD units in smaller batches; consequently, they require more production orders than the CD units.

The company has always used direct labor-hours as the base for assigning overhead costs to its products.

With these data in hand, the ABC team was prepared to begin the design of the new activity-based costing system. But first, they wanted to compute the cost of each product using the company's existing cost system.

Direct Labor-Hours as a Base

Under the company's existing costing system, the predetermined overhead rate would be $20 per direct labor-hour, computed as follows:

$$\text{Predetermined overhead rate} = \frac{\text{Estimated total manufacturing overhead}}{\text{Estimated total amount of the allocation base}}$$

$$= \frac{\$10,000,000}{500,000 \text{ DLHs}} = \$20 \text{ per DLH}$$

Using this rate, the ABC team computed the unit product costs as given below:

	DVD Units	CD Units
Direct materials (above).	$ 90	$ 50
Direct labor (above)	20	20
Manufacturing overhead (2 DLHs × $20 per DLH)	40	40
Unit product cost	$150	$110

The problem with this costing approach is that it relies entirely on direct labor-hours to assign overhead cost to products and does not consider the impact of other factors—such as setups and testing—on the overhead costs of the company. Even though these other factors suggest that the two products place different demands on overhead resources, under the company's traditional costing system, the two products are assigned the same overhead cost per unit because they require equal amounts of direct labor time.

While this method of computing costs is fast and simple, it is accurate only in those situations where other factors affecting overhead costs are not significant. These other factors *are* significant in the case of Comtek Sound, Inc.

Computing Activity Rates

The ABC team then analyzed Comtek Sound, Inc.'s operations and identified six major activities to include in the new activity-based costing system. (These six activities are identical to those illustrated earlier in Exhibit 3–3.) Cost and other data relating to the activities are presented in Exhibit 3–4. That exhibit shows the amount of overhead cost for each activity cost pool, along with the expected amount of activity for the current year. The machine setups activity cost pool, for example, was assigned $1,600,000 in overhead cost. The company expects to complete 4,000 setups during the year, of which 3,000 will be for DVD units and 1,000 will be for CD units. Data for other activities are also shown in the exhibit.

The ABC team then computed an activity rate for each activity. (See the middle panel in Exhibit 3–4.) The activity rate of $400 per machine setup, for example, was computed

EXHIBIT 3–4 Comtek Sound's Activity-Based Costing System

Basic Data

Activities and Activity Measures	Estimated Overhead Cost	Expected Activity		
		DVD Units	CD Units	Total
Labor related (direct labor-hours).........	$ 800,000	100,000	400,000	500,000
Machine related (machine-hours)	2,100,000	300,000	700,000	1,000,000
Machine setups (setups)	1,600,000	3,000	1,000	4,000
Production orders (orders).............	3,150,000	800	400	1,200
Parts administration (part types)	350,000	400	300	700
General factory (machine-hours).........	2,000,000	300,000	700,000	1,000,000
	$10,000,000			

Computation of Activity Rates

Activities	(a) Estimated Overhead Cost	(b) Total Expected Activity	(a) ÷ (b) Activities Rate
Labor related	$800,000	500,000 DLHs	$1.60 per DLH
Machine related	$2,100,000	1,000,000 MHs	$2.10 per MH
Machine setups	$1,600,000	4,000 setups	$400.00 per setup
Production orders..........	$3,150,000	1,200 orders	$2,625.00 per order
Parts administration	$350,000	700 part types	$500.00 per part type
General factory............	$2,000,000	1,000,000 MHs	$2.00 per MH

Computation of the Overhead Cost per Unit of Product

Activities and Activity Rates	DVD Units		CD Units	
	Expected Activity	Amount	Expected Activity	Amount
Labor related, at $1.60 per DLH.............	100,000	$ 160,000	400,000	$ 640,000
Machine related, at $2.10 per MH	300,000	630,000	700,000	1,470,000
Machine setups, at $400 per setup	3,000	1,200,000	1,000	400,000
Production orders, at $2,625 per order	800	2,100,000	400	1,050,000
Parts administration, at $500 per part type	400	200,000	300	150,000
General factory, at $2.00 per MH............	300,000	600,000	700,000	1,400,000
Total overhead costs assigned (a)		$4,890,000		$5,110,000
Number of units produced (b)		50,000		200,000
Overhead cost per unit (a) ÷ (b)............		$97.80		$25.55

EXHIBIT 3–5
Comparison of Unit Product Costs

	Activity-Based Costing		Direct-Labor-Based Costing	
	DVD Units	CD Units	DVD Units	CD Units
Direct materials	$ 90.00	$50.00	$ 90.00	$ 50.00
Direct labor.	20.00	20.00	20.00	20.00
Manufacturing overhead.	97.80	25.55	40.00	40.00
Unit product cost	$207.80	$95.55	$150.00	$110.00

by dividing the total estimated overhead cost in the activity cost pool, $1,600,000, by the expected amount of activity, 4,000 setups. This process was repeated for each of the other activities in the activity-based costing system.

Computing Product Costs

Once the activity rates were calculated, it was easy to compute the overhead cost that would be allocated to each product. (See the bottom panel of Exhibit 3–4.) For example, the amount of machine setup cost allocated to DVD units was determined by multiplying the activity rate of $400 per setup by the 3,000 expected setups for DVD units during the year. This yielded a total of $1,200,000 in machine setup costs to be assigned to the DVD units.

Note from the exhibit that the use of an activity approach has resulted in $97.80 in overhead cost being assigned to each DVD unit and $25.55 to each CD unit. The ABC team then used these amounts to determine unit product costs under activity-based costing, as presented in Exhibit 3–5. For comparison, the exhibit also shows the unit product costs derived earlier when direct labor-hours were used as the base for assigning overhead costs to the products.

The ABC team members summarized their findings as follows in the team's report:

> In the past, the company has been charging $40.00 in overhead cost to a unit of either product, whereas it should have been charging $97.80 in overhead cost to each DVD unit and only $25.55 to each CD unit. Thus, unit costs have been badly distorted as a result of using direct labor-hours as the allocation base. The company may even have been suffering a loss on the DVD units without knowing it because the cost of these units has been so vastly understated. Through activity-based costing, we have been able to more accurately assign overhead costs to each product.
>
> Although in the past we thought our competitors were pricing below their cost on the CD units, it turns out that we were overcharging for these units because our costs were overstated. Similarly, we always used to believe that our competitors were overpricing the DVD units, but now we realize that our prices have been way too low because the cost of our DVD units was being understated. It turns out that we, not our competitors, had everything backwards.

The pattern of cost distortion shown by the ABC team's findings is quite common. Such distortion can happen in any company that relies on direct labor-hours or machine-hours in assigning overhead cost to products and ignores other significant causes of overhead costs.

IN BUSINESS   **Finding That Golden Top 20%**

According to Meridien Research of Newton, Massachusetts, 20% of a bank's customers generate about 150% of its profits. At the other end of the spectrum, 30% of a bank's customers drain 50% of its profits. The question becomes how do banks identify which customers are in that golden top 20%? For many banks, the answer is revealed through customer relationship management software that provides activity-based costing capability.

"We had some customers that we thought, on the surface, would be very profitable, with an average of $300,000 in business accounts," said Jerry Williams, chairman and chief executive officer of First Bancorp. "What we didn't pull out was the fact that some write more than 275 checks a month. Once you apply the labor costs, it's not a profitable customer."

Meridien Research estimates that large commercial banks are increasing their spending on customer profitability systems by 14% a year with total annual expenditures exceeding $6 billion dollars.

Source: Joseph McKendrick, "Your Best Customers May Be Different Tomorrow," *Bank Technology News,* July 2001, pp. 1–4.

Shifting of Overhead Cost

When a company implements activity-based costing, overhead cost often shifts from high-volume products to low-volume products, with a higher unit product cost resulting for the low-volume products. We saw this happen in the example above, where the product cost of the low-volume DVD units increased from $150.00 to $207.80 per unit. This increase in cost resulted from batch-level and product-level costs, which shifted from the high-volume product to the low-volume product. For example, consider the cost of issuing production orders, which is a batch-level activity. As shown in Exhibit 3–4, the average cost to Comtek Sound to issue a single production order is $2,625. This cost is assigned to a production order regardless of how many units are processed in that order. The key here is to realize that fewer DVD units (the low-volume product) are processed per production order than CD units:

LEARNING OBJECTIVE 4

Contrast the product costs computed under activity-based costing and conventional costing methods.

	DVD Units	CD Units
Number of units produced per year (a)	50,000	200,000
Number of production orders issued per year (b)	800	400
Number of units processed per production order (a) ÷ (b)	62.5	500

Spreading the $2,625 cost to issue a production order over the number of units processed per order results in the following average cost per unit:

	DVD Units	CD Units
Cost to issue a production order (a).	$2,625	$2,625
Average number of units processed per production order (above) (b).	62.5	500
Production order cost per unit (a) ÷ (b)	$42.00	$5.25

Thus, the production order cost for a DVD unit (the low-volume product) is $42, which is *eight times* the $5.25 cost for a CD unit.

Product-level costs—such as parts administration—have a similar impact. In a conventional costing system, these costs are spread more or less uniformly across all units that are produced. In an activity-based costing system, these costs are assigned more accurately to products. Since product-level costs are fixed with respect to the number of units processed, the average cost per unit of an activity such as parts administration will be higher for low-volume products than for high-volume products.

Process Improvements Help Nurses

Providence Portland Medical Center (PPMC) used ABC to improve one of the most expensive and error-prone processes within its nursing units—ordering, distributing, and administering medications to patients. To the surprise of everyone involved, the ABC data showed that "medication-related activities made up 43% of the nursing unit's total operating costs." The ABC team members knew that one of the root causes of this time-consuming process was the illegibility of physician orders that are faxed to the pharmacy. Replacing the standard fax machine with a much better $5,000 machine virtually eliminated unreadable orders and decreased follow-up telephone calls by more than 90%—saving the hospital $500,000 per year. In total, the ABC team generated improvement ideas that offered $1 million of net savings in redeployable resources. "This amount translates to additional time that nurses and pharmacists can spend on direct patient care."

Source: "How ABC Analysis Will Save PPMC Over $1 Million a Year," *Financial Analysis, Planning & Reporting,* November 2003, pp. 6–10.

TARGETING PROCESS IMPROVEMENTS

Activity-based costing can be used to identify activities that would benefit from process improvements. Indeed, this is the most widely cited benefit of activity-based costing by managers.[1] When used in this way, activity-based costing is often called *activity-based management*. Basically, **activity-based management** involves focusing on activities to eliminate waste, decrease processing time, and reduce defects. Activity-based management is used in organizations as diverse as manufacturing companies, hospitals, and the U.S. Marine Corps. When "40 percent of the cost of running a hospital involves storing, collecting and moving information," there is obviously a great deal of room for eliminating waste.[2]

The first step in any improvement program is to decide what to improve. The Theory of Constraints approach discussed in the Prologue is a powerful tool for targeting the area in an organization whose improvement will yield the greatest benefit. Activity-based management provides another approach. The activity rates computed in activity-based costing can provide valuable clues concerning where there is waste and opportunity for improvement. For example, looking at the activity rates in Exhibit 3–4, Comtek's managers may conclude that $2,625 to process a production order is far too expensive for an activity that adds no value to the product. As a consequence, they may target production-order processing for process improvement using Six Sigma as discussed in the Prologue.

Benchmarking is another way to leverage the information in activity rates. **Benchmarking** is a systematic approach to identifying the activities with the greatest room for improvement. It is based on comparing the performance in an organization with the performance of other, similar organizations known for their outstanding performance. If a particular part of the organization performs far below the world-class standard, managers will target that area for improvement.

---

[1]Dan Swenson, "The Benefits of Activity-Based Cost Management to the Manufacturing Industry," *Journal of Management Accounting Research* 7, pp. 167–180.
[2]Kambiz Foroohar, "Rx: Software," *Forbes,* April 7, 1997, p. 114.

Comparing Activity-Based and Traditional Product Costs

Airco Heating and Air Conditioning (Airco), located in Van Buren, Arkansas, implemented an ABC system to better understand the profitability of its products. The ABC system assigned $4,458,605 of overhead costs to eight activities as follows:

Activity Cost Pool	Total Cost	Total Activity	Activity Rate
Machines	$ 435,425	73,872 machine-hours	$5.89
Data record maintenance	132,597	14 products administered	$9,471.21
Material handling	1,560,027	16,872 products	$92.46
Product changeover	723,338	72 setup hours	$10,046.36
Scheduling	24,877	2,788 production runs	$8.92
Raw material receiving	877,107	2,859 receipts	$306.79
Product shipment	561,014	13,784,015 miles	$0.04
Customer service	144,220	2,533 customer contacts	$56.94
Total	$4,458.605		

Airco's managers were surprised by the fact that 55% [($1,560,027 + $877,107) ÷ $4,458,605] of its overhead resources were consumed by material handling and receiving activities. They responded by reducing the raw material and part transport distances within the facility. In addition, they compared the traditional and ABC product margin percentages (computed by dividing each product's margin by the sales of the product) for the company's seven product lines of air conditioners as summarized below:

	Product						
	5-ton	6-ton	7.5 ton	10-ton	12.5 ton	15-ton	20-ton
Traditional product margin % . .	−20%	4%	40%	−4%	20%	42%	70%
ABC product margin %.	−15%	−8%	50%	1%	−6%	40%	69%

In response to the ABC data, Airco decided to explore the possibility of raising prices on 5-ton, 6-ton, and 12.5-ton air conditioners while at the same time seeking to reduce overhead consumption by these products.

Source: Copyright 2004 from "An Application of Activity-Based Costing in the Air Conditioner Manufacturing Industry," *The Engineering Economist*, Volume 49, Issue 3, 2004, pp. 221–236, by Heather Nachtmann and Mohammad Hani Al-Rifai. Reproduced by permission of Taylor & Francis Group, LLC., http://www.taylorand francis.com.

EVALUATION OF ACTIVITY-BASED COSTING

Activity-based costing improves the accuracy of product costs, helps managers to understand the nature of overhead costs, and helps target areas for improvement through benchmarking and other techniques. These benefits are discussed in this section.

The Benefits of Activity-Based Costing

Activity-based costing improves the accuracy of product costs in three ways. First, activity-based costing usually increases the number of cost pools used to accumulate overhead costs. Rather than accumulating all overhead costs in a single, plantwide pool, or accumulating them in departmental pools, the company accumulates costs for each major activity. Second, the activity cost pools are more homogeneous than departmental cost pools. In principle, all of the costs in an activity cost pool pertain to a single activity. In contrast, departmental cost pools contain the costs of many different activities carried out in the department. Third, activity-based costing uses a variety of activity measures to assign overhead costs to products, some of which are correlated with volume and some of which are not. This differs from conventional approaches that rely exclusively on direct labor-hours or other measures of volume such as machine-hours to assign overhead costs to products.

Because conventional costing systems typically apply overhead costs to products using direct labor-hours, it may appear to managers that overhead costs are caused by direct labor-hours. Activity-based costing makes it clear that batch setups, engineering change orders, and other activities cause overhead costs rather than just direct labor. Managers thus have a better understanding of the causes of overhead costs, which should lead to better decisions and better cost control.

Finally, activity-based costing highlights the activities that could benefit most from Six Sigma and other improvement initiatives. Thus, activity-based costing can be used as a part of programs to improve operations.

IN BUSINESS   Costs in Health Care

Owens & Minor, a $3 billion medical supplies distributor, offers an activity-based billing option to its customers. Instead of charging a fixed amount for items that are ordered by customers, the charges are based on activities required to fill the order as well as on the cost of the item ordered. For example, Owens & Minor charges extra for weekend deliveries. These charges encourage customers to reduce their weekend delivery requests. This results in decreased costs for Owens & Minor, which can then be passed on to customers in the form of lower charges for the specific items that are ordered. As many as 25% of Owens & Minor's 4,000 health care customers have used this billing option to identify and realize cost reduction opportunities. For example, Bill Wright of Sutter Health in Sacramento, California, said that Owens & Minor's activity-based billing has motivated his company to eliminate weekend deliveries, place more items per order, align purchase quantities with prepackaged specifications, and transmit orders electronically. The end result is that one Sutter affiliate decreased its purchasing costs from 4.25% of product costs to 3.75%. In all, Owens & Minor has identified about 250 activity-driven procurement costs that hospitals can manage more efficiently to reduce costs.

Source: Todd Shields, "Hospitals Turning to Activity-Based Costing to Save and Measure Distribution Costs," *Healthcare Purchasing News*, November 2001, pp. 14–15.

Limitations of Activity-Based Costing

Any discussion of activity-based costing is incomplete without some cautionary warnings. First, the cost of implementing and maintaining an activity-based costing system may outweigh the benefits. Second, it would be naïve to assume that product costs provided even by an activity-based costing system are always relevant when making decisions. These limitations are discussed below.

The Cost of Implementing Activity-Based Costing   Implementing ABC is a major project that involves a great deal of effort. First, the cost system must be designed—preferably by a cross-functional team. This requires taking valued employees away from other tasks for a major project. In addition, the data used in the activity-based costing system must be collected and verified. In some cases, this requires collecting data that has never been collected before. In short, implementing and maintaining an activity-based costing system can present a formidable challenge, and management may decide that the costs are too great to justify the expected benefits. Nevertheless, it should be kept in mind that the costs of collecting and processing data have dropped dramatically over the last several decades due to bar coding and other technologies, and these costs can be expected to continue to fall.

When are the benefits of activity-based costing most likely to be worth the cost? Companies that have some of the following characteristics are most likely to benefit from activity-based costing:

1. Products differ substantially in volume, batch size, and in the activities they require.
2. Conditions have changed substantially since the existing cost system was established.
3. Overhead costs are high and increasing and no one seems to understand why.
4. Management does not trust the existing cost system and ignores cost data from the system when making decisions.

Limitations of the ABC Model The activity-based costing model relies on a number of critical assumptions.[3] Perhaps the most important of these assumptions is that the cost in each activity cost pool is strictly proportional to its activity measure. What little evidence we have on this issue suggests that overhead costs are less than proportional to activity.[4] Economists call this increasing returns to scale—as activity increases, the average cost drops. As a practical matter, this means that product costs computed by a traditional or activity-based costing system will be overstated for the purposes of making decisions. The product costs generated by activity-based costing are almost certainly more accurate than those generated by a conventional costing system, but they should nevertheless be viewed with caution. Managers should be particularly alert to product costs that contain allocations of facility-level costs. As we shall see later in the book, product costs that include facility-level or organization-sustaining costs can easily lead managers astray.

Bakery Owner

YOU DECIDE

You are the owner of a bakery that makes a complete line of specialty breads, pastries, cakes, and pies for the retail and wholesale markets. A summer intern has just completed an activity-based costing study that concluded, among other things, that one of your largest recurring jobs is losing money. A local luxury hotel orders the same assortment of desserts every week for its Sunday brunch buffet for a fixed price of $975 per week. The hotel is quite happy with the quality of the desserts the bakery has been providing, but it would seek bids from other local bakeries if the price were increased.

The activity-based costing study conducted by the intern revealed that the cost to the bakery of providing these desserts is $1,034 per week, resulting in an apparent loss of $59 per week or over $3,000 per year. Scrutinizing the intern's report, you find that the weekly cost of $1,034 includes facility-level costs of $329. These facility-level costs include portions of the rent on the bakery's building, your salary, depreciation on the office personal computer, and so on. The facility-level costs were arbitrarily allocated to the Sunday brunch job on the basis of direct labor-hours.

Should you demand an increase in price from the luxury hotel for the Sunday brunch desserts to at least $1,034? If an increase is not forthcoming, should you withdraw from the agreement and discontinue providing the desserts?

Modifying the ABC Model The discussion in this chapter has assumed that the primary purpose of an activity-based costing system is to provide more accurate product costs for external reports. If the product costs are to be used by managers for internal decisions, some modifications should be made. For example, for decision-making

---

[3]Eric Noreen, "Conditions under Which Activity-Based Cost Systems Provide Relevant Costs," *Journal of Management Accounting Research,* Fall 1991, pp. 159–168.
[4]Eric Noreen and Naomi Soderstrom, "The Accuracy of Proportional Cost Models: Evidence from Hospital Service Departments," *Review of Accounting Studies* 2, 1997; and Eric Noreen and Naomi Soderstrom, "Are Overhead Costs Proportional to Activity? Evidence from Hospital Service Departments," *Journal of Accounting and Economics,* January 1994, pp. 253–278.

purposes, the distinction between manufacturing costs on the one hand and selling and administrative expenses on the other hand is unimportant. Managers need to know what costs a product causes, and it doesn't matter whether the costs are manufacturing costs or selling and administrative expenses. Consequently, for decision-making purposes, some selling and administrative expenses should be assigned to products as well as manufacturing costs. Moreover, as mentioned above, facility-level and organization-sustaining costs should be removed from product costs when making decisions. Nevertheless, the techniques covered in this chapter provide a good basis for understanding the mechanics of activity-based costing. For a more complete coverage of the use of activity-based costing in decisions, see more advanced texts.[5]

Activity-Based Costing and Service Industries

Although initially developed as a tool for manufacturing companies, activity-based costing is also being used in service industries. Successful implementation of an activity-based costing system depends on identifying the key activities that generate costs and tracking how many of those activities are performed for each service the organization provides. Activity-based costing has been implemented in a wide variety of service industries including railroads, hospitals, banks, and data services companies.

DECISION MAKER

Legal Firm Business Manager

You have been hired to manage the business aspects of a local legal firm with a staff of 6 attorneys, 10 paralegals, and 5 staffpersons. Clients of the firm are billed a fixed amount per hour of attorney time. The fixed hourly charge is determined each year by dividing the total cost of the legal office for the preceding year by the total billed hours of attorney time for that year. A markup of 25% is then added to this average cost per hour of billed attorney time to provide for a profit and for inflation.

The firm's partners are concerned because the firm has been unprofitable for several years. The firm has been losing its smaller clients to other local firms—largely because the firm's fees have become uncompetitive. And the firm has been attracting larger clients with more complex legal problems from its competitors. To serve these demanding larger clients, the firm must subscribe to expensive on-line legal reference services, hire additional paralegals and staffpersons, and lease additional office space.

What do you think might be the reason for the unprofitable operations in recent years? What might be done to improve the situation for the coming year?

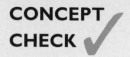

CONCEPT CHECK ✔

2. Which of the following statements is false? (You may select more than one answer.)
   a. Activity-based costing systems usually shift costs from low-volume products to high-volume products.
   b. Benchmarking can be used to identify activities with the greatest potential for improvement.
   c. Activity-based costing is most valuable to companies that manufacture products that are similar in terms of their volume of production, batch size, and complexity.
   d. Activity-based costing systems are based on the assumption that the costs included in each activity cost pool are strictly proportional to the cost pool's activity measure.

---

[5]See, for example, Chapter 8 and its appendix in Ray Garrison, Eric Noreen, and Peter Brewer, *Managerial Accounting*, 12th edition, McGraw-Hill/Irwin © 2008.

COST FLOWS IN AN ACTIVITY-BASED COSTING SYSTEM

In Chapter 2, we discussed the flow of costs in a job-order costing system. The flow of costs through Raw Materials, Work in Process, and other accounts is the same under activity-based costing. The only difference in activity-based costing is that more than one predetermined overhead rate is used to apply overhead costs to products. Our purpose in this section is to provide a detailed example of cost flows in an activity-based costing system.

> **LEARNING OBJECTIVE 5**
>
> Record the flow of costs in an activity-based costing system.

An Example of Cost Flows

The company in the following example has five activity cost pools and therefore must compute five predetermined overhead rates (i.e., activity rates). Except for that detail, the journal entries, T-accounts, and general cost flows are the same as described in Chapter 2.

Basic Data Sarvik Company uses activity-based costing for its external financial reports. The company has five activity cost pools, which are listed below along with relevant data for the coming year.

Activity Cost Pool	Activity Measure	Estimated Overhead Cost	Expected Activity
Machine related	Machine-hours	$175,000	5,000 MHs
Purchase orders.	Number of orders	$63,000	700 orders
Machine setups	Number of setups	$92,000	460 setups
Product testing.	Number of tests	$160,000	200 tests
General factory.	Direct labor-hours	$300,000	25,000 DLHs

At the beginning of the year, the company had inventory balances as follows:

Raw materials	$3,000
Work in process	$4,000
Finished goods	$0

Selected transactions recorded by the company during the year are given below:

a. Raw materials were purchased on account, $915,000.
b. Raw materials were requisitioned for use in production, $900,000 ($810,000 direct and $90,000 indirect).
c. Labor costs were incurred in the factory, $370,000 ($95,000 direct labor and $275,000 indirect labor).
d. Depreciation was recorded on factory assets, $180,000.
e. Miscellaneous manufacturing overhead costs were incurred, $230,000.
f. Manufacturing overhead cost was applied to production. Actual activity during the year was as follows:

Activity Cost Pool	Actual Activity
Machine related	4,600 MHs
Purchase orders.	800 orders
Machine setups	500 setups
Product testing.	190 tests
General factory.	23,000 DLHs

g. Goods costing $1,650,000 to manufacture according to the activity-based costing system were completed during the year.

Tracking the Flow of Costs   The predetermined overhead rates (i.e., activity rates) for the activity cost pools would be computed as follows:

Activity Cost Pools	(a) Estimated Overhead Cost	(b) Total Expected Activity	(a) ÷ (b) Activity Rate
Machine related	$175,000	5,000 machine-hours	$35 per machine-hour
Purchase orders.	$63,000	700 orders	$90 per order
Machine setups	$92,000	460 setups	$200 per setup
Product testing.	$160,000	200 tests	$800 per test
General factory.	$300,000	25,000 direct labor-hours	$12 per direct labor-hour

The following journal entries would be used to record transactions (a) through (g) above:

a.	Raw Materials	915,000	
	Accounts Payable*		915,000
b.	Work in Process.	810,000	
	Manufacturing Overhead	90,000	
	Raw Materials.		900,000
c.	Work in Process.	95,000	
	Manufacturing Overhead	275,000	
	Salaries and Wages Payable*.		370,000
d.	Manufacturing Overhead	180,000	
	Accumulated Depreciation		180,000
e.	Manufacturing Overhead	230,000	
	Accounts Payable*		230,000

From Chapter 2 the formula for computing applied overhead cost is:

Predetermined overhead rate × Actual activity = Applied overhead cost

In activity-based costing, this formula is applied for each activity cost pool using its own predetermined overhead rate (i.e., activity rate). The computations are as follows:

Activities	(1) Activity Rate	(2) Actual Activity	(1) × (2) Applied Overhead Cost
Machine related	$35 per MH	4,600 MHs	$161,000
Purchase orders.	$90 per order	800 orders	72,000
Machine setups	$200 per setup	500 setups	100,000
Product testing.	$800 per test	190 tests	152,000
General factory.	$12 per DLH	23,000 DLHs	276,000
Total			$761,000

By totaling these five applied overhead cost figures, we find that the company applied $761,000 in overhead cost to products during the year. The following entry would be used to record this application of overhead cost:

---

*Other accounts, such as Cash, may be credited.

f. | Work in Process. . . . . | 761,000
    | Manufacturing Overhead . . . . | 761,000

Finally, the following journal entry would be used to record the completion of work in process as described in transaction (g) above:

g. | Finished Goods . . . . | 1,650,000
    | Work in Process . . . . | 1,650,000

The T-accounts corresponding to the above journal entries appear below:

Raw Materials		
Bal. 3,000	(b) 900,000
(a) 915,000	
Bal. 18,000	

Work in Process		
Bal. 4,000	(g) 1,650,000
(b) 810,000	
(c) 95,000	
(f) 761,000	
Bal. 20,000	

Finished Goods		
Bal. 0	
(g) 1,650,000	

Accumulated Depreciation	
	(d) 180,000

Accounts Payable	
	(a) 915,000
	(e) 230,000

Salaries and Wages Payable	
	(c) 370,000

Manufacturing Overhead		
(b) 90,000	(f) 761,000
(c) 275,000	
(d) 180,000	
(e) 230,000	
775,000	761,000
Bal. 14,000	

The overhead is underapplied by $14,000. This can be determined directly, as shown below, or by reference to the balance in the Manufacturing Overhead T-account above.

Actual manufacturing overhead incurred	$775,000
Manufacturing overhead applied	761,000
Overhead underapplied	$ 14,000

SUMMARY

LO1 Understand the basic approach in activity-based costing and how it differs from conventional costing.

Activity-based costing was developed to more accurately assign overhead costs to products. Activity-based costing differs from conventional costing as described in Chapter 2 in two major ways. First, in activity-based costing, each major activity that consumes overhead resources has its own cost pool and its own activity rate, whereas in Chapter 2 there was only a single overhead cost pool and a single predetermined overhead rate. Second, the allocation bases (or activity measures) in activity-based costing are diverse. They may include machine setups, purchase orders, engineering change orders, and so on, in addition to direct labor-hours or machine-hours. Nevertheless, within each activity cost pool, the mechanics of computing overhead rates and of applying overhead to products are the same as described in Chapter 2. However, the increase in the number of cost pools and the use of better activity measures generally result in more accurate product costs.

LO2   Compute activity rates for an activity-based costing system.

Each activity in an activity-based costing system has its own cost pool and its own activity measure. The activity rate for a particular activity is computed by dividing the total cost in the activity's cost pool by the total amount of activity.

LO3   Compute product costs using activity-based costing.

Product costs in activity-based costing, as in conventional costing systems, consist of direct materials, direct labor, and overhead. In both systems, overhead is applied to products using predetermined overhead rates. In the case of an activity-based costing system, each activity has its own predetermined overhead rate (i.e., activity rate). The activities required by a product are multiplied by their respective activity rates to determine the amount of overhead that is applied to the product.

LO4   Contrast the product costs computed under activity-based costing and conventional costing methods.

Under conventional costing methods, overhead costs are applied to products using some measure of volume such as direct labor-hours or machine-hours. This results in most of the overhead cost being applied to high-volume products. In contrast, under activity-based costing, some overhead costs are applied on the basis of batch-level or product-level activities. This change in allocation bases shifts overhead costs from high-volume products to low-volume products. Accordingly, product costs for high-volume products are commonly lower under activity-based costing than under conventional costing methods, and product costs for low-volume products are higher.

LO5   Record the flow of costs in an activity-based costing system.

The journal entries and general flow of costs in an activity-based costing system are the same as they are in a conventional costing system. The only difference is the use of more than one predetermined overhead rate (i.e., activity rate) to apply overhead to products.

GUIDANCE ANSWERS TO *DECISION MAKER* AND *YOU DECIDE*

Bakery Owner (p. 135)

The bakery really isn't losing money on the weekly order of desserts from the luxury hotel. By definition, facility-level costs are not affected by individual products and jobs—these costs would continue unchanged even if the weekly order were dropped. Recalling the discussion in Chapter 1 concerning decision making, only those costs and benefits that differ between alternatives in a decision are relevant. Since the facility-level costs would be the same whether the dessert order is kept or dropped, they are not relevant in this decision and should be ignored. Hence, the real cost of the job is $705 ($1,034 − $329), which reveals that the job actually yields a weekly profit of $270 ($975 − $705) rather than a loss.

No, the bakery owner should not press for a price increase—particularly if that would result in the hotel seeking bids from competitors. And no, the bakery owner certainly should not withdraw from the agreement to provide the desserts.

Legal Firm Business Manager (p. 136)

The recent problems the firm has been facing can probably be traced to its simplified billing system. Rather than carefully tracing costs to clients, costs are arbitrarily allocated to clients on the basis of attorney hours. Large, demanding clients require much more overhead resources than smaller clients, but the costs of these overhead resources are arbitrarily allocated to all clients on the basis of attorney hours. This results in shifting overhead costs to the smaller, less demanding clients and increasing their charges. It also results in undercharging larger, more demanding clients. Consequently, the firm has been losing smaller clients to competitors and has been attracting larger, demanding clients. Unfortunately, this change in the mix of clients has led to much higher costs and reduced profits.

The situation can be improved by using activity-based costing to trace more costs directly to clients. This should result in shifting costs from the smaller, less demanding clients to the larger, more demanding clients that cause those costs. Smaller clients will face lower charges and hence will be more likely to stay with the firm. Larger, more demanding clients will face higher charges that will fully cover the costs they impose on the firm.

GUIDANCE ANSWERS TO CONCEPT CHECKS

1. **Choice d.** Product-level costs are unrelated to the amount of a product that is made.
2. **Choices a and c.** Activity-based costing systems usually shift costs from high-volume products to low-volume products. Activity-based costing is most valuable for companies with highly diverse products rather than with similar products.

REVIEW PROBLEM: ACTIVITY-BASED COSTING

Aerodec, Inc., manufactures and sells two types of wooden deck chairs: Deluxe and Tourist. Annual sales in units, direct labor-hours (DLHs) per unit, and total direct labor-hours per year are provided below:

Deluxe deck chair: 2,000 units × 5 DLHs per unit	10,000
Tourist deck chair: 10,000 units × 4 DLHs per unit.	40,000
Total direct labor-hours.	50,000

Costs for direct materials and direct labor for one unit of each product are given below:

	Deluxe	Tourist
Direct materials	$25	$17
Direct labor (at $12 per DLH).....................	$60	$48

Manufacturing overhead costs total $800,000 each year. The breakdown of these costs among the company's six activity cost pools is given below. The activity measures are shown in parentheses.

Activities and Activity Measures	Estimated Overhead Cost	Expected Activity		
		Deluxe	Tourist	Total
Labor related (direct labor-hours)	$ 80,000	10,000	40,000	50,000
Machine setups (number of setups)	150,000	3,000	2,000	5,000
Parts administration (number of parts)	160,000	50	30	80
Production orders (number of orders).............	70,000	100	300	400
Material receipts (number of receipts).............	90,000	150	600	750
General factory (machine-hours)	250,000	12,000	28,000	40,000
	$800,000			

Required:

1. Classify each of Aerodec's activities as either a unit-level, batch-level, product-level, or facility-level activity.
2. Assume that the company applies overhead cost to products on the basis of direct labor-hours.
   a. Compute the predetermined overhead rate.
   b. Determine the unit product cost of each product, using the predetermined overhead rate computed in (2)(a) above.
3. Assume that the company uses activity-based costing to compute overhead rates.
   a. Compute the activity rate (i.e., predetermined overhead rate) for each of the six activities listed above.
   b. Using the rates developed in (3)(a) above, determine the amount of overhead cost that would be assigned to a unit of each product.
   c. Determine the unit product cost of each product and compare this cost to the cost computed in (2) (b) above.

Solution to Review Problem

1.

Activity Cost Pool	Type of Activity
Labor related	Unit level
Machine setups	Batch level
Parts administration.......................	Product level
Production orders.........................	Batch level
Material receipts..........................	Batch level
General factory...........................	Facility level

2. a.

$$\text{Predetermined overhead rate} = \frac{\text{Estimated total manufacturing overhead}}{\text{Estimated total amount of the allocation base}}$$

$$= \frac{\$800,000}{50,000 \text{ DLHs}} = \$16 \text{ per DLH}$$

b.

	Deluxe	Tourist
Direct materials	$ 25	$ 17
Direct labor............................	60	48
Manufacturing overhead applied:		
Deluxe: 5 DLHs × $16 per DLH	80	
Tourist: 4 DLHs × $16 per DLH.........		64
Unit product cost	$165	$129

3. a.

Activities	(a) Estimated Overhead Cost	(b) Total Expected Activity	(a) ÷ (b) Activity Rate
Labor related	$80,000	50,000 DLHs	$1.60 per DLH
Machine setups	$150,000	5,000 setups	$30.00 per setup
Parts administration................................	$160,000	80 parts	$2,000.00 per part
Production orders....................................	$70,000	400 orders	$175.00 per order
Material receipts....................................	$90,000	750 receipts	$120.00 per receipt
General factory.....................................	$250,000	40,000 MHs	$6.25 per MH

b.

Activities and Activity Rates	Deluxe Expected Activity	Deluxe Amount	Tourist Expected Activity	Tourist Amount
Labor related, at $1.60 per DLH......................	10,000	$ 16,000	40,000	$ 64,000
Machine setups, at $30 per setup	3,000	90,000	2,000	60,000
Parts administration, at $2,000 per part..............	50	100,000	30	60,000
Production orders, at $175 per order..................	100	17,500	300	52,500
Material receipts, at $120 per receipt................	150	18,000	600	72,000
General factory, at $6.25 per MH.....................	12,000	75,000	28,000	175,000
Total overhead cost assigned (a)		$316,500		$483,500
Number of units produced (b)		2,000		10,000
Overhead cost per unit, (a) ÷ (b)....................		$158.25		$48.35

c.

	Deluxe	Tourist
Direct materials........................	$ 25.00	$ 17.00
Direct labor	60.00	48.00
Manufacturing overhead (see above)	158.25	48.35
Unit product cost.......................	$243.25	$113.35

Under activity-based costing, the unit product cost of the Deluxe deck chair is much greater than the cost computed in (2)(b) above, and the unit product cost of the Tourist deck chair is much less. Using volume (direct labor-hours) in (2)(b) to apply overhead cost to products results in too little overhead cost being applied to the Deluxe deck chair (the low-volume product) and too much overhead cost being applied to the Tourist deck chair (the high-volume product).

GLOSSARY

Activity   An event that causes the consumption of overhead resources. (p. 121)

Activity-based costing (ABC)   A two-stage costing method in which overhead costs are applied to products on the basis of the activities they require. (p. 121)

Activity-based management   A management approach that focuses on managing activities as a way of eliminating waste and reducing delays and defects. (p. 132)

Activity cost pool   A "bucket" in which costs are accumulated that relate to a single activity measure in an activity-based costing system. (p. 122)

Activity measure   An allocation base in an activity-based costing system; ideally, a measure of whatever causes the costs in an activity cost pool. (p. 122)

Activity rate   A predetermined overhead rate in activity-based costing. Each activity cost pool has its own activity rate which is used to apply overhead to products and services. (p. 122)

Batch-level activities   Activities that are performed each time a batch of goods is handled or processed, regardless of how many units are in a batch. The amount of resources consumed depends on the number of batches run rather than on the number of units in the batch. (p. 124)

Benchmarking   A systematic approach to identifying the activities with the greatest room for improvement. It is based on comparing the performance in an organization with the performance of other, similar organizations known for their outstanding performance. (p. 132)

Facility-level activities   Activities that relate to the overall costs of maintaining and managing productive capacity and that can't be traced to specific products. (p. 125)

Product-level activities   Activities that relate to specific products that must be carried out regardless of how many units are produced and sold or batches run. (p. 124)

Unit-level activities   Activities that arise as a result of the total volume of goods and services that are produced, and that are performed each time a unit is produced. (p. 124)

Quiz 3

Multiple-choice questions are provided on the text website at www.mhhe.com/brewer4e.

QUESTIONS

3–1   What are the three common approaches for assigning overhead costs to products?
3–2   Why is activity-based costing growing in popularity?
3–3   Why do departmental overhead rates sometimes result in inaccurate product costs?
3–4   What are the four hierarchical levels of activity discussed in the chapter?
3–5   Why is activity-based costing described as a "two-stage" costing method?
3–6   Why do overhead costs often shift from high-volume products to low-volume products when a company switches from a conventional costing method to activity-based costing?
3–7   What are the three major ways in which activity-based costing improves the accuracy of product costs?
3–8   What are the major limitations of activity-based costing?

 BRIEF EXERCISES

BRIEF EXERCISE 3–1   ABC Cost Hierarchy (LO1)
The following activities occur at Greenwich Corporation, a company that manufactures a variety of products.

a.   Various individuals manage the parts inventories.
b.   A clerk in the factory issues purchase orders for a job.
c.   The personnel department trains new production workers.
d.   The factory's general manager meets with other department heads to coordinate plans.
e.   Direct labor workers assemble products.
f.   Engineers design new products.

g. The materials storekeeper issues raw materials to be used in jobs.
h. The maintenance department performs periodic preventive maintenance on general-use equipment.

Required:
Classify each of the activities above as either a unit-level, batch-level, product-level, or facility-level activity.

BRIEF EXERCISE 3–2   Compute Activity Rates (LO2)
Rustafson Corporation is a diversified manufacturer of consumer goods. The company's activity-based costing system has the following seven activity cost pools:

Activity Cost Pool	Estimated Overhead Cost	Expected Activity
Labor related	$52,000	8,000 direct labor-hours
Machine related	$15,000	20,000 machine-hours
Machine setups	$42,000	1,000 setups
Production orders.	$18,000	500 orders
Product testing	$48,000	2,000 tests
Packaging.	$75,000	5,000 packages
General factory.	$108,800	8,000 direct labor-hours

Required:
1. Compute the activity rate for each activity cost pool.
2. Compute the company's predetermined overhead rate, assuming that the company uses a single plantwide predetermined overhead rate based on direct labor-hours.

BRIEF EXERCISE 3–3   Compute ABC Product Costs (LO3)
Larner Corporation is a diversified manufacturer of industrial goods. The company's activity-based costing system contains the following six activity cost pools and activity rates:

Activity Cost Pool	Activity Rates
Labor related.	$7.00 per direct labor-hour
Machine related.	$3.00 per machine-hour
Machine setups.	$40.00 per setup
Production orders	$160.00 per order
Shipments.	$120.00 per shipment
General factory	$4.00 per direct labor-hour

Cost and activity data have been supplied for the following products:

	J78	B52
Direct materials cost per unit	$6.50	$31.00
Direct labor cost per unit	$3.75	$6.00
Number of units produced per year	4,000	100

	Total Expected Activity	
	J78	B52
Direct labor-hours.	1,000	40
Machine-hours.	3,200	30
Machine setups	5	1
Production orders.	5	1
Shipments	10	1

Required:
Compute the unit product cost of each of the products listed above.

BRIEF EXERCISE 3–4   Contrast ABC and Conventional Product Costs (LO4)

Pacifica Industrial Products Corporation makes two products, Product H and Product L. Product H is expected to sell 40,000 units next year and Product L is expected to sell 8,000 units. A unit of either product requires 0.4 direct labor-hours.

The company's total manufacturing overhead for the year is expected to be $1,632,000.

Required:

1. The company currently applies manufacturing overhead to products using direct labor-hours as the allocation base. If this method is followed, how much overhead cost would be applied to each product? Compute both the overhead cost per unit and the total amount of overhead cost that would be applied to each product. (In other words, how much overhead cost is applied to a unit of Product H? Product L? How much overhead cost is applied in total to all the units of Product H? Product L?)

2. Management is considering an activity-based costing system and would like to know what impact this change might have on product costs. For purposes of discussion, it has been suggested that all of the manufacturing overhead be treated as a product-level cost. The total manufacturing overhead would be divided in half between the two products, with $816,000 assigned to Product H and $816,000 assigned to Product L.

   If this suggestion is followed, how much overhead cost per unit would be applied to each product?

3. Explain the impact on unit product costs of the switch in costing systems.

BRIEF EXERCISE 3–5   Cost Flows in an ABC System (LO5)

Masters Corporation implemented activity-based costing several years ago and uses it for its external financial reports. The company has four activity cost pools, which are listed below.

Activity Cost Pool	Activity Rate
Machine related	$18 per MH
Purchase orders.	$78 per order
Machine setups	$63 per setup
General factory.	$14 per DLH

At the beginning of the year, the company had inventory balances as follows:

Raw materials	$25,000
Work in process	$44,000
Finished goods.	$86,000

Selected transactions recorded by the company during the year are given below:

a. Raw materials were purchased on account, $928,000.
b. Raw materials were requisitioned for use in production, $931,000 ($822,000 direct and $109,000 indirect).
c. Labor costs were incurred in the factory, $468,000 ($396,000 direct labor and $72,000 indirect labor).
d. Depreciation was recorded on factory assets, $284,000.
e. Miscellaneous manufacturing overhead costs were incurred, $175,000.
f. Manufacturing overhead cost was applied to production. Actual activity during the year was as follows:

Activity Cost Pool	Actual Activity
Machine related	15,000 MHs
Purchase orders.	900 orders
Machine setups	1,300 setups
General factory.	12,000 DLHs

g. Completed products were transferred to the company's finished goods warehouse. According to the company's costing system, these products cost $1,830,000.

Required:

1. Prepare journal entries to record transactions (a) through (g) above.
2. Post the entries in (1) above to T-accounts.
3. Compute the underapplied or overapplied overhead cost in the Manufacturing Overhead account.

Manufacturing overhead is applied to products on the basis of direct labor-hours. The rate of $16.50 per hour was determined by dividing the total manufacturing overhead cost for a month by the direct labor-hours:

$$\text{Predetermined overhead rate} = \frac{\text{Manufacturing overhead}}{\text{Direct labor-hours}}$$

$$= \frac{\$99,000}{6,000 \text{ DLHs}} = \$16.50 \text{ per DLH}$$

The following additional information is available about the company and its products:

a. Standard briefcases are produced in batches of 1,000 units, and specialty briefcases are produced in batches of 100 units. Thus, the company does 10 setups for the standard items each month and 25 setups for the specialty items. A setup for the standard items requires one hour, whereas a setup for the specialty items requires two hours.

b. All briefcases are inspected to ensure that quality standards are met. Each month a total of 200 hours is spent inspecting the standard briefcases and 400 hours is spent inspecting the specialty briefcases.

c. A standard briefcase requires 0.5 hours of machine time, and a specialty briefcase requires 1.2 hours of machine time.

d. The company is considering the use of activity-based costing as an alternative to its traditional costing system for computing unit product costs. Since these unit product costs will be used for external financial reporting, all manufacturing overhead costs are to be allocated to products and nonmanufacturing costs are to be excluded from product costs. The activity-based costing system has already been designed and costs have been allocated to the activity cost pools. The activity cost pools and activity measures are detailed below:

Activity Cost Pool	Activity Measure	Estimated Overhead Cost
Purchasing	Number of orders	$15,000
Material handling	Number of receipts	16,000
Production orders and setups.	Setup-hours	6,000
Inspection.	Inspection-hours	18,000
Frame assembly	Assembly-hours	12,000
Machine-related	Machine-hours	32,000
		$99,000

	Expected Activity		
Activity Measure	Standard Briefcases	Specialty Briefcases	Total
Number of orders:			
Leather	50	10	60
Fabric	70	20	90
Synthetic material	0	150	150
Number of receipts:			
Leather	70	10	80
Fabric	85	20	105
Synthetic material	0	215	215
Setup-hours	?	?	?
Inspection-hours.	200	400	600
Assembly-hours	700	800	1,500
Machine-hours	?	?	?

Required:

1. Using activity-based costing, determine the amount of manufacturing overhead cost that would be applied to each standard briefcase and each specialty briefcase.

2. Using the data computed in part (1) above and other data from the case as needed, determine the unit product cost of each product line from the perspective of activity-based costing.

3. Within the limitations of the data that have been provided, evaluate the president's concern about the profitability of the two product lines. Would you recommend that the company shift its resources entirely to the production of specialty briefcases? Explain.

4. Beth Mersey stated that "the competition hasn't been able to touch our price on specialty business." Why do you suppose the competition hasn't been able to touch FirstLine Cases' price?

CASE (LO2, LO3, LO4)

CHECK FIGURE
(2c) Mona Loa unit product cost: $4.83

Coffee Bean, Inc. (CBI), is a processor and distributor of a variety of blends of coffee. The company buys coffee beans from around the world and roasts, blends, and packages them for resale. CBI offers a large variety of different coffees that it sells to gourmet shops in one-pound bags. The major cost of the coffee is raw materials. However, the company's predominantly automated roasting, blending, and packing processes require a substantial amount of manufacturing overhead. The company uses relatively little direct labor.

Some of CBI's coffees are very popular and sell in large volumes, while a few of the newer blends sell in very low volumes. CBI prices its coffees at manufacturing cost plus a markup of 30% with some adjustments made to keep the company's prices competitive.

For the coming year, CBI's budget includes estimated manufacturing overhead cost of $3,000,000. CBI assigns manufacturing overhead to products on the basis of direct labor-hours. The expected direct labor cost totals $600,000, which represents 50,000 hours of direct labor time. On the basis of the sales budget and expected raw materials costs, the company will purchase and use $6,000,000 of raw materials (mostly coffee beans) during the year.

The expected costs for direct materials and direct labor for one-pound bags of two of the company's coffee products appear below.

	Mona Loa	Malaysian
Direct materials...	$4.20	$3.20
Direct labor (0.025 hours per bag)	$0.30	$0.30

CBI's controller believes that the company's traditional costing system may be providing misleading cost information. To determine whether or not this is correct, the controller has prepared an analysis of the year's expected manufacturing overhead costs, as shown in the following table:

Activity Cost Pool	Activity Measure	Expected Activity for the Year	Expected Cost for the Year
Purchasing	Purchase orders	1,710 orders	$ 513,000
Material handling......	Number of setups	1,800 setups	720,000
Quality control........	Number of batches	600 batches	144,000
Roasting	Roasting hours	96,100 roasting hours	961,000
Blending	Blending hours	33,500 blending hours	402,000
Packaging	Packaging hours	26,000 packaging hours	260,000
Total manufacturing overhead cost			$3,000,000

Data regarding the expected production of Mona Loa and Malaysian coffee are presented below. There will be no raw materials inventory for either of these coffees at the beginning of the year.

	Mona Loa	Malaysian
Expected sales	100,000 pounds	2,000 pounds
Batch size	10,000 pounds	500 pounds
Setups..................................	3 per batch	3 per batch
Purchase order size	20,000 pounds	500 pounds
Roasting time per 100 pounds..............	1.0 roasting hours	1.0 roasting hours
Blending time per 100 pounds..............	0.5 blending hours	0.5 blending hours
Packaging time per 100 pounds.............	0.1 packaging hours	0.1 packaging hours

As explained in Chapter 2, job-order costing and process costing are two common methods for determining unit product costs. A job-order costing system is used when many different jobs or products are worked on each period. Examples of industries that use job-order costing include furniture manufacturing, special-order printing, shipbuilding, and many types of service organizations.

By contrast, **process costing** is most commonly used in industries that convert raw materials into homogeneous (i.e., uniform) products, such as bricks, soda, or paper, on a continuous basis. Examples of companies that would use process costing include Reynolds Aluminum (aluminum ingots), Scott Paper (toilet paper), General Mills (flour), Exxon (gasoline and lubricating oils), Coppertone (sunscreens), and Kellogg (breakfast cereals). In addition, process costing is sometimes used in companies with assembly operations. A form of process costing may also be used in utilities that produce gas, water, and electricity.

Our purpose in this chapter is to explain how product costing works in a process costing system.

COMPARISON OF JOB-ORDER AND PROCESS COSTING

In some ways process costing is very similar to job-order costing, and in some ways it is very different. In this section, we focus on these similarities and differences to provide a foundation for the detailed discussion of process costing that follows.

Similarities between Job-Order and Process Costing

Much of what you learned in Chapter 2 about costing and cost flows applies equally well to process costing in this chapter. That is, we are not throwing out all that we have learned about costing and starting from "scratch" with a whole new system. The similarities between job-order and process costing can be summarized as follows:

1. Both systems have the same basic purposes—to assign material, labor, and manufacturing overhead costs to products and to provide a mechanism for computing unit product costs.
2. Both systems use the same basic manufacturing accounts, including Manufacturing Overhead, Raw Materials, Work in Process, and Finished Goods.
3. The flow of costs through the manufacturing accounts is basically the same in both systems.

As can be seen from this comparison, much of the knowledge that you have already acquired about costing is applicable to a process costing system. Our task now is to refine and extend your knowledge to process costing.

Differences between Job-Order and Process Costing

There are three differences between job-order and process costing. First, process costing is used when a company produces a continuous flow of units that are indistinguishable from one another. Job-order costing is used when a company produces many different jobs that have unique production requirements. Second, under process costing, it makes no sense to try to identify materials, labor, and overhead costs with a particular customer order (as we did with job-order costing), since each order is just one of many that are filled from a continuous flow of virtually identical units from the production line. Accordingly, process costing accumulates costs by department (rather than by order) and assigns these costs uniformly to all units that pass through the department during a period. Job cost sheets (which we used for job-order costing) are not used to accumulate costs. Third, process costing systems compute unit costs by department. This differs from job-order costing where unit costs are computed by job on the job cost sheet. Exhibit 4–1 summarizes the differences just described.

Job-Order Costing	Process Costing
1. Many different jobs are worked on during each period, with each job having different production requirements.	1. A single product is produced either on a continuous basis or for long periods of time. All units of product are identical.
2. Costs are accumulated by individual job.	2. Costs are accumulated by department.
3. Unit costs are computed *by job* on the job cost sheet.	3. Unit costs are computed *by department*.

EXHIBIT 4–1
Differences between Job-Order and Process Costing

Cost Analyst

DECISION MAKER

Your company is planning a new production facility that will process wood chips into standard rolls of newsprint for sale to printers. Would you recommend that the company use job-order costing or process costing to account for the costs of producing the rolls of newsprint?

COST FLOWS IN PROCESS COSTING

Before we go through a detailed example of process costing, it will be helpful to see how manufacturing costs flow through a process costing system.

Processing Departments

A **processing department** is an organizational unit where work is performed on a product and where materials, labor, or overhead costs are added to the product. For example, a Nalley's potato chip factory might have three processing departments—one for preparing potatoes, one for cooking, and one for inspecting and packaging. A brick factory might have two processing departments—one for mixing and molding clay into brick form and one for firing the molded brick. Some products may go through a number of processing departments, while others may go through only one or two. Regardless of the number, the processing departments all have two essential features. First, the activity in the processing department must be performed uniformly on all of the units passing through it. Second, the output of the processing department must be homogeneous—that is, all units produced should be identical.

Products in a process costing environment such as bricks or potato chips typically flow in sequence from one department to another as in Exhibit 4–2.

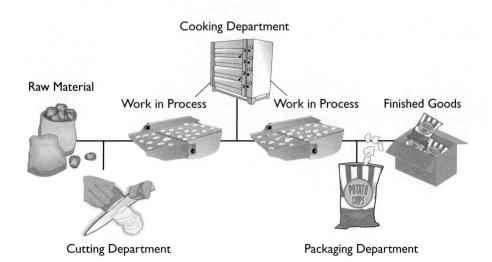

Cooking Department

Raw Material

Work in Process

Work in Process

Finished Goods

Cutting Department

Packaging Department

EXHIBIT 4–2
Sequential Processing Departments

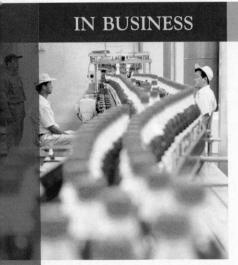

IN BUSINESS   Coca-Cola's Processing Departments

In 2004, the Coca-Cola Company sold more than $21 billion of products in over 200 countries. Some of the company's key processing steps include washing and rinsing bottles, mixing and blending ingredients, filling and capping bottles, and labeling and packaging bottles. Raw material costs are added at various stages during this process. For example, sugar, filtered water, carbon dioxide, and syrup are added during the mixing and blending stage of the process. Bottle caps are added during the filling and capping step and paper labels are added during the labeling and packaging stage.

Coca-Cola's manufacturing process is well suited for process costing because it produces a continuous stream of identical bottles of soda. The material costs and conversion costs that are incurred at the various stages of the production process can be assigned to products by spreading them evenly over the total volume of production.

Source: The Coca-Cola Company 2004 annual report.

The Flow of Materials, Labor, and Overhead Costs

Cost accumulation is simpler in a process costing system than in a job-order costing system. In a process costing system, instead of having to trace costs to perhaps hundreds of different jobs, costs are traced to only a few processing departments.

A T-account model of materials, labor, and overhead cost flows in a process costing system is presented in Exhibit 4–3. Several key points should be noted from this exhibit. First, note that a separate Work in Process account is maintained for *each processing department*. In contrast, in a job-order costing system the entire company may have only one Work in Process account. Second, note that the completed production of the first processing

EXHIBIT 4–3 T-Account Model of Process Costing Flows

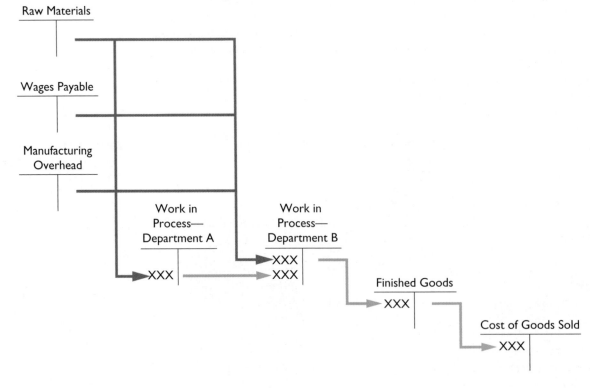

department (Department A in the exhibit) is transferred to the Work in Process account of the second processing department (Department B). After further work in Department B, the completed units are transferred to Finished Goods. (In Exhibit 4–3, we show only two processing departments, but a company can have many processing departments.)

Finally, note that materials, labor, and overhead costs can be added in *any* processing department—not just the first. Costs in Department B's Work in Process account would consist of the materials, labor, and overhead costs incurred in Department B plus the costs attached to partially completed units transferred in from Department A (called **transferred-in costs**).

Materials, Labor, and Overhead Cost Entries

To complete our discussion of cost flows in a process costing system, in this section we show journal entries relating to materials, labor, and overhead costs at Megan's Classic Cream Soda, a company that has two processing departments—Formulating and Bottling. In the Formulating Department, ingredients are checked for quality and then mixed and injected with carbon dioxide to create bulk cream soda. In the Bottling Department, bottles are checked for defects, filled with cream soda, capped, visually inspected again for defects, and then packed for shipping.

LEARNING OBJECTIVE 1

Record the flow of materials, labor, and overhead through a process costing system.

Materials Costs   As in job-order costing, materials are drawn from the storeroom using a materials requisition form. Materials can be added in any processing department, although it is not unusual for materials to be added only in the first processing department, with subsequent departments adding only labor and overhead costs as the partially completed units move along toward completion.

At Megan's Classic Cream Soda, some materials (i.e., water, flavors, sugar, and carbon dioxide) are added in the Formulating Department and some materials (i.e., bottles, caps, and packing materials) are added in the Bottling Department. The journal entry to record the materials used in the first processing department, the Formulating Department, is as follows:

Work in Process—Formulating.	XXX	
Raw Materials		XXX

The journal entry to record the materials used in the second processing department, the Bottling Department, appears below:

Work in Process—Bottling	XXX	
Raw Materials		XXX

Labor Costs   In process costing, labor costs are traced to departments—not to individual jobs. The following journal entry records the labor costs in the Formulating Department at Megan's Classic Cream Soda:

Work in Process—Formulating.	XXX	
Salaries and Wages Payable.		XXX

A similar entry would be made to record labor costs in the Bottling Department.

Overhead Costs   In process costing, as in job-order costing, predetermined overhead rates are usually used. Manufacturing overhead cost is applied to units of product as they move through the department. The following journal entry records the overhead cost for the Formulating Department:

Work in Process—Formulating.	XXX	
Manufacturing Overhead.		XXX

A similar entry would be made to record manufacturing overhead costs in the Bottling Department.

Completing the Cost Flows   Once processing has been completed in a department, the units are transferred to the next department for further processing, as illustrated in the T-accounts in Exhibit 4–3. The following journal entry transfers the cost of partially completed units from the Formulating Department to the Bottling Department:

Work in Process—Bottling	XXX	
Work in Process—Formulating		XXX

After processing has been completed in the Bottling Department, the costs of the completed units are transferred to the Finished Goods inventory account:

Finished Goods	XXX	
Work in Process—Bottling.		XXX

Finally, when a customer's order is filled and units are sold, the cost of the units is transferred to Cost of Goods Sold:

Cost of Goods Sold	XXX	
Finished Goods.		XXX

To summarize, the cost flows between accounts are basically the same in a process costing system as they are in a job-order costing system. The only difference at this point is that in a process costing system each department has a separate Work in Process account.

EQUIVALENT UNITS OF PRODUCTION

Video 4–1

Double Diamond Skis, a company that manufactures a high-performance deep-powder ski, uses process costing to determine its unit product costs. The production process is illustrated in Exhibit 4–4. Skis go through a sequence of five processing departments, starting with the Shaping and Milling Department and ending with the Finishing and Pairing Department. The basic idea in process costing is to add together all of the costs incurred in a department in a period and then spread those costs uniformly across the units processed in that department during that period. For example, if $80,000 in costs are incurred in a department to produce 2,000 units, the cost per unit in the department would be $40. However, units that have only been partially completed pose a problem. It does not seem reasonable to count partially completed units as equivalent to fully completed units when counting the department's output. Therefore, in process costing, partially completed units are mathematically translated into an equivalent number of fully completed units. This translation is accomplished using the following formula:

Equivalent units = Number of partially completed units × Percentage completion

As the formula states, **equivalent units** is defined as the product of the number of partially completed units and the percentage completion of those units. Roughly speaking, the equivalent units is the number of complete units that could have been obtained from the materials and effort that went into the partially complete units.

For example, suppose the Molding Department at Double Diamond has 500 units in its ending work in process inventory that are 60% complete. These 500 partially complete units are equivalent to 300 fully complete units (500 × 60% = 300). Therefore, the ending work in process inventory contains 300 equivalent units. These equivalent units would be added to any units completed during the period to determine the department's output for the period—called the *equivalent units of production*.

EXHIBIT 4-4   The Production Process at Double Diamond Skis*

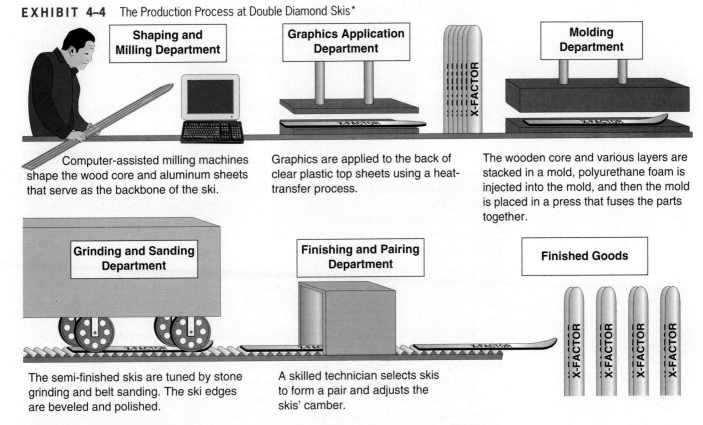

Shaping and Milling Department

Computer-assisted milling machines shape the wood core and aluminum sheets that serve as the backbone of the ski.

Graphics Application Department

Graphics are applied to the back of clear plastic top sheets using a heat-transfer process.

Molding Department

The wooden core and various layers are stacked in a mold, polyurethane foam is injected into the mold, and then the mold is placed in a press that fuses the parts together.

Grinding and Sanding Department

The semi-finished skis are tuned by stone grinding and belt sanding. The ski edges are beveled and polished.

Finishing and Pairing Department

A skilled technician selects skis to form a pair and adjusts the skis' camber.

Finished Goods

*Adapted from Bill Gout, Jesse James Doquilo, and Studio M D, "Capped Crusaders," *Skiing*, October 1993, pp. 138–144.

The equivalent units of production can be computed using either the *weighted-average method* or the *FIFO method*. The weighted-average method is a little simpler, and for that reason, it is the method used in this chapter. The details of the FIFO method are contained in a supplement to this chapter that can be downloaded at www.mhhe.com/brewer4e. In broad terms, in the **FIFO method** the equivalent units and unit costs relate only to work done during the current period. In contrast, the **weighted-average method** blends together units and costs from the current period with units and costs from the prior period. In the weighted-average method, the **equivalent units of production** for a department are the number of units transferred to the next department (or to finished goods) plus the equivalent units in the department's ending work in process inventory.

Weighted-Average Method

Under the weighted-average method, a department's equivalent units are computed as follows:

> Weighted-Average Method
> (a separate calculation is made for each cost category
> in each processing department)
>
> Equvalents units = Units transferred to the next department or to finished goods
> of production   + Equivalent units in ending work in process inventory

Note that the computation of the equivalent units of production involves adding the number of units transferred out of the department to the equivalent units in the department's ending inventory. There is no need to compute the equivalent units for the units transferred out of the department—they are 100% complete with respect to the work done in that department or they would not be transferred out. In other words, each unit transferred out of the department is counted as one equivalent unit.

Consider the Shaping and Milling Department at Double Diamond. This department uses computerized milling machines to precisely shape the wooden core and metal sheets that will be used to form the backbone of the ski. (See Exhibit 4–4 for an overview of the production process at Double Diamond.) The following activity took place in the department in May:

Shaping and Milling Department			
		Percent Completed	
	Units	Materials	Conversion
Beginning work in process.................	200	55%	30%
Units started into production during May.............................	5,000		
Units completed during May and transferred to the next department...........	4,800	100%*	100%*
Ending work in process	400	40%	25%

*It is always assumed that units transferred out of a department are 100% complete with respect to the processing done in that department.

Note the use of the term *conversion* in the table above. **Conversion cost,** as defined in Chapter 1, is direct labor cost plus manufacturing overhead cost. In process costing, conversion cost may be treated as a single element of product cost.

Note that the beginning work in process inventory was 55% complete with respect to materials costs and 30% complete with respect to conversion costs. This means that 55% of the materials costs required to complete the units in the department had already been incurred. Likewise, 30% of the conversion costs required to complete the units had already been incurred.

Two equivalent unit figures must be computed—one for materials and one for conversion. These computations are shown in Exhibit 4–5.

Note that the computations in Exhibit 4–5 ignore the fact that the units in the beginning work in process inventory were partially complete. For example, the 200 units in beginning inventory were already 30% complete with respect to conversion costs. Nevertheless, the weighted-average method is concerned only with the 4,900 equivalent units that are in ending inventories and in units transferred to the next department; it is not concerned with the fact that the beginning inventory was already partially complete. In other words, the 4,900 equivalent units computed using the weighted-average method include work that was accomplished in prior periods. This is a key point in the weighted-average method and it is easy to overlook.

Exhibit 4–6 provides an alternative way of looking at the computation of equivalent units of production. Study this exhibit carefully before going on.

IN BUSINESS   Cutting Conversion Costs

Cemex SA, the world's third largest cement maker, owns 54 plants. Each of these plants consumes 800 tons of fuel a day heating kilns to 2,700 degrees Fahrenheit. Not surprisingly, energy costs account for 40% of the company's overall conversion costs. Historically, Cemex relied exclusively on coal to heat its kilns; however, faced with soaring coal prices and shrinking profits, the company desperately needed a cheaper fuel. Cemex turned its attention to an oil industry waste product called petroleum coke that burns hotter than coal and costs half as much. The company spent about $150 million to convert its kilns to burn petroleum coke. Overall, Cemex has cut its energy bills by 17%, helping it earn higher profit margins than its biggest rivals.

Source: John Lyons, "Expensive Energy? Burn Other Stuff, One Firm Decides," *The Wall Street Journal,* September 1, 2004, pp. A1 and A8.

EXHIBIT 4–5
Equivalent Units of Production:
Weighted-Average Method

Shaping and Milling Department	Materials	Conversion
Units transferred to the next department	4,800	4,800
Ending work in process:		
Materials: 400 units × 40% complete..................	160	
Conversion: 400 units × 25% complete		100
Equivalent units of production	4,960	4,900

EXHIBIT 4–6
Visual Perspective of Equivalent
Units of Production

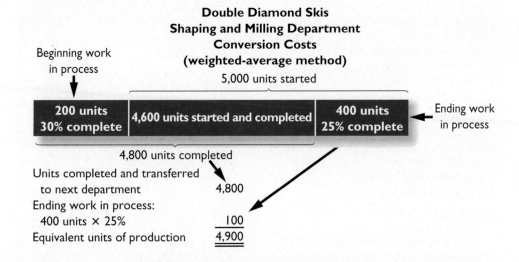

Double Diamond Skis
Shaping and Milling Department
Conversion Costs
(weighted-average method)

Beginning work in process

5,000 units started

| 200 units 30% complete | 4,600 units started and completed | 400 units 25% complete |

Ending work in process

4,800 units completed

Units completed and transferred to next department	4,800
Ending work in process:	
400 units × 25%	100
Equivalent units of production	4,900

Term Paper Writer

Assume your professors assigned four separate five-page papers that were all due on the same day. You turned in two complete papers and two incomplete papers—one of which was two pages long and the other was three pages long. Assuming that each page requires the same time and effort, how many complete papers could you have turned in with the same expenditure of time and effort?

Home Runs Galore

In 1999 Rawlings, the baseball manufacturer, was forced to open its Turrialba facility in Costa Rica to a delegation from Major League Baseball to dispel rumors that Rawlings balls were behind the record numbers of home runs.

    The delegation found that the production process was unchanged from earlier years. The red pills (rubber-coated corks purchased from a company in Mississippi) are wound three times with wool yarn and then once with cotton string. The balls are weighed, measured, and inspected after each wind. The covers, cut from sheets of rawhide, are hand-stitched and then machine-rolled. After a trip through a drying room to remove the moisture that keeps the leather soft during the sewing process, the balls are stamped with logos. After they are weighed, measured, and inspected once again, the balls are wrapped in tissue and packed in boxes. Balls that don't meet Major League specifications (5–5$\frac{1}{4}$ ounces and 9–9$\frac{1}{4}$ inches in circumference) are sold elsewhere.

Source: "Behind-the-Seams Look: Rawlings Throws Open Baseball Plant Door," *USA Today*, May 24, 2000, pp. 1C–2C.

COMPUTE AND APPLY COSTS

LEARNING OBJECTIVE 3

Compute the cost per equivalent unit using the weighted-average method.

In the last section we computed the equivalent units of production for materials and for conversion at Double Diamond Skis. In this section we will compute the cost per equivalent unit for materials and for conversion. We will then use these costs to value ending work in process and finished goods inventories. Exhibit 4–7 displays all of the data concerning May's operations in the Shaping and Milling Department that we will need to complete these tasks.

EXHIBIT 4–7
Shaping and Milling Department Data for May Operations

Topic Tackler

PLUS

Concept 4–2

Beginning work in process:	
Units in process..	200
Stage of completion with respect to materials.....................	55%
Stage of completion with respect to conversion	30%
Costs in the beginning inventory:	
Materials cost..	$ 9,600
Conversion cost...	5,575
Total cost in the beginning inventory	$15,175
Units started into production during the period.....................	5,000
Units completed and transferred out................................	4,800
Costs added to production during the period:	
Materials cost	$368,600
Conversion cost...	350,900
Total cost added in the department.................................	$719,500
Ending work in process:	
Units in process..	400
Stage of completion with respect to materials.....................	40%
Stage of completion with respect to conversion	25%

Cost per Equivalent Unit—Weighted-Average Method

In the weighted-average method, the cost per equivalent unit is computed as follows:

Weighted-Average Method
(a separate calculation is made for each cost
category in each processing department)

$$\text{Cost per equivalent unit} = \frac{\begin{array}{c}\text{Cost of beginning} \\ \text{work in process inventory}\end{array} + \begin{array}{c}\text{Cost added} \\ \text{during the period}\end{array}}{\text{Equivalent units of production}}$$

Note that the numerator is the sum of the cost of beginning work in process inventory and of the cost added during the period. Thus, the weighted-average method blends together costs from the prior and current periods. That is why it is called the weighted-average method; it averages together units and costs from both the prior and current periods.

The costs per equivalent unit for materials and for conversion are computed below for the Shaping and Milling Department for May:

Shaping and Milling Department Costs per Equivalent Unit	Materials	Conversion
Cost of beginning work in process inventory	$ 9,600	$ 5,575
Costs added during the period.........................	368,600	350,900
Total cost (a)..	$378,200	$356,475
Equivalent units of production (see Exhibit 4-5) (b)	4,960	4,900
Cost per equivalent unit (a) ÷ (b)......................	$76.25	$72.75

Applying Costs—Weighted-Average Method

LEARNING OBJECTIVE 4

Assign costs to units using the weighted-average method.

The costs per equivalent unit are used to value units in ending inventory and units that are transferred to the next department. For example, each unit transferred out of Double Diamond's Shaping and Milling Department to the Graphics Application Department as depicted in Exhibit 4–4 will carry with it a cost of $149 ($76.25 for materials cost and $72.75 for conversion cost). Since 4,800 units were transferred out in May to the next department, the total cost assigned to those units would be $715,200 (4,800 units × $149 per unit).

A complete accounting of the costs of both ending work in process inventory and the units transferred out appears below:

Shaping and Milling Department Costs of Ending Work in Process Inventory and the Units Transferred Out	Materials	Conversion	Total
Ending work in process inventory:			
Equivalent units of production (materials: 400 units × 40% complete; conversion: 400 units × 25% complete) (a)........................	160	100	
Cost per equivalent unit (see above) (b).........	$76.25	$72.75	
Cost of ending work in process inventory (a) × (b)	$12,200	$7,275	$19,475
Units completed and transferred out:			
Units transferred to the next department (a)......	4,800	4,800	
Cost per equivalent unit (see above) (b).........	$76.25	$72.75	
Cost of units transferred out (a) × (b)...........	$366,000	$349,200	$715,200

In each case, the equivalent units are multiplied by the cost per equivalent unit to determine the cost assigned to the units. This is done for each cost category—in this case, materials and conversion. The equivalent units for the units completed and transferred out are simply the number of units transferred to the next department because they would not have been transferred unless they were complete.

The costs assigned to ending work in process inventory and to the units transferred out reconcile with the costs we started with in Exhibit 4–7 as shown below:

Shaping and Milling Department Cost Reconciliation	
Costs to be accounted for:	
Cost of beginning work in process inventory (Exhibit 4–7).............	$ 15,175
Costs added to production during the period (Exhibit 4–7)	719,500
Total cost to be accounted for..................................	$734,675
Costs accounted for as follows:	
Cost of ending work in process inventory (see above)...............	$ 19,475
Cost of units transferred out (see above)	715,200
Total cost accounted for	$734,675

The $715,200 cost of the units transferred to the next department, Graphics Application, will be accounted for in that department as "costs transferred in." It will be treated in the process costing system as just another category of costs like materials or conversion costs. The only difference is that the costs transferred in will always be 100% complete with respect to the work done in the Graphics Applications Department. Costs are passed on from one department to the next in this fashion, until they reach the last processing department, Finishing and Pairing. When the products are completed in this last department, their costs are transferred to finished goods.

**CONCEPT
CHECK**

1. Beginning work in process includes 400 units that are 20% complete with respect to conversion and 30% complete with respect to materials. Ending work in process includes 200 units that are 40% complete with respect to conversion and 50% complete with respect to materials. If 2,000 units were started during the period, what are the equivalent units of production for the period according to the weighted-average method?
    a.   Conversion equivalent units = 2,280 units; Material equivalent units = 2,100 units
    b.   Conversion equivalent units = 1,980 units; Material equivalent units = 2,080 units
    c.   Conversion equivalent units = 2,480 units; Material equivalent units = 1,980 units
    d.   Conversion equivalent units = 2,280 units; Material equivalent units = 2,300 units
2. Assume the same facts as above in Concept Check 1. Also, assume that $9,900 of material costs and $14,880 of conversion costs were in the beginning inventory and $180,080 of materials and $409,200 of conversion costs were added to production during the period. What is the total cost per equivalent unit using the weighted-average method?
    a. $268.60
    b. $267.85
    c. $280.00
    d. $265.00

SUMMARY

LO1   Record the flow of materials, labor, and overhead through a process costing system.
The journal entries to record the flow of costs in process costing are basically the same as in job-order costing. Direct materials costs are debited to Work in Process when the materials are released for use in production. Direct labor costs are debited to Work in Process as incurred. Manufacturing overhead costs are applied to Work in Process by debiting Work in Process. Costs are accumulated by department in process costing and by job in job-order costing.

LO2   Compute the equivalent units of production using the weighted-average method.
To compute unit costs for a department, the department's output in terms of equivalent units must be determined. In the weighted-average method, the equivalent units for a period are the sum of the units transferred out of the department during the period and the equivalent units in ending work in process inventory at the end of the period.

LO 3   Compute the cost per equivalent unit using the weighted-average method.
The cost per equivalent unit for a particular cost category in a department is computed by dividing the sum of the cost of beginning work in process inventory and the cost added during the period by the equivalent units of production for the period.

LO 4   Assign costs to units using the weighted-average method.
The cost per equivalent unit is used to value units in ending inventory and units transferred to the next department. The cost assigned to ending inventory is determined by multiplying the cost per equivalent unit by the equivalent units in ending inventory. The cost assigned to the units transferred to the next department is determined by multiplying the cost per equivalent unit by the number of units transferred.

GUIDANCE ANSWERS TO *DECISION MAKER* AND *YOU DECIDE*

Cost Analyst (p. 163)
The new production facility will convert a raw material (wood chips) into a homogeneous product (newsprint) produced in a continuous process. Therefore, a process costing system should be used.

Term Paper Writer (p. 169)
Each complete paper is five pages long and, by assumption, each page requires the same time and effort to write. Therefore, the time and effort that went into writing one incomplete two-page paper and one incomplete three-page paper could have been used to write one complete five-page paper. Added to the two complete papers that were turned in, this would have resulted in three complete papers.

GUIDANCE ANSWERS TO CONCEPT CHECKS

1. **Choice d.** Material equivalent units are 2,200 units completed and transferred to the next department + 100 equivalent units in ending work in process inventory (200 units × 50%). Conversion equivalent units are 2,200 units completed and transferred to the next department plus 80 equivalent units in ending work in process inventory (200 units × 40%).
2. **Choice a.** ($189,980 ÷ 2,300 equivalent units) + ($424,080 ÷ 2,280 equivalent units) = $268.60.

REVIEW PROBLEM: PROCESS COST FLOWS AND COSTING UNITS

Luxguard Home Paint Company produces exterior latex paint, which it sells in one-gallon containers. The company has two processing departments—Base Fab and Finishing. White paint, which is used as a base for all the company's paints, is mixed from raw ingredients in the Base Fab Department. Pigments are added to the basic white paint, the pigmented paint is squirted under pressure into one-gallon containers, and the containers are labeled and packed for shipping in the Finishing Department. Information relating to the company's operations for April follows:

a. Issued raw materials for use in production: Base Fab Department, $851,000; and Finishing Department, $629,000.
b. Incurred direct labor costs: Base Fab Department, $330,000; and Finishing Department, $270,000.
c. Applied manufacturing overhead cost: Base Fab Department, $665,000; and Finishing Department $405,000.
d. Transferred the cost of basic white paint from the Base Fab Department to the Finishing Department, $1,850,000.
e. Transferred paint that had been prepared for shipping from the Finishing Department to Finished Goods. Its cost according to the company's cost system was $3,200,000.

Required:

1. Prepare journal entries to record items (a) through (e) above.
2. Post the journal entries from (1) above to T-accounts. The balance in the Base Fab Department's Work in Process account on April 1 was $150,000; the balance in the Finishing Department's Work in Process account was $70,000. After posting entries to the T-accounts, find the ending balance in each department's Work in Process account.
3. Determine the cost of ending work in process inventories and of units transferred out of the Base Fab Department in April. The following additional information is available regarding production in the Base Fab Department during April:

Production data:	
Units (gallons) in process, April 1: materials 100% complete, labor and overhead 60% complete	30,000
Units (gallons) started into production during April	420,000
Units (gallons) completed and transferred to the Finishing Department	370,000
Units (gallons) in process, April 30: materials 50% complete, labor and overhead 25% complete	80,000
Cost data:	
Work in process inventory, April 1:	
Materials	$ 92,000
Labor	21,000
Overhead	37,000
Total cost of work in process	$ 150,000
Cost added during April:	
Materials	$ 851,000
Labor	330,000
Overhead	665,000
Total cost added during April	$1,846,000

Solution to Review Problem

1.   a. | Work in Process—Base Fab Department .... | 851,000 | |
         | Work in Process—Finishing Department .... | 629,000 | |
         | Raw Materials .... | | 1,480,000 |

     b. | Work in Process—Base Fab Department .... | 330,000 | |
         | Work in Process—Finishing Department .... | 270,000 | |
         | Salaries and Wages Payable .... | | 600,000 |

     c. | Work in Process—Base Fab Department .... | 665,000 | |
         | Work in Process—Finishing Department .... | 405,000 | |
         | Manufacturing Overhead .... | | 1,070,000 |

     d. | Work in Process—Finishing Department .... | 1,850,000 | |
         | Work in Process—Base Fab Department .... | | 1,850,000 |

     e. | Finished Goods .... | 3,200,000 | |
         | Work in Process—Finishing Department .... | | 3,200,000 |

2.

Raw Materials			
Bal.	XXX	(a)	1,480,000

Salaries and Wages Payable		
	(b)	600,000

Work in Process—Base Fab Department			
Bal.	150,000	(d)	1,850,000
(a)	851,000		
(b)	330,000		
(c)	665,000		
Bal.	146,000		

Manufacturing Overhead			
(Various actual costs)		(c)	1,070,000

Work in Process—Finishing Department			
Bal.	70,000	(e)	3,200,000
(a)	629,000		
(b)	270,000		
(c)	405,000		
(d)	1,850,000		
Bal.	24,000		

Finished Goods		
Bal.	XXX	
(e)	3,200,000	

3.   First, we must compute the equivalent units of production for each cost category:

Base Fab Department Equivalent Units of Production			
	Materials	Labor	Overhead
Units transferred to the next department	370,000	370,000	370,000
Ending work in process inventory (materials: 80,000 units × 50% complete; labor: 80,000 units × 25% complete; overhead: 80,000 units × 25% complete)	40,000	20,000	20,000
Equivalent units of production	410,000	390,000	390,000

Then we must compute the cost per equivalent unit for each cost category:

Base Fab Department Costs per Equivalent Unit	Materials	Labor	Overhead
Cost of beginning work in process inventory	$ 92,000	$ 21,000	$ 37,000
Costs added during the period.	851,000	330,000	665,000
Total cost	$943,000	$351,000	$702,000
Equivalent units of production	410,000	390,000	390,000
Cost per equivalent unit	$2.30	$0.90	$1.80

The costs per equivalent unit can then be applied to the units in ending work in process inventory and the units transferred out as follows:

Base Fab Department Costs of Ending Work in Process Inventory and the Units Transferred Out	Materials	Labor	Overhead	Total
Ending work in process inventory:				
Equivalent units of production (a)	40,000	20,000	20,000	
Cost per equivalent unit (b)	$2.30	$0.90	$1.80	
Cost of ending work in process inventory (a) × (b) . . .	$92,000	$18,000	$36,000	$146,000
Units completed and transferred out:				
Units transferred to the next department (a).	370,000	370,000	370,000	
Cost per equivalent unit (b)	$2.30	$0.90	$1.80	
Cost of units completed and transferred out (a) × (b) .	$851,000	$333,000	$666,000	$1,850,000

GLOSSARY

Conversion cost   Direct labor cost plus manufacturing overhead cost. (p. 168)

Equivalent units   The product of the number of partially completed units and their percentage of completion with respect to a particular cost. Equivalent units are the number of complete whole units one could obtain from the materials and effort contained in partially completed units. (p. 166)

Equivalent units of production (weighted-average method)   The units transferred to the next department (or to finished goods) during the period plus the equivalent units in the department's ending work in process inventory. (p. 167)

FIFO method   A method of accounting for cost flows in a process costing system in which equivalent units and unit costs relate only to work done during the current period. (p. 167)

Process costing   A costing method used when essentially homogeneous products are produced on a continuous basis. (p. 162)

Processing department   An organizational unit where work is performed on a product and where materials, labor, or overhead costs are added to the product. (p. 163)

Transferred-in cost   The cost attached to products that have been received from a prior processing department. (p. 165)

Weighted-average method   A method of process costing that blends together units and costs from both the current and prior periods. (p. 167)

Multiple-choice questions are provided on the text website at www.mhhe.com/brewer4e.

Quiz 4

QUESTIONS

4–1   Under what conditions would it be appropriate to use a process costing system?

4–2   In what ways are job-order and process costing similar?

4–3   Why is cost accumulation easier under a process costing system than it is under a job-order costing system?

4-4   How many Work in Process accounts are maintained in a company that uses process costing?

4-5   Assume that a company has two processing departments, Mixing and Firing. Prepare a journal entry to show a transfer of partially completed units from the Mixing Department to the Firing Department.

4-6   Assume that a company has two processing departments, Mixing and Firing. Explain what costs might be added to the Firing Department's Work in Process account during a period.

4-7   What is meant by the term *equivalent units of production* when the weighted-average method is used?

BRIEF EXERCISES

BRIEF EXERCISE 4-1   Process Costing Journal Entries (LO1)

Arizona Brick Corporation produces bricks in two processing departments—Molding and Firing. Information relating to the company's operations in March follows:

a. Raw materials were issued for use in production: Molding Department, $28,000; and Firing Department, $5,000.

b. Direct labor costs were incurred: Molding Department, $18,000; and Firing Department, $5,000.

c. Manufacturing overhead was applied: Molding Department, $24,000; and Firing Department, $37,000.

d. Unfired, molded bricks were transferred from the Molding Department to the Firing Department. According to the company's process costing system, the cost of the unfired, molded bricks was $67,000.

e. Finished bricks were transferred from the Firing Department to the finished goods warehouse. According to the company's process costing system, the cost of the finished bricks was $108,000.

f. Finished bricks were sold to customers. According to the company's process costing system, the cost of the finished bricks sold was $106,000.

Required:
Prepare journal entries to record items (a) through (f) above.

BRIEF EXERCISE 4-2   Computation of Equivalent Units—Weighted-Average Method (LO2)

Lindex Company manufactures a product that goes through three departments. Information relating to activity in the first department during October is given below:

	Units	Percent Completed	
		Materials	Conversion
Work in process, October 1	50,000	90%	60%
Work in process, October 31	30,000	70%	50%

The department started 390,000 units into production during the month and transferred 410,000 completed units to the next department.

Required:
Compute the equivalent units of production for October, assuming that the company uses the weighted-average method for accounting for units and costs.

BRIEF EXERCISE 4-3   Cost Per Equivalent Unit—Weighted-Average Method (LO3)

Billinstaff Industries uses the weighted-average method in its process costing system. Data for the Assembly Department for May appear below:

	Materials	Labor	Overhead
Work in process, May 1	$14,550	$23,620	$118,100
Cost added during May	$88,350	$14,330	$71,650
Equivalent units of production	1,200	1,100	1,100

Required:
Compute the cost per equivalent unit for materials, for labor, for overhead, and in total.

BRIEF EXERCISE 4–4   Applying Costs to Units—Weighted-Average Method (LO4)

Data concerning a recent period's activity in the Prep Department, the first processing department in a company that uses process costing, appear below:

	Materials	Conversion
Equivalent units of production in ending work in process	300	100
Cost per equivalent unit	$31.56	$9.32

A total of 1,300 units were completed and transferred to the next processing department during the period.

Required:
Compute the cost of the units transferred to the next department during the period and the cost of ending work in process inventory.

 EXERCISES

EXERCISE 4–5   Equivalent Units—Weighted-Average Method (LO2)

Gulf Fisheries, Inc., processes tuna for various distributors. Two departments are involved—Cleaning and Packing. Data relating to pounds of tuna processed in the Cleaning Department during May are given below:

	Pounds of Tuna	Percent Completed*
Work in process, May 1	30,000	55%
Work in process, May 31	20,000	90%

*Labor and overhead only.

A total of 480,000 pounds of tuna were started into processing during May. All materials are added at the beginning of processing in the Cleaning Department.

Required:
Determine the equivalent units for May for the Cleaning Department, assuming that the company uses the weighted-average method.

EXERCISE 4–6   Equivalent Units and Cost per Equivalent Unit—Weighted-Average Method (LO2, LO3)

Kalox, Inc., manufactures a product that passes through two departments. Data for May for the first department follow:

	Gallons	Materials	Labor	Overhead
Work in process, May 1	80,000	$68,600	$30,000	$48,000
Gallons started in process	760,000			
Gallons transferred out.	790,000			
Work in process, May 31	50,000			
Cost added during May		$907,200	$370,000	$592,000

The beginning work in process inventory was 80% complete with respect to materials and 75% complete with respect to labor and overhead. The ending work in process inventory was 60% complete with respect to materials and 20% complete with respect to labor and overhead.

Required:
Assume that the company uses the weighted-average method of accounting for units and costs.

1. Determine the equivalent units for May's activity for the first department.
2. Determine the costs per equivalent unit for May.

EXERCISE 4–7 Process Costing Journal Entries (LO1)

Schneider Brot is a bread-baking company located in Aachen, Germany, near the Dutch border. The company uses a process costing system for its single product—a popular pumpernickel bread. Schneider Brot has two processing departments—Mixing and Baking. The T-accounts below show the flow of costs through the two departments in April (all amounts are in the currency euros):

Work in Process—Mixing			
Balance 4/1	10,000	Transferred out	760,000
Direct materials	330,000		
Direct labor	260,000		
Overhead	190,000		

Work in Process—Baking			
Balance 4/1	20,000	Transferred out	980,000
Transferred in	760,000		
Direct labor	120,000		
Overhead	90,000		

Required:

Prepare journal entries showing the flow of costs through the two processing departments during April.

EXERCISE 4–8 Equivalent Units and Cost per Equivalent Unit—Weighted-Average Method (LO2, LO3, LO4)

Solex Company produces a high-quality insulation material that passes through two production processes. Data for June for the first process follow:

	Units	Completion with Respect to Materials	Completion with Respect to Conversion
Work in process inventory, June 1	60,000	75%	40%
Work in process inventory, June 30	40,000	50%	25%

Materials cost in work in process inventory, June 1	$56,600
Conversion cost in work in process inventory, June 1	$14,900
Units started into production	280,000
Units transferred to the next process	300,000
Materials cost added during June	$385,000
Conversion cost added during June.	$214,500

Required:

1. Assume that the company uses the weighted-average method of accounting for units and costs. Determine the equivalent units for June for the first process.
2. Compute the costs per equivalent unit for June for the first process.
3. Determine the total cost of ending work in process inventory and the total cost of units transferred to the next process in June.

PROBLEMS

CHECK FIGURE
May 31 Bending
Department WIP: $34,317

PROBLEM 4–9A Cost Flows (LO1)

Techno Co. produces a special kind of tool that is widely used by construction. The tool is produced in two production departments: Bending and Drilling. Raw materials are introduced at various points in the Bending Department.

The following incomplete Work in Process account has been provided for the Bending Department for May:

Work in Process—Bending Department

May 1 balance	45,369	Completed and transferred to Drilling (? units)	?
May costs added:			
Raw materials (270,000 units)	394,210		
Direct labor	638,144		
Overhead	493,584		
May 31 balance	?		

The May 1 work in process inventory in the Bending Department consists of the following elements: raw materials, $13,385; direct labor, $18,880; and overhead, $13,104. Costs incurred during May in the Drilling Department were: materials used, $100,800; direct labor, $250,600; and overhead cost applied to production, $189,000.

Required:

1. Prepare journal entries to record the costs incurred in both the Bending Department and Drilling Department during May. Key your entries to the items (a) through (g) below.
   a. Raw materials were issued for use in production.
   b. Direct labor costs were incurred.
   c. Manufacturing overhead costs for the entire factory were incurred, $685,000. (Credit Accounts Payable.)
   d. Manufacturing overhead cost was applied to production using a predetermined overhead rate.
   e. Units that were complete with respect to processing in the Bending Department were transferred to the Drilling Department, $1,536,990.
   f. Units that were complete with respect to processing in the Drilling Department were transferred to Finished Goods, $1,650,000.
   g. Completed units were sold on account, $2,700,000. The Cost of Goods Sold was $1,600,000.

2. Post the journal entries from (1) above to T-accounts. The following account balances existed at the beginning of May. (The beginning balance in the Bending Department's Work in Process account is given above.)

Raw Materials	$500,000
Work in Process—Drilling Department	$10,000
Finished Goods	$110,000

After posting the entries to the T-accounts, find the ending balances in the inventory accounts and the manufacturing overhead accounts.

PROBLEM 4–10A   Equivalent Units; Applying Costs—Weighted-Average Method (LO2, LO3, LO4)
Laura Houldsworth Co. manufactures porcelain dolls that go through three processing departments prior to completion. Information about work in the first department, Molding, is given below for July:

CHECK FIGURE
(2) Materials: $0.96 per unit
(3) July 31 WIP: $11,000

Production data:	
Units in process, July 1 (materials 100% complete; conversion 90% complete)	15,000
Units started into production during July	160,000
Units completed and transferred out.	155,000
Units in process, July 31 (materials 40% complete; conversion 10% complete)	?
Cost data:	
Work in process inventory, July 1:	
Materials cost	$14,100
Conversion cost	$22,680
Cost added during July:	
Materials cost	$142,380
Conversion cost	$237,940

Materials are added at several stages during the molding process, whereas conversion costs are incurred uniformly. The company uses the weighted-average method.

Required:

1. Compute the equivalent units of production.
2. Compute the costs per equivalent unit for the month.
3. Determine the total cost of ending work in process inventory and of the units transferred to the next department.
4. Prepare a cost reconciliation between the costs determined in part (3) above and the cost of beginning work in process inventory and costs added in July.

CHECK FIGURE
(1) Materials: 102,500
    equivalent units;
(2) Conversion: $2.50 per
    unit;
(3) 86,000 units

PROBLEM 4–11A   Interpreting a Report—Weighted-Average Method (LO2, LO3, LO4)

Cooperative Santa Maria of southern Sonora state in Mexico makes a unique syrup using cane sugar and local herbs. The syrup is sold in small bottles and is prized as a flavoring for drinks and for use in desserts. The bottles are sold for $13 each. (The Mexican currency is the peso and is denoted by $.) The first stage in the production process is carried out in the Mixing Department, which removes foreign matter from the raw materials and mixes them in the proper proportions in large vats. The company uses the weighted-average method in its process costing system.

A hastily prepared report for the Mixing Department for May appears below:

Quantity Schedule

Units to be accounted for:	
Work in process, May 1 (materials 90% complete; conversion 70% complete)	6,000
Started into production	100,000
Total units to be accounted for	106,000
Units accounted for as follows:	
Transferred to the next department	92,000
Work in process, May 30 (materials 75% complete, conversion 50% complete)	14,000
Total units accounted for	106,000

Cost Reconciliation

Cost to be accounted for:	
Work in process, May 1	$ 16,400
Cost added during the month	431,200
Total cost	$447,600
Cost accounted for as follows:	
Work in process, May 30	$ 37,975
Transferred to the next department	409,400
Total cost	$447,375

Cooperative Santa Maria has just been acquired by another company, and the management of the acquiring company wants some additional information about Cooperative Santa Maria's operations.

Required:

1. What were the equivalent units for the month?
2. What were the costs per equivalent unit for the month? The beginning inventory consisted of the following costs: materials, $5,900; and conversion cost, $10,500. The costs added during the month consisted of: materials, $194,200; and conversion cost, $237,000.
3. How many of the units transferred to the next department were started and completed during the month?
4. The manager of the Mixing Department, anxious to make a good impression on the new owner, stated, "Materials prices jumped from about $1.10 per unit in April to $2.00 per unit in May, but due to good cost control I was able to hold our materials cost to less than $2.00 per unit for the month." Should this manager be rewarded for good cost control? Explain.

PROBLEM 4–12A   Cost Flows (LO1)

Seaside Company produces a dried fish product that goes through two departments—Drying and Salting. The company has prepared the following summary of production and costs for the Drying Department for December.

CHECK FIGURE
December 31 Drying
Department WIP: $44,000

Drying Department costs:	
Work in process inventory, December 1	$ 97,400
Materials added during December	540,460
Labor added during December	397,970
Overhead applied during December	208,170
Total departmental costs	$1,244,000

The general ledger also shows the following costs incurred in the Salting Department during December: materials used, $295,000; direct labor cost incurred, $201,000; and overhead cost applied to products, $340,000.

Required:

1. Prepare journal entries as follows to record activity in the company during December. Key your entries to the letters (a) through (g) below.
    a. Raw materials were issued to the two departments for use in production.
    b. Direct labor costs were incurred in the two departments.
    c. Manufacturing overhead costs were incurred, $542,000. (Credit Accounts Payable.) The company maintains a single Manufacturing Overhead account for the entire plant.
    d. Manufacturing overhead cost was applied to production in each department using predetermined overhead rates.
    e. Units completed with respect to processing in the Drying Department were transferred to the Salting Department, $1,200,000.
    f. Units completed with respect to processing in the Salting Department were transferred to Finished Goods, $1,980,000.
    g. Units were sold on account, $2,500,000. The Cost of Goods Sold was $1,930,000.

2. Post the journal entries from (1) above to T-accounts. Balances in selected accounts on December 1 are given below:

Raw Materials	$850,000
Work in Process—Salting Department	$33,000
Finished Goods	$57,000

After posting the entries to the T-accounts, find the ending balance in the inventory accounts and the Manufacturing Overhead accounts.

PROBLEM 4–13A   Equivalent Units; Cost per Equivalent Unit; Applying Costs—Weighted-Average Method (LO2, LO3, LO4)

CHECK FIGURE
April 30 WIP: $14,430

Tropical Break, Ltd., of Fiji makes blended tropical fruit drinks in two stages. Fruit juices are extracted from fresh fruits and then blended in the Blending Department. The blended juices are then bottled and packed for shipping in the Bottling Department. The following information pertains to the operations of the Blending Department for April. (The currency in Fiji is the Fijian dollar.)

		Percent Completed	
	Units	Materials	Conversion
Work in process, beginning	7,000	85%	60%
Started into production	88,000		
Completed and transferred out	82,000		
Work in process, ending	13,000	60%	20%
		Materials	Conversion
Work in process, beginning		$6,800	$8,000
Cost added during April		$105,450	$144,280

Required:

Assume that the company uses the weighted-average method.

1. Determine the equivalent units for April for the Blending Department.
2. Compute the costs per equivalent unit for April for the Blending Department.
3. Determine the total cost of ending work in process inventory and the total cost of units transferred to the next department in April.
4. Prepare a report that reconciles the total costs assigned to the ending work in process inventory and the units transferred out with the costs in beginning inventory and costs added during the month.

CHECK FIGURE
(1) Materials: $2.00 per unit; March 31 WIP $8,439

PROBLEM 4–14A   Analysis of Work in Process Account—Weighted-Average Method (LO1, LO2, LO3, LO4)

Dillon Corporation manufactures an industrial cleaning compound that goes through three processing departments—Grinding, Mixing, and Cooking. All raw materials are introduced at the start of work in the Grinding Department. The Work in Process T-account for the Grinding Department for a recent month is given below:

Work in Process—Grinding Department		
Inventory, March 1 (4,500 units; Conversion 60% complete) 12,365	Completed and transferred to mixing (? units)	?
March costs added:		
Raw material (56,800 units) 113,475		
Labor and overhead 75,319		
Inventory, March 31 (2,900 units; Conversion 70% complete) ?		

The March 1 work in process inventory consists of $9,125 in materials cost and $3,240 in conversion cost. The company uses the weighted-average method.

Required:

1. Determine the equivalent units of production for March.
2. Determine the costs per equivalent unit for March.
3. Determine the total cost of the units completed and transferred to the next department during March and the total cost of ending work in process inventory.
4. What criticism can be made of the unit costs that you have computed if they are used to evaluate how well costs have been controlled?

CHECK FIGURES
(1) Labor: $0.95 per equivalent unit
(2) December 31 WIP: $86,040
(4) COGS: $1,999,830

PROBLEM 4–15A   Equivalent Units; Costing Inventories; Journal Entries; Cost of Goods Sold—Weighted-Average Method (LO1, LO2, LO3, LO4)

You are employed by Tuff Soles Corporation, a manufacturer of boots. The company's chief financial officer is trying to verify the accuracy of the ending Work in Process and Finished Goods inventories prior to closing the books for the year. You have been asked to assist in this verification. The year-end balances shown on Tuff Soles Corporation's books are as follows:

	Units	Costs
Work in process, December 31 (labor and overhead 80% complete)	30,000	$85,000
Finished goods, December 31.	12,000	$60,000

Materials are added to production at the beginning of the manufacturing process, and overhead is applied to each product at the rate of 80% of direct labor cost. There was no finished goods inventory at the beginning of the year. A review of Tuff Soles Corporation's inventory and cost records has disclosed the following data:

		Costs	
	Units	Materials	Labor
Work in process, January 1 (labor and overhead 70% complete).	15,000	$18,000	$9,555
Units started into production	650,000		
Cost added during the year:			
Materials cost.................		$979,500	
Labor cost....................			$616,495
Units completed during the year	635,000		

The company uses the weighted-average cost method.

Required:

1. Determine the equivalent units and costs per equivalent unit for materials, labor, and overhead for the year.
2. Determine the amount of cost that should be assigned to the ending Work in Process and Finished Goods inventories.
3. Prepare the necessary correcting journal entry to adjust the Work in Process and Finished Goods inventories to the correct balances as of December 31.
4. Determine the cost of goods sold for the year assuming there is no underapplied or overapplied overhead.

(CPA, adapted)

BUILDING YOUR SKILLS

ETHICS CASE (LO2, LO4)

Thad Kostowski and Carol Lee are production managers in the Appliances Division of Mesger Corporation, which has several dozen plants scattered in locations throughout the world. Carol manages the plant located in Kansas City, Missouri, while Thad manages the plant in Roseville, Oregon. Production managers are paid a salary and get an additional bonus equal to 10% of their base salary if the entire division meets or exceeds its target profits for the year. The bonus is determined in March after the company's annual report has been prepared and issued to stockholders.

Late in February, Carol received a phone call from Thad that went like this:

Thad: How's it going, Carol?

Carol: Fine, Thad. How's it going with you?

Thad: Great! I just got the preliminary profit figures for the division for last year and we are within $62,500 of making the year's target profits. All we have to do is pull a few strings, and we'll be over the top!

Carol: What do you mean?

Thad: Well, one thing that would be easy to change is your estimate of the percentage completion of your ending work in process inventories.

Carol: I don't know if I should do that, Thad. Those percentage completion numbers are supplied by Jean Jackson, my lead supervisor. I have always trusted her to provide us with good estimates. Besides, I have already sent the percentage completion figures to corporate headquarters.

Thad: You can always tell them there was a mistake. Think about it, Carol. All of us managers are doing as much as we can to pull this bonus out of the hat. You may not want the bonus check, but the rest of us sure could use it.

The final processing department in Carol's production facility began the year with no work in process inventories. During the year, 270,000 units were transferred in from the prior processing department and 250,000 units were completed and sold. Costs transferred in from the prior department totaled $49,221,000. No materials are added in the final processing department. A total of $16,320,000 of conversion cost was incurred in the final processing department during the year.

Required:

1. Jean Jackson estimated that the units in ending inventory in the final processing department were 25% complete with respect to the conversion costs of the final processing department. If this estimate of the percentage completion is used, what would be the cost of goods sold for the year?

2. Does Thad Kostowski want the estimated percentage completion to be increased or decreased? Explain why.

3. What percentage completion would result in increasing the reported net operating income by $62,500 over the net operating income that would be reported if the 25% figure were used?

4. Do you think Carol Lee should go along with the request to alter estimates of the percentage completion?

  ANALYTICAL THINKING   (LO2, LO3, LO4)

Durall Company manufactures a plastic gasket that is used in automobile engines. The gaskets go through three processing departments: Mixing, Forming, and Stamping. The company's accountant (who is very inexperienced) has prepared a summary of production and costs for the Forming Department as follows for October:

Forming Department costs:	
Work in process inventory, October 1, 8,000 units;	
materials 100% complete; conversion $^7/_8$ complete..............	$ 22,420*
Costs transferred in from the Mixing Department..................	81,480
Material added during October (added when processing	
is 50% complete in the Forming Department)	27,600
Conversion costs added during October	96,900
Total departmental costs..................................	$228,400
Forming Department costs assigned to:	
Units completed and transferred to the Stamping	
Department, 100,000 units at $2.284 each.................	$228,400
Work in process inventory, October 31, 5,000 units;	
materials 0% complete; conversion $^2/_5$ complete	0
Total departmental costs assigned............................	$228,400

*Consists of cost transferred in, $8,820; materials cost, $3,400; and conversion costs, $10,200.

After mulling over the data above, Durall's president commented, "I can't understand what's happening here. Despite a concentrated effort at cost reduction, our unit cost actually went up in the Forming Department last month. With that kind of performance, year-end bonuses are out of the question for the people in that department."

The company uses the weighted-average method in its process costing.

Required:

1. Prepare a revised report for the Forming Department for October showing how much cost should have been assigned to the units completed and transferred to the Stamping Department and to the ending work in process inventory.

2. Explain to the president why the unit cost appearing on the report prepared by the accountant is so high.

5

Cost Behavior: Analysis and Use

<< A LOOK BACK

We provided overviews of the systems that are used to accumulate product costs in Chapters 2 (job-order costing), 3 (activity-based costing), and 4 (process costing).

A LOOK AT THIS CHAPTER

After reviewing the behavior of variable and fixed costs, in Chapter 5 we discuss mixed costs, which are a combination of variable and fixed costs, and describe the methods that can be used to break a mixed cost into its variable and fixed components. We also introduce the contribution format income statement, which is designed to aid decision making. In the appendix, we compare variable costing and absorption costing net operating incomes.

A LOOK AHEAD >>

Chapter 6 describes the basics of cost-volume-profit analysis, a tool that helps managers understand the interrelationships among cost, volume, and profit.

CHAPTER OUTLINE

Types of Cost Behavior Patterns

- Variable Costs
- True Variable versus Step-Variable Costs
- The Linearity Assumption and the Relevant Range
- Fixed Costs
- Types of Fixed Costs
- Fixed Costs and the Relevant Range
- Mixed Costs

The Analysis of Mixed Costs

- Diagnosing Cost Behavior with a Scattergraph Plot
- The High-Low Method
- The Least-Squares Regression Method

The Contribution Format Income Statement

- Why a New Income Statement Format?
- The Contribution Approach

Appendix 5A: Variable Costing

- Absorption Costing Income Statement
- Variable Costing Contribution Format Income Statement
- Reconciliation of Variable Costing with Absorption Costing Income

LEARNING OBJECTIVES

LP 5

After studying Chapter 5, you should be able to:

LO1 Understand how fixed and variable costs behave and how to use them to predict costs.

LO2 Use a scattergraph plot to diagnose cost behavior.

LO3 Analyze a mixed cost using the high-low method.

LO4 Prepare an income statement using the contribution format.

LO5 (Appendix) Use variable costing to prepare a contribution format income statement and contrast absorption costing and variable costing.

DECISION FEATURE

The Business of Art Sculpture

Shidoni Foundry, located in Tesuque, New Mexico, is a fine art casting and fabrication facility. The process of creating a bronze or other metal sculpture is complex. The artist creates the sculpture using modeling clay. The artist then hires a foundry such as Shidoni to produce the actual metal sculpture. Shidoni craftspeople make a rubber mold from the clay model then use that mold to make a wax version of the original. The wax is in turn used to make a ceramic casting mold and then finally the bronze version is cast. Both the wax and the ceramic casting mold are destroyed in the process of making the metal casting, but the rubber mold is not and can be reused to make additional castings.

The surface of the metal sculpture can be treated with various patinas. One of the accompanying photos shows Harry Gold, the shop's patina artist, applying a patina to a metal sculpture with brush and blowtorch. The other photo shows a finished sculpture with patinas applied.

The artist is faced with a difficult business decision. The rubber mold for a small figure such as the seated Indian in the accompanying photo costs roughly $500; the mold for a life-size figure such as the cowboy costs $3,800 to $5,000. This is just for the mold! Fortunately, as discussed above, a number of metal castings can be made from each mold. However, each life-size casting costs $8,500 to $11,000. In contrast, a casting of the much smaller Indian sculpture would cost about $750. Given the fixed costs of the mold and variable costs of the casting, finish treatments, and bases, the artist must decide how many castings to produce and how to price them. The fewer the castings, the greater the rarity factor, and hence the higher the price that can be charged to art lovers. However, in that case, the fixed costs of making the mold must be spread across fewer items. The artist must make sure not to price the sculptures so high that the investment in molds and in the castings cannot be recovered.

Source: Conversations with Shidoni personnel, including Bill Rogers and Harry Gold, and Shidoni literature. See www.shidoni.com for more information concerning the company.

In Chapter 1, we stated that costs can be classified by behavior. Cost behavior refers to how a cost will change as the level of activity changes. Managers who understand how costs behave can predict how costs will change under various alternatives. Conversely, attempting to make decisions without a thorough understanding of cost behavior patterns can lead to disaster. For example, cutting back production of a product might result in far less cost savings than managers assume if they confuse fixed costs with variable costs—leading to a drop in profits. To avoid such problems, managers must be able to accurately predict what costs will be at various activity levels.

This chapter briefly reviews the definitions of variable and fixed costs and then discusses the behavior of these costs in greater depth than in Chapter 1. The chapter also introduces the concept of a mixed cost, which is a cost that has both variable and fixed cost elements. The chapter concludes by introducing a new income statement format—called the *contribution format*—in which costs are organized by behavior rather than by the traditional functions of production, sales, and administration.

TYPES OF COST BEHAVIOR PATTERNS

Topic Tackler

PLUS

Concept 5-1

In Chapter 1 we mentioned only variable and fixed costs. In this chapter we will examine a third cost behavior pattern, known as a *mixed* or *semivariable* cost. All three cost behavior patterns—variable, fixed, and mixed—are found in most organizations. The relative proportion of each type of cost present in an organization is known as the organization's **cost structure.** For example, an organization might have many fixed costs but few variable or mixed costs. Alternatively, it might have many variable costs but few fixed or mixed costs. In this chapter we will concentrate on gaining a fuller understanding of the behavior of each type of cost. In the next chapter we explore how cost structure impacts decisions.

LEARNING OBJECTIVE 1

Understand how fixed and variable costs behave and how to use them to predict costs.

Variable Costs

We explained in Chapter 1 that a variable cost is a cost whose total dollar amount varies in direct proportion to changes in the activity level. If the activity level doubles, the total variable cost also doubles. If the activity level increases by only 10%, then the total variable cost increases by 10% as well.

Advertising on the Web

Many companies spend a growing portion of their advertising budgets on web-based contextual advertising. Here is an example of how it works. A tour company specializing in trips to Belize would like to steer consumers interested in Belize vacations to its website. The tour company partners with National Geographic and Quigo Technologies, a software company, to ensure that every time a visitor reads a National Geographic article mentioning the word Belize, a pop-up advertisement contains a link to the tour company's website. The tour company pays 50 cents each time a visitor clicks on that link. The 50 cents is split between iExplore.com, National Geographic's on-line business, and Quigo Technologies. For the tour company, this form of advertising is a clear example of a variable cost. The cost per click is constant at 50 cents per unit, but the total advertising cost rises as the number of clicks increases.

The challenge for software developers at companies such as Quigo Technologies, Google, and Yahoo is to write programs that intelligently select ads that are relevant to the context of a given web page. Providing superior contextual relevance increases the likelihood that web surfers will click on an advertisement, which in turn increases the revenue generated. Quigo Technologies' Michael Yavonditte claims that his company's ads are clicked on 0.7% of the time versus 0.2% for competitors.

Source: Chana R. Schoenberger, "Out of Context," *Forbes*, November 29, 2004, pp. 64–68.

We also found in Chapter 1 that a variable cost remains constant if expressed on a *per unit* basis. To provide an example, consider Nooksack Expeditions, a small company that provides daylong whitewater rafting excursions on rivers in the North Cascade Mountains. The company provides all of the necessary equipment and experienced guides, and it serves gourmet meals to its guests. The meals are purchased from an exclusive caterer for $30 a person for a daylong excursion. If we look at the cost of the meals on a *per person* basis, it remains constant at $30. This $30 cost per person will not change, regardless of how many people participate in a daylong excursion. The behavior of this variable cost, on both a per unit and a total basis, is tabulated below:

Number of Guests	Cost of Meals per Guest	Total Cost of Meals
250	$30	$7,500
500	$30	$15,000
750	$30	$22,500
1,000	$30	$30,000

The idea that a variable cost is constant per unit but varies in total with the activity level is crucial to understanding cost behavior patterns. We shall rely on this concept repeatedly in this chapter and in chapters ahead.

Exhibit 5–1 illustrates variable cost behavior. Note that the graph of the total cost of the meals slants upward to the right. This is because the total cost of the meals is directly proportional to the number of guests. In contrast, the graph of the per unit cost of meals is flat because the cost of the meal per guest is constant at $30.

The Activity Base   For a cost to be variable, it must be variable *with respect to something*. That "something" is its *activity base*. An **activity base** is a measure of whatever causes the incurrence of variable cost. An activity base is also sometimes referred to as a *cost driver*. Some of the most common activity bases are direct labor-hours, machine-hours, units produced, and units sold. Other examples of activity bases (cost drivers) include the number of miles driven by salespersons, the number of pounds of laundry

EXHIBIT 5–1 Variable Cost Behavior

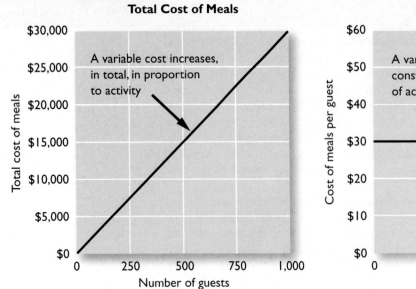

Total Cost of Meals

A variable cost increases, in total, in proportion to activity

(y-axis: Total cost of meals — $0, $5,000, $10,000, $15,000, $20,000, $25,000, $30,000)
(x-axis: Number of guests — 0, 250, 500, 750, 1,000)

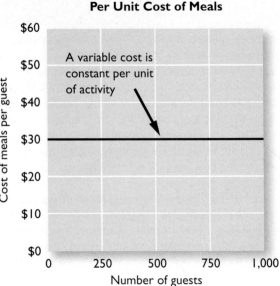

Per Unit Cost of Meals

A variable cost is constant per unit of activity

(y-axis: Cost of meals per guest — $0, $10, $20, $30, $40, $50, $60)
(x-axis: Number of guests — 0, 250, 500, 750, 1,000)

cleaned by a hotel, the number of calls handled by technical support staff at a software company, and the number of beds occupied in a hospital.

People sometimes get the notion that if a cost doesn't vary with production or with sales, then it is not a variable cost. This is not correct. As suggested by the range of bases listed above, costs are caused by many different activities within an organization. Whether a cost is variable or fixed depends on whether it is caused by the activity under consideration. For example, when analyzing the cost of service calls under a product warranty, the relevant activity measure is the number of service calls made. Those costs that vary in total with the number of service calls made are the variable costs of making service calls.

Nevertheless, unless it is stated otherwise, you can assume that the activity base under consideration is the total volume of goods and services provided by the organization. So, for example, if we ask whether direct materials at Ford is a variable cost, the answer is yes, since the cost of direct materials is variable with respect to Ford's total volume of output. We will specify the activity base only when it is something other than total output.

Extent of Variable Costs   The number and type of variable costs in an organization will depend in large part on the organization's structure and purpose. A public utility like Florida Power and Light, with large investments in equipment, will tend to have few variable costs. Most of the costs are associated with its plant, and these costs tend to be insensitive to changes in levels of service provided. A manufacturing company like Black and Decker, by contrast, will often have many variable costs; these costs will be associated with both manufacturing and distributing its products to customers.

A merchandising company like Wal-Mart or J. K. Gill will usually have a high proportion of variable costs in its cost structure. In most merchandising companies, the cost of merchandise purchased for resale, a variable cost, constitutes a very large component of total cost. Service companies, by contrast, have diverse cost structures. Some service companies, such as the Skippers restaurant chain, have fairly large variable costs because of the costs of their raw materials. On the other hand, service companies involved in consulting, auditing, engineering, dental, medical, and architectural activities have very large fixed costs in the form of expensive facilities and highly trained salaried employees.

Some of the more frequently encountered variable costs are listed in Exhibit 5–2. This exhibit is not a complete listing of all costs that can be considered variable. Moreover,

EXHIBIT 5–2
Examples of Variable Costs

Type of Organization	Costs that Are Normally Variable with Respect to Volume of Output
Merchandising company	Cost of goods (merchandise) sold
Manufacturing company	Direct materials
	Direct labor*
	Variable elements of manufacturing overhead:
	Indirect materials
	Lubricants
	Supplies
Both merchandising and manufacturing companies	Variable elements of selling and administrative costs:
	Commissions
	Shipping costs
Service organizations	Supplies, travel

*Direct labor may or may not be variable in practice. See the discussion later in this chapter.

some of the costs listed in the exhibit may behave more like fixed than variable costs in some organizations and in some circumstances. We will see examples of this later in the chapter. Nevertheless, Exhibit 5–2 provides a useful listing of many of the costs that normally would be considered variable with respect to the volume of output.

True Variable versus Step-Variable Costs

Not all variable costs have exactly the same behavior pattern. Some variable costs behave in a *true variable* or *proportionately variable* pattern. Other variable costs behave in a *step-variable* pattern.

True Variable Costs   Direct materials is a true or proportionately variable cost because the amount used during a period will vary in direct proportion to the level of production activity. Moreover, any amounts purchased but not used can be stored and carried forward to the next period as inventory.

What Goes Up Doesn't Necessarily Come Down

IN BUSINESS

The traditional view of variable costs is that they behave similarly in response to either increases or decreases in activity. However, the results of a research study using data from 7,629 companies spanning a 20-year period suggests otherwise. In this study, a 1% increase in sales corresponded with a 0.55% increase in selling and administrative costs, while a 1% decrease in sales corresponded with a 0.35% decrease in selling and administrative costs. These results suggest that many costs do not mechanistically increase or decrease in response to changes in the activity base; rather, they change in response to managers' decisions about how to react to changes in the level of the activity base.

"When volume falls, managers must decide whether to maintain committed resources and bear the costs of operating with unutilized capacity or reduce committed resources and incur the adjustment costs of retrenching and, if volume is restored, replacing committed resources at a later date." Managers faced with these choices are less likely to reduce expenses when they perceive that a decrease in activity level is temporary or when the cost of adjusting committed resources is high.

Source: Mark C. Anderson, Rajiv D. Banker, and Surya N. Janakiraman, "Are Selling, General, and Administrative Costs 'Sticky'?" *Journal of Accounting Research,* March 2003, pp. 47–63.

EXHIBIT 5–3
True Variable versus
Step-Variable Costs

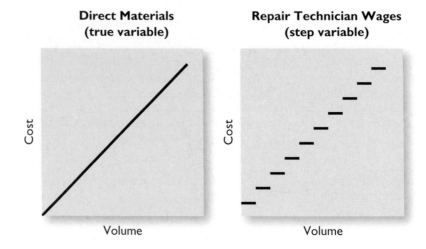

Direct Materials (true variable)

Repair Technician Wages (step variable)

EXHIBIT 5–3
True Variable versus
Step-Variable Costs

Step-Variable Costs

The cost of a resource that is obtainable only in large chunks and that increases or decreases only in response to fairly wide changes in activity is known as a **step-variable cost.** For example, the wages of skilled repair technicians are often considered to be a step-variable cost. Such a technician's time can only be obtained in large chunks—it is difficult to hire a skilled technician on anything other than a full-time basis. Moreover, any technician's time not currently used cannot be stored as inventory and carried forward to the next period. If the time is not used effectively, it is gone forever. Furthermore, a repair technician can work at a leisurely pace if pressures are light but intensify his or her efforts if pressures build up. For this reason, small changes in the level of production may have no effect on the number of technicians employed by the company.

Exhibit 5–3 contrasts the behavior of a step-variable cost with the behavior of a true variable cost. Notice that the cost of repair technicians changes only with fairly wide changes in volume and that additional technicians come in large, indivisible chunks. Great care must be taken in working with these kinds of costs to prevent "fat" from building up in an organization. There may be a tendency to employ additional help more quickly than needed, and there is a natural reluctance to lay people off when volume declines.

IN BUSINESS

How Many Guides?

Majestic Ocean Kayaking, of Ucluelet, British Columbia, is owned and operated by Tracy Morben-Eeftink. The company offers a number of guided kayaking excursions ranging from 3-hour tours of the Ucluelet harbor to 6-day kayaking and camping trips in Clayoquot Sound. One of the company's excursions is a 4-day kayaking and camping trip to The Broken Group Islands in the Pacific Rim National Park. Special regulations apply to trips in the park—including a requirement that one certified guide must be assigned for every five guests or fraction thereof. For example, a trip with 12 guests must have at least three certified guides. Guides are not salaried and are paid on a per-day basis. Therefore, the cost to the company of the guides for a trip is a step-variable cost rather than a fixed cost or a strictly variable cost. One guide is needed for 1 to 5 guests, two guides for 6 to 10 guests, three guides for 11 to 15 guests, and so on.

Sources: Tracy Morben-Eeftink, owner, and Kevin Bradshaw, guide, Majestic Ocean Kayaking. For more information about the company, see www.oceankayaking.com.

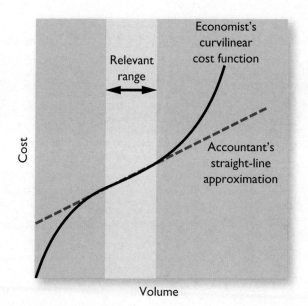

EXHIBIT 5–4
Curvilinear Costs and the
Relevant Range

The Linearity Assumption and the Relevant Range

Except in the case of step-variable costs, we ordinarily assume a strictly linear relationship between cost and volume. Economists correctly point out that many costs that the accountant classifies as variable actually behave in a *curvilinear* fashion; that is, the relation between cost and activity is a curve. A curvilinear cost is illustrated in Exhibit 5–4.

Although many costs are not strictly linear, a curvilinear cost can be satisfactorily approximated with a straight line within a narrow band of activity known as the *relevant range*. The **relevant range** is that range of activity within which the assumptions made about cost behavior are reasonably valid. For example, note that the dashed line in Exhibit 5–4 approximates the curvilinear cost with very little loss of accuracy within the shaded relevant range. However, outside of the relevant range this particular straight line is a poor approximation to the curvilinear cost relationship. Managers should always keep in mind that assumptions made about cost behavior may be invalid if activity falls outside of the relevant range.

Coping with the Fallout from September 11

IN BUSINESS

Costs can change for reasons having nothing to do with changes in volume. Filterfresh company services office coffee machines, providing milk, sugar, cups, and coffee. The company's operations were profoundly affected by the security measures many companies initiated after the terrorist attacks on the World Trade Center and the Pentagon on September 11, 2001. Heightened security at customer locations means that Filterfresh's 250 deliverymen can no longer casually walk through a customer's lobby with a load of supplies. Now a guard typically checks the deliveryman's identification and paperwork at the loading dock and may search the van before permitting the deliveryman access to the customer's building. These delays have added an average of about an hour per day to each route, which means that Filterfresh needs 24 more delivery people to do the same work it did prior to September 11. That's a 10% increase in cost without any increase in the amount of coffee sold.

Source: Anna Bernasek, "The Friction Economy," *Fortune*, February 18, 2002, pp. 104–112.

EXHIBIT 5–5 Fixed Cost Behavior

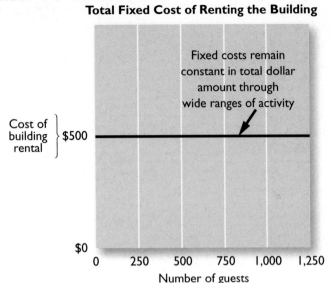

Total Fixed Cost of Renting the Building

Fixed costs remain constant in total dollar amount through wide ranges of activity

Cost of building rental $500

$0

0   250   500   750   1,000   1,250
Number of guests

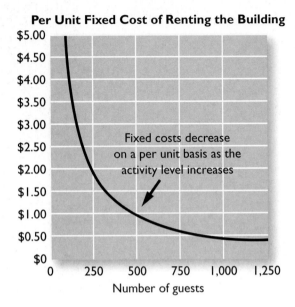

Per Unit Fixed Cost of Renting the Building

$5.00
$4.50
$4.00
$3.50
$3.00
$2.50
$2.00
$1.50
$1.00
$0.50
$0

Fixed costs decrease on a per unit basis as the activity level increases

0   250   500   750   1,000   1,250
Number of guests

Fixed Costs

In our discussion of cost behavior patterns in Chapter 2, we stated that total fixed costs remain constant within the relevant range of activity. To continue the Nooksack Expeditions example, assume the company rents a building for $500 per month to store its equipment. Within the relevant range, the total amount of rent paid is the same regardless of the number of guests the company takes on its expeditions during any given month. Exhibit 5–5 depicts this cost behavior pattern.

Since fixed costs remain constant in total, the average fixed cost *per unit* becomes progressively smaller as the level of activity increases. If Nooksack Expeditions has only 250 guests in a month, the $500 fixed rental cost would amount to an average of $2 per guest. If there are 1,000 guests, the fixed rental cost would average only 50 cents per guest. Exhibit 5–5 illustrates this aspect of the behavior of fixed costs. Note that as the number of guests increases, the average fixed cost per unit drops, but it drops at a decreasing rate. The first guests have the biggest impact on the average fixed cost per unit.

It is necessary in some contexts to express fixed costs on an average per unit basis. For example, in Chapter 2 we showed how unit product costs computed for use in external financial statements contain both variable and fixed costs. As a general rule, however, we caution against expressing fixed costs on an average per unit basis in internal reports because it creates the false impression that fixed costs are like variable costs and that total fixed costs actually change as the level of activity changes. To avoid confusion in internal reporting and decision-making situations, fixed costs should be expressed in total rather than on a per unit basis.

IN BUSINESS   Costing the Trek

Jackson Hole Llamas is owned and operated by Jill Aanonsen/Hodges and David Hodges. The company provides guided tours to remote areas of Yellowstone National Park and the Jedediah Smith Wilderness, with the llamas carrying the baggage for the multiday treks.

Jill and David operate out of their ranch in Jackson Hole, Wyoming, leading about 10 trips each summer season. All food is provided as well as tents and sleeping pads. On the basis of the number of guests on a trip, Jill and David will decide how many llamas will go on the trip and how many will remain on the ranch. Llamas are transported to the trailhead in a special trailer.

The company has a number of costs, some of which are listed below:

Cost	Cost Behavior
Food and beverage costs	Variable with respect to the number of guests and the length of the trip in days.
Truck and trailer operating costs	Variable with respect to the number of miles to the trailhead.
Guide wages	Step variable; Jill and David serve as the guides on most trips and hire guides only for larger groups.
Costs of providing tents	Variable with respect to the number of guests and length of the trip in days. Jackson Hole Llamas owns its tents, but they wear out through use and must be repaired or eventually replaced.
Cost of feeding llamas	Variable with respect to the number of guests, and hence the number of llamas, on a trip. [Actually, the cost of feeding llamas may *decrease* with the number of guests on a trip. When a llama is on a trek, it lives off the land—eating grasses and other vegetation found in meadows and along the trail. When a llama is left on the ranch, it may have to be fed purchased feed.]
Property taxes	Fixed.

Source: Jill Aanonsen/Hodges and David Hodges, owners and operators of Jackson Hole Llamas, www.jhllamas.com.

Types of Fixed Costs

Fixed costs are sometimes referred to as capacity costs, since they result from outlays made for buildings, equipment, skilled professional employees, and other items needed to provide the basic capacity for sustained operations. For planning purposes, fixed costs can be viewed as being either *committed* or *discretionary*.

Committed Fixed Costs Investments in facilities, equipment, and the basic organization that can't be significantly reduced even for short periods of time without making fundamental changes are referred to as **committed fixed costs.** Examples of such costs include depreciation of buildings and equipment, real estate taxes, insurance expenses, and salaries of top management and operating personnel. Even if operations are interrupted or cut back, committed fixed costs remain largely unchanged in the short term. During a recession, for example, a company won't usually eliminate key executive positions or sell off key facilities—the basic organizational structure and facilities ordinarily are kept intact. The costs of restoring them later are likely to be far greater than any short-run savings that might be realized.

Once a decision is made to acquire committed fixed resources, the company may be locked into that decision for many years to come. Consequently, such commitments should be made only after careful analysis of the available alternatives. Investment decisions involving committed fixed costs will be examined in Chapter 14.

Discretionary Fixed Costs **Discretionary fixed costs** (often referred to as *managed fixed costs*) usually arise from *annual* decisions by management to spend on certain fixed cost items. Examples of discretionary fixed costs include advertising, research, public relations, management development programs, and internships for students.

Two key differences exist between discretionary fixed costs and committed fixed costs. First, the planning horizon for a discretionary fixed cost is short term—usually a single year. By contrast, committed fixed costs have a planning horizon that encompasses many

Committed vs. Discretionary Fixed Costs

years. Second, discretionary fixed costs can be cut for short periods of time with minimal damage to the long-run goals of the organization. For example, spending on management development programs can be reduced because of poor economic conditions. Although some unfavorable consequences may result from the cutback, it is doubtful that these consequences would be as great as those that would result if the company decided to economize by laying off key personnel.

Whether a particular cost is regarded as committed or discretionary may depend on management's strategy. For example, during recessions when the level of home building is down, many construction companies lay off most of their workers and virtually disband operations. Other construction companies retain large numbers of employees on the payroll, even though the workers have little or no work to do. While these latter companies may be faced with short-term cash flow problems, it will be easier for them to respond quickly when economic conditions improve. And the higher morale and loyalty of their employees may give these companies a significant competitive advantage.

The most important characteristic of discretionary fixed costs is that management is not locked into its decisions regarding such costs. Discretionary costs can be adjusted from year to year or even perhaps during the course of a year if necessary.

IN BUSINESS   A Twist on Fixed and Variable Costs

Mission Controls designs and installs automation systems for food and beverage manufacturers. At most companies, when sales drop and cost cutting is necessary, top managers lay off workers. The founders of Mission Controls decided to do something different when sales drop—they slash their own salaries before they even consider letting any of their employees go. This makes their own salaries somewhat variable, while the wages and salaries of workers act more like fixed costs. The payoff is a loyal and committed workforce.

Source: Christopher Caggiano, "Employment, Guaranteed for Life," *Inc* magazine, October 15, 2002, p. 74.

The Trend toward Fixed Costs   The trend in many industries is toward greater fixed costs relative to variable costs. Chores that used to be performed by hand have been taken over by machines. For example, grocery clerks at stores like Safeway and Kroger used to key in prices by hand on cash registers. Now, stores are equipped with barcode readers that enter price and other product information automatically. In general, competition has created pressure to give customers more value for their money—a demand that often can only be satisfied by automating business processes. For example, an H & R Block employee used to fill out tax returns for customers by hand and the advice given to a customer largely depended on the knowledge of that particular employee. Now, sophisticated computer software based on the accumulated knowledge of many experts is used to complete tax returns, and the software provides tax planning and other advice tailored to the customer's needs.

As automation intensifies, the demand for "knowledge" workers—those who work primarily with their minds rather than their muscles—has grown tremendously. Since knowledge workers tend to be salaried, highly trained, and difficult to replace, the costs of compensating these workers are often relatively fixed and are committed rather than discretionary.

A New Twist on Sending Jobs Offshore

SeaCode (www.sea-code.com) is a San Diego based company that offers a new twist on the popular practice of outsourcing jobs from the United States to foreign countries with lower labor costs. The company houses 600 computer programmers from around the world on a cruise ship three miles off the coast of Los Angeles. This "floating tech factory" is subject to the labor laws of whatever flag the boat chooses to fly rather than to U.S. labor laws. SeaCode pays its "knowledge workers" $1,500 to $1,800 per month, which is below prevailing salaries on the U.S. mainland but exceeds the salaries in many countries. The company claims that it has been inundated with resumes of college graduates from across the globe.

SeaCode's clients get access to highly skilled labor at a lower cost than would have to be paid for similar jobs housed on U.S. soil. In addition, rather than having to fly halfway around the world to places such as India or China to oversee projects, U.S. managers can fly to Los Angeles and in a brief time be three miles off the California coast checking on the status of "offshore" operations.

Source: Reed Tucker, "Will a Floating Tech Factory Fly?" *Fortune*, September 5, 2005, p. 28.

Is Labor a Variable or a Fixed Cost?   As the preceding discussion suggests, wages and salaries may be fixed or variable. The behavior of wage and salary costs will differ from one country to another, depending on labor regulations, labor contracts, and custom. In some countries, such as France, Germany, and Japan, management has little flexibility in adjusting the labor force to changes in business activity. In countries such as the United States and the United Kingdom, management typically has much greater latitude. However, even in these less restrictive environments, managers may choose to treat employee compensation as a fixed cost for several reasons.

First, many managers are reluctant to decrease their workforce in response to short-term declines in sales. These managers realize that the success of their businesses hinges on retaining highly skilled and trained employees. If these valuable workers are laid off, it is unlikely that they would ever return or be easily replaced. Furthermore, laying off workers undermines the morale of those employees who remain.

Second, managers do not want to be caught with a bloated payroll in an economic downturn. Therefore, managers are reluctant to add employees in response to short-term increases in sales. Instead, more and more companies rely on temporary and part-time workers to take up the slack when their permanent, full-time employees are unable to handle all of the demand for their products and services. In such companies, labor costs are a complex mixture of fixed and variable costs.

The Regulatory Burden

The late Peter F. Drucker, a renowned observer of business and society, claimed that "the driving force behind the steady growth of temps [and outsourcing of work] ... is the growing burden of rules and regulations for employers." U.S. laws and regulations concerning employees require companies to file multiple reports—and any breach, even if unintentional, can result in punishment. According to the Small Business Administration, the owner of a small or midsize business spends up to a quarter of his or her time on employment-related paperwork and the cost of complying with government regulations (including tax report preparation) is over $5,000 per employee per year. "No wonder that employers ... complain bitterly that they have no time to work on products and services.... They no longer chant the old mantra 'People are our greatest asset.' Instead, they claim 'People are our greatest liability.'" To the extent that the regulatory burden leads to a decline in permanent full-time employees and an increase in the use of temporary employees and outsourcing, labor costs are converted from fixed to variable costs. While this is not the intent of the regulations, it is a consequence.

Source: Peter F. Drucker, "They're Not Employees, They're People," *Harvard Business Review*, February 2002.

Many major companies have undergone waves of downsizing in recent years in which large numbers of employees, including managers, have lost their jobs. This downsizing may seem to suggest that even management salaries should be regarded as variable costs, but this would not be a valid conclusion. Downsizing has largely been the result of attempts to streamline business processes and cut costs rather than a response to a decline in sales activity. This underscores an important, but subtle, point. Fixed costs can change—they just don't change in response to small changes in activity.

In sum, there is no clear-cut answer to the question "Is labor a variable or fixed cost?" It depends on how much flexibility management has to adjust the workforce and management's strategy. Nevertheless, unless otherwise stated, we will assume in this text that direct labor is a variable cost. This assumption is more likely to be valid for companies in the United States than in countries where employment laws permit much less flexibility.

Labor at Southwest Airlines

Starting with a $10,000 investment in 1966, Herb Kelleher built Southwest Airlines into the most profitable airline in the United States. Prior to stepping down as president and CEO of the airline in 2001, Kelleher wrote: "The thing that would disturb me most to see after I'm no longer CEO is layoffs at Southwest. Nothing kills your company's culture like layoffs. Nobody has ever been furloughed here, and that is unprecedented in the airline industry. It's been a huge strength of ours... We could have furloughed at various times and been more profitable, but I always thought that was shortsighted. You want to show your people that you value them and you're not going to hurt them just to get a little money in the short run."

Because of this commitment by management to the company's employees, all wages and salaries are basically committed fixed costs at Southwest Airlines.

Source: Herb Kelleher, "The Chairman of the Board Looks Back," *Fortune*, May 28, 2001, pp. 63–76.

Fixed Costs and the Relevant Range

The concept of the relevant range, which was introduced in the discussion of variable costs, is also important in understanding fixed costs—particularly discretionary fixed costs. The levels of discretionary fixed costs are typically decided at the beginning of the year and depend on the needs of planned programs such as advertising and training. The scope of these programs will depend, in turn, on the overall anticipated level of activity for the year. At very high levels of activity, programs are often broadened or expanded. For example, if the company hopes to increase sales by 25%, it would probably plan for much larger advertising costs than if no sales increase were planned. So the *planned* level of activity might affect total discretionary fixed costs. However, once the total discretionary fixed costs have been

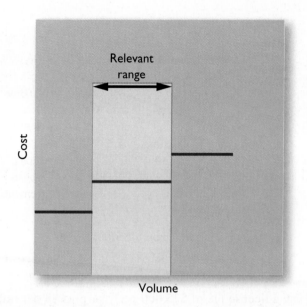

EXHIBIT 5–6
Fixed Costs and the
Relevant Range

budgeted, they are unaffected by the *actual* level of activity. For example, once the advertising budget has been established and spent, it will not be affected by how many units are actually sold. Therefore, the cost is fixed with respect to the *actual* number of units sold.

Discretionary fixed costs are easier to adjust than committed fixed costs. They also tend to be less "lumpy." Committed fixed costs consist of costs such as buildings, equipment, and the salaries of key personnel. It is difficult to buy half a piece of equipment or to hire a quarter of a product-line manager, so the step pattern depicted in Exhibit 5–6 is typical for such costs. The relevant range of activity for a fixed cost is the range of activity over which the graph of the cost is flat as in Exhibit 5–6. As a company expands its level of activity, it may outgrow its present facilities, or the key management team may need to be expanded. The result, of course, will be increased committed fixed costs as larger facilities are built and as new management positions are created.

One reaction to the step pattern depicted in Exhibit 5–6 is to conclude that discretionary and committed fixed costs are really just step-variable costs. To some extent this is true, since *almost* all costs can be adjusted in the long run. There are two major differences, however, between the step-variable costs depicted earlier in Exhibit 5–3 and the fixed costs depicted in Exhibit 5–6.

The first difference is that the step-variable costs can often be adjusted quickly as conditions change, whereas once fixed costs have been set, they usually can't be changed easily. A step-variable cost such as the wages of repair technicians, for example, can be adjusted upward or downward by hiring and laying off technicians. By contrast, once a company has signed a lease for a building, it is locked into that level of lease cost for the life of the contract.

The second difference is that the *width of the steps* depicted for step-variable costs is much narrower than the width of the steps depicted for the fixed costs in Exhibit 5–6. The width of the steps relates to volume or level of activity. For step-variable costs, the width of a step might be 40 hours of activity per week in the case of repair technicians. For fixed costs, however, the width of a step might be *thousands* or even *tens of thousands* of hours of activity. In essence, the width of the steps for step-variable costs is generally so narrow that these costs can be treated essentially as variable costs for most purposes. The width of the steps for fixed costs, on the other hand, is so wide that these costs should be treated as entirely fixed within the relevant range.

Mixed Costs

A **mixed cost** contains both variable and fixed cost elements. Mixed costs are also known as semivariable costs. To continue the Nooksack Expeditions example, the

EXHIBIT 5–7
Mixed Cost Behavior

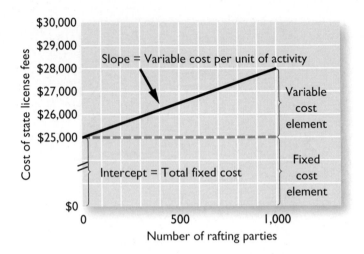

company must pay a license fee of $25,000 per year plus $3 per rafting party to the state's Department of Natural Resources. If the company runs 1,000 rafting parties this year, the total fees paid to the state would be $28,000, made up of $25,000 in fixed cost plus $3,000 in variable cost. Exhibit 5–7 depicts the behavior of this mixed cost.

Even if Nooksack fails to attract any customers, the company still must pay the license fee of $25,000. This is why the cost line in Exhibit 5–7 intersects the vertical cost axis at the $25,000 point. For each rafting party the company organizes, the total cost of the state fees will increase by $3. Therefore, the total cost line slopes upward as the variable cost of $3 per party is added to the fixed cost of $25,000 per year.

Since the mixed cost in Exhibit 5–7 is represented by a straight line, the following equation for a straight line can be used to express the relationship between a mixed cost and the level of activity:

$$Y = a + bX$$

In this equation,

Y = The total mixed cost
a = The total fixed cost (the vertical intercept of the line)
b = The variable cost per unit of activity (the slope of the line)
X = The level of activity

In the case of the state fees paid by Nooksack Expeditions, the equation is written as follows:

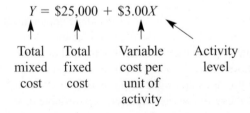

$$Y = \$25,000 + \$3.00X$$

| Total mixed cost | Total fixed cost | Variable cost per unit of activity | Activity level |

This equation makes it easy to calculate the total mixed cost for any level of activity within the relevant range. For example, suppose that the company expects to organize 800 rafting parties in the next year. The total state fees would be calculated as follows:

$$Y = \$25,000 + (\$3.00 \text{ per rafting party} \times 800 \text{ rafting parties})$$

$$= \$27,400$$

DECISION MAKER

Cost Analyst

You have been hired to analyze costs for a caterer that provides and serves refreshments for wedding receptions. Costs incurred by the caterer include administrative salaries, rental of the central kitchen, the salary of the full-time chef, wages of part-time cooks, the costs of groceries and kitchen supplies, delivery vehicle depreciation and operating expenses, the wages of part-time food servers, depreciation of silverware and dinnerware, and the costs of cleaning table linens. Which of these costs are likely to be variable with respect to the number of guests at a wedding reception? Which are likely to be fixed? Which are likely to be mixed?

THE ANALYSIS OF MIXED COSTS

Mixed costs are very common. For example, the cost of providing X-ray services to patients at the Harvard Medical School Hospital is a mixed cost. The costs of equipment depreciation and radiologists' and technicians' salaries are fixed, but the costs of X-ray film, power, and supplies are variable. At Southwest Airlines, maintenance costs are a mixed cost. The company incurs fixed costs for renting maintenance facilities and for keeping skilled mechanics on the payroll, but the costs of replacement parts, lubricating oils, tires, and so forth, are variable with respect to how often and how far the company's aircraft are flown.

The fixed portion of a mixed cost represents the minimum cost of having a service *ready and available* for use. The variable portion represents the cost incurred for *actual consumption* of the service, thus it varies in proportion to the amount of service actually consumed.

How does management go about actually estimating the fixed and variable components of a mixed cost? The most common methods used in practice are *account analysis* and the *engineering approach.*

In **account analysis,** an account is classified as either variable or fixed based on the analyst's prior knowledge of how the cost in the account behaves. For example, direct materials would be classified as variable and a building lease cost would be classified as fixed because of the nature of those costs. The total fixed cost of an organization is the sum of the costs for the accounts that have been classified as fixed. The variable cost per unit is estimated by dividing the sum of the costs for the accounts that have been classified as variable by the total activity.

The **engineering approach** to cost analysis involves a detailed analysis of what cost behavior should be, based on an industrial engineer's evaluation of the production methods to be used, the materials specifications, labor requirements, equipment usage, production efficiency, power consumption, and so on. For example, Pizza Hut might use the engineering approach to estimate the cost of preparing and serving a particular take-out pizza. The cost of the pizza would be estimated by carefully costing the specific ingredients used to make the pizza, the power consumed to cook the pizza, and the cost of the container the pizza is delivered in. The engineering approach must be used in those situations where no past experience is available concerning activity and costs. In addition, it is sometimes used together with other methods to improve the accuracy of cost analysis.

Account analysis works best when analyzing costs at a fairly aggregated level, such as the cost of serving patients in the emergency room (ER) of Swedish Hospital. The costs of drugs, supplies, forms, wages, equipment, and so on can be roughly classified as variable or fixed and a mixed cost formula for the overall cost of the emergency room can be estimated fairly quickly. However, this method does not recognize that some of the accounts may contain both fixed and variable costs. For example, the cost of electricity for the ER is a mixed cost. Most of the electricity is a fixed cost because it is used for heating and lighting. However, the consumption of electricity increases with activity in the ER since diagnostic equipment, operating theater lights, defibrillators, and so on all consume electricity. The most effective way to estimate the fixed and variable elements of such a mixed cost may be to analyze past records of cost and activity data. These records

EXHIBIT 5–8
Scattergraph Method of
Cost Analysis

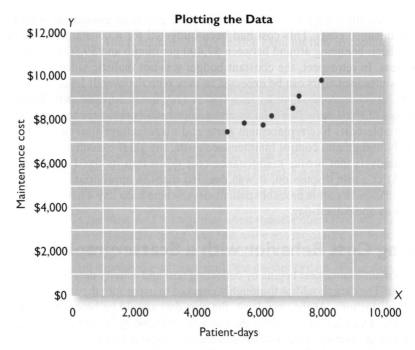

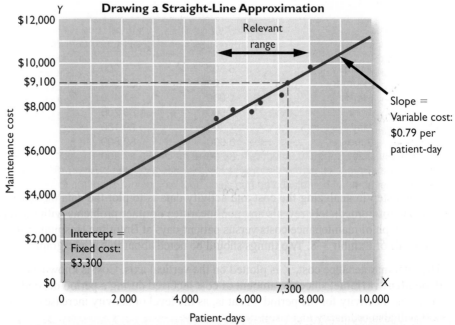

estimated by subtracting the estimated fixed cost from the total cost at the point lying on the straight line.

Total maintenance cost for 7,300 patient-days (a point falling on the straight line)	$9,100
Less estimated fixed cost (the vertical intercept)	3,300
Estimated total variable cost for 7,300 patient-days	$5,800

The average variable cost per unit at 7,300 patient-days is computed as follows:

$$\text{Variable cost per unit} = \$5,800 \div 7,300 \text{ patient-days}$$

$$= \$0.79 \text{ per patient-day (rounded)}$$

Combining the estimate of the fixed cost and the estimate of the variable cost per patient-day, we can express the relation between cost and activity as follows:

$$Y = 3,300 + \$0.79X$$

where X is the number of patient-days.

  We hasten to add that this *is* a quick-and-dirty method of estimating the fixed and variable cost elements of a mixed cost; it is seldom used in practice when the financial implications of a decision based on the analysis are significant. However, setting aside the estimates of the fixed and variable cost elements, plotting the data on a scattergraph is an essential diagnostic step that is too often overlooked. Suppose, for example, we had been interested in the relation between total nursing wages and the number of patient-days at the hospital. The permanent, full-time nursing staff can handle up to 7,000 patient-days in a month. Beyond that level of activity, part-time nurses must be called in to help out. The cost and activity data for nurses are plotted on the scattergraph in Exhibit 5–9. Looking at

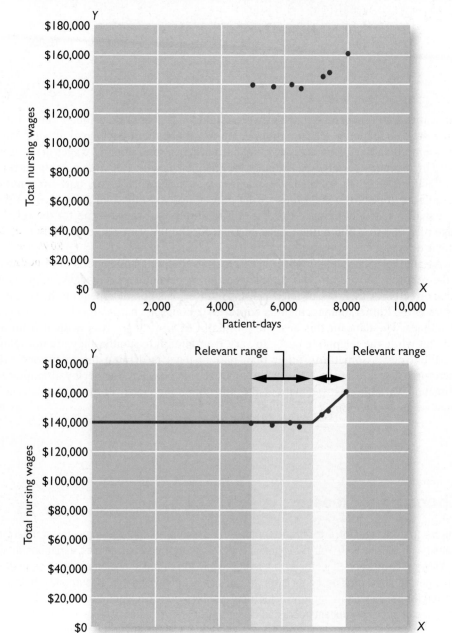

EXHIBIT 5–9
More than One Relevant Range

EXHIBIT 5–10
A Diagnostic Scattergraph Plot

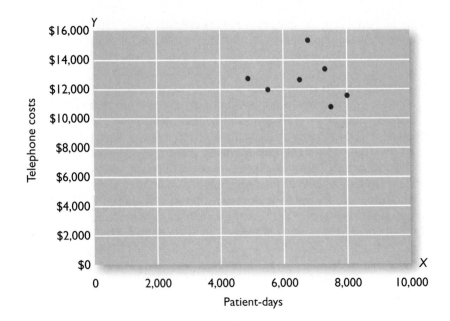

that scattergraph, it is evident that two straight lines would do a much better job of fitting the data than a single straight line. Up to 7,000 patient-days, total nursing wages are essentially a fixed cost. Above 7,000 patient-days, total nursing wages are a mixed cost. This happens because, as stated above, the permanent, full-time nursing staff can handle up to 7,000 patient-days in a month. Above that level, part-time nurses are called in to help, which adds to the cost. Consequently, two straight lines (and two equations) would be used to represent total nursing wages—one for the relevant range of 5,000 to 7,000 patient-days and one for the relevant range of 7,000 to 8,000 patient-days.

As another example, suppose that Brentline Hospital's management is interested in the relation between the hospital's telephone costs and patient-days. Patients are billed directly for their use of telephones, so those costs do not appear on the hospital's cost records. Rather, management is concerned about the charges for the staff's use of telephones. The data for this cost are plotted in Exhibit 5–10. It is evident from that plot that while the telephone costs do vary from month to month, they are not related to patient-days. Something other than patient-days is driving the telephone bills. Therefore, it would not make sense to analyze this cost any further by attempting to estimate a variable cost per patient-day for telephone costs. Plotting the data helps diagnose such situations.

YOU DECIDE	**Choosing a Measure of Activity**

You are the manager of a for-profit company that helps students prepare for standardized exams such as the SAT. You have been trying to figure out what causes variations in your monthly electrical costs. Electricity is used primarily to run office equipment such as personal computers and to provide lighting for the business office and for classrooms. Below are scattergraphs that show monthly electrical costs plotted against two different possible measures of activity—student-hours and classroom-hours. A student who takes a course involving 10 hours of classroom time would be counted as 10 student-hours. Each hour a classroom is used is counted as one classroom-hour, regardless of the number of students in the classroom at the time.

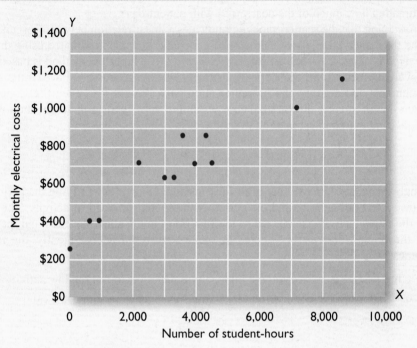

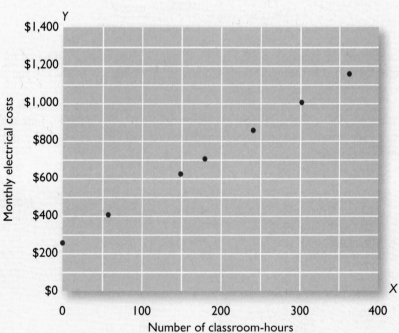

Which measure of activity—student-hours or classroom-hours—best explains variations in monthly electrical costs and should therefore be used to estimate its variable cost component?

The High-Low Method

In addition to the quick-and-dirty method described in the preceding section, more precise methods are available for estimating fixed and variable costs. However, it must be emphasized that fixed and variable costs should be computed only if a scattergraph plot confirms that the relation is approximately linear. In the case of maintenance costs at

LEARNING OBJECTIVE 3

Analyze a mixed cost using the high-low method.

Brentline Hospital, the relation does appear to be linear. In the case of telephone costs, there isn't any clear relation between telephone costs and patient-days, so there is no point in estimating how much of the cost varies with patient-days.

Assuming that the scattergraph plot indicates a linear relation between cost and activity, the fixed and variable cost elements of a mixed cost can be estimated using the *high-low method* or the *least-squares regression method*. The high-low method is based on the rise-over-run formula for the slope of a straight line. As discussed above, if the relation between cost and activity can be represented by a straight line, then the slope of the straight line is equal to the variable cost per unit of activity. Consequently, the following formula can be used to estimate the variable cost.

$$\text{Variable cost} = \text{Slope of the line} = \frac{\text{Rise}}{\text{Run}} = \frac{Y_2 - Y_1}{X_2 - X_1}$$

To analyze mixed costs with the **high-low method,** begin by identifying the period with the lowest level of activity and the period with the highest level of activity. The period with the lowest activity is selected as the first point in the above formula and the period with the highest activity is selected as the second point. Consequently, the formula becomes:

$$\frac{\text{Variable}}{\text{cost}} = \frac{Y_2 - Y_1}{X_2 - X_1} = \frac{\text{Cost at the high activity level} - \text{Cost at the low activity level}}{\text{High activity level} - \text{Low activity level}}$$

or

$$\text{Variable cost} = \frac{\text{Change in cost}}{\text{Change in activity}}$$

Therefore, when the high-low method is used, the variable cost is estimated by dividing the difference in cost between the high and low levels of activity by the change in activity between those two points.

To return to the Brentline Hospital example, using the high-low method, we first identify the periods with the highest and lowest *activity*—in this case, June and March. We then use the activity and cost data from these two periods to estimate the variable cost component as follows:

	Patient-Days	Maintenance Cost Incurred
High activity level (June)	8,000	$9,800
Low activity level (March)	5,000	7,400
Change	3,000	$2,400

$$\text{Variable cost} = \frac{\text{Change in cost}}{\text{Change in activity}} = \frac{\$2,400}{3,000 \text{ patient-days}} = \$0.80 \text{ per patient-day}$$

Having determined that the variable maintenance cost is 80 cents per patient-day, we can now determine the amount of fixed cost. This is done by taking total cost at *either* the high or the low activity level and deducting the variable cost element. In the computation below, total cost at the high activity level is used in computing the fixed cost element:

$$\text{Fixed cost element} = \text{Total cost} - \text{Variable cost element}$$

$$= \$9,800 - (\$0.80 \text{ per patient-day} \times 8,000 \text{ patient-days})$$

$$= \$3,400$$

Both the variable and fixed cost elements have now been isolated. The cost of maintenance can be expressed as $3,400 per month plus 80 cents per patient-day or as:

$$Y = \$3,400 + \$0.80X$$

Total
maintenance
cost

Total
patient-days

The data used in this illustration are shown graphically in Exhibit 5–11. Notice that a straight line has been drawn through the points corresponding to the low and high levels of activity. In essence, that is what the high-low method does—it draws a straight line through those two points.

Sometimes the high and low levels of activity don't coincide with the high and low amounts of cost. For example, the period that has the highest level of activity may not have the highest amount of cost. Nevertheless, the highest and lowest levels of *activity* are always used to analyze a mixed cost under the high-low method. The reason is that the analyst would like to use data that reflect the greatest possible variation in activity.

The high-low method is very simple to apply, but it suffers from a major (and sometimes critical) defect—it utilizes only two data points. Generally, two data points are not enough to produce accurate results. Additionally, the periods with the highest and lowest activity tend to be unusual. A cost formula that is estimated solely using data from these unusual periods may misrepresent the true cost behavior during normal periods. Such a distortion is evident in Exhibit 5–11. The straight line should probably be shifted down somewhat so that it is closer to more of the data points. For these reasons, other methods of cost analysis that use all of the data will generally be more accurate than the high-low method. A manager who chooses to use the high-low method should do so with a full awareness of its limitations.

Fortunately, computer software makes it very easy to use sophisticated statistical methods, such as *least-squares regression,* that use all of the data and that are capable of

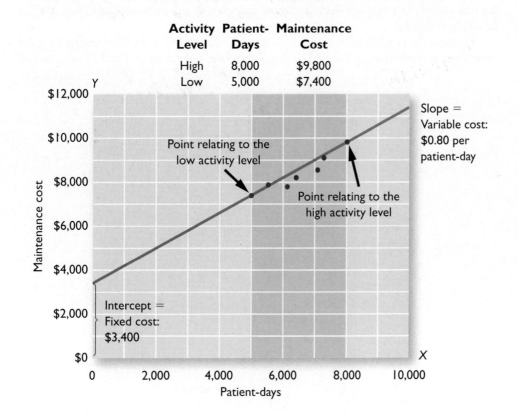

Activity Level	Patient-Days	Maintenance Cost
High	8,000	$9,800
Low	5,000	$7,400

EXHIBIT 5–11
High-Low Method of Cost Analysis

providing much more information than just the estimates of variable and fixed costs. The details of these statistical methods are beyond the scope of this text, but the basic approach is discussed below. Nevertheless, even if the least-squares regression approach is used, it is always a good idea to plot the data in a scattergraph. By simply looking at the scattergraph, you can quickly verify whether it makes sense to fit a straight line to the data using least-squares regression or some other method.

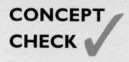

CONCEPT CHECK

3. Assume a hotel rented 400, 480, and 420 rooms in the months of April, May, and June, respectively; and the total housekeeping costs for the three months in question were $6,000, $6,800, and $6,200. With use of the high-low method, what is the amount of monthly fixed housekeeping costs?
   a. $1,000
   b. $1,500
   c. $2,000
   d. $2,500

The Least-Squares Regression Method

The **least-squares regression method,** unlike the high-low method, uses all of the data to separate a mixed cost into its fixed and variable components. A *regression line* of the form $Y = a + bX$ is fitted to the data, where a represents the total fixed cost and b represents the variable cost per unit of activity. The basic idea underlying the least-squares regression method is illustrated in Exhibit 5–12 using hypothetical data points. Notice from the exhibit that the deviations from the plotted points to the regression line are measured vertically on the graph. These vertical deviations are called the regression errors. There is nothing mysterious about the least-squares regression method. It simply computes the regression line that minimizes the sum of these squared errors. The formulas that accomplish this are fairly complex and involve numerous calculations, but the principle is simple.

Fortunately, computers are adept at carrying out the computations required by the least-squares regression formulas. The data—the observed values of X and Y—are entered

EXHIBIT 5–12
The Concept of Least-Squares Regression

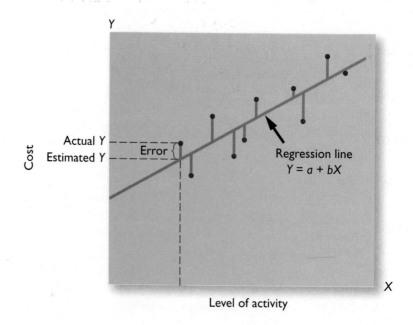

into the computer, and software does the rest. In the case of the Brentline Hospital maintenance cost data, a statistical software package on a personal computer can calculate the following least-squares regression estimates of the total fixed cost (a) and the variable cost per unit of activity (b):

$$a = \$3,431$$

$$b = \$0.759$$

Therefore, by the least-squares regression method, the fixed element of the maintenance cost is \$3,431 per month and the variable portion is 75.9 cents per patient-day.

In terms of the linear equation $Y = a + bX$, the cost formula can be written as

$$Y = \$3,431 + \$0.759X$$

where activity (X) is expressed in patient-days.

Notice the least-squares regression estimates (variable cost per patient day = 75.9 cents; fixed cost per month = \$3,431) differ from those obtained using the scattergraph method (variable cost per patient-day = 79 cents; fixed cost per month = \$3,300) and the high-low method (variable cost per patient-day = 80 cents; fixed cost per month = \$3,400). These differences are to be expected given that each method used different amounts of data and in different ways. While any of these three cost formulas can be used to predict costs or establish benchmarks, the method that uses the most data (e.g., least-squares regression) is usually the most accurate. So, if Brentline Hospital wants to estimate next month's maintenance costs based on an estimated activity level of 7,800 patient-days, it would most likely rely on the cost formula derived using least-squares regression. Rounded to the nearest whole dollar, this formula estimates maintenance costs of \$9,351, calculated as follows:

$$Y = \$3,431 + \$0.759X$$

$$= \$3,431 + \$0.759 \times 7,800$$

$$= \$3,431 + \$5,920$$

$$= \$9,351$$

Suppose that it turns out that next month the actual level of activity is 7,810 patient-days and the actual maintenance cost is \$9,427. Is this cost too high or too low, given the actual level of activity for the period? According to the cost formula, the maintenance cost should be \$9,359 (to the nearest whole dollar), determined as follows:

$$Y = \$3,431 + \$0.759X$$

$$= \$3,431 + \$0.759 \times 7,810$$

$$= \$3,431 + \$5,928$$

$$= \$9,359$$

Since the actual maintenance cost was \$9,427, the cost formula suggests that too much was spent on maintenance cost. We will revisit this method of setting benchmarks to compare to actual spending in later chapters.

THE CONTRIBUTION FORMAT INCOME STATEMENT

Separating costs into fixed and variable elements helps to predict costs and provide benchmarks. As we will see in later chapters, separating costs into fixed and variable elements is also often crucial in making decisions. This crucial distinction between fixed and variable costs is at the heart of the **contribution approach** to the construction of income statements. The unique thing about the contribution approach is that it provides managers

LEARNING OBJECTIVE 4

Prepare an income statement using the contribution format.

with an income statement that clearly distinguishes between fixed and variable costs and therefore facilitates planning, control, and decision making.

Why a New Income Statement Format?

An income statement prepared using the *traditional approach,* as illustrated in Chapter 1, is organized in a "functional" format—emphasizing the functions of production, administration, and sales. No attempt is made to distinguish between fixed and variable costs. Under the heading "Administrative expense," for example, both variable and fixed costs are lumped together.

Although an income statement prepared in the functional format may be useful for external reporting purposes, it has serious limitations when used for internal purposes. Internally, managers need cost data organized in a format that will facilitate planning, control, and decision making. As we shall see in chapters ahead, these tasks are much easier when cost data are available in a fixed and variable format. The contribution format income statement has been developed in response to these needs.

The Contribution Approach

Topic Tackler

PLUS

Concept 5-2

Exhibit 5–13 uses a simple example to compare the contribution approach to the income statement with the traditional approach discussed in Chapter 1. Notice that the net operating income shown in both income statements in the exhibit is $1,000. In this portion of the chapter, we focus solely on situations where both income statements report the same net operating income. It is possible, and indeed quite common, for a traditional income statement, which is based on absorption costing, and a contribution format income statement, which is based on variable costing, to report different amounts of net operating income. We explore this phenomenon in Appendix 5A: Variable Costing and explain in detail the differences between absorption costing and variable costing.

Notice that the contribution approach separates costs into fixed and variable categories, first deducting variable expenses from sales to obtain what is known as the *contribution margin.* The **contribution margin** is the amount remaining from sales revenues after

EXHIBIT 5–13 Comparison of the Contribution Income Statement with the Traditional Income Statement

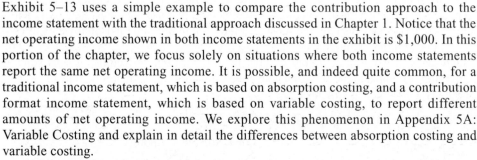

Traditional Approach (costs organized by function)			Contribution Approach (costs organized by behavior)			
Sales		$12,000	Sales			$12,000
Cost of goods sold		6,000*	Less variable expenses:			
Gross margin		6,000	Variable production	$2,000		
Selling and administrative expenses:			Variable selling	600		
Selling	$3,100*		Variable administrative	400	3,000	
Administrative	1,900*	5,000	Contribution margin			9,000
Net operating income		$ 1,000	Less fixed expenses:			
			Fixed production	4,000		
			Fixed selling	2,500		
			Fixed administrative	1,500	8,000	
			Net operating income			$ 1,000

*Contains both variable and fixed expenses. This is the income statement for a manufacturing company; thus, when the income statement is placed in the contribution format, the "cost of goods sold" is divided between variable production costs and fixed production costs. If this were the income statement for a *merchandising* company (which simply purchases completed goods from a supplier), then the cost of goods sold would be *all* variable.

variable expenses have been deducted. This amount *contributes* toward covering fixed expenses and then toward profits for the period.

The contribution format income statement is used as an internal planning, controlling, and decision-making tool. Its emphasis on cost behavior facilitates cost-volume-profit analysis (such as we shall be doing in the next chapter), management performance appraisals, and budgeting. Moreover, the contribution approach helps managers organize data pertinent to numerous decisions such as product-line analysis, pricing, use of scarce resources, and make or buy analysis. All of these topics are covered in later chapters.

4. A company's contribution approach income statement showed net operating income of $4,000, and fixed expenses of $10,000. How much contribution margin did the company earn?
   a. $29,000
   b. $15,000
   c. $19,000
   d. $14,000

CONCEPT CHECK ✓

SUMMARY

LO1 Understand how fixed and variable costs behave and how to use them to predict costs.
The total amount of a variable cost is proportional to the level of activity within the relevant range. The variable cost per unit of activity is constant as the level of activity changes.

The total amount of a fixed cost is constant as the level of activity changes within the relevant range. The fixed cost per unit of activity decreases as the level of activity increases because a constant amount is divided by a larger number.

To predict costs at a new level of activity, multiply the variable cost per unit by the new level of activity and then add to the result the total fixed cost.

LO2 Use a scattergraph plot to diagnose cost behavior.
A scattergraph plot helps provide insight into the behavior of a cost. In the scattergraph, activity is plotted on the horizontal, X, axis and total cost is plotted on the vertical, Y, axis. If the relation between cost and activity appears to be linear based on the scattergraph plot, then the variable and fixed components of a mixed cost can be estimated using the quick-and-dirty method, the high-low method, or the least-squares regression method.

LO3 Analyze a mixed cost using the high-low method.
To use the high-low method, first identify the periods with the highest and the lowest levels of activity. Second, estimate the variable cost element by dividing the change in total cost by the change in activity for these two periods. Third, estimate the fixed cost element by subtracting the total variable cost from the total cost at either the highest or the lowest level of activity.

The high-low method relies on only two, often unusual, data points rather than all of the available data and therefore may provide misleading estimates of variable and fixed costs.

LO4 Prepare an income statement using the contribution format.
Managers use costs organized by behavior in many decisions. To help managers make such decisions, the income statement can be prepared in a contribution format. The traditional income statement format emphasizes the purposes for which costs were incurred (i.e., to manufacture the product, to sell the product, or to administer the organization). In contrast, the contribution format income statement classifies costs by cost behavior (i.e., variable versus fixed).

Note that even though sales were exactly the same in January and February and the cost structure did not change, net operating income was $35,000 higher in February than in January under absorption costing.

Variable Costing Contribution Format Income Statement

As discussed earlier, the only reason that absorption costing income differs from variable costing income is that each method accounts for fixed manufacturing overhead differently. Under absorption costing, fixed manufacturing overhead is included in product costs. In variable costing, fixed manufacturing overhead is not included in product costs and instead is treated as a period expense, just like selling and administrative costs.

Under variable costing, product costs consist solely of variable production costs. At Weber Light Aircraft, the variable production cost per unit is $25,000, determined as follows:

Variable Production Cost	
Direct materials	$19,000
Direct labor	5,000
Variable manufacturing overhead	1,000
Variable production cost	$25,000

Since the variable production cost is $25,000 per aircraft, the variable costing cost of goods sold can be easily computed as follows:

Variable Costing Cost of Goods Sold	January	February	March
Variable production cost (a)	$25,000	$25,000	$25,000
Units sold (b)	1	1	3
Variable cost of goods sold (a) × (b)	$25,000	$25,000	$75,000

The selling and administrative expenses will exactly equal the amounts reported using absorption costing. The only difference will be how those costs appear on the income statement.

The variable costing income statements for January, February, and March appear below. The contribution approach discussed in the chapter has been used in these income statements.

Variable Costing Contribution Format Income Statements			
	January	February	March
Sales	$100,000	$100,000	$300,000
Less variable expenses:			
Variable cost of goods sold..............	25,000	25,000	75,000
Variable selling and administrative			
expense	10,000	10,000	30,000
Total variable expenses	35,000	35,000	105,000
Contribution margin	65,000	65,000	195,000
Less fixed expenses:			
Fixed manufacturing overhead...........	70,000	70,000	70,000
Fixed selling and administrative expense...	20,000	20,000	20,000
Total fixed expenses....................	90,000	90,000	90,000
Net operating income...................	$ (25,000)	$ (25,000)	$105,000

First, note that net operating income is the same in January under absorption costing and variable costing, but differs in the other two months. We will discuss this in some depth shortly.

Second, note that the format of the variable costing income statement differs from the absorption costing income statement. An absorption costing income statement categorizes costs by function—manufacturing versus selling and administrative. All of the manufacturing costs flow through the absorption costing cost of goods sold and all of the selling and administrative costs are listed separately as period expenses. In contrast, in the contribution approach above, costs are categorized according to how they behave. All of the variable expenses are listed together and all of the fixed expenses are listed together. The variable expenses category includes manufacturing costs (i.e., variable cost of goods sold) as well as selling and administrative expenses. The fixed expenses category also includes both manufacturing costs and selling and administrative expenses.

Reconciliation of Variable Costing with Absorption Costing Income

As noted earlier, variable costing and absorption costing net operating incomes may not be the same. In the case of Weber Light Aircraft, the net operating incomes were the same in January, but differed in the other two months. These differences occur because under absorption costing some fixed manufacturing overhead is capitalized in inventories (i.e., included in product costs) rather than currently expensed on the income statement. If inventories increase during a period, under absorption costing some of the fixed manufacturing overhead of the current period will be *deferred* in ending inventories. For example, in February two aircraft were produced and each carried with it $35,000 ($70,000 ÷ 2 aircraft produced) in fixed manufacturing overhead. Since only one aircraft was sold, $35,000 of this fixed manufacturing overhead was on the absorption costing income statement as part of cost of goods sold, but $35,000 would have been on the balance sheet as part of finished goods inventories. In contrast, under variable costing *all* of the $70,000 of fixed manufacturing overhead appeared on the income statement as a period expense. Consequently, net operating income was higher under absorption costing than under variable costing by $35,000 in February. This was reversed in March when two units were produced, but three were sold. In March, under absorption costing $105,000 of fixed manufacturing overhead was included in cost of goods sold ($35,000 for the unit produced in February and sold in March plus $35,000 for each of the two units produced and sold in March), but only $70,000 was recognized as a period expense under variable costing. Hence, the net operating income in March was $35,000 lower under absorption costing than under variable costing.

In general, when production exceeds sales and hence inventories increase, net operating income is higher under absorption costing than under variable costing. This occurs because some of the fixed manufacturing overhead of the period is *deferred* in inventories under absorption costing. In contrast, when sales exceed production and hence inventories decrease, net operating income is lower under absorption costing than under variable costing. This occurs because some of the fixed manufacturing overhead of previous periods is *released* from inventories under absorption costing. When production and sales are equal, no change in inventories occurs and absorption costing and variable costing net operating incomes are the same.[2]

Variable costing and absorption costing net operating incomes can be reconciled by determining how much fixed manufacturing overhead was deferred in, or released from, inventories during the period.

Fixed Manufacturing Overhead Deferred in, or Released from, Inventories under Absorption Costing			
	January	February	March
Fixed manufacturing overhead in beginning inventories	$0	$ 0	$ 35,000
Fixed manufacturing overhead in ending inventories	0	35,000	0
Fixed manufacturing overhead deferred in (released from) inventories	$0	$35,000	$(35,000)

The reconciliation would then be reported as follows:

Reconciliation of Variable Costing and Absorption Costing Net Operating Incomes			
	January	February	March
Variable costing net operating income	$(25,000)	$(25,000)	$105,000
Add (deduct) fixed manufacturing overhead deferred in (released from) ending inventory under absorption costing	0	35,000	(35,000)
Absorption costing net operating income	$(25,000)	$ 10,000	$ 70,000

Again note that the difference between variable costing net operating income and absorption costing net operating income is entirely due to the amount of fixed manufacturing overhead that is deferred in, or released from, inventories during the period under absorption costing. Changes in inventories affect absorption costing net operating income—they do not affect variable costing net operating income, providing that the cost structure is stable.

---

[2]These general statements about the relation between variable costing and absorption costing net operating income assume LIFO is used to value inventories. Even when LIFO is not used, the general statements tend to be correct.

SUMMARY OF APPENDIX 5A

LO5   (Appendix) Use variable costing to prepare a contribution format income statement and contrast absorption costing and variable costing.

Under variable costing, only the variable costs of making a product are assigned to the product. All other costs are treated as period costs and taken directly to the income statement as expenses.

Absorption costing treats fixed manufacturing overhead as a product cost. When units of product are sold these overhead costs flow from finished goods inventory through the income statement as part of cost of goods sold. In variable costing, fixed manufacturing overhead costs are treated as period costs and recorded immediately on the income statement.

GLOSSARY (APPENDIX 5A)

Variable costing   A costing approach under which only the variable costs of making a product are assigned to the product. All other costs are treated as period costs and taken directly to the income statement as expenses. (p. 217)

Multiple-choice questions are provided on the text website at www.mhhe.com/brewer4e.

Quiz 5

QUESTIONS

5–1   Distinguish between (a) a variable cost, (b) a fixed cost, and (c) a mixed cost.
5–2   What effect does an increase in volume have on—
    a. Unit fixed costs?
    b. Unit variable costs?
    c. Total fixed costs?
    d. Total variable costs?
5–3   Define the following terms: (a) cost behavior, and (b) relevant range.
5–4   What is meant by an *activity base* when dealing with variable costs? Give several examples of activity bases.
5–5   Distinguish between (a) a variable cost, (b) a mixed cost, and (c) a step-variable cost. Chart the three costs on a graph, with activity plotted horizontally and cost plotted vertically.
5–6   Managers often assume a strictly linear relationship between cost and volume. How can this practice be defended in light of the fact that many costs are curvilinear?
5–7   Distinguish between discretionary fixed costs and committed fixed costs.
5–8   Classify the following fixed costs as normally being either committed or discretionary:
    a. Depreciation on buildings.
    b. Advertising.
    c. Research.
    d. Long-term equipment leases.
    e. Pension payments to the company's retirees.
    f. Management development and training.
5–9   Does the concept of the relevant range apply to fixed costs? Explain.
5–10   What is the major disadvantage of the high-low method?
5–11   What methods are available for separating a mixed cost into its fixed and variable elements using past records of cost and activity data? Which method is considered to be most accurate? Why?
5–12   Give the general formula for a mixed cost. Which term represents the variable cost? The fixed cost?
5–13   Once a line has been drawn in the quick-and-dirty method, how does one determine the fixed cost element? The variable cost element?
5–14   What is meant by the term *least-squares regression*?
5–15   What is the difference between the contribution approach to the income statement and the traditional approach to the income statement?
5–16   What is the contribution margin?
5–17   (Appendix 5A) What is the basic difference between absorption costing and variable costing?
5–18   (Appendix 5A) Are selling and administrative expenses accounted for as product costs or as period costs under variable costing?
5–19   (Appendix 5A) Explain how fixed manufacturing overhead costs are shifted from one period to another under absorption costing.

5–20   (Appendix 5A) If production exceeds sales, which method would you expect to show the higher net operating income, variable costing or absorption costing? Why?

5–21   (Appendix 5A) If fixed manufacturing overhead costs are released from inventory under absorption costing, what does this tell you about the level of production in relation to the level of sales?

5–22   (Appendix 5A) Under absorption costing, how is it possible to increase net operating income without increasing sales?

BRIEF EXERCISES

BRIEF EXERCISE 5–1   Fixed and Variable Cost Behavior (LO1)

Koffee Express operates a number of espresso coffee stands in busy suburban malls. The fixed weekly expense of a coffee stand is $1,100 and the variable cost per cup of coffee served is $0.26.

Required:

1. Fill in the following table with your estimates of total costs and cost per cup of coffee at the indicated levels of activity for a coffee stand. Round off the cost of a cup of coffee to the nearest tenth of a cent.

	Cups of Coffee Served in a Week		
	1,800	**1,900**	**2,000**
Fixed cost.	?	?	?
Variable cost.	?	?	?
Total cost	?	?	?
Cost per cup of coffee served	?	?	?

2. Does the cost per cup of coffee served increase, decrease, or remain the same as the number of cups of coffee served in a week increases? Explain.

BRIEF EXERCISE 5–2   Scattergraph Analysis (LO2)

The data below have been taken from the cost records of the Atlanta Processing Company. The data relate to the cost of operating one of the company's processing facilities at various levels of activity:

Month	Units Processed	Total Cost
January	8,000	$14,000
February.	4,500	$10,000
March.	7,000	$12,500
April	9,000	$15,500
May	3,750	$10,000
June	6,000	$12,500
July.	3,000	$8,500
August	5,000	$11,500

Required:

1. Prepare a scattergraph using the above data. Plot cost on the vertical axis and activity on the horizontal axis. Fit a line to your plotted points using a ruler.

2. Using the quick-and-dirty method, what is the approximate monthly fixed cost? The approximate variable cost per unit processed? Show your computations.

BRIEF EXERCISE 5–3   High-Low Method (LO3)

The Edelweiss Hotel in Vail, Colorado, has accumulated records of the total electrical costs of the hotel and the number of occupancy-days over the last year. An occupancy-day represents a room rented out for one day. The hotel's business is highly seasonal, with peaks occurring during the ski season and in the summer.

Month	Occupancy-Days	Electrical Costs
January	2,604	$6,257
February.....................	2,856	$6,550
March.......................	3,534	$7,986
April	1,440	$4,022
May	540	$2,289
June........................	1,116	$3,591
July.........................	3,162	$7,264
August	3,608	$8,111
September	1,260	$3,707
October	186	$1,712
November....................	1,080	$3,321
December....................	2,046	$5,196

Required:
1. Using the high-low method, estimate the fixed cost of electricity per month and the variable cost of electricity per occupancy-day. Round off the fixed cost to the nearest whole dollar and the variable cost to the nearest whole cent.
2. What factors other than occupancy-days are likely to affect the variation in electrical costs from month to month?

BRIEF EXERCISE 5–4   Contribution Format Income Statement (LO4)

Haaki Shop, Inc., is a large retailer of water sports equipment. An income statement for the company's surfboard department for a recent quarter is presented below:

The Haaki Shop, Inc.
Income Statement—Surfboard Department
For the Quarter Ended May 31

Sales		$800,000
Cost of goods sold...............................		300,000
Gross margin		500,000
Selling and administrative expenses:		
Selling expenses	$250,000	
Administrative expenses.......................	160,000	410,000
Net operating income............................		$ 90,000

Surfboards sell, on the average, for $400 each. Variable selling expenses are $50 per surfboard sold. The remaining selling expenses are fixed. The administrative expenses are 25% variable and 75% fixed. The company does not manufacture its own surfboards; it purchases them from a supplier at a cost of $150 per surfboard.

Required:
1. Prepare an income statement for the quarter using the contribution approach.
2. For every surfboard sold this quarter, what was the contribution toward fixed expenses and toward earning profits.

BRIEF EXERCISE 5–5   (Appendix 5A) Variable and Absorption Costing Unit Product Costs and Income Statements (LO5)

Maxwell Company manufactures and sells a single product. The following costs were incurred during the company's first year of operations:

EXERCISE 5–10   High-Low Method; Predicting Cost (LO1, LO3)

The number of X-rays taken and X-ray costs over the last nine months at Beverly Hospital are given below:

Month	X-Rays Taken	X-Ray Costs
January	6,250	$28,000
February	7,000	$29,000
March	5,000	$23,000
April	4,250	$20,000
May	4,500	$22,000
June	3,000	$17,000
July	3,750	$18,000
August	5,500	$24,000
September	5,750	$26,000

Required:

1. Using the high-low method, estimate a cost formula for X-ray costs.
2. Using the cost formula you derived above, what X-ray costs would you expect to be incurred during a month in which 4,600 X-rays are taken?

EXERCISE 5–11   Scattergraph Analysis; High-Low Method (LO2, LO3)

Refer to the data in Exercise 5–10 for Beverly Hospital.

Required:

1. Prepare a scattergraph using the data from Exercise 5–10. Plot cost on the vertical axis and activity on the horizontal axis. Using a ruler, fit a line to your plotted points.
2. Using the quick-and-dirty method, what is the approximate monthly fixed cost? The approximate variable cost per X-ray taken?
3. Scrutinize the points on your graph and explain why the high-low method would or would not yield an accurate cost formula in this situation.

EXERCISE 5–12 (APPENDIX 5A)   Variable and Absorption Costing Unit Product Costs (LO5)

Shastri Bicycle of Bombay, India, produces an inexpensive, yet rugged, bicycle for use on the city's crowded streets that it sells for 500 rupees. (Indian currency is denominated in rupees, denoted by R.) Selected data for the company's operations last year follow (all currency values are in thousands of rupees):

Units in beginning inventory	0
Units produced	10,000
Units sold	8,000
Units in ending inventory	2,000
Variable costs per unit:	
Direct materials	R120
Direct labor	R140
Variable manufacturing overhead	R50
Variable selling and administrative	R20
Fixed costs:	
Fixed manufacturing overhead	R600,000
Fixed selling and administrative	R400,000

Required:

1. Assume that the company uses absorption costing. Compute the unit product cost for one bicycle.
2. Assume that the company uses variable costing. Compute the unit product cost for one bicycle.

EXERCISE 5–13   (Appendix 5A) Variable Costing Income Statement; Explanation of Difference in Net Operating Income (LO5)

Refer to the data in Exercise 5–12 for Shastri Bicycle. An absorption costing income statement prepared by the company's accountant appears below (all currency values are in thousands of rupees):

Sales (8,000 units × R500 per unit)...................	R4,000,000
Cost of goods sold (8,000 units × R? per unit)	2,960,000
Gross margin	1,040,000
Selling and administrative expenses:	
Variable selling and administrative R160,000	
Fixed selling and administrative 400,000	560,000
Net operating income................................	R 480,000

Required:
1. Determine how much of the ending inventory consists of fixed manufacturing overhead cost deferred in inventory to the next period.
2. Prepare an income statement for the year using the variable costing method. Explain the difference in net operating income between the two costing methods.

EXERCISE 5–14 Cost Behavior; Contribution Format Income Statement (LO1, LO4)

Parker Company manufactures and sells a single product. A partially completed schedule of the company's total and per unit costs over the relevant range of 60,000 to 100,000 units produced and sold each year is given below:

	Units Produced and Sold		
	60,000	80,000	100,000
Total costs:			
Variable costs	$150,000	?	?
Fixed costs	360,000	?	?
Total costs..........................	$510,000	?	?
Cost per unit:			
Variable cost	?	?	?
Fixed cost	?	?	?
Total cost per unit	?	?	?

Required:
1. Complete the schedule of the company's total and unit costs above.
2. Assume that the company produces and sells 90,000 units during the year at a selling price of $7.50 per unit. Prepare a contribution format income statement.

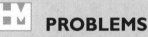

PROBLEMS

PROBLEM 5–15A Contribution Format versus Traditional Income Statement (LO4)

The Fun Store, Inc., purchases very large and heavy toys from a large manufacturer and sells them at the retail level. The toys cost, on the average, $9 each from the manufacturer. The Fun Store, Inc., sells the toys to its customers at an average price of $40 each. The selling and administrative costs that the company incurs in a typical month are presented below:

CHECK FIGURE
(1) Net operating income is $(400)

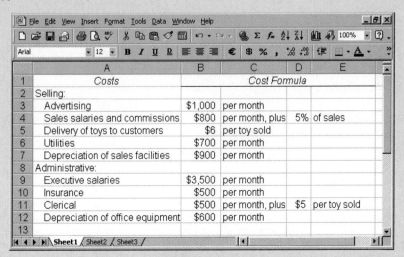

During October, The Fun Store, Inc., sold and delivered 450 toys.

Required:

1. Prepare an income statement for The Fun Store, Inc., for October. Use the traditional format, with costs organized by function.
2. Redo (1) above, using the contribution format, with costs organized by behavior. Show costs and revenues on both a total and a per unit basis down through contribution margin.
3. Refer to the income statement you prepared in (2) above. Why might it be misleading to show the fixed costs on a per unit basis?

CHECK FIGURE
(1) $303,450 per month plus $5.00 per bed-day

PROBLEM 5–16A   High-Low Method; Predicting Cost (LO1, LO3)

Black Forest Clinic contains 340 beds. The average occupancy rate is 85% per month. In other words, on average, 85% of the clinic's beds are occupied by patients. At this level of occupancy, the clinic's operating costs are $40 per occupied bed per day, assuming a 30-day month. This $40 cost contains both variable and fixed cost elements.

During November, the clinic's occupancy rate was only 70%. A total of $339,150 in operating cost was incurred during the month.

Required:

1. Using the high-low method, estimate:
   a. The variable cost per occupied bed on a daily basis.
   b. The total fixed operating costs per month.
2. Assume an occupancy rate of 80% per month. What amount of total operating cost would you expect the clinic to incur?

CHECK FIGURE
(1) $4,590 per month plus $29.00 per scan

PROBLEM 5–17A   High-Low and Scattergraph Analysis (LO2, LO3)

Sinai Cedars Hospital of San Francisco has just hired a new chief administrator who is anxious to employ sound management and planning techniques in the business affairs of the hospital. Accordingly, she has directed her assistant to summarize the cost structure of the various departments so that data will be available for planning purposes.

The assistant is unsure how to classify the utilities costs in the Radiology Department since these costs do not exhibit either strictly variable or fixed cost behavior. Utilities costs are very high in the department due to a CAT scanner that draws a large amount of power and is kept running at all times. The scanner can't be turned off due to the long warm-up period required for its use. When the scanner is used to scan a patient, it consumes an additional burst of power. The assistant has accumulated the following data on utilities costs and use of the scanner since the first of the year.

Month	Number of Scans	Utilities Cost
January	20	$5,000
February	50	$6,000
March	80	$7,000
April	60	$6,450
May	100	$7,490
June	70	$6,500
July	30	$5,500
August	10	$4,880
September	40	$5,550
October	90	$7,000

The chief administrator has informed her assistant that the utilities cost is probably a mixed cost that will have to be broken down into its variable and fixed cost elements by use of a scattergraph. The assistant feels, however, that if an analysis of this type is necessary, then the high-low method should be used, since it is easier and quicker. The controller has suggested that there may be a better approach.

Required:

1. Using the high-low method, estimate a cost formula for utilities. Express the formula in the form $Y = a + bX$. (The variable rate should be stated in terms of cost per scan.)
2. Prepare a scattergraph using the above data. (The number of scans should be placed on the horizontal axis, and utilities cost should be placed on the vertical axis.) Fit a straight line to the plotted points using a ruler and estimate a cost formula for utilities using the quick-and-dirty method.

PROBLEM 5–18A   (Appendix 5A) Variable Costing Income Statement; Reconciliation (LO5)

CHECK FIGURE
(1) Year 2 net operating
   income: $210,000

During Denton Company's first two years of operations, the company reported absorption costing net operating income as follows:

	Year 1	Year 2
Sales (@ $50 per unit)	$1,000,000	$1,500,000
Cost of goods sold	680,000	1,020,000
Gross margin	320,000	480,000
Selling and administrative expenses*	310,000	340,000
Net operating income	$ 10,000	$ 140,000

*$3 per unit variable; $250,000 fixed each year.

The company's $34 unit product cost is computed as follows:

Direct materials	$ 8
Direct labor	10
Variable manufacturing overhead	2
Fixed manufacturing overhead ($350,000 ÷ 25,000 units)	14
Unit product cost	$34

Production and cost data for the two years are given below:

	Year 1	Year 2
Units produced	25,000	25,000
Units sold	20,000	30,000

Required:
1. Prepare a variable costing income statement for each year.
2. Reconcile the absorption costing and the variable costing net operating income figures for each year.

PROBLEM 5–19A   Identifying Cost Behavior Patterns (LO1)

A number of graphs displaying cost behavior patterns are shown below. The vertical axis on each graph represents total cost, and the horizontal axis represents the level of activity (volume).

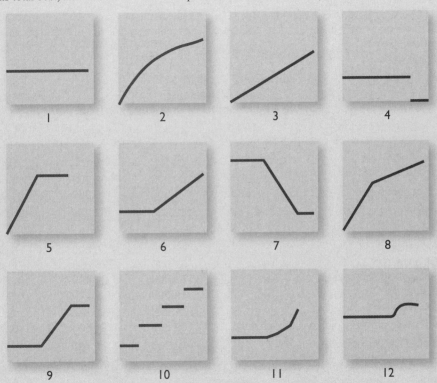

Required:

1. For each of the following situations, identify the graph that illustrates the cost behavior pattern involved. Any graph may be used more than once.

    a. Salaries of maintenance workers, where one maintenance worker is needed for every 1,200 hours of machine-hours or less (that is, 0 to 1,200 hours requires one maintenance worker, 1,201 to 2,400 hours requires two maintenance workers, etc.).

    b. Rent on a factory building donated by the city, where the agreement calls for a fixed fee payment unless 120,000 labor-hours or more are worked, in which case no rent need be paid.

    c. Electricity bill—a flat fixed charge, plus a variable cost after a certain number of kilowatt-hours are used.

    d. Depreciation of equipment, where the amount is computed by the straight-line method. When the depreciation rate was established, it was anticipated that the obsolescence factor would be greater than the wear and tear factor.

    e. Use of a machine under a lease, where a minimum charge of $5,000 is paid for up to 1,000 hours of machine time. After 1,000 hours of machine time, an additional charge of $3 per hour is paid up to a maximum charge of $7,000 per period.

    f. Cost of raw materials, where the cost starts at $9 per unit and then decreases by 5 cents per unit for each of the first 100 units purchased, after which it remains constant at $6 per unit.

    g. City water bill, which is computed as follows:

First 500,000 gallons or less	$750 flat fee
Next 8,000 gallons	$0.005 per gallon used
Next 8,000 gallons	$0.010 per gallon used
Next 8,000 gallons	$0.015 per gallon used
Etc.	Etc.

    h. Cost of raw materials used.

    i. Rent on a factory building donated by the county, where the agreement calls for rent of $230,000 less $1 for each direct labor-hour worked in excess of 90,000 hours, but a minimum rental payment of $45,000 must be paid.

2. How would knowledge of cost behavior patterns such as those above be of help to a manager in analyzing the cost structure of his or her company?

(CPA, adapted)

CHECK FIGURE
(2) Shipping: P9,000 per month plus P9.00 per unit

PROBLEM 5–20A Cost Behavior; High-Low Method; Contribution Format Income Statement (LO1, LO3, LO4)

Compania Maritima S.A., of Santiago de Chile, is a merchandising company that supplies a variety of American products to the Chilean market. The company's income statements for the three most recent months follow:

Compania Maritima S.A. Income Statements For the Three Months Ending June 30			
	April	May	June
Sales in units	6,500	7,400	7,000
Sales revenue	P260,000	P296,000	P280,000
Cost of goods sold	78,000	88,800	84,000
Gross margin	182,000	207,200	196,000
Selling and administrative expenses:			
Advertising	5,000	5,000	5,000
Shipping	67,500	75,600	72,000
Salaries and commissions	30,800	34,400	32,800
Insurance	4,000	4,000	4,000
Depreciation	2,500	2,500	2,500
Total selling and administrative expenses	109,800	121,500	116,300
Net operating income	P 72,200	P 85,700	P 79,700

(Note: Compania Maritima S.A.'s Chilean-formatted income statement has been recast in the format common in the United States. The Chilean dollar is denoted by P.)

Required:
1. Identify each of the company's expenses (including cost of goods sold) as either variable, fixed, or mixed.
2. Using the high-low method, separate each mixed expense into variable and fixed elements. State the cost formula for each mixed expense.
3. Redo the company's income statement at the 7,000-unit level of activity using the contribution format.

PROBLEM 5–21A (APPENDIX 5A) Variable and Absorption Costing Unit Product Costs and Income Statements; Explanation of Difference in Net Operating Income (LO5)

Wiengot Antennas, Inc., produces and sells a unique type of TV antenna. The company has just opened a new plant to manufacture the antenna. The following cost and revenue data have been provided for the first month of the plant's operation:

Beginning inventory	0
Units produced	40,000
Units sold	35,000
Selling price per unit	$60
Selling and administrative expenses:	
Variable per unit	$2
Fixed (total)	$560,000
Manufacturing costs:	
Direct materials cost per unit	$15
Direct labor cost per unit	$7
Variable manufacturing overhead cost per unit	$2
Fixed manufacturing overhead cost (total)	$640,000

Management is anxious to see how profitable the new antenna will be and has asked that an income statement be prepared for the month.

Required:
1. Assume that the company uses absorption costing.
   a. Determine the unit product cost.
   b. Prepare an income statement for the month.
2. Assume that the company uses the contribution approach with variable costing.
   a. Determine the unit product cost.
   b. Prepare an income statement for the month.
3. Explain the reason for any difference in the ending inventory balance under the two costing methods and the impact of this difference on reported net operating income.

PROBLEM 5–22A High-Low Method; Cost of Goods Manufactured (LO1, LO3)

Carlyle Company manufactures a single product. The company keeps careful records of manufacturing activities from which the following information has been extracted:

eXcel

	Level of Activity	
	January—Low	April—High
Number of units produced	12,000	15,000
Cost of goods manufactured	$250,000	$300,000
Work in process inventory, beginning	$5,000	$16,000
Work in process inventory, ending	$6,000	$9,000
Direct materials cost per unit	$4.00	$4.00
Direct labor cost per unit	$8.00	$8.00
Manufacturing overhead cost, total	?	?

The company's manufacturing overhead cost consists of both variable and fixed cost elements. To have data available for planning, management wants to determine how much of the overhead cost is variable with units produced and how much of it is fixed per month.

Required:
1. For both January and April, estimate the amount of manufacturing overhead cost added to production. The company had no underapplied or overapplied overhead in either month. (*Hint:* A useful way to proceed might be to construct a schedule of cost of goods manufactured.)
2. Using the high-low method, estimate a cost formula for manufacturing overhead. Express the variable portion of the formula in terms of a variable rate per unit of product.
3. If 13,500 units are produced during a month, what would the cost of goods manufactured be? (Assume that work in process inventories do not change and that overhead cost is neither underapplied nor overapplied for the month.)

CHECK FIGURE
(2) $47,500 per month plus
$1.50 per machine-hour

PROBLEM 5–23A   High-Low Analysis and Predicting Cost (LO1, LO3)

Prospero Corporation's total overhead costs at various levels of activity are presented below:

Month	Machine-Hours	Total Overhead Costs
August	10,000	$99,500
September	15,000	$119,000
October	20,000	$138,500
November.	5,000	$80,000

Assume that the total overhead costs above consist of utilities, supervisory salaries, and maintenance. The breakdown of these costs at the 5,000 machine-hour level of activity is:

Utilities (variable)	$12,000
Supervisory salaries (fixed)	13,000
Maintenance (mixed)	55,000
Total overhead costs	$80,000

Prospero Corporation's management wants to break down the maintenance cost into its variable and fixed cost elements.

Required:
1. Estimate how much of the $138,500 of overhead cost in October was maintenance cost. (*Hint:* To do this, it may be helpful to first determine how much of the $138,500 consisted of utilities and supervisory salaries. Think about the behavior of variable and fixed costs!)
2. Using the high-low method, estimate a cost formula for maintenance.
3. Express the company's *total* overhead costs in the linear equation form $Y = a + bX$.
4. What *total* overhead costs would you expect to be incurred at an operating activity level of 17,000 machine-hours?

CHECK FIGURE
(2) ¥750,000 per year plus
¥375 per DLH

PROBLEM 5–24A   High-Low Method; Predicting Cost (LO1, LO3)

Susumi Corporation of Japan is a manufacturing company whose total factory overhead costs fluctuate considerably from year to year according to increases and decreases in the number of direct labor-hours worked in the factory. Total factory overhead costs (in Japanese yen, denoted by ¥) at high and low levels of activity for recent years are given below:

	Level of Activity	
	Low	High
Direct labor-hours.	4,000	5,000
Total factory overhead costs.	¥15,250,000	¥17,625,000

The factory overhead costs above consist of indirect materials, rent, and maintenance. The company has analyzed these costs at the 4,000-hour level of activity as follows:

Indirect materials (variable)	¥ 8,000,000
Rent (fixed)	5,000,000
Maintenance (mixed)	2,250,000
Total factory overhead costs	¥15,250,000

To have data available for planning, the company wants to break down the maintenance cost into its variable and fixed cost elements.

Required:
1. Estimate how much of the ¥17,625,000 factory overhead cost at the high level of activity consists of maintenance cost. (*Hint:* To do this, it may be helpful to first determine how much of the ¥17,625,000 consists of indirect materials and rent. Think about the behavior of variable and fixed costs!)
2. Using the high-low method, estimate a cost formula for maintenance.
3. What total factory overhead costs would you expect the company to incur at an operating level of 4,800 direct labor-hours?

BUILDING YOUR SKILLS

TEAMWORK IN ACTION   (LO1)

Assume that your team is going to form a company that will manufacture chocolate chip cookies. The team is responsible for preparing a list of all product components and costs necessary to make this product.

Required:
Prepare a list of all product components and costs necessary to manufacture your cookies and identify each of the product costs as direct materials, direct labor, or factory overhead. Identify each of those costs as variable, fixed, or mixed.

COMMUNICATING IN PRACTICE   (LO1, LO4)

Jasmine Lee owns a catering company that serves food and beverages at parties and business functions. Lee's business is seasonal, with a heavy schedule during the summer months and holidays and a lighter schedule at other times.

One of the major events requested by Lee's customers is a cocktail party. She offers a standard cocktail party and has estimated the total cost per guest as follows:

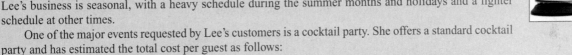

Food and beverages	$17.00
Labor (0.5 hours @ $10.00 per hour)	5.00
Overhead (0.5 hours @ $18.63 per hour)	9.32
Total cost per guest	$31.32

The standard cocktail party lasts three hours and Lee hires one worker for every six guests, which works out to one-half hour of direct labor per guest. These workers are hired only as needed and are paid only for the hours they actually work.

Lee ordinarily charges $45 per guest. She is confident about her estimates of the costs of foods and beverages and labor, but is not as comfortable with the estimate of overhead cost. The $18.63 overhead cost per labor-hour was determined by dividing the total overhead expenses for the last 12 months by the total labor-hours for the same period. Her overhead includes costs such as the annual rent for office space, administrative salaries, the costs of hiring and writing paychecks for temporary workers, and so on.

Lee has received a request to bid on a large fund-raising cocktail party to be given next month by an important local charity. (The party would last the usual three hours.) She would like to win this contract because the guest list for this charity event includes many prominent individuals that she would like to land as future clients. Other caterers have also been invited to bid on the event, and she believes that one, if not more, of those companies will bid less than $45 per guest. She is not willing to lose money on the event and needs your input before making any decisions.

Required:

Write a memo to Ms. Lee that addresses her concern about her estimate of overhead costs and whether or not she should base her bid on the estimated cost of $31.32 per guest. (*Hint:* Start by discussing the need to consider cost behavior when estimating costs. You can assume that she will not incur any additional fixed costs if she wins the bid on the cocktail party.)   (CMA, adapted)

ANALYTICAL THINKING (LO2)

Mapleleaf Sweepers of Toronto manufactures replacement rotary sweeper brooms for the large sweeper trucks that clear leaves and snow from city streets. The business is seasonal, with the largest demand during and just preceding the fall and winter months. Since there are so many different kinds of sweeper brooms used by its customers, Mapleleaf Sweepers makes all of its brooms to order.

The company has been analyzing its overhead accounts to determine fixed and variable components for planning purposes. Below are data for the company's janitorial labor costs over the last nine months. (Cost data are in Canadian dollars.)

	Number of Units Produced	Number of Janitorial Workdays	Janitorial Labor Cost
January	115	21	$3,840
February.	109	19	$3,648
March	102	23	$4,128
April	76	20	$3,456
May	69	23	$4,320
June	108	22	$4,032
July.	77	16	$2,784
August	71	14	$2,688
September	127	21	$3,840

The number of workdays varies from month to month due to the number of weekdays, holidays, days of vacation, and sick leave taken in the month. The number of units produced in a month varies depending on demand and the number of workdays in the month.

There are two janitors who each work an eight-hour shift each workday. They each can take up to 10 days of paid sick leave each year. Their wages on days they call in sick and their wages during paid vacations are charged to miscellaneous overhead rather than to the janitorial labor cost account.

Required:

1. Prepare a scattergraph and plot the janitorial labor cost and units produced. (Place cost on the vertical axis and units produced on the horizontal axis.)
2. Prepare a scattergraph and plot the janitorial labor cost and number of workdays. (Place cost on the vertical axis and the number of workdays on the horizontal axis.)
3. Which measure of activity—number of units produced or janitorial workdays—should be used as the activity base for explaining janitorial labor cost?

RESEARCH AND APPLICATION [LO1, LO2, LO3, LO4, LO5]

The questions in this exercise are based on Blue Nile, Inc. To answer the questions, you will need to download Blue Nile's Form 10-K for the fiscal year ended January 5, 2005 at www.sec.gov/edgar/searchedgar/companysearch.html. Once at this website, input CIK code 1091171 and hit enter. In the gray box on the right-hand side of your computer screen define the scope of your search by inputting 10-K and then pressing enter. Select the 10-K/A with a filing date of March 25, 2005. You do not need to print this document to answer the questions. You will need the information below to answer the questions.

	2004				2005	
	Quarter 1	Quarter 2	Quarter 3	Quarter 4	Quarter 1	Quarter 2
Net sales	?	?	?	?	$44,116	$43,826
Cost of sales	?	?	?	?	$34,429	$33,836
Gross profit.	?	?	?	?	$9,687	$9,990
Selling, general, and administrative expense	$5,308	$5,111	$5,033	$7,343	$6,123	$6,184
Operating income. . .	?	?	?	?	$3,564	$3,806

REQUIRED:

1. What is Blue Nile's strategy for success in the marketplace? Does the company rely primarily on a customer intimacy, operational excellence, or product leadership customer value proposition? What evidence from the 10-K supports your conclusion?
2. What business risks does Blue Nile face that may threaten its ability to satisfy stockholder expectations? What are some examples of control activities that the company could use to reduce these risks? (*Hint:* Focus on pages 8–19 of the 10-K.) Are some of the risks faced by Blue Nile difficult to reduce through control activities? Explain.
3. Is Blue Nile a merchandiser or a manufacturer? What information contained in the 10-K supports your answer?
4. Using account analysis, would you label cost of sales and selling, general, and administrative expense as variable, fixed, or mixed costs? Why? (*Hint:* focus on pages 24–26 and 38 of the 10-K.) Cite one example of a variable cost, step-variable cost, discretionary fixed cost, and committed fixed cost for Blue Nile.
5. Fill in the blanks in the table above based on information contained in the 10-K. Using the high-low method, estimate the variable and fixed cost elements of the quarterly selling, general, and administrative expense. Express Blue Nile's variable and fixed selling, general, and administrative expenses in the form $Y = a + bX$.
6. Prepare a contribution format income statement for the third quarter of 2005 assuming that Blue Nile's net sales were $45,500 and its cost of sales as a percentage of net sales remained unchanged from the prior quarter.
7. How would you describe Blue Nile's cost structure? Is Blue Nile's cost of sales as a percentage of sales higher or lower than competitors with bricks-and-mortar jewelry stores?

6

Cost-Volume-Profit Relationships

<< A LOOK BACK

In Chapter 5 we described variable, fixed, and mixed costs and covered the methods that can be used to break a mixed cost into its variable and fixed components. We also introduced the contribution format income statement.

A LOOK AT THIS CHAPTER

Chapter 6 describes the basics of cost-volume-profit analysis, an essential tool for decision making. Cost-volume-profit analysis helps managers understand the interrelationships among cost, volume, and profit.

A LOOK AHEAD >>

Chapter 7 describes the budgeting process.

CHAPTER OUTLINE

LEARNING OBJECTIVES

LP 6

After studying Chapter 6, you should be able to:

LO1 Explain how changes in activity affect contribution margin and net operating income.

LO2 Prepare and interpret a cost-volume-profit (CVP) graph.

LO3 Use the contribution margin ratio (CM ratio) to compute changes in contribution margin and net operating income resulting from changes in sales volume.

LO4 Show the effects on contribution margin of changes in variable costs, fixed costs, selling price, and volume.

LO5 Compute the break-even point in unit sales and dollar sales.

LO6 Determine the level of sales needed to achieve a desired target profit.

LO7 Compute the margin of safety and explain its significance.

LO8 Compute the degree of operating leverage at a particular level of sales and explain how it can be used to predict changes in net operating income.

LO9 Compute the break-even point for a multiproduct company and explain the effects of shifts in the sales mix on contribution margin and the break-even point.

DECISION FEATURE

Forget the Theater—Make Money on Cable TV

"Several years ago, Hollywood experienced a phenomenon known as the 'straight-to-cable' era. What this phrase referred to was a well used (and abused!) movie-making principle that hinted that if anyone (and many times it really was just *anyone*) could produce a movie (quality was never an issue) for under a million dollars, it'd automatically turn a profit from the sale of its cable TV rights. In essence, the 'movie' would bypass the theaters all together [*sic*] and still turn a profit. From a business stand-point, what this money-making scheme illustrates is [that] every product has a break-even point. Make more money than this and you turn a profit. Make less than this, and, well, you get the picture (pardon the pun)."

Source: Ben Chiu, "The Last Big-Budget Combat Sim," *Computer Games,* June 1999, p. 40.

ost-volume-profit (CVP) analysis is a powerful tool that helps managers understand the relationships among cost, volume, and profit. CVP analysis focuses on how profits are affected by the following five factors:

1. Selling prices.
2. Sales volume.
3. Unit variable costs.
4. Total fixed costs.
5. Mix of products sold.

Because CVP analysis helps managers understand how profits are affected by these key factors, it is a vital tool in many business decisions. These decisions include what products and services to offer, what prices to charge, what marketing strategy to use, and what cost structure to implement.

To help understand the role of CVP analysis in business decisions, consider the case of Acoustic Concepts, Inc., a company founded by Prem Narayan, a graduate student in electrical engineering, to market a radically new speaker he has designed for automobile sound systems. The speaker, called the Sonic Blaster, uses an advanced microprocessor to boost amplification to awesome levels. Prem contracted with a Taiwanese electronics manufacturer to produce the speaker. With seed money provided by his family, Prem placed an order with the manufacturer and ran advertisements in auto magazines.

The Sonic Blaster was an immediate success, and sales grew to the point that Prem moved the company's headquarters out of his apartment and into rented office space in a nearby industrial park. He also hired a receptionist, an accountant, a sales manager, and a small sales staff to sell the speakers to retail stores. Prem is concerned about the financial risks of rapidly expanding his company. He also wonders how much sales would have to increase to justify a new marketing campaign proposed by his sales manager. The answers to these and other questions can be found using CVP analysis.

THE BASICS OF COST-VOLUME-PROFIT (CVP) ANALYSIS

Video 6–1

To help Prem Narayan answer the questions he has raised, we begin by looking at the contribution format income statement for Acoustic Concepts, Inc., that is shown below. The contribution format income statement classifies costs according to their behavior. Although this type of income statement would not ordinarily be made available to people outside the company, its focus on cost behavior helps managers inside the company by enabling them to judge the impact on profits of changes in selling price, cost, or volume.

Acoustic Concepts, Inc. Contribution Income Statement For the Month of June		
	Total	**Per Unit**
Sales (400 speakers)	$100,000	$250
Variable expenses	60,000	150
Contribution margin	40,000	$100
Fixed expenses	35,000	
Net operating income	$ 5,000	

Notice that sales, variable expenses, and contribution margin are expressed on a per-unit basis as well as in total on this income statement. The per unit figures will be very helpful in the following pages as we answer some of Prem's questions.

Contribution Margin

As explained in the previous chapter, contribution margin is the amount remaining from sales revenue after variable expenses have been deducted. Thus, it is the amount available to cover fixed expenses and then to provide profits for the period. Notice the sequence here—contribution margin is used *first* to cover the fixed expenses, and then whatever remains goes toward profits. If the contribution margin is not sufficient to cover the fixed expenses, then a loss occurs for the period. To illustrate with an extreme example, assume that Acoustic Concepts sells only one speaker during a particular month. The company's income statement would appear as follows:

> **LEARNING OBJECTIVE 1**
>
> Explain how changes in activity affect contribution margin and net operating income.

Contribution Income Statement Sales of 1 Speaker	Total	Per Unit
Sales (1 speaker)	$ 250	$250
Variable expenses.	150	150
Contribution margin.	100	$100
Fixed expenses.	35,000	
Net operating loss.	$(34,900)	

For each additional speaker the company sells during the month, $100 more in contribution margin becomes available to help cover the fixed expenses. If a second speaker is sold, for example, then the total contribution margin will increase by $100 (to a total of $200) and the company's loss will decrease by $100, to $34,800:

Contribution Income Statement Sales of 2 Speakers	Total	Per Unit
Sales (2 speakers)	$ 500	$250
Variable expenses.	300	150
Contribution margin.	200	$100
Fixed expenses.	35,000	
Net operating loss.	$(34,800)	

If enough speakers can be sold to generate $35,000 in contribution margin, then all of the fixed expenses will be covered and the company will have managed to at least *break even* for the month—that is, it will show neither profit nor loss but just cover all of its costs. To reach the break-even point, the company will have to sell 350 speakers in a month, since each speaker sold yields $100 in contribution margin:

Contribution Income Statement Sales of 350 Speakers	Total	Per Unit
Sales (350 speakers)	$87,500	$250
Variable expenses	52,500	150
Contribution margin	35,000	$100
Fixed expenses	35,000	
Net operating income.	$ 0	

Computation of the break-even point is discussed in detail later in the chapter; for the moment, note that the **break-even point** is the level of sales at which profit is zero.

Once the break-even point has been reached, net operating income will increase by the amount of the unit contribution margin for each additional unit sold. For example, if 351 speakers are sold in a month, then the net operating income for the month will be $100, since the company will have sold 1 speaker more than the number needed to break even:

	Total	Per Unit
Contribution Income Statement		
Sales of 351 Speakers		
Sales (351 speakers)	$87,750	$250
Variable expenses	52,650	150
Contribution margin	35,100	$100
Fixed expenses	35,000	
Net operating income.	$ 100	

If 352 speakers are sold (2 speakers above the break-even point), the net operating income for the month will be $200. If 353 speakers are sold (3 speakers above the break-even point), the net operating income for the month will be $300, and so forth. To estimate the profit at any sales volume above the break-even point, simply multiply the number of units sold in excess of the break-even point by the unit contribution margin. The result represents the anticipated profits for the period. Or, to estimate the effect of a planned increase in sales on profits, simply multiply the increase in units sold by the unit contribution margin. The result will be the expected increase in profits. To illustrate, if Acoustic Concepts is currently selling 400 speakers per month and plans to increase sales to 425 speakers per month, the anticipated impact on profits can be computed as follows:

Increased number of speakers to be sold	25
Contribution margin per speaker	× $100
Increase in net operating income.	$2,500

These calculations can be verified as follows:

	Sales Volume			
	400 Speakers	425 Speakers	Difference (25 Speakers)	Per Unit
Sales (@ $250 per speaker).	$100,000	$106,250	$6,250	$250
Variable expenses (@ $150 per speaker)	60,000	63,750	3,750	150
Contribution margin	40,000	42,500	2,500	$100
Fixed expenses	35,000	35,000	0	
Net operating income.	$ 5,000	$ 7,500	$2,500	

To summarize, if sales are zero, the company's loss would equal its fixed expenses. Each unit that is sold reduces the loss by the amount of the unit contribution margin. Once the break-even point has been reached, each additional unit sold increases the company's profit by the amount of the unit contribution margin.

CVP Relationships in Graphic Form

The relations among revenue, cost, profit, and volume can be illustrated by a **cost-volume-profit (CVP) graph.** A CVP graph highlights CVP relationships over wide ranges of activity.

Preparing the CVP Graph   In a CVP graph (sometimes called a *break-even chart*), unit volume is represented on the horizontal (X) axis and dollars on the vertical (Y) axis. Preparing a CVP graph involves three steps as depicted in Exhibit 6–1:

1. Draw a line parallel to the volume axis to represent total fixed expense. For Acoustic Concepts, total fixed expense is $35,000.
2. Choose some volume of sales and plot the point representing total expense (fixed and variable) at the activity level you have selected. In Exhibit 6–1, a volume of 600 speakers has been selected. Total expense at that activity level is:

Fixed expense.	$ 35,000
Variable expense (600 speakers × $150 per speaker).	90,000
Total expense	$125,000

After the point has been plotted, draw a line through it back to the point where the fixed expense line intersects the dollars axis.

3. Again choose some volume of unit sales and plot the point representing total sales dollars at the activity level you have selected. In Exhibit 6–1, a volume of 600 speakers has again been selected. Sales at that activity level total $150,000 (600 speakers × $250 per speaker). Draw a line through this point back to the origin.

The interpretation of the completed CVP graph is given in Exhibit 6–2. The anticipated profit or loss at any given level of sales is measured by the vertical distance between the total revenue line (sales) and the total expense line (variable expense plus fixed expense).

The break-even point is where the total revenue and total expense lines cross. The break-even point of 350 speakers in Exhibit 6–2 agrees with the break-even point computed earlier.

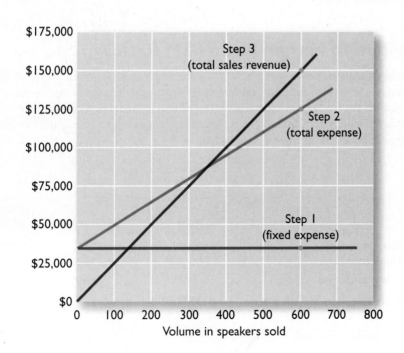

EXHIBIT 6–1
Preparing the CVP Graph

EXHIBIT 6–2
The Completed CVP Graph

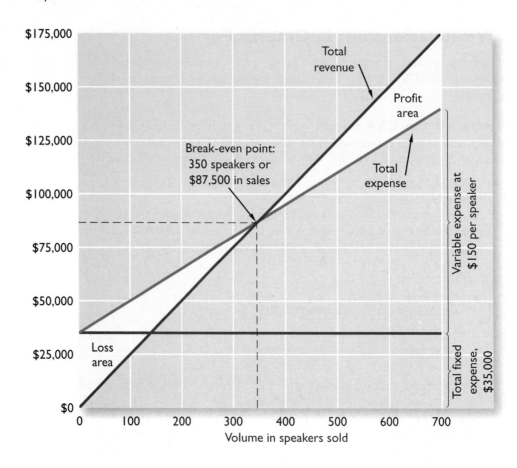

As discussed earlier, when sales are below the break-even point—in this case, 350 units—the company suffers a loss. Note that the loss (represented by the vertical distance between the total expense and total revenue lines) gets bigger as sales decline. When sales are above the break-even point, the company earns a profit and the size of the profit (represented by the vertical distance between the total revenue and total expense lines) increases as sales increase.

LEARNING OBJECTIVE 3

Use the contribution margin ratio (CM ratio) to compute changes in contribution margin and net operating income resulting from changes in sales volume.

Contribution Margin Ratio (CM Ratio)

In the previous section, we explored how cost-volume-profit relations can be visualized. In this section, we show how the *contribution margin ratio* can be used in cost-volume-profit calculations. As the first step, we have added a column to Acoustic Concepts' contribution format income statement in which sales revenues, variable expenses, and contribution margin are expressed as a percentage of sales:

	Total	Per Unit	Percent of Sales
Sales (400 speakers)...............	$100,000	$250	100%
Variable expenses	60,000	150	60
Contribution margin	40,000	$100	40
Fixed expenses	35,000		
Net operating income..............	$ 5,000		

The contribution margin as a percentage of sales is referred to as the **contribution margin ratio (CM ratio).** This ratio is computed as follows:

$$\text{CM ratio} = \frac{\text{Contribution margin}}{\text{Sales}}$$

For Acoustic Concepts, the computations are:

$$\text{CM ratio} = \frac{\text{Total contribution margin}}{\text{Total sales}} = \frac{\$40,000}{\$100,000} = 40\%$$

In a company such as Acoustic Concepts that has only one product, the CM ratio can also be computed on a per unit basis as follows:

$$\text{CM ratio} = \frac{\text{Unit contribution margin}}{\text{Unit selling price}} = \frac{\$100}{\$250} = 40\%$$

The CM ratio shows how the contribution margin will be affected by a change in total sales. Acoustic Concepts' CM ratio of 40% means that for each dollar increase in sales, total contribution margin will increase by 40 cents ($1 sales × CM ratio of 40%). Net operating income will also increase by 40 cents, assuming that fixed costs are not affected by the increase in sales.

As this illustration suggests, *the impact on net operating income of any given dollar change in total sales can be computed by simply applying the CM ratio to the dollar change.* For example, if Acoustic Concepts plans a $30,000 increase in sales during the coming month, the contribution margin should increase by $12,000 ($30,000 increase in sales × CM ratio of 40%). As we noted above, net operating income will also increase by $12,000 if fixed costs do not change. This is verified by the following table:

	Sales Volume			Percent of Sales
	Present	**Expected**	**Increase**	
Sales	$100,000	$130,000	$30,000	100%
Variable expenses	60,000	78,000*	18,000	60
Contribution margin	40,000	52,000	12,000	40%
Fixed expenses	35,000	35,000	0	
Net operating income.	$ 5,000	$ 17,000	$12,000	

*$130,000 expected sales ÷ $250 per unit = 520 units.
520 units × $150 per unit = $78,000.

The CM ratio is particularly valuable in situations where trade-offs must be made between more dollar sales of one product versus more dollar sales of another. In this situation, products that yield the greatest amount of contribution margin per dollar of sales should be emphasized.

Some Applications of CVP Concepts

The concepts developed on the preceding pages can be used in a variety of decision-making situations such as the five considered below.

Change in Fixed Cost and Sales Volume   Acoustic Concepts is currently selling 400 speakers per month at $250 per speaker for total monthly sales of $100,000. The sales manager feels that a $10,000 increase in the monthly advertising budget would increase monthly sales by $30,000 to a total of 520 units. Should the advertising budget

LEARNING OBJECTIVE 4

Show the effects on contribution margin of changes in variable costs, fixed costs, selling price, and volume.

Topic Tackler

PLUS

Concept 6-1

be increased? The following table shows the financial impact of the proposed change in the monthly advertising budget:

	Current Sales	Sales with Additional Advertising Budget	Difference	Percent of Sales
Sales	$100,000	$130,000	$30,000	100%
Variable expenses	60,000	78,000*	18,000	60
Contribution margin	40,000	52,000	12,000	40%
Fixed expenses	35,000	45,000†	10,000	
Net operating income	$ 5,000	$ 7,000	$ 2,000	

*520 units × $150 per unit = $78,000.
†$35,000 + additional $10,000 monthly advertising budget = $45,000.

Assuming no other factors need to be considered, the increase in the advertising budget should be approved because it would increase net operating income by $2,000. There are two shorter ways to arrive at this solution. The first alternative solution follows:

Alternative Solution I

Expected total contribution margin:	
$130,000 × 40% CM ratio	$52,000
Present total contribution margin:	
$100,000 × 40% CM ratio	40,000
Incremental contribution margin.	12,000
Change in fixed expenses:	
Less incremental advertising expense	10,000
Increased net operating income.	$ 2,000

Because in this case only the fixed costs and the sales volume change, the solution can be presented in an even shorter format, as follows:

Alternative Solution 2

Incremental contribution margin:	
$30,000 × 40% CM ratio	$12,000
Less incremental advertising expense.	10,000
Increased net operating income.	$ 2,000

Notice that this approach does not depend on knowledge of previous sales. Also note that it is unnecessary under either shorter approach to prepare an income statement. Both of the alternative solutions involve an **incremental analysis**—they consider only those items of revenue, cost, and volume that will change if the new program is implemented. Although in each case a new income statement could have been prepared, the incremental approach is simpler and more direct and focuses attention on the specific changes that would occur as a result of the decision.

Change in Variable Cost and Sales Volume

Refer to the original data. Recall that Acoustic Concepts is currently selling 400 speakers per month. Prem is considering the use of higher-quality components, which would increase his variable costs (and thereby reduce the contribution margin) by $10 per speaker. However, his sales manager predicts that using higher-quality components would increase sales to 480 speakers per month. Should the higher-quality components be used?

The $10 increase in variable costs would decrease the unit contribution margin by $10—from $100 down to $90.

Solution

Expected total contribution margin with higher-quality components:	
480 speakers × $90 per speaker.....................	$43,200
Present total contribution margin:	
400 speakers × $100 per speaker	40,000
Increase in total contribution margin	$ 3,200

According to this analysis, the higher-quality components should be used. Since fixed costs would not change, the $3,200 increase in contribution margin shown above should result in a $3,200 increase in net operating income.

Growing Sales at Amazon.com

IN BUSINESS

Amazon.com was deciding between two tactics for growing sales and profits. The first approach was to invest in television advertising. The second approach was to introduce free shipping on orders over a designated amount of sales. To evaluate the first option, Amazon.com invested in television ads in two markets—Minneapolis, Minnesota, and Portland, Oregon. The company quantified the profit impact of this choice by subtracting the increase in fixed advertising costs from the increase in contribution margin resulting from the advertising campaign. The advertising results paled in comparison to the free "super saver shipping" program, which the company introduced on orders over $99. In fact, the free shipping option proved to be so popular and profitable that within two years Amazon.com dropped its qualifying threshold to $49 and then again to a mere $25. At each stage of this progression, Amazon.com used cost-volume-profit analysis to determine whether the extra revenue from liberalizing the free shipping offer more than offset the associated increase in shipping costs.

Source: Rob Walker, "Because 'Optimism is Essential,'" *Inc.* magazine, April 2004, pp. 149–150.

Change in Fixed Cost, Sales Price, and Sales Volume

Refer to the original data and recall again that Acoustics Concepts is currently selling 400 speakers per month. To increase sales, Prem's sales manager would like to cut the selling price by $20 per speaker and increase the advertising budget by $15,000 per month. The sales manager believes that if these two steps are taken, unit sales will increase by 50% to 600 speakers per month. Should the changes be made?

A decrease in the selling price of $20 per speaker would decrease the unit contribution margin by $20 down to $80.

Solution

Expected total contribution margin with lower selling price:	
600 speakers × $80 per speaker....................	$48,000
Present total contribution margin:	
400 speakers × $100 per speaker...................	40,000
Incremental contribution margin......................	8,000
Change in fixed expenses:	
Less incremental advertising expense...............	15,000
Reduction in net operating income....................	$ (7,000)

According to this analysis, the changes should not be made. The $7,000 reduction in net operating income that is shown above can be verified by preparing comparative income statements as follows:

	Present 400 Speakers per Month		Expected 600 Speakers per Month		
	Total	Per Unit	Total	Per Unit	Difference
Sales	$100,000	$250	$138,000	$230	$38,000
Variable expenses.......	60,000	150	90,000	150	30,000
Contribution margin......	40,000	$100	48,000	$ 80	8,000
Fixed expenses.........	35,000		50,000*		15,000
Net operating income (loss).........	$ 5,000		$ (2,000)		$ (7,000)

*35,000 + Additional monthly advertising budget of $15,000 = $50,000.

IN BUSINESS

Delta Attempts to Boost Ticket Sales

The United States Transportation Department ranked the Cincinnati/Northern Kentucky International Airport (CNK) as the second most expensive airport in the country. Because of its high ticket prices, CNK airport officials estimated that they were losing 28% of Cincinnati-area travelers—about 2,500 people per day—to five surrounding airports that offered lower fares. Delta Airlines, which has 90% of the traffic at CNK, attempted to improve the situation by introducing SimpliFares. The program, which Delta touted with a $2 million media campaign, not only lowered fares but also reduced the ticket change fee from $100 to $50. From a cost-volume-profit standpoint, Delta was hoping that the increase in discretionary fixed advertising costs and the decrease in sales revenue realized from lower ticket prices would be more than offset by an increase in sales volume.

Source: James Pilcher, "New Delta Fares Boost Ticket Sales," *The Cincinnati Enquirer*, September 3, 2004, pp. A1 and A12.

Change in Variable Cost, Fixed Cost, and Sales Volume   Refer to Acoustic Concepts' original data. As before, the company is currently selling 400 speakers per month. The sales manager would like to pay a sales commission of $15 per speaker sold, rather than the flat salaries that now total $6,000 per month. The sales manager is confident that the change would increase monthly sales by 15% to 460 speakers per month. Should the change be made?

Solution

Changing the sales staff's compensation from salaries to commissions would affect both fixed and variable expenses. Fixed expenses would decrease by $6,000, from $35,000 to $29,000. Variable expenses would increase by $15, from $150 to $165, and the unit contribution margin would decrease from $100 to $85.

Expected total contribution margin with sales staff on commissions:	
460 speakers × $85 per speaker	$39,100
Present total contribution margin:	
400 speakers × $100 per speaker	40,000
Decrease in total contribution margin	(900)
Change in fixed expenses:	
Add salaries avoided if a commission is paid	6,000
Increase in net operating income	$ 5,100

According to this analysis, the changes should be made. Again, the same answer can be obtained by preparing comparative income statements:

	Present 400 Speakers per Month		Expected 460 Speakers per Month		
	Total	Per Unit	Total	Per Unit	Difference
Sales	$100,000	$250	$115,000	$250	$15,000
Variable expenses	60,000	150	75,900	165	15,900
Contribution margin	40,000	$100	39,100	$ 85	900
Fixed expenses	35,000		29,000		(6,000)*
Net operating income	$ 5,000		$ 10,100		$ 5,100

*Note: A *reduction* in fixed expenses has the effect of *increasing* net operating income.

Change in Selling Price   Refer to the original data where Acoustic Concepts is currently selling 400 speakers per month. The company has an opportunity to make a bulk sale of 150 speakers to a wholesaler if an acceptable price can be negotiated. This sale would not disturb the company's regular sales and would not affect the company's total fixed expenses. What price per speaker should be quoted to the wholesaler if Acoustic Concepts wants to increase its total monthly profits by $3,000?

Solution

Variable cost per speaker.	$150
Desired profit per speaker:	
$3,000 ÷ 150 speakers.	20
Quoted price per speaker.	$170

Notice that fixed expenses are not included in the computation. This is because fixed expenses are not affected by the bulk sale, so all of the additional contribution margin increases profits.

IN BUSINESS

The eToys Saga

The company eToys, which sells toys over the Internet, lost $190 million in 1999 on sales of $151 million. One big cost was advertising. eToys spent about $37 on advertising for each $100 of sales. (Other e-tailers were spending even more—in some cases, up to $460 on advertising for each $100 in sales!)

eToys did have some advantages relative to bricks-and-mortar stores such as Toys "R" Us. eToys had much lower inventory costs since it needed to keep on hand only one or two of a slow-moving item, whereas a traditional store has to fully stock its shelves. And bricks-and-mortar retail spaces in malls and elsewhere do cost money—on average, about 7% of sales. However, e-tailers such as eToys have their own set of disadvantages. Customers "pick and pack" their own items at a bricks-and-mortar outlet, but e-tailers have to pay employees to carry out this task. This costs eToys about $33 for every $100 in sales. And the technology to sell over the net is not free. eToys paid about $29 for its website and related technology for every $100 in sales. However, many of these costs of selling over the net are fixed. Toby Lenk, the CEO of eToys, estimated that the company would pass its break-even point somewhere between $750 and $900 million in sales—representing less than 1% of the market for toys. eToys didn't make it and laid off 70% of its employees in January 2001. Subsequently, eToys was acquired by KBToys.com.

Sources: Erin Kelly, "The Last e-Store on the Block," *Fortune*, September 18, 2000, pp. 214–220; and Jennifer Couzin, *The Industry Standard*, January 4, 2001.

BREAK-EVEN ANALYSIS

Video 6–1　　　Concept 6-2

Break-even analysis is an aspect of CVP analysis that is designed to answer questions such as how far could sales drop before the company begins to lose money?

Break-Even Computations

Earlier in the chapter we defined the break-even point as the level of sales at which the company's profit is zero. The break-even point can be computed using either the *equation method* or the *contribution margin method*—the two methods are equivalent.

LEARNING OBJECTIVE 5
Compute the break-even point in unit sales and dollar sales.

The Equation Method The **equation method** translates the contribution format income statement illustrated earlier in the chapter into equation form as follows:

$$\text{Profits} = (\text{Sales} - \text{Variable expenses}) - \text{Fixed expenses}$$

Rearranging this equation slightly yields the following equation, which is widely used in CVP analysis:

$$\text{Sales} = \text{Variable expenses} + \text{Fixed expenses} + \text{Profits}$$

At the break-even point, profits are zero. Therefore, the break-even point can be computed by finding the point where sales equal the total of the variable expenses plus the fixed expenses. For Acoustic Concepts, the break-even point in unit sales, Q, can be computed as follows:

$$\text{Sales} = \text{Variable expenses} + \text{Fixed expenses} + \text{Profits}$$

$$\$250Q = \$150Q + \$35,000 + \$0$$

$$\$100Q = \$35,000$$

$$Q = \$35,000 \div \$100 \text{ per speaker}$$

$$Q = 350 \text{ speakers}$$

where:

$$Q = \text{Quantity of speakers sold}$$
$$\$250 = \text{Unit selling price}$$
$$\$150 = \text{Unit variable expenses}$$
$$\$35,000 = \text{Total fixed expenses}$$

The break-even point in total sales dollars can be computed by multiplying the break-even level of unit sales by the selling price per unit:

$$350 \text{ speakers} \times \$250 \text{ per speaker} = \$87,500$$

The break-even point in total sales dollars, X, can also be computed as follows:

$$\text{Sales} = \text{Variable expenses} + \text{Fixed expenses} + \text{Profits}$$

$$X = 0.60X + \$35,000 + \$0$$

$$0.40X = \$35,000$$

$$X = \$35,000 \div 0.40$$

$$X = \$87,500$$

where:

$$X = \text{Total sales dollars}$$
$$0.60 = \text{Variable expense ratio (Variable expenses} \div \text{Sales)}$$
$$\$35,000 = \text{Total fixed expenses}$$

Note that in the above analysis the *variable expense ratio* is used. The **variable expense ratio** is the ratio of variable expense to sales. It can be computed by dividing the total variable expense by the total sales or, in a single product analysis, it can be computed by dividing the variable cost per unit by the unit selling price.

Also note that the use of the ratios in the above analysis yields a break-even point expressed in sales dollars rather than in units sold. If desired, the break-even point in units sold can be computed as follows:

$$\$87,500 \div \$250 \text{ per speaker} = 350 \text{ speakers}$$

Recruit

YOU DECIDE

Assume that you are being recruited by the ConneXus Corp. and have an interview scheduled later this week. You are interested in working for this company for a variety of reasons. In preparation for the interview, you did some research at your local library and gathered the following information about the company. ConneXus is a company set up by two young engineers, George Searle and Humphrey Chen, to allow consumers to order music CDs on their cell phones. Suppose you hear on the radio a cut from a CD that you would like to own. If you subscribe to their service, you would pick up your cell phone, punch ".CD," and enter the radio station's frequency and the time you heard the song, and the CD would be on its way to you.

ConneXus charges about $17 for a CD, including shipping. The company pays its supplier about $13 for the CD, leaving a contribution margin of $4 per CD. Because of the fixed costs of running the service (about $1,850,000 a year), Searle expects the company to lose about $1.5 million in its first year of operations on sales of 88,000 CDs.

What are your initial impressions of this company based on the information you gathered? What other information would you want to obtain during the job interview?

Source: Adapted from Peter Kafka, "Play It Again," *Forbes*, July 26, 1999, p. 94.

The Contribution Margin Method The **contribution margin method** is a shortcut version of the equation method already described. The approach centers on the idea discussed earlier that each unit sold provides a certain amount of contribution margin that goes toward covering fixed costs. To find how many units must be sold to break even, divide the total fixed expenses by the unit contribution margin:

$$\text{Break-even point in units sold} = \frac{\text{Fixed expenses}}{\text{Unit contribution margin}}$$

Each speaker generates a contribution margin of $100 ($250 selling price, less $150 variable expenses). Since the total fixed expenses are $35,000, the break-even point in unit sales is computed as follows:

$$\frac{\text{Fixed expenses}}{\text{Unit contribution margin}} = \frac{\$35,000}{\$100 \text{ per speaker}} = 350 \text{ speakers}$$

A variation of this method uses the CM ratio instead of the unit contribution margin. The result is the break-even point in total sales dollars rather than in total units sold.

$$\text{Break-even point in total sales dollars} = \frac{\text{Fixed expenses}}{\text{CM ratio}}$$

In the Acoustic Concepts example, the calculation is as follows:

$$\frac{\text{Fixed expenses}}{\text{CM ratio}} = \frac{\$35,000}{0.40} = \$87,500$$

This approach, based on the CM ratio, is particularly useful when a company has multiple products and wishes to compute a single break-even point for the company as a whole. More is said on this point later in the chapter.

What Happened to the Profit?

Chip Conley is CEO of Joie de Vivre Hospitality, a company that owns and operates 28 hospitality businesses in northern California. Conley summed up the company's experience after the dot.com crash and 9/11 as follows: "In the history of American hotel markets, no hotel market has ever seen a drop in revenues as precipitous as the one in San Francisco and Silicon Valley in the last two years. On average, hotel revenues . . . dropped 40% to 45%. . . . We've been fortunate that our breakeven point is lower than our competition's. . . . But the problem is that the hotel business is a fixed-cost business. So in an environment where you have those precipitous drops and our costs are moderately fixed, our net incomes—well, they're not incomes anymore, they're losses."

Source: Karen Dillon, "Shop Talk," *Inc.* magazine, December 2002, pp. 111–114.

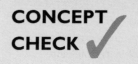

2. Assume the selling price per unit is $30, the contribution margin ratio is 40%, and the total fixed cost is $60,000. What is the break-even point in unit sales?
   a. 2,000
   b. 3,000
   c. 4,000
   d. 5,000

Target Profit Analysis

CVP formulas can be used to determine the sales volume needed to achieve a target profit. Suppose that Acoustic Concepts wishes to earn a target profit of $40,000 per month. How many speakers would have to be sold?

> **LEARNING OBJECTIVE 6**
>
> Determine the level of sales needed to achieve a desired target profit.

The Equation Approach One approach is to use the equation method. Instead of solving for the unit sales where profits are zero, solve for the unit sales where profits are $40,000.

$$\text{Sales} = \text{Variable expenses} + \text{Fixed expenses} + \text{Profits}$$

$$\$250Q = \$150Q + \$35,000 + \$40,000$$

$$\$100Q = \$75,000$$

$$Q = \$75,000 \div \$100 \text{ per speaker}$$

$$Q = 750 \text{ speakers}$$

where:

$$Q = \text{Quantity of speakers sold}$$

$$\$250 = \text{Unit selling price}$$

$$\$150 = \text{Unit variable expenses}$$

$$\$35,000 = \text{Total fixed expenses}$$

$$\$40,000 = \text{Target profit}$$

Thus, the target profit can be achieved by selling 750 speakers per month, which represents $187,500 in total sales ($250 per speaker × 750 speakers).

The Contribution Margin Approach A second approach involves expanding the contribution margin formula to include the target profit:

$$\text{Unit sales to attain the target profit} = \frac{\text{Fixed expenses} + \text{Target profit}}{\text{Unit contribution margin}}$$

$$= \frac{\$35,000 + \$40,000}{\$100 \text{ per speaker}}$$

$$= 750 \text{ speakers}$$

This approach gives the same answer as the equation method because it is simply a shortcut version of the equation method. Similarly, the dollar sales needed to attain the target profit can be computed as follows:

$$\text{Dollar sales to attain target profit} = \frac{\text{Fixed expenses} + \text{Target profit}}{\text{CM ratio}}$$

$$= \frac{\$35,000 + \$40,000}{0.40}$$

$$= \$187,500$$

The Margin of Safety

LEARNING OBJECTIVE 7

Compute the margin of safety and explain its significance.

The **margin of safety** is the excess of budgeted (or actual) sales dollars over the break-even volume of sales dollars. It is the amount by which sales can drop before losses are incurred. The higher the margin of safety, the lower the risk of not breaking even and incurring a loss. The formula for its calculation is:

$$\text{Margin of safety} = \text{Total budgeted (or actual) sales} - \text{Break-even sales}$$

The margin of safety can also be expressed in percentage form by dividing the margin of safety in dollars by total dollar sales:

$$\text{Margin of safety percentage} = \frac{\text{Margin of safety in dollars}}{\text{Total budgeted (or actual) sales dollars}}$$

The calculation of the margin of safety for Acoustic Concepts is:

Sales (at the current volume of 400 speakers) (a)	$100,000
Break-even sales (at 350 speakers)	87,500
Margin of safety (in dollars) (b)	$ 12,500
Margin of safety as a percentage of sales, (b) ÷ (a)	12.5%

This margin of safety means that at the current level of sales and with the company's current prices and cost structure, a reduction in sales of $12,500, or 12.5%, would result in just breaking even.

In a single-product company like Acoustic Concepts, the margin of safety can also be expressed in terms of the number of units sold by dividing the margin of safety in dollars by the selling price per unit. In this case, the margin of safety is 50 speakers ($12,500 ÷ $250 per speaker = 50 speakers).

DECISION MAKER

Loan Officer

Sam Calagione owns Dogfish Head Craft Brewery, a microbrewery in Rehoboth Beach, Delaware. He charges his distributors $100 per case for premium beers such as World Wide Stout. The distributors tack on 25% when selling to retailers who in turn add a 30% markup before selling the beer to consumers. In the most recent year, Dogfish's revenue was $7 million and its net operating income was $800,000. Calagione reports that the costs of making one case of World Wide Stout are $30 for raw ingredients, $16 for labor, $6 for bottling and packaging, and $10 for utilities.

Assume that Calagione has approached your bank for a loan. As the loan officer you should consider a variety of factors, including the company's margin of safety. Assuming that the information related to World Wide Stout is representative of all Dogfish microbrews and that other information about the company is favorable, would you consider Dogfish's margin of safety to be comfortable enough to extend a loan?

Source: Patricia Huang, "Château Dogfish," *Forbes*, February 28, 2005, pp. 57–59.

CONCEPT CHECK ✓

3. Assume a company produces one product that sells for $55, has a variable cost per unit of $35, and has fixed costs of $100,000. How many units must the company sell to earn a target profit of $50,000?
   a. 7,500 units
   b. 10,000 units
   c. 12,500 units
   d. 15,000 units

CONCEPT CHECK ✓

(continued)

4. Given the same facts as in question 3 above, if the company exactly meets its target profit, what will be its margin of safety in sales dollars?
   a. $110,000
   b. $127,500
   c. $137,500
   d. $150,000

CVP CONSIDERATIONS IN CHOOSING A COST STRUCTURE

Cost structure refers to the relative proportion of fixed and variable costs in an organization. Managers often have some latitude in trading off between these two types of costs. For example, fixed investments in automated equipment can reduce variable labor costs. In this section, we discuss the choice of a cost structure. We introduce the concept of *operating leverage,* which plays a key role in determining the impact of cost structure on profit stability.

Video 6–1

Cost Structure and Profit Stability

Which cost structure is better—high variable costs and low fixed costs, or the opposite? No single answer to this question is possible; each approach has its advantages. To show what we mean, refer to the income statements given below for two blueberry farms. Bogside Farm depends on migrant workers to pick its berries by hand, whereas Sterling Farm has invested in expensive berry-picking machines. Consequently, Bogside Farm has higher variable costs, but Sterling Farm has higher fixed costs:

	Bogside Farm		Sterling Farm	
	Amount	Percent	Amount	Percent
Sales	$100,000	100%	$100,000	100%
Variable expenses	60,000	60	30,000	30
Contribution margin	40,000	40%	70,000	70%
Fixed expenses	30,000		60,000	
Net operating income	$ 10,000		$ 10,000	

Which farm has the better cost structure? The answer depends on many factors, including the long-run trend in sales, year-to-year fluctuations in the level of sales, and the attitude of the owners toward risk. If sales are expected to exceed $100,000 in the future, then Sterling Farm probably has the better cost structure. The reason is that its CM ratio is higher, and its profits will therefore increase more rapidly as sales increase. To illustrate, assume that each farm experiences a 10% increase in sales without any increase in fixed costs. The new income statements would be as follows:

	Bogside Farm		Sterling Farm	
	Amount	Percent	Amount	Percent
Sales	$110,000	100%	$110,000	100%
Variable expenses	66,000	60	33,000	30
Contribution margin	44,000	40%	77,000	70%
Fixed expenses	30,000		60,000	
Net operating income	$ 14,000		$ 17,000	

Sterling Farm has experienced a greater increase in net operating income due to its higher CM ratio even though the increase in sales was the same for both farms.

What if sales drop below $100,000? What are the farms' break-even points? What are their margins of safety? The computations needed to answer these questions are shown below using the contribution margin method:

	Bogside Farm	Sterling Farm
Fixed expenses	$ 30,000	$ 60,000
Contribution margin ratio	÷ 0.40	÷ 0.70
Break-even in total sales dollars	$ 75,000	$ 85,714
Total current sales (a)	$100,000	$100,000
Break-even sales	75,000	85,714
Margin of safety in sales dollars (b)	$ 25,000	$ 14,286
Margin of safety as a percentage of sales, (b) ÷ (a)	25.0%	14.3%

Bogside Farm's margin of safety is greater and its contribution margin ratio is lower than Sterling Farm. Therefore Bogside Farm is less vulnerable to downturns than Sterling Farm. Due to its lower contribution margin ratio, Bogside Farm will not lose contribution margin as rapidly as Sterling Farm when sales decline. Thus, Bogside Farm's profit will be less volatile. We saw earlier that this is a drawback when sales increase, but it provides more protection when sales drop. And because its break-even point is lower, Bogside Farm can suffer a larger sales decline before losses emerge.

To summarize, without knowing the future, it is not obvious which cost structure is better. Both have advantages and disadvantages. Sterling Farm, with its higher fixed costs and lower variable costs, will experience wider swings in net operating income as sales fluctuate, with greater profits in good years and greater losses in bad years. Bogside Farm, with its lower fixed costs and higher variable costs, will enjoy greater profit stability and will be more protected from losses during bad years, but at the cost of lower net operating income in good years.

IN BUSINESS

A Losing Cost Structure

Both JetBlue and United Airlines use an Airbus 235 to fly from Dulles International Airport near Washington, DC, to Oakland, California. Both planes have a pilot, copilot, and four flight attendants. That is where the similarity ends. Based on 2002 data, the pilot on the United flight earned $16,350 to $18,000 a month compared to $6,800 per month for the JetBlue pilot. United's senior flight attendants on the plane earned more than $41,000 per year; whereas the JetBlue attendants were paid $16,800 to $27,000 per year. Largely because of the higher labor costs at United, its costs of operating the flight were more than 60% higher than JetBlue's costs. Due to intense fare competition from JetBlue and other low-cost carriers, United was unable to cover its higher operating costs on this and many other flights. Consequently, United went into bankruptcy at the end of 2002.

Source: Susan Carey, "Costly Race in the Sky," *The Wall Street Journal*, September 9, 2002, pp. B1 and B3.

LEARNING OBJECTIVE 8

Compute the degree of operating leverage at a particular level of sales and explain how it can be used to predict changes in net operating income.

Operating Leverage

A lever is a tool for multiplying force. With use of a lever, a massive object can be moved with only a modest amount of force. In business, *operating leverage* serves a similar purpose. **Operating leverage** is a measure of how sensitive net operating income is to a given percentage change in sales. Operating leverage acts as a multiplier. If operating leverage is high, a small percentage increase in sales can produce a much larger percentage increase in net operating income.

Operating leverage can be illustrated by returning to the data for the two blueberry farms. We previously showed that a 10% increase in sales (from $100,000 to $110,000 in each farm) results in a 70% increase in the net operating income of Sterling Farm (from $10,000 to $17,000) and only a 40% increase in the net operating income of Bogside Farm (from $10,000 to $14,000). Thus, for a 10% increase in sales, Sterling Farm experiences a much greater percentage increase in profits than does Bogside Farm. Therefore, Sterling Farm has greater operating leverage than Bogside Farm.

The **degree of operating leverage** at a given level of sales is computed by the following formula:

$$\text{Degree of operating leverage} = \frac{\text{Contribution margin}}{\text{Net operating income}}$$

The degree of operating leverage is a measure, at a given level of sales, of how a percentage change in sales volume will affect profits. To illustrate, the degree of operating leverage for the two farms at $100,000 sales would be computed as follows:

$$\text{Bogside Farm: } \frac{\$40,000}{\$10,000} = 4$$

$$\text{Sterling Farm: } \frac{\$70,000}{\$10,000} = 7$$

Since the degree of operating leverage for Bogside Farm is 4, the farm's net operating income grows four times as fast as its sales. Similarly, Sterling Farm's net operating income grows seven times as fast as its sales. Thus, if sales increase by 10%, then we can expect the net operating income of Bogside Farm to increase by four times this amount, or by 40%, and the net operating income of Sterling Farm to increase by seven times this amount, or by 70%.

	(1) Percent Increase in Sales	(2) Degree of Operating Leverage	Percent Increase in Net Operating Income (1) × (2)
Bogside Farm.............	10%	4	40%
Sterling Farm	10%	7	70%

What is responsible for the higher operating leverage at Sterling Farm? The only difference between the two farms is their cost structure. If two companies have the same total revenue and same total expense but different cost structures, then the company with the higher proportion of fixed costs in its cost structure will have higher operating leverage. Referring back to the original example on page 255, when both farms have sales of $100,000 and total expenses of $90,000, one-third of Bogside Farm's costs are fixed but two-thirds of Sterling Farm's costs are fixed. As a consequence, Sterling's degree of operating leverage is higher than Bogside's.

The degree of operating leverage is not constant; it is greatest at sales levels near the break-even point and decreases as sales and profits rise. The following table shows the degree of operating leverage for Bogside Farm at various sales levels. (Data used earlier for Bogside Farm are shown in color.)

Sales................	$75,000	$80,000	$100,000	$150,000	$225,000
Variable expenses.......	45,000	48,000	60,000	90,000	135,000
Contribution margin (a) ...	30,000	32,000	40,000	60,000	90,000
Fixed expenses.........	30,000	30,000	30,000	30,000	30,000
Net operating income (b) ..	$ 0	$ 2,000	$ 10,000	$ 30,000	$ 60,000
Degree of operating leverage, (a) ÷ (b).....	∞	16	4	2	1.5

Thus, a 10% increase in sales would increase profits by only 15% (10% × 1.5) if sales were previously $225,000, as compared to the 40% increase we computed earlier at the $100,000 sales level. The degree of operating leverage will continue to decrease the farther the company moves from its break-even point. At the break-even point, the degree of operating leverage is infinitely large ($30,000 contribution margin ÷ $0 net operating income = ∞).

The degree of operating leverage can be used to quickly estimate what impact various percentage changes in sales will have on profits, without the necessity of preparing detailed income statements. As shown by our examples, the effects of operating leverage can be dramatic. If a company is near its break-even point, then even small percentage increases in sales can yield large percentage increases in profits. *This explains why management will often work very hard for only a small increase in sales volume.* If the degree of operating leverage is 5, then a 6% increase in sales would translate into a 30% increase in profits.

STRUCTURING SALES COMMISSIONS

Companies usually compensate salespeople by paying them a commission based on sales, a salary, or a combination of the two. Commissions based on sales dollars can lead to lower profits. To illustrate, consider Pipeline Unlimited, a producer of surfing equipment. Salespeople for the company sell the company's products to retail sporting goods stores throughout North America and the Pacific Basin. Data for two of the company's surfboards, the XR7 and Turbo models, appear below:

	Model	
	XR7	Turbo
Selling price	$695	$749
Variable expenses	344	410
Contribution margin	$351	$339

Which model will salespeople push hardest if they are paid a commission of 10% of sales revenue? The answer is the Turbo, since it has the higher selling price and hence the larger commission. On the other hand, from the standpoint of the company, profits will be greater if salespeople steer customers toward the XR7 model since it has the higher contribution margin.

To eliminate such conflicts, commissions can be based on contribution margin rather than on selling price. If this is done, the salespersons will want to sell the mix of products that will maximize contribution margin. Providing that fixed costs are not affected by the sales mix, maximizing the contribution margin will also maximize the company's profit. In effect, by maximizing their own compensation, salespersons will also maximize the company's profit.

An Alternative Approach to Sales Commissions   IN BUSINESS

Thrive Networks, located in Concord, Massachusetts, used to pay its three salesmen based on individually-earned commissions. This system seemed to be working fine as indicated by the company's sales growth from $2.7 million in 2002 to $3.6 million in 2003. However, the company felt there was a better way to motivate and compensate its salesmen. It pooled commissions across the three salesmen and compensated them collectively. The new approach was designed to build teamwork and leverage each salesman's individual strengths. Jim Lippie, the Director of Business Development, was highly skilled at networking and generating sales leads. John Barrows, the Sales Director, excelled at meeting with prospective clients and producing compelling proposals. Nate Wolfson, the CEO and final member of the sales team, was the master at closing the deal. The new approach has worked so well that Wolfson plans to use three-person sales teams in his offices nationwide.

Source: Cara Cannella, "Kill the Commissions," *Inc.* magazine, August 2004, p. 38.

SALES MIX

Before concluding our discussion of CVP concepts, we need to consider the impact of changes in *sales mix* on a company's profit.

The Definition of Sales Mix

The term **sales mix** refers to the relative proportions in which a company's products are sold. The idea is to achieve the combination, or mix, that will yield the greatest amount of profits. Most companies have many products, and often these products are not equally profitable. Hence, profits will depend to some extent on the company's sales mix. Profits will be greater if high-margin rather than low-margin items make up a relatively large proportion of total sales.

Changes in the sales mix can cause perplexing variations in a company's profits. A shift in the sales mix from high-margin items to low-margin items can cause total profits to decrease even though total sales may increase. Conversely, a shift in the sales mix from low-margin items to high-margin items can cause the reverse effect—total profits may increase even though total sales decrease. It is one thing to achieve a particular sales volume; it is quite another thing to sell the most profitable mix of products.

> **LEARNING OBJECTIVE 9**
>
> Compute the break-even point for a multiproduct company and explain the effects of shifts in the sales mix on contribution margin and the break-even point.

Kodak: Going Digital   IN BUSINESS

Kodak dominates the film industry in the U.S., selling two out of every three rolls of film. It also processes 40% of all film dropped off for developing. Unfortunately for Kodak, this revenue stream is rapidly declining due to competition from digital cameras, which do not use film at all. To counter this threat, Kodak has moved into the digital market with its own line of digital cameras and various services, but sales of digital products undeniably cut into the company's film business. "Chief Financial Officer Robert Brust has 'stress-tested' profit models based on how quickly digital cameras may spread. If half of homes go digital, . . . Kodak's sales would rise 10% a year—but profits would go up only 8% a year. Cost cuts couldn't come fast enough to offset a slide in film sales and the margin pressure from selling cheap digital cameras." The sales mix is moving in the wrong direction, given the company's current cost structure and competitive prices.

Source: Bruce Upbin, "Kodak's Digital Moment," *Forbes*, August 21, 2000, pp. 106–112.

Sales Mix and Break-Even Analysis

If a company sells more than one product, break-even analysis is more complex than discussed to this point. The reason is that different products will have different selling prices, different costs, and different contribution margins. Consequently, the break-even point depends on the mix in which the various products are sold. To illustrate, consider Sound Unlimited, a small company that imports DVDs from France. At present, the company sells two DVDs: the Le Louvre DVD, a multimedia free-form tour of the famous art museum in Paris; and the Le Vin DVD, which features the wines and wine-growing regions of France. The company's September sales, expenses, and break-even point are shown in Exhibit 6–3.

As shown in the exhibit, the break-even point is $60,000 in sales, which was computed by dividing the company's fixed expenses of $27,000 by its overall CM ratio of 45%. However, this is the break-even only if the company's sales mix does not change. Currently, the Le Louvre DVD is responsible for 20% and the Le Vin DVD for 80% of the company's dollar sales. Assuming this sales mix does not change, then if total sales are $60,000, the sales of the Le Louvre DVD would be $12,000 (20% of $60,000) and the sales of the Le Vin DVD would be $48,000 (80% of $60,000). As shown in Exhibit 6–3, at these levels of sales, the company would indeed break even. But $60,000 in sales represents the break-even point for the company only if the sales mix does not change. *If the*

EXHIBIT 6–3   Multiproduct Break-Even Analysis

Sound Unlimited
Contribution Income Statement
For the Month of September

	Le Louvre DVD		Le Vin DVD		Total	
	Amount	Percent	Amount	Percent	Amount	Percent
Sales	$20,000	100%	$80,000	100%	$100,000	100%
Variable expenses	15,000	75	40,000	50	55,000	55
Contribution margin	$ 5,000	25%	$40,000	50%	45,000	45%
Fixed expenses					27,000	
Net operating income					$ 18,000	

Computation of the break-even point:

$$\frac{\text{Fixed expenses}}{\text{Overall CM ratio}} = \frac{\$27,000}{0.45} = \$60,000$$

Verification of the break-even:

	Le Louvre DVD	Le Vin DVD	Total
Current dollar sales	$20,000	$80,000	$100,000
Percentage of total dollar sales	20%	80%	100%
Sales at break-even	$12,000	$48,000	$ 60,000

	Le Louvre DVD		Le Vin DVD		Total	
	Amount	Percent	Amount	Percent	Amount	Percent
Sales	$12,000	100%	$48,000	100%	$ 60,000	100%
Variable expenses	9,000	75	24,000	50	33,000	55
Contribution margin	$ 3,000	25%	$24,000	50%	27,000	45%
Fixed expenses					27,000	
Net operating income					$ 0	

EXHIBIT 6-4 Multiproduct Break-Even Analysis: A Shift in Sales Mix (see Exhibit 6-3)

Sound Unlimited
Contribution Income Statement
For the Month of October

	Le Louvre DVD		Le Vin DVD		Total	
	Amount	Percent	Amount	Percent	Amount	Percent
Sales	$80,000	100%	$20,000	100%	$100,000	100%
Variable expenses	60,000	75	10,000	50	70,000	70
Contribution margin	$20,000	25%	$10,000	50%	30,000	30%
Fixed expenses					27,000	
Net operating income					$ 3,000	

Computation of the break-even point:

$$\frac{\text{Fixed expenses}}{\text{Overall CM ratio}} = \frac{\$27,000}{0.30} = \$90,000$$

sales mix changes, then the break-even point will also usually change. This is illustrated by the results for October in which the sales mix shifted away from the more profitable Le Vin DVD (which has a 50% CM ratio) toward the less profitable Le Louvre DVD (which has a 25% CM ratio). These results appear in Exhibit 6–4.

Although sales have remained unchanged at $100,000, the sales mix is exactly the reverse of what it was in Exhibit 6–3, with the bulk of the sales now coming from the less profitable Le Louvre DVD. Notice that this shift in the sales mix has caused both the overall CM ratio and total profits to drop sharply from the prior month even though total sales are the same. The overall CM ratio has dropped from 45% in September to only 30% in October, and net operating income has dropped from $18,000 to only $3,000. In addition, with the drop in the overall CM ratio, the company's break-even point is no longer $60,000 in sales. Since the company is now realizing less average contribution margin per dollar of sales, it takes more sales to cover the same amount of fixed costs. Thus, the break-even point has increased from $60,000 to $90,000 in sales per year.

In preparing a break-even analysis, some assumption must be made concerning the sales mix. Usually the assumption is that it will not change. However, if the sales mix is expected to change, then this must be explicitly considered in any CVP computations.

Playing the CVP Game   IN BUSINESS

In 2002, General Motors (GM) gave away almost $2,600 per vehicle in customer incentives such as price cuts and 0% financing. "The pricing sacrifices have been more than offset by volume gains, most of which have come from trucks and SUVs, like the Chevy Suburban and the GMC Envoy, which generate far more profit for the company than cars. Lehman Brothers analysts estimate that GM will sell an additional 395,000 trucks and SUVs and an extra 75,000 cars in 2002. The trucks, however, are the company's golden goose, hauling in an average [contribution margin] . . . of about $7,000, compared with just $4,000 for the cars. All told, the volume gains could bring in an additional $3 billion [in profits]."

Source: Janice Revell, "GM's Slow Leak," *Fortune*, October 28, 2002, pp. 105–110.

ASSUMPTIONS OF CVP ANALYSIS

A number of assumptions commonly underlie CVP analysis:

1. Selling price is constant. The price of a product or service will not change as volume changes.
2. Costs are linear and can be accurately divided into variable and fixed elements. The variable element is constant per unit, and the fixed element is constant in total over the entire relevant range.
3. In multiproduct companies, the sales mix is constant.
4. In manufacturing companies, inventories do not change. The number of units produced equals the number of units sold.

While these assumptions may be violated in practice, the results of CVP analysis are often "good enough" to be quite useful. Perhaps the greatest danger lies in relying on simple CVP analysis when a manager is contemplating a large change in volume that lies outside of the relevant range. For example, a manager might contemplate increasing the level of sales far beyond what the company has ever experienced before. However, even in these situations the model can be adjusted as we have done in this chapter to take into account anticipated changes in selling prices, fixed costs, and the sales mix that would otherwise violate the assumptions mentioned above. For example, in a decision that would affect fixed costs, the change in fixed costs can be explicitly taken into account as illustrated earlier in the chapter in the Acoustic Concepts example on page 245.

Assumptions of CVP Analysis

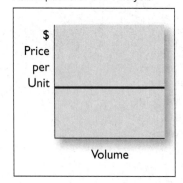

Selling price is constant

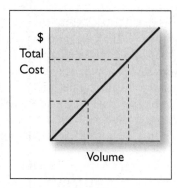

Variable cost per unit is constant

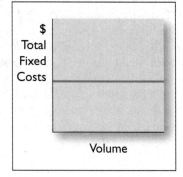

Fixed costs are constant

Sales mix is constant

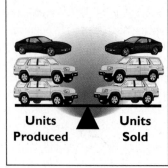

Inventory levels are constant

SUMMARY

LO1   Explain how changes in activity affect contribution margin and net operating income.

The unit contribution margin, which is the difference between a unit's selling price and its variable cost, indicates how net operating income will change as the result of selling one more or one less unit. For example, if a product's unit contribution margin is $10, then selling one more unit will add $10 to the company's profit.

LO2   Prepare and interpret a cost-volume-profit (CVP) graph.

A cost-volume-profit graph displays sales revenues and expenses as a function of unit sales. Revenue is depicted as a straight line slanting upward to the right from the origin. Total expenses include fixed costs and variable costs. The fixed costs are flat on the graph. The variable cost slants upward to the right. The break-even point is the point at which the total sales revenue and total expense lines intersect on the graph.

LO3   Use the contribution margin ratio (CM ratio) to compute changes in contribution margin and net operating income resulting from changes in sales volume.

The contribution margin ratio is computed by dividing the unit contribution margin by the unit selling price, or by dividing the total contribution margin by the total sales.

The contribution margin shows how much a dollar increase in sales affects the total contribution margin and net operating income. For example, if a product has a 40% contribution margin ratio, then a $100 increase in sales should result in a $40 increase in contribution margin and in net operating income.

LO4   Show the effects on contribution margin of changes in variable costs, fixed costs, selling price, and volume.

Contribution margin concepts can be used to estimate the effects of changes in various parameters such as variable costs, fixed costs, selling prices, and volume on the total contribution margin and net operating income.

LO5   Compute the break-even point in unit sales and dollar sales.

The break-even point is the level of sales at which profits are zero. It can be computed using several methods. The break-even point in units can be determined by dividing total fixed expenses by the unit contribution margin. The break-even point in sales dollars can be determined by dividing total fixed expenses by the contribution margin ratio.

LO6   Determine the level of sales needed to achieve a desired target profit.

The sales, in units, required to attain a desired target profit can be determined by summing the total fixed expenses and the desired target profit and then dividing the result by the unit contribution margin.

LO7   Compute the margin of safety and explain its significance.

The margin of safety is the difference between the total budgeted (or actual) sales dollars of a period and the break-even sales dollars. It expresses how much cushion there is in the current level of sales above the break-even point.

LO8   Compute the degree of operating leverage at a particular level of sales and explain how it can be used to predict changes in net operating income.

The degree of operating leverage is computed by dividing the total contribution margin by net operating income. The degree of operating leverage can be used to determine the impact a given percentage change in sales would have on net operating income. For example, if a company's degree of operating leverage is 2.5, then a 10% increase in sales from the current level of sales should result in a 25% increase in net operating income.

LO9   Compute the break-even point for a multiproduct company and explain the effects of shifts in the sales mix on contribution margin and the break-even point.

The break-even point for a multiproduct company can be computed by dividing the company's total fixed expenses by the overall contribution margin ratio.

This method for computing the break-even point assumes that the sales mix is constant. If the sales mix shifts toward products with a lower contribution margin ratio, then more total sales are required to attain any given level of profits.

GUIDANCE ANSWERS TO *DECISION MAKER AND YOU DECIDE*

Recruit (p. 251)

You can get a feel for the challenges that this company will face by determining its break-even point.

$$\text{Sales} = \text{Variable expenses} + \text{Fixed expenses} + \text{Profits}$$

$$\$17Q = \$13Q + \$1,850,000 + \$0$$

$$\$4Q = \$1,850,000$$

$$Q = 462,500$$

Assuming that its cost structure stays the same, ConneXus needs to increase its sales by 426%—from 88,000 to 462,500 CDs—just to break even. After it reaches that break-even point, net operating income will increase by $4 (the contribution margin) for each additional CD that it sells. Joining the company would be a risky proposition; you should be prepared with some probing questions when you arrive for your interview. (For example, what steps does the company plan to take to increase sales? How might the company reduce its fixed and/or variable expenses so as to lower its break-even point?)

Loan Officer (p. 254)

To determine the company's margin of safety, you need to determine its break-even point. Start by estimating the company's variable expense ratio:

$$\text{Variable cost per unit} \div \text{Selling price per unit} = \text{Variable expense ratio}$$

$$\$62 \div \$100 = 62\%$$

Then, estimate the company's variable expenses:

$$\text{Sales} \times \text{Variable expense ratio} = \text{Estimated amount of variable expenses}$$

$$\$7,000,000 \times 0.62 = \$4,340,000$$

Next, estimate the company's current level of fixed expenses as follows:

$$\text{Sales} = \text{Variable expenses} + \text{Fixed expenses} + \text{Profits}$$

$$\$7,000,000 = \$4,340,000 + X + \$800,000$$

$$X = \$7,000,000 - \$4,340,000 - \$800,000$$

$$X = \$1,860,000$$

Use the equation approach to estimate the company's break-even point:

$$\text{Sales} = \text{Variable expenses} + \text{Fixed expenses} + \text{Profits}$$

$$X = 0.62X + \$1,860,000 + \$0$$

$$0.38X = \$1,860,000$$

$$X = \$4,894,737$$

Finally, compute the company's margin of safety:

$$\text{Margin of safety} = (\text{Sales} - \text{Break-even sales}) \div \text{Sales}$$

$$= (\$7,000,000 - \$4,894,737) \div \$7,000,000$$

$$= 30\%$$

The margin of safety appears to be adequate, so if the other information about the company is favorable, a loan would seem to be justified.

GUIDANCE ANSWERS TO CONCEPT CHECKS

1. **Choice d.** The contribution margin ratio equals 1.0 − Variable costs as a percent of sales.
2. **Choice d.** The contribution margin per unit is $12 (40% of $30). Therefore, the break-even point in units sold = $60,000 ÷ $12 = 5,000.
3. **Choice a.** ($100,000 + $50,000) ÷ $20 contribution margin per unit = 7,500 units.
4. **Choice c.** 7,500 units is 2,500 units above the break-even point. Therefore, the margin of safety is 2,500 units × $55 per unit = $137,500.

REVIEW PROBLEM: CVP RELATIONSHIPS

Voltar Company manufactures and sells a specialized cordless telephone for high electromagnetic radiation environments. The company's contribution format income statement for the most recent year is given below:

	Total	Per Unit	Percent of Sales
Sales (20,000 units)	$1,200,000	$60	100%
Variable expenses	900,000	45	?
Contribution margin	300,000	$15	? %
Fixed expenses	240,000		
Net operating income	$ 60,000		

Management is anxious to increase the company's profit and has asked for an analysis of a number of items.

Required:
1. Compute the company's CM ratio and variable expense ratio.
2. Compute the company's break-even point in both units and sales dollars. Use the equation method.
3. Assume that sales increase by $400,000 next year. If cost behavior patterns remain unchanged, by how much will the company's net operating income increase? Use the CM ratio to compute your answer.
4. Refer to the original data. Assume that next year management wants the company to earn a profit of at least $90,000. How many units will have to be sold to meet this target profit?
5. Refer to the original data. Compute the company's margin of safety in both dollar and percentage form.
6. a. Compute the company's degree of operating leverage at the present level of sales.
   b. Assume that through a more intense effort by the sales staff the company's sales increase by 8% next year. By what percentage would you expect net operating income to increase? Use the degree of operating leverage to obtain your answer.
   c. Verify your answer to part (b) by preparing a new contribution format income statement showing an 8% increase in sales.
7. In an effort to increase sales and profits, management is considering the use of a higher quality speaker. The higher quality speaker would increase variable costs by $3 per unit, but management could eliminate one quality inspector who is paid a salary of $30,000 per year. The sales manager estimates that the higher quality speaker would increase annual sales by at least 20%.
   a. Assuming that changes are made as described above, prepare a projected contribution format income statement for next year. Show data on a total, per unit, and percentage basis.
   b. Compute the company's new break-even point in both units and dollars of sales. Use the contribution margin method.
   c. Would you recommend that the changes be made?

Solution to Review Problem

1.
$$\text{CM ratio} = \frac{\text{Unit contribution margin}}{\text{Selling price}} = \frac{\$15}{\$60} = 25\%$$

$$\text{Variable expense ratio} = \frac{\text{Variable expense}}{\text{Selling price}} = \frac{\$45}{\$60} = 75\%$$

2.
$$\text{Sales} = \text{Variable expenses} + \text{Fixed expenses} + \text{Profits}$$

$$\$60Q = \$45Q + \$240,000 + \$0$$

$$\$15Q = \$240,000$$

$$Q = \$240,000 \div \$15 \text{ per unit}$$

$$Q = 16,000 \text{ units; or at } \$60 \text{ per unit, } \$960,000$$

Alternative solution:

$$X = 0.75X + \$240,000 + \$0$$

$$0.25X = \$240,000$$

$$X = \$240,000 \div 0.25$$

$$X = \$960,000; \text{ or at } \$60 \text{ per unit, } 16,000 \text{ units}$$

3.

Increase in sales	$400,000
Multiply by the CM ratio	×25%
Expected increase in contribution margin	$100,000

Since the fixed expenses are not expected to change, net operating income will increase by the entire $100,000 increase in contribution margin computed above.

4. Equation method:

$$\text{Sales} = \text{Variable expenses} + \text{Fixed expenses} + \text{Profits}$$

$$\$60Q = \$45Q + \$240,000 + \$90,000$$

$$\$15Q = \$330,000$$

$$Q = \$330,000 \div \$15 \text{ per unit}$$

$$Q = 22,000 \text{ units}$$

Contribution margin method:

$$\frac{\text{Fixed expenses} + \text{Target profit}}{\text{Contribution margin per unit}} = \frac{\$240,000 + \$90,000}{\$15 \text{ per unit}} = 22,000 \text{ units}$$

5. Margin of safety in dollars = Total sales − Break-even sales

$$= \$1,200,000 - \$960,000 = \$240,000$$

$$\text{Margin of safety percentage} = \frac{\text{Margin of safety in dollars}}{\text{Total sales}} = \frac{\$240,000}{\$1,200,000} = 20\%$$

6. a. Degree of operating leverage $= \dfrac{\text{Contribution margin}}{\text{Net operating income}} = \dfrac{\$300,000}{\$60,000} = 5$

b.

Expected increase in sales	8%
Degree of operating leverage	×5
Expected increase in net operating income	40%

c. If sales increase by 8%, then 21,600 units (20,000 × 1.08 = 21,600) will be sold next year. The new contribution format income statement would be as follows:

	Total	Per Unit	Percent of Sales
Sales (21,600 units)	$1,296,000	$60	100%
Variable expenses	972,000	45	75
Contribution margin	324,000	$15	25%
Fixed expenses	240,000		
Net operating income	$ 84,000		

Thus, the $84,000 expected net operating income for next year represents a 40% increase over the $60,000 net operating income earned during the current year:

$$\frac{\$84,000 - \$60,000}{\$60,000} = \frac{\$24,000}{\$60,000} = 40\% \text{ increase}$$

Note from the income statement above that the increase in sales from 20,000 to 21,600 units has increased *both* total sales and total variable expenses. It is a common error to overlook the increase in variable expenses when preparing a projected contribution format income statement.

7. a.   A 20% increase in sales would result in 24,000 units being sold next year: 20,000 units × 1.20 = 24,000 units.

	Total	Per Unit	Percent of Sales
Sales (24,000 units)	$1,440,000	$60	100%
Variable expenses	1,152,000	48*	80
Contribution margin	288,000	$12	20%
Fixed expenses	210,000†		
Net operating income	$ 78,000		

*$45 + $3 = $48; $48 ÷ $60 = 80%.
†$240,000 − $30,000 = $210,000.

Note that the change in per unit variable expenses results in a change in both the per unit contribution margin and the CM ratio.

b.

$$\text{Break-even point in unit sales} = \frac{\text{Fixed expenses}}{\text{Unit contribution margin}}$$

$$= \frac{\$210,000}{\$12 \text{ per unit}} = 17,500 \text{ units}$$

$$\text{Break-even point in dollar sales} = \frac{\text{Fixed expenses}}{\text{CM ratio}}$$

$$= \frac{\$210,000}{0.20} = \$1,050,000$$

c.   Yes, based on these data the changes should be made. The changes increase the company's net operating income from the present $60,000 to $78,000 per year. Although the changes also result in a higher break-even point (17,500 units as compared to the present 16,000 units), the company's margin of safety actually becomes greater than before:

$$\text{Margin of safety in dollars} = \text{Total sales} - \text{Break-even sales}$$

$$= \$1,440,000 - \$1,050,000 = \$390,000$$

As shown in (5) above, the company's present margin of safety is only $240,000. Thus, several benefits will result from the proposed changes.

GLOSSARY

Break-even point   The level of sales at which profit is zero. The break-even point can also be defined as the point where total sales equals total expenses or as the point where total contribution margin equals total fixed expenses. (p. 242)

Contribution margin method   A method of computing the break-even point in which the fixed expenses are divided by the contribution margin per unit. (p. 252)

Contribution margin ratio (CM ratio)   A ratio computed by dividing contribution margin by dollar sales. (p. 245)

Cost-volume-profit (CVP) graph   A graphical representation of the relationships between an organization's revenues, costs, and profits on the one hand and its sales volume on the other hand. (p. 243)

Degree of operating leverage   A measure, at a given level of sales, of how a percentage change in sales will affect profits. The degree of operating leverage is computed by dividing contribution margin by net operating income. (p. 257)

Equation method   A method of computing the break-even point that relies on the equation Sales = Variable expenses + Fixed expenses + Profits. (p. 250)

Incremental analysis   An analytical approach that focuses only on those costs and revenues that change as a result of a decision. (p. 246)

Margin of safety   The excess of budgeted (or actual) dollar sales over the break-even dollar sales. (p. 254)

Operating leverage   A measure of how sensitive net operating income is to a given percentage change in dollar sales. It is computed by dividing the contribution margin by net operating income. (p. 256)

Sales mix   The relative proportions in which a company's products are sold. Sales mix is computed by expressing the sales of each product as a percentage of total sales. (p. 259)

Variable expense ratio   A ratio computed by dividing variable expenses by dollar sales (p. 251)

Quiz 1   Multiple-choice questions are provided on the text website at www.mhhe.com/brewer4e.

QUESTIONS

6–1   What is meant by a product's contribution margin ratio? How is this ratio useful in planning business operations?

6–2   Often the most direct route to a business decision is to make an incremental analysis based on the information available. What is meant by an *incremental analysis*?

6–3   Company A's costs are mostly variable, whereas Company B's costs are mostly fixed. When sales increase, which company will tend to realize the greatest increase in profits? Explain.

6–4   What is meant by the term *operating leverage*?

6–5   What is meant by the term *break-even point*?

6–6   Name three approaches to break-even analysis. Briefly explain how each approach works.

6–7   In response to a request from your immediate supervisor, you have prepared a CVP graph portraying the cost and revenue characteristics of your company's product and operations. Explain how the lines on the graph and the break-even point would change if (a) the selling price per unit decreased, (b) the fixed cost increased throughout the entire range of activity portrayed on the graph, and (c) the variable cost per unit increased.

6–8   What is meant by the margin of safety?

6–9   What is meant by the term *sales mix*? What assumption is usually made concerning sales mix in CVP analysis?

6–10   Explain how a shift in the sales mix could result in both a higher break-even point and a lower net operating income.

BRIEF EXERCISES

BRIEF EXERCISE 6–1   Preparing a Contribution Format Income Statement (LO1)

Wheeler Corporation's most recent income statement is shown below:

	Total	Per Unit
Sales (8,000 units)	$208,000	$26.00
Variable expenses	144,000	18.00
Contribution margin	64,000	$ 8.00
Fixed expenses	56,000	
Net operating income	$ 8,000	

Required:

Prepare a new contribution format income statement under each of the following conditions (consider each case independently):

1. The sales volume increases by 50 units.
2. The sales volume decreases by 50 units.
3. The sales volume is 7,000 units.

BRIEF EXERCISE 6–2   Prepare a Cost-Volume-Profit (CVP) Graph (LO2)

Katara Enterprises has a single product whose selling price is $36 and whose variable cost is $24 per unit. The company's monthly fixed expense is $12,000.

Required:

1. Prepare a cost-volume-profit graph for the company up to a sales level of 2,000 units.
2. Estimate the company's break-even point in unit sales using your cost-volume-profit graph.

BRIEF EXERCISE 6–3   Computing and Using the CM Ratio (LO3)

Last month when Harrison Creations, Inc., sold 40,000 units, total sales were $300,000, total variable expenses were $240,000, and total fixed expenses were $45,000.

Required:
1. What is the company's contribution margin (CM) ratio?
2. Estimate the change in the company's net operating income if it were to increase its total sales by $1,500.

BRIEF EXERCISE 6–4   Changes in Variable Costs, Fixed Costs, Selling Price, and Volume (LO4)

Data for Herron Corporation are shown below:

	Per Unit	Percent of Sales
Selling price	$75	100%
Variable expenses	45	60
Contribution margin	$30	40%

Fixed expenses are $75,000 per month and the company is selling 3,000 units per month.

Required:
1. The marketing manager argues that an $8,000 increase in the monthly advertising budget would increase monthly sales by $15,000. Should the advertising budget be increased?
2. Refer to the original data. Management is considering using higher quality components that would increase the variable cost by $3 per unit. The marketing manager believes the higher quality product would increase sales by 15% per month. Should the higher quality components be used?

BRIEF EXERCISE 6–5   Compute the Break-Even Point (LO5)

Maxson Products has a single product, a woven basket whose selling price is $8 and whose variable cost is $6 per unit. The company's monthly fixed expense is $5,500.

Required:
1. Solve for the company's break-even point in unit sales using the equation method.
2. Solve for the company's break-even point in sales dollars using the equation method and the CM ratio.
3. Solve for the company's break-even point in unit sales using the contribution margin method.
4. Solve for the company's break-even point in sales dollars using the contribution margin method and the CM ratio.

BRIEF EXERCISE 6–6   Compute the Level of Sales Required to Attain a Target Profit (LO6)

Liman Corporation has a single product whose selling price is $140 and whose variable cost is $60 per unit. The company's monthly fixed expense is $40,000.

Required:
1. Using the equation method, solve for the unit sales that are required to earn a target profit of $6,000.
2. Using the contribution margin approach, solve for the dollar sales that are required to earn a target profit of $8,000.

BRIEF EXERCISE 6–7   Compute the Margin of Safety (LO7)

Mohan Corporation distributes a sun umbrella used at resort hotels. Data concerning the next month's budget appear below:

Selling price	$25 per unit
Variable expense	$15 per unit
Fixed expense	$8,500 per month
Unit sales	1,000 units per month

Required:

1. Compute the company's margin of safety.
2. Compute the company's margin of safety as a percentage of its sales.

BRIEF EXERCISE 6–8   Compute and Use the Degree of Operating Leverage (LO8)

Eneliko Company installs home theater systems. The company's most recent monthly contribution format income statement follows:

	Amount	Percent of Sales
Sales	$120,000	100%
Variable expenses	84,000	70
Contribution margin	36,000	30%
Fixed expenses	24,000	
Net operating income	$ 12,000	

Required:

1. Compute the company's degree of operating leverage.
2. Using the degree of operating leverage, estimate the impact on net operating income of a 10% increase in sales.
3. Verify your estimate from part (2) above by constructing a new contribution format income statement for the company assuming a 10% increase in sales.

BRIEF EXERCISE 6–9   Compute the Break-Even Point for a Multiproduct Company (LO9)

Lucky Products markets two computer games: Predator and Runway. A contribution format income statement for a recent month for the two games appears below:

	Predator	Runway	Total
Sales	$100,000	$50,000	$150,000
Variable expenses.	25,000	5,000	30,000
Contribution margin	$ 75,000	$45,000	120,000
Fixed expenses.			90,000
Net operating income			$ 30,000

Required:

1. Compute the overall contribution margin (CM) ratio for the company.
2. Compute the overall break-even point for the company in sales dollars.
3. Verify the overall break-even point for the company by constructing a contribution format income statement showing the appropriate levels of sales for the two products.

EXERCISES

EXERCISE 6–10   Break-Even Analysis and CVP Graphing (LO2, LO4, LO5)

Chi Omega Sorority is planning its annual Riverboat Extravaganza. The Extravaganza committee has assembled the following expected costs for the event:

Dinner (per person)	$7
Favors and program (per person).	$3
Band.	$1,500
Tickets and advertising	$700
Riverboat rental	$4,800
Floorshow and strolling entertainers	$1,000

The committee members would like to charge $30 per person for the evening's activities.

Required:
1. Compute the break-even point for the Extravaganza (in terms of the number of persons who must attend).
2. Assume that last year only 250 persons attended the Extravaganza. If the same number attend this year, what price per ticket must be charged to break even?
3. Refer to the original data ($30 ticket price per person). Prepare a CVP graph for the Extravaganza from a zero level of activity up to 600 tickets sold. Number of persons should be placed on the horizontal (X) axis, and dollars should be placed on the vertical (Y) axis.

EXERCISE 6–11 Using a Contribution Format Income Statement (LO1, LO4)

Porter Company's most recent contribution format income statement is shown below:

	Total	Per Unit
Sales (30,000 units)	$150,000	$5.00
Variable expenses	90,000	3.00
Contribution margin	60,000	$2.00
Fixed expenses	50,000	
Net operating income	$ 10,000	

Required:

Prepare a new contribution format income statement under each of the following conditions (consider each case independently):
1. The number of units sold increases by 15%.
2. The selling price decreases by 50 cents per unit, and the number of units sold increases by 20%.
3. The selling price increases by 50 cents per unit, fixed expenses increase by $10,000, and the number of units sold decreases by 5%.
4. Variable expenses increase by 20 cents per unit, the selling price increases by 12%, and the number of units sold decreases by 10%.

EXERCISE 6–12 Break-Even and Target Profit Analysis (LO3, LO4, LO5, LO6)

Super Sales Company is the exclusive distributor for a revolutionary bookbag that sells for $60 per unit and has a CM ratio of 40%. The company's fixed expenses are $360,000 per year.

Required:
1. What are the variable expenses per unit?
2. Using the equation method:
   a. What is the break-even point in units and in sales dollars?
   b. What sales level in units and in sales dollars is required to earn an annual profit of $90,000?
   c. Assume that through negotiation with the manufacturer the Super Sales Company is able to reduce its variable expenses by $3 per unit. What is the company's new break-even point in units and in sales dollars?
3. Repeat (2) above using the contribution margin method.

EXERCISE 6–13 Break-Even Analysis; Target Profit; Margin of Safety; CM Ratio (LO1, LO3, LO5, LO6, LO7)

Pringle Company distributes a single product. The company's sales and expenses for a recent month follow:

	Total	Per Unit
Sales	$600,000	$40
Variable expenses	420,000	28
Contribution margin	180,000	$12
Fixed expenses	150,000	
Net operating income	$ 30,000	

Required:
1. What is the monthly break-even point in units sold and in sales dollars?
2. Without resorting to computations, what is the total contribution margin at the break-even point?

SCHEDULE 1

	A	B	C	D	E	F
1		**Hampton Freeze, Inc.**				
2		**Sales Budget**				
3		**For the Year Ended December 31, 2008**				
4						
5				*Quarter*		
6		*1*	*2*	*3*	*4*	*Year*
7	Budgeted sales in cases	10,000	30,000	40,000	20,000	100,000
8	Selling price per case	$ 20.00	$ 20.00	$ 20.00	$ 20.00	$ 20.00
9	Total sales	$200,000	$600,000	$800,000	$400,000	$2,000,000
10						
11	Percentage of sales collected in the period of the sale		70%			
12	Percentage of sales collected in the period after the sale		30%			
13		70%	30%			
14		**Schedule of Expected Cash Collections**				
15	Accounts receivable, beginning balance[1]	$ 90,000				$ 90,000
16	First-quarter sales[2]	140,000	$ 60,000			200,000
17	Second-quarter sales[3]		420,000	$180,000		600,000
18	Third-quarter sales[4]			560,000	$240,000	800,000
19	Fourth-quarter sales[5]	-	-	-	280,000	280,000
20	Total cash collections[6]	$230,000	$480,000	$740,000	$520,000	$1,970,000
21						
22						

[1]Cash collections from last year's fourth-quarter sales. See the beginning-of-year balance sheet on page 306.

[2]$200,000 × 70%; $200,000 × 30%.

[3]$600,000 × 70%; $600,000 × 30%.

[4]$800,000 × 70%; $800,000 × 30%.

[5]$400,000 × 70%.

[6]Uncollected fourth-quarter sales appear as accounts receivable on the company's end-of-year balance sheet (see Schedule 10 on page 307).

Note that production requirements are influenced by the desired level of the ending inventory. Inventories should be carefully planned. Excessive inventories tie up funds and create storage problems. Insufficient inventories can lead to lost sales or last-minute, high-cost production efforts. At Hampton Freeze, management believes that an ending inventory equal to 20% of the next quarter's sales strikes the appropriate balance.

Schedule 2 contains the production budget for Hampton Freeze. The first row in the production budget contains the budgeted sales, which have been taken directly from the sales budget (Schedule 1). The total needs for the first quarter are determined by adding together the budgeted sales of 10,000 cases for the quarter and the desired ending inventory of 6,000 cases. As discussed above, the ending inventory is intended to provide some cushion in case problems develop in production or sales increase unexpectedly. Since the budgeted sales for the second quarter are 30,000 cases and management would

SCHEDULE 2

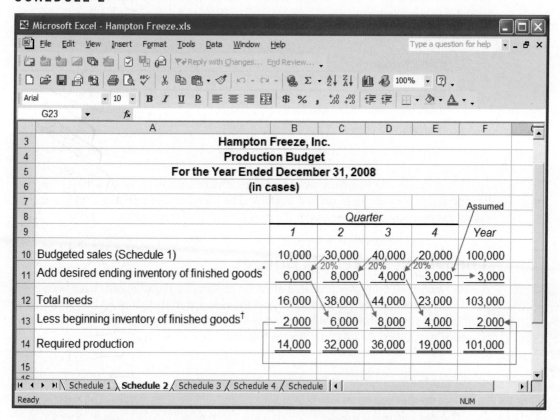

*Twenty percent of the next quarter's sales. The ending inventory of 3,000 cases is assumed.

†The beginning inventory in each quarter is the same as the prior quarter's ending inventory.

like the ending inventory in each quarter to equal 20% of the following quarter's sales, the desired ending inventory is 6,000 cases (20% of 30,000 cases). Consequently, the total needs for the first quarter are 16,000 cases. However, since the company already has 2,000 cases in beginning inventory, only 14,000 cases need to be produced in the first quarter.

Pay particular attention to the Year column to the right of the production budget in Schedule 2. In some cases (e.g., budgeted sales and required production), the amount listed for the year is the sum of the quarterly amounts for the item. In other cases (e.g., desired ending inventory of finished goods and beginning inventory of finished goods), the amount listed for the year is not simply the sum of the quarterly amounts. From the standpoint of the entire year, the beginning finished goods inventory is the same as the beginning finished goods inventory for the first quarter—it is *not* the sum of the beginning finished goods inventories for all quarters. Similarly, from the standpoint of the entire year, the ending finished goods inventory is the same as the ending finished goods inventory for the fourth quarter—it is *not* the sum of the ending finished goods inventories for all four quarters. It is important to pay attention to such distinctions in all of the schedules that follow.

Inventory Purchases—Merchandising Company

Hampton Freeze prepares a production budget because it is a *manufacturing* company. If it were a *merchandising* company, it would prepare instead a **merchandise purchases budget** showing the amount of goods to be purchased from suppliers during the period.

The merchandise purchases budget follows the same basic format as the production budget, as shown below:

Budgeted sales	XXXXX
Add desired ending merchandise inventory	XXXXX
Total needs	XXXXX
Less beginning merchandise inventory	XXXXX
Required purchases	XXXXX

A merchandising company would prepare a merchandise purchases budget such as the one above for each item carried in stock. The merchandise purchases budget can be expressed in terms of either units or the purchase cost of those units.

The Direct Materials Budget

A *direct materials budget* is prepared after the production requirements have been computed. The **direct materials budget** details the raw materials that must be purchased to fulfill the production budget and to provide for adequate inventories. The required purchases of raw materials are computed as follows:

Raw materials needed to meet the production schedule	XXXXX
Add desired ending inventory of raw materials	XXXXX
Total raw materials needs	XXXXX
Less beginning inventory of raw materials	XXXXX
Raw materials to be purchased	XXXXX

Schedule 3 contains the direct materials budget for Hampton Freeze. The only raw material included in that budget is high fructose sugar, which is the major ingredient in popsicles other than water. The remaining raw materials are relatively insignificant and are included in variable manufacturing overhead. As with finished goods, management would like to maintain some raw materials inventories to act as a cushion in case of supply disruptions or other potential problems. In this case, management would like to maintain ending inventories of sugar equal to 10% of the following quarter's production needs.

The first line in the direct materials budget contains the required production for each quarter, which is taken directly from the production budget (Schedule 2). Looking at the first quarter, since the production schedule calls for production of 14,000 cases of popsicles and each case requires 15 pounds of sugar, the total production needs are 210,000 pounds of sugar (14,000 cases × 15 pounds per case). In addition, management wants to have ending inventories of 48,000 pounds of sugar, which is 10% of the following quarter's needs of 480,000 pounds. Consequently, the total needs are 258,000 pounds (210,000 pounds for the current quarter's production plus 48,000 pounds for the desired ending inventory). However, since the company already has 21,000 pounds in beginning inventory, only 237,000 pounds of sugar (258,000 pounds − 21,000 pounds) will need to be purchased. Finally, the cost of the raw materials purchases is determined by multiplying the amount of raw material to be purchased by its unit cost. In this case, since 237,000 pounds of sugar will need to be purchased during the first quarter and sugar costs $0.20 per pound, the total cost will be $47,400 (237,000 pounds × $0.20 per pound).

SCHEDULE 3

					Assumed
	Hampton Freeze, Inc.				
	Direct Materials Budget				
	For the Year Ended December 31, 2008				
			Quarter		
	1	**2**	**3**	**4**	**Year**
Required production in cases (Schedule 2)	14,000	32,000	36,000	19,000	101,000
Raw materials needed per case (pounds)	15	15	15	15	15
Production needs (pounds)	210,000	480,000	540,000	285,000	1,515,000
Add desired ending inventory of raw materials[1]	48,000	54,000	28,500	22,500	22,500
Total needs	258,000	534,000	568,500	307,500	1,537,500
Less beginning inventory of raw materials	21,000	48,000	54,000	28,500	21,000
Raw materials to be purchased	237,000	486,000	514,500	279,000	1,516,500
Cost of raw materials per pound	$ 0.20	$ 0.20	$ 0.20	$ 0.20	$ 0.20
Cost of raw materials to be purchased	$ 47,400	$ 97,200	$ 102,900	$ 55,800	$ 303,300
Percentage of purchases paid for in the period of the purchase			50%		
Percentage of purchases paid for in the period after purchase			50%		
	50%	50%			
Schedule of Expected Cash Disbursements for Materials					
Accounts payable, beginning balance[2]	$ 25,800				$ 25,800
First-quarter purchases[3]	23,700	$ 23,700			47,400
Second-quarter purchases[4]		48,600	$ 48,600		97,200
Third-quarter purchases[5]			51,450	$ 51,450	102,900
Fourth-quarter purchases[6]	-	-	-	27,900	27,900
Total cash disbursements for materials	$ 49,500	$ 72,300	$ 100,050	$ 79,350	$ 301,200

[1]Ten percent of the next quarter's production needs. For example, the second-quarter production needs are 480,000 pounds. Therefore, the desired ending inventory for the first quarter would be 10% × 480,000 pounds = 48,000 pounds. The ending inventory of 22,500 pounds for the fourth quarter is assumed.

[2]Cash payments for last year's fourth-quarter material purchases. See the beginning-of-year balance sheet on page 306.

[3]$47,400 × 50%; $47,400 × 50%.

[4]$97,200 × 50%; $97,200 × 50%.

[5]$102,900 × 50%; $102,900 × 50%.

[6]$55,800 × 50%. Unpaid fourth-quarter purchases appear as accounts payable on the company's end-of-year balance sheet.

As with the production budget, the amounts listed under the Year column are not always the sum of the quarterly amounts. The desired ending raw materials inventory for the year is the same as the desired ending raw materials inventory for the fourth quarter. Likewise, the beginning raw materials inventory for the year is the same as the beginning raw materials inventory for the first quarter.

The direct materials budget (or the merchandise purchases budget for a merchandising company) is usually accompanied by a schedule of expected cash disbursements for raw materials (or merchandise purchases). This schedule is needed to prepare the overall cash budget. Disbursements for raw materials (or merchandise purchases) consist of payments for purchases on account in prior periods plus any payments for purchases in the current budget period. Schedule 3 contains such a schedule of cash disbursements for Hampton Freeze.

Ordinarily, companies do not immediately pay their suppliers. At Hampton Freeze, the policy is to pay for 50% of purchases in the quarter in which the purchase is made and 50% in the following quarter, so while the company intends to purchase $47,400 worth of sugar in the first quarter, the company will only pay for half, $23,700, in the first quarter and the other half will be paid in the second quarter. The company will also pay $25,800 in the first quarter for sugar that was purchased on account in the previous quarter, but not yet paid for. This is the beginning balance in the accounts payable. Therefore, the total cash disbursements for sugar in the first quarter are $49,500—the $25,800 payment for sugar acquired in the previous quarter plus the $23,700 payment for sugar acquired during the first quarter.

The Direct Labor Budget

The **direct labor budget** shows the direct labor-hours required to satisfy the production budget. By knowing in advance how much labor time will be needed throughout the budget year, the company can develop plans to adjust the labor force as the situation requires. Companies that neglect to budget run the risk of facing labor shortages or having to hire and lay off workers at awkward times. Erratic labor policies lead to insecurity, low morale, and inefficiency.

The direct labor budget for Hampton Freeze is shown in Schedule 4. The first line in the direct labor budget consists of the required production for each quarter, which is taken directly from the production budget (Schedule 2). The direct labor requirement for each quarter is computed by multiplying the number of units to be produced in that quarter by the number of direct labor-hours required to make a unit. For example, 14,000 cases are to be produced in the first quarter and each case requires 0.40 direct labor-hours, so a total

SCHEDULE 4

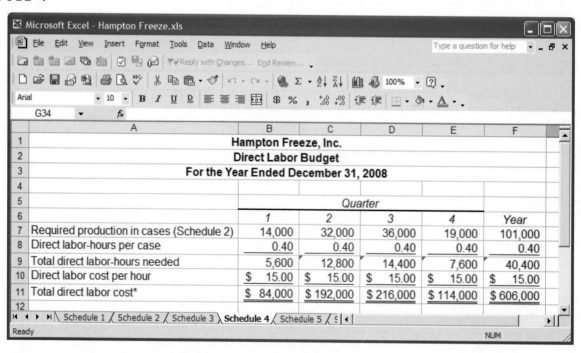

Hampton Freeze, Inc.
Direct Labor Budget
For the Year Ended December 31, 2008

	Quarter				
	1	2	3	4	Year
7 Required production in cases (Schedule 2)	14,000	32,000	36,000	19,000	101,000
8 Direct labor-hours per case	0.40	0.40	0.40	0.40	0.40
9 Total direct labor-hours needed	5,600	12,800	14,400	7,600	40,400
10 Direct labor cost per hour	$ 15.00	$ 15.00	$ 15.00	$ 15.00	$ 15.00
11 Total direct labor cost*	$ 84,000	$ 192,000	$ 216,000	$ 114,000	$ 606,000

*This schedule assumes that the direct labor workforce will be fully adjusted to the total direct labor-hours needed each quarter.

of 5,600 direct labor-hours (14,000 cases × 0.40 direct labor-hours per case) will be required in the first quarter. The direct labor requirements can then be translated into budgeted direct labor costs. How this is done will depend on the company's labor policy. In Schedule 4, Hampton Freeze has assumed that the direct labor force will be adjusted as the work requirements change from quarter to quarter. In that case, the direct labor cost is computed by simply multiplying the direct labor-hour requirements by the direct labor rate per hour. For example, the direct labor cost in the first quarter is $84,000 (5,600 direct labor-hours × $15 per direct labor-hour).

However, many companies have employment policies or contracts that prevent them from laying off and rehiring workers as needed. Suppose, for example, that Hampton Freeze has 25 workers who are classified as direct labor, but each of them is guaranteed at least 480 hours of pay each quarter at a rate of $15 per hour. In that case, the minimum direct labor cost for a quarter would be computed as follows:

$$25 \text{ workers} \times 480 \text{ hours per worker} \times \$15 \text{ per hour} = \$180,000$$

Note that in this case the direct labor costs for the first and fourth quarters would have to be increased to $180,000.

The Manufacturing Overhead Budget

The **manufacturing overhead budget** lists all costs of production other than direct materials and direct labor. Schedule 5 shows the manufacturing overhead budget for Hampton Freeze. At Hampton Freeze, manufacturing overhead is separated into variable and fixed components. The variable component is $4 per direct labor-hour and the fixed component is $60,600 per quarter. Because the variable component of manufacturing overhead depends on direct labor, the first line in the manufacturing overhead budget consists of the budgeted direct labor-hours from the direct labor budget (Schedule 4). The budgeted

> **LEARNING OBJECTIVE 6**
>
> Prepare a manufacturing overhead budget.

SCHEDULE 5

Microsoft Excel - Hampton Freeze.xls

Hampton Freeze, Inc.
Manufacturing Overhead Budget
For the Year Ended December 31, 2008

	A		Quarter				Year
			1	2	3	4	
7	Budgeted direct labor-hours (Schedule 4)		5,600	12,800	14,400	7,600	40,400
8	Variable manufacturing overhead rate		$ 4.00	$ 4.00	$ 4.00	$ 4.00	$ 4.00
9	Variable manufacturing overhead		$ 22,400	$ 51,200	$ 57,600	$ 30,400	$ 161,600
10	Fixed manufacturing overhead		60,600	60,600	60,600	60,600	242,400
11	Total manufacturing overhead		83,000	111,800	118,200	91,000	404,000
12	Less depreciation		15,000	15,000	15,000	15,000	60,000
13	Cash disbursements for manufacturing overhead		$ 68,000	$ 96,800	$ 103,200	$ 76,000	$ 344,000
14							
15	Total manufacturing overhead (a)						$ 404,000
16	Budgeted direct labor-hours (b)						40,400
17	Predetermined overhead rate for the year (a)÷(b)						$ 10.00

Schedule 5 / Schedule 6 / Schedule 7 / Schedule 8 / Schedule 9 / Sched

direct labor-hours in each quarter are multiplied by the variable rate to determine the variable component of manufacturing overhead. For example, the variable manufacturing overhead for the first quarter is $22,400 (5,600 direct labor-hours × $4.00 per direct labor-hour). This is added to the fixed manufacturing overhead for the quarter to determine the total manufacturing overhead for the quarter of $83,000 ($22,400 + $60,600).

A few words about fixed costs and the budgeting process are in order. In most cases, fixed costs are the costs of supplying capacity to make products, process purchase orders, handle customer calls, and so on. The amount of capacity that will be required depends on the expected level of activity for the period. If the expected level of activity is greater than the company's current capacity, then fixed costs may have to be increased. Or, if the expected level of activity is appreciably below the company's current capacity, then it may be desirable to decrease fixed costs if possible. However, once the level of the fixed costs has been determined in the budget, the costs really are fixed. The time to adjust fixed costs is during the budgeting process. An activity-based costing system can help to determine the appropriate level of fixed costs at budget time by answering questions like, "How many clerks will we need to hire to process the anticipated number of purchase orders next year?" For simplicity, all of the budgeting examples in this book assume that the appropriate levels of fixed costs have already been determined.

The last line of Schedule 5 for Hampton Freeze shows its budgeted cash disbursements for manufacturing overhead. Since some of the overhead costs are not cash outflows, the total budgeted manufacturing overhead costs must be adjusted to determine the cash disbursements for manufacturing overhead. At Hampton Freeze, the only significant noncash manufacturing overhead cost is depreciation, which is $15,000 per quarter. These noncash depreciation charges are deducted from the total budgeted manufacturing overhead to determine the expected cash disbursements. Hampton Freeze pays all overhead costs involving cash disbursements in the quarter incurred. Note that the company's predetermined overhead rate for the year is $10 per direct labor-hour, which is determined by dividing the total budgeted manufacturing overhead for the year by the total budgeted direct labor-hours for the year.

The Ending Finished Goods Inventory Budget

After completing Schedules 1–5, all of the data needed to compute unit product costs have been compiled. The unit product costs are needed for two reasons: first, to determine cost of goods sold on the budgeted income statement; and second, to determine the value of ending inventory on the balance sheet. The carrying cost of unsold units is computed on the **ending finished goods inventory budget.**

The new financial manager considered using variable costing to prepare Hampton Freeze's budget statements, but she decided to use absorption costing instead because the bank would very likely require absorption costing financial statements. She also knew that it would be easy to convert the absorption costing financial statements to a variable costing basis later. At this point, the primary concern was to determine what financing, if any, would be required in 2008 and then to arrange for that financing from the bank.

The unit product cost computations are shown in Schedule 6. For Hampton Freeze, the absorption costing unit product cost is $13 per case of popsicles—consisting of $3 of direct materials, $6 of direct labor, and $4 of manufacturing overhead. Manufacturing overhead is applied to units of product at the rate of $10 per direct labor-hour. The budgeted carrying cost of the ending inventory is $39,000.

The Selling and Administrative Expense Budget

LEARNING OBJECTIVE 7

Prepare a selling and administrative expense budget.

The **selling and administrative expense budget** lists the budgeted expenses for areas other than manufacturing. In large organizations, this budget would be a compilation of many smaller, individual budgets submitted by department heads and other persons responsible for selling and administrative expenses. For example, the marketing manager would submit a budget detailing the advertising expenses for each budget period.

SCHEDULE 6

Microsoft Excel - Hampton Freeze.xls

File Edit View Insert Format Tools Data Window Help

	A	B	C	D	E	F	G	H
1			Hampton Freeze, Inc.					
2			Ending Finished Goods Inventory Budget					
3			(absorption costing basis)					
4			For the Year Ended December 31, 2008					
5								
6	Item	Quantity			Cost			Total
7	Production cost per case:							
8	Direct materials	15.00	pounds		$ 0.20	per pound		$ 3.00
9	Direct labor	0.40	hours		$15.00	per hour		6.00
10	Manufacturing overhead	0.40	hours		$10.00	per hour		4.00
11	Unit product cost							$ 13.00
12								
13	Budgeted finished goods inventory:							
14	Ending finished goods inventory in cases (Schedule 2)							3,000
15	Unit product cost (see above)							$ 13.00
16	Ending finished goods inventory in dollars							$ 39,000
17								

Schedule 5 \ Schedule 6 / Schedule 7 / Schedule 8 / Schedule

Ready   NUM

Schedule 7 contains the selling and administrative expense budget for Hampton Freeze. Like the manufacturing overhead budget, the selling and administrative expense budget is divided into variable and fixed cost components. In the case of Hampton Freeze, the variable selling and administrative expense is $1.80 per case. Consequently, budgeted sales in cases for each quarter are entered at the top of the schedule. These data are taken from the sales budget (Schedule 1). The budgeted variable selling and administrative expenses are determined by multiplying the budgeted cases sold by the variable selling and administrative expense per case. For example, the budgeted variable selling and administrative expense for the first quarter is $18,000 (10,000 cases × $1.80 per case). The fixed selling and administrative expenses (all given data) are then added to the variable selling and administrative expenses to arrive at the total budgeted selling and administrative expenses. Finally, to determine the cash disbursements for selling and administrative expenses, the total budgeted selling and administrative expense is adjusted by subtracting any noncash selling and administrative expenses (in this case, just depreciation).

Budget Analyst   YOU DECIDE

You have been hired as a budget analyst by a regional chain of Italian restaurants with attached bars. Management has had difficulty in the past predicting some of its costs; the assumption has always been that all operating costs are variable with respect to gross restaurant sales. What would you suggest doing to improve the accuracy of the budget forecasts?

SCHEDULE 7

Microsoft Excel - Hampton Freeze.xls

File Edit View Insert Format Tools Data Window Help

Type a question for help

Arial   10   B I U

J34

	A	B	C	D	E	F
1		Hampton Freeze, Inc.				
2		Selling and Administrative Expense Budget				
3		For the Year Ended December 31, 2008				
4						
5			Quarter			
6		1	2	3	4	Year
7	Budgeted sales in cases (Schedule 1)	10,000	30,000	40,000	20,000	100,000
8	Variable selling and administrative expense per case	$ 1.80	$ 1.80	$ 1.80	$ 1.80	$ 1.80
9	Variable selling and administrative expense	$ 18,000	$ 54,000	$ 72,000	$ 36,000	$180,000
10	Fixed selling and administrative expenses:					
11	Advertising	20,000	20,000	20,000	20,000	80,000
12	Executive salaries	55,000	55,000	55,000	55,000	220,000
13	Insurance	10,000	10,000	10,000	10,000	40,000
14	Property taxes	4,000	4,000	4,000	4,000	16,000
15	Depreciation	10,000	10,000	10,000	10,000	40,000
16	Total fixed selling and administrative expenses	99,000	99,000	99,000	99,000	396,000
17	Total selling and administrative expenses	117,000	153,000	171,000	135,000	576,000
18	Less depreciation	10,000	10,000	10,000	10,000	40,000
19	Cash disbursements for selling and administrative expenses	$107,000	$143,000	$161,000	$125,000	$536,000
20						

Schedule 5 / Schedule 6 \ Schedule 7 / Schedule 8 / Schedule 9 / Schedule 10

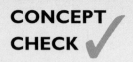

CONCEPT CHECK ✓

1. If a company has a beginning merchandise inventory of $50,000, a desired ending merchandise inventory of $30,000, and a budgeted cost of goods sold of $300,000, what is the amount of required inventory purchases?
   a. $320,000
   c. $380,000
   b. $280,000
   d. $300,000

2. Budgeted unit sales for March, April, and May are 75,000, 80,000, and 90,000 units. Management desires to maintain an ending inventory equal to 30% of the next month's unit sales. How many units should be produced in April?
   a. 80,000 units
   c. 77,000 units
   b. 83,000 units
   d. 85,000 units

IN BUSINESS

Keeping Current

Jim Bell, Hunstman Corp.'s director of corporate finance, says that his company must frequently update its budgets and its forecasts to meet the demands of investors, creditors, and others. The company updates its annual budget each month, using the most recent data, to provide greater accuracy as the year unfolds. The budget is also used together with sophisticated modeling software to evaluate what effects decisions and various changes in input prices and other parameters might have on future results.

Source: Tim Reason, "Partial Clearing," *CFO*, December 2002, pp. 73–76.

The Cash Budget

As illustrated in Exhibit 7–2, the cash budget combines much of the data developed in the preceding steps. It is a good idea to review Exhibit 7–2 to get the big picture firmly in mind before moving on.

The cash budget is composed of four major sections:

1. The receipts section.
2. The disbursements section.
3. The cash excess or deficiency section.
4. The financing section.

Topic Tackler

PLUS

Concept 7-2

The receipts section lists all of the cash inflows, except from financing, expected during the budget period. Generally, the major source of receipts are from sales.

The disbursements section summarizes all cash payments that are planned for the budget period. These payments include raw materials purchases, direct labor payments, manufacturing overhead costs, and so on, as contained in their respective budgets. In addition, other cash disbursements such as equipment purchases and dividends are listed.

The cash excess or deficiency section is computed as follows:

Cash balance, beginning	XXXX
Add receipts	XXXX
Total cash available	XXXX
Less disbursements	XXXX
Excess (deficiency) of cash available over disbursements	XXXX

If a cash deficiency exists during any budget period, the company will need to borrow funds. If there is a cash excess during any budget period, funds borrowed in previous periods can be repaid or the excess funds can be invested.

The financing section details the borrowings and repayments projected to take place during the budget period. It also lists interest payments that will be due on money borrowed.[1]

The cash balances at both the beginning and end of the year may be adequate even though a serious cash deficit occurs at some point during the year. Consequently, the cash budget should be broken down into time periods that are short enough to capture major fluctuations in cash balances. While a monthly cash budget is most common, some organizations budget cash on a weekly or even daily basis. Larry Giano has prepared a quarterly cash budget for Hampton Freeze that can be further refined as necessary. This budget appears in Schedule 8. The cash budget builds on the earlier schedules and on additional data that are provided below:

- The beginning cash balance is $42,500.

- Management plans to spend $130,000 during the year on equipment purchases: $50,000 in the first quarter; $40,000 in the second quarter; $20,000 in the third quarter; and $20,000 in the fourth quarter.

- The board of directors has approved cash dividends of $8,000 per quarter.

- Management would like to have a cash balance of at least $30,000 at the beginning of each quarter for contingencies.

- Hampton Freeze has an agreement with a local bank that allows the company to borrow in increments of $10,000 at the beginning of each quarter, up to a total loan balance of $250,000. The interest rate on these loans is 1% per month and for simplicity we will assume that interest is not compounded. The company would, as far as it is able, repay the loan plus accumulated interest at the end of the year.

---

[1]The format for the statement of cash flows, which is discussed in Chapter 13, may also be used for the cash budget.

SCHEDULE 8

	Microsoft Excel - Hampton Freeze.xls							
	File Edit View Insert Format Tools Data Window Help							

	A	B	C	D	E	F	G	H
1	Hampton Freeze, Inc.							
2	Cash Budget							
3	For the Year Ended December 31, 2008							
4								
5					Quarter			
6		Schedule	1	2	3	4	Year	
7	Cash balance, beginning		$42,500	$36,000	$ 33,900	$165,650	$ 42,500	
8	Add receipts:							
9	Collections from customers	1	230,000	480,000	740,000	520,000	1,970,000	
10	Total cash available		272,500	516,000	773,900	685,650	2,012,500	
11	Less disbursements:							
12	Direct materials	3	49,500	72,300	100,050	79,350	301,200	
13	Direct labor	4	84,000	192,000	216,000	114,000	606,000	
14	Manufacturing overhead	5	68,000	96,800	103,200	76,000	344,000	
15	Selling and administrative	7	107,000	143,000	161,000	125,000	536,000	
16	Equipment purchases		50,000	40,000	20,000	20,000	130,000	
17	Dividends		8,000	8,000	8,000	8,000	32,000	
18	Total disbursements		366,500	552,100	608,250	422,350	1,949,200	
19	Excess (deficiency) of cash available over disbursements		(94,000)	(36,100)	165,650	263,300	63,300	
20	Financing:							
21	Borrowings (at the beginnings of quarters)		130,000	70,000	-	-	200,000	
22	Repayments (at end of the year)		-	-	-	(200,000)	(200,000)	
23	Interest		-	-	-	(21,900)	(21,900)	
24	Total financing		130,000	70,000	-	(221,900)	(21,900)	
25	Cash balance, ending		$36,000	$33,900	$165,650	$ 41,400	$ 41,400	
26								
27								

Schedule 3 / Schedule 4 / Schedule 5 / Schedule 6 / Schedule 7 \ **Schedule 8** / Sche

The cash budget is prepared one quarter at a time, starting with the first quarter. The cash budget was begun by entering the beginning balance of cash for the first quarter of $42,500—a number that is given above. Receipts—in this case, just the $230,000 in cash collections from customers—are added to the beginning balance to arrive at the total cash available of $272,500. Because the total disbursements are 366,500 and the total cash available is only $272,500, there is a shortfall of 94,000. Because management would like to have a beginning cash balance of at least $30,000 for the second quarter, the company will need to borrow at least $124,000.

Required Borrowings at the Beginning of the First Quarter	
Desired ending cash balance.	$ 30,000
Plus deficiency of cash available over disbursements	94,000
Minimum required borrowings	$124,000

Recall that the bank requires that loans be made in increments of $10,000. Because Hampton Freeze needs to borrow at least $124,000, it will have to borrow $130,000.

The second quarter of the cash budget is handled similarly. Note that the ending cash balance for the first quarter is brought forward as the beginning cash balance for the second quarter. Also note that additional borrowing is required in the second quarter because of the continued cash shortfall.

Required Borrowings at the Beginning of the Second Quarter	
Desired ending cash balance.	$30,000
Plus deficiency of cash available over disbursements	36,100
Minimum required borrowings	$66,100

Again, recall that the bank requires that loans be made in increments of $10,000. Because Hampton Freeze needs to borrow at least $66,100 at the beginning of the second quarter, the company will have to borrow $70,000 from the bank.

In the third quarter, the cash flow situation improves dramatically and the excess of cash available over disbursements is $165,650. Therefore, the company will end the quarter with ample cash and no further borrowing is necessary.

At the end of the fourth quarter, the loan and accumulated interest must be repaid. The accumulated interest can be computed as follows:

Interest on $130,000 borrowed at the beginning of the first quarter:	
$130,000 × 0.01 per month × 12 months*	$15,600
Interest on $70,000 borrowed at the beginning of the second quarter:	
$70,000 × 0.01 per month × 9 months*	6,300
Total interest accrued to the end of the fourth quarter	$21,900

*Simple, rather than compounded, interest is assumed for simplicity.

Note that the loan repayment of $200,000 (=$130,000 + $70,000) appears in the financing section for the fourth quarter along with the interest payment of $21,900 computed above.

As with the production and direct materials budgets, the amounts under the Year column in the cash budget are not always the sum of the amounts for the four quarters. In particular, the beginning cash balance for the year is the same as the beginning cash balance for the first quarter, and the ending cash balance for the year is the same as the ending cash balance for the fourth quarter. Also note the beginning cash balance in any quarter is the same as the ending cash balance for the previous quarter.

The Budgeted Income Statement

A budgeted income statement can be prepared from the data developed in Schedules 1–8. *The budgeted income statement is one of the key schedules in the budget process.* It shows the company's planned profit, and serves as a benchmark to compare to subsequent performance.

Schedule 9 contains the budgeted income statement for Hampton Freeze.

LEARNING OBJECTIVE 9

Prepare a budgeted income statement.

SCHEDULE 9

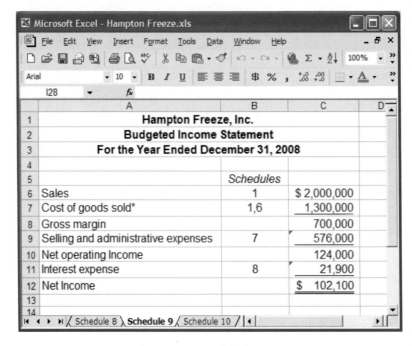

*100,000 cases sold × $13 per case = $1,300,000.

The Budgeted Balance Sheet

The budgeted balance sheet is developed using data from the balance sheet from the beginning of the budget period and data contained in the various schedules. Hampton Freeze's budgeted balance sheet is presented in Schedule 10. Some of the data on the budgeted balance sheet have been taken from the company's previous end-of-year balance sheet for 2007, which appears below:

Hampton Freeze, Inc.
Balance Sheet
December 31, 2007

Assets

Current assets:		
Cash...	$ 42,500	
Accounts receivable	90,000	
Raw materials inventory (21,000 pounds) ...	4,200	
Finished goods inventory (2,000 cases).....	26,000	
Total current assets		$162,700
Plant and equipment:		
Land	80,000	
Buildings and equipment	700,000	
Accumulated depreciation	(292,000)	
Plant and equipment, net...................		488,000
Total assets		$650,700

Liabilities and Stockholders' Equity

Current liabilities:		
Accounts payable (raw materials)...........		$ 25,800
Stockholders' equity:		
Common stock, no par	$175,000	
Retained earnings	449,900	
Total stockholders' equity		624,900
Total liabilities and stockholders' equity ..		$650,700

SCHEDULE 10

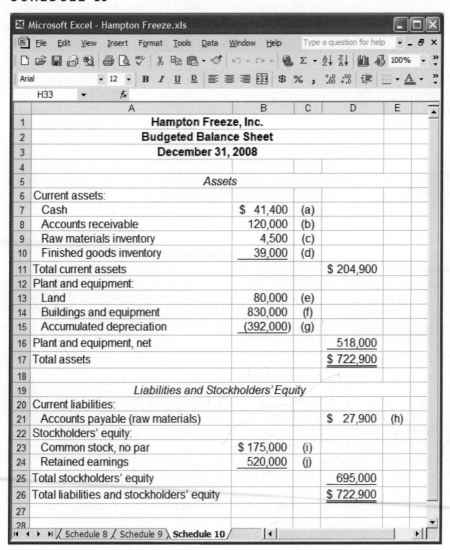

Explanation of December 31, 2008, balance sheet figures:

(a) The ending cash balance, as projected by the cash budget in Schedule 8.

(b) Thirty percent of fourth-quarter sales, from Schedule 1 ($400,000 × 30% = $120,000).

(c) From Schedule 3, the ending raw materials inventory will be 22,500 pounds. This material costs $0.20 per pound. Therefore, the ending inventory in dollars will be 22,500 pounds × $0.20 = $4,500.

(d) From Schedule 6.

(e) From the December 31, 2007 balance sheet (no change).

(f) The December 31, 2007 balance sheet indicated a balance of $700,000. During 2008, $130,000 of additional equipment will be purchased (see Schedule 8), bringing the December 31, 2008 balance to $830,000.

(g) The December 31, 2007 balance sheet indicated a balance of $292,000. During 2008, $100,000 of depreciation will be taken ($60,000 on Schedule 5 and $40,000 on Schedule 7), bringing the December 31, 2008 balance to $392,000.

(h) One-half of the fourth-quarter raw materials purchases, from Schedule 3.

(i) From the December 31, 2007 balance sheet (no change).

(j) December 31, 2007, balance $449,900
   Add net income, from Schedule 9   102,100
                                                                                  552,000

   Deduct dividends paid, from Schedule 8   32,000
   December 31, 2008, balance $520,000

IN BUSINESS

Cash Crisis at a Start-Up Company

Good Home Co., headquartered in New York City, sells home cleaning and laundry products through merchandisers such as Restoration Hardware and Nordstrom. In 2001, the company's sales were $2.1 million. Then in September 2002, the company's founder Christine Dimmick appeared on the cable shopping network QVC and in a few hours she sold more than $300,000 worth of merchandise. However, euphoria turned to panic when Christine realized that she needed $200,000 in short-term financing to fill those orders. When attempts to renegotiate payment terms with suppliers failed, Christine realized that she needed to hire a finance professional. Jerry Charlup, who was hired as Good Home's part-time CFO, spent $6,000 to create a cash flow forecasting system using Excel. As Good Home's annual sales have grown to $4 million, Charlup says the new forecasting system is giving the company "a far clearer fix on how much operating capital it needs at any given time."

Source: Susan Hansen, "The Rent-To-Own CFO Program," *Inc. magazine*, February 2004, pp. 28–29.

IN BUSINESS

Concentrating on the Cash Flow

Burlington Northern Santa Fe (BNSF) operates the second largest railroad in the United States. The company's senior vice president, CFO, and treasurer is Tom Hunt, who reports that "As a general theme, we've become very cash-flow-oriented." After the merger of the Burlington Northern and Santa Fe railroads, the company went through a number of years in which they were investing heavily and consequently had negative cash flows. To keep on top of the company's cash position, Hunt has a cash forecast prepared every month. "Everything falls like dominoes from free cash flow," Hunt says. "It provides us with alternatives. Right now, the alternative of choice is buying back our own stock . . . [b]ut it could be increasing dividends or making acquisitions. All those things are not even on the radar screen if you don't have free cash flow."

Source: Randy Myers, "Cash Crop: The 2000 Working Capital Survey," *CFO*, August 2000, pp. 59–82.

CONCEPT CHECK ✓

3. March, April, and May sales are $100,000, $120,000, and $125,000, respectively. A total of 80% of all sales are credit sales and 20% are cash sales. A total of 60% of credit sales are collected in the month of the sale and 40% are collected in the next month. There are no bad debt expenses. What is the amount of cash collections for April?
    a. $89,600
    b. $111,600
    c. $113,600
    d. $132,600

4. Referring to the facts in question 3 above, what is the accounts receivable balance at the end of May?
    a. $40,000
    b. $50,000
    c. $72,000
    d. $80,000

Assuming that the company's plans unfold as expected, the master budget indicates that the company will be profitable, its balance sheet will be sound, but that the company will need to borrow in the short term to make payments to employees and suppliers. Armed with these data, the company can approach a bank to arrange for a line of credit or other form of loan. It is much easier to arrange for a loan before it is needed than to show up at the bank begging for a loan in an emergency situation. With the master budget, the company can show the bank a solid plan for repaying any loans. This is not the primary purpose of budgeting. As discussed previously, the primary purposes of budgeting include communicating plans, coordinating efforts, allocating resources, and setting benchmarks. Nevertheless, budgets also help managers uncover potential problems such as cash shortfalls.

Bank Manager

DECISION MAKER

You are the manager of a branch of a state bank located in a medium-sized community. The owner of a small manufacturing company in the community wants to apply for an unsecured line of credit for the upcoming year. The company has been in business for several years but has experienced seasonal cash shortages as it has grown. What documents would you request from the owner to back up the loan request and what tests would you apply to the documents to ensure that they are realistic?

Moving beyond Excel to the Web

IN BUSINESS

While research shows that two-thirds of U.S. companies still rely on Microsoft Excel for their budgeting process, some companies are evolving to a more technologically advanced approach. For example, Hendrick Motorsports has vaulted to the top of the NASCAR racing circuit thanks in part to its new budgeting process. Scott Lampe, Hendrick's CFO, discarded Excel in favor of Forecaster, a Web-based budgeting program. He commented "with a spreadsheet, you can build the model the way you want it. . . . The problem is, only you understand that model. Then you have to explain it to everyone, one at a time." The Web-based approach enables Lampe to involve his crew chiefs, chassis guys, and engine guys in the budgeting process.

The Facilities & Operations (F&O) Business Office of the Battelle, Pacific Northwest National Laboratory has over 130 budget activities—each of which requires the preparation of an annual budget. In 2001, F&O replaced its spreadsheet-driven budget with a Web-based approach. The new system enables F&O "management and their support staff to directly input their business plan and budget requests, eliminating the need for central business planning and budgeting staff to upload the numerous budget requests and subsequent changes." The Web-based budgeting system saves F&O personnel more than 500 hours that were previously spent preparing Excel spreadsheets and uploading data.

Source: John Goff, "In The Fast Lane," *CFO*, December 2004, pp. 53–58; and Peter T. Smith, Craig A. Goranson, and Mary F. Astley, "Intranet Budgeting Does the Trick," *Strategic Finance*, May 2003, pp. 30–33.

SUMMARY

LOI Understand why organizations budget and the processes they use to create budgets.
Organizations budget for a variety of reasons, including to communicate management's plans throughout the organization, to force managers to think about and plan for the future, to allocate resources within the organization, to identify bottlenecks before they occur, to coordinate activities, and to provide benchmarks for evaluating subsequent performance.

Budgets should be developed with the full participation of all managers who will be subject to budgetary controls.

LO2 Prepare a sales budget, including a schedule of expected cash collections.

The sales budget forms the foundation for the master budget. It provides details concerning the anticipated unit and dollar sales.

The schedule of expected cash collections is based on the sales budget, the expected breakdown between cash and credit sales, and the expected pattern of collections on credit sales.

LO3 Prepare a production budget.

The production budget details how many units must be produced each budget period to satisfy expected sales and to provide for adequate levels of finished goods inventories.

LO4 Prepare a direct materials budget, including a schedule of expected cash disbursements for purchases of materials.

The direct materials budget shows the materials that must be purchased each budget period to meet anticipated production requirements and to provide for adequate levels of materials inventories.

Cash disbursements for purchases of materials will depend on the amount of materials purchased in each budget period and the company's policies concerning payments to suppliers for materials bought on credit.

LO5 Prepare a direct labor budget.

The direct labor budget shows the direct labor-hours that are required to meet the production schedule as detailed in the production budget. The direct labor-hour requirements are used to determine the direct labor cost in each budget period.

LO6 Prepare a manufacturing overhead budget.

Manufacturing overhead consists of both variable and fixed manufacturing overhead. The variable manufacturing overhead depends on the number of units produced from the production budget. The variable and fixed manufacturing overhead costs are combined to determine the total manufacturing overhead. Any noncash manufacturing overhead such as depreciation is deducted from the total manufacturing overhead to determine the cash disbursements for manufacturing overhead.

LO7 Prepare a selling and administrative expense budget.

Like manufacturing overhead, selling and administrative expenses consist of both variable and fixed expenses. The variable expenses depend on the number of units sold or some other measure of activity. The variable and fixed expenses are combined to determine the total selling and administrative expense. Any noncash selling and administrative expenses such as depreciation are deducted from the total to determine the cash disbursements for selling and administrative expenses.

LO8 Prepare a cash budget.

The cash budget is a critical piece of the master budget. It permits managers to anticipate and plan for cash shortfalls.

The cash budget is organized into a receipts section, a disbursements section, a cash excess or deficiency section, and a financing section. The cash budget draws on information taken from nearly all of the other budgets and schedules including the schedule of cash collections, the schedule of cash disbursements for purchases of materials, the direct labor budget, the manufacturing overhead budget, and the selling and administrative expense budget.

LO9 Prepare a budgeted income statement.

The budgeted income statement is constructed using data from the sales budget, the ending finished goods inventory budget, the manufacturing overhead budget, the selling and administrative budget, and the cash budget.

LO10 Prepare a budgeted balance sheet.

The budgeted balance sheet is constructed using data from virtually all other parts of the master budget.

GUIDANCE ANSWERS TO *DECISION MAKER* AND *YOU DECIDE*

Budget Analyst (p. 301)

Not all costs are variable with respect to gross restaurant sales. For example, assuming no change in the number of restaurant sites, rental costs are probably fixed. To more accurately forecast costs for the budget, costs should be separated into variable and fixed components. Furthermore, more appropriate activity measures should be selected for the variable costs. For example, gross restaurant sales may be divided into food sales and bar sales—each of which could serve as an activity measure for some costs. In addition, some costs (such as the costs of free dinner rolls) may be variable with respect to the number of diners rather than with respect to food or bar sales. Other activity measures may permit even more accurate cost predictions.

Bank Manager (p. 309)

At minimum, you should request a cash budget with supporting documents including a sales budget, production budget, direct materials budget, direct labor budget, manufacturing overhead budget, selling and administrative expense budget, budgeted income statement, and budgeted balance sheet. You should check that the cash budget provides for repayment of the loan, plus interest, and that it leaves the company with sufficient cash reserves to start the new year. You should also check that assumptions concerning sales growth and fixed and variable costs are consistent with the company's recent experience.

GUIDANCE ANSWERS TO CONCEPT CHECKS

1. **Choice b.** Required inventory purchases are calculated as follows: Cost of goods sold of $300,000 + Ending inventory of $30,000 − Beginning inventory of $50,000 = $280,000.
2. **Choice b.** 80,000 units sold in April + 27,000 units of desired ending inventory − 24,000 units of beginning inventory = 83,000 units.
3. **Choice c.** Cash collections for April are calculated as follows: ($100,000 × 80% × 40%) + ($120,000 × 20%) + ($120,000 × 80% × 60%) = $113,600.
4. **Choice a.** The May 31 accounts receivable balance is $125,000 × 80% × 40% = $40,000.

REVIEW PROBLEM: BUDGET SCHEDULES

Mynor Corporation manufactures and sells a seasonal product that has peak sales in the third quarter. The following information concerns operations for Year 2—the coming year—and for the first two quarters of Year 3:

a. The company's single product sells for $8.00 per unit. Budgeted sales in units for the next six quarters are as follows (all sales are on credit):

	Year 2 Quarter				Year 3 Quarter	
	1	**2**	**3**	**4**	**1**	**2**
Budgeted unit sales	40,000	60,000	100,000	50,000	70,000	80,000

b. Sales are collected in the following pattern: 75% in the quarter the sales are made, and the remaining 25% in the following quarter. On January 1, Year 2, the company's balance sheet showed $65,000 in accounts receivable, all of which will be collected in the first quarter of the year. Bad debts are negligible and can be ignored.

c. The company desires an ending finished goods inventory at the end of each quarter equal to 30% of the budgeted unit sales for the next quarter. On December 31, Year 1, the company had 12,000 units on hand.

d. Five pounds of raw materials are required to complete one unit of product. The company requires ending raw materials inventory at the end of each quarter equal to 10% of the following quarter's production needs. On December 31, Year 1, the company had 23,000 pounds of raw materials on hand.

e. The raw material costs $0.80 per pound. Raw material purchases are paid for in the following pattern: 60% paid in the quarter the purchases are made, and the remaining 40% paid in the following quarter. On January 1, Year 2, the company's balance sheet showed $81,500 in accounts payable for raw material purchases, all of which will be paid for in the first quarter of the year.

Required:
Prepare the following budgets and schedules for the year, showing both quarterly and total figures:

1. A sales budget and a schedule of expected cash collections.
2. A production budget.
3. A direct materials budget and a schedule of expected cash payments for purchases of materials.

Solution to Review Problem

1. The sales budget is prepared as follows:

	Year 2 Quarter				
	1	2	3	4	Year
Budgeted unit sales	40,000	60,000	100,000	50,000	250,000
Selling price per unit.	× $8	× $8	× $8	× $8	× $8
Total sales	$320,000	$480,000	$800,000	$400,000	$2,000,000

Based on the budgeted sales above, the schedule of expected cash collections is prepared as follows:

	Year 2 Quarter				
	1	2	3	4	Year
Accounts receivable, beginning balance	$ 65,000				$ 65,000
First-quarter sales ($320,000 × 75%, 25%)	240,000	$ 80,000			320,000
Second-quarter sales ($480,000 × 75%, 25%).		360,000	$120,000		480,000
Third-quarter sales ($800,000 × 75%, 25%).			600,000	$200,000	800,000
Fourth-quarter sales ($400,000 × 75%)				300,000	300,000
Total cash collections.	$305,000	$440,000	$720,000	$500,000	$1,965,000

2. Based on the sales budget in units, the production budget is prepared as follows:

	Year 2 Quarter					Year 3 Quarter	
	1	2	3	4	Year 2	1	2
Budgeted unit sales.	40,000	60,000	100,000	50,000	250,000	70,000	80,000
Add desired ending finished goods inventory*	18,000	30,000	15,000	21,000†	21,000	24,000	
Total needs	58,000	90,000	115,000	71,000	271,000	94,000	
Less beginning finished goods inventory	12,000	18,000	30,000	15,000	12,000	21,000	
Required production	46,000	72,000	85,000	56,000	259,000	73,000	

*30% of the following quarter's budgeted sales in units.
†30% of the budgeted Year 3 first-quarter sales.

3. Based on the production budget, raw materials will need to be purchased during the year as follows:

	Year 2 Quarter					Year 3 Quarter
	1	2	3	4	Year 2	1
Required production (units)	46,000	72,000	85,000	56,000	259,000	73,000
Raw materials needed per unit (pounds)	× 5	× 5	× 5	× 5	× 5	× 5
Production needs (pounds).	230,000	360,000	425,000	280,000	1,295,000	365,000
Add desired ending inventory of raw materials (pounds)*.	36,000	42,500	28,000	36,500†	36,500	
Total needs (pounds).	266,000	402,500	453,000	316,500	1,331,500	
Less beginning inventory of raw materials (pounds).	23,000	36,000	42,500	28,000	23,000	
Raw materials to be purchased (pounds)	243,000	366,500	410,500	288,500	1,308,500	

*10% of the following quarter's production needs in pounds.
†10% of the Year 3 first-quarter production needs in pounds.

Based on the raw material purchases above, expected cash payments are computed as follows:

| | Year 2 Quarter | | | | |
	1	2	3	4	Year
Cost of raw materials to be purchased at $0.80 per pound	$194,400	$293,200	$328,400	$230,800	$1,046,800
Accounts payable, beginning balance....................	$ 81,500				$ 81,500
First-quarter purchases ($194,400 × 60%, 40%)...........	116,640	$ 77,760			194,400
Second-quarter purchases ($293,200 × 60%, 40%)........		175,920	$117,280		293,200
Third-quarter purchases ($328,400 × 60%, 40%).........			197,040	$131,360	328,400
Fourth-quarter purchases ($230,800 × 60%).............				138,480	138,480
Total cash disbursements	$198,140	$253,680	$314,320	$269,840	$1,035,980

GLOSSARY

Budget   A quantitative plan for acquiring and using resources over a specified time period. (p. 286)
Budget committee   A group of key managers who are responsible for overall budgeting policy and for coordinating the preparation of the budget. (p. 289)
Cash budget   A detailed plan showing how cash resources will be acquired and used over a specific time period. (p. 290)
Control   Those steps taken by management to increase the likelihood that all parts of the organization are working together to achieve the goals set down at the planning stage. (p. 286)
Direct labor budget   A detailed plan that shows the direct labor-hours required to fulfill the production budget. (p. 298)
Direct materials budget   A detailed plan showing the amount of raw materials that must be purchased to fulfill the production budget and to provide for adequate inventories. (p. 296)
Ending finished goods inventory budget   A budget showing the dollar amount of unsold finished goods inventory that will appear on the ending balance sheet. (p. 300)
Manufacturing overhead budget   A detailed plan showing the production costs other than direct materials and direct labor that will be incurred over a specified time period. (p. 299)
Master budget   A summary of a company's plans that sets specific targets for sales, production, and financing activities and that generally culminates in a cash budget, budgeted income statement, and budgeted balance sheet. (p. 286)
Merchandise purchases budget   A detailed plan used by a merchandising company that shows the amount of goods that must be purchased from suppliers during the period. (p. 295)
Participative budget   See *Self-imposed budget*. (p. 287)
Planning   Developing goals and preparing budgets to achieve those goals. (p. 286)
Production budget   A detailed plan showing the number of units that must be produced during a period in order to satisfy both sales and inventory needs. (p. 293)
Responsibility accounting   A system of accountability in which managers are held responsible for those items of revenue and cost—and only those items—over which they can exert significant control. The managers are held responsible for differences between budgeted and actual results. (p. 286)
Sales budget   A detailed schedule showing expected sales expressed in both dollars and units. (p. 290)
Self-imposed budget   A method of preparing budgets in which managers prepare their own budgets. These budgets are then reviewed by higher-level managers, and any issues are resolved by mutual agreement. (p. 287)
Selling and administrative expense budget   A detailed schedule of planned expenses that will be incurred in areas other than manufacturing during a budget period. (p. 300)

Multiple-choice questions are provided on the text website at www.mhhe.com/brewer4e.

Quiz 7

QUESTIONS

7–1   What is a budget? What is budgetary control?
7–2   What are some of the major benefits to be gained from budgeting?
7–3   What is meant by the term *responsibility accounting*?
7–4   What is a master budget? Briefly describe its contents.

The selling price of the lamp shades is $30 per unit.

b.   All sales are on account. Based on past experience, sales are collected in the following pattern:

20%	in the month of sale
76%	in the month following sale
4%	uncollectible

Sales for June totaled $420,000.

c.   The company maintains finished goods inventories equal to 30% of the following month's sales. This requirement will be met at the end of June.

d.   Each lamp shade requires 2.0 feet of PTX, a material that is sometimes hard to acquire. Therefore, the company requires that the ending inventory of PTX be equal to 40% of the following month's production needs. The inventory of PTX on hand at the beginning and end of the quarter will be:

June 30	14,240 feet
September 30	? feet

e.   The PTX costs $5.00 per foot. 50% of a month's purchases of PTX is paid for in the month of purchase; the remainder is paid for in the following month. The accounts payable on July 1 for purchases of PTX during June will be $91,000.

Required:

1.   Prepare a sales budget, by month and in total, for the third quarter. (Show your budget in both units and dollars.) Also prepare a schedule of expected cash collections, by month and in total, for the third quarter.

2.   Prepare a production budget for each of the months of July, August, September, and October.

3.   Prepare a direct materials budget for PTX, by month and in total, for the third quarter. Also prepare a schedule of expected cash disbursements for PTX, by month and in total, for the third quarter.

CHECK FIGURE
(1) May 31 cash balance:
$4,200
(2) Net income: $15,800

PROBLEM 7–20A   Cash Budget; Income Statement; Balance Sheet (LO4, LO8, LO9, LO10)
Quinten Company is a wholesale distributor of soft drinks. The company's balance sheet as of April 30 is given below:

Quinten Company
Balance Sheet
April 30

Assets

Cash.	$ 11,000
Accounts receivable.	75,000
Inventory	42,000
Buildings and equipment, net of depreciation	338,000
Total assets	$466,000

Liabilities and Stockholders' Equity

Accounts payable.	$ 89,000
Note payable	35,000
Capital stock, no par	280,000
Retained earnings	62,000
Total liabilities and stockholders' equity	$466,000

The company is in the process of preparing budget data for May. A number of budget items have already been prepared, as stated below:

a.   Sales are budgeted at $300,000 for May. Of these sales, $120,000 will be for cash; the remainder will be credit sales. 35% of a month's credit sales are collected in the month the sales are made, and the remainder are collected in the following month. All of the April 30 accounts receivable will be collected in May.

b. Purchases of inventory are expected to total $216,000 during May. These purchases will all be on account. 60% of all purchases are paid for in the month of purchase; the remainder are paid in the following month. All of the April 30 accounts payable to suppliers will be paid during May.

c. The May 31 inventory balance is budgeted at $50,000.

d. Selling and administrative expenses for May are budgeted at $71,000, exclusive of depreciation. These expenses will be paid in cash. Depreciation is budgeted at $5,000 for the month.

e. The note payable on the April 30 balance sheet will be paid during May, with $200 in interest. (All of the interest relates to May.)

f. New refrigerating equipment costing $10,000 will be purchased for cash during May.

g. During May, the company will borrow $70,000 from its bank by giving a new note payable to the bank for that amount. The new note will be due in one year.

Required:

1. Prepare a cash budget for May. Support your budget with a schedule of expected cash collections from sales and a schedule of expected cash disbursements for merchandise purchases.

2. Prepare a budgeted income statement for May. Use the absorption income statement format as shown in Schedule 9.

3. Prepare a budgeted balance sheet as of May 31.

PROBLEM 7–21A   Cash Budget with Supporting Schedules (LO2, LO4, LO8)

Fowkes & Sons sells bicycles. Management is planning its cash needs for the second quarter. The company usually has to borrow money during this quarter to support peak sales of dirt bikes, which occur during May. The following information has been assembled to assist in preparing a cash budget for the quarter:

a. Budgeted monthly absorption costing income statements for April–July are:

CHECK FIGURE
(2a) May purchases: $395,500
(3)   June 30 cash balance: $42,070

	April	May	June	July
Sales	$550,000	$580,000	$520,000	$480,000
Cost of goods sold	385,000	406,000	364,000	336,000
Gross margin	165,000	174,000	156,000	144,000
Less selling and administrative expenses:				
Selling expense	72,000	74,000	75,000	73,000
Administrative expense*	53,000	54,000	56,000	55,000
Total selling and administrative expenses	125,000	128,000	131,000	128,000
Net operating income	$ 40,000	$ 46,000	$ 25,000	$ 16,000

*Includes $14,000 of depreciation each month.

b. Sales are 30% for cash and 70% on account.

c. Sales on account are collected over a three-month period with 20% collected in the month of sale; 60% collected in the first month following the month of sale; and the remaining 20% collected in the second month following the month of sale. February's sales totaled $340,000, and March's sales totaled $380,000.

d. Forty percent of a month's inventory purchases are paid for in the month of purchase; the remaining 60% are paid in the following month. Accounts payable at March 31 for inventory purchases during March total $177,450.

e. Each month's ending inventory must equal 25% of the cost of the merchandise to be sold in the following month. The merchandise inventory at March 31 is $96,250.

f. Dividends of $39,000 will be declared and paid in April.

g. Land costing $60,000 will be purchased for cash in May.

h. The cash balance at March 31 is $52,000; the company must maintain a cash balance of at least $30,000 at the end of each month.

i. The company has an agreement with a local bank that allows the company to borrow in increments of $1,000 at the beginning of each month, up to a total loan balance of $50,000. The interest rate on these loans is 1% per month. For simplicity, we will assume that the interest is not compounded. The company will, as far as it is able, repay the loan plus accumulated interest at the end of the quarter.

Required:

1. Prepare a schedule of expected cash collections for April, May, and June, and for the quarter in total.
2. Prepare the following for merchandise inventory:
    a. A merchandise purchases budget for April, May, and June.
    b. A schedule of expected cash disbursements for merchandise purchases for April, May, and June, and for the quarter in total.
3. Prepare a cash budget for the third quarter by month as well as in total for the quarter.

CHECK FIGURE
(2a) February purchases: $159,000
(4) February ending cash balance: $5,200

PROBLEM 7–22A   Completing a Master Budget (LO2, LO4, LO7, PO8, PO9, PO10)

Spektra Company, a home furnishings store, prepares its master budget on a quarterly basis. The following data have been assembled to assist in preparing the master budget for the first quarter:

a. As of December 31 (the end of the prior quarter), the company's general ledger showed the following account balances:

	Debits	Credits
Cash	$ 26,000	
Accounts Receivable.	50,000	
Inventory	86,400	
Building and Equipment (net)	80,000	
Accounts Payable		$102,000
Capital Stock.		45,000
Retained Earnings		95,400
	$242,400	$242,400

b. Actual sales for December and budgeted sales for the next four months are as follows:

December (actual)	$200,000
January	$240,000
February.	$250,000
March.	$275,000
April	$260,000

c. Sales are 75% for cash and 25% on credit. All payments on credit sales are collected in the month following sale. The accounts receivable at December 31 are a result of December credit sales.
d. The company's gross margin is 40% of sales. (In other words, cost of goods sold is 60% of sales.)
e. Monthly expenses are budgeted as follows: salaries and wages, $14,000 per month: advertising, $25,000 per month; shipping, 5% of sales; other expense, 15% of sales. Depreciation will be $8,000 for the quarter.
f. Each month's ending inventory should equal 60% of the following month's cost of goods sold.
g. 30% of a month's inventory purchases is paid for in the month of purchase; the remainder is paid for in the following month.
h. During February, the company will purchase land for $8,000 cash. During March, land will be purchased for cash at a cost of $2,000.
i. During January, the company will declare and pay $30,000 in cash dividends.
j. Management wants to maintain a minimum cash balance of $5,000. The company has an agreement with a local bank that allows the company to borrow in increments of $1,000 at the beginning of each month, up to a total loan balance of $20,000. The interest rate on these loans is 1% per month. For simplicity, we will assume that the interest is not compounded. The company will, as far as it is able, repay the loan plus accumulated interest at the end of the quarter.

Required:

Using the data above, complete the following statements and schedules for the first quarter:

1. Schedule of expected cash collections:

	January	February	March	Quarter
Cash sales	$180,000			
Credit sales	50,000			
Total cash collections	$230,000			

2. a. Merchandise purchases budget:

	January	February	March	Quarter
Budgeted cost of goods sold	$144,000*	$150,000		
Add desired ending inventory.	90,000†			
Total needs.	234,000			
Less beginning inventory	86,400			
Required purchases.	$147,600			

*$240,000 sales × 60% cost ratio = $144,000
†150,000 × 60% = $90,000

b. Schedule of expected cash disbursements for merchandise purchases:

	January	February	March	Quarter
December purchases.	$102,000			$102,000
January purchases.	44,280	$103,320		147,600
February purchases.				
March purchases	———			
Total cash disbursements for purchases	$146,280			

3. Schedule of expected cash disbursements for selling and administrative expenses:

	January	February	March	Quarter
Salaries and wages	$14,000			
Advertising.	25,000			
Shipping.	12,000			
Other expenses	36,000			
Total cash disbursements for selling and administrative expenses	$87,000			

4. Cash budget:

	January	February	March	Quarter
Cash balance, beginning	$ 26,000			
Add cash collections	230,000			
Total cash available	256,000			
Less cash disbursements:				
Purchases of inventory.	146,280			
Selling and administrative expenses	87,000			
Purchases of land.	0			
Cash dividends.	30,000			
Total cash disbursements	263,280			
Excess (deficiency) of cash	(7,280)			
Financing:				
Etc.				

5. Prepare an absorption costing income statement for the quarter ending March 31 as shown in Schedule 9 in the chapter.
6. Prepare a balance sheet as of March 31.

PROBLEM 7–23A   Cash Budget with Supporting Schedules (LO2, LO4, LO7, LO8)

Colormania is a wholesale distributor of dyes and pigments. When the treasurer of Colormania approached the company's bank late in the current year seeking short-term financing, he was told that money was very tight and that any borrowing over the next year would have to be supported by a detailed statement of cash collections and disbursements. The treasurer also was told that it would be very helpful to the bank if borrowers would indicate the quarters in which they would be needing funds, as well as the amounts that would be needed, and the quarters in which repayments could be made.

Since the treasurer is unsure as to the particular quarters in which the bank financing will be needed, he has assembled the following information to assist in preparing a detailed cash budget:

a. Budgeted sales and merchandise purchases for next year, as well as actual sales and purchases for the last quarter of the current year are:

	Sales	Merchandise Purchases
Current Year:		
Fourth quarter actual	$700,000	$528,000
Next Year:		
First quarter estimated	$720,000	$544,500
Second quarter estimated	$750,000	$561,000
Third quarter estimated	$740,000	$549,000
Fourth quarter estimated	$700,000	$528,000

b. The company normally collects 80% of a quarter's sales before the quarter ends and another 15% in the following quarter. The remainder is uncollectible. This pattern of collections is now being experienced in the current year's fourth-quarter actual data.

c. 85% of a quarter's merchandise purchases are paid for within the quarter. The remainder is paid in the following quarter.

d. Selling and administrative expenses for next year are budgeted at $60,000 per quarter plus 10% of sales. Of the fixed amount, $15,000 each quarter is depreciation.

e. The company will pay $18,000 in dividends each quarter.

f. Land purchases of $20,000 will be made in the second quarter, and purchases of $18,000 will be made in the third quarter. These purchases will be for cash.

g. The Cash account contained $20,000 at the end of the current year. The treasurer feels that this represents a minimum balance that must be maintained.

h. The company has an agreement with a local bank that allows the company to borrow in increments of $1,000 at the beginning of each quarter, up to a total loan balance of $10,000. The interest rate on these loans is 1% per month. For simplicity, we will assume that the interest is not compounded. The company will, as far as it is able, repay the loan plus accumulated interest at the end of the year.

i. At present, the company has no loans outstanding.

Required:

1. Prepare the following by quarter and in total for next year:
   a. A schedule of expected cash collections.
   b. A schedule of expected cash disbursements for merchandise purchases.

2. Compute the expected cash payments for selling and administrative expenses, by quarter and in total, for next year.
3. Prepare a cash budget, by quarter and in total, for next year.

PROBLEM 7–24A Completing a Master Budget (LO2, LO4, LO7, LO8, LO9, LO10)
The following data relate to the operations of Andros Company, a magazine distributor:

CHECK FIGURE
(2) May purchases:
    $83,825
(4) May 31 cash balance:
    $23,970

Current assets as of March 31:	
Cash	$15,200
Accounts receivable	$40,000
Inventory	$20,125
Buildings and equipment (net)	$120,000
Accounts payable	$62,250
Capital stock	$40,000
Retained earnings	$93,075

a. The gross margin is 30% of sales.
b. Actual and budgeted sales data:

March (actual)	$100,000
April	$115,000
May	$118,000
June	$125,000
July	$130,000

c. Sales are 60% for cash and 40% on credit. Credit sales are collected in the month following sale. The accounts receivable at March 31 are the result of March credit sales.
d. Each month's ending inventory should equal 25% of the following month's budgeted cost of goods sold.
e. 20% of a month's inventory purchases is paid for in the month of purchase; the remainder is paid for in the following month. The accounts payable at March 31 are a result of March purchases of inventory.
f. Monthly expenses are as follows: commissions $17,000; rent, $6,000; other expenses (excluding depreciation), 3% of sales. These expenses are paid monthly. Depreciation is $4,000 per month and includes depreciation on new assets.
g. Equipment costing $22,000 will be purchased for cash in April.
h. Management wants to maintain a minimum cash balance of $15,000 at the end of each month. The company has an agreement with a local bank that allows the company to borrow in increments of $1,000 at the beginning of each month, up to a total loan balance of $20,000. The interest rate on these loans is 1% per month. For simplicity, we will assume that the interest is not compounded. The company will, as far as it is able, repay the loan plus accumulated interest at the end of the quarter.

Required:
Using the preceding data:

1. Complete the following schedule:

	Schedule of Expected Cash Collections			
	April	May	June	Quarter
Cash sales	$ 69,000			
Credit sales	40,000	_____	_____	_____
Total collections	$109,000	_____	_____	_____

2. Complete the following:

Merchandise Purchases Budget

	April	May	June	Quarter
Budgeted cost of goods sold*	$ 80,500	$82,600		
Add desired ending inventory†	20,650			
Total needs.....................	101,150			
Less beginning inventory	20,125			
Required purchases..............	$ 81,025			

*$115,000 sales × 70% cost ratio = $80,500
†$82,600 × 25% = $20,650

Schedule of Expected Cash Disbursements—Merchandise Purchases

	April	May	June	Quarter
March purchases	$62,250			$62,250
April purchases	16,205	$64,820		81,025
May purchases				
June purchases				
Total disbursements	$78,455			

3. Complete the following:

Schedule of Expected Cash Disbursements—Selling and Administrative Expenses

	April	May	June	Quarter
Commissions	$17,000			
Rent	6,000			
Other expenses	3,450			
Total disbursements..............	$26,450			

4. Complete the following cash budget:

Cash Budget

	April	May	June	Quarter
Cash balance, beginning	$ 15,200			
Add cash collections	109,000			
Total cash available	124,200			
Less cash disbursements:				
Purchases of inventory...........	78,455			
Selling and administrative expenses	26,450			
Purchase of equipment...........	22,000			
Total disbursements..............	126,905			
Excess (deficiency) of cash	(2,705)			
Financing:				
Etc.				

5. Prepare an absorption costing income statement for the quarter ending June 30 similar to Schedule 9 in the text.
6. Prepare a balance sheet as of June 30.

BUILDING YOUR SKILLS

CASE   (LO2, LO4, LO8, LO9, LO10)

You have just been hired as a management trainee by Cravat Sales Company, a nationwide distributor of a designer's silk ties. The company has an exclusive franchise on the distribution of the ties, and sales have grown so rapidly over the last few years that it has become necessary to add new members to the management team. You have been given direct responsibility for all planning and budgeting. Your first assignment is to prepare a master budget for the next three months, starting April 1. You are anxious to make a favorable impression on the president and have assembled the information below.

CHECK FIGURE
(1d) April cash disburse-
      ments: $195,750
(2)   June ending cash
      balance: $10,730

The company desires a minimum ending cash balance each month of $10,000. The ties are sold to retailers for $8.00 each. Recent actual sales and forecasted sales in units are as follows:

January (actual)	20,000	June	60,000
February (actual)	24,000	July	40,000
March (actual)	28,000	August	36,000
April	35,000	September	32,000
May	45,000		

The large buildup in sales before and during June is due to Father's Day. Ending inventories are supposed to equal 90% of the next month's sales in units. The ties cost the company $5.00 each.

Purchases are paid for as follows: 50% in the month of purchase and the remaining 50% in the following month. All sales are on credit, with no discount, and payable within 15 days. The company has found, however, that only 25% of a month's sales are collected by month-end. An additional 50% is collected in the month following, and the remaining 25% is collected in the second month following. Bad debts have been negligible.

The company's monthly operating expenses are given below:

Variable:	
Sales commissions	$1 per tie
Fixed:	
Wages and salaries	$22,000
Utilities	$14,000
Insurance expired	$1,200
Depreciation	$1,500
Miscellaneous	$3,000

All operating expenses are paid during the month, in cash, with the exception of depreciation and insurance expired. Land will be purchased during May for $25,000 cash. The company declares dividends of $12,000 each quarter, payable in the first month of the following quarter. The company's balance sheet at March 31 is given below:

Assets	
Cash	$ 14,000
Accounts receivable ($48,000 February sales; $168,000 March sales)	216,000
Inventory (31,500 units)	157,500
Prepaid insurance	14,400
Fixed assets, net of depreciation	172,700
Total assets	$574,600

Liabilities and Stockholders' Equity	
Accounts payable	$ 85,750
Dividends payable	12,000
Capital stock	300,000
Retained earnings	176,850
Total liabilities and stockholders' equity	$574,600

The company has an agreement with a local bank that allows the company to borrow in increments of $1,000 at the beginning of each month, up to a total loan balance of $40,000. The interest rate on these loans is 1% per month. For simplicity, we will assume that the interest is not compounded. At the end of the quarter, the company would pay the bank all of the accumulated interest on the loan and as much of the loan as possible (in increments of $1,000), while still retaining at least $10,000 in cash.

Required:

Prepare a master budget for the three-month period ending June 30. Include the following detailed budgets:

1. a. A sales budget by month and in total.
   b. A schedule of expected cash collections, by month and in total.
   c. A merchandise purchases budget in units and in dollars. Show the budget by month and in total.
   d. A schedule of budgeted cash disbursements for merchandise purchases, by month and in total.
2. A cash budget. Show the budget by month and in total.
3. A budgeted income statement for the three-month period ending June 30. Use the contribution approach.
4. A budgeted balance sheet as of June 30.

COMMUNICATING IN PRACTICE (LO1)

In the late 1980s and early 1990s, public universities found that they were no longer immune to the financial stress faced by their private sister institutions and corporate America. Budget cuts were in the air across the land. When the budget ax hit, the cuts often came without warning and their size was sometimes staggering. State support for some institutions dropped by 40% or more. Most university administrators had only experienced budget increases, never budget cuts. Also, the budget setbacks usually occurred at the most inopportune time—during the school year when contractual commitments with faculty and staff had been signed, programs had been planned, and students were enrolled and taking classes.

Required:

1. Should the administration be "fair" to all affected and institute a round of across-the-board cuts whenever the state announces another subsidy reduction?
2. If not across-the-board cutbacks in programs, then would you recommend more focused reductions, and if so, what priorities would you establish for bringing spending in line with revenues?
3. Since these usually are not one-time-only cutbacks, how would you manage continuous, long-term reductions in budgets extending over a period of years?
4. Should the decision-making process be top-down (centralized with top administrators) or bottom-up (participative)? Why?
5. How should issues such as protect-your-turf mentality, resistance to change, and consensus building be dealt with?

ETHICS CHALLENGE (LO1)

Granger Stokes, managing partner of the venture capital firm of Halston and Stokes, was dissatisfied with the top management of PrimeDrive, a manufacturer of computer disk drives. Halston and Stokes had invested $20 million in PrimeDrive, and the return on their investment had been below expectations for several years. In a tense meeting of the board of directors of PrimeDrive, Stokes exercised his firm's rights as the major equity investor in PrimeDrive and fired PrimeDrive's chief executive officer (CEO). He then quickly moved to have the board of directors of PrimeDrive appoint himself as the new CEO.

Stokes prided himself on his hard-driving management style. At the first management meeting, he asked two of the managers to stand and fired them on the spot, just to show everyone who was in control of the company. At the budget review meeting that followed, he ripped up the departmental budgets that had been submitted for his review and yelled at the managers for their "wimpy, do nothing targets." He then ordered everyone to submit new budgets calling for at least a 40% increase in sales volume and announced that he would not accept excuses for results that fell below budget.

Keri Kalani, an accountant working for the production manager at PrimeDrive, discovered toward the end of the year that her boss had not been scrapping defective disk drives that had been returned by customers. Instead, he had been shipping them in new cartons to other customers to avoid booking losses. Quality control had deteriorated during the year as a result of the push for increased volume, and returns of defective disk drives were running as high as 15% of the new drives shipped. When she confronted her boss with her discovery, he told her to mind her own business. And then, in the way of a justification for his actions, he said, "All of us managers are finding ways to hit Stokes's targets."

Required:
1. Is Granger Stokes using budgets as a planning and control tool?
2. What are the behavioral consequences of the way budgets are being used at PrimeDrive?
3. What, if anything, do you think Keri Kalani should do?

TEAMWORK IN ACTION   (LO2, LO4, LO6, LO8)

Roller, Ltd., of Melbourne, Australia, is the exclusive distributor in Australia and the South Pacific of a popular brand of in-line skates manufactured in Mexico. The company is in the process of putting together its cash budget for the second quarter—April, May, and June—of next year. The president of the company suspects that some financing will be required in the second quarter because sales are expanding and the company intends to make several major equipment purchases in that quarter. The president is confident that the company will be able to meet or exceed the following budgeted sales figures (all in Australian dollars) next year:

CHECK FIGURE
June excess of cash available over disbursements: $41,800

January	$158,000	July	$190,000
February	$160,000	August	$192,000
March	$164,000	September	$210,000
April	$172,000	October	$230,000
May	$176,000	November	$260,000
June	$184,000	December	$180,000

The following additional information will be used in formulating the cash budget:

a. All of the company's sales are on credit. The company collects 30% of its billings in the month after the sale and the remaining 70% in the second month after the sale. Uncollectible accounts are negligible.

b. The cost of goods sold is 75% of sales. Because of the shipping time from Mexico, the company orders skates from the manufacturer one month in advance of their expected sale. Roller, Ltd., desires to maintain little or no inventory.

c. The company orders skates on credit from the manufacturer. The company pays half of its bill in the month after it orders the skates and the other half in the second month after it places the order.

d. Operating expenses, other than cost of goods sold, are budgeted to be $178,800 for the year. The composition of these expenses is given below. All of these expenses are incurred evenly throughout the year except for the property taxes. Property taxes are paid in four equal installments in the last month of each quarter.

Salaries and wages	$120,000
Advertising and promotion	12,000
Property taxes	18,000
Insurance	4,800
Utilities	6,000
Depreciation	18,000
Total operating expenses	$178,800

e. Income tax payments are made by the company in the first month of each quarter based on the taxable income for the prior quarter. The income tax payment due in April is $16,000.

f. Because of expanding sales, the company plans to make equipment purchases of $22,300 in April and $29,000 in May. These purchases will not affect depreciation for the year.

g. The company has a policy of maintaining an end-of-month cash balance of $20,000. Cash is borrowed or invested monthly, as needed, to maintain this balance. All borrowing is done at the beginning of the month, and all investments and repayments are made at the end of the month. As of March 31, there are no investments of excess cash and no outstanding loans.

h. The annual interest rate on loans from the bank is 12%. Compute interest on whole months ($\frac{1}{12}$, $\frac{2}{12}$, and so forth). The company will pay off any loans, including accumulated interest, at the end of the second quarter if sufficient cash is available.

Required:

The team should discuss and then respond to the following two questions:

1. Prepare a cash budget for Roller, Ltd., by month and in total for the second quarter.
2. Discuss why cash budgeting is particularly important for an expanding company like Roller, Ltd.

RESEARCH AND APPLICATION [LO1]

The questions in this exercise give you an appreciation for the complexity of budgeting in a large multinational corporation. To answer the questions, you will need to download the Procter & Gamble (P&G) 2005 Annual Report at www.pg.com/investors/annualreports.jhtml and briefly refer to "Item 2: Properties" in P&G's Form 10-K for the fiscal year ended June 30, 2005. To access the 10-K report, go to www.sec.gov/edgar/searchedgar/companysearch.html. Input CIK code 80424 and hit enter. In the gray box on the right-hand side of your computer screen define the scope of your search by inputting 10-K and then pressing enter. Select the 10-K with a filing date of August 29, 2005. You will also need to briefly refer to Macy's Inc.'s Form 10-K for the fiscal year ended January 29, 2005. Macy's CIK code is 794367 and its filing date is March 28, 2005. You do not need to print any documents to answer the questions.

REQUIRED:

1. What is P&G's strategy for success in the marketplace? Does the company rely primarily on a customer intimacy, operational excellence, or product leadership customer value proposition? What evidence supports your conclusion?

2. What business risks does P&G face that may threaten its ability to satisfy stockholder expectations? What are some examples of control activities that the company could use to reduce these risks? (*Hint:* Focus on page 28 of the annual report).

3. What were P&G's quarterly net sales for the fiscal year ended June 30, 2005? What were Federated Department Stores' quarterly net sales for 2004? (*Hint:* see page 79 of its 10-K.) How does P&G's quarterly sales trend compare to Federated Department Stores' quarterly sales trend? Which of the two quarterly sales trends is likely to cause greater cash budgeting concerns? Why?

4. Describe the scope of P&G's business in three respects—physical facilities, products, and customers. More specifically, how many manufacturing facilities does P&G operate globally? What are P&G's three Global Business Units (GBUs)? Which of P&G's 17 "billion dollar brands" are included in each of these GBUs? How many brands does P&G offer in total and in how many countries does it sell these brands? How many countries does P&G's Market Development Organization operate in?

5. Describe five uncertainties that complicate P&G's efforts to accurately forecast its sales and expenses.

6. Although not specifically discussed in P&G's annual report, how could an Enterprise System as described in Chapter 1 help a globally dispersed, highly complex company such as P&G improve its budgeting process?

7. P&G's annual report briefly discusses the acquisition of Gillette (see pages 10–11). It acknowledges that Gillette has some different cultural norms in terms of how it defines accountability and communicates internally. Although not discussed in the annual report, how could differences in two organization's budgeting practices be responsible for these types of divergent cultural norms?

8 Standard Costs

<< A LOOK BACK

In Chapter 7, we discussed the budgeting process and each of the budgets in the master budget.

A LOOK AT THIS CHAPTER

In Chapter 8, we begin a discussion of management control and performance measures by focusing on standard costing systems. Management by exception and variance analysis are described, as are the computations of material, labor, and overhead variances.

A LOOK AHEAD >>

In Chapter 9, we compare and contrast the static budget approach to a flexible budget approach and discuss the preparation of performance reports, using a flexible budget approach, to analyze overhead variances.

CHAPTER OUTLINE

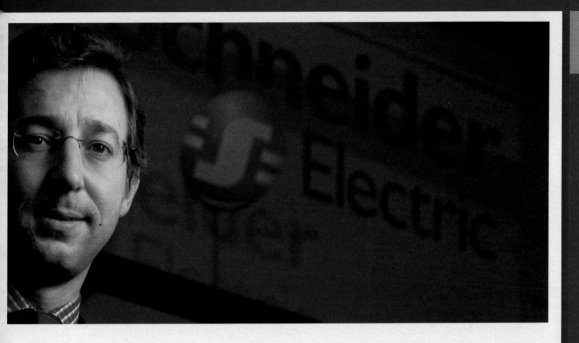

LEARNING
OBJECTIVES

LP 8
*After studying Chapter 8, you
should be able to:*

LO1 Explain how direct
materials standards and
direct labor standards
are set.

LO2 Compute the direct
materials price and
quantity variances
and explain their
significance.

LO3 Compute the direct
labor rate and
efficiency variances
and explain their
significance.

LO4 Compute the variable
manufacturing
overhead spending and
efficiency variances.

LO5 (Appendix 8A) Prepare
journal entries to
record standard costs
and variances.

DECISION FEATURE

Managing Materials and Labor

Schneider Electric's Oxford, Ohio, plant manufactures metal-housed units (Busways) that transport electricity from its point of entry into a building to remote locations throughout the building. The plant's managers pay close attention to direct material costs because they constitute the majority of the plant's total manufacturing costs. To help control scrap rates for direct material inputs, such as copper, steel, and aluminum, the accounting department prepares direct materials quantity variances. These variances compare the standard quantity of direct materials that should have been used to make a product (according to computations made by the plant's engineers) to the amount of direct materials that were actually used. Quantifying these differences helps employees identify and deal with the causes of excessive scrap, such as an inadequately trained machine operator, poor quality raw material inputs, or a malfunctioning machine.

Because direct labor is also a significant component of the plant's total manufacturing costs, the management team also keeps daily tabs on its direct labor efficiency variance. This variance compares the standard amount of labor time allowed to make a product to the actual amount of labor time used. When idle workers cause an unfavorable labor efficiency variance, managers react to this information by temporarily moving workers from departments experiencing slack to those that are constraining production.

Source: Conversation with Doug Taylor, Plant Controller, Schneider Electric's Oxford, Ohio, plant.

I n this chapter we begin our study of management control and performance measures. As explained in the following quotation, performance measurement serves a vital function in both personal life and in organizations:

> Imagine you want to improve your basketball shooting skill. You know that practice will help, so you [go] to the basketball court. There you start shooting toward the hoop, but as soon as the ball gets close to the rim your vision goes blurry for a second, so that you cannot observe where the ball ended up in relation to the target (left, right, in front, too far back, inside the hoop?). It would be pretty difficult to improve under those conditions … (And by the way, how long would [shooting baskets] sustain your interest if you couldn't observe the outcome of your efforts?)
>
> Or imagine someone engaging in a weight loss program. A normal step in such programs is to purchase a scale to be able to track one's progress: Is this program working? Am I losing weight? A positive answer would be encouraging and would motivate me to keep up the effort, while a negative answer might lead me to reflect on the process: Am I working on the right diet and exercise program? Am I doing everything I am supposed to? etc. Suppose you don't want to set up a sophisticated measurement system and decide to forgo the scale. You would still have some idea of how well you are doing from simple methods such as clothes feeling looser, a belt that fastens at a different hole, or simply via observation in a mirror! Now, imagine trying to sustain a weight loss program without *any* feedback on how well you are doing.
>
> In these … examples, availability of quantitative measures of performance can yield two types of benefits: First, performance feedback can help improve the "production process" through a better understanding of what works and what doesn't; e.g., shooting this way works better than shooting that way. Secondly, feedback on performance can sustain motivation and effort, because it is encouraging and/or because it suggests that more effort is required for the goal to be met.[1]

In the same way, performance measurement can be helpful in an organization. It can provide feedback concerning what works and what does not work, and it can help motivate people to sustain their efforts.

IN BUSINESS

Focusing on the Numbers

Joe Knight is the CEO of Setpoint, a company that designs and builds factory-automation equipment. Knight uses a large whiteboard, with about 20 rows and 10 columns, to focus worker attention on key factors involved in managing projects. A visitor to the plant, Steve Petersen, asked Knight to explain the board, but Knight instead motioned one of his workers to come over. The young man, with a baseball cap turned backward on his head, proceeded to walk the visitor through the board, explaining the calculation of gross margin and other key indicators on the board.

"'I was just amazed,' Petersen recalls. 'He knew that board inside and out. He knew every number on it. He knew exactly where the company was and where they had to focus their attention. There was no hesitation.... I was so impressed... that the people on the shop floor had it down like that. It was their scoreboard. It was the way they could tell if they were winning or losing. I talked to several of them, and I just couldn't get over the positive attitude they had and their understanding of the numbers.'"

Source: Bo Burlingham, "What's Your Culture Worth?," *Inc.* magazine, September 2001, pp. 124–133.

Companies in highly competitive industries like FedEx, Southwest Airlines, Dell, and Toyota must be able to provide high-quality goods and services at low cost. If they do not,

---

[1]Soumitra Dutta and Jean-François Manzoni, *Process Reengineering, Organizational Change and Performance Improvement* (New York: McGraw-Hill), Chapter IV.

their customers will buy from more efficient competitors. Stated in the starkest terms, managers must obtain inputs such as raw materials and electricity at the lowest possible prices and must use them as effectively as possible—while maintaining or increasing the quality of what they sell. If inputs are purchased at prices that are too high or more input is used than is really necessary, higher costs will result.

How do managers control the prices that are paid for inputs and the quantities that are used? They could examine every transaction in detail, but this obviously would be an inefficient use of management time. For many companies, the answer to this control problem lies at least partially in *standard costs.*

STANDARD COSTS—MANAGEMENT BY EXCEPTION

A *standard* is a benchmark or "norm" for measuring performance. Standards are found everywhere. Your doctor evaluates your weight using standards for individuals of your age, height, and gender. The food we eat in restaurants is prepared under specified standards of cleanliness. The buildings we live in conform to standards set in building codes. Standards are also widely used in managerial accounting where they relate to the *quantity* and *cost* (or acquisition price) of inputs used in manufacturing goods or providing services.

Video 8–1

Quantity and cost standards are set for each major input such as raw materials and labor time. *Quantity standards* specify how much of an input should be used to make a product or provide a service. *Cost (price) standards* specify how much should be paid for each unit of the input. Actual quantities and actual costs of inputs are compared to these standards. If either the quantity or the cost of inputs departs significantly from the standards, managers investigate the discrepancy to find the cause of the problem and eliminate it. This process is called **management by exception.**

In our daily lives, we operate in a management by exception mode most of the time. Consider what happens when you sit down in the driver's seat of your car. You put the key in the ignition, you turn the key, and your car starts. Your expectation (standard) that the car will start is met; you do not have to open the car hood and check the battery, the connecting cables, the fuel lines, and so on. If you turn the key and the car does not start, then you have a discrepancy (variance). Your expectations are not met, and you need to investigate why. Note that even if the car starts after a second try, it still would be wise to investigate. The fact that the expectation was not met should be viewed as an opportunity to uncover the cause of the problem rather than as simply an annoyance. If the underlying cause is not discovered and corrected, the problem may recur and become much worse.

Management by Exception

EXHIBIT 8–1
The Variance Analysis Cycle

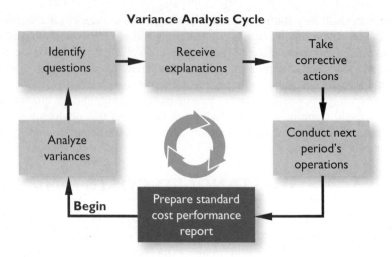

Variance Analysis Cycle

This basic approach to identifying and solving problems is the essence of the *variance analysis cycle,* which is illustrated in Exhibit 8–1. The cycle begins with the preparation of standard cost performance reports in the accounting department. These reports highlight the *variances,* which are the differences between actual results and what should have occurred according to the standards. The variances raise questions. Why did this variance occur? Why is this variance larger than it was last period? The significant variances are investigated to discover their root causes. Corrective actions are taken. And then next period's operations are carried out. The cycle begins again with the preparation of a new standard cost performance report for the latest period. The emphasis should be on highlighting problems, finding their root causes, and then taking corrective action. The goal is to improve operations—not to assign blame.

Standard Costing at Parker Brass

The Brass Products Division at Parker Hannifin Corporation, known as Parker Brass, is a world-class manufacturer of tube and brass fittings, valves, hose and hose fittings. Management at the company uses variances from its standard costing system to target problem areas for improvement. If a production variance exceeds 5% of sales, the responsible manager is required to explain the variance and propose a plan of action to correct the detected problems. In the past, variances were reported at the end of the month—often several weeks after a particular job had been completed. Now, a variance report is generated the day after a job is completed and summary variance reports are prepared weekly. These more frequent reports help managers take more timely corrective action.

Source: David Johnsen and Parvez Sopariwala, "Standard Costing Is Alive and Well at Parker Brass," *Management Accounting Quarterly,* Winter 2000, pp. 12–20.

Who Uses Standard Costs?

Manufacturing, service, food, and not-for-profit organizations all make use of standards to some extent. Auto service centers like Firestone and Sears, for example, often set specific labor time standards for the completion of certain tasks, such as installing a carburetor or doing a valve job, and then measure actual performance against these standards. Fast-food outlets such as McDonald's have exacting standards for the quantity of meat going into a sandwich, as well as standards for the cost of the meat. Hospitals have standard costs for food, laundry, and other items, as well as standard time allowances for certain routine activities, such as laboratory tests. In short, you are likely to run into standard costs in virtually any line of business.

Manufacturing companies often have highly developed standard costing systems in which standards for direct materials, direct labor, and overhead are created for each product. A **standard cost card** shows the standard quantities and costs of the inputs required to produce a unit. In the following section, we provide a detailed example of setting standard costs and preparing a standard cost card.

SETTING STANDARD COSTS

Setting price and quantity standards ideally combines the expertise of everyone who has responsibility for purchasing and using inputs. In a manufacturing setting, this might include accountants, purchasing managers, engineers, production supervisors, line managers, and production workers. Past records of purchase prices and input usage can be helpful in setting standards. However, the standards should be designed to encourage efficient *future* operations, not just a repetition of past operations that may or may not have been efficient.

Video 8–1

Ideal versus Practical Standards

Should standards be attainable all of the time, part of the time, or almost none of the time? Opinions vary, but standards tend to fall into one of two categories—either ideal or practical.

Ideal standards can be attained only under the best circumstances. They allow for no machine breakdowns or other work interruptions, and they call for a level of effort that can be attained only by the most skilled and efficient employees working at peak effort 100% of the time. Some managers feel that such standards spur continual improvement. These managers argue that even though employees know they will rarely meet the standard, it is a constant reminder of the need for ever-increasing efficiency and effort. Few organizations use ideal standards. Most managers feel that ideal standards tend to discourage even the most diligent workers. Moreover, variances from ideal standards are difficult to interpret. Large variances from the ideal are normal and it is therefore difficult to "manage by exception."

Practical standards are standards that are "tight but attainable." They allow for normal machine downtime and employee rest periods, and they can be attained through reasonable, though highly efficient, efforts by the average worker. Variances from practical standards typically signal a need for management attention because they represent deviations that fall outside of normal operating conditions. Furthermore, practical standards can serve multiple purposes. In addition to signaling abnormal conditions, they can also be used in forecasting cash flows and in planning inventory. By contrast, ideal standards cannot be used for these purposes because they do not allow for normal inefficiencies and result in unrealistic forecasts.

Throughout the remainder of this chapter, we will assume that practical rather than ideal standards are in use.

Owner of a Painting Company

YOU DECIDE

Having painted a relative's house last summer, you have decided to start your own housepainting company this summer and have hired several of your friends. An uncle who is in the construction business has suggested that you use time standards for various tasks such as preparing wood siding, painting wood trim, and painting wood siding. A table of such standards for professional painters has been published in a recent issue of a trade magazine for painting contractors. What advantages and disadvantages do you see in using such standards? How do you think they should be used in your business, if at all?

We now turn our attention to a one-year-old company called the Colonial Pewter Company to explain many of the key concepts in this chapter. The company's only product is a reproduction of an 18th-century pewter bookend that is made largely by hand, using traditional metalworking tools. Consequently, the manufacturing process is labor intensive and requires a high level of skill.

Colonial Pewter has recently expanded its workforce to take advantage of unexpected demand for the bookends. The company started with a small group of experienced pewter workers but has had to hire less experienced workers as a result of the expansion. Recently, production problems have been encountered with iron-contaminated pewter that was acquired several months ago by the purchasing department for a bargain price. The combination of inexperienced workers and contaminated raw materials seems to have caused an unusual amount of waste and higher than expected costs. To better understand the root causes of his company's problems, the president has directed his controller to install a standard costing system.

Setting Direct Materials Standards

LEARNING OBJECTIVE 1

Explain how direct materials standards and direct labor standards are set.

The controller's first task was to prepare price and quantity standards for the company's only significant raw material, pewter ingots. The **standard price per unit** for direct materials should reflect the final, delivered cost of the materials, net of any discounts taken. After consulting with the purchasing manager, the controller calculated the following standard price of a pound of pewter in ingot form:

Purchase price, top-grade pewter ingots, in 40-pound ingots	$3.85
Freight, by truck, from the supplier's warehouse	0.24
Less purchase discount	(0.09)
Standard price per pound	$4.00

Notice that the standard price reflects a particular grade of material (top grade), purchased in particular lot sizes (40-pound ingots), and delivered by a particular type of carrier (truck). Allowances have also been made for discounts. If everything proceeds according to these expectations, the net cost of a pound of pewter should be $4.00.

The **standard quantity per unit** for direct materials should reflect the amount of material required for each unit of finished product, as well as an allowance for unavoidable waste, spoilage, and other normal inefficiencies. After consulting with the production manager, the controller prepared the following documentation for the standard quantity of pewter in a pair of bookends:

Material requirements as specified in the bill of materials for a pair of bookends, in pounds	2.7
Allowance for waste and spoilage, in pounds	0.2
Allowance for rejects, in pounds	0.1
Standard quantity per pair of bookends, in pounds	3.0

As discussed in Chapter 2, the bill of materials details the quantity of each type of material that should be used in a product. As shown above, the material requirements listed on the bill of materials should be adjusted for waste and other factors when determining the standard quantity per unit of product. "Waste and spoilage" refers to materials that are wasted as a normal part of the production process or that spoil before they are used. "Rejects" refers to the direct material contained in defective units that must be scrapped.

Although allowances for waste, spoilage, and rejects are often built into standards, this practice is now often criticized because it contradicts the zero defects goal that underlies improvement programs such as Six Sigma. If allowances for waste, spoilage, and rejects are built into the standard cost, those allowances should be periodically reviewed and reduced over time to reflect improved processes, better training, and better equipment.

Once the price and quantity standards have been set, the standard cost of material per unit of the finished product can be computed as follows:

$$3.0 \text{ pounds per unit} \times \$4.00 \text{ per pound} = \$12.00 \text{ per unit}$$

This $12.00 cost will appear on the product's standard cost card.

Setting Direct Labor Standards

Direct labor price and quantity standards are usually expressed in terms of a labor rate and labor-hours. The **standard rate per hour** for direct labor should include wages, employment taxes, and fringe benefits. Using wage records and in consultation with the production manager, the controller determined the standard rate per direct labor-hour at the Colonial Pewter Company as follows:

Basic wage rate per hour	$10.00
Employment taxes at 10% of the basic rate	1.00
Fringe benefits at 30% of the basic rate	3.00
Standard rate per direct labor-hour	$14.00

Many companies prepare a single standard rate per hour for all employees in a department. This standard rate reflects the expected "mix" of workers, even though the actual wage rates may vary somewhat from individual to individual due to differing skills or seniority. According to the standard computed above, the direct labor rate for Colonial Pewter should average $14.00 per hour.

The standard direct labor time required to complete a unit of product (called the **standard hours per unit**) is perhaps the single most difficult standard to determine. One approach is to break down each task into elemental body movements (such as reaching, pushing, and turning over). Published tables of standard times for such movements can be used to estimate the total time required to complete the task. Another approach is for an industrial engineer to do a time and motion study, actually clocking the time required for each task. As stated earlier, the standard time should include allowances for breaks, personal needs of employees, cleanup, and machine downtime.

After consulting with the production manager, the controller prepared the following documentation for the standard hours per unit:

Basic labor time per unit, in hours	1.9
Allowance for breaks and personal needs	0.1
Allowance for cleanup and machine downtime	0.3
Allowance for rejects	0.2
Standard labor-hours per unit of product	2.5

Once the rate and time standards have been set, the standard labor cost per unit of product can be computed as follows:

$$2.5 \text{ direct labor-hours per unit} \times \$14.00 \text{ per direct labor-hour} = \$35.00 \text{ per unit}$$

This $35.00 per unit standard labor cost appears along with direct materials on the standard cost card for a pair of pewter bookends.

EXHIBIT 8–2
Standard Cost Card—Variable
Manufacturing Costs

Inputs	(1) Standard Quantity or Hours	(2) Standard Price or Rate	Standard Cost (1) × (2)
Direct materials	3.0 pounds	$4.00 per pound	$12.00
Direct labor	2.5 hours	$14.00 per hour	35.00
Variable manufacturing overhead	2.5 hours	$3.00 per hour	7.50
Total standard cost per unit			$54.50

Setting Variable Manufacturing Overhead Standards

As with direct labor, the price and quantity standards for variable manufacturing overhead are usually expressed in terms of rate and hours. The rate represents *the variable portion of the predetermined overhead rate* discussed in Chapter 2; the hours represent whatever base is used to apply overhead to units of product (usually machine-hours or direct labor-hours, as we learned in Chapter 2). At Colonial Pewter, the variable portion of the predetermined overhead rate is $3.00 per direct labor-hour. Therefore, the standard variable manufacturing overhead cost per unit is computed as follows:

2.5 direct labor-hours per unit × $3.00 per direct labor-hour = $7.50 per unit

This $7.50 per unit cost for variable manufacturing overhead appears along with direct materials and direct labor on the standard cost card in Exhibit 8–2. Observe that the **standard cost per unit** for direct materials, direct labor, and variable manufacturing overhead is computed the same way—by multiplying the standard quantity or hours by the standard price or rate.

Are Standards the Same as Budgets?

Standards and budgets are very similar. The major distinction between the two terms is that a standard is a *unit* amount, whereas a budget is a *total* amount. The standard cost for direct materials at Colonial Pewter is $12.00 per pair of bookends. If 1,000 pairs of bookends are to be made, then the budgeted cost of direct materials would be $12,000. In effect, *a standard can be viewed as the budgeted cost for one unit of product.*

A GENERAL MODEL FOR VARIANCE ANALYSIS

Video 8–1

Why are standards separated into two categories—price and quantity? Different managers are usually responsible for buying and for using inputs. For example, in the case of a raw material, a purchasing manager is responsible for its price. However, the production manager is responsible for the amount of the raw material actually used to make products. As we shall see, setting up separate standards for price and quantity allows us to better separate the responsibilities of these two managers. It also allows us to prepare more timely reports. The purchasing manager's tasks are completed when the material is delivered for use in the factory. A performance report for the purchasing manager can be prepared at that point. However, the production manager's responsibilities have just begun at that point. A performance report for the production manager must be delayed until production is completed and it is known how much raw material was used in the final product. Therefore, it is important to clearly distinguish between deviations from price standards (the responsibility of the purchasing manager) and deviations from quantity standards (the responsibility of the production manager). Differences between *standard* prices and *actual* prices and between *standard* quantities and *actual* quantities are called **variances.** The act of computing and interpreting variances is called *variance analysis.*

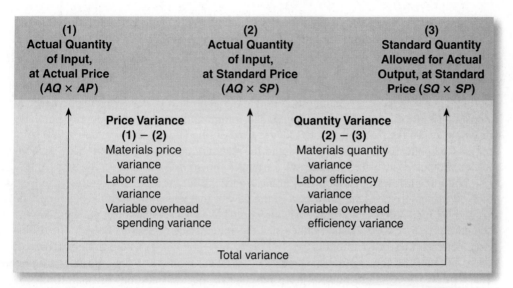

EXHIBIT 8–3
A General Model for Variance Analysis—Variable Manufacturing Costs

Price and Quantity Variances

Exhibit 8–3 presents a general model for computing standard cost variances for variable costs. This model isolates price variances from quantity variances and shows how each of these variances is computed.[2] We will be using this model throughout the chapter to compute variances for direct materials, direct labor, and variable manufacturing overhead.

Three things should be noted from Exhibit 8–3. First, a price variance and a quantity variance can be computed for each of the three variable costs—direct materials, direct labor, and variable manufacturing overhead—even though the variances have different names. For example, a price variance is called a *materials price variance* in the case of direct materials but a *labor rate variance* in the case of direct labor and an *overhead spending variance* in the case of variable manufacturing overhead.

Second, the price variance—regardless of what it is called—is computed in exactly the same way regardless of whether one is dealing with direct materials, direct labor, or variable manufacturing overhead. The same is true of the quantity variance.

Third, the input is the actual quantity of direct materials, direct labor, and variable manufacturing overhead used; the output is the good production of the period, expressed in terms of the *standard quantity (or the standard hours) allowed for the actual output* (see column 3 in Exhibit 8–3). The **standard quantity allowed** or **standard hours allowed** means the amount of an input *that should have been used* to produce the actual output of the period. This could be more or less than the actual amount of the input depending on the efficiency or inefficiency of operations. The standard quantity allowed is computed by multiplying the actual output in units by the standard input allowed per unit of output.

With this general model as the foundation, we will now calculate Colonial Pewter's price and quantity variances.

USING STANDARD COSTS—DIRECT MATERIALS VARIANCES

After determining Colonial Pewter Company's standard costs for direct materials, direct labor, and variable manufacturing overhead, the next step was to compute the company's variances for June, the most recent month. As discussed in the preceding section, variances

LEARNING OBJECTIVE 2

Compute the direct materials price and quantity variances and explain their significance.

---

[2]Variance analysis of fixed costs is discussed in the next chapter.

are computed by comparing standard costs to actual costs. The controller referred to the standard cost card in Exhibit 8–2 that shows that the standard cost of direct materials per pair of bookends is as follows:

$$3.0 \text{ pounds per unit} \times \$4.00 \text{ per pound} = \$12.00 \text{ per unit}$$

Colonial Pewter's records for June showed that 6,500 pounds of pewter were purchased at a cost of $3.80 per pound. This cost included freight and was net of a quantity purchase discount. All of the material purchased was used during June to manufacture 2,000 pairs of pewter bookends. Using these data and the standard costs from Exhibit 8–2, the controller computed the price and quantity variances shown in Exhibit 8–4.

The three arrows in Exhibit 8–4 point to three different total cost figures. The first, $24,700, refers to the actual total cost of the pewter that was purchased during June. The second, $26,000, refers to what the pewter would have cost if it had been purchased at the standard price of $4.00 a pound rather than the actual price of $3.80 a pound. The difference between these two amounts, $1,300 ($26,000 − $24,700), is the price variance. It exists because the actual purchase price was $0.20 per pound less than the standard purchase price. Since 6,500 pounds were purchased, the total amount of the variance is $1,300 ($0.20 per pound × 6,500 pounds). This variance is labeled favorable (denoted by F), since the actual purchase price was less than the standard purchase price. A price variance is labeled unfavorable (denoted by U) if the actual purchase price exceeds the standard purchase price.

The third arrow in Exhibit 8–4 points to $24,000—the cost if the pewter had been purchased at the standard price *and* only the standard quantity allowed per unit had been used. The standards call for 3 pounds of pewter per unit. Since 2,000 units were produced, 6,000 pounds of pewter should have been used. This is referred to as the standard quantity allowed for the actual output. If this 6,000 pounds of pewter had been purchased at the standard price of $4.00 per pound, the company would have spent $24,000. The difference between this amount, $24,000, and the amount at the end of the middle arrow in Exhibit 8–4, $26,000, is the quantity variance of $2,000.

To understand this quantity variance, note that the actual amount of pewter used in production was 6,500 pounds. However, the standard amount of pewter allowed for the actual output is 6,000 pounds. Therefore, a total of 500 pounds too much pewter was used to produce the actual output. To express this in dollar terms, the 500 pounds is multiplied by the standard price of $4.00 per pound to yield the quantity variance of $2,000. Why is the standard price, rather than the actual price, of the pewter used in this calculation? The production manager is ordinarily responsible for the quantity variance. If the actual price were used in the calculation of the quantity variance, the production manager would be held responsible for the efficiency or inefficiency of the purchasing manager. Apart from that being unfair, fruitless arguments between the production manager and purchasing manager

EXHIBIT 8–4
Variance Analysis—Direct Materials

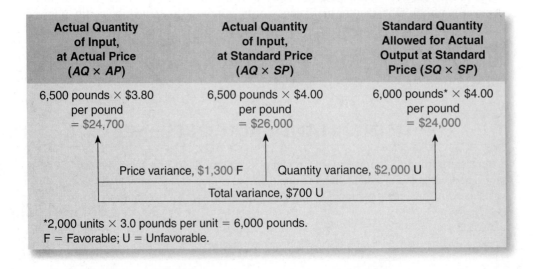

Actual Quantity of Input, at Actual Price (AQ × AP)	Actual Quantity of Input, at Standard Price (AQ × SP)	Standard Quantity Allowed for Actual Output at Standard Price (SQ × SP)
6,500 pounds × $3.80 per pound = $24,700	6,500 pounds × $4.00 per pound = $26,000	6,000 pounds* × $4.00 per pound = $24,000

Price variance, $1,300 F   Quantity variance, $2,000 U

Total variance, $700 U

*2,000 units × 3.0 pounds per unit = 6,000 pounds.
F = Favorable; U = Unfavorable.

would occur every time the actual price of an input is above its standard price. To avoid these arguments, the standard price is used when computing the quantity variance.

The quantity variance in Exhibit 8–4 is labeled unfavorable (denoted by U). This is because more pewter was used to produce the actual output than the standard allows. A quantity variance is labeled favorable (F) if the actual quantity is less than the standard quantity.

The computations in Exhibit 8–4 reflect the fact that all of the material purchased during June was also used during June. How are the variances computed if the amount of material purchased differs from the amount used? To illustrate, assume that during June the company purchased 6,500 pounds of materials, as before, but that it used only 5,000 pounds of material during the month and produced only 1,600 units. In this case, the price variance and quantity variance would be computed as shown in Exhibit 8–5.

Most companies compute the materials price variance when materials are *purchased* rather than when they are used in production. There are two reasons for this practice. First, delaying the computation of the price variance until the materials are used would result in less timely variance reports. Second, computing the price variance when the materials are purchased allows materials to be carried in the inventory accounts at their standard cost. This greatly simplifies bookkeeping. (See Appendix 8A at the end of the chapter for an explanation of how the bookkeeping works in a standard costing system.)

Note from the exhibit that the price variance is computed on the entire amount of material purchased (6,500 pounds), as before, whereas the quantity variance is computed only on the portion of this material used in production during the month (5,000 pounds). What about the other 1,500 pounds of material that were purchased during the period, but that have not yet been used? When those materials are used in future periods, a quantity variance will be computed. However, a price variance will not be computed when the materials are finally used because the price variance was computed when the materials were purchased. The situation illustrated in Exhibit 8–5 is common for companies that purchase materials well before they are used in production.

Materials Price Variance—A Closer Look

A **materials price variance** measures the difference between what is paid for a given quantity of materials and what should have been paid according to the standard. From

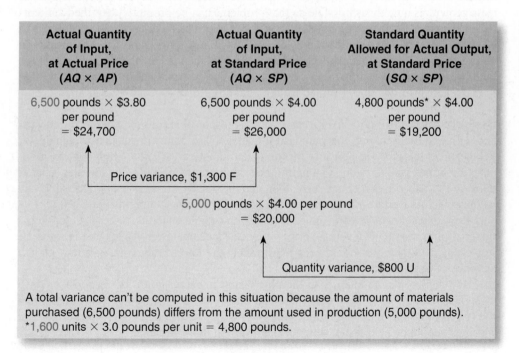

EXHIBIT 8–5
Variance Analysis—Direct Materials, When the Amount Purchased Differs from the Amount Used

Actual Quantity of Input, at Actual Price (AQ × AP)	Actual Quantity of Input, at Standard Price (AQ × SP)	Standard Quantity Allowed for Actual Output, at Standard Price (SQ × SP)
6,500 pounds × $3.80 per pound = $24,700	6,500 pounds × $4.00 per pound = $26,000	4,800 pounds* × $4.00 per pound = $19,200

Price variance, $1,300 F

5,000 pounds × $4.00 per pound = $20,000

Quantity variance, $800 U

A total variance can't be computed in this situation because the amount of materials purchased (6,500 pounds) differs from the amount used in production (5,000 pounds).
*1,600 units × 3.0 pounds per unit = 4,800 pounds.

Exhibit 8–4, this difference can be expressed by the following formula:

$$\text{Materials price variance} = (AQ \times AP) - (AQ \times SP)$$

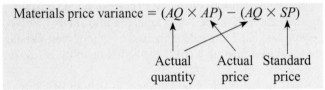

Actual   Actual Standard
quantity   price   price

The formula can be factored as follows:

$$\text{Materials price variance} = AQ(AP - SP)$$

Using the data from Exhibit 8–4 in this formula, we have the following:

$$6{,}500 \text{ pounds } (\$3.80 \text{ per pound} - \$4.00 \text{ per pound}) = \$1{,}300 \text{ F}$$

Notice that the answer is the same as that shown in Exhibit 8–4. Also note that when using this formula approach, a negative variance is always labeled as favorable (F) and a positive variance is always labeled as unfavorable (U). This will be true of all variance formulas in this and later chapters.

Variance reports are often presented in the form of a table. An excerpt from Colonial Pewter's variance report is shown below along with the purchasing manager's explanation for the materials price variance.

Colonial Pewter Company
Performance Report—Purchasing Department

Item Purchased	(1) Quantity Purchased	(2) Actual Price	(3) Standard Price	(4) Difference in Price (2) − (3)	Total Price Variance (1) × (4)	Explanation
Pewter	6,500 pounds	$3.80	$4.00	$0.20	$1,300 F	Bargained for an especially good price

F = Favorable; U = Unfavorable.

Isolation of Variances   Variances should be isolated and brought to the attention of management as quickly as possible so that problems can be promptly identified and corrected. The most significant variances should be viewed as "red flags"; an exception has occurred that requires explanation by the responsible manager and perhaps follow-up effort. The performance report itself may contain explanations for the variances, as illustrated above. In the case of Colonial Pewter Company, the purchasing manager said that the favorable price variance resulted from bargaining for an especially good price.

Responsibility for the Variance   Who is responsible for the materials price variance? Generally speaking, the purchasing manager has control over the price paid for goods and is therefore responsible for the materials price variance. Many factors influence the prices paid for goods including how many units are ordered, how the order is delivered, whether the order is a rush order, and the quality of materials purchased. If any of these factors deviates from what was assumed when the standards were set, a price variance can result. For example, purchasing second-grade materials rather than top-grade materials may result in a favorable price variance, since the lower-grade materials may be less costly. However, we should keep in mind that the lower-grade materials may be less suitable for production.

However, someone other than the purchasing manager could be responsible for a materials price variance. Production may be scheduled in such a way, for example, that the purchasing manager must request express delivery. In these cases, the production manager should be held responsible for the resulting price variances.

A word of caution is in order. Variance analysis should not be used to assign blame. The emphasis should be on *supporting* the line managers and *assisting* them in meeting the goals that they have participated in setting for the company. In short, the emphasis should be positive rather than negative. Excessive dwelling on what has already happened, particularly in terms of trying to find someone to blame, can destroy morale and kill any cooperative spirit.

Materials Quantity Variance—A Closer Look

The **materials quantity variance** measures the difference between the quantity of materials used in production and the quantity that should have been used according to the standard. Although the variance is concerned with the physical usage of materials, as shown in Exhibit 8–4, it is generally stated in dollar terms to help judge its importance. The formula for the materials quantity variance is as follows:

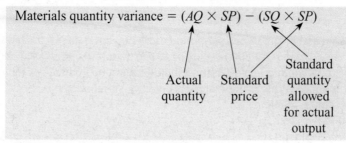

$$\text{Materials quantity variance} = (AQ \times SP) - (SQ \times SP)$$

Actual quantity   Standard price   Standard quantity allowed for actual output

Again, the formula can be factored as follows:

$$\text{Materials quantity variance} = SP(AQ - SQ)$$

Using the data from Exhibit 8–4 in the formula, we have the following:

$$\$4.00 \text{ per pound } (6{,}500 \text{ pounds} - 6{,}000 \text{ pounds}^*) = \$2{,}000 \text{ U}$$

*2,000 units $\times$ 3.0 pounds per unit = 6,000 pounds.

The answer, of course, is the same as that shown in Exhibit 8–4. The data might appear as follows if a formal performance report were prepared:

	(1)	(2)	(3)	(4)		
Colonial Pewter Company Performance Report—Production Department						
Type of Materials	Standard Price	Actual Quantity	Standard Quantity Allowed	Difference in Quantity (2) − (3)	Total Quantity Variance (1) × (4)	Explanation
Pewter	$4.00	6,500 pounds	6,000 pounds	500 pounds	$2,000 U	Low-quality materials unsuitable for production
F = Favorable; U = Unfavorable.						

The materials quantity variance is best isolated when materials are used in production. Materials are drawn for the number of units to be produced, according to the standard bill of materials for each unit. Any additional materials are usually drawn with an excess materials requisition slip, which is different in color from the normal requisition slips. This procedure calls attention to the excessive usage of materials *while production is still in process* and provides an opportunity to correct any developing problem.

Excessive materials usage can result from many factors, including faulty machines, inferior materials quality, untrained workers, and poor supervision. Generally speaking, it is the responsibility of the production department to see that material usage is kept in line with standards. There may be times, however, when the *purchasing* department is responsible for an unfavorable materials quantity variance. For example, if the purchasing department buys inferior materials at a lower price, the materials may be unsuitable for use and may result in excessive waste. Thus, purchasing rather than production would be responsible for the quantity variance. At Colonial Pewter, the production manager claimed on the Production Department's Performance Report that low-quality materials were the cause of the unfavorable materials quantity variance for June.

CONCEPT CHECK

1. The standard and actual prices per pound of raw material are $4.00 and $4.50, respectively. A total of 10,500 pounds of raw material was purchased and then used to produce 5,000 units. The quantity standard allows two pounds of the raw material per unit produced. What is the materials quantity variance?
   a. $5,000 unfavorable
   b. $5,000 favorable
   c. $2,000 favorable
   d. $2,000 unfavorable
2. Referring to the facts in question 1 above, what is the material price variance?
   a. $5,250 favorable
   b. $5,250 unfavorable
   c. $5,000 unfavorable
   d. $5,000 favorable

IN BUSINESS

What Happened to the Raisins?

Management at an unnamed breakfast cereal company became concerned about the apparent waste of raisins in one of its products. A box of the product was supposed to contain 10 ounces of cereal and 2 ounces of raisins. However, the production process had been using an average of 2.5 ounces of raisins per box. To correct the problem, a bonus was offered to employees if the consumption of raisins dropped to 2.1 ounces per box or less—which would allow for about 5% waste. Within a month, the target was hit and bonuses were distributed. However, another problem began to appear. Market studies indicated that customers had become dissatisfied with the amount of raisins in the product. Workers had hit the 2.1-ounce per box target by drastically reducing the amount of raisins in rush orders. Boxes of the completed product are ordinarily weighed and if the weight is less than 12 ounces, the box is rejected. However, rush orders aren't weighed since that would slow down the production process. Consequently, workers were reducing the raisins in rush orders so as to hit the overall target of 2.1 ounces of raisins per box. This resulted in substandard boxes of cereal in rush orders and customer complaints. Clearly, managers need to be very careful when they set targets and standards. They may not get what they bargained for. Subsequent investigation by an internal auditor revealed that, due to statistical fluctuations, an average of about 2.5 ounces of raisins must be used to ensure that every box contains at least 2 ounces of raisins.

Source: Harper A. Roehm and Joseph R. Castellano, "The Danger of Relying on Accounting Numbers Alone," *Management Accounting Quarterly*, Fall 1999, pp. 4–9.

USING STANDARD COSTS—DIRECT LABOR VARIANCES

The next step in determining Colonial Pewter's variances for June is to compute the direct labor variances for the month. Recall from Exhibit 8–2 that the standard direct labor cost per unit of product is $35, computed as follows:

LEARNING OBJECTIVE 3

Compute the direct labor rate and efficiency variances and explain their significance.

2.5 hours per unit × $14.00 per hour = $35.00 per unit

During June, the company paid its direct labor workers $74,250, including employment taxes and fringe benefits, for 5,400 hours of work. This was an average of $13.75 per hour. Using these data and the standard costs from Exhibit 8–2, the direct labor rate and efficiency variances are computed in Exhibit 8–6.

Notice that the column headings in Exhibit 8–6 are the same as those used in the prior two exhibits, except that in Exhibit 8–6 the terms *hours* and *rate* are used in place of the terms *quantity* and *price*.

Topic Tackler

PLUS

Concept 8-2

Labor Rate Variance—A Closer Look

As explained earlier, the price variance for direct labor is commonly termed a **labor rate variance.** This variance measures any deviation from standard in the average hourly rate paid to direct labor workers. The formula for the labor rate variance is expressed as follows:

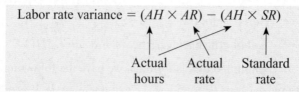

Labor rate variance = (AH × AR) − (AH × SR)

   Actual Actual Standard
   hours rate rate

The formula can be factored as follows:

Labor rate variance = AH(AR − SR)

Using the data from Exhibit 8–6 in the formula, the labor rate variance can be computed as follows:

5,400 hours ($13.75 per hour − $14.00 per hour) = $1,350 F

In most companies, the wage rates paid to workers are quite predictable. Nevertheless, rate variances can arise because of the way labor is used. Skilled workers with high hourly rates of pay may be given duties that require little skill and call for lower hourly rates of pay. This will result in an unfavorable labor rate variance, since the actual hourly

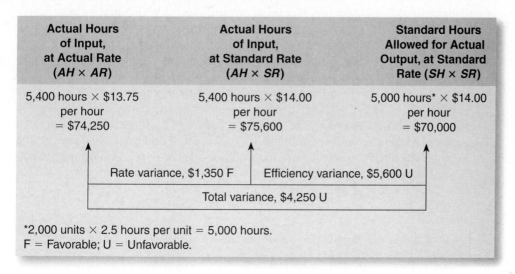

Actual Hours of Input, at Actual Rate (AH × AR)	Actual Hours of Input, at Standard Rate (AH × SR)	Standard Hours Allowed for Actual Output, at Standard Rate (SH × SR)
5,400 hours × $13.75 per hour = $74,250	5,400 hours × $14.00 per hour = $75,600	5,000 hours* × $14.00 per hour = $70,000

Rate variance, $1,350 F   Efficiency variance, $5,600 U

Total variance, $4,250 U

*2,000 units × 2.5 hours per unit = 5,000 hours.
F = Favorable; U = Unfavorable.

EXHIBIT 8–6
Variance Analysis—Direct Labor

rate of pay will exceed the standard rate specified for the particular task. In contrast, a favorable rate variance would result when workers who are paid at a rate lower than specified in the standard are assigned to the task. However, the lower paid workers may not be as efficient. Finally, overtime work at premium rates will result in an unfavorable rate variance if the overtime premium is charged to the direct labor account.

    Who is responsible for controlling the labor rate variance? Since labor rate variances generally arise as a result of how labor is used, production supervisors are usually responsible for seeing that labor rate variances are kept under control.

Labor Efficiency Variance—A Closer Look

The **labor efficiency variance** attempts to measure the productivity of direct labor. No variance is more closely watched by management, since it is widely believed that increasing direct labor productivity is vital to reducing costs. The formula for the labor efficiency variance is expressed as follows:

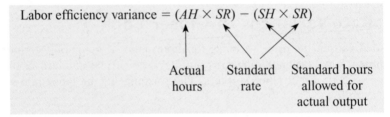

$$\text{Labor efficiency variance} = (AH \times SR) - (SH \times SR)$$

Actual hours   Standard rate   Standard hours allowed for actual output

The formula can be factored as follows:

$$\text{Labor efficiency variance} = SR(AH - SH)$$

Using the data from Exhibit 8–6 in this formula, we have the following:

$$\$14.00 \text{ per hour } (5{,}400 \text{ hours } - 5{,}000 \text{ hours}^*) = \$5{,}600 \text{ U}$$

*2,000 units × 2.5 hours per unit = 5,000 hours.

    Possible causes of an unfavorable labor efficiency variance include poorly trained or motivated workers; poor quality materials, requiring more labor time; faulty equipment, causing breakdowns and work interruptions; poor supervision of workers; and inaccurate standards. The managers in charge of production would usually be responsible for control of the labor efficiency variance. However, the purchasing manager could be held responsible if purchase of poor quality materials resulted in excessive labor processing time.

    Another important cause of an unfavorable labor efficiency variance may be insufficient demand for the company's products. Managers in some companies argue that it is difficult, and perhaps unwise, to constantly adjust the workforce in response to changes in the amount of work that needs to be done. In such companies, the direct labor workforce is essentially fixed in the short run. If demand is insufficient to keep everyone busy, workers are not laid off. In this case, if demand falls below the level needed to keep everyone busy, an unfavorable labor efficiency variance will often be recorded.

    If customer orders are insufficient to keep the workers busy, the work center manager has two options—either accept an unfavorable labor efficiency variance or build inventory.[3] A central lesson of Lean Production is that building inventory with no immediate prospect of sale is a bad idea. Excessive inventory—particularly work in process inventory—leads to high defect rates, obsolete goods, and inefficient operations. As a consequence, when the workforce is basically fixed in the short term, managers must be cautious about how labor efficiency variances are used. Some experts advocate eliminating labor efficiency variances entirely in such situations—at least for the purposes of motivating and controlling workers on the shop floor.

---

[3]For further discussion, see Eliyahu M. Goldratt and Jeff Cox, *The Goal,* 2nd rev. ed. (Croton-on-Hudson, NY: North River Press).

Does Direct Labor Variance Reporting Increase Productivity?

Professors Rajiv Banker, Sarv Devaraj, Roger Schroeder, and Kingshuk Sinha studied the direct labor variance reporting practices at 18 plants of a Fortune 500 manufacturing company. Seven of the plants eliminated direct labor variance reporting and the other 11 plants did not. The group of seven plants that eliminated direct labor variance reporting experienced an 11% decline in labor productivity, which was significantly greater than the decline experienced by the other 11 plants. The authors estimated that the annual loss due to the decline in labor productivity across the seven plants of $1,996,000 was only partially offset by the $200,000 saved by eliminating the need to track direct labor variances.

While these findings suggest that direct labor variance reporting is a useful tool for monitoring direct labor workers, advocates of Lean Production would argue otherwise. They would claim that direct labor variance reporting is a non-value-added activity that encourages excessive production and demoralizes direct labor workers. The two points-of-view provide an interesting opportunity to debate the appropriate role of management accounting within organizations.

Source: Rajiv Banker, Sarv Devaraj, Roger Schroeder, and Kingshuk Sinha, "Performance Impact of the Elimination of Direct Labor Variance Reporting: A Field Study," *Journal of Accounting Research*, September 2002, pp. 1013–1036.

Department Resources Manager

You are the manager of the computer-generated special effects department for a company that produces special effects for high-profile films. You receive a copy of this month's performance report for your department and discover a large labor efficiency variance that is unfavorable. What factors might have contributed to this unfavorable variance?

USING STANDARD COSTS—VARIABLE MANUFACTURING OVERHEAD VARIANCES

LEARNING OBJECTIVE 4

Compute the variable manufacturing overhead spending and efficiency variances.

The final step in the analysis of Colonial Pewter's variances for June is to compute the variable manufacturing overhead variances. The variable portion of manufacturing overhead can be analyzed using the same basic formulas that are used to analyze direct materials and direct labor. Recall from Exhibit 8–2 that the standard variable manufacturing overhead is $7.50 per unit of product, computed as follows:

$$2.5 \text{ hours per unit} \times \$3.00 \text{ per hour} = \$7.50 \text{ per unit}$$

Colonial Pewter's cost records showed that the total actual variable manufacturing overhead cost for June was $15,390. Recall from the earlier discussion of the direct labor variances that 5,400 hours of direct labor time were recorded during the month and that the company produced 2,000 pairs of bookends. The analysis of this overhead data appears in Exhibit 8–7.

Notice the similarities between Exhibits 8–6 and 8–7. These similarities arise from the fact that direct labor-hours are being used as the base for allocating overhead cost to units of product; thus, the same hourly figures appear in Exhibit 8–7 for variable manufacturing overhead as in Exhibit 8–6 for direct labor. The main difference between the two exhibits is in the standard hourly rate being used, which in this company is much lower for variable manufacturing overhead than for direct labor.

EXHIBIT 8–7
Variance Analysis—Variable
Manufacturing Overhead

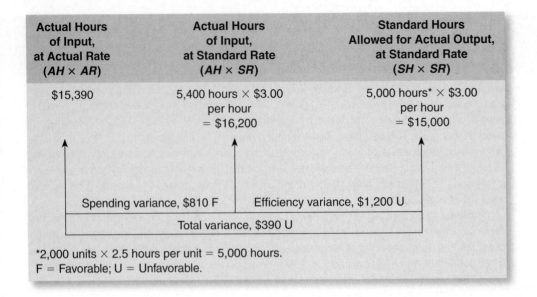

Actual Hours of Input, at Actual Rate (AH × AR)	Actual Hours of Input, at Standard Rate (AH × SR)	Standard Hours Allowed for Actual Output, at Standard Rate (SH × SR)
$15,390	5,400 hours × $3.00 per hour = $16,200	5,000 hours* × $3.00 per hour = $15,000

Spending variance, $810 F   Efficiency variance, $1,200 U

Total variance, $390 U

*2,000 units × 2.5 hours per unit = 5,000 hours.
F = Favorable; U = Unfavorable.

Manufacturing Overhead Variances—A Closer Look

The formula for the **variable overhead spending variance** is expressed as follows:

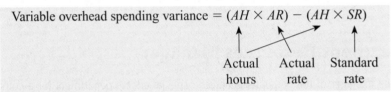

$$\text{Variable overhead spending variance} = (AH \times AR) - (AH \times SR)$$

Actual hours   Actual rate   Standard rate

This formula can be factored as follows:

$$\text{Variable overhead spending variance} = AH(AR - SR)$$

Using the data from Exhibit 8–7 in the formula, the variable overhead spending variance can be computed as follows:

$$5,400 \text{ hours } (\$2.85 \text{ per hour*} - \$3.00 \text{ per hour}) = \$810 \text{ F}$$

*$15,390 ÷ 5,400 hours = $2.85 per hour.

The formula for the **variable overhead efficiency variance** is expressed as follows:

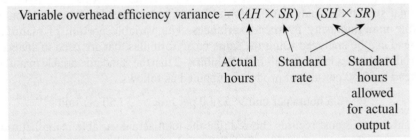

$$\text{Variable overhead efficiency variance} = (AH \times SR) - (SH \times SR)$$

Actual hours   Standard rate   Standard hours allowed for actual output

This formula can be factored as follows:

$$\text{Variable overhead efficiency variance} = SR(AH - SH)$$

Again using the data from Exhibit 8–7, the variance can be computed as follows:

$$\$3.00 \text{ per hour } (5,400 \text{ hours } - 5,000 \text{ hours*}) = \$1,200 \text{ U}$$

*2,000 units × 2.5 hours per unit = 5,000 hours.

We will reserve further discussion of the variable overhead spending and efficiency variances until the next chapter, where overhead analysis is discussed in depth.

Before proceeding further, we suggest that you pause at this point and go back and review the data contained in Exhibits 8–2 through 8–7. These exhibits and the accompanying text discussion provide a comprehensive, integrated illustration of standard setting and variance analysis.

CONCEPT CHECK ✓

3. The actual direct labor wage rate is $8.50 and 4,500 direct labor-hours were actually worked during the month. The standard direct labor wage rate is $8.00 and the standard quantity of hours allowed for the actual level of output was 5,000 direct labor-hours. What is the direct labor efficiency variance?
   a. $4,000 favorable
   b. $4,000 unfavorable
   c. $4,500 unfavorable
   d. $4,500 favorable
4. Referring to the facts in question 3 above, what is the variable overhead efficiency variance if the standard variable overhead per direct labor-hour is $5.00?
   a. $5,000 favorable
   b. $5,000 unfavorable
   c. $2,500 unfavorable
   d. $2,500 favorable

To review Colonial Pewter's standard cost variances, the largest variances are the unfavorable materials quantity variance of $2,000 and the unfavorable labor efficiency variance of $5,600. These variances were thoroughly discussed by the responsible managers, with the conclusion that the variances were probably due to the new inexperienced workers. The unfavorable labor efficiency variance was probably due to the inability of the inexperienced workers to work as fast or as effectively as the company's seasoned workforce. The materials quantity variance was traced to an unusually large number of rejected bookends that resulted from faulty workmanship. The production manager reported that efforts were already under way to correct these problems. The newer workers were being teamed with more experienced workers to show them more efficient and effective ways of doing their jobs.

VARIANCE ANALYSIS AND MANAGEMENT BY EXCEPTION

Variance analysis and performance reports are important elements of *management by exception*, which is an approach that emphasizes focusing on those areas of responsibility where goals and expectations are not being met.

The budgets and standards discussed in this chapter and in the preceding chapter reflect management's plans. If all goes according to plan, there will be little difference between actual results and the results that would be expected according to the budgets and standards. If this happens, managers can concentrate on other issues. However, if actual results do not conform to the budget and to standards, the performance reporting system sends a signal to the manager that an "exception" has occurred. This signal is in the form of a variance from the budget or standards.

However, are all variances worth investigating? The answer is no. Differences between actual results and what was expected will almost always occur. If every variance were investigated, management would waste a great deal of time tracking down nickel-and-dime differences. Variances may occur for a variety of reasons—only some of which are significant and worthy of management's attention. For example, hotter-than-normal weather in the summer may result in higher-than-expected electrical bills for air conditioning. Or, workers may work slightly faster or slower on a particular day. Because of

Video 8–1

unpredictable random factors, one can expect that virtually every cost category will produce a variance of some kind.

How should managers decide which variances are worth investigating? One clue is the size of the variance. A variance of $5.00 is probably not big enough to warrant attention, whereas a variance of $5,000 might well be worth tracking down. Another clue is the size of the variance relative to the amount of spending. A variance that is only 0.1% of spending on an item is likely to be well within the bounds one would normally expect due to random factors. On the other hand, a variance of 10% of spending is much more likely to be a signal that something is wrong.

In addition to watching for unusually large variances, the pattern of the variances should be monitored. For example, a run of steadily mounting variances should trigger an investigation even though none of the variances is large enough by itself to warrant investigation.

EVALUATION OF CONTROLS BASED ON STANDARD COSTS

Advantages of Standard Costs

Standard cost systems have a number of advantages.

1. Standard costs are a key element in a management by exception approach. If costs conform to the standards, managers can focus on other issues. When costs are significantly outside the standards, managers are alerted that there may be problems requiring attention. This approach helps managers focus on important issues.
2. Standards that are viewed as reasonable by employees can promote economy and efficiency. They provide benchmarks that individuals can use to judge their own performance.
3. Standard costs can greatly simplify bookkeeping. Instead of recording actual costs for each job, the standard costs for direct materials, direct labor, and overhead can be charged to jobs.
4. Standard costs fit naturally in an integrated system of "responsibility accounting." The standards establish what costs should be, who should be responsible for them, and whether actual costs are under control.

Potential Problems with the Use of Standard Costs

The improper use of standard costs can present a number of potential problems.

1. Standard cost variance reports are usually prepared on a monthly basis and often are released days or even weeks after the end of the month. As a consequence, the information in the reports may be so outdated that it is almost useless. Timely, frequent reports that are approximately correct are better than infrequent reports that are very precise but out of date by the time they are released. Some companies are now reporting variances and other key operating data daily or even more frequently.
2. If managers are insensitive and use variance reports as a club, morale will suffer. Employees should receive positive reinforcement for work well done. Management by exception, by its nature, tends to focus on the negative. If variances are used as a club, subordinates may be tempted to cover up unfavorable variances or take actions that are not in the best interests of the company to make sure the variances are favorable. For example, workers may put on a crash effort to increase output at the end of the month to avoid an unfavorable labor efficiency variance. In the rush to produce more output, quality may suffer.
3. Labor quantity standards and efficiency variances make two important assumptions. First, they assume that the production process is labor-paced; if labor works faster, output will go up. However, output in many companies is not determined by how fast labor works; rather, it is determined by the processing speed of machines. Second, the computations assume that labor is a variable cost. However, direct labor may be essentially fixed. If labor is fixed, then an undue emphasis on labor efficiency variances creates pressure to build excess inventories.

4. In some cases, a "favorable" variance can be as bad or worse than an "unfavorable" variance. For example, McDonald's has a standard for the amount of hamburger meat that should be in a Big Mac. A "favorable" variance would mean that less meat was used than the standard specifies. The result is a substandard Big Mac and possibly a dissatisfied customer.

5. Too much emphasis on meeting the standards may overshadow other important objectives such as maintaining and improving quality, on-time delivery, and customer satisfaction. This tendency can be reduced by using supplemental performance measures that focus on these other objectives.

6. Just meeting standards may not be sufficient; continual improvement may be necessary to survive in a competitive environment. For this reason, some companies focus on the trends in the standard cost variances—aiming for continual improvement rather than just meeting the standards. In other companies, engineered standards are replaced either by a rolling average of actual costs, which is expected to decline, or by very challenging target costs.

In sum, managers should exercise considerable care when using a standard cost system. It is particularly important that managers go out of their way to focus on the positive, rather than just on the negative, and to be aware of possible unintended consequences.

Nevertheless, standard costs are found in the vast majority of manufacturing companies and in many service companies, although their use is changing. For evaluating performance, standard cost variances are often complemented by a performance measurement system called the *balanced scorecard,* which is discussed in the next section. The balanced scorecard concept has been eagerly embraced by a wide variety of organizations, including Analog Devices, KPMG, Tenneco, Allstate, AT&T, Elf Atochem, Conair-Franklin, CIGNA Corporation, London Life Insurance Co., Southern Gardens Citrus Processing, Duke Children's Hospital, JP Morgan Chase, 3COM, Rockwater, Apple Computer, Advanced Micro Devices (AMD), FMC, the Bank of Montreal, the Massachusetts Special Olympics, United Way of Southeastern New England, Boston Lyric Opera, Bridgeport Hospital and Healthcare Services, and the Housing Authority of Fiji.

When Improvement Isn't Better

IN BUSINESS

Mark Graham Brown, a performance-measurement consultant, warns managers to focus on the right metrics when measuring performance. He relates the following story: "A fast-food chain gave lip service to many objectives, but what senior managers watched most rigorously was how much chicken its restaurants had to throw away... What happened? As one restaurant operator explained, it was easy to hit your... targets: just don't cook any chicken until somebody orders it. Customers might have to wait 20 minutes for their meal, and would probably never come back—but you'd sure make your numbers. Moral: a measurement may look good on paper, but you need to ask what behavior it will drive."

Source: "Using Measurement to Boost Your Unit's Performance," *Harvard Management Update*, October 1998.

BALANCED SCORECARD

A **balanced scorecard** consists of an integrated set of performance measures that are derived from and support the company's strategy. A strategy is essentially a theory about how to achieve the organization's goals. For example, Southwest Airlines' strategy is to offer an *operational excellence* customer value proposition that has three key components—low ticket prices, convenience, and reliability. The company operates only one type of aircraft, the Boeing 737, to reduce maintenance and training costs and simplify scheduling. It further reduces costs by not offering meals, seat assignments, or baggage transfers and by booking a large portion of its passenger revenue over the Internet. Southwest also uses point-to-point flights rather than the hub-and-spoke approach of its larger competitors, thereby providing customers convenient, nonstop service to their final destination. Since Southwest serves many less congested airports such as Chicago Midway, Burbank, Manchester, Oakland, and Providence, it offers quicker passenger check-ins and reliable departures, while maintaining high asset utilization (i.e., the company's average gate turn-around time of 25 minutes enables it to function with fewer planes and gates). Overall, the company's strategy has worked. At a time when Southwest Airlines' larger competitors are struggling, it continues to earn substantial profits.

IN BUSINESS   **A Picture Is Worth a Thousand Numbers**

Graphics are routinely integrated in Balanced Scorecard reports, with data often displayed on a "dashboard" with representations of gauges and digital readouts. At Beverage Can Americas Co. in Chicago, a division of London-based Rexam Plc., executive dashboards and scorecards are being rolled out to thousands of employees. "Each worker sees a handful of metrics that pertain to his or her job, which are represented as green, yellow, or red icons depending on whether they are satisfactory, borderline, or subpar."

Source: Scott Leibs, "Now You See It," *CFO*, July 2002, pp. 61–66.

Under the balanced scorecard approach, top management translates its strategy into performance measures that employees can understand and influence. For example, the amount of time passengers have to wait in line to have their baggage checked might be a performance measure for the supervisor in charge of the Southwest Airlines check-in counter at the Burbank airport. This performance measure is easily understood by the supervisor and can be improved by the supervisor's actions. Under the balanced scorecard approach, nonfinancial measures of performance—such as the amount of time passengers must wait to check bags—are used in addition to financial measures of performance such as standard cost variances. Nonfinancial measures of performance of quality and customer satisfaction are particularly important since they typically tie directly to the company's strategy in a cause-and-effect manner and they serve as leading indicators of the company's success.

SUMMARY

LO1   Explain how direct materials standards and direct labor standards are set.
Each direct cost has both a price and a quantity standard. The standard price for an input is the price that should be paid for a single unit of the input. In the case of direct materials, the price should include shipping costs and should be net of quantity and other discounts. In the case of direct labor, the standard rate should include wages, fringe benefits, and employment taxes.

LO2   Compute the direct materials price and quantity variances and explain their significance.
The materials price variance is the difference between the actual price paid for materials and the standard price, multiplied by the quantity purchased. An unfavorable variance occurs whenever the actual price exceeds the standard price. A favorable variance occurs when the actual price is less than the standard price for the input.

The materials quantity variance is the difference between the amount of materials actually used and the amount that should have been used to produce the actual good output of the period, multiplied by the standard price per unit of the input. An unfavorable materials quantity variance occurs when the amount of materials actually used exceeds the amount that should have been used according to the materials quantity standard. A favorable variance occurs when the amount of materials actually used is less than the amount that should have been used according to the standard.

LO3   Compute the direct labor rate and efficiency variances and explain their significance.
The direct labor rate variance is the difference between the actual wage rate paid and the standard wage rate, multiplied by the hours worked. An unfavorable variance occurs whenever the actual wage rate exceeds the standard wage rate. A favorable variance occurs when the actual wage rate is less than the standard wage rate.

The labor efficiency variance is the difference between the hours actually worked and the hours that should have been used to produce the actual good output of the period, multiplied by the standard wage rate. An unfavorable labor efficiency variance occurs when the hours actually worked exceed the hours allowed for the actual output. A favorable variance occurs when the hours actually worked are less than hours allowed for the actual output.

LO4 Compute the variable manufacturing overhead spending and efficiency variances.
The variable manufacturing overhead spending variance is the difference between the actual variable manufacturing overhead cost incurred and the actual hours worked multiplied by the standard variable manufacturing overhead rate. The variable manufacturing overhead efficiency variance is the difference between the hours actually worked and the hours that should have been used to produce the actual good output of the period, multiplied by the standard variable manufacturing overhead rate.

GUIDANCE ANSWERS TO *DECISION MAKER* AND *YOU DECIDE*

Owner of a Painting Company (p. 339)
The standards published in the trade magazine are for professional painters; at least initially, these standards would not be realistic for your inexperienced painting crew. Therefore, the standards would not be particularly useful for bidding on jobs or for setting budgets. Nevertheless, the standards would provide important feedback about how well the painting crew is performing relative to the professional competition. Setting a goal of beating the professional painters (as represented by the standards) might energize your painting crew and motivate them to work harder and to think of innovative ways of improving the painting process.

Psychologically, it might be best not to use the labels *unfavorable* and *favorable* for the variances since almost all of them will initially be unfavorable. Instead, you might focus on the ratio of the actual time to the standard time, with the idea that this ratio should decline over time and eventually should be less than 1.0. This ratio could be plotted on a weekly or daily basis and displayed in a prominent location so that everyone in the painting crew can see how well the crew is doing relative to professional painters.

Department Resources Manager (p. 351)
An unfavorable labor efficiency variance in the computer-generated special effects department might have been caused by inexperienced, poorly trained, or unmotivated employees, faulty hardware and/or software that may have caused work interruptions, and/or poor supervision of the employees in this department. In addition, it is possible that there was insufficient demand for the output of this department—resulting in idle time—or that the standard (or benchmark) for this department is inaccurate.

GUIDANCE ANSWERS TO CONCEPT CHECKS

1. **Choice d.** The materials quantity variance is (10,500 pounds used − 10,000 pounds allowed) × $4.00 per pound = $2,000 unfavorable.
2. **Choice b.** The materials price variance is ($4.50 actual price per pound − $4.00 standard price per pound) × 10,500 pounds purchased = $5,250 unfavorable.
3. **Choice a.** The direct labor efficiency variance is (4,500 hours − 5,000 hours) × $8.00 standard hourly rate = $4,000 favorable.
4. **Choice d.** The variable overhead efficiency variance is (4,500 hours − 5,000 hours) × $5.00 per hour = $2,500 favorable.

REVIEW PROBLEM: STANDARD COSTS

Xavier Company produces a single product. Variable manufacturing overhead is applied to products on the basis of direct labor-hours. The standard costs for one unit of product are as follows:

Direct material: 6 ounces at $0.50 per ounce	$ 3.00
Direct labor: 1.8 hours at $10 per hour	18.00
Variable manufacturing overhead: 1.8 hours at $5 per hour	9.00
Total standard variable cost per unit.	$30.00

During June, 2,000 units were produced. The costs associated with June's operations were as follows:

Material purchased: 18,000 ounces at $0.60 per ounce	$10,800
Material used in production: 14,000 ounces	—
Direct labor: 4,000 hours at $9.75 per hour	$39,000
Variable manufacturing overhead costs incurred	$20,800

Required:

Compute the direct materials, direct labor, and variable manufacturing overhead variances.

Solution to Review Problem

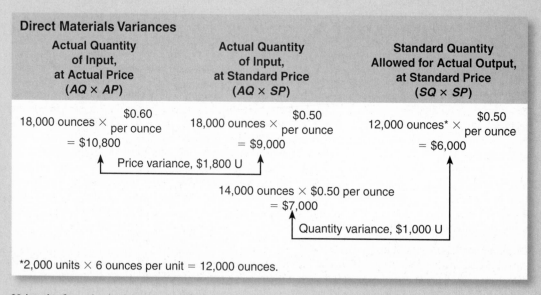

Direct Materials Variances

Actual Quantity of Input, at Actual Price ($AQ \times AP$)	Actual Quantity of Input, at Standard Price ($AQ \times SP$)	Standard Quantity Allowed for Actual Output, at Standard Price ($SQ \times SP$)
18,000 ounces × $0.60 per ounce = $10,800	18,000 ounces × $0.50 per ounce = $9,000	12,000 ounces* × $0.50 per ounce = $6,000

Price variance, $1,800 U

14,000 ounces × $0.50 per ounce = $7,000

Quantity variance, $1,000 U

*2,000 units × 6 ounces per unit = 12,000 ounces.

Using the formulas in the chapter, the same variances would be computed as follows:

$$\text{Materials price variance} = AQ(AP - SP)$$
$$18,000 \text{ ounces } (\$0.60 \text{ per ounce} - \$0.50 \text{ per ounce}) = \$1,800 \text{ U}$$

$$\text{Materials quantity variance} = SP(AQ - SQ)$$
$$\$0.50 \text{ per ounce } (14,000 \text{ ounces} - 12,000 \text{ ounces}) = \$1,000 \text{ U}$$

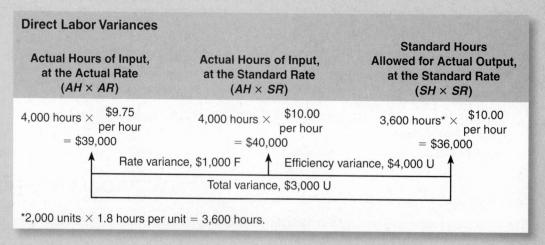

Direct Labor Variances

Actual Hours of Input, at the Actual Rate ($AH \times AR$)	Actual Hours of Input, at the Standard Rate ($AH \times SR$)	Standard Hours Allowed for Actual Output, at the Standard Rate ($SH \times SR$)
4,000 hours × $9.75 per hour = $39,000	4,000 hours × $10.00 per hour = $40,000	3,600 hours* × $10.00 per hour = $36,000

Rate variance, $1,000 F   Efficiency variance, $4,000 U

Total variance, $3,000 U

*2,000 units × 1.8 hours per unit = 3,600 hours.

Using the formulas in the chapter, the same variances would be computed as follows:

$$\text{Labor rate variance} = AH(AR - SR)$$
$$4,000 \text{ hours } (\$9.75 \text{ per hour} - \$10.00 \text{ per hour}) = \$1,000 \text{ F}$$

$$\text{Labor efficiency variance} = SR(AH - SH)$$
$$\$10.00 \text{ per hour } (4,000 \text{ hours} - 3,600 \text{ hour}) = \$4,000 \text{ U}$$

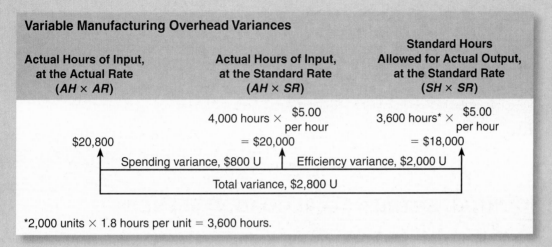

Variable Manufacturing Overhead Variances

Actual Hours of Input, at the Actual Rate ($AH \times AR$)	Actual Hours of Input, at the Standard Rate ($AH \times SR$)	Standard Hours Allowed for Actual Output, at the Standard Rate ($SH \times SR$)
	4,000 hours × $\$5.00$ per hour = $\$20,000$	3,600 hours* × $\$5.00$ per hour = $\$18,000$
$\$20,800$		

Spending variance, $800 U   Efficiency variance, $2,000 U

Total variance, $2,800 U

*2,000 units × 1.8 hours per unit = 3,600 hours.

Using the formulas in the chapter, the same variances would be computed as:

$$\text{Variable overhead spending variance} = AH(AR - SR)$$
$$4,000 \text{ hours } (\$5.20 \text{ per hour*} - \$5.00 \text{ per hour}) = \$800 \text{ U}$$

*$20,800 ÷ 4,000 hours = $5.20 per hour.

$$\text{Variable overhead efficiency variance} = SR(AH - SH)$$
$$\$5.00 \text{ per hour } (4,000 \text{ hours } - 3,600 \text{ hours }) = \$2,000 \text{ U}$$

GLOSSARY

Balanced scorecard   An integrated set of performance measures that are derived from and support the organization's strategy. (p. 355)

Ideal standards   Standards that assume peak efficiency at all times. (p. 339)

Labor efficiency variance   The difference between the actual hours taken to complete a task and the standard hours allowed, multiplied by the standard hourly labor rate. (p. 350)

Labor rate variance   The difference between the actual hourly labor rate and the standard rate, multiplied by the number of hours worked during the period. (p. 349)

Management by exception   A management system in which standards are set for various activities, with actual results compared to these standards. Significant deviations from standards are flagged as exceptions. (p. 337)

Materials price variance   The difference between the actual unit price paid for an item and the standard price, multiplied by the quantity purchased. (p. 345)

Materials quantity variance   The difference between the actual quantity of materials used in production and the standard quantity allowed for the actual output, multiplied by the standard price per unit of materials. (p. 347)

Practical standards   Standards that allow for normal machine downtime and other work interruptions and that can be attained through reasonable, though highly efficient, efforts by the average worker. (p. 339)

Standard cost card   A detailed listing of the standard amounts of inputs and their costs that are required to produce a unit of a specific product. (p. 339)

Standard cost per unit   The standard quantity allowed of an input per unit of a specific product, multiplied by the standard price of the input. (p. 342)

Standard hours allowed   The time that should have been taken to complete the period's output. It is computed by multiplying the actual number of units produced by the standard hours per unit. (p. 343)

Standard hours per unit   The amount of direct labor time that should be required to complete a single unit of product, including allowances for breaks, machine downtime, cleanup, rejects, and other normal inefficiencies. (p. 341)

Standard price per unit   The price that should be paid for an input. The price should be net of discounts and should include any shipping costs. (p. 340)

Standard quantity allowed   The amount of an input that should have been used to complete the period's actual output. It is computed by multiplying the actual number of units produced by the standard quantity per unit. (p. 343)

Standard quantity per unit   The amount of an input that should be required to complete a single unit of product, including allowances for normal waste, spoilage, rejects, and other normal inefficiencies. (p. 340)

Standard rate per hour   The labor rate that should be incurred per hour of labor time, including employment taxes and fringe benefits. (p. 341)

Variable overhead efficiency variance   The difference between the actual level of activity (direct labor-hours, machine-hours, or some other base) and the standard activity allowed, multiplied by the variable part of the predetermined overhead rate. (p. 352)

Variable overhead spending variance   The difference between the actual variable overhead cost incurred during a period and the standard cost that should have been incurred based on the actual activity of the period. (p. 352)

Variance   The differences between standard prices and actual prices and between standard quantities and actual quantities. (p. 342)

APPENDIX 8A: JOURNAL ENTRIES TO RECORD VARIANCES

> **LEARNING OBJECTIVE 5**
>
> Prepare journal entries to record standard costs and variances.

Although standard costs and variances can be computed and used without being formally entered into the accounting records, many organizations prefer to make formal journal entries. Formal entry tends to give variances a greater emphasis than informal, off-the-record computations. This emphasis signals management's desire to keep costs within the limits that have been set. In addition, formal use of standard costs simplifies the bookkeeping process enormously. Inventories and cost of goods sold can be valued at their standard costs—eliminating the need to keep track of the actual cost of each unit.

Direct Materials Variances

To illustrate the journal entries needed to record standard cost variances, we will return to the data contained in the review problem at the end of the chapter. The entry to record the purchase of direct materials would be as follows:

Raw Materials (18,000 ounces at $0.50 per ounce)......	9,000	
Materials Price Variance (18,000 ounces at $0.10 per ounce U)...............................	1,800	
Accounts Payable (18,000 ounces at $0.60 per ounce)..		10,800

Notice that the price variance is recognized when purchases are made, rather than when materials are actually used in production and that the materials are carried in the inventory account at standard cost. As direct materials are later drawn from inventory and used in production, the quantity variance is recorded as follows:

Work in Process (12,000 ounces at $0.50 per ounce).....	6,000	
Materials Quantity Variance (2,000 ounces U at $0.50 per ounce)................................	1,000	
Raw Materials (14,000 ounces at $0.50 per ounce)..		7,000

Thus, direct materials are added to the Work in Process account at the standard cost of the materials that should have been used to produce the actual output.

Notice that both the price variance and the quantity variance above are unfavorable and are debit entries. If either of these variances had been favorable, it would have appeared as a credit entry.

Direct Labor Variances

Referring again to the cost data in the review problem at the end of the chapter, the journal entry to record the incurrence of direct labor cost would be:

Work in Process (3,600 hours at $10.00 per hour)	36,000	
Labor Efficiency Variance (400 hours U at $10.00 per hour) ..	4,000	
Labor Rate Variance (4,000 hours at $0.25 per hour F)..		1,000
Wages Payable (4,000 hours at $9.75 per hour)......		39,000

Thus, as with direct materials, direct labor costs enter into the Work in Process account at standard, both in terms of the rate and in terms of the hours allowed for the actual production of the period. Note that the unfavorable labor efficiency variance is a debit entry whereas the favorable labor rate variance is a credit entry.

Variable Manufacturing Overhead Variances

Variable manufacturing overhead variances are usually not recorded in the accounts separately but rather are determined as part of the general analysis of overhead, which is discussed in the next chapter.

Cost Flows in a Standard Cost System

The flows of costs through the company's accounts are illustrated in Exhibit 8A–1. Note that entries into the various inventory accounts are made at standard cost—not actual cost. The differences between actual and standard costs are entered into special accounts that accumulate the various standard cost variances. Ordinarily, these standard cost variance accounts are closed out to Cost of Goods Sold at the end of the period. Unfavorable variances increase Cost of Goods Sold, and favorable variances decrease Cost of Goods Sold.

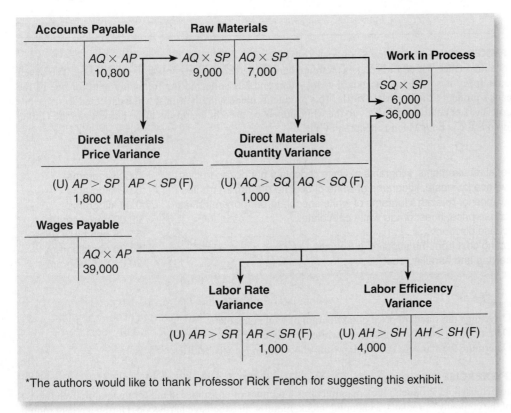

EXHIBIT 8A–1
Cost Flows in a Standard Cost System*

*The authors would like to thank Professor Rick French for suggesting this exhibit.

SUMMARY FOR APPENDIX 8A

LO5 (Appendix 8A) Prepare journal entries to record standard costs and variances.
Raw materials, work in process, and finished goods inventories are all carried at their standard costs. Differences between actual and standard costs are recorded as variances. Favorable variances are credit entries and unfavorable variances are debit entries.

3. Post the entries you have prepared to the following T-accounts:

Raw Materials			Work in Process			Labor Rate Variance
?	?		Materials used ?			
Bal. ?			Labor cost ?			

Materials Price Variance			Accounts Payable			Labor Efficiency Variance
			40,250			

Materials Quantity Variance			Wages Payable	
			8,120	

PROBLEMS

PROBLEM 8–12A   Comprehensive Variance Analysis (LO2, LO3, LO4)
Kramer Toy Company manufactures a plastic swimming pool at its East Crest Plant. The plant has been experiencing problems as shown by its September contribution format income statement below:

	Budgeted	Actual
Sales (15,000 pools)	$495,000	$495,000
Variable expenses:		
Variable cost of goods sold*	220,050	227,120
Variable selling expenses	24,000	24,000
Total variable expenses	244,050	251,120
Contribution margin	250,950	243,880
Fixed expenses:		
Manufacturing overhead	128,000	128,000
Selling and administrative	85,000	85,000
Total fixed expenses	213,000	213,000
Net operating income	$ 37,950	$ 30,880

*Contains direct materials, direct labor, and variable manufacturing overhead.

Janet Wilson, who has just been appointed general manager of the East Crest Plant, has been given instructions to "get things under control." Upon reviewing the plant's income statement, Ms. Wilson has concluded that the major problem lies in the variable cost of goods sold. She has been provided with the following standard cost per swimming pool:

	Standard Quantity or Hours	Standard Price or Rate	Standard Cost
Direct materials	3.2 pounds	$1.80 per pound	$ 5.76
Direct labor	0.8 hours	$9.20 per hour	7.36
Variable manufacturing overhead	0.5 hours*	$3.10 per hour	1.55
Total standard cost			$14.67

*Based on machine-hours.

Ms. Wilson has determined that during September the plant produced 15,000 pools and incurred the following costs:

a. Purchased 62,000 pounds of materials at a cost of $1.75 per pound.
b. Used 51,000 pounds of materials in production. (Finished goods and work in process inventories are insignificant and can be ignored.)
c. Worked 11,800 direct labor-hours at a cost of $10.10 per hour.
d. Incurred variable manufacturing overhead cost totaling $19,240 for the month. A total of 7,400 machine-hours was recorded.

It is the company's policy to close all variances to cost of goods sold on a monthly basis.

Required:
1. Compute the following variances for September:
    a. Direct materials price and quantity variances.
    b. Direct labor rate and efficiency variances.
    c. Variable overhead spending and efficiency variances.
2. Summarize the variances that you computed in (1) above by showing the net overall favorable or unfavorable variance for the month. What impact did this figure have on the company's income statement? Show computations.
3. Pick out the two most significant variances that you computed in (1) above. Explain to Ms. Wilson possible causes of these variances.

PROBLEM 8–13A Basic Variance Analysis (LO2, LO3, LO4)

Riley Labs produces various chemical compounds for industrial use. One compound, called Lundor, is prepared using an elaborate distilling process. The company has developed standard costs for one unit of Lundor as follows:

CHECK FIGURE
(1a) Materials price
     variance: $16,100 F
(2a) Labor efficiency
     variance: $3,600 U

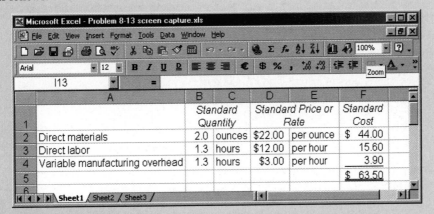

	Standard Quantity	Standard Price or Rate	Standard Cost
Direct materials	2.0 ounces	$22.00 per ounce	$ 44.00
Direct labor	1.3 hours	$12.00 per hour	15.60
Variable manufacturing overhead	1.3 hours	$3.00 per hour	3.90
			$ 63.50

During November, the following activity was recorded by the company relative to production of Lundor:

a. Materials purchased, 11,500 ounces at a cost of $236,900.
b. There was no beginning inventory of materials; however, at the end of the month, 3,000 ounces of material remained in ending inventory.
c. The company employs 36 lab technicians to work on the production of Lundor. During November, each worked an average of 160 hours at an average rate of $11.90 per hour.
d. Variable manufacturing overhead is assigned to Lundor on the basis of direct labor-hours. Variable manufacturing overhead costs during November totaled $16,416.
e. During November, 4,200 good units of Lundor were produced.

The company's management is anxious to determine the efficiency of the Lundor production activities.

Required:
1. For direct materials used in the production of Lundor:
    a. Compute the price and quantity variances.
    b. The materials were purchased from a new supplier who is anxious to enter into a long-term purchase contract. Would you recommend that the company sign the contract? Explain.
2. For direct labor employed in the production of Lundor:
    a. Compute the rate and efficiency variances.
    b. In the past, the 36 technicians employed in the production of Lundor consisted of 21 senior technicians and 15 assistants. During November, the company experimented with fewer senior

technicians and more assistants in order to save costs. Would you recommend that the new labor mix be continued? Explain.

3. Compute the variable overhead spending and efficiency variances. What relation can you see between this efficiency variance and the labor efficiency variance?

PROBLEM 8–14A   (Appendix 8A) Comprehensive Variance Analysis; Journal Entries (LO2, LO3, LO4, LO5)

Pemberly Athletics produces a broad line of sports equipment and uses a standard cost system for control purposes. Last year the company produced 8,400 varsity basketballs. The standard costs associated with this basketball, along with the actual costs incurred last year, are given below (per basketball):

	Standard Cost	Actual Cost
Direct materials:		
Standard: 3.8 feet at $5.00 per foot	$19.00	
Actual: 4.0 feet at $4.90 per foot.		$19.60
Direct labor:		
Standard: 1.1 hours at $7.50 per hour	8.25	
Actual: 1.0 hours at $8.20 per hour		8.20
Variable manufacturing overhead:		
Standard: 1.1 hours at $2.60 per hour	2.86	
Actual: 1.0 hours at $2.80 per hour		2.80
Total cost per basketball.	$30.11	$30.60

The president was elated when he saw that actual costs exceeded standard costs by only $0.49 per basketball. He stated, "I was afraid that our unit cost might get out of hand when we gave out those raises last year in order to stimulate output. But it's obvious our costs are well under control."

There was no inventory of materials on hand to start the year. During the year, 33,600 feet of materials were purchased and used in production.

Required:
1. For direct materials:
   a.   Compute the price and quantity variances for the year.
   b.   Prepare journal entries to record all activity relating to direct materials for the year.
2. For direct labor:
   a.   Compute the rate and efficiency variances.
   b.   Prepare a journal entry to record the incurrence of direct labor cost for the year.
3. Compute the variable overhead spending and efficiency variances.
4. Was the president correct in his statement that "our costs are well under control"? Explain.
5. State possible causes of each variance that you have computed.

PROBLEM 8–15A   Variance Analysis in a Hospital (LO2, LO3, LO4)

Joan Cortez, chief administrator for Ocean Crest Hospital, is concerned about the costs for tests in the hospital's lab. Charges for lab tests are consistently higher at Ocean Crest than at other hospitals and have resulted in many complaints. Also, because of strict regulations on amounts reimbursed for lab tests, payments received from insurance companies and governmental units have not been high enough to cover lab costs.

Ms. Cortez has asked you to evaluate costs in the hospital's lab for the past month. The following information is available:

a.   Two types of tests are performed in the lab—blood tests and smears. During the past month, 1,500 blood tests and 1,900 smears were performed in the lab.
b.   Small glass plates are used in both types of tests. During the past month, the hospital purchased 11,450 plates at a cost of $24,045. This cost is net of a $0.10 per plate quantity discount. 1,400 of these plates were unused at the end of the month; no plates were on hand at the beginning of the month.
c.   During the past month, 1,200 hours of labor time were recorded in the lab at a cost of $11,400.
d.   The lab's variable overhead cost last month totaled $6,840.

Ocean Crest Hospital has never used standard costs. By searching industry literature, however, you have determined the following nationwide averages for hospital labs:

a. *Plates:* Two plates are required per lab test. These plates cost $2.20 each and are disposed of after the test is completed.

b. *Labor:* Each blood test should require 0.40 hours to complete, and each smear should require 0.10 hours to complete. The average cost of this lab time is $12.00 per hour.

c. *Overhead:* Overhead cost is based on direct labor-hours. The average rate for variable overhead is $5.50 per hour.

Required:

1. Compute a materials price variance for the plates purchased last month and a materials quantity variance for the plates used last month.

2. For labor cost in the lab:
    a. Compute a labor rate variance and a labor efficiency variance.
    b. In most hospitals, one-half of the workers in the lab are senior technicians and one-half are assistants. In an effort to reduce costs, Ocean Crest Hospital employs only one-fourth senior technicians and three-fourths assistants. Would you recommend that this policy be continued? Explain.

3. Compute the variable overhead spending and efficiency variances. Is there any relation between the variable overhead efficiency variance and the labor efficiency variance? Explain.

PROBLEM 8–16A Comprehensive Variance Problem (LO1, LO2, LO3, LO4)

Celtron Inc. produces a lightweight backpack that is popular with college students. Standard variable costs relating to a single backpack are given below:

CHECK FIGURE
(1) Standard cost: $33.75
(3) 2.70 yards per
    backpack

	Standard Quantity or Hours	Standard Price or Rate	Standard Cost
Direct materials	?	$6.50 per yard	$?
Direct labor.	?	?	?
Variable manufacturing overhead.	?	$2.80 per direct labor-hour	?
Total standard cost.			?

Overhead is applied to production on the basis of direct labor-hours. During September, 1,000 backpacks were manufactured and sold. Selected information relating to the month's production is given below:

	Materials Used	Direct Labor	Variable Manufacturing Overhead
Total standard cost allowed for the month's production	$17,550	$12,000	$4,200
Actual costs incurred	$14,700	?	$3,500
Materials price variance.	?		
Materials quantity variance	$650 U		
Labor rate variance		?	
Labor efficiency variance.		?	
Variable overhead spending variance . . .			?
Variable overhead efficiency variance . . .			?

The following additional information is available for September's production:

Actual direct labor-hours	1,600
Difference between standard and actual cost per backpack produced during September.	$2.15 F

There were no beginning or ending inventories of raw materials.

Required:

1. What is the standard cost of a single backpack?
2. What was the actual cost per backpack produced during September?
3. How many yards of material are required at standard per backpack?
4. What was the materials price variance for September?
5. What is the standard direct labor rate per hour?
6. What was the labor rate variance for September? The labor efficiency variance?
7. What was the variable overhead spending variance for September? The variable overhead efficiency variance?
8. Prepare a standard cost card for one backpack.

CHECK FIGURE
(1) Actual hours: 200

PROBLEM 8–17A   Working Backwards from Labor Variances (LO3)

The auto repair shop of Mechanics World uses standards to control the labor time and labor cost in the shop. The standard labor cost for a motor tune-up is given below:

Job	Standard Hours	Standard Rate	Standard Cost
Motor tune-up........	3.0 labor-hours	$9.50 per labor-hour	$28.50

The record showing the time spent in the shop last week on motor tune-ups has been misplaced. However, the shop supervisor recalls that 60 tune-ups were completed during the week, and the controller recalls the following variance data relating to tune-ups:

Labor rate variance	$90 F
Total labor variance	$100 U

Required:

1. Determine the number of actual labor-hours spent on tune-ups during the week.
2. Determine the actual hourly rate of pay for tune-ups last week.

(*Hint:* A useful way to proceed would be to work from known to unknown data either by using the variance formulas or by using the columnar format shown in Exhibit 8–6.)

CHECK FIGURE
(1) Oxotate: 24.0 kilograms
(3) Standard cost: $119.40

PROBLEM 8–18A   Setting Standards (LO1)

Brighton Labs is a chemical manufacturer that supplies various products to industrial users. The company plans to introduce a new chemical solution, called Toric, for which it needs to develop a standard product cost. The following information is available on the production of Toric:

a.   Toric is made by combining a chemical compound (Oxotate) and a solution (Mayol), and boiling the mixture. A 30% loss in volume occurs for both the Mayol and the Oxotate during boiling. After boiling, the mixture consists of 9.1 liters of Mayol and 14.0 kilograms of Oxotate per 12-liter batch of Toric.

b.   After the boiling process is complete, the solution is cooled slightly before 6 kilograms of Gretat are added per 12-liter batch of Toric. The addition of Gretat does not affect the total liquid volume. The resulting solution is then bottled in 12-liter containers.

c.   The finished product is highly unstable, and one 12-liter batch out of 6 is rejected at final inspection. Rejected batches have no commercial value and are thrown out.

d.   It takes a worker 35 minutes to process one 12-liter batch of Toric. Employees work an 8-hour day, including 1 hour per day for rest breaks and cleanup.

Required:

1. Determine the standard quantity for each of the raw materials needed to produce an acceptable 12-liter batch of Toric.
2. Determine the standard labor time to produce an acceptable 12-liter batch of Toric.
3. Assuming the following purchase prices and costs, prepare a standard cost card for direct materials and direct labor for one acceptable 12-liter batch of Toric:

Mayol	$1.50 per liter
Oxotate.............................	$2.80 per kilogram
Gretat...............................	$3.00 per kilogram
Direct labor cost.......................	$9.00 per hour

(CMA, adapted)

PROBLEM 8–19A Developing Standard Costs (LO1)

FlashFresh Corporation is a small producer of fruit-flavored frozen desserts. For many years, FlashFresh's products have had strong regional sales on the basis of brand recognition; however, other companies have begun marketing similar products in the area, and price competition has become increasingly intense. Becky Nomura, the company's controller, is planning to implement a standard cost system for FlashFresh and has gathered considerable information from her co-workers on production and material requirements for FlashFresh's products. Nomura believes that the use of standard costing will allow FlashFresh to improve cost control and make better pricing decisions.

FlashFresh's most popular product is strawberry sherbet. The sherbet is produced in 10-gallon batches, and each batch requires 5 quarts of good strawberries. (If you are unfamiliar with gallons and quarts as measures, one gallon equals four quarts.) The fresh strawberries are sorted by hand before they enter the production process. Because of imperfections in the strawberries and normal spoilage, 1 quart of berries is discarded for every 9 quarts of acceptable berries. The standard direct labor time for the sorting to obtain 1 quart of acceptable strawberries is 3 minutes. The acceptable strawberries are then blended with the other ingredients; blending requires 10 minutes of direct labor time per batch. After blending, the sherbet is packaged in quart containers. Nomura has gathered the following pricing information:

a. FlashFresh purchases strawberries at a cost of $0.90 per quart. All other ingredients cost a total of $1.60 per gallon of sherbet.
b. Direct labor is paid at the rate of $10.00 per hour.
c. The total cost of direct material and direct labor required to package the sherbet is $0.30 per quart.

Required:
1. Develop the standard cost for the direct cost components (materials, labor, and packaging) of a 10-gallon batch of strawberry sherbet. The standard cost should identify the standard quantity, standard rate, and standard cost per batch for each direct cost component of a batch of strawberry sherbet.
2. As part of the implementation of a standard cost system at FlashFresh, Becky Nomura plans to train those responsible for maintaining the standards on how to use variance analysis. Nomura is particularly concerned with the causes of unfavorable variances.
    a. Discuss possible causes of unfavorable materials price variances and identify the individual(s) who should be held responsible for these variances.
    b. Discuss possible causes of unfavorable labor efficiency variances and identify the individual(s) who should be held responsible for these variances.

(CMA, adapted)

PROBLEM 8–20A Direct Materials and Direct Labor Variances; Computations from Incomplete Data (LO2, LO3)

Cramer Company manufactures a product for which the following standards have been set:

	Standard Quantity or Hours	Standard Price or Rate	Standard Cost
Direct materials	2.00 feet	$8.00 per foot	$16.00
Direct labor	? hours	? per hour	?

During June, the company purchased direct materials at a cost of $49,770, all of which were used in the production of 3,000 units of product. There were no beginning inventories of raw materials. In addition, 5,400 hours of direct labor time were worked on the product during the month. The cost of this labor time was $38,340. The following variances have been computed for the month:

Materials quantity variance	$2,400 U
Total labor variance	$90 U
Labor efficiency variance	$2,250 U

Required:
1. For direct materials:
    a. Compute the actual cost per foot for materials for June.
    b. Compute the materials price variance and a total variance for materials.

2. For direct labor:
   a. Compute the standard direct labor rate per hour.
   b. Compute the standard hours allowed for the month's production.
   c. Compute the standard hours allowed per unit of product.

(*Hint:* In completing the problem, it may be helpful to move from known to unknown data either by using the columnar format shown in Exhibits 8–4 and 8–6 or by using the variance formulas.)

CHECK FIGURE
(1a) Materials price
       variance: $12,400 F
(3) Variable overhead
       spending variance:
       $4,080 F

eXcel

PROBLEM 8–21A   (Appendix 8A) Comprehensive Variance Analysis with Incomplete Data; Journal Entries (LO1, LO2, LO3, LO4, LO5)

Far North Sporting, Ltd., manufactures a premium hockey stick. The standard cost of one hockey stick is:

	Standard Quantity or Hours	Standard Price or Rate	Standard Cost
Direct materials	? feet	$5.00 per foot	$?
Direct labor.	1.5 hours	? per hour	?
Variable manufacturing overhead. . . .	? hours	$2.50 per hour	?
Total standard cost.			$45.75

Last year, 12,000 hockey sticks were produced and sold. Selected cost data relating to last year's operations follow:

	Dr.	Cr.
Accounts payable—direct materials purchased (62,000 feet)		$297,600
Wages payable (? hours)		$236,640*
Work in process—direct materials	$288,000	
Direct labor rate variance.		$8,160
Variable overhead efficiency variance	$6,000	
*Relates to the actual direct labor cost for the year.		

The following additional information is available for last year's operations:

a. No materials were on hand at the start of last year. Some of the materials purchased during the year were still on hand in the warehouse at the end of the year.
b. The variable manufacturing overhead rate is based on direct labor-hours. Total actual variable manufacturing overhead cost for last year was $46,920.
c. Actual direct materials usage for last year exceeded the standard by 0.2 feet per stick.

Required:
1. For direct materials:
   a. Compute the price and quantity variances for last year.
   b. Prepare journal entries to record all activities relating to direct materials for last year.
2. For direct labor:
   a. Verify the rate variance given above and compute the efficiency variance for last year.
   b. Prepare a journal entry to record activity relating to direct labor for last year.
3. Compute the variable overhead spending variance for last year and verify the variable overhead efficiency variance given above.
4. State possible causes of each variance that you have computed.
5. Prepare a standard cost card for one hockey stick.

BUILDING YOUR SKILLS

TEAMWORK IN ACTION   (LO1)

Terry Travers is the manufacturing supervisor of Aurora Manufacturing Company, which produces a variety of plastic products. Some of these products are standard items that are listed in the company's catalog, while others are made to customer specifications. Each month, Travers receives a performance report showing the budget for the month, the actual activity, and the variance between budget and actual. Part of Travers's annual performance evaluation is based on his department's performance against budget. Aurora's purchasing manager, Sally Christensen, also receives monthly performance reports and she, too, is evaluated in part on the basis of these reports.

The monthly reports for June had just been distributed when Travers met Christensen in the hallway outside their offices. Scowling, Travers began the conversation, "I see we have another set of monthly performance reports hand-delivered by that not very nice junior employee in the budget office. He seemed pleased to tell me that I'm in trouble with my performance again."

Christensen: I got the same treatment. All I ever hear about are the things I haven't done right. Now I'll have to spend a lot of time reviewing the report and preparing explanations. The worst part is that it's now the 21st of July so the information is almost a month old, and we have to spend all this time on history.

Travers: My biggest gripe is that our production activity varies a lot from month to month, but we're given an annual budget that's written in stone. Last month we were shut down for three days when a strike delayed delivery of the basic ingredient used in our plastic formulation, and we had already exhausted our inventory. You know about that problem, though, because we asked you to call all over the country to find an alternate source of supply. When we got what we needed on a rush basis, we had to pay more than we normally do.

Christensen: I expect problems like that to pop up from time to time—that's part of my job—but now we'll both have to take a careful look at our reports to see where the charges are reflected for that rush order. Every month I spend more time making sure I should be charged for each item reported than I do making plans for my department's daily work. It's really frustrating to see charges for things I have no control over.

Travers: The way we get information doesn't help, either. I don't get copies of the reports you get, yet a lot of what I do is affected by your department, and by most of the other departments we have. Why do the budget and accounting people assume that I should be told only about my operations even though the president regularly gives us pep talks about how we all need to work together as a team?

Christensen: I seem to get more reports than I need, and I am never asked to comment on them until top management calls me on the carpet about my department's shortcomings. Do you ever hear comments when your department shines?

Travers: I guess they don't have time to review the good news. One of my problems is that all the reports are in dollars and cents. I work with people, machines, and materials. I need information to help me *this* month to solve *this* month's problems—not another report of the dollars expended *last* month or the month before.

Required:

Your team should discuss and then respond to the following questions. All team members should agree with and understand the answers and be prepared to report on those answers in class. (Each teammate can assume responsibility for a different part of the presentation.)

1. On the basis of the conversation between Terry Travers and Sally Christensen, describe the likely motivation and behavior of these two employees as a result of the standard cost and variance reporting system that is used by Aurora Manufacturing Company.

2. List the recommendations that your team would make to Aurora Manufacturing Company to enhance employee motivation as it relates to the company's standard cost and variance reporting system.

(CMA, adapted)

COMMUNICATING IN PRACTICE (LO1)

Make an appointment to meet with the manager of an auto repair shop that uses standards. In most cases, this would be an auto repair shop that is affiliated with a national chain such as Firestone or Sears or the service department of a new-car dealer.

Required:

At the scheduled meeting, find out the answers to the following questions and write a memo to your instructor describing the information obtained during your meeting.

1. How are standards set?
2. Are standards practical or ideal?
3. Is the actual time taken to complete a task compared to the standard time?
4. What are the consequences of unfavorable variances? Of favorable variances?
5. Do the standards and variances create any potential problems?

ETHICS CASE   (LO1)

Stacy Cummins, the newly hired controller at Merced Home Products, Inc., was disturbed by what she had discovered about the standard costs at the Home Security Division. In looking over the past several years of quarterly earnings reports at the Home Security Division, she noticed that the first-quarter earnings were always poor, the second-quarter earnings were slightly better, the third-quarter earnings were again slightly better, and the fourth quarter always ended with a spectacular performance in which the Home Security Division managed to meet or exceed its target profit for the year. She also was concerned to find letters from the company's external auditors to top management warning about an unusual use of standard costs at the Home Security Division.

When Ms. Cummins ran across these letters, she asked the assistant controller, Gary Farber, if he knew what was going on at the Home Security Division. Gary said that it was common knowledge in the company that the vice president in charge of the Home Security Division, Preston Lansing, had rigged the standards at his division in order to produce the same quarterly earnings pattern every year. According to company policy, variances are taken directly to the income statement as an adjustment to cost of goods sold.

Favorable variances have the effect of increasing net operating income, and unfavorable variances have the effect of decreasing net operating income. Lansing had rigged the standards so that there were always large favorable variances. Company policy was a little vague about when these variances have to be reported on the divisional income statements. While the intent was clearly to recognize variances on the income statement in the period in which they arise, nothing in the company's accounting manuals actually explicitly required this. So for many years Lansing had followed a practice of saving up the favorable variances and using them to create a nice smooth pattern of earnings growth in the first three quarters, followed by a big "Christmas present" of an extremely good fourth quarter. (Financial reporting regulations forbid carrying variances forward from one year to the next on the annual audited financial statements, so all of the variances must appear on the divisional income statement by the end of the year.)

Ms. Cummins was concerned about these revelations and attempted to bring up the subject with the president of Merced Home Products but was told that "we all know what Lansing's doing, but as long as he continues to turn in such good reports, don't bother him." When Ms. Cummins asked if the board of directors was aware of the situation, the president somewhat testily replied, "Of course they are aware."

Required:
1. How did Preston Lansing probably "rig" the standard costs—are the standards set too high or too low? Explain.
2. Should Preston Lansing be permitted to continue his practice of managing reported earnings?
3. What should Stacy Cummins do in this situation?

9

Flexible Budgets and Overhead Analysis

<< A LOOK BACK

We discussed budgeting in Chapter 7—the process that is used by organizations to plan the financial aspects of their operations. We introduced management control and performance measures in Chapter 8 with a discussion of standard costs and variance analysis.

A LOOK AT THIS CHAPTER

Chapter 9 continues our coverage of the budgeting process by presenting the flexible approach to budgeting, including the use of a flexible budget to control overhead costs.

A LOOK AHEAD >>

We continue the discussion of management control and performance measures in Chapter 10 by focusing on how decentralized organizations are managed.

CHAPTER OUTLINE

Flexible Budgets

- Characteristics of a Flexible Budget

- Deficiencies of the Static Budget

- How a Flexible Budget Works

- Using the Flexible Budgeting Concept in Performance Evaluation

- The Measure of Activity—A Critical Choice

Variable Overhead Variances—A Closer Look

- Actual versus Standard Hours

- Spending Variance Alone

- Both Spending and Efficiency Variances

- Activity-Based Costing and the Flexible Budget

Overhead Rates and Fixed Overhead Analysis

- Flexible Budgets and Overhead Rates

- Overhead Application in a Standard Cost System

- The Fixed Overhead Variances

- The Budget Variance—A Closer Look

- The Volume Variance—A Closer Look

- Graphic Analysis of Fixed Overhead Variances

- Cautions in Fixed Overhead Analysis

- Overhead Variances and Underapplied or Overapplied Overhead Cost

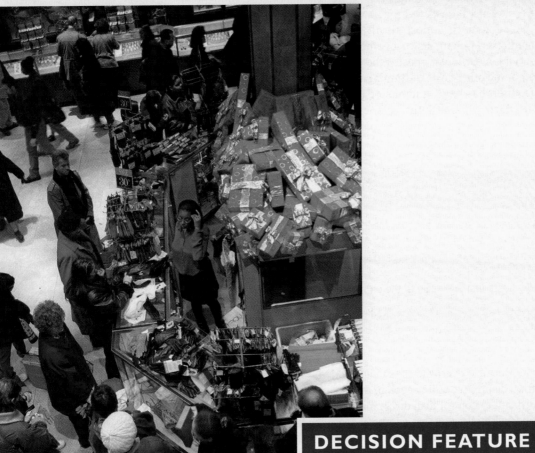

LEARNING OBJECTIVES

LP 9

After studying Chapter 9, you should be able to:

LO1 Prepare a flexible budget and explain the advantages of the flexible budget approach over the static budget approach.

LO2 Prepare a performance report for both variable and fixed overhead costs using the flexible budget approach.

LO3 Use a flexible budget to prepare a variable overhead performance report containing only a spending variance.

LO4 Use a flexible budget to prepare a variable overhead performance report containing both a spending and an efficiency variance.

LO5 Compute the predetermined overhead rate and apply overhead to products in a standard cost system.

LO6 Compute and interpret the fixed overhead budget and volume variances.

DECISION FEATURE

Controlling Costs—Rain or Shine

Totes»Isotoner Corporation is the world's largest marketer of umbrellas, gloves, rainwear, and other weather-related accessories. One of the company's costs is a "flex advertising" fee that it pays to department stores based on the stores' sales of totes»Isotoner products. The company prepares a management report that compares actual flex advertising costs *as a percentage of actual sales* to budgeted flex advertising costs *as a percentage of budgeted sales*. This is done because management expects a variable cost, such as flex advertising, to stay constant on a per sales dollar basis.

The company purposely does not compare its actual and budgeted *total dollar amounts* of flex advertising expense because it provides misleading feedback about managerial performance. For example, if actual sales exceed budgeted sales, a highly efficient manager could be naïvely penalized for incurring actual variable costs that exceed budgeted variable costs. Conversely, if actual sales are less than budgeted sales, an inefficient manager could be naïvely rewarded for incurring actual variable costs that are less than budgeted variable costs.

When it comes to fixed costs, totes»Isotoner monitors total dollar amounts rather than percentages. For example, the Information Technology (IT) Department incurs numerous costs that are not affected by sales variation within the relevant range. If percentages were used to manage these costs, an increase in sales would decrease the IT Department's total fixed costs as a percentage of sales, thereby sending misleading signals about managerial efficiency.

In addition to cost information, totes»Isotoner uses other nonfinancial performance measures to ensure its employees do not fixate on minimizing costs to the detriment of customers.

Source: Author's conversation with Donna Deye, Senior Vice-President and CFO, totes»Isotoner Corporation.

Overhead is a major cost, if not *the* major cost, in many organizations. For example, it costs Microsoft very little to make copies of its software for sale to customers; almost all of Microsoft's costs are in research and development and marketing—elements of overhead. Or consider Disney World. The only direct cost of serving a particular guest is the cost of the food the guest consumes at the park; virtually all of the other costs of running the amusement park are overhead. Even Boeing, a manufacturer, has huge amounts of overhead in the form of engineering salaries, buildings, insurance, administrative salaries, and marketing costs. Not surprisingly, controlling overhead costs is a major preoccupation of managers.

IN BUSINESS   **Focus on Overhead Costs**

Overhead costs now account for as much as 66% of the costs incurred by companies in service industries and up to 37% of the total costs of manufacturers. Consequently, overhead reduction is a recurring theme in many organizations. However, the extent of the reductions must be considered in light of competitive pressures to improve services and product quality. Managers must avoid cutting costs that add value to the organization.

Source: Nick Develin, "Unlocking Overhead Value," *Management Accounting*, December 1999, pp. 22–34.

Because overhead is usually made up of many separate costs, including everything from disposable coffee cups in the visitors' waiting area to the president's salary, it is more difficult to control than direct materials and direct labor. Overhead control is further complicated by the fact that overhead costs can be variable, fixed, or a mixture of variable and fixed. However, these complications can be largely overcome by using flexible budgets. In this chapter, we learn how to prepare flexible budgets and how they can be used to control costs. We also expand the study of overhead variances that we started in Chapter 8.

Let's start with a simple example. Imagine that you work as a baggage handler for an airline. Your boss has said that you should be able to unload 20 pieces of luggage from an airplane per minute. Flight 2707 from Boston carries *on average* 300 pieces of luggage. Today Flight 2707 is scheduled to arrive from Boston and your boss has decided that you should be able to unload the luggage on the flight in 15 minutes (300 pieces of luggage ÷ 20 pieces per minute). However, it takes you 20 minutes instead of 15 minutes to unload the luggage and consequently your boss yells at you. But, the flight actually contained 460 pieces of luggage. How would you feel? You might do some quick math as follows. Since there were 460 pieces of luggage on this flight and you are expected to unload 20 pieces per minute, then you should have been expected to unload the luggage on this flight in 23 minutes (460 pieces of luggage ÷ 20 pieces per minute). You did it in just 20 minutes instead of 23 minutes. Therefore, you should be getting a pat on the back, not yelled at! Notice, your natural inclination was to "flex" the budget of 15 minutes, which was based on 300 pieces of luggage, to reflect what the budget should be for 460 pieces of luggage—23 minutes. Now, let's proceed by applying dollars and cents to this concept.

FLEXIBLE BUDGETS

Video 9–1

Characteristics of a Flexible Budget

The budgets that we studied in Chapter 7 were *static budgets*. A **static budget** is prepared at the beginning of the budgeting period and is valid for only the planned level of activity. A static budget is suitable for planning but is inappropriate for evaluating how well costs are controlled. If the actual level of activity differs from what was planned, it would be

Static vs. Flexible Budgets

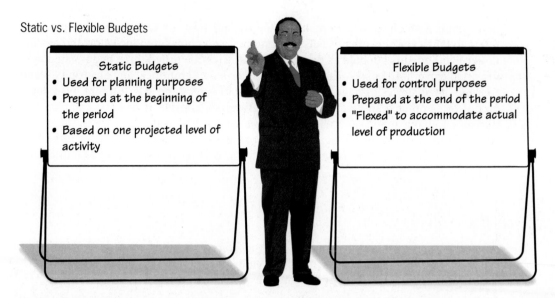

Static Budgets
- Used for planning purposes
- Prepared at the beginning of the period
- Based on one projected level of activity

Flexible Budgets
- Used for control purposes
- Prepared at the end of the period
- "Flexed" to accommodate actual level of production

misleading to compare actual costs to the static budget. If activity is higher than expected, variable costs should be higher than expected; and if activity is lower than expected, variable costs should be lower than expected.

Flexible budgets take into account how changes in activity affect costs. A **flexible budget** makes it easy to estimate what costs should be for any level of activity within a specified range. When a flexible budget is used in performance evaluation, actual costs are compared to what the *costs should have been for the actual level of activity during the period* rather than to the budgeted costs from the original budget. This is a very important distinction—particularly for variable costs. If adjustments for the level of activity are not made, it is very difficult to interpret discrepancies between budgeted and actual costs.

Deficiencies of the Static Budget

To illustrate the difference between a static budget and a flexible budget, consider the case of Rick's Hairstyling, an upscale hairstyling salon located in Beverly Hills that is owned and managed by Rick Manzi. The salon has very loyal customers—many of whom are associated with the film industry. Recently Rick has been attempting to get better control of his overhead costs by preparing monthly budgets.

At the end of February, Rick carefully prepared the March budget for overhead items that appears in Exhibit 9–1. Rick believes that the number of customers served in a month is the best way to measure the overall level of activity in his salon. He refers to these visits as client-visits. A customer who comes into the salon and has his or her hair styled is counted as one client-visit. Rick identified three major categories of variable overhead costs—hairstyling supplies, client gratuities, and electricity—and four major categories of fixed costs—support staff wages and salaries, rent, insurance, and utilities other than electricity. Client gratuities consist of flowers, candies, and glasses of champagne that Rick gives to his customers while they are in the salon. Rick considers electricity to be a variable cost, because almost all of the electricity in the salon is consumed by running blow-dryers, curling irons, and other hairstyling equipment.

EXHIBIT 9–1

RICK'S
hairstyling salon

Rick's Hairstyling
Static Budget
For the Month Ended March 31

Budgeted number of client-visits	5,000
Budget variable overhead costs:	
Hairstyling supplies ($1.20 per client-visit)	$ 6,000
Client gratuities ($4.00 per client-visit)	20,000
Electricity ($0.20 per client-visit)	1,000
Total variable overhead cost	27,000
Budgeted fixed overhead costs:	
Support staff wages and salaries	8,000
Rent	12,000
Insurance	1,000
Utilities other than electricity	500
Total fixed overhead cost	21,500
Total Budgeted Overhead Cost	$48,500

To develop the budget for variable overhead, Rick estimated that the average cost per client-visit should be $1.20 for hairstyling supplies, $4.00 for client gratuities, and $0.20 for electricity. On the basis of his estimate of 5,000 client-visits in March, Rick budgeted for $6,000 ($1.20 per client-visit × 5,000 client-visits) in hairstyling supplies, $20,000 ($4.00 per client-visit × 5,000 client-visits) in client gratuities, and $1,000 ($0.20 per client-visit × 5,000 client-visits) in electricity.

Rick's fixed overhead budget was based on records of how much he had spent on these items in the past. The budget included $8,000 for support staff wages and salaries, $12,000 for rent, $1,000 for insurance, and $500 for utilities other than electricity.

At the end of March, Rick prepared a report comparing actual to budgeted costs. That report appears in Exhibit 9–2. The problem with that report, as Rick immediately realized, is that it compares costs at one level of activity (5,200 client-visits) to costs at a different level of activity (5,000 client-visits). Since Rick had 200 more client-visits than expected, some of his costs *should* be higher than budgeted. From Rick's standpoint, although the increase in client-visits is desirable, it is having a negative impact on the variable overhead variances shown in his report. He knows that to make the report more meaningful he needs to separate the portion of his variable overhead variances that is caused by the extra 200 client-visits from the portion that relates to his cost control efforts.

EXHIBIT 9–2

Rick's Hairstyling
Static Budget Performance Report
For the Month Ended March 31

	Actual	Budgeted	Variance
Client-visits	5,200	5,000	200 F
Variable overhead costs:			
Hairstyling supplies	$ 6,400	$ 6,000	$ 400 U*
Client gratuities	22,300	20,000	2,300 U*
Electricity	1,020	1,000	20 U*
Total variable overhead cost	29,720	27,000	2,720 U*
Fixed overhead costs:			
Support staff wages and salaries	8,100	8,000	100 U
Rent	12,000	12,000	0
Insurance	1,000	1,000	0
Utilities other than electricity	470	500	30 F
Total fixed overhead cost	21,570	21,500	70 U
Total overhead cost	$51,290	$48,500	$2,790 U*

*The cost variances for variable costs and for total overhead are useless for evaluating how well costs were controlled since they have been derived by comparing actual costs at one level of activity to budgeted costs at a different level of activity.

How a Flexible Budget Works

Exhibit 9–3 illustrates how flexible budgets work. It shows how overhead costs should be expected to change, depending on the monthly level of activity. Within the activity range of 4,900 to 5,200 client-visits, the fixed costs are expected to remain the same. For the variable overhead costs, the per client costs ($1.20 for hairstyling supplies, $4.00 for client gratuities, and $0.20 for electricity) are multiplied by the appropriate number of

LEARNING OBJECTIVE 2

Prepare a performance report for both variable and fixed overhead costs using the flexible budget approach.

EXHIBIT 9–3   Illustration of the Flexible Budgeting Concept

Rick's Hairstyling
Flexible Budget
For the Month Ended March 31

Budgeted number of client-visits   5,000

Overhead Costs	Cost Formula (per client-visit)	Activity (in client-visits)			
		4,900	5,000	5,100	5,200
Variable overhead costs:					
Hairstyling supplies	$1.20	$ 5,880	$ 6,000	$ 6,120	$ 6,240
Client gratuities	4.00	19,600	20,000	20,400	20,800
Electricity	0.20	980	1,000	1,020	1,040
Total variable overhead cost	$5.40	26,460	27,000	27,540	28,080
Fixed overhead costs:					
Support staff wages and salaries		8,000	8,000	8,000	8,000
Rent		12,000	12,000	12,000	12,000
Insurance		1,000	1,000	1,000	1,000
Utilities other than electricity		500	500	500	500
Total fixed overhead cost		21,500	21,500	21,500	21,500
Total overhead cost		$47,960	$48,500	$49,040	$49,580

client-visits in each column. For example, the $1.20 cost of hairstyling supplies was multiplied by 4,900 client-visits to give the total cost of $5,880 for hairstyling supplies at that level of activity.

Using the Flexible Budgeting Concept in Performance Evaluation

To get a better idea of how well variable overhead costs were controlled in March, the flexible budgeting concept was used to create a new performance report based on the *actual* number of client-visits for the month (Exhibit 9–4). This new budget is prepared by multiplying the actual level of activity by the cost formula for each of the variable cost categories. For example, using the $1.20 per client-visit for hairstyling supplies, the total cost for this item *should be* $6,240 for 5,200 client-visits ($1.20 per client-visit × 5,200 client-visits). Since the actual cost for hairstyling supplies was $6,400, the unfavorable variance is $160. This differs from the $400 unfavorable variance shown for hairstyling supplies in Exhibit 9–2. The difference arises because Exhibit 9–2 uses a static budget approach that compares actual costs at one level of activity to budgeted costs at a different level of activity. This is like comparing apples to oranges. Because actual activity was higher by 200 client-visits than budgeted activity, the total cost of hairstyling supplies *should* have been $240 ($1.20 per client-visit × 200 client-visits) higher than budgeted. As a result, $240 of the $400 "unfavorable" variance in the static budget performance report in Exhibit 9–2 was spurious.

The flexible budget performance report in Exhibit 9–4 provides a more valid assessment of performance because actual costs are compared to what costs should have been at the actual level of activity. In other words, apples are compared to apples. When this is done, we see that the hairstyling supplies variance is $160 unfavorable rather than $400 unfavorable as it was in the original static budget performance report. In some cases, as with electricity, an unfavorable static budget variance may be transformed into a favorable variance when an increase in activity is properly taken into account.

EXHIBIT 9–4

Rick's Hairstyling
Flexible Budget Performance Report
For the Month Ended March 31

Budgeted number of client-visits 5,000
Actual number of client-visits 5,200

Overhead Costs	Cost Formula (per client-visit)	Actual Costs Incurred for 5,200 Client-Visits	Flexible Budget Based on 5,200 Client-Visits	Variance
Variable overhead costs:				
Hairstyling supplies	$1.20	$ 6,400	$ 6,240	$ 160 U
Client gratuities	4.00	22,300	20,800	1,500 U
Electricity	0.20	1,020	1,040	20 F
Total variable overhead cost	$5.40	29,720	28,080	1,640 U
Fixed overhead costs:				
Support staff wages and salaries		8,100	8,000	100 U
Rent		12,000	12,000	0
Insurance		1,000	1,000	0
Utilities other than electricity		470	500	30 F
Total fixed overhead cost		21,570	21,500	70 U
Total overhead cost		$51,290	$49,580	$1,710 U

1. Which of the following statements is false? (You may select more than one answer.)
   a. A flexible budget is used for control purposes and a static budget is used for planning purposes.
   b. A flexible budget is prepared at the end of the period and a static budget is prepared at the beginning of the period.
   c. A flexible budget is not useful for controlling variable costs.
   d. A static budget provides budgeted estimates for one level of activity.

2. A company's static budget estimate of total overhead costs was $100,000 based on the assumption that 10,000 units would be produced and sold. The company estimates that 30% of its overhead is variable and the remainder is fixed. What would be the total overhead cost according to the flexible budget if 12,000 units were produced and sold?
   a. $96,000
   b. $100,000
   c. $106,000
   d. $116,000

CONCEPT CHECK ✓

Focus on Opportunities

IN BUSINESS

The late management guru Peter F. Drucker cautioned managers that "almost without exception, the first page of the [monthly] report presents the areas in which results fall below expectations or in which expenditures exceed the budget. It focuses on problems. Problems cannot be ignored. But… enterprises have to focus on opportunities. That requires a small but fundamental procedural change: a new first page to the monthly report, one that precedes the page that shows the problems. The new page should focus on where results are better than expected. As much time should be spent on that new first page as traditionally was spent on the problem page."

Source: Peter F. Drucker, "Change Leaders," *Inc.* magazine, June 1999, pp. 65–72.

The largest variance on the flexible budget performance report is the $1,500 unfavorable variance for client gratuities. Rick had suspected that these expenses had gotten a little out of control, and the report confirmed those suspicions. He resolved to watch these expenses more closely in the coming months.

Confusion often arises concerning the fixed costs on a performance report. Actual fixed costs can differ from budgeted fixed costs. Costs are called fixed because they shouldn't be affected by changes in the level of activity within the relevant range. However, that does not mean that fixed costs can't change for other reasons. For example, Rick's utility bill, which includes natural gas for heating, varies with the weather. Additionally, the use of the term *fixed* may suggest that the cost can't be controlled, but that isn't true. It is often easier to control fixed costs than variable costs. For example, it would be fairly easy for Rick to control his insurance costs, which are fixed, by adjusting the amount of his insurance protection. It would be much more difficult for Rick to have much impact on the variable cost of electricity, which is a necessary cost of serving customers.

To reiterate, it is important to remember that a cost is variable if it is proportional to activity; it is fixed if it does not depend on the level of activity. However, fixed costs can change for reasons having nothing to do with changes in the level of activity. And controllability has little to do with whether a cost is variable or fixed. Fixed costs are often more controllable than variable costs.

Using the flexible budget approach, Rick Manzi now has a better way of assessing whether overhead costs are under control. The analysis is not so simple, however, in companies that provide a variety of products and services. The number of units produced or customers served may not be an adequate measure of overall activity. For example, does it make sense to count a Sony CD player, worth less than $50, as equivalent to a large-screen Sony HDTV? If the number of units produced is used as a measure of overall activity, then the CD player and the large-screen HDTV would be counted as equivalent. Clearly, the number of units produced (or customers served) may not be appropriate as an overall measure of activity when the organization has a variety of products or services; a common denominator may be needed.

The Measure of Activity—A Critical Choice

What should be used as the measure of activity when a company produces a variety of products and services? At least three factors are important in selecting an activity base for an overhead flexible budget:

1. Changes in the activity base should cause, or at least be highly correlated with, changes in the variable overhead costs in the flexible budget. Ideally, the variable overhead costs in the flexible budget should vary in direct proportion to changes in the activity base. For example, in a carpentry shop specializing in handmade wood furniture, the costs of miscellaneous supplies such as glue, wooden dowels, and sandpaper should vary with the number of direct labor-hours. Direct labor-hours would therefore be a good measure of activity to use in a flexible budget for the costs of such supplies.
2. The activity base should not be expressed in dollars or some other currency. For example, direct labor cost is usually a poor choice for an activity base in flexible budgets because changes in wage rates affect the activity base but do not usually result in a proportionate change in overhead. For example, we would not ordinarily expect to see a 5% increase in the consumption of glue in a carpentry shop if the workers receive a 5% increase in pay. Therefore, it is best to use physical rather than financial measures of activity in flexible budgets.
3. The activity base should be simple and easily understood, otherwise it will result in confusion and misunderstanding. It is difficult to control costs if people don't understand the reports or do not accept them as valid.

IN BUSINESS   **Gas Stations**

Generally, convenience store and car wash sales are directly related to the volume of gas sold by a gas station. Consequently, the gas sales budget would be the starting point for the entire budgeting process. Factors that should be considered when forecasting gas sales might include: the prior year's sales, changes in the volume of traffic in the area, changes in the environment that impact access to the station (for example, road construction or the installation of median barriers that impede access), and changes in the number or type of gas stations that are operating in the immediate vicinity.

When a flexible budgeting approach is used, the manager of a gas station might choose to prepare one overhead budget or separate overhead budgets for each of its segments (gas station, convenience store, and car wash). The decision would be based on whether or not the same activity base could be used for the three segments.

Source: Steven P. Smalley, "Measuring the Convenience of Gas Stations," *Appraisal Journal*, October 1999, p. 339.

VARIABLE OVERHEAD VARIANCES—A CLOSER LOOK

When the flexible budget is based on *hours* of activity (such as direct labor-hours) rather than on units of product or number of customers served, the flexible budget on the performance report can be based on either the actual hours used *or* the standard hours allowed for the actual output. Which should be used?

Actual versus Standard Hours

To explain these two options, we will use an example involving MicroDrive Corporation, a manufacturer of precision computer disk-drive motors for military applications. Data concerning the company's variable manufacturing overhead costs are shown in Exhibit 9–5.

MicroDrive uses machine-hours as the activity base in its flexible budget because its managers believe most of the company's overhead costs are driven by machine-hours. At the beginning of the year, MicroDrive estimated that it would produce 25,000 motors. Since the company's standard allowance is 2 machine-hours per motor, the budgeted level of activity for the year was 50,000 machine-hours. During the year the company actually produced 20,000 motors that *should* have been produced in 40,000 machine-hours (2 machine-hours allowed per motor × 20,000 motors); however, the company actually used 42,000 machine-hours to makes these motors.

In preparing an overhead performance report for the year, MicroDrive could use the 42,000 machine-hours actually worked during the year *or* the 40,000 machine-hours that should have been worked according to the standard. If the actual hours are used, only a spending variance will be computed. If the standard hours are used, both a spending *and* an efficiency variance will be computed. Both of these approaches are illustrated in the following sections.

Spending Variance Alone

If MicroDrive Corporation bases its overhead performance report on the 42,000 machine-hours actually worked during the year, then the performance report will show only a spending variance for variable overhead. Exhibit 9–6 shows a performance report prepared in this way.

Topic Tackler PLUS

Concept 9-2

Video 9–1

Video 9–2

LEARNING OBJECTIVE 3

Use a flexible budget to prepare a variable overhead performance report containing only a spending variance.

EXHIBIT 9–5
MicroDrive Corporation Data

Budgeted production	25,000	motors
Actual production	20,000	motors
Standard machine-hours per motor	2	machine-hours
Budgeted machine-hours (2 × 25,000)	50,000	machine-hours
Standard machine-hours allowed for the actual output (2 × 20,000)	40,000	machine-hours
Actual machine-hours	42,000	machine-hours
Variable overhead costs per machine-hour:		
Indirect labor.	$0.80	per machine-hour
Lubricants.	$0.30	per machine-hour
Power	$0.40	per machine-hour
Actual total variable overhead costs:		
Indirect labor.	$36,000	
Lubricants.	11,000	
Power	24,000	
Total actual variable overhead cost.	$71,000	

EXHIBIT 9–6

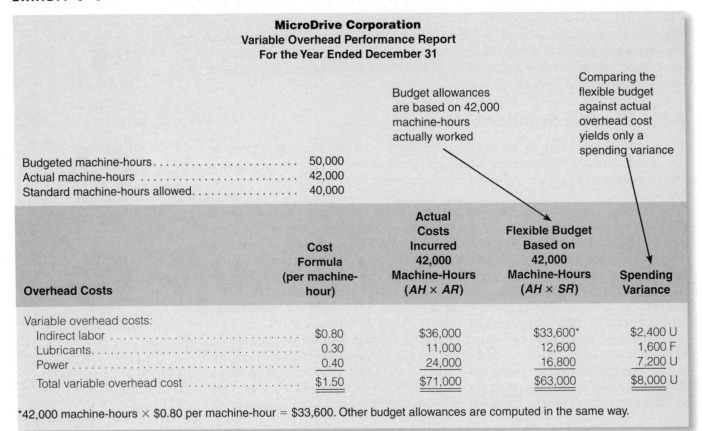

MicroDrive Corporation
Variable Overhead Performance Report
For the Year Ended December 31

Budget allowances are based on 42,000 machine-hours actually worked

Comparing the flexible budget against actual overhead cost yields only a spending variance

Budgeted machine-hours. 50,000
Actual machine-hours 42,000
Standard machine-hours allowed. 40,000

Overhead Costs	Cost Formula (per machine-hour)	Actual Costs Incurred 42,000 Machine-Hours (AH × AR)	Flexible Budget Based on 42,000 Machine-Hours (AH × SR)	Spending Variance
Variable overhead costs:				
Indirect labor	$0.80	$36,000	$33,600*	$2,400 U
Lubricants.	0.30	11,000	12,600	1,600 F
Power	0.40	24,000	16,800	7,200 U
Total variable overhead cost	$1.50	$71,000	$63,000	$8,000 U

*42,000 machine-hours × $0.80 per machine-hour = $33,600. Other budget allowances are computed in the same way.

The formula for the spending variance was introduced in the preceding chapter. That formula is:

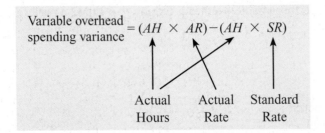

$$\text{Variable overhead spending variance} = (AH \times AR) - (AH \times SR)$$

Actual Hours　　Actual Rate　　Standard Rate

Or, in factored form:

$$\text{Variable overhead spending variance} = AH(AR - SR)$$

The report in Exhibit 9–6 is structured around the first, or unfactored, format.

Interpreting the Spending Variance　The variable overhead spending variance is useful only to the extent that the cost driver for variable overhead really is the actual hours worked. Then the flexible budget based on the actual hours worked is a valid benchmark that tells us how much *should* have been spent in total on variable overhead items during the period. The actual overhead costs are larger than this benchmark, resulting in an unfavorable variance, if either (1) the variable overhead items cost more to purchase than the standards allow or (2) more variable overhead items were used than the standards allow. So the spending variance includes both price and quantity variances.

Both Spending and Efficiency Variances

If management of MicroDrive Corporation wants to compute variable overhead spending and efficiency variances, then it should compute budget allowances for *both* the 40,000 machine-hour and the 42,000 machine-hour levels of activity. Exhibit 9–7 shows a performance report prepared in this way.

Note that the spending variance in Exhibit 9–7 is the same as the spending variance shown in Exhibit 9–6. The performance report in Exhibit 9–7 has simply been expanded to also include an efficiency variance. Together, the spending and efficiency variances make up the total variance.

Interpreting the Efficiency Variance   Like the variable overhead spending variance, the variable overhead efficiency variance is useful only to the extent that the cost driver for variable overhead really is the actual hours worked. Then any increase in hours actually worked should result in additional variable overhead costs. Consequently, if too many hours were used to create the actual output, this is likely to result in an increase in variable overhead. The variable overhead efficiency variance is an estimate of the effect on variable overhead costs of inefficiency in the use of the base (i.e., hours). In a sense, the term *variable overhead efficiency variance* is a misnomer. It seems to suggest that it measures the efficiency with which variable overhead resources were used. It does not. It is an estimate of the indirect effect on variable overhead costs of inefficiency in the use of the activity base.

EXHIBIT 9–7

MicroDrive Corporation
Variable Overhead Performance Report
For the Year Ended December 31

Budget allowances are based on 40,000 machine-hours—the time it *should have taken* to produce the year's actual output of 20,000 motors—as well as on the 42,000 *actual* machine-hours worked

This approach yields both a spending and an efficiency variance

Budgeted machine-hours	50,000
Actual machine-hours	42,000
Standard machine-hours allowed	40,000

Overhead Costs	Cost Formula (per machine-hour)	(1) Actual Costs Incurred 42,000 Machine-Hours (AH × AR)	(2) Flexible Budget Based on 42,000 Machine-Hours (AH × SR)	(3) Flexible Budget Based on 40,000 Machine-Hours (SH × SR)	Total Variance (1) − (3)	Spending Variance (1) − (2)	Efficiency Variance (2) − (3)
Variable overhead costs:							
Indirect labor	$0.80	$36,000	$33,600*	$32,000	$ 4,000 U	$2,400 U	$1,600 U
Lubricants	0.30	11,000	12,600	12,000	1,000 F	1,600 F	600 U
Power	0.40	24,000	16,800	16,000	8,000 U	7,200 U	800 U
Total variable overhead cost	$1.50	$71,000	$63,000	$60,000	$11,000 U	$8,000 U	$3,000 U

*42,000 machine-hours × $0.80 per machine-hour = $33,600. Other budget allowances are computed in the same way.

Recall from the preceding chapter that the variable overhead efficiency variance is a function of the difference between the actual hours incurred and the hours that should have been used to produce the period's output:

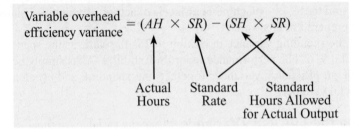

Or, in factored form:

$$\text{Variable overhead efficiency variance} = SR(AH - SH)$$

If more hours are worked than are allowed at standard, then the overhead efficiency variance will be unfavorable. However, as discussed above, the inefficiency is not in the use of overhead *but rather in the use of the base itself.*

This point can be illustrated by looking again at Exhibit 9–7. Two thousand more machine-hours were used during the period than should have been used to produce the period's output. Each of these hours presumably required the incurrence of $1.50 of variable overhead cost, resulting in an unfavorable variance of $3,000 (2,000 machine-hours × $1.50 per machine-hour). Although this $3,000 variance is called an overhead efficiency variance, it could better be called a machine-hours efficiency variance, since it results from using too many machine-hours rather than from inefficient use of overhead resources.

Control of the Efficiency Variance   Who is responsible for control of the overhead efficiency variance? Since the variance reflects efficiency in the utilization of the base underlying the flexible budget, whoever is responsible for control of this base is responsible for control of the variance. If the base is direct labor-hours, then the supervisor responsible for the use of labor time is responsible for any overhead efficiency variance.

Activity-Based Costing and the Flexible Budget

It is unlikely that all of the variable overhead in a complex organization is driven by a single factor such as the number of units produced or the number of labor-hours or machine-hours. The flexible budgeting approach can be easily adapted to accommodate a number of cost drivers. The cost formula for each variable cost element can depend on its own cost driver rather than on a single organization-wide measure of activity. For example, in a medical clinic the variable overhead cost of providing clinic staff with latex gloves might be driven by the number of patient-visits whereas the variable overhead cost of sterile wiping pads to prepare injection sites might be driven by the number of injections administered. In the flexible budget, the cost formula for latex gloves would be stated in terms of patient-visits whereas the cost formula for sterile wiping pads would be stated in terms of injections administered.

OVERHEAD RATES AND FIXED OVERHEAD ANALYSIS

As we shall see, fixed overhead variances are fundamentally different from variable overhead variances. To understand fixed overhead variances, we will need to review how predetermined overhead rates are established and used.

Flexible Budgets and Overhead Rates

LEARNING OBJECTIVE 5

Compute the predetermined overhead rate and apply overhead to products in a standard cost system.

Fixed costs come in large chunks that by definition do not vary with changes in the level of activity within the relevant range. This creates a problem in product costing, since the average fixed cost per unit will vary with the level of activity. Consider the data in the following table:

Month	(1) Total Fixed Overhead Cost	(2) Number of Units Produced	Average Fixed Cost per Unit (1) ÷ (2)
January	$6,000	1,000	$6.00
February	$6,000	1,500	$4.00
March	$6,000	800	$7.50

Notice that the large number of units produced in February results in a low unit cost ($4.00), whereas the smaller number of units produced in March results in a higher unit cost ($7.50). This occurs because the fixed cost is spread across more units in February than in March. One of the major reasons for using a predetermined overhead rate is to avoid such fluctuations in unit costs. A predetermined overhead rate can be set for an entire year, resulting in the same unit cost being recorded in the accounting system throughout the year.

Throughout the remainder of this chapter, we will be analyzing the fixed overhead costs of MicroDrive Corporation. To assist us in that task, the flexible budget of the company—including fixed costs—is displayed in Exhibit 9–8. Note that the total fixed overhead costs amount to $300,000 within the range of activity in the flexible budget.

Denominator Activity   The formula that we used in Chapter 2 to compute the predetermined overhead rate was:

$$\text{Predetermined overhead rate} = \frac{\text{Estimated total manufacturing overhead cost}}{\text{Estimated total amount of the allocation base (MH, DLH, etc.)}}$$

EXHIBIT 9–8

MicroDrive Corporation
Flexible Budgets at Various Levels of Activity

Overhead Costs	Cost Formula (per machine-hour)	Activity (in machine-hours)			
		40,000	45,000	50,000	55,000
Variable overhead costs:					
Indirect labor	$0.80	$ 32,000	$ 36,000	$ 40,000	$ 44,000
Lubricants	0.30	12,000	13,500	15,000	16,500
Power	0.40	16,000	18,000	20,000	22,000
Total variable overhead cost	$1.50	60,000	67,500	75,000	82,500
Fixed overhead costs:					
Depreciation		100,000	100,000	100,000	100,000
Supervisory salaries		160,000	160,000	160,000	160,000
Insurance		40,000	40,000	40,000	40,000
Total fixed overhead cost		300,000	300,000	300,000	300,000
Total overhead cost		$360,000	$367,500	$375,000	$382,500

The estimated total amount of the allocation base in the formula for the predetermined overhead rate is called the **denominator activity.** Recall from our discussion in Chapter 2 that once an estimated activity level (denominator activity) has been chosen, it remains unchanged throughout the year, even if the actual level of activity differs from what was estimated. The reason for not changing the denominator is to keep the amount of overhead applied to each unit of product the same regardless of when it is produced during the year.

Computing the Overhead Rate When we discussed predetermined overhead rates in Chapter 2, we didn't explain how the estimated total manufacturing overhead cost was determined. This figure can be derived using a flexible budget. The flexible budget can be used to determine the total amount of overhead cost that should be incurred at the denominator level of activity. The predetermined overhead rate can then be computed using the following variation on the basic formula for the predetermined overhead rate:

$$\text{Predetermined overhead rate} = \frac{\text{Overhead from the flexible budget at the denominaor level of activity}}{\text{Denominator level of activity}}$$

To illustrate, refer to MicroDrive Corporation's flexible budget for manufacturing overhead in Exhibit 9–8. Suppose that the budgeted activity level for the year is 50,000 machine-hours and that this will be used as the denominator activity in the formula for the predetermined overhead rate. The numerator in the formula is the estimated total overhead cost of $375,000 when the level of activity is 50,000 machine-hours. This amount is taken from the flexible budget in Exhibit 9–8. Thus, the predetermined overhead rate for MicroDrive Corporation is computed as follows:

$$\text{Predetermined overhead rate} = \frac{\$375,000}{50,000 \text{ MHs}} = \$7.50 \text{ per machine-hour (MH)}$$

Or the company can break its predetermined overhead rate down into its variable and fixed components:

$$\text{Variable component: } \frac{\$75,000}{50,000 \text{ MHs}} = \$1.50 \text{ per machine-hour (MH)}$$

$$\text{Fixed component: } \frac{\$300,000}{50,000 \text{ MHs}} = \$6.00 \text{ per machine-hour (MH)}$$

For every standard machine-hour recorded, work in process will be charged with $7.50 of overhead, of which $1.50 is variable overhead and $6.00 is fixed overhead. Since a disk-drive motor should take two machine-hours to complete, its cost will include $3.00 of variable overhead and $12.00 of fixed overhead, as shown on the following standard cost card:

Standard Cost Card—Per Motor	
Direct materials (assumed)	$14.00
Direct labor (assumed)	6.00
Variable overhead (2 machine-hours at $1.50 per machine-hour)	3.00
Fixed overhead (2 machine-hours at $6.00 per machine-hour).	12.00
Total standard cost per motor	$35.00

In sum, the flexible budget provides the estimated overhead cost needed to compute the predetermined overhead rate. Thus, the flexible budget plays a key role in determining the amount of fixed and variable overhead cost that will be charged to units of product.

Overhead Application in a Standard Cost System

To understand fixed overhead variances, we first have to understand how overhead is applied to work in process in a standard cost system. Recall from Chapter 2 that we applied overhead to work in process on the basis of the actual level of activity. This procedure was correct, since at the time we were dealing with a normal cost system.[1] However, we are now dealing with a standard cost system. In such a system, overhead is applied to work in process on the basis of the *standard hours allowed for the output of the period* rather than on the basis of the actual number of hours worked. Exhibit 9–9 illustrates this point. In a standard cost system, every unit of a particular product is charged with the same amount of overhead cost, regardless of how much time the unit actually requires for processing.

The Fixed Overhead Variances

To illustrate the computation of fixed overhead variances, we will refer again to the data for MicroDrive Corporation.

> **LEARNING OBJECTIVE 6**
> Compute and interpret the fixed overhead budget and volume variances.

Denominator activity in machine-hours	50,000
Budgeted fixed overhead costs	$300,000
Fixed portion of the predetermined overhead rate (computed earlier)	$6 per machine-hour

Normal Cost System	Standard Cost System
Manufacturing Overhead	Manufacturing Overhead
Actual overhead costs incurred | Applied overhead costs: Actual hours × Predetermined overhead rate	Actual overhead costs incurred | Applied overhead costs: Standard hours allowed for actual output × Predetermined overhead rate
Underapplied or overapplied overhead	Underapplied or overapplied overhead

EXHIBIT 9–9
Applied Overhead Costs: Normal Cost System versus Standard Cost System

---

[1]Normal cost systems are discussed in Chapter 2.

Let's assume that the following actual operating results were recorded for the year:

Actual machine-hours	42,000
Standard machine-hours allowed*	40,000
Actual fixed overhead costs:	
Depreciation	$100,000
Supervisory salaries	172,000
Insurance	36,000
Total actual fixed overhead cost	$308,000

*For the actual production of the year.

From these data, two variances are computed for fixed overhead—a *budget variance* and a *volume variance.* The variances are shown in Exhibit 9–10.

Notice from the exhibit that overhead has been applied to work in process on the basis of 40,000 standard hours allowed for the actual output of the year rather than on the basis of 42,000 actual hours worked. This keeps unit costs from being affected by variations in efficiency.

The Budget Variance—A Closer Look

The **budget variance** is the difference between the actual fixed overhead costs incurred during the period and the original budgeted fixed overhead costs for the period. It can be computed as shown in Exhibit 9–10 or by using the following formula:

$$\frac{\text{Budget}}{\text{variance}} = \frac{\text{Actual fixed}}{\text{overhead cost}} - \frac{\text{Budgeted}}{\text{fixed overhead cost}}$$

Applying this formula to MicroDrive Corporation, the budget variance would be computed as follows:

$$\$308,000 - \$300,000 = \$8,000 \text{ U}$$

The variances computed for the fixed costs at Rick's Hairstyling in Exhibit 9–4 are all budget variances, since they represent the difference between the actual fixed overhead cost and the budgeted fixed overhead cost.

An expanded overhead performance report for MicroDrive Corporation appears in Exhibit 9–11. This report includes the budget variances for fixed overhead as well as the spending variances for variable overhead from Exhibit 9–6.

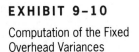

EXHIBIT 9–10

Computation of the Fixed Overhead Variances

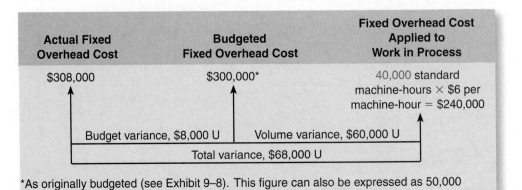

Actual Fixed Overhead Cost	Budgeted Fixed Overhead Cost	Fixed Overhead Cost Applied to Work in Process
$308,000	$300,000*	40,000 standard machine-hours × $6 per machine-hour = $240,000

Budget variance, $8,000 U   Volume variance, $60,000 U

Total variance, $68,000 U

*As originally budgeted (see Exhibit 9–8). This figure can also be expressed as 50,000 denominator machine-hours × $6 per machine-hour = $300,000.

EXHIBIT 9-11
Fixed Overhead Costs on the
Overhead Performance Report

MicroDrive Corporation
Overhead Performance Report
For the Year Ended December 31

Budgeted machine-hours 50,000
Actual machine-hours 42,000
Standard machine-hours allowed 40,000

Overhead Costs	Cost Formula (per machine-hour)	Actual Costs 42,000 Machine-Hours	Flexible Budget Based on 42,000 Machine-Hours	Spending or Budget Variance
Variable overhead costs:				
Indirect labor.	$0.80	$ 36,000	$ 33,600	$ 2,400 U
Lubricants.	0.30	11,000	12,600	1,600 F
Power	0.40	24,000	16,800	7,200 U
Total variable overhead cost	$1.50	71,000	63,000	8,000 U
Fixed overhead costs:				
Depreciation		100,000	100,000	0
Supervisory salaries.		172,000	160,000	12,000 U
Insurance		36,000	40,000	4,000 F
Total fixed overhead cost		308,000	300,000	8,000 U
Total overhead cost		$379,000	$363,000	$16,000 U

The budget variances for fixed overhead can be very useful, since they represent the difference between how much *should* have been spent (according to the original budget) and how much was actually spent. For example, Exhibit 9–11 shows that supervisory salaries has a $12,000 unfavorable variance. This large variance should be explained. Was it due to an increase in salaries? Was it due to overtime? Was another supervisor hired? If so, why was another supervisor hired?

The Volume Variance—A Closer Look

The **volume variance** is a measure of facility utilization. The variance arises whenever the standard hours allowed for the output of a period are different from the denominator activity level that was planned when the period began. It can be computed as shown in Exhibit 9–10 or by using the following formula:

$$\begin{array}{l} \text{Volume} \\ \text{variance} \end{array} = \begin{array}{l} \text{Fixed component} \\ \text{of the predetermined} \\ \text{overhead rate} \end{array} \times \left(\begin{array}{l} \text{Denominator} \\ \text{hours} \end{array} - \begin{array}{l} \text{Standard hours} \\ \text{allowed} \end{array} \right)$$

Applying this formula to MicroDrive Corporation, the volume variance would be computed as follows:

$6.00 per MH (50,000 MHs − 40,000 MHs) = $60,000 U

Note that this computation agrees with the volume variance shown in Exhibit 9–10. As stated earlier, the volume variance is a measure of facility utilization. Or, to be more precise, it is a measure of how much actual output departed from the planned output that determined the denominator level of activity. An unfavorable variance, as above, means that the company's actual output was *less* than planned. A favorable variance would mean that the company's actual output was *greater* than planned.

It is important to note that the volume variance does not measure over- or under-spending. A company normally would incur the same dollar amount of fixed overhead cost regardless of whether the period's activity was above or below the planned (denominator) level. In short, the volume variance is an activity-related variance. It is explainable only by activity and is controllable only through activity.

To summarize:

1. If the denominator activity and the standard hours allowed for the actual output of the period are the same, the volume variance is zero.
2. If the denominator activity is greater than the standard hours allowed for the actual output of the period, then the volume variance is unfavorable. This indicates that facilities were utilized less than was planned.
3. If the denominator activity is less than the standard hours allowed for the actual output of the period, then the volume variance is favorable. This indicates that facilities were utilized more than was planned.

DECISION MAKER   Vice President of Production

One of the company's factories produces a single product. The factory recently reported a significant unfavorable volume variance for the year. Sales for that product were less than anticipated. What should you do?

Graphic Analysis of Fixed Overhead Variances

Exhibit 9–12 shows a graphic analysis that offers insights into the budget and volume variances. As shown in the graph, fixed overhead cost is applied to work in process at the predetermined rate of $6.00 for each standard hour of activity. (The applied-cost line is the upward-sloping line on the graph.) Since a denominator level of 50,000 machine-hours was used in computing the $6.00 rate, the applied-cost line crosses the budget-cost line at exactly 50,000 machine-hours. If the denominator hours and the standard hours allowed for the output are the same, there is no volume variance. It is only when the standard hours differ from the denominator hours that a volume variance arises.

In MicroDrive's case, the standard hours allowed for the actual output (40,000 hours) are less than the denominator hours (50,000 hours). The result is an unfavorable volume variance, because less cost was applied to production than was originally budgeted. If the situation had been reversed and the standard hours allowed for the actual output had exceeded the denominator hours, then the volume variance on the graph would have been favorable.

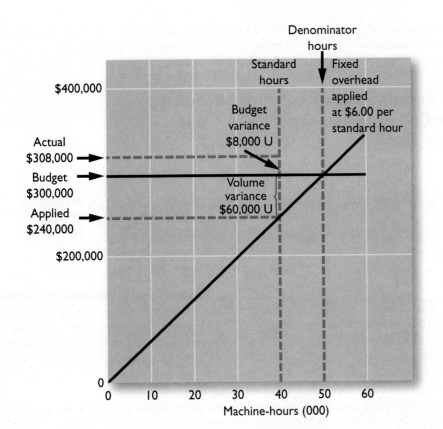

EXHIBIT 9–12
Graphic Analysis of Fixed
Overhead Variances

3. A company's actual and budgeted fixed overhead are $220,000 and $200,000, respectively. The fixed portion of the predetermined overhead rate is $8 per unit. How many units was the predetermined overhead rate based on?

CONCEPT CHECK ✓

   a. 20,000 units
   b. 25,000 units
   c. 30,000 units
   d. 35,000 units

4. Referring to the facts in question 3 above, what is the fixed overhead volume variance if 32,000 units were actually produced?

   a. $56,000 favorable
   b. $56,000 unfavorable
   c. $75,000 unfavorable
   d. $75,000 favorable

Cautions in Fixed Overhead Analysis

A volume variance for fixed overhead arises because when applying the costs to work in process, we act *as if* the fixed costs are variable. The graph in Exhibit 9–12 illustrates this point. Notice from the graph that fixed overhead costs are applied to work in process at a rate of $6.00 per hour *as if* they are variable. Treating these costs as if they are variable is necessary for product costing purposes, but some real dangers lurk here. Managers can easily be misled into thinking that fixed costs are *in fact* variable.

Keep clearly in mind that fixed overhead costs come in large chunks. Expressing fixed costs on a unit or per hour basis, though necessary for product costing for external reports, is artificial. Increases or decreases in activity in fact have no effect on total fixed costs within the relevant range of activity. Even though fixed costs are expressed on a unit or per hour basis, they are *not* proportional to activity. In a sense, the volume variance is the error that occurs as a result of treating fixed costs as variable costs in the costing system.

Overhead Variances and Underapplied or Overapplied Overhead Cost

Four variances relating to overhead cost have been computed for MicroDrive Corporation in this chapter. These four variances are as follows:

Variable overhead spending variance (p. 387)	$ 8,000 U
Variable overhead efficiency variance (p. 387)	3,000 U
Fixed overhead budget variance (p. 392)	8,000 U
Fixed overhead volume variance (p. 392)	60,000 U
Total overhead variance	$79,000 U

Recall from Chapter 2 that underapplied or overapplied overhead is the difference between the amount of overhead applied to products and the actual overhead costs incurred during a period. Basically, the overhead variances we have computed in this chapter break the underapplied or overapplied overhead down into variances that can be used by managers for control purposes. *The sum of the overhead variances equals the underapplied or overapplied overhead cost for a period.*

Furthermore, in a standard cost system, unfavorable variances are equivalent to underapplied overhead and favorable variances are equivalent to overapplied overhead. Unfavorable variances occur because more was spent on overhead than the standards allow. Underapplied overhead occurs when more was spent on overhead than was applied to products during the period. But in a standard costing system, the standard amount of overhead allowed is exactly the same as the amount of overhead applied to products. Therefore, in a standard costing system, unfavorable variances and underapplied overhead are the same thing, as are favorable variances and overapplied overhead.

For MicroDrive Corporation, the total overhead variance is $79,000 unfavorable. Therefore, its overhead cost is underapplied by $79,000 for the year. To solidify this point in your mind, *carefully study the review problem at the end of the chapter!* This review problem provides a comprehensive summary of overhead analysis, including the computation of underapplied or overapplied overhead cost in a standard cost system.

IN BUSINESS   Overhead Accounts: Fertile Ground for Fraud

Particularly in small companies, no one but the controller may understand concepts such as overhead variances and overapplied and underapplied overhead. Furthermore, a small company controller may be able to both authorize cash disbursements and account for them. Since small, closely held companies often do not hire external auditors, these circumstances create an ideal environment for fraud.

Such was the case in a small manufacturing company with 100 employees and $30 million in annual sales. The controller embezzled nearly $1 million from the company over three years by writing checks to himself. The consultant who uncovered the fraud was tipped off by the unusually high overhead variances that resulted from the controller recording fictitious expenses in the overhead accounts to offset the fraudulent cash disbursements. After the fraud was exposed, the company implemented various controls to reduce the risk of future problems, such as hiring an internal auditor and requiring periodic review of overhead variances to identify and explain significant discrepancies.

Source: John B. MacArthur, Bobby E. Waldrup, and Gary R. Fane, "Caution: Fraud Overhead," *Strategic Finance*, October 2004, pp. 28–32.

Production Manager

You are the production manager at a factory that makes decorator ceramic tiles. Your company's top management has adopted Lean Production as a guiding principle. During the last month, you filled all orders for tiles completely with no defects and on time, and you started and ended the month with no work in process inventories. You feel that the factory was working extremely effectively during the month and were surprised to be asked by top management to explain a very large unfavorable volume variance. What would have caused the unfavorable volume variance? How can such an unfavorable volume variance be avoided in the future?

SUMMARY

LO1   Prepare a flexible budget and explain the advantages of the flexible budget approach over the static budget approach.

A flexible budget shows what costs should be as a function of the level of activity. A flexible budget provides a better benchmark for evaluating how well costs have been controlled than the static budget approved at the beginning of the period. Some costs should be different from the amounts budgeted at the beginning of the period simply because the level of activity is different from what was expected. The flexible budget takes this fact into account, whereas the static budget does not.

LO2   Prepare a performance report for both variable and fixed overhead costs using the flexible budget approach.

A flexible budget performance report compares actual costs to what the costs should have been, given the actual level of activity for the period. Variable costs are flexed (i.e., adjusted) for the actual level of activity. This is done by multiplying the cost per unit of activity by the actual level of activity. Fixed costs, at least within the relevant range, are not adjusted for the level of activity. The total cost for a fixed cost item is carried over from the static budget without adjustment.

LO3   Use a flexible budget to prepare a variable overhead performance report containing only a spending variance.

The spending variance for a variable overhead expense is computed by comparing the actual cost incurred to the amount that should have been spent, based on the actual direct labor-hours or machine-hours of the period.

LO4   Use a flexible budget to prepare a variable overhead performance report containing both a spending and an efficiency variance.

As stated above, the spending variance for a variable overhead expense is computed by comparing the actual cost incurred to the amount that should have been spent, based on the actual direct labor-hours or machine-hours of the period. The efficiency variance is computed by comparing the cost that should have been incurred for the actual direct labor-hours or machine-hours of the period to the cost that should have been incurred for the actual level of *output* of the period.

LO5   Compute the predetermined overhead rate and apply overhead to products in a standard cost system.

In a standard cost system, overhead is applied to products based on the standard hours allowed for the actual output of the period. This differs from a normal cost system in which overhead is applied to products based on the actual hours of the period.

LO6   Compute and interpret the fixed overhead budget and volume variances.

The fixed overhead budget variance is the difference between the actual total fixed overhead costs incurred for the period and the budgeted total fixed overhead costs. This variance measures how well fixed overhead costs were controlled.

The fixed overhead volume variance is the difference between the fixed overhead applied to production using the predetermined overhead rate and the budgeted total fixed overhead. A favorable variance occurs when the standard hours allowed for the actual output exceed the hours assumed when the predetermined overhead rate was computed. An unfavorable variance occurs when the standard hours allowed for the actual output are less than the hours assumed when the predetermined overhead rate was computed.

GUIDANCE ANSWERS TO *DECISION MAKER* AND *YOU DECIDE*

Vice President of Production (p. 394)

An unfavorable fixed overhead volume variance means that the factory is operating below the activity level that was planned for the year. You should meet with the vice president of sales to determine why demand was less than planned. Was production part of the problem? Were orders delivered late? Were customers quoted lead times that were too long? Could production help increase demand by improving the quality of the product and the services provided to customers? If sales are declining and are not expected to rebound, you should consider how to make use of the excess capacity in this factory. You might consider whether the factory could be reconfigured to produce another product or if a section of the factory could be leased to another company.

Production Manager (p. 397)

The unfavorable volume variance was caused by the actual level of activity in the factory being less than the denominator level of activity. Since the factory produced only what was ordered, which is exactly what it should do in a Lean Production environment, the production manager should not be held responsible for this variance. Given the denominator level of activity, the production manager could have avoided the unfavorable volume variance only by producing more than was ordered—which would have violated Lean Production principles.

The easiest way to avoid an unfavorable volume variance is to set the denominator level of activity at a much lower level so that it is unlikely that it would exceed the actual level of activity. Unfortunately, the production manager is unlikely to have the authority to change the denominator level of activity. If the denominator level of activity is not changed, then the only way to avoid an unfavorable volume variance is to produce at a higher level than the denominator level of activity—which again would be a violation of lean principles if sales are less than the denominator level of activity.

GUIDANCE ANSWERS TO CONCEPT CHECKS

1. **Choice c.** A flexible budget is useful for controlling variable costs.
2. **Choice c.** The flexible budget at 12,000 units would be (12,000 units × $3.00 per unit variable overhead) + $70,000 of fixed overhead = $106,000.
3. **Choice b.** Budgeted fixed overhead of $200,000 ÷ $8.00 per unit fixed overhead rate = 25,000 units.
4. **Choice a.** The fixed overhead volume variance is (32,000 units − 25,000 units) × $8.00 per unit = $56,000 favorable.

REVIEW PROBLEM: OVERHEAD ANALYSIS

(This problem provides a comprehensive review of Chapter 9, including the computation of underapplied or overapplied overhead and its breakdown into the four overhead variances.)

Data for the manufacturing overhead of Aspen Company are given below:

Overhead Costs	Cost Formula (per machine-hour)	Machine-Hours		
		5,000	6,000	7,000
Variable overhead costs:				
Supplies	$0.20	$ 1,000	$ 1,200	$ 1,400
Indirect labor.	0.30	1,500	1,800	2,100
Total variable overhead cost.	$0.50	2,500	3,000	3,500
Fixed overhead costs:				
Depreciation		4,000	4,000	4,000
Supervision.		5,000	5,000	5,000
Total fixed overhead cost		9,000	9,000	9,000
Total overhead cost		$11,500	$12,000	$12,500

Five machine-hours are required per unit of product. The company has set its denominator activity for the coming period at 6,000 machine-hours (or 1,200 units). The predetermined overhead rate is computed as follows:

$$\text{Total: } \frac{\$12,000}{6,000 \text{ MHs}} = \$2.00 \text{ per machine-hour}$$

$$\text{Variable component: } \frac{\$3,000}{6,000 \text{ MHs}} = \$0.50 \text{ per machine-hour}$$

$$\text{Fixed component: } \frac{\$9,000}{6,000 \text{ MHs}} = \$1.50 \text{ per machine-hour}$$

Assume the following *actual* results for the period:

Number of units produced	1,300 units
Actual machine-hours	6,800 machine-hours
Standard machine-hours allowed*	6,500 machine-hours
Actual variable overhead cost	$4,200
Actual fixed overhead cost	$9,400

*1,300 units × 5 machine-hours per unit.

Therefore, the company's Manufacturing Overhead account would appear as follows at the end of the period:

Manufacturing Overhead

Actual overhead costs	13,600*	13,000†	Applied overhead costs
Underapplied overhead	600		

*$4,200 variable + $9,400 fixed = $13,600.
†6,500 standard machine-hours × $2 per machine-hour = $13,000.
In a standard cost system, overhead is applied on the basis of standard hours, not actual hours.

Required:
Analyze the $600 underapplied overhead in terms of:

1. The variable overhead spending variance.
2. The variable overhead efficiency variance.
3. The fixed overhead budget variance.
4. The fixed overhead volume variance.

Solution to Review Problem

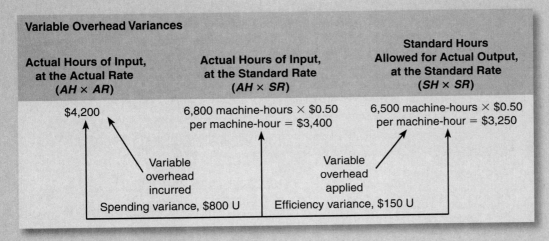

Variable Overhead Variances

Actual Hours of Input, at the Actual Rate (AH × AR)	Actual Hours of Input, at the Standard Rate (AH × SR)	Standard Hours Allowed for Actual Output, at the Standard Rate (SH × SR)
$4,200	6,800 machine-hours × $0.50 per machine-hour = $3,400	6,500 machine-hours × $0.50 per machine-hour = $3,250

Variable overhead incurred

Variable overhead applied

Spending variance, $800 U   Efficiency variance, $150 U

These same variances can be computed as follows:
Variable overhead spending variance:

$$\text{Spending variance} = (AH \times AR) - (AH \times SR)$$

$$= \frac{\text{Total actual}}{\text{variable overhead}} - (AH \times SR)$$

$$\$4{,}200 - (6{,}800 \text{ machine-hours} \times \$0.50 \text{ per machine-hour}) = \$800 \text{ U}$$

Variable overhead efficiency variance:

$$\text{Efficiency variance} = SR(AH - SH)$$

$$\$0.50 \text{ per machine-hour } (6{,}800 \text{ machine-hours} - 6{,}500 \text{ machine-hours}) = \$150 \text{ U}$$

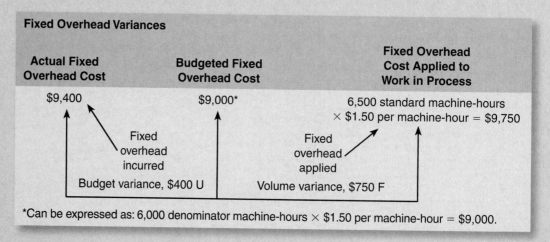

Fixed Overhead Variances

Actual Fixed Overhead Cost	Budgeted Fixed Overhead Cost	Fixed Overhead Cost Applied to Work in Process
$9,400	$9,000*	6,500 standard machine-hours × $1.50 per machine-hour = $9,750

Fixed overhead incurred

Fixed overhead applied

Budget variance, $400 U   Volume variance, $750 F

*Can be expressed as: 6,000 denominator machine-hours × $1.50 per machine-hour = $9,000.

These same variances can be computed as follows:
Fixed overhead budget variance:

$$\frac{\text{Budget}}{\text{variance}} = \frac{\text{Actual fixed}}{\text{overhead cost}} - \frac{\text{Budgeted fixed}}{\text{overhead cost}}$$

$$= \$9{,}400 - \$9{,}000 = \$400 \text{ U}$$

Fixed overhead volume variance:

$$\text{Volume variance} = \begin{array}{c}\text{Fixed portion}\\ \text{of the predetermined}\\ \text{overhead rate}\end{array} \times \left(\begin{array}{c}\text{Denominator}\\ \text{hours}\end{array} - \begin{array}{c}\text{Standard}\\ \text{hours}\end{array}\right)$$

$$\$1.50 \text{ per machine-hour } (6{,}000 \text{ machine-hours} - 6{,}500 \text{ machine-hours}) = \$750 \text{ F}$$

Summary of Variances

The four overhead variances are summarized below:

Variable overhead:	
Spending variance.............	$800 U
Efficiency variance............	150 U
Fixed overhead:	
Budget variance...............	400 U
Volume variance	750 F
Underapplied overhead..........	$600

Notice that the sum of the variances agrees with the underapplied balance in the company's Manufacturing Overhead account.

GLOSSARY

Budget variance   The difference between the actual fixed overhead costs incurred and the budgeted fixed overhead costs in the flexible budget. (p. 392)

Denominator activity   The level of activity used to compute the predetermined overhead rate. (p. 390)

Flexible budget   A budget that can be used to estimate what costs should be for any level of activity within a specified range. (p. 379)

Static budget   A budget created at the beginning of the budgeting period that is valid only for the planned level of activity. (p. 378)

Volume variance   The variance that arises whenever the standard hours allowed for the output of a period are different from the denominator activity level that was used to compute the predetermined overhead rate. It is computed by multiplying the fixed component of the predetermined overhead rate by the difference between the denominator hours and the standard hours allowed for the actual output. (p. 393)

QUESTIONS

9–1	What is a static budget?
9–2	What is a flexible budget and how does it differ from a static budget?
9–3	In our comparing of flexible budget data with actual data in a performance report for variable overhead, what variance(s) will be produced if the flexible budget data are based on actual hours worked? On both actual hours worked and standard hours allowed?
9–4	What is meant by the term *standard hours allowed*?
9–5	How does the variable manufacturing overhead spending variance differ from the materials price variance?
9–6	Why is the term *overhead efficiency variance* potentially misleading?
9–7	What is meant by the term *denominator level of activity*?
9–8	Why do we apply overhead to work in process on the basis of standard hours allowed in this chapter when we applied it on the basis of actual hours in Chapter 2? What is the difference in costing systems between the two chapters?
9–9	What does the fixed overhead budget variance measure?
9–10	Under what circumstances would you expect the volume variance to be favorable? Unfavorable? Does the variance measure deviations in spending for fixed overhead items? Explain.
9–11	Underapplied or overapplied overhead can be broken down into what four variances?
9–12	If factory overhead is overapplied for August, would you expect the total of the overhead variances to be favorable or unfavorable?

Multiple-choice questions are provided on the text website at www.mhhe.com/brewer4e.

Quiz 9

 BRIEF EXERCISES

BRIEF EXERCISE 9–1   Preparing a Flexible Budget   (LO1)

An incomplete flexible budget for overhead is given below for AutoPutz, Gmbh, a German company that owns and operates a large automatic carwash facility near Köln. The German currency is the euro, which is denoted by €.

Autoputz, Gmbh
Flexible Budget

Overhead Costs	Cost Formula (per car)	Activity (cars) 7,000	8,000	9,000
Variable overhead costs:				
Cleaning supplies	?	?	€ 6,000	?
Electricity	?	?	4,800	?
Maintenance	?	?	1,200	?
Total variable overhead cost	?	?	?	?
Fixed overhead costs:				
Operator wages		?	10,000	?
Depreciation		?	20,000	?
Rent		?	8,000	?
Total fixed overhead cost		?	?	?
Total overhead cost		?	?	?

Required:
Fill in the missing data.

BRIEF EXERCISE 9–2   Using a Flexible Budget   (LOI)
Refer to the data in Brief Exercise 9–1. AutoPutz, Gmbh's owner-manager would like to prepare a budget for August assuming an activity level of 8,200 cars.

Required:
Prepare a static budget for August. Use Exhibit 9–1 in the chapter as your guide.

BRIEF EXERCISE 9–3   Flexible Budget Performance Report   (LO2)
Refer to the data in Brief Exercise 9–1. AutoPutz, Gmbh's actual level of activity during August was 8,300 cars, although the owner had constructed his static budget for the month assuming the level of activity would be 8,200 cars. The actual overhead costs incurred during August are given below:

	Actual Costs Incurred for 8,300 Cars
Variable overhead costs:	
Cleaning supplies	€6,350
Electricity	€4,865
Maintenance	€1,600
Fixed overhead costs:	
Operator wages	€10,050
Depreciation	€20,200
Rent	€8,000

Required:
Prepare a flexible budget performance report for both the variable and fixed overhead costs for August. Use Exhibit 9–4 in the chapter as your guide.

BRIEF EXERCISE 9–4   Variable Overhead Performance Report with Just a Spending Variance   (LO3)
Jessel Corporation bases its variable overhead performance report on the actual direct labor-hours of the period. Data concerning the most recent year that ended on December 31 appear below:

Budgeted direct labor-hours	42,000
Actual direct labor-hours	44,000
Standard direct labor-hours allowed	45,000
Cost formula (per direct labor-hour):	
Indirect labor	$0.90
Supplies	$0.15
Electricity	$0.05
Actual costs incurred:	
Indirect labor	$42,000
Supplies	$6,900
Electricity	$1,800

Required:
Prepare a variable overhead performance report using the format in Exhibit 9–6. Compute just the variable overhead spending variances (do not compute the variable overhead efficiency variances).

BRIEF EXERCISE 9–5   Variable Overhead Performance Report with Both Spending and Efficiency Variances   (LO4)
Refer to the data for Jessel Corporation in Brief Exercise 9–4. Management would like to compute both spending and efficiency variances for variable overhead in the company's variable overhead performance report.

Required:
Prepare a variable overhead performance report using the format in Exhibit 9–7. Compute both the variable overhead spending variances and the variable overhead efficiency variances.

BRIEF EXERCISE 9–6   Applying Overhead in a Standard Costing System   (LO5)
Mosbach Corporation has a standard cost system in which it applies overhead to products based on the standard direct labor-hours allowed for the actual output of the period. Data concerning the most recent year appear below:

Variable overhead cost per direct labor-hour	$3.50
Total fixed overhead cost per year	$600,000
Budgeted standard direct labor-hours (denominator level of activity)	80,000
Actual direct labor-hours	84,000
Standard direct labor-hours allowed for the actual output	82,000

Required:

1. Compute the predetermined overhead rate for the year.
2. Determine the amount of overhead that would be applied to the output of the period.

BRIEF EXERCISE 9–7   Fixed Overhead Variances   (LO6)
Lusive Corporation has a standard cost system in which it applies overhead to products based on the standard direct labor-hours allowed for the actual output of the period. Data concerning the most recent year appear below:

Total budgeted fixed overhead cost for the year.	$400,000
Actual fixed overhead cost for the year	$394,000
Budgeted standard direct labor-hours (denominator level of activity)	50,000
Actual direct labor-hours	51,000
Standard direct labor-hours allowed for the actual output	48,000

Required:

1. Compute the fixed portion of the predetermined overhead rate for the year.
2. Compute the fixed overhead budget variance and volume variance.

 **EXERCISES**

EXERCISE 9–8   Predetermined Overhead Rate; Overhead Variances   (LO4, LO5, LO6)
Weller Company's flexible budget for manufacturing overhead (in condensed form) is given below:

Overhead Costs	Cost Formula (per machine-hour)	Machine-Hours		
		8,000	9,000	10,000
Variable cost	$1.05	$ 8,400	$ 9,450	$10,500
Fixed cost.		24,800	24,800	24,800
Total overhead cost		$33,200	$34,250	$35,300

The following information is available for a recent period:

a.   The denominator activity of 8,000 machine-hours is used to compute the predetermined overhead rate.

b.   At the 8,000 standard machine-hours level of activity, the company should produce 3,200 units of product.

c. The company's actual operating results were:

Number of units produced	3,500
Actual machine-hours	8,500
Actual variable overhead costs	$9,860
Actual fixed overhead costs	$25,100

Required:

1. Compute the predetermined overhead rate and break it down into variable and fixed cost components.
2. Compute the standard hours allowed for the actual production.
3. Compute the variable overhead spending and efficiency variances and the fixed overhead budget and volume variances.

EXERCISE 9–9   Prepare a Flexible Budget   (LO1)

The cost formulas for Swan Company's manufacturing overhead costs are given below. These cost formulas cover a relevant range of 8,000 to 10,000 machine-hours each year.

Overhead Costs	Cost Formula
Supplies	$0.20 per machine-hour
Indirect labor	$10,000 plus $0.25 per machine-hour
Utilities	$0.15 per machine-hour
Maintenance.	$7,000 plus $0.10 per machine-hour
Depreciation.	$8,000

Required:

Prepare a flexible budget in increments of 1,000 machine-hours. Include all costs in your budget.

EXERCISE 9–10   Variable Overhead Performance Report   (LO4)

Ronson Products, Ltd., an Australian company, has the following cost formulas (expressed in Australian dollars) for variable overhead costs in one of its machine shops:

Variable Overhead Cost	Cost Formula (per machine-hour)
Supplies	$0.70
Power	1.20
Lubrication	0.50
Wearing tools	3.10
Total variable overhead cost.	$5.50

During July, the machine shop was scheduled to work 3,200 machine-hours (MHs) and to produce 16,000 units of product. The standard machine time per unit of product is 0.2 hours. A severe storm during the month forced the company to close for several days, which reduced the level of output for the month. Actual results for July were:

Actual machine-hours worked	2,700
Actual number of units produced	14,000

Actual costs for July were:

Variable Overhead Cost	Total Actual Cost	Per Machine-Hour
Supplies	$1,836	$0.68
Power	3,348	1.24
Lubrication	1,485	0.55
Wearing tools	8,154	3.02
Total variable overhead cost.	$14,823	$5.49

Required:
Prepare an overhead performance report for the machine shop for July. Use column headings in your report as shown below:

Overhead Costs	Cost Formula (per MH)	Actual Costs Incurred, 2,700 MHs	Flexible Budget Based on ? MHs	Flexible Budget Based on ? MHs	Total Variance	Breakdown of the Total Variance	
						Spending Variance	Efficiency Variance

EXERCISE 9–11 Variable Overhead Performance Report (LO2, LO3)
The variable portion of Whaley Company's flexible budget for manufacturing overhead is given below:

Variable Overhead Costs	Cost Formula (per machine-hour)	Machine-Hours 10,000	Machine-Hours 18,000	Machine-Hours 24,000
Utilities	$1.20	$12,000	$21,600	$ 28,800
Supplies	0.30	3,000	5,400	7,200
Maintenance.	2.40	24,000	43,200	57,600
Rework	0.60	6,000	10,800	14,400
Total variable overhead cost.	$4.50	$45,000	$81,000	$108,000

During a recent period, the company recorded 16,000 machine-hours of activity. The variable overhead costs incurred were:

Utilities	$20,000
Supplies	$4,700
Maintenance.	$35,100
Rework	$12,300

The budgeted activity for the period had been 18,000 machine-hours.

Required:

1. Prepare a variable overhead performance report for the period. Indicate whether variances are favorable (F) or unfavorable (U). Show only a spending variance on your report.
2. Discuss the significance of the variances. Might some variances be the result of others? Explain.

EXERCISE 9–12   Fixed Overhead Variances   (LO6)

Selected operating information on three different companies for a recent year is given below:

	Company		
	X	**Y**	**Z**
Full-capacity direct labor-hours	20,000	9,000	10,000
Budgeted direct labor-hours*	19,000	8,500	8,000
Actual direct labor-hours.	19,500	8,000	9,000
Standard direct labor-hours allowed for actual output	18,500	8,250	9,500

*Denominator activity for computing the predetermined overhead rate.

Required:

For each company, state whether the company would have a favorable or unfavorable volume variance and why.

EXERCISE 9–13   Predetermined Overhead Rates   (LO5)

Operating at a normal level of 24,000 direct labor-hours, Trone Company produces 8,000 units of product each period. The direct labor wage rate is $12.60 per hour. Two pounds of direct materials go into each unit of product; the material costs $4.20 per pound. The flexible budget used to plan and control manufacturing overhead costs is given below in condensed form.

Flexible Budget Data

Overhead Costs	Cost Formula (per direct labor-hour)	Direct Labor-Hours		
		20,000	**22,000**	**24,000**
Variable cost.	$1.60	$ 32,000	$ 35,200	$ 38,400
Fixed cost		84,000	84,000	84,000
Total overhead cost.		$116,000	$119,200	$122,400

Required:

1. Using 24,000 direct labor-hours as the denominator activity, compute the predetermined overhead rate and break it down into variable and fixed elements.
2. Complete the standard cost card below for one unit of product:

Direct materials, 2 pounds at $4.20 per pound.	$8.40
Direct labor, ?	?
Variable overhead, ?.	?
Fixed overhead, ?.	?
Total standard cost per unit	$?

EXERCISE 9–14   Variable Overhead Performance Report with Both Spending and Efficiency Variances   (LO4)

The check-clearing office of San Juan Bank is responsible for processing all checks that come to the bank for payment. Managers at the bank believe that variable overhead costs are essentially proportional to the number of labor-hours worked in the office, so labor-hours are used as the activity base in the preparation of variable overhead budgets and performance reports. Data for October, the most recent month, appear below:

Budgeted labor-hours	865
Actual labor-hours	860
Standard labor-hours allowed for the actual number of checks processed	880

	Cost Formula (per labor-hour)	Actual Costs Incurred in October
Variable overhead costs:		
Office supplies	$0.15	$ 146
Staff coffee lounge	0.05	124
Indirect labor	3.25	2,790
Total variable overhead cost	$3.45	$3,060

Required:
Prepare a variable overhead performance report for October for the check-clearing office that includes both spending and efficiency variances. Use Exhibit 9–7 as a guide.

 PROBLEMS

PROBLEM 9–15A   Preparing a Performance Report   (LO2, LO3)
The Antigua Blood Bank, a private charity partly supported by government grants, is located on the Caribbean island of Antigua. The blood bank has just finished its operations for September, which was a particularly busy month due to a powerful hurricane that hit neighboring islands causing many injuries. The hurricane largely bypassed Antigua, but residents of Antigua willingly donated their blood to help people on other islands. As a consequence, the blood bank collected and processed over 10% more blood than had been originally planned for the month.

A report prepared by a government official comparing actual costs to budgeted costs for the blood bank appears below. (The currency on Antigua is the East Caribbean dollar.) Continued support from the government depends on the blood bank's ability to demonstrate control over its costs.

CHECK FIGURE
(1) Flexible budget total cost at 950 liters: $56,810

Antigua Blood Bank
Cost Control Report
For the Month Ended September 30

	Actual	Budget	Variance
Liters of blood collected	950	820	130
Variable costs:			
Medical supplies	$12,500	$10,660	$1,840 U
Lab tests	7,900	7,790	110 U
Refreshments for donors	6,700	5,740	960 U
Administrative supplies	2,300	2,050	250 U
Total variable cost	29,400	26,240	3,160 U
Fixed costs:			
Staff salaries	15,000	15,000	0
Equipment depreciation	6,800	6,600	200 U
Rent	4,000	4,000	0
Utilities	880	810	70 U
Total fixed cost	26,680	26,410	270 U
Total cost	$56,080	$52,650	$3,430 U

The managing director of the blood bank was very unhappy with this report, claiming that his costs were higher than expected due to the emergency on the neighboring islands. He also pointed out that the additional costs had been fully covered by payments from grateful recipients on the other islands. The government official who prepared the report countered that all of the figures had been submitted by the blood bank to the government; he was just pointing out that actual costs were a lot higher than promised in the budget.

Required:

1. Prepare a new performance report for September using the flexible budget approach. (Note: Even though some of these costs might be classified as direct costs rather than as overhead, the flexible budget approach can still be used to prepare a flexible budget performance report.)
2. Do you think any of the variances in the report you prepared should be investigated? Why?

CHECK FIGURE
(3) Spending variance:
€ 5,700 U
Budget variance:
€ 13,200 F

PROBLEM 9–16A Applying Overhead; Overhead Variances (LO4, LO5, LO6)

Pawdewski, S.A., of Cracow, Poland, is a major producer of classic Polish sausage. The company uses a standard cost system to help control costs. Manufacturing overhead is applied to production on the basis of standard direct labor-hours. According to the company's flexible budget, the following manufacturing overhead costs should be incurred at an activity level of 74,000 labor-hours (the denominator activity level):

Variable manufacturing overhead cost	€229,400
Fixed manufacturing overhead cost	414,400
Total manufacturing overhead cost.	€643,800

The currency in Poland is the euro, which is denoted here by €.

During the most recent year, the following operating results were recorded:

Activity:	
Actual labor-hours worked	66,000
Standard labor-hours allowed for output.	68,000
Cost:	
Actual variable manufacturing overhead cost incurred	€210,300
Actual fixed manufacturing overhead cost incurred	€401,200

At the end of the year, the company's Manufacturing Overhead account contained the following data:

Manufacturing Overhead			
Actual	611,500	Applied	591,600
	19,900		

Management would like to determine the cause of the €19,900 underapplied overhead.

Required:

1. Compute the predetermined overhead rate. Break the rate down into variable and fixed cost components.
2. Show how the €591,600 applied in the Manufacturing Overhead account was computed.
3. Analyze the €19,900 underapplied overhead in terms of the variable overhead spending and efficiency variances and the fixed overhead budget and volume variances.
4. Explain the meaning of each variance that you computed in (3) above.

CHECK FIGURE
(3) Volume variance:
$5,600 U

PROBLEM 9–17A Relations among Fixed Overhead Variances (LO5, LO6)

Selected information relating to East Shore Inc.'s operations for the most recent year is given below:

Activity:	
Denominator activity (machine-hours).	84,000
Standard machine-hours allowed per unit	8.0
Number of units produced	10,400
Costs:	
Actual fixed overhead costs incurred.	$584,000
Fixed overhead budget variance	$4,000 F

The company applies overhead cost to products on the basis of standard machine-hours.

Required:

1. What were the standard machine-hours allowed for the actual production?
2. What was the fixed portion of the predetermined overhead rate?
3. What was the volume variance?

PROBLEM 9–18A   Preparing an Overhead Performance Report   (LO2, LO3, LO6)

Several years ago, Edwards Inc. developed a comprehensive budgeting system for profit planning and control purposes. The line supervisors have been very happy with the system and with the reports being prepared on their performance, but both middle and upper management have expressed considerable dissatisfaction with the information being generated by the system. A typical manufacturing overhead performance report for a recent period follows:

CHECK FIGURE
(3) Total of spending and budget variances: $6,300 U

Edwards Inc.
Overhead Performance Report—Machining Department
For the Quarter Ended June 30

	Actual	Budget	Variance
Machine-hours	20,000	24,000	
Variable overhead costs:			
Indirect materials	$ 15,200	$ 16,800	$1,600 F
Rework	4,200	4,800	600 F
Utilities	34,200	36,000	1,800 F
Machine setup	9,400	9,600	200 F
Total variable overhead cost	63,000	67,200	4,200 F
Fixed overhead costs:			
Maintenance	64,300	65,000	700 F
Inspection	54,000	54,000	0
Total fixed overhead cost	118,300	119,000	700 F
Total overhead cost	$181,300	$186,200	$4,900 F

After receiving a copy of this overhead performance report, the supervisor of the Machining Department stated, "These reports are super. It makes me feel really good to see how well things are going in my department. I can't understand why those people upstairs complain so much."

The budget data above are for the original planned level of activity for the quarter.

Required:

1. The company's vice president is uneasy about the performance reports being prepared and would like you to evaluate their usefulness to the company.
2. What changes, if any, should be made in the overhead performance report to give better insight into how well the supervisor is controlling costs?
3. Prepare a new overhead performance report for the quarter, incorporating any changes you suggested in (2) above. (Include both the variable and the fixed costs in your report.)

PROBLEM 9–19A   Comprehensive Standard Cost Variances   (LO4, LO6)

"Wonderful! Not only did our salespeople do a good job in meeting the sales budget this year, but our production people did a good job in controlling costs as well," said Anna Jones, president of Hess Inc. "Our $34,110 overall manufacturing cost variance is only 1.47% of the $2,320,000 standard cost of products made during the year. That's well within the 3% limit set by management for acceptable variances. It looks like everyone will be in line for a bonus this year."

The company produces and sells a single product. The standard cost card for the product follows:

CHECK FIGURE
(3a) Efficiency variance: $4,560 U
(3b) Volume variance: $37,950 F

Standard Cost Card—per Unit of Product

Direct materials, 1.3 feet at $8.00 per foot	$10.40
Direct labor, 1.5 DLHs at $13.00 per DLH	19.50
Variable overhead, 1.5 DLHs at $1.20 per DLH	1.80
Fixed overhead, 1.5 DLHs at $3.30 per DLH	4.95
Standard cost per unit	$36.65

The following additional information is available for the year just completed:

a.　The company manufactured 64,000 units of product during the year.

b.　A total of 87,400 feet of material was purchased during the year at a cost of $8.05 per foot. All of this material was used to manufacture the 64,000 units. There were no beginning or ending inventories for the year.

c.　The company worked 99,800 direct labor-hours during the year at a cost of $12.80 per direct labor-hour (DLH).

d.　Overhead is applied to products on the basis of standard direct labor-hours. Data relating to manufacturing overhead costs follow:

Denominator activity level (direct labor-hours)	84,500
Budgeted fixed overhead costs (from the overhead flexible budget)	$278,850
Actual variable overhead costs incurred	$117,300
Actual fixed overhead costs incurred	$281,400

Required:

1.　Compute the direct materials price and quantity variances for the year.
2.　Compute the direct labor rate and efficiency variances for the year.
3.　For manufacturing overhead compute:
　　a.　The variable overhead spending and efficiency variances for the year.
　　b.　The fixed overhead budget and volume variances for the year.
4.　Total the variances you have computed, and compare the net amount with the $34,110 mentioned by the president. Do you agree that bonuses should be given to everyone for good cost control during the year? Explain.

CHECK FIGURE
(2) Materials quantity variance: $4,680 U
(3) Volume variance: $17,850 F

PROBLEM 9–20A　Comprehensive Standard Cost Variances　(LO4, LO5, LO6)
Luque Corporation uses a standard cost system and sets predetermined overhead rates on the basis of direct labor-hours. The following data are taken from the company's budget for the current year:

Denominator activity (direct labor-hours)	65,000
Variable manufacturing overhead cost	$143,000
Fixed manufacturing overhead cost	$341,250

The standard cost card for the company's only product is given below:

Direct materials, 4 yards at $7.80 per yard	$31.20
Direct labor, 4 DLHs at $8.40 per DLH	33.60
Manufacturing overhead 4 DLHs at $7.45 per DLH	29.80
Standard cost per unit	$94.60

During the year, the company produced 17,100 units of product and incurred the following costs:

Materials purchased, 69,200 yards at $8.00 per yard	$553,600
Materials used in production (in yards)	69,000
Direct labor cost incurred, 66,500 DLHs at $8.60 per DLH	$571,900
Variable manufacturing overhead cost incurred	$141,800
Fixed manufacturing overhead cost incurred	$345,700

Required:

1.　Redo the standard cost card in a clearer, more usable format by detailing the variable and fixed overhead cost components.
2.　Prepare an analysis of the variances for materials and labor for the year.
3.　Prepare an analysis of the variances for variable and fixed overhead for the year.
4.　What effect, if any, does the choice of a denominator activity level have on unit standard costs? Is the volume variance a controllable variance from a spending point of view? Explain.

PROBLEM 9–21A   Using Fixed Overhead Variances   (LO6)

The standard cost card for the single product manufactured by Bailey Industries is given below:

CHECK FIGURE
(1) Standard DLHs
     allowed: 48,500 DLHs

Standard Cost Card—per Unit

Direct materials, 80.0 yards at $0.50 per yard	$ 40.00
Direct labor, 5.0 DLHs at $12.50 per DLH	62.50
Variable overhead, 5.0 DLHs at $8.50 per DLH	42.50
Fixed overhead, 5.0 DLHs at $12.00 per DLH	60.00
Total standard cost per unit	$205.00

Manufacturing overhead is applied to production on the basis of standard direct labor-hours. During the year, the company worked 47,500 direct labor-hours and manufactured 9,700 units of product. Selected data relating to the company's fixed manufacturing overhead cost for the year are shown below:

Actual Fixed Overhead Cost	Budgeted Fixed Overhead Cost	Fixed Overhead Cost Applied to Work in Process
$591,400	?	__?__ DLHs × $ __?__ per DLH = $ __?__
	Budget variance, $__?__	Volume variance, $18,000 U

Required:

1. What were the standard direct labor-hours allowed for the year's production?
2. What was the amount of fixed overhead cost contained in the flexible budget for the year?
3. What was the fixed overhead budget variance for the year?
4. What denominator activity level did the company use in setting the predetermined overhead rate for the year?

PROBLEM 9–22A   Applying Overhead; Overhead Variances   (LO4, LO5, LO6)

Thomas Corporation manufactures a single product that requires a great deal of hand labor. Overhead cost is applied on the basis of standard direct labor-hours. The company's condensed flexible budget for manufacturing overhead is given below:

CHECK FIGURE
(2) Standard cost: $216.00
(4) Volume variance:
     $20,000 F

Overhead Costs	Cost Formula (per direct labor-hour)	Direct Labor-Hours 16,000	Direct Labor-Hours 24,000	Direct Labor-Hours 32,000
Variable manufacturing overhead cost	$6.00	$ 96,000	$ 144,000	$ 192,000
Fixed manufacturing overhead cost		120,000	120,000	120,000
Total manufacturing overhead cost		$216,000	$264,000	$312,000

The company's product requires 4 pounds of material that has a standard cost of $8.00 per pound and 8 hours of direct labor time that has a standard rate of $12.00 per hour.

The company planned to operate at a denominator activity level of 24,000 direct labor-hours and to produce 3,000 units of product during the most recent year. Actual activity and costs for the year were as follows:

Number of units produced	3,500
Actual direct labor-hours worked	29,600
Actual variable manufacturing overhead cost incurred	$168,800
Actual fixed manufacturing overhead cost incurred	$124,000

Required:

1. Compute the predetermined overhead rate for the year. Break the rate down into variable and fixed components.
2. Prepare a standard cost card for the company's product; show the details for all manufacturing costs on your standard cost card.
3. Do the following:
   a. Compute the standard direct labor-hours allowed for the year's production.
   b. Complete the following Manufacturing Overhead T-account for the year:

Manufacturing Overhead	
?	?
?	?

4. Determine the reason for any underapplied or overapplied overhead for the year by computing the variable overhead spending and efficiency variances and the fixed overhead budget and volume variances.
5. Suppose the company had chosen 30,000 direct labor-hours as the denominator activity rather than 24,000 hours. State which, if any, of the variances computed in (4) above would have changed and explain how the variance(s) would have changed. No computations are necessary.

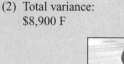

PROBLEM 9–23A   Evaluating an Overhead Performance Report   (LO2, LO4)
Debra Herman, supervisor of the Assembly Department for Greenlake Industries, was visibly upset after being reprimanded for her department's poor performance over the prior month. The department's performance report is given below:

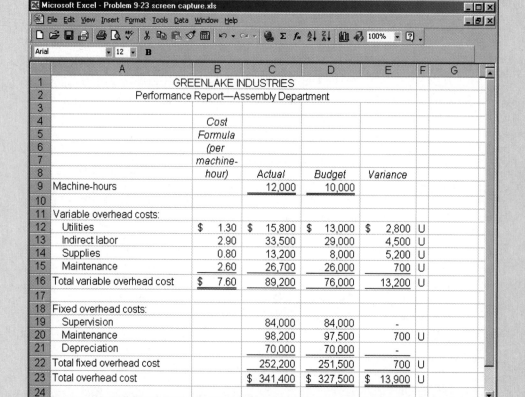

Microsoft Excel - Problem 9-23 screen capture.xls

File Edit View Insert Format Tools Data Window Help

Arial   12   B

	A	B	C	D	E	F	G
1		GREENLAKE INDUSTRIES					
2		Performance Report—Assembly Department					
3							
4		Cost					
5		Formula					
6		(per					
7		machine-					
8		hour)	Actual	Budget	Variance		
9	Machine-hours		12,000	10,000			
10							
11	Variable overhead costs:						
12	Utilities	$ 1.30	$ 15,800	$ 13,000	$ 2,800 U		
13	Indirect labor	2.90	33,500	29,000	4,500 U		
14	Supplies	0.80	13,200	8,000	5,200 U		
15	Maintenance	2.60	26,700	26,000	700 U		
16	Total variable overhead cost	$ 7.60	89,200	76,000	13,200 U		
17							
18	Fixed overhead costs:						
19	Supervision		84,000	84,000	-		
20	Maintenance		98,200	97,500	700 U		
21	Depreciation		70,000	70,000	-		
22	Total fixed overhead cost		252,200	251,500	700 U		
23	Total overhead cost		$ 341,400	$ 327,500	$ 13,900 U		
24							

Sheet1 Sheet2 Sheet3

"I just can't understand all the red ink," said Debra Herman to Keith Johnson, supervisor of another department. "When the boss called me in, I thought he was going to give me a pat on the back because I know for a fact that my department worked more efficiently last month than it has ever worked before. Instead, he tore me apart. I thought for a minute that it might be over the supplies that were stolen out of our warehouse last month. But they only amounted to a couple of thousand dollars, and just look at this report. *Everything* is unfavorable."

The budget for the Assembly Department had called for production of 2,000 units last month, which is equal to a budgeted activity level of 10,000 machine-hours (at a standard time of 5.0 hours per unit). Actual production in the Assembly Department for the month was 2,600 units.

Required:

1. Evaluate the overhead performance report given above and explain why the variances are all unfavorable.
2. Prepare a new overhead performance report that will help Ms. Herman's superiors assess efficiency and cost control in the Assembly Department. (*Hint:* Exhibit 9–7 may be helpful in structuring your report; however, the report you prepare should include both variable and fixed costs.)
3. Would the supplies stolen out of the warehouse be included as part of the variable overhead spending variance or as part of the variable overhead efficiency variance for the month? Explain.

PROBLEM 9–24A   Flexible Budget and Overhead Performance Report   (LO1, LO2, LO3, LO4)

You have just been hired by Seward Corporation, the manufacturer of a revolutionary new garage door opening device. Sam Ballard, the president, has asked that you review the company's costing system and "do what you can to help us get better control of our manufacturing overhead costs." You find that the company has never used a flexible budget, and you suggest that preparing such a budget would be an excellent first step in overhead planning and control.

After much effort and analysis, you are able to determine the following cost formulas for the company's normal operating range of 15,000 to 25,000 machine-hours each month:

CHECK FIGURE
(2) Total of spending and
budget variances:
$400 F

Overhead Costs	Cost Formula
Utilities.	$2.40 per machine-hour
Maintenance	$1.20 per machine-hour plus $65,000 per month
Machine setup	$0.50 per machine-hour
Indirect labor	$1.10 per machine-hour plus $210,000 per month
Depreciation	$60,000 per month

To show the president how the flexible budget concept works, you have gathered the following actual manufacturing overhead cost data for the most recent month, June, in which the company worked 18,000 machine-hours and produced 32,000 units:

Utilities.	$ 42,600
Maintenance	88,100
Machine setup	9,200
Indirect labor	228,100
Depreciation	60,200
Total manufacturing overhead cost	$428,200

The only variance in the fixed costs for the month was for depreciation, which increased as a result of purchasing new equipment.

The company had originally planned to work 25,000 machine-hours during June.

Required:

1. Prepare a flexible budget for the company in increments of 5,000 machine-hours.
2. Prepare an overhead performance report for the company for June. (Use the format illustrated in Exhibit 9–11.)
3. What additional information would you need to compute a variable overhead efficiency variance for the company?

got a call from Maria over at Sanchez and she said they would be sending us a final bill for the project before the end of the year. The total bill, including the reimbursements for the additional work, is going to be . . .

Kapp: I am not sure I want to hear this.

Prating: $176,000.

Kapp: Ouch!

Prating: The additional work we asked them to do added $16,000 to the cost of the project.

Kapp: No way can I turn in a performance report with an overall unfavorable variance. They'll kill me at corporate headquarters. Call up Maria at Sanchez and ask her not to send the bill until after the first of the year. We have to have that $6,000 favorable variance for industrial engineering on the performance report.

Required:

What should Lance Prating do?

10 Decentralization

<< A LOOK BACK

We introduced management control and performance measures in Chapter 8 with a discussion of standard costs and variance analysis. Chapter 9 extended that discussion to overhead costs.

A LOOK AT THIS CHAPTER

Chapter 10 continues our coverage of performance measurement by introducing return on investment and residual income measures to motivate managers and monitor progress toward achieving the company's goals.

A LOOK AHEAD >>

After introducing the concept of relevant costs and benefits, we discuss in Chapter 11 how effective decision making depends on the correct use of relevant data.

CHAPTER OUTLINE

Centralizing Communications

Ingersoll-Rand, a global conglomerate that traces its roots to the early 1870s, has about 46,000 employees. The company has received numerous recognitions and awards, including being named the *Industryweek* Best Managed Company for several years in a row. Even so, the company decided that it needed to restructure its organization to effectively compete in the current economic environment.

Previously comprising 8 autonomous companies, Ingersoll-Rand now operates as 13 separate business units. To improve communications, its computer systems were integrated to provide information to managers and headquarters in real time. The company continues to operate in a decentralized fashion. Even though many of its functions have been centralized, such as purchasing, payroll, and accounts receivable and payable, decision making is still spread throughout the organization. For example, factory managers continue to be responsible for deciding what must be purchased. However, instead of directly issuing purchase orders to vendors, requisitions are communicated to headquarters, which then issues the purchase orders. As a result of this centralized approach to purchasing, the company has been able to negotiate better discounts with suppliers.

Analysts estimate the cost of the restructuring at $50 million. Don Janson, director of common administrative resources implementations at Ingersoll-Rand, predicts that the changes will pay for themselves within three years.

Sources: Ingersoll-Rand Company website; and Steve Konicki, "A Company Merges Its Many Units—Successfully," *Informationweek*, May 8, 2000, pp. 174–178.

It is impossible for the top manager to make decisions about everything except in very small organizations. For example, the CEO of the Hyatt Hotel chain cannot be expected to decide whether a particular hotel guest at the Hyatt Hotel on Maui should be allowed to check out later than the normal checkout time. It makes sense for the CEO to authorize employees at Maui to make this decision. As in this example, managers in large organizations have to delegate some decisions to those who are at lower levels in the organization.

DECENTRALIZATION IN ORGANIZATIONS

In a **decentralized organization**, decision-making authority is spread throughout the organization rather than being confined to a few top executives. All large organizations are decentralized to some extent out of necessity. At one extreme, a strongly decentralized organization empowers even the lowest-level managers and employees to make decisions. At the other extreme, a strongly centralized organization provides lower-level managers with little freedom to make a decision. Most organizations fall somewhere between these two extremes.

Advantages and Disadvantages of Decentralization

The major advantages of decentralization include:

1. By delegating day-to-day problem solving to lower-level managers, top management can concentrate on bigger issues such as overall strategy.
2. Empowering lower-level managers to make decisions puts the decision-making authority in the hands of those who tend to have the most detailed and up-to-date information about day-to-day operations.
3. By eliminating layers of decision making and approvals, organizations can respond more quickly to customers and to changes in the operating environment.
4. Granting decision-making authority helps train lower-level managers for higher-level positions.
5. Empowering lower-level managers to make decisions can increase their motivation and job satisfaction.

The major disadvantages of decentralization include:

1. Lower-level managers may make decisions without fully understanding the big picture.
2. If lower-level managers make their own decisions, coordination may be lacking.
3. Lower-level managers may have objectives that clash with the objectives of the entire organization.[1] For example, a manager may be more interested in increasing the size of his or her department, leading to more power and prestige, than in increasing the department's effectiveness.
4. Spreading innovative ideas may be difficult in a decentralized organization. Someone in one part of the organization may have a terrific idea that would benefit other parts of the organization, but without strong central direction the idea may not be

---

[1] Similar problems exist with top-level managers as well. The shareholders of the company delegate their decision-making authority to the top managers. Unfortunately, top managers may abuse that trust by rewarding themselves and their friends too generously, spending too much company money on palatial offices, and so on. The issue of how to ensure that top managers act in the best interests of the company's owners continues to puzzle experts. To a large extent, the owners rely on performance evaluation using return on investment and residual income measures as discussed later in the chapter and on bonuses and stock options. The stock market is also an important disciplining mechanism. If top managers squander the company's resources, the price of the company's stock will almost surely fall—resulting in a loss of prestige, bonuses, and possibly a job. And, of course, particularly outrageous self-dealing may land a CEO in court, as recent events have demonstrated.

shared with, and adopted by, other parts of the organization. This problem can be reduced by effective use of intranet systems that make it easier to share information across departments.

Decentralization: A Delicate Balance

IN BUSINESS

Decentralization has its advantages and disadvantages. Bed Bath & Beyond, a specialty retailer headquartered in Union, New Jersey, benefits from decentralizing its merchandise stocking decisions to local store managers, who choose 70% of their store's merchandise based on local customer tastes. For example, the company's Manhattan stores stock wall paint, but its suburban stores do not because home improvement giants in the suburbs, such as Home Depot, meet this customer need.

On the other hand, Nestlé, a consumer food products company with $60 billion in annual sales, has been working to overcome glaring inefficiencies arising from its decentralized management structure. For example, in Switzerland "each candy and ice cream factory was ordering its own sugar. Moreover, different factories were using different names for the identical grade of sugar, making it almost impossible for bosses at headquarters to track costs." Nestlé hopes to significantly reduce costs and simplify recordkeeping by centralizing its raw materials purchases.

Sources: Nanette Byrnes, "What's Beyond for Bed Bath & Beyond?" *BusinessWeek*, January 19, 2004, pp. 44–50; and Carol Matlack, "Nestle Is Starting to Slim Down at Last," *BusinessWeek*, October 27, 2003, pp. 56–57.

RESPONSIBILITY ACCOUNTING

Decentralized organizations need *responsibility accounting systems* that link lower-level managers' decision-making authority with accountability for the outcomes of those decisions. The term **responsibility center** is used for any part of an organization whose manager has control over and is accountable for cost, profit, or investments. The three primary types of responsibility centers are *cost centers, profit centers,* and *investment centers.*[2]

Cost, Profit, and Investment Centers

Cost Center   The manager of a **cost center** has control over costs, but not over revenue or the use of investment funds. Service departments such as accounting, finance, general administration, legal, and personnel are usually classified as cost centers. In addition, manufacturing facilities are often considered to be cost centers. The managers of cost centers are expected to minimize costs while providing the level of products and services demanded by other parts of the organization. For example, the manager of a manufacturing facility would be evaluated at least in part by comparing actual costs to how much costs should have been for the actual level of output during the period. Standard cost variances and flexible budget variances, such as those discussed in Chapters 8 and 9, are often used to evaluate cost center performance.

Profit Center   The manager of a **profit center** has control over both costs and revenue, but not over the use of investment funds. For example, the manager in charge of a Six Flags amusement park would be responsible for both the revenues and costs, and hence the profits, of the amusement park, but may not have control over major investments in the park. Profit center managers are often evaluated by comparing actual profit to targeted or budgeted profit.

---

[2]Some companies classify business segments that are responsible mainly for generating revenue, such as an insurance sales office, as *revenue centers.* Other companies would consider this to be just another type of profit center, since costs of some kind (salaries, rent, utilities) are usually deducted from the revenues in the segment's income statement.

Responsibility Accounting: A Chinese Perspective

For years Han Dan Iron and Steel Company was under Chinese government control. As a market-oriented economy began to emerge, the company realized that its management accounting system was ill-equipped for the future because of its focus on responding to government mandates rather than market demands. For example, the outdated management accounting system had no incentive programs to encourage people to be productive. Managers were preoccupied with meeting production quotas imposed by their government rather than meeting profitability targets. The company overcame these weaknesses by implementing what it called a *responsibility cost control system* that (1) set cost and profit targets that reflected market pressures, (2) assigned target costs to responsibility center managers, (3) evaluated the performance of responsibility center managers based on their ability to meet preestablished targets, and (4) established an incentive program to motivate productivity improvements.

Source: Z. Jun Lin and Zengbiao Yu, "Responsibility Cost Control System in China: A Case of Management Accounting Application, *Management Accounting Research,* December 2002, pp. 447–467.

Investment Center The manager of an **investment center** has control over cost, revenue, and investments in operating assets. For example, the vice president of the Truck Division at General Motors would have a great deal of discretion over investments in the division. This vice president would be responsible for initiating investment proposals, such as funding research into more fuel-efficient engines for sport-utility vehicles. Once the proposal has been approved by General Motors' top-level managers and board of directors, the vice president of the Truck Division would then be responsible for making sure that the investment pays off. Investment center managers are usually evaluated using return on investment (ROI) or residual income measures, as discussed later in the chapter.

Extreme Incentives

In 2003, Tyco International, Ltd., was rocked by a series of scandals including disclosure of $2 billion of accounting-related problems, investigations by the Securities and Exchange Commission, and a criminal trial of its ex-CEO, Dennis Kozlowski, on charges of more than $600 million in unauthorized compensation and fraudulent stock sales. Was any of this foreseeable? Well, in a word, yes.

BusinessWeek reported in 1999 that the CEO of Tyco International, Ltd., was putting unrelenting pressure on his managers to deliver growth. "Each year, [the CEO] sets targets for how much each manager must increase his or her unit's earnings in the coming year. The targets are coupled with a powerful incentive system. If they meet or exceed these targets, managers are promised a bonus that can be many times their salary. But if they fall even a bit short, the bonus plummets." This sounds good, but "to many accounting experts, the sort of all-or-nothing bonus structure set up at Tyco is a warning light. If top executives set profit targets too high or turn a blind eye to how managers achieve them, the incentive for managers to cut corners is enormous. Indeed, a blue-ribbon panel of accounting experts who were trying to improve corporate auditing standards several years ago . . . identified just such extreme incentives as a red flag. 'If you're right under the target, there's a tremendous economic interest to accelerate earnings,' says David F. Larcker, a professor of accounting at the Wharton School. 'If you're right over it, there is an incentive to push earnings into the next period.'"

Sources: *Reuters,* "Tyco Says to Restate Several Years of Results," June 16, 2003; Jeanne King, *Reuters,* "New York Trial of ex-Tyco CEO Kozlowski Can Proceed," June 23, 2003; and William C. Symonds, Diane Brady, Geoffrey Smith, and Lorraine Woellert, "Tyco: Aggressive or Out of Line?" *BusinessWeek,* November 1, 1999, pp. 160–165.

EXHIBIT 10-1   Business Segments Classified as Cost, Profit, and Investment Centers

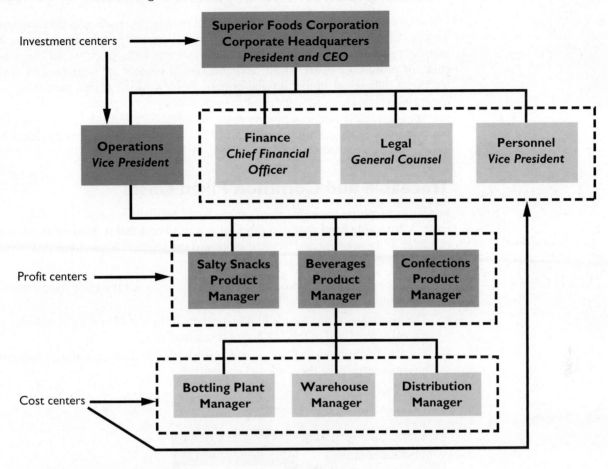

An Organizational View of Responsibility Centers

Superior Foods Corporation, a company that manufactures and distributes snack foods and beverages, provides an example of the various kinds of responsibility centers. Exhibit 10–1 shows a partial organization chart for Superior Foods that displays its cost, profit, and investment centers. The departments and work centers that do not generate significant revenues by themselves are classified as cost centers. These are staff departments—such as finance, legal, and personnel—and operating units—such as the bottling plant, warehouse, and beverage distribution center. The profit centers generate revenues, and they include the salty snacks, beverages, and confections product families. The vice president of operations oversees the allocation of investment funds across the product families and is responsible for the profits of those product families. And finally, corporate headquarters is an investment center, since it is responsible for all revenues, costs, and investments.

Meeting Targets the Wrong Way   IN BUSINESS

Putting too much emphasis on meeting financial targets can lead to undesirable behavior. Michael C. Jensen reports, "I once watched the management of a manufacturing company struggle to reach their year-end targets. In late fall, they announced a price increase of 10% effective January 2. Now it may be that a price increase was needed, but it was not in line with the competition, nor was it likely that January 2, of all dates, was the best time for the increase. A price increase on January 2, would, however, cause customers to order before year-end and thereby help managers reach their targets." The short-term boost in sales comes at the cost of lost future sales and possible customer ill will.

Source: Michael C. Jensen, "Why Pay People to Lie?" *The Wall Street Journal*, January 8, 2001, p. A32.

Decentralization and Segment Reporting

Effective decentralization requires *segmented reporting.* In addition to the companywide income statement, reports are needed for individual segments of the organization. A **segment** is a part or activity of an organization about which managers would like cost, revenue, or profit data. Cost, profit, and investment centers are segments as are sales territories, individual stores, service centers, manufacturing plants, marketing departments, individual customers, and product lines. A company's operations can be segmented in many ways. For example, a grocery store chain like Safeway or Kroger can segment its business by geographic region, by individual store, by the nature of the merchandise (i.e., green groceries, canned goods, paper goods), by brand name, and so on.

Traceable and Common Fixed Costs

In segment reports, *traceable fixed costs* should be distinguished from *common fixed costs.* A **traceable fixed cost** of a segment is a fixed cost that is incurred because of the existence of the segment and would disappear if the segment were eliminated. Examples of traceable fixed costs include the following:

*   The salary of the Fritos product manager at PepsiCo is a traceable fixed cost of the Fritos business segment of PepsiCo.
*   The maintenance cost for the building in which Boeing 747s are assembled is a traceable fixed cost of the 747 business segment of Boeing.
*   The liability insurance at Disney World is a traceable fixed cost of the Disney World business segment of the Disney Corporation.

Segmenting a Company

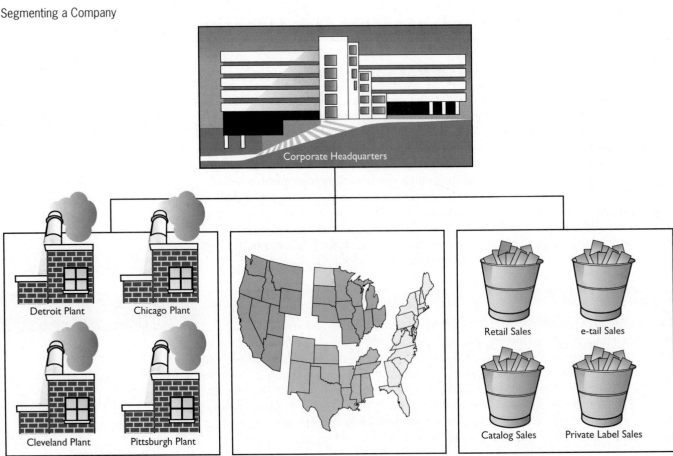

Corporate Headquarters

Detroit Plant   Chicago Plant

Cleveland Plant   Pittsburgh Plant

Segmenting by Plant

Segmenting by Geographic Territory

Retail Sales   e-tail Sales

Catalog Sales   Private Label Sales

Segmenting by Customer Channel

A **common fixed cost** is a fixed cost that supports the operations of more than one segment, but is not traceable in whole or in part to any one segment. Even if the segment were entirely eliminated, there would be no change in a common fixed cost. Examples of common fixed costs include the following:

- The salary of the CEO of General Motors is a common fixed cost of the various divisions of General Motors.
- The cost of the checkout equipment at a Safeway or Kroger grocery store is a common fixed cost of the store's various departments—such as groceries, produce, bakery.
- The cost of the receptionist's salary at an office shared by a number of doctors is a common fixed cost of the doctors. The cost is traceable to the office, but not to individual doctors.

In general, traceable costs should be assigned to segments, but common fixed costs should not. Assigning common fixed costs to segments would overstate the costs that are actually caused by the segments and that could be avoided by eliminating the segments. The details of how to deal with traceable and common fixed costs in segment reports are covered in more advanced texts. For example, see Chapter 12 of Ray Garrison, Eric Noreen, and Peter Brewer, *Managerial Accounting,* 12th edition, McGraw-Hill/Irwin, 2008.

1. Managers in which of the following responsibility centers are held responsible for profits? (You may select more than one answer.)
   a. Revenue centers
   b. Cost centers
   c. Profit centers
   d. Investment centers

2. Which of the following statements is false? (You may select more than one answer.)
   a. The same cost can be traceable or common depending on how the segment is defined.
   b. In general, common fixed costs should be assigned to segments.
   c. If a company eliminates a segment of its business, the costs that were traceable to that segment should disappear.
   d. If four segments share $1 million in common fixed costs and one segment is eliminated, the common fixed costs will decrease by $250,000.

RATE OF RETURN FOR MEASURING MANAGERIAL PERFORMANCE

When a company is truly decentralized, managers are given a great deal of autonomy. Profit and investment centers are often virtually independent businesses, with their managers having about the same control over decisions as if they were in fact running their own independent companies. With this autonomy, fierce competition often develops among managers, with each striving to make his or her segment the "best" in the company.

Competition between investment centers is particularly keen for investment funds. How do top managers in corporate headquarters go about deciding who gets new investment funds as they become available, and how do these managers decide which investment centers are most profitably using the funds that they have already been given? One of the most popular ways of making these judgments is to measure the rate of return that investment center managers are able to generate on their assets. This rate of return is called the *return on investment (ROI).*

LEARNING OBJECTIVE 1

Compute the return on investment (ROI) and show how changes in sales, expenses, and assets affect an organization's ROI.

The Return on Investment (ROI) Formula

Return on investment (ROI) is defined as net operating income divided by average operating assets:

$$\text{ROI} = \frac{\text{Net operating income}}{\text{Average operating assets}}$$

The higher a business segment's return on investment (ROI), the greater the profit earned per dollar invested in the segment's operating assets.

Net Operating Income and Operating Assets Defined

Note that *net operating income,* rather than net income, is used in the ROI formula. **Net operating income** is income before interest and taxes and is sometimes referred to as EBIT (earnings before interest and taxes). Net operating income is used in the formula because the base (i.e., denominator) consists of *operating assets.* To be consistent, we use net operating income in the numerator.

Operating assets include cash, accounts receivable, inventory, plant and equipment, and all other assets held for operating purposes. Examples of assets that are not included in operating assets (i.e., examples of nonoperating assets) include land held for future use, an investment in another company, or a building rented to someone else. These assets are not held for operating purposes and therefore are excluded from operating assets. The operating assets base used in the formula is typically computed as the average of the operating assets between the beginning and the end of the year.

Most companies use the net book value (i.e., acquisition cost less accumulated depreciation) of depreciable assets to calculate average operating assets. This approach has drawbacks. An asset's net book value decreases over time as the accumulated depreciation increases. This decreases the denominator in the ROI calculation, thus increasing ROI. Consequently, ROI mechanically increases over time. Moreover, replacing old depreciated equipment with new equipment increases the book value of depreciable assets and decreases ROI. Hence, using net book value in the calculation of average operating assets results in a predictable pattern of increasing ROI over time as accumulated depreciation grows and discourages replacing old equipment with new, updated equipment. An alternative to using net book value is the gross cost of the asset, which ignores accumulated depreciation. Gross cost stays constant over time because depreciation is ignored; therefore, ROI does not grow automatically over time, and replacing a fully depreciated asset with a comparably priced new asset will not adversely affect ROI.

Nevertheless, most companies use the net book value approach to computing average operating assets because it is consistent with their financial reporting practices of recording the net book value of assets on the balance sheet and including depreciation as an operating expense on the income statement. In this text, we will use the net book value approach unless a specific exercise or problem directs otherwise.

Understanding ROI

The equation for ROI, net operating income divided by average operating assets, does not provide much help to managers interested in taking actions to improve their ROI. It only offers two levers for improving performance—net operating income and average operating assets. Fortunately, ROI can also be expressed in terms of **margin** and **turnover** as follows:

$$\text{ROI} = \text{Margin} \times \text{Turnover}$$

where

$$\text{Margin} = \frac{\text{Net operating income}}{\text{Sales}}$$

and

$$\text{Turnover} = \frac{\text{Sales}}{\text{Average operating assets}}$$

Note that the sales terms in the margin and turnover formulas cancel out when they are multiplied together, yielding the original formula for ROI stated in terms of net operating income and average operating assets. So either formula for ROI will give the same answer. However, the margin and turnover formulation provides some additional insights.

From a manager's perspective, margin and turnover are very important concepts. Margin is ordinarily improved by increasing sales or reducing operating expenses, including cost of goods sold and selling and administrative expenses. The lower the operating expenses per dollar of sales, the higher the margin earned. Some managers tend to focus too much on margin and ignore turnover. However, turnover incorporates a crucial area of a manager's responsibility—the investment in operating assets. Excessive funds tied up in operating assets (e.g., cash, accounts receivable, inventories, plant and equipment, and other assets) depress turnover and lower ROI. In fact, inefficient use of operating assets can be just as much of a drag on profitability as excessive operating expenses, which depress margin.

E.I. du Pont de Nemours and Company (better known as DuPont) pioneered the use of ROI and recognized the importance of looking at both margin and turnover in assessing a manager's performance. ROI is now widely used as the key measure of investment center performance. ROI reflects in a single figure many aspects of the manager's responsibilities. It can be compared to the returns of other investment centers in the organization, the returns of other companies in the industry, and to the past returns of the investment center itself.

Insuring the Bottom Line   IN BUSINESS

Insurance companies have begun to offer managers a radical way to avoid some of the risk of having to report bad financial results. For example, the Reliance Group has created a product called Enterprise Earnings Protection Insurance that covers any operating earnings shortfall due to events beyond management's control. If a company buys an insurance policy guaranteeing $5 million in profits, but it posted only a $3 million profit, then Reliance would have to make up the difference of $2 million. Reliance reports that a company may have to pay as little as 5% of its estimated profit to insure against a 20% shortfall.

Source: Diane Brady, "Is Your Bottom Line Covered?" *BusinessWeek*, February 8, 1999, pp. 85–86.

DuPont also developed the diagram that appears in Exhibit 10–2. This exhibit helps managers understand how they can work to improve ROI. Any increase in ROI must involve at least one of the following:

1. Increased sales
2. Reduced operating expenses
3. Reduced operating assets

Many actions involve combinations of changes in sales, expenses, and operating assets. For example, a manager may make an investment in (i.e., increase) operating assets to reduce operating expenses or increase sales. Whether the net effect is favorable or not is judged in terms of its overall impact on ROI.

To illustrate how ROI is impacted by various actions, we will use the Monthaven outlet of the Burger Grill chain as an example. Burger Grill is a small chain of upscale

EXHIBIT 10–2   Elements of Return on Investment (ROI)

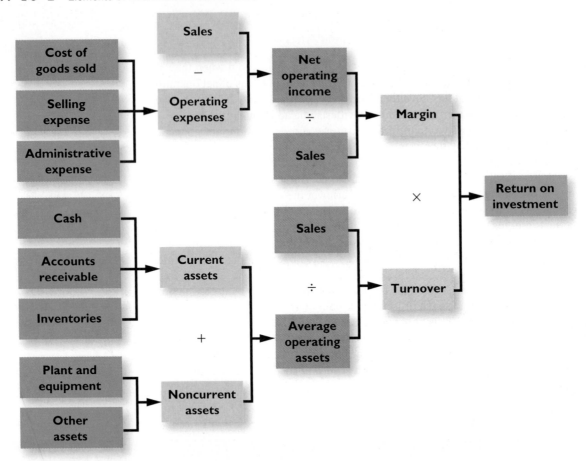

casual restaurants that has been rapidly adding outlets via franchising. The Monthaven franchise is owned by a group of local surgeons who have little time to devote to management and little expertise in business matters. Therefore, they delegate operating decisions—including decisions concerning investments in operating assets such as inventories—to a professional manager they have hired. The manager is evaluated largely based on the ROI the franchise generates.

The following data represent the results of operations for the most recent month:

Sales	$100,000
Operating expenses	$90,000
Net operating income	$10,000
Average operating assets	$50,000

IN BUSINESS   J. Crew Pulls the ROI Levers

J. Crew has adopted an interesting strategy for improving its ROI. The company has started selling "super-premium products—such as $1,500 cashmere coats and $1,500 beaded tunics—in limited editions, sometimes no more than 100 pieces nationwide." The intentional creation of scarcity causes many items to sell out within weeks as shoppers snatch them up before they are gone for good.

This strategy is helping boost J. Crew's ROI in two ways. First, the company earns higher margins on premium-priced products where customer demand dramatically exceeds supply. Second, the company is slashing its inventories because such small quantities of each item are purchased from suppliers. While J. Crew sacrifices some sales from customers who would have purchased sold out items, the overall effect on profits has been favorable. "Tighter inventories mean that J. Crew is no longer putting reams of clothes on sale, a move that kills profit margins and trains shoppers to wait for discounts. At one point . . . half of J. Crew's clothing sold at a discount. Today only a small percentage of it does."

Source: Julia Boorstin, "Mickey Drexler's Second Coming," *Fortune*, May 2, 2005, pp. 101–104.

The rate of return generated by the Monthaven Burger Grill investment center is as follows:

$$\text{ROI} = \text{Margin} \times \text{Turnover}$$

$$= \frac{\text{Net operating income}}{\text{Sales}} \times \frac{\text{Sales}}{\text{Average operating assets}}$$

$$= \frac{\$10,000}{\$100,000} \times \frac{\$100,000}{\$50,000}$$

$$= 10\% \times 2 = 20\%$$

Example 1: Increased Sales without Any Increase in Operating Assets Assume that the manager of the Monthaven Burger Grill can increase sales by 10% without any increase in operating assets. The increase in sales will require additional operating expenses. However, operating expenses include some fixed expenses, which would probably not be affected by a 10% increase in sales. Therefore, the increase in operating expenses would probably be less than 10%; let's assume the increase is 7.8%. Under those assumptions, the new net operating income would be $12,980, an increase of 29.8%, determined as follows:

Sales (1.10 × $100,000)	$110,000
Operating expenses (1.078 × $90,000)	97,020
Net operating income	$ 12,980

In this case, the new ROI would be:

$$\text{ROI} = \frac{\text{Net operating income}}{\text{Sales}} \times \frac{\text{Sales}}{\text{Average operating assets}}$$

$$= \frac{\$12,980}{\$110,000} \times \frac{\$110,000}{\$50,000}$$

$$= 11.8\% \times 2.2 = 25.96\% \text{ (as compared to 20\% originally)}$$

Note that the key to improved ROI in the case of an increase in sales is that the percentage increase in operating expenses must be less than the percentage increase in sales.

Example 2: Decreased Operating Expenses with No Change in Sales or Operating Assets Assume that by improving business processes, the manager of the Monthaven Burger Grill can reduce operating expenses by $1,000 without any effect on sales or operating assets. This reduction in operating expenses would increase net operating income by $1,000, from $10,000 to $11,000. The new ROI would be:

$$\text{ROI} = \frac{\text{Net operating income}}{\text{Sales}} \times \frac{\text{Sales}}{\text{Average operating assets}}$$

$$= \frac{\$11,000}{\$100,000} \times \frac{\$100,000}{\$50,000}$$

$$= 11\% \times 2 = 22\% \text{ (as compared to 20\% originally)}$$

When margins or profits are being squeezed, the first line of attack is often to cut costs. Discretionary fixed costs are particularly vulnerable to cuts. However, managers must be careful not to cut too much or in the wrong place. Inappropriate cost cutting can lead to decreased sales, increased costs elsewhere, and a drop in morale.

Example 3: Decreased Operating Assets with No Change in Sales or Operating Expenses   Assume that the manager of the Monthaven Burger Grill uses Lean Production techniques to reduce inventories by $10,000. This might actually have a positive effect on sales (through fresher ingredients) and on operating expenses (through reduced inventory spoilage), but for the sake of illustration, suppose the reduction in inventories has no effect on sales or operating expenses. The reduction in inventories will reduce average operating assets by $10,000, from $50,000 down to $40,000. The new ROI would be:

$$\text{ROI} = \frac{\text{Net operating income}}{\text{Sales}} \times \frac{\text{Sales}}{\text{Average operating assets}}$$

$$= \frac{\$10,000}{\$100,000} \times \frac{\$100,000}{\$40,000}$$

$$= 10\% \times 2.5 = 25\% \text{ (as compared to 20\% originally)}$$

In this example, Lean Production was used to reduce operating assets. Another common tactic for reducing operating assets is to speed up the collection of accounts receivable. For example, many companies encourage customers to pay electronically rather than by mail.

Example 4: Invest in Operating Assets to Increase Sales   Assume that the manager of the Monthaven Burger Grill invests $2,000 in a state-of-the-art soft-serve ice cream machine that can dispense a number of different flavors. This new machine will boost sales by $4,000, but will require additional operating expenses of $1,000. Thus, net operating income will increase by $3,000, to $13,000. The new ROI would be:

$$\text{ROI} = \frac{\text{Net operating income}}{\text{Sales}} \times \frac{\text{Sales}}{\text{Average operating assets}}$$

$$= \frac{\$13,000}{\$104,000} \times \frac{\$104,000}{\$52,000}$$

$$= 12.5\% \times 2 = 25\% \text{ (as compared to 20\% originally)}$$

In this particular example, the investment had no effect on turnover, which remained at 2, so there had to be an increase in margin in order to improve the ROI.

IN BUSINESS

McDonald Chic

McDonald's France has been spending lavishly to remodel its restaurants to blend with local architecture and to make their interiors less uniform and sterile. For example, some outlets in the Alps have wood-and-stone interiors similar to those of alpine chalets. The idea is to defuse the negative feelings many of the French people have toward McDonald's as a symbol of American culture and, perhaps more importantly, to try to entice customers to linger over their meals and spend more. This investment in operating assets has apparently been successful—even though a Big Mac costs about the same in Paris as in New York, the average French customer spends about $9 per visit versus only about $4 in the U.S.

Source: Carol Matlack and Pallavi Gogoi, "What's This? The French Love McDonald's?" *BusinessWeek*, January 13, 2003, p. 50.

ROI and the Balanced Scorecard

The DuPont scheme, which is illustrated in Exhibit 10–2, provides managers with *some* guidance about how to increase ROI. Generally speaking, ROI can be increased by increasing sales, decreasing costs, and/or decreasing investments in operating assets. However, it may not be obvious to managers how they are supposed to increase sales, decrease costs, and decrease investments in a way that is consistent with the company's strategy. For example, a manager who is given inadequate guidance may cut back on investments that are critical to implementing the company's strategy.

For that reason, as discussed in Chapter 8, managers should be evaluated using a balanced scorecard approach. ROI, or residual income (discussed below), is typically included as one of the financial performance measures on a company's balanced scorecard. However, this measure is supplemented by other measures that indicate *how* the company intends to improve its financial performance. A well-constructed balanced scorecard should answer questions like: "What internal business processes should be improved?" and "Which customer should be targeted and how will they be attracted and retained at a profit?" In short, a well-constructed balanced scorecard provides managers with a road map that indicates how the company intends to increase its ROI. In the absence of such a road map of the company's strategy, managers may have difficulty understanding what they are supposed to do to increase ROI and they may work at cross-purposes rather than in harmony with the overall strategy of the company.

Criticisms of ROI

Although ROI is widely used in evaluating performance, it is subject to the following criticisms:

1. Just telling managers to increase ROI may not be enough. Managers may not know how to increase ROI; they may increase ROI in a way that is inconsistent with the company's strategy; or they may take actions that increase ROI in the short run but harm the company in the long run (such as cutting back on research and development). This is why ROI is best used as part of a balanced scorecard. A balanced scorecard can provide concrete guidance to managers, making it more likely that their actions are consistent with the company's strategy, and reducing the likelihood that they will boost short-run performance at the expense of long-term performance.
2. A manager who takes over a business segment typically inherits many committed costs over which the manager has no control. These committed costs make it difficult to fairly assess the performance of the manager.
3. As discussed in the next section, a divisional manager who is evaluated based on ROI may reject investment opportunities that are profitable for the company as a whole but that would negatively impact the division's ROI.

Let the Buyer Beware

IN BUSINESS

Those who sell products and services to businesses are well aware that many potential customers look very carefully at the impact the purchase would have on ROI before making a purchase. Unfortunately, some salespersons make extravagant ROI claims. For example, businesspeople complain that software salespersons routinely exaggerate the impact that new software will have on ROI. Some of the tricks used by salespersons include: inflating the salaries of workers who are made redundant by productivity gains; omitting costs such as training costs and implementation costs; inflating expected sales increases; and using former clients as examples of ROI gains when the clients were given the software for free or for nominal cost. The message? Be skeptical of salespersons' claims with respect to ROI gains from purchasing their products and services.

Source: Scott Leibs, "All Hail the ROI," *CFO*, April 2002, pp. 27–28.

Jewelry Store Manager

You were recently hired as the manager of a chain of jewelry stores that are located in downtown Chicago. You are excited about the high level of autonomy that you have been given to run the stores but are nervous because you've heard rumors that the previous manager was let go because the return on investment (ROI) of the stores was unacceptable. What steps should you consider to improve ROI?

RESIDUAL INCOME—ANOTHER MEASURE OF PERFORMANCE

LEARNING OBJECTIVE 2

Compute residual income and understand its strengths and weaknesses.

Topic Tackler

PLUS

Concept 10-2

Residual income is another approach to measuring an investment center's performance. **Residual income** is the net operating income that an investment center earns above the minimum required return on its operating assets. In equation form, residual income is calculated as follows:

$$\frac{\text{Residual}}{\text{income}} = \frac{\text{Net operating}}{\text{income}} - \left(\frac{\text{Average operating}}{\text{assets}} \times \frac{\text{Minimum required}}{\text{rate of return}}\right)$$

Economic Value Added (EVA®) is an adaptation of residual income that has been adopted by many companies.[3] Under EVA, companies often modify their accounting principles in various ways. For example, funds used for research and development are often treated as investments rather than as expenses.[4] These complications are best dealt with in a more advanced course; in this text we will not draw any distinction between residual income and EVA.

When residual income or EVA is used to measure performance, the objective is to maximize the total amount of residual income or EVA, not to maximize ROI. This is an important distinction. If the objective were to maximize ROI, then every company should divest all of its products except the single product with the highest ROI.

A wide variety of organizations have embraced some version of residual income or EVA, including Bausch & Lomb, Best Buy, Boise Cascade, Coca-Cola, Dun and Bradstreet, Eli Lilly, Federated Mogul, Georgia-Pacific, Guidant Corporation, Hershey Foods, Husky Injection Molding, J.C. Penney, Kansas City Power & Light, Olin, Quaker Oats, Silicon Valley Bank, Sprint, Toys Я Us, Tupperware, and the United States Postal Service. In addition, financial institutions such as Credit Suisse First Boston now use EVA—and its allied concept, market value added—to evaluate potential investments in other companies.

Heads I Win, Tails You Lose

A number of companies, including AT&T, Armstrong Holdings, and Baldwin Technology, have stopped using residual income measures of performance after trying them. Why? Reasons differ, but "bonus evaporation is often seen as the Achilles' heel of value-based metrics [like residual income and EVA]— and a major cause of plans being dropped." Managers tend to love residual income and EVA when their bonuses are big, but clamor for changes in performance measures when bonuses shrink.

Source: Bill Richard and Alix Nyberg, "Do EVA and Other Value Metrics Still Offer a Good Mirror of Company Performance?" *CFO*, March 2001, pp. 56–64.

---

[3]The basic idea underlying residual income and economic value added has been around for over 100 years. In recent years, economic value added has been popularized and trademarked by the consulting firm Stern, Stewart & Co.

[4]Over 100 different adjustments could be made for deferred taxes, LIFO reserves, provisions for future liabilities, mergers and acquisitions, gains or losses due to changes in accounting rules, operating leases, and other accounts, but most companies make only a few. For further details, see John O'Hanlon and Ken Peasnell, "Wall Street's Contribution to Management Accounting: The Stern Stewart EVA® Financial Management System," *Management Accounting Research* 9 (1998), pp. 421–444.

For purposes of illustration, consider the following data for an investment center—the Ketchikan Division of Alaskan Marine Services Corporation.

Alaskan Marine Services Corporation **Ketchikan Division** **Basic Data for Performance Evaluation**	
Average operating assets	$100,000
Net operating income	$20,000
Minimum required rate of return	15%

Alaskan Marine Services Corporation has long had a policy of using ROI to evaluate its investment center managers, but it is considering switching to residual income. The controller of the company, who is in favor of the change to residual income, has provided the following table that shows how the performance of the division would be evaluated under each of the two methods:

Alaskan Marine Services Corporation **Ketchikan Division**	Alternative Performance Measures	
	ROI	**Residual Income**
Average operating assets (a)	$100,000	$100,000
Net operating income (b)	$ 20,000	$ 20,000
ROI, (b) ÷ (a)	20%	
Minimum required return (15% × $ 100,000)		15,000
Residual income		$ 5,000

The reasoning underlying the residual income calculation is straightforward. The company is able to earn a rate of return of at least 15% on its investments. Since the company has invested $100,000 in the Ketchikan Division in the form of operating assets, the company should be able to earn at least $15,000 (15% × $100,000) on this investment. Because the Ketchikan Division's net operating income is $20,000, the residual income above and beyond the minimum required return is $5,000. If residual income is adopted as the performance measure to replace ROI, the manager of the Ketchikan Division would be evaluated based on the growth in residual income from year to year.

Motivation and Residual Income

One of the primary reasons why the controller of Alaskan Marine Services Corporation would like to switch from ROI to residual income relates to how managers view new investments under the two performance measurement schemes. The residual income approach encourages managers to make investments that are profitable for the entire company but that would be rejected by managers who are evaluated using the ROI formula.

To illustrate this problem with ROI, suppose that the manager of the Ketchikan Division is considering purchasing a computerized diagnostic machine to aid in servicing marine diesel engines. The machine would cost $25,000 and is expected to generate additional operating income of $4,500 a year. From the standpoint of the company, this would be a good investment because it promises a rate of return of 18% ($4,500 ÷ $25,000), which exceeds the company's minimum required rate of return of 15%.

If the manager of the Ketchikan Division is evaluated based on residual income, she would be in favor of the investment in the diagnostic machine as shown below:

Alaskan Marine Services Corporation
Ketchikan Division
Performance Evaluated Using Residual Income

	Present	New Project	Overall
Average operating assets	$100,000	$25,000	$125,000
Net operating income	$ 20,000	$ 4,500	$ 24,500
Minimum required return.	15,000	3,750*	18,750
Residual income	$ 5,000	$ 750	$ 5,750

*$25,000 × 15% = $3,750.

Since the project would increase the residual income of the Ketchikan Division by $750, the manager would choose to invest in the new diagnostic machine.

Now suppose that the manager of the Ketchikan Division is evaluated based on ROI. The effect of the diagnostic machine on the division's ROI is computed below:

Alaskan Marine Services Corporation
Ketchikan Division
Performance Evaluated Using ROI

	Present	New Project	Overall
Average operating assets (a)	$100,000	$25,000	$125,000
Net operating income (b)	$20,000	$4,500	$24,500
ROI, (b) ÷ (a)	20%	18%	19.6%

The new project reduces the division's ROI from 20% to 19.6%. This happens because the 18% rate of return on the new diagnostic machine, while above the company's 15% minimum required rate of return, is below the division's current ROI of 20%. Therefore, the new diagnostic machine would decrease the division's ROI even though it would be a good investment from the standpoint of the company as a whole. If the manager of the division is evaluated based on ROI, she will be reluctant to even propose such an investment.

Generally, managers who are evaluated based on ROI will reject any project whose rate of return is below their division's current ROI even if the rate of return on the project is above the company's minimum required rate of return. In contrast, managers who are evaluated using residual income will pursue any project whose rate of return is above the minimum required rate of return because it will increase their residual income. Because it is in the best interests of the company as a whole to accept any project whose rate of return is above the minimum required rate of return, managers who are evaluated based on residual income will tend to make better decisions concerning investment projects than managers who are evaluated based on ROI.

IN BUSINESS | Shoring Up Return on Capital

Shoe Store Manager

You are the manager of a shoe store in a busy shopping mall. The store is part of a national chain that evaluates its store managers on the basis of return on investment (ROI). As the manager of the store, you have control over costs, pricing, and the inventory you carry. The ROI of your store was 17.21% last year and is projected to be 17.00% this year unless some action is taken. The projected ROI has been computed as follows:

Average operating assets (a)	$2,000,000
Net operating income (b)	$340,000
ROI, (b) ÷ (a)	17.00%

Your bonus this year will depend on improving your ROI performance over last year. The minimum required rate of return on investment for the national chain is 15%.

You are considering two alternatives for improving this year's ROI:

a. Cut inventories (and average operating assets) by $500,000. This will unfortunately result in a reduction in sales, with a negative impact on net operating income of $79,000.
b. Add a new product line that would increase average operating assets by $200,000, but would increase net operating income by $33,000.

Which alternative would result in your earning a bonus for the year? Which alternative is in the best interests of the national chain?

Divisional Comparison and Residual Income

The residual income approach has one major disadvantage. It can't be used to compare the performance of divisions of different sizes. Larger divisions often have more residual income than smaller divisions, not necessarily because they are better managed but simply because they are bigger.

As an example, consider the following residual income computations for the Wholesale Division and the Retail Division of Sisal Marketing Corporation:

	Wholesale Division	Retail Division
Average operating assets (a)	$1,000,000	$250,000
Net operating income	$ 120,000	$ 40,000
Minimum required return: 10% × (a)	100,000	25,000
Residual income	$ 20,000	$ 15,000

Observe that the Wholesale Division has slightly more residual income than the Retail Division, but that the Wholesale Division has $1,000,000 in operating assets as compared to only $250,000 in operating assets for the Retail Division. Thus, the Wholesale Division's greater residual income is probably due to its larger size rather than the quality of its management. In fact, it appears that the smaller division may be better managed, since it has been able to generate nearly as much residual income with only one-fourth as much in operating assets. When comparing investment centers, it is probably better to focus on the percentage change in residual income from year to year rather than on the absolute amount of the residual income.

CONCEPT CHECK

3. Last year sales were $300,000, net operating income was $75,000, and average operating assets were $500,000. If sales next year remain the same as last year and expenses and average operating assets are reduced by 5%, what will be the return on investment next year?

   a.   12.2%
   b.   18.2%
   c.   20.2%
   d.   25.2%

4. Referring to the facts in question 3 above, if the minimum required rate of return is 12%, what will be the residual income next year?

   a. $26,250
   b. $27,250
   c. $28,250
   d. $29,250

Transfer Prices

A problem arises in evaluating segments of a company when one segment provides a good or service to another segment. For example, the truck division of Ford provides trucks to the passenger car division to use in its operations. If both the truck and passenger car divisions are evaluated based on their profits, disputes are likely to arise over the *transfer price* charged for the trucks used by the passenger car division. A **transfer price** is the price charged when one segment of an organization provides a good or service to another segment in the organization. The selling segment, in this case the truck division, would naturally like the transfer price to be as high as possible whereas the buying segment, in this case the passenger car division, would like the price to be as low as possible.

The question of what transfer price to charge is one of the most difficult problems in managerial accounting. The objective in transfer pricing should be to motivate the segment managers to do what is in the best interests of the overall organization. For example, if we want the manager of the passenger car division of Ford to make decisions that are in the best interests of the overall organization, the transfer price charged to the passenger car division for trucks must be the cost incurred by the entire organization up to the point of transfer—including any opportunity costs. If the transfer price is less than this cost, then the manager of the passenger car division will think that the cost of the trucks is lower than it really is and will tend to demand more trucks than would be optimal for the entire company. If the transfer price is greater than the cost incurred by the entire organization up to the point of the transfer, then the passenger car division manager will think the cost of the trucks is higher than it really is and will tend to demand fewer trucks than would be optimal for the entire organization. While this principle may seem clear-cut, as a practical matter, implementing it is very difficult for a variety of reasons. In practice, companies usually adopt a simplified transfer pricing policy based on variable cost, absorption cost, or market prices. All of these approaches have flaws, which are covered in more advanced texts.

SUMMARY

LO1   Compute the return on investment (ROI) and show how changes in sales, expenses, and assets affect an organization's ROI.

Return on investment (ROI) is defined as net operating income divided by average operating assets. Alternatively, it can be defined as the product of margin and turnover, where margin is net operating income divided by sales and turnover is sales divided by average operating assets.

The relations among sales, expenses, assets, and ROI are complex. The effect of a change in any one variable on the others will depend on the specific circumstances. Nevertheless, an increase in sales often leads to an increase in ROI via the effect of sales on net operating income. If the organization has significant fixed costs, then a given percentage increase in sales is likely to have an even larger percentage effect on net operating income.

LO2   Compute residual income and understand its strengths and weaknesses.
Residual income is the difference between net operating income and the minimum required return on average operating assets. The minimum required return on average operating assets is computed by applying the minimum rate of return to the average operating assets.

A major advantage of residual income over ROI is that it encourages investment in projects whose rates of return are above the minimum required rate of return for the entire organization, but below the segment's current ROI.

GUIDANCE ANSWERS TO DECISION MAKER AND YOU DECIDE

Jewelry Store Manager (p. 432)
Three approaches can be used to increase ROI:

1. Increase sales—An increase in sales will positively impact the margin if expenses increase proportionately less than sales. An increase in sales will also favorably affect turnover if there is not a proportionate increase in operating assets.
2. Reduce expenses—This approach is often the first path selected by managers to increase profitability and ROI. You should start by reviewing the stores' discretionary fixed costs (such as advertising). It may be possible to cut some discretionary fixed costs with minimal damage to the long-run goals of the organization. You should also investigate whether there are adequate physical controls over the inventory of jewelry items. Thefts result in an increase in cost of goods sold without a corresponding increase in sales!
3. Reduce operating assets—An excessive investment in operating assets (such as inventory) reduces turnover and hurts ROI. Given the nature of the operations of retail jewelry stores, inventory must be in sufficient quantities at specific times during the year (such as Christmas, Valentine's Day, and Mother's Day) or sales will suffer. However, those levels do not need to be maintained throughout the year.

Shoe Store Manager (p. 435)
The effects of the two alternatives on your store's ROI for the year can be computed as follows:

	Present	Alternative (a)	Overall
Average operating assets (a).	$2,000,000	$(500,000)	$1,500,000
Net operating income (b).	$340,000	$(79,000)	$261,000
ROI, (b) ÷ (a)	17.00%	15.80%	17.40%

	Present	Alternative (b)	Overall
Average operating assets (a)	$2,000,000	$200,000	$2,200,000
Net operating income (b).	$340,000	$33,000	$373,000
ROI, (b) ÷ (a)	17.00%	16.50%	16.95%

Alternative (a) would increase your store's ROI to 17.40%—beating last year's ROI and hence earning you a bonus. Alternative (b) would actually decrease your store's ROI and would result in no bonus for the year. So to earn the bonus, you would select Alternative (a). However, this alternative is not in the best interests of the national chain since the ROI of the lost sales is 15.8%, which exceeds the national chain's minimum required rate of return of 15%. Rather, it would be in the national chain's interests to adopt Alternative (b)—the addition of a new product line. The ROI on these sales would be 16.5%, which exceeds the minimum required rate of return of 15%.

GUIDANCE ANSWERS TO CONCEPT CHECKS

1. **Choices c and d.** Both profit and investment center managers are held responsible for profits. In addition, an investment center manager is held responsible for earning an adequate return on investment or residual income.
2. **Choices b and d.** Common fixed costs should not be assigned to segments. Common fixed costs will not decrease if a segment is discontinued.
3. **Choice b.** The net operating income would be $300,000 − ($225,000 × 95%) = $86,250. The return on investment would be ($86,250 ÷ ($500,000 × 95%) = 18.2%.
4. **Choice d.** The residual income would be $86,250 − ($475,000 × 12%) = $29,250.

REVIEW PROBLEM: RETURN ON INVESTMENT (ROI) AND RESIDUAL INCOME

The Magnetic Imaging Division of Medical Diagnostics, Inc., has reported the following results for last year's operations:

Sales	$25 million
Net operating income	$ 3 million
Average operating assets	$10 million

Required:

1. Compute the Magnetic Imaging Division's margin, turnover, and ROI.
2. Top management of Medical Diagnostics, Inc., has set a minimum required rate of return on average operating assets of 25%. What is the Magnetic Imaging Division's residual income for the year?

Solution to Review Problem

1. The required calculations appear below:

$$\text{Margin} = \frac{\text{Net operating income}}{\text{Sales}}$$

$$= \frac{\$3,000,000}{\$25,000,000}$$

$$= 12\%$$

$$\text{Turnover} = \frac{\text{Sales}}{\text{Average operating assets}}$$

$$= \frac{\$25,000,000}{\$10,000,000}$$

$$= 2.5$$

$$\text{ROI} = \text{Margin} \times \text{Turnover}$$

$$= 12\% \times 2.5$$

$$= 30\%$$

2. The Magnetic Imaging Division's residual income is computed as follows:

Average operating assets	$10,000,000
Net operating income	$ 3,000,000
Minimum required return (25% × $10,000,000)	2,500,000
Residual income	$ 500,000

GLOSSARY

Common fixed cost   A fixed cost that supports more than one business segment, but is not traceable in whole or in part to any one of the business segments. (p. 425)

Cost center   A business segment whose manager has control over cost but has no control over revenue or investments in operating assets. (p. 421)

Decentralized organization   An organization in which decision making authority is not confined to a few top executives but rather is spread throughout the organization. (p. 420)

Economic Value Added (EVA)   A concept similar to residual income in which a variety of adjustments may be made to GAAP financial statements for performance evaluation purposes. (p. 432)

Investment center   A business segment whose manager has control over cost, revenue, and investments in operating assets. (p. 422)

Margin   Net operating income divided by sales. (p. 426)

Net operating income   Income before interest and income taxes have been deducted. (p. 426)

Operating assets   Cash, accounts receivable, inventory, plant and equipment, and all other assets held for operating purposes. (p. 426)

Profit center   A business segment whose manager has control over cost and revenue but has no control over investments in operating assets. (p. 421)

Residual income   The net operating income that an investment center earns above the minimum required return on its operating assets. (p. 432)

Responsibility center   Any business segment whose manager has control over costs, revenues, or investments in operating assets. (p. 421)

Return on investment (ROI)   Net operating income divided by average operating assets. It also equals margin multiplied by turnover. (p. 424)

Segment   Any part or activity of an organization about which managers seek cost, revenue, or profit data. (p. 424)

Traceable fixed cost   A fixed cost that is incurred because of the existence of a particular business segment and that would be eliminated if the segment were eliminated. (p. 424)

Transfer price   The price charged when one division or segment provides goods or services to another division or segment of an organization. (p. 436)

Turnover   Sales divided by average operating assets. (p. 426)

Multiple-choice questions are provided on the text website at www.mhhe.com/brewer4e.

Quiz 10

QUESTIONS

10–1   What is meant by the term *decentralization*?
10–2   What benefits result from decentralization?
10–3   Distinguish between a cost center, a profit center, and an investment center.
10–4   What is a segment of an organization? Give several examples of segments.
10–5   What is meant by the terms *margin* and *turnover*?
10–6   What is meant by residual income?
10–7   In what way can the use of ROI as a performance measure for investment centers lead to bad decisions? How does the residual income approach overcome this problem?
10–8   What is meant by the term *transfer price,* and why are transfer prices needed?

BRIEF EXERCISES

BRIEF EXERCISE 10-1   Compute the Return on Investment (ROI) (LO1)

Tundra Services Company, a division of a major oil company, provides various services to the operators of the North Slope oil field in Alaska. Data concerning the most recent year appear below:

Sales............................	$18,000,000
Net operating income	$5,400,000
Average operating assets	$36,000,000

Required

1. Compute the margin for Tundra Services Company.
2. Compute the turnover for Tundra Services Company.
3. Compute the return on investment (ROI) for Tundra Services Company.

BRIEF EXERCISE 10-2   Effects of Changes in Sales, Expenses, and Assets on ROI (LO1)

BusServ.com Corporation provides business-to-business services on the Internet. Data concerning the most recent year appear below:

Sales	$8,000,000
Net operating income	$800,000
Average operating assets	$3,200,000

Required

Consider each question below independently. Carry out all computations to two decimal places.

1. Compute the company's return on investment (ROI).
2. The entrepreneur who founded the company is convinced that sales will increase next year by 150% and that net operating income will increase by 400%, with no increase in average operating assets. What would be the company's ROI?
3. The chief financial officer of the company believes a more realistic scenario would be a $2,000,000 increase in sales, requiring an $800,000 increase in average operating assets, with a resulting $250,000 increase in net operating income. What would be the company's ROI in this scenario?

BRIEF EXERCISE 10-3   Residual Income (LO2)

Midlands Design Ltd. of Manchester, England, is a company specializing in providing design services to residential developers. Last year the company had net operating income of £400,000 on sales of £2,000,000. The company's average operating assets for the year were £2,200,000 and its minimum required rate of return was 16%. (The currency used in England is the pound, denoted by £.)

Required

Compute the company's residual income for the year.

EXERCISES

EXERCISE 10-4   Effects of Changes in Profits and Assets on Return on Investment (ROI) (LO1)

The Abs Shoppe is a regional chain of health clubs. The managers of the clubs, who have authority to make investments as needed, are evaluated based largely on return on investment (ROI). The Kirkland Abs Shoppe club reported the following results for the past year:

Sales	$800,000
Net operating income	$16,000
Average operating assets	$100,000

Required

The following questions are to be considered independently. Carry out all computations to two decimal places.

1. Compute the Kirkland club's return on investment (ROI).
2. Assume that the manager of the Kirkland club is able to increase sales by $80,000 and that, as a result, net operating income increases by $6,000. Further assume that this is possible without any increase in operating assets. What would be the club's return on investment (ROI)?
3. Assume that the manager of the Kirkland club is able to reduce expenses by $3,200 without any change in sales or operating assets. What would be the club's return on investment (ROI)?
4. Assume that the manager of the Kirkland club is able to reduce operating assets by $20,000 without any change in sales or net operating income. What would be the club's return on investment (ROI)?

EXERCISE 10-5   Evaluating New Investments Using Return on Investment (ROI) and Residual Income (LO1, LO2)

Selected sales and operating data for three divisions of three different service companies follow:

	Division A	Division B	Division C
Sales	$6,000,000	$10,000,000	$8,000,000
Average operating assets	$1,500,000	$5,000,000	$2,000,000
Net operating income	$300,000	$900,000	$180,000
Minimum required rate of return	15%	18%	12%

Required

1. Compute the return on investment (ROI) for each division using the formula stated in terms of margin and turnover.
2. Compute the residual income for each division.
3. Assume that each division is presented with an investment opportunity that would yield a rate of return of 17%.

   a. If performance is being measured by ROI, which division or divisions will probably accept the opportunity? Reject? Why?
   b. If performance is being measured by residual income, which division or divisions will probably accept the opportunity? Reject? Why?

EXERCISE 10-6   Computing and Interpreting Return on Investment (ROI) (LO1)

Selected operating data for two divisions of York Company are given below:

	Division	
	Eastern	Western
Sales	$1,000,000	$1,750,000
Average operating assets	$500,000	$500,000
Net operating income	$90,000	$105,000
Property, plant, and equipment (net)	$250,000	$200,000

Required

1. Compute the rate of return for each division using the return on investment (ROI) formula stated in terms of margin and turnover.
2. Which divisional manager seems to be doing the better job? Why?

EXERCISE 10-7   Contrasting Return on Investment (ROI) and Residual Income (LO1, LO2)

Rains Nickless Ltd. of Australia has two engineering consulting divisions that operate in Perth and Darwin. Selected data on the two divisions follow:

	Division	
	Perth	Darwin
Sales	$9,000,000	$20,000,000
Net operating income	$630,000	$1,800,000
Average operating assets	$3,000,000	$10,000,000

Required

1. Compute the return on investment (ROI) for each division in terms of margin and turnover.
2. Assume that the company evaluates performance using residual income and that the minimum required rate of return is 16%. Compute the residual income for each division.
3. Is the Darwin Division's greater amount of residual income an indication that it is better managed? Explain.

EXERCISE 10-8   Cost-Volume-Profit Analysis and Return on Investment (ROI) (LO1)

Images.com is a small Internet retailer of high-quality posters. The company has $800,000 in operating assets and fixed expenses of $160,000 per year. With this level of operating assets and fixed expenses, the company can support sales of up to $5,000,000 per year. The company's contribution margin ratio is 10%, which means that an additional dollar of sales results in additional contribution margin, and net operating income, of 10 cents.

Required

1. Complete the following table showing the relation between sales and return on investment (ROI).

Sales	Net Operating Income	Average Operating Assets	ROI
$4,500,000	$290,000	$800,000	?
$4,600,000	?	$800,000	?
$4,700,000	?	$800,000	?
$4,800,000	?	$800,000	?
$4,900,000	?	$800,000	?
$5,000,000	?	$800,000	?

2. What happens to the company's return on investment (ROI) as sales increase? Explain.

PROBLEMS

CHECK FIGURE
(1) Total ROI: 23.8%

PROBLEM 10-9A   Return on Investment (ROI) and Residual Income (LO1, LO2)

"I know headquarters wants us to add that new product line," said Clem Baker, manager of Westwood Inc.'s Office Products Division. "But I want to see the numbers before I make any move. Our division's return on investment (ROI) has led the company for three years, and I don't want any letdown."

Westwood Inc. is a decentralized organization with five autonomous divisions. The divisions are evaluated on the basis of ROI, with year-end bonuses given to the divisional managers who have the highest ROIs. Operating results for the company's Office Products Division for the most recent year are given below:

Sales.	$9,000,000
Variable expenses.	5,400,000
Contribution margin.	3,600,000
Fixed expenses.	2,520,000
Net operating income	$1,080,000
Divisional operating assets	$4,500,000

The company had an overall ROI of 18% last year (considering all divisions). The Office Products Division has an opportunity to add a new product line that would require an additional investment in operating assets of $250,000. The cost and revenue characteristics of the new product line per year would be:

Sales	$1,000,000
Variable expenses.	60% of sales
Fixed expenses.	$350,000

Required

1. Compute the Office Products Division's ROI for the most recent year; also compute the ROI as it would appear if the new product line is added.
2. If you were in Clem Baker's position, would you be inclined to accept or reject the new product line? Explain.

3. Why do you suppose headquarters is anxious for the Office Products Division to add the new product line?

4. Suppose that the company's minimum required rate of return on operating assets is 15% and that performance is evaluated using residual income.

   a. Compute the Office Products Division's residual income for the most recent year; also compute the residual income as it would appear if the new product line is added.

   b. Under these circumstances, if you were in Clem Baker's position, would you accept or reject the new product line? Explain.

PROBLEM 10-10A Return on Investment (ROI) and Residual Income (LO1, LO2)

Financial data for Pierce Industries for last year follow:

Pierce Industries
Balance Sheet

	Ending Balance	Beginning Balance
Assets		
Cash.	$ 140,000	$ 170,000
Accounts receivable	360,000	330,000
Inventory	360,000	350,000
Plant and equipment, net	610,000	680,000
Investment in Salem Service Corp.	270,000	230,000
Land (undeveloped)	180,000	190,000
Total assets	$1,920,000	$1,950,000
Liabilities and Stockholders' Equity		
Accounts payable	$ 446,000	$ 200,000
Long-term debt	1,400,000	1,700,000
Stockholders' equity	74,000	50,000
Total liabilities and stockholders' equity	$1,920,000	$1,950,000

Pierce Industries
Income Statement

Sales		$6,000,000
Less operating expenses		5,760,000
Net operating income		240,000
Less interest and taxes:		
Interest expense	$170,000	
Tax expense	30,000	200,000
Net income		$ 40,000

The company paid dividends of $16,000 last year. The "Investment in Salem Service Corp.," on the balance sheet, represents an investment in the stock of another company.

Required

1. Compute the company's margin, turnover, and return on investment (ROI) for last year.

2. The board of directors of Pierce Industries has set a minimum required rate of return of 14%. What was the company's residual income last year?

PROBLEM 10-11A   Return on Investment (ROI) (LO1)

Provide the missing data in the following table for the divisions of a service company:

	Division		
	Juneau	Kodiak	Leafton
Sales.	?	$11,750,000	?
Net operating income	?	$940,000	$210,000
Average operating assets	$650,000	?	?
Margin.	4.0%	?	7.0%
Turnover	4.0	?	?
Return on investment (ROI)	?	16.0 %	14.0%

PROBLEM 10-12A   Return on Investment (ROI) and Residual Income Relations (LO1, LO2)

A family friend has asked for your help in analyzing the operations of three anonymous companies that operate in the same service sector. Supply the missing data in the table below:

	Company		
	A	B	C
Sales.	$9,400,000	$6,800,000	$4,600,000
Net operating income	?	$260,000	?
Average operating assets	$3,100,000	?	$1,900,000
Return on investment (ROI)	19%	16%	?
Minimum required rate of return:			
Percentage	15%	?	13%
Dollar amount	?	$325,000	?
Residual income	?	?	$95,000

PROBLEM 10-13A   Return on Investment (ROI) and Residual Income; Decentralization (LO1, LO2)

Kramer Industries produces tool and die machinery for manufacturers. Several years ago the company acquired Douglas Steel Company, one of its suppliers of alloy steel plates. Kramer Industries decided to maintain Douglas's separate identity and therefore established the Douglas Steel Division as one of its investment centers.

Kramer Industries evaluates its divisions on the basis of ROI. Management bonuses are also based on ROI. All investments in operating assets are expected to earn a minimum required rate of return of 16%.

Douglas's ROI has ranged from 19% to 22% since it was acquired by Kramer Industries. During the past year, Douglas had an investment opportunity that would yield an estimated rate of return of 18%. Douglas's management decided against the investment because it believed the investment would decrease the division's overall ROI.

Last year's absorption costing income statement for Douglas Steel Division is given below. The division's operating assets were $16,800,000 at the end of the year, which represents an increase of 5% over the previous year-end balance.

Douglas Steel Division
Divisional Income Statement
For the Year Ended December 31

Sales.		$41,000,000
Cost of goods sold		20,863,000
Gross margin.		20,137,000
Selling and administrative expenses:		
Selling expenses	$7,385,000	
Administrative expenses	9,472,000	16,857,000
Net operating income		$ 3,280,000

Required

1. Compute the following performance measures for the Douglas Steel Division:
   a. ROI. (Remember, ROI is based on the *average* operating assets, computed from the beginning-of-year and end-of-year balances.) State ROI in terms of margin and turnover.
   b. Residual income.
2. Would the management of Douglas Steel Division have been more likely to accept the investment opportunity it had last year if residual income were used as a performance measure instead of ROI? Explain.
3. The Douglas Steel Division is a separate investment center within Kramer Industries. Identify the items Douglas must be free to control if it is to be evaluated fairly by either the ROI or residual income performance measures.

(CMA, adapted)

PROBLEM 10-14A   Return on Investment Analysis (LO1)
The contribution format income statement for Williamson Inc. for last year is given below:

CHECK FIGURE
(3) ROI: 21.2%
(6) ROI: 18.4%

e**X**cel

```
Microsoft Excel - Problem 10-14 screen capture.xls
File  Edit  View  Insert  Format  Tools  Data  Window  Help

Arial        12    I  U  D    €  $  , .00

         A                  B       C          D
  1                                Total       Unit
  2   Sales                       $8,000,000  $160.00
  3   Less variable expenses       5,600,000   112.00
  4   Contribution margin          2,400,000    48.00
  5   Less fixed expenses          1,600,000    32.00
  6   Net operating income           800,000    16.00
  7   Less income taxes @    40%     320,000     6.40
  8   Net income                  $ 480,000  $   9.60
  9
    Sheet1  Sheet2  Sheet3
```

The company had average operating assets of $4,000,000 during the year.

Required

1. Compute the company's return on investment (ROI) for the period using the ROI formula stated in terms of margin and turnover.

For each of the following questions, indicate whether the margin and turnover will increase, decrease, or remain unchanged as a result of the events described, and then compute the new ROI. Consider each question separately, starting in each case from the data used to compute the original ROI in (1) above.

2. Using Lean Production, the company is able to reduce the average level of inventory by $800,000. (The released funds are used to pay off short-term creditors.)
3. The company achieves a cost savings of $48,000 per year by using less costly materials.
4. The company issues bonds and uses the proceeds to purchase $1,000,000 in machinery and equipment at the beginning of the period. Interest on the bonds is $120,000 per year. Sales remain unchanged. The new, more efficient equipment reduces production costs by $160,000 per year.
5. As a result of a more intense effort by salespeople, sales are increased by 10%; operating assets remain unchanged.
6. Obsolete inventory carried on the books at a cost of $80,000 is scrapped and written off as a loss.
7. The company uses $180,000 of cash (received on accounts receivable) to repurchase and retire some of its common stock.

PROBLEM 10-15A   Comparison of Performance Using Return on Investment (ROI) (LO1)

Comparative data on three companies in the same service industry are given below:

	Company		
	A	**B**	**C**
Sales	$650,000	$580,000	?
Net operating income	$84,500	$75,400	?
Average operating assets	$325,000	?	$725,000
Margin	?	?	4.0%
Turnover	?	?	2.6
Return on investment ROI	?	10.4%	?

Required

1. What advantages are there to breaking down the ROI computation into two separate elements, margin and turnover?
2. Fill in the missing information above, and comment on the relative performance of the three companies in as much detail as the data permit. Make specific recommendations about how to improve the return on investment.

> (Adapted from National Association of Accountants, *Research Report No. 35*, p. 34)

BUILDING YOUR SKILLS

eXcel

ANALYTICAL THINKING   (LO1, LO2)

The Bearing Division of Timkin Company produces a small bearing that is used by a number of companies as a component part in their products. Timkin Company operates its divisions as autonomous units, giving its divisional managers great discretion in pricing and other decisions. Each division is expected to generate a return on its operating assets of at least 12%. The Bearing Division has operating assets of $300,000. The bearings are sold for $4 each. Variable costs are $2.50 per bearing, and fixed costs total $234,000 per year. The division's annual capacity is 200,000 bearings.

Required

1. How many bearings must be sold each year to obtain the desired rate of return on operating assets of 12%?

   a.   What is the margin earned at this level of sales?
   b.   What is the turnover at this level of sales?

2. Assume that the Bearing Division's current ROI is 12%. In order to increase the division's ROI, the divisional manager wants to increase the selling price to $4.25 per bearing. Market studies indicate that this increase in price would result in sales dropping to 160,000 units per year. However, operating assets could be reduced by $10,000 due to the decreased needs for inventories and accounts receivable. Compute the margin, turnover, and ROI if these changes are made.

3. Refer to the original data. Assume again that the Bearing Division's current ROI is 12%. Rather than increase the selling price, the sales manager wants to reduce the selling price to $3.75 per bearing. Market studies indicate that the demand at this lower price would result in annual sales of 200,000 bearings. However, this would require an increase in operating assets of $10,000 due to larger inventories and receivables. Compute the margin, turnover, and ROI if these changes are made.

4. Refer to the original data. Assume that the normal volume of sales is 180,000 bearings each period at a price of $4.00 per bearing. Another division of Timkin Company is currently purchasing 20,000 bearings each period from an overseas supplier at a price of $3.25 per bearing. The manager of the Bearing Division has refused to meet this price, pointing out that it would result in a loss for her division as follows:

Selling price per bearing		$ 3.25
Cost per bearing:		
Variable cost	$2.50	
Fixed cost ($234,000 ÷ 200,000 bearings)	1.17	3.67
Net loss per bearing		$(0.42)

The manager of the Bearing Division also points out that the normal $4.00 selling price barely allows her division to earn the 12% required rate of return. "If we take on some business at only $3.25 per bearing, then our ROI is obviously going to suffer," she reasons, "and maintaining that ROI figure is the key to our division's future. Besides, taking on these extra units would require us to increase our operating assets by at least $25,000 due to the larger inventories and accounts receivable we would be carrying." Would you recommend that the Bearing Division sell the bearings to the other division for $3.25? Show ROI computations to support your answer.

COMMUNICATING IN PRACTICE (LO1, LO2)

How do the performance measurement and compensation systems of service companies compare with those of manufacturers? Ask the manager of your local McDonald's, Wendy's, Burger King, or other fast-food chain if he or she could spend some time discussing the performance measures that the company uses to evaluate store managers and how the performance measures tie in with their compensation.

Required

After asking the following questions, write a brief memorandum to your instructor that summarizes what you discovered during your interview with the manager of the franchise.

1. What are the national chain's goals, that is, the broad, long-range plans of the company (e.g., to increase market share)?
2. What performance measures are used to help motivate the store managers and monitor progress toward achieving the corporation's goals?
3. Are the performance measures consistent with the store manager's compensation plan?

TEAMWORK IN ACTION (LO2)

Divide your team into two groups—one will play the part of the managers of the Consumer Products Division of Highstreet Enterprises, Inc., and the other will play the part of the managers of the Industrial Products Division of the same company.

The Consumer Products Division would like to acquire an advanced electric motor from the Industrial Products Division that would be used to make a state-of-the-art sorbet maker. At the expected selling price of $89, the Consumer Products Division would sell 50,000 sorbet makers per year. Each sorbet maker would require one of the advanced electric motors. The only possible source for the advanced electric motor is the Industrial Products Division, which holds a critical patent. The variable cost of the sorbet maker (not including the cost of the electric motor) would be $54. The sorbet maker project would require additional fixed costs of $180,000 per year and additional operating assets of $3,000,000.

The Industrial Products Division has plenty of spare capacity to make the electric motors requested by the Consumer Products Division. The variable cost of producing the motors would be $13 per unit. The additional fixed costs that would have to be incurred to fill the order from the Consumer Products Division would amount to $30,000 per year and the additional operating assets would be $400,000.

The division managers of Highstreet Enterprises are evaluated based on residual income, with a minimum required rate of return of 20%.

Required

The two groups—those representing the managers of the Consumer Products Division and those representing the managers of the Industrial Products Division—should negotiate concerning the transfer price for the 50,000 advanced electric motors per year. (The groups may or may not be able to come to an agreement.) Whatever the outcome of the negotiations, each group should write a memo to the instructor justifying the outcome in terms of what would be in the best interests of their division.

RESEARCH AND APPLICATION [LO1, LO2]

The questions in this exercise are based on FedEx Corporation. To answer the questions you will need to download FedEx's Form 10-K for the fiscal year ended May 31, 2005 at www.sec.gov/edgar/searchedgar/companysearch.html. Once at this website, input CIK code 1048911 and hit enter. In the gray box on the right-hand side of your computer screen define the scope of your search by inputting 10-K and then pressing enter. Select the 10-K with a filing date of July 14, 2005. You do not need to print this document to answer the questions.

REQUIRED:

1. What is FedEx's strategy for success in the marketplace? Does the company rely primarily on a customer intimacy, operational excellence, or product leadership customer value proposition? What evidence supports your conclusion?
2. What are FedEx's four main business segments? Provide two examples of traceable fixed costs for each of FedEx's four business segments. Provide two examples of common costs that are not traceable to the four business segments.
3. Identify one example of a cost center, a profit center, and an investment center for FedEx.
4. Provide three examples of fixed costs that can be traceable or common depending on how FedEx defines its business segments.
5. Compute the margin, turnover, and return on investment (ROI) in 2005 for each of FedEx's four business segments. (*Hint*: page 99 reports total segment assets for each business segment).
6. Assume that FedEx established a minimum required rate of return of 15% for each of its business segments. Compute the residual income earned in 2005 in each of FedEx's four segments.
7. Assume that the senior managers of FedEx Express and FedEx Ground each have an investment opportunity that would require $20 million of additional operating assets and that would increase operating income by $4 million. If FedEx evaluates all of its senior managers using ROI, would the managers of both segments pursue the investment opportunity? If FedEx evaluates all of its senior managers using residual income, would the managers of both segments pursue the investment opportunity?

11

Relevant Costs for Decision Making

<< A LOOK BACK

We concluded our coverage of performance measures in Chapter 10 by focusing on decentralized organizations. Return on investment (ROI) and residual income are used to motivate the managers of investment centers and to monitor the performance of these centers.

A LOOK AT THIS CHAPTER

We continue our coverage of decision-making in Chapter 11 by focusing on the use of relevant cost data when analyzing alternatives. In general, only those costs and benefits that differ between alternatives are relevant in a decision. This basic idea is applied in a wide variety of situations in this chapter.

A LOOK AHEAD >>

Common approaches to making major investment decisions, which can have significant long-term implications for any organization, are discussed in Chapter 12.

CHAPTER OUTLINE

DECISION FEATURE

Massaging the Numbers

Building and expanding convention centers appears to be an obsession with politicians. Indeed, in 44 cities across the United States, billions of dollars are being spent to build or expand convention centers—adding more than 7 million square feet of convention space to the 64 million square feet that already exists. Given that trade show attendance across the country has been steadily declining, how do politicians justify these enormous investments? Politicians frequently rely on consultants who produce studies that purport to show the convention center will have a favorable economic impact on the area.

These economic impact studies are bogus in two respects. First, a large portion of the so-called favorable economic impact that is cited by consultants would be realized by a city even if it did not invest in a new or expanded convention center. For example, Portland, Oregon, voters overwhelmingly opposed spending $82 million to expand their city's convention center. Nonetheless, local politicians proceeded with the project. After completing the expansion, more than 70% of the people spending money at trade shows in Portland were from the Portland area. How much of the money spent by these locals would have been spent in Portland anyway if the convention center had not been expanded? We don't know, but in all likelihood much of this money would have been spent anyway at the zoo, the art museum, the theater, local restaurants, and so on. This portion of the "favorable" economic impact cited by consultants and used by politicians to justify expanding convention centers should be ignored because of its irrelevance. Second, since the supply of convention centers throughout the United States substantially exceeds demand, convention centers must offer substantial economic incentives, such as waiving rental fees, to attract trade shows. The cost of these concessions, although often excluded from consultants' projections, further erodes the genuine economic viability of building or expanding a convention center.

Source: Victoria Murphy, "The Answer Is Always Yes," *Forbes,* February, 28, 2005, pp. 82–84.

M anagers must decide what products to sell, whether to make or buy component parts, what prices to charge, what channels of distribution to use, whether to accept special orders at special prices, and so forth. Making such decisions is often a difficult task that is complicated by numerous alternatives and massive amounts of data, only some of which may be relevant.

Every decision involves choosing from among at least two alternatives. In making a decision, the costs and benefits of one alternative must be compared to the costs and benefits of other alternatives. Costs that differ between alternatives are called **relevant costs.** Distinguishing between relevant and irrelevant cost and benefit data is critical for two reasons. First, irrelevant data can be ignored—saving decision makers tremendous amounts of time and effort. Second, bad decisions can easily result from erroneously including irrelevant costs and benefits when analyzing alternatives. To be successful in decision making, managers must be able to tell the difference between relevant and irrelevant data and must be able to correctly use the relevant data in analyzing alternatives. The purpose of this chapter is to develop these skills by illustrating their use in a wide range of decision-making situations. These decision-making skills are as important in your personal life as they are to managers. After completing your study of this chapter, you should be able to think more clearly about decisions in many facets of your life.

COST CONCEPTS FOR DECISION MAKING

Video 11–1

Four cost terms discussed in Chapter 1 are particularly applicable to this chapter. These terms are *differential costs, incremental costs, opportunity costs,* and *sunk costs.* You may find it helpful to turn back to Chapter 1 and refresh your memory concerning these terms before reading on.

Identifying Relevant Costs and Benefits

Only those costs and benefits that differ in total between alternatives are relevant in a decision. If the total amount of a cost will be the same regardless of the alternative selected, then the decision has no effect on the cost, so the cost can be ignored. For example, if you are trying to decide whether to go to a movie or to rent a videotape for the evening, the rent on your apartment is irrelevant. Whether you go to a movie or rent a videotape, the rent on your apartment will be exactly the same and is therefore irrelevant to the decision. On the other hand, the cost of the movie ticket and the cost of renting the videotape would be relevant in the decision because they are *avoidable costs.*

An **avoidable cost** is a cost that can be eliminated in whole or in part by choosing one alternative over another. By choosing the alternative of going to the movie, the cost of renting the videotape can be avoided. By choosing the alternative of renting the video-tape, the cost of the movie ticket can be avoided. Therefore, the cost of the movie ticket and the cost of renting the videotape are both avoidable costs. On the other hand, the rent on the apartment is not an avoidable cost of either alternative. You would continue to rent your apartment under either alternative. Avoidable costs are relevant costs. Unavoidable costs are irrelevant costs.

Two broad categories of costs are never relevant in decisions. These irrelevant costs are:

1. Sunk costs.
2. Future costs that do not differ between the alternatives.

As we learned in Chapter 1, a **sunk cost** is a cost that has already been incurred and cannot be avoided regardless of what a manager decides to do. For example, suppose a used car dealer purchased a five-year-old Toyota Camry for $12,000. The amount paid for the Camry is a sunk cost because it has already been incurred and the transaction cannot be undone. Sunk costs are always the same no matter what alternatives are being considered; therefore, they are irrelevant and should be ignored when making decisions. Future costs that do not differ between alternatives should also be ignored when making decisions. Continuing with the example discussed earlier, suppose you intend to order a pizza after you go to the movie theater or you rent a video. In that case, if you are going to buy the same pizza regardless of your choice of entertainment, its cost is irrelevant to the choice of whether you go to the movie theater or rent a video. Notice, the cost of the pizza is not a sunk cost because it has not yet been incurred. Nonetheless, the cost of the pizza is irrelevant to the entertainment decision because it is a future cost that does not differ between the alternatives.

The term **differential cost** was also introduced in Chapter 1. In managerial accounting, the terms *avoidable cost, differential cost, incremental cost,* and *relevant cost* are often used interchangeably. To identify the costs that are avoidable in a particular decision and are therefore relevant, these steps should be followed:

1. Eliminate costs and benefits that do not differ between alternatives. These irrelevant costs consist of (a) sunk costs and (b) future costs that do not differ between alternatives.
2. Use the remaining costs and benefits that do differ between alternatives in making the decision. The costs that remain are the differential, or avoidable, costs.

The Sunk Cost Trap

IN BUSINESS

Hal Arkes, a psychologist at Ohio University, asked 61 college students to assume they had mistakenly purchased tickets for both a $50 and a $100 ski trip for the same weekend. They could go on only one of the ski trips and would have to throw away the unused ticket. He further asked them to assume that they would actually have more fun on the $50 trip. Most of the students reported that they would go on the less enjoyable $100 trip. The larger cost mattered more to the students than having more fun. However, the sunk costs of the tickets should have been totally irrelevant in this decision. No matter which trip was selected, the actual total cost was $150—the cost of both tickets. And since this cost does not differ between the alternatives, it should be ignored. Like these students, most people have a great deal of difficulty ignoring sunk costs when making decisions.

Source: John Gourville and Dilip Soman, "Pricing and the Psychology of Consumption," *Harvard Business Review*, September 2002, pp. 92–93.

Different Costs for Different Purposes

We need to recognize a fundamental concept of managerial accounting from the outset of our discussion—costs that are relevant in one decision situation are not necessarily relevant in another. This means that *managers need different costs for different purposes*. For one purpose, a particular group of costs may be relevant; for another purpose, an entirely different group of costs may be relevant. Thus, *each* decision situation must be carefully analyzed to isolate the relevant costs. Otherwise, irrelevant data may cloud the situation and lead to a bad decision.

The concept of "different costs for different purposes" is basic to managerial accounting; we shall frequently see its application in the pages that follow.

An Example of Identifying Relevant Costs and Benefits

Cynthia is currently a student in an MBA program in Boston and would like to visit a friend in New York City over the weekend. She is trying to decide whether to drive or take the train. Because she is on a tight budget, she wants to carefully consider the costs of the two alternatives. If one alternative is far less expensive than the other, that may be decisive in her choice. By car, the distance between her apartment in Boston and her friend's apartment in New York City is 230 miles. Cynthia has compiled the following list of items to consider:

Automobile Costs		
Item	**Annual Cost of Fixed Items**	**Cost per Mile (based on 10,000 miles per year)**
(a) Annual straight-line depreciation on car [($24,000 original cost − $10,000 estimated resale value in 5 years)/5 years]	$2,800	$0.280
(b) Cost of gasoline ($1.60 per gallon ÷ 32 miles per gallon)		0.050
(c) Annual cost of auto insurance and license	$1,380	0.138
(d) Maintenance and repairs		0.065
(e) Parking fees at school ($45 per month × 8 months) . . .	$360	0.036
(f) Total average cost per mile		$0.569
Other Data		
(g) Reduction in the resale value of car due solely to wear and tear	$0.026 per mile	
(h) Cost of round-trip Amtrak ticket from Boston to New York City.	$104	
(i) Benefit of relaxing and being able to study during the train ride rather than having to drive	?	
(j) Cost of putting the dog in a kennel while gone	$40	
(k) Benefit of having a car available in New York City.	?	
(l) Hassle of parking the car in New York City	?	
(m) Cost of parking the car in New York City.	$25 per day	

Which costs and benefits are relevant in this decision? Remember, only those costs and benefits that differ between alternatives are relevant. Everything else is irrelevant and can be ignored.

Start at the top of the list with item (a): the original cost of the car is a sunk cost. This cost has already been incurred and therefore can never differ between alternatives. Consequently, it is irrelevant and should be ignored. The same is true of the accounting depreciation of $2,800 per year, which simply spreads the sunk cost across five years.

Item (b), the cost of gasoline consumed by driving to New York City, is a relevant cost. If Cynthia takes the train, this cost would not be incurred. Hence, the cost differs between alternatives and is therefore relevant.

Item (c), the annual cost of auto insurance and license, is not relevant. Whether Cynthia takes the train or drives on this particular trip, her annual auto insurance premium and her auto license fee will remain the same.[1]

Item (d), the cost of maintenance and repairs, is relevant. While maintenance and repair costs have a large random component, over the long run they should be more or less proportional to the number of miles the car is driven. Thus, the average cost of $0.065 per mile is a reasonable estimate to use.

---

[1]If Cynthia has an accident while driving to New York City or back, this might affect her insurance premium when the policy is renewed. The increase in the insurance premium would be a relevant cost of this particular trip, but the normal amount of the insurance premium is not relevant in any case.

Item (e), the monthly fee that Cynthia pays to park at her school during the academic year is not relevant. Regardless of which alternative she selects—driving or taking the train—she will still need to pay for parking at school.

Item (f) is the total average cost of $0.569 per mile. As discussed above, some elements of this total are relevant, but some are not relevant. Since it contains some irrelevant costs, it would be incorrect to estimate the cost of driving to New York City and back by simply multiplying the $0.569 by 460 miles (230 miles each way × 2). This erroneous approach would yield a cost of driving of $261.74. Unfortunately, such mistakes are often made in both personal life and in business. Since the total cost is stated on a per-mile basis, people are easily misled. Often people think that if the cost is stated as $0.569 per mile, the cost of driving 100 miles is $56.90. But it is not. Many of the costs included in the $0.569 cost per mile are sunk and/or fixed and will not increase if the car is driven another 100 miles. The $0.569 is an average cost, not an incremental cost. Beware of such unitized costs (i.e., costs stated in terms of a dollar amount per unit, per mile, per direct labor-hour, per machine-hour, and so on)—they are often misleading.

Item (g), the decline in the resale value of the car that occurs as a consequence of driving more miles, is relevant in the decision. Because she uses the car, its resale value declines, which is a real cost of using the car that should be taken into account. Cynthia estimated this cost by accessing the *Kelly Blue Book* website at www.kbb.com. The reduction in resale value of an asset through use or over time is often called *real* or *economic depreciation*. This is different from accounting depreciation, which attempts to match the sunk cost of an asset with the periods that benefit from that cost.

Item (h), the $104 cost of a round-trip ticket on Amtrak, is relevant in this decision. If she drives, she would not have to buy the ticket.

Item (i) is relevant to the decision, even if it is difficult to put a dollar value on relaxing and being able to study while on the train. It is relevant because it is a benefit that is available under one alternative but not under the other.

Item (j), the cost of putting Cynthia's dog in the kennel while she is gone, is irrelevant in this decision. Whether she takes the train or drives to New York City, she will still need to put her dog in a kennel.

Like item (i), items (k) and (l) are relevant to the decision even if it is difficult to measure their dollar impacts.

Item (m), the cost of parking in New York City for two days, is relevant to the decision.

Bringing together all of the relevant data, Cynthia would estimate the relevant costs of driving and taking the train as follows:

Relevant financial cost of driving to New York City:	
Gasoline (460 miles at $0.050 per mile)	$23.00
Maintenance and repairs (460 miles @ $0.065 per mile)	29.90
Reduction in the resale value of car due solely to wear and tear (460 miles @ $0.026 per mile)	11.96
Cost of parking the car in New York City (2 days @ $25 per day)	50.00
Total	$114.86

Relevant financial cost of taking the train to New York City:	
Cost of round-trip Amtrak ticket from Boston to New York City	$104.00

What should Cynthia do? From a purely financial standpoint, it would be cheaper by $10.86 ($114.86 − $104.00) to take the train than to drive. Cynthia has to decide if the convenience of having a car in New York City outweighs the additional cost and the disadvantages of being unable to relax and study on the train and the hassle of finding parking in the city.

In this example, we focused on identifying the relevant costs and benefits—everything else was ignored. In the next example, we include all of the costs and benefits—relevant or not. Nonetheless, we'll still get the correct answer because the irrelevant costs and benefits will cancel out when we compare the alternatives.

IN BUSINESS

Cruising on the Cheap

Cruise ship operators such as Princess Cruises sometimes offer deep discounts on popular cruises. For example, a 10-day Mediterranean cruise on the Norwegian Dream was once offered at up to 75% off the list price. A seven-day cruise to Alaska could be booked for a $499–$700 discount. The cause? "An ambitious fleet expansion left the cruise industry grappling with a tidal wave of capacity . . . Most cruise costs are fixed whether all the ship's berths are filled or not, so it is better to sell cheap than not at all . . . In the current glut, discounting has made it possible for the cruise lines to keep berths nearly full."

Source: Martin Brannigan, *The Wall Street Journal,* July 17, 2000, pp. B1 and B4.

Reconciling the Total and Differential Approaches

Oak Harbor Woodworks is considering a new labor-saving machine that rents for $3,000 per year. The machine will be used on the company's butcher block production line. Data concerning the company's annual sales and costs of butcher blocks with and without the new machine are shown below:

	Current Situation	Situation with the New Machine
Units produced and sold	5,000	5,000
Selling price per unit	$40	$40
Direct materials cost per unit	$14	$14
Direct labor cost per unit	$8	$5
Variable overhead cost per unit	$2	$2
Fixed costs, other	$62,000	$62,000
Fixed costs, rental of new machine	—	$3,000

Given the data above, the net operating income for the product under the two alternatives can be computed as shown in Exhibit 11–1.

Note that the net operating income is $12,000 higher with the new machine, so that is the better alternative. Note also that the $12,000 advantage for the new machine can be obtained in two different ways. It is the difference between the $30,000 net operating income with the new machine and the $18,000 net operating income for the current situation. It is also the sum of the differential costs and benefits as shown in the last column of Exhibit 11–1. A positive number in the Differential Costs and Benefits column indicates that the difference between the alternatives favors the new machine; a negative number indicates that the difference favors the current situation. A zero in that column simply means that the total amount for the item is exactly the same for both alternatives. Thus, since the difference in the net operating incomes equals the sum of the differences for the individual items, any cost or benefit that is the same for both alternatives will have no impact on which alternative is preferred. This is the reason that costs and benefits that do not differ between alternatives are irrelevant and can be ignored. If we properly account for them, they will cancel out when we compare the alternatives.

We could have arrived at the same solution much more quickly by completely ignoring the irrelevant costs and benefits.

EXHIBIT 11–1
Total and Differential Costs

	Current Situation	Situation with New Machine	Differential Costs and Benefits
Sales (5,000 units @ $40 per unit).............	$200,000	$200,000	$ 0
Variable expenses:			
Direct materials (5,000 units at $14 per unit)	70,000	70,000	0
Direct labor (5,000 units at $8 and $5 per unit)	40,000	25,000	15,000
Variable overhead (5,000 units at $2 per unit)	10,000	10,000	0
Total variable expenses	120,000	105,000	
Contribution margin	80,000	95,000	
Fixed expenses:			
Other.......................................	62,000	62,000	0
Rent of new machine	0	3,000	(3,000)
Total fixed expenses.......................	62,000	65,000	
Net operating income......................	$ 18,000	$ 30,000	$12,000

- The selling price per unit and the number of units sold do not differ between the alternatives. Therefore, the total sales revenues are exactly the same for the two alternatives as shown in Exhibit 11–1. Since the sales revenues are exactly the same, they have no effect on the difference in net operating income between the two alternatives. That is shown in the last column in Exhibit 11–1, which shows a $0 differential benefit.

- The direct materials cost per unit, the variable overhead cost per unit, and the number of units produced and sold do not differ between the alternatives. Consequently, the total direct materials cost and the total variable overhead cost will be the same for the two alternatives and can be ignored.

- The "other" fixed expenses do not differ between the alternatives, so they can be ignored as well.

Indeed, the only costs that do differ between the alternatives are direct labor costs and the fixed rental cost of the new machine. Hence, the two alternatives can be compared based only on these relevant costs:

Net advantage of renting the new machine:	
Decrease in direct labor costs (5,000 units at a cost savings of $3 per unit)...	$15,000
Increase in fixed expenses.......................................	(3,000)
Net annual cost savings from renting the new machine................	$12,000

If we focus on just the relevant costs and benefits, we get exactly the same answer as when we listed all of the costs and benefits—including those that do not differ between the alternatives and hence are irrelevant. We get the same answer because the only costs and benefits that matter in the final comparison of the net operating incomes are those that differ between the two alternatives and hence are not zero in the last column of Exhibit 11–1. Those two relevant costs are both listed in the above analysis showing the net advantage of renting the new machine.

Why Isolate Relevant Costs?

In the preceding example, we used two different approaches to analyze the alternatives. First, we considered all costs, both those that were relevant and those that were not; and second, we considered only the relevant costs. We obtained the same answer under both approaches. It would be natural to ask, "Why bother to isolate relevant costs when total costs will do the job just as well?" Isolating relevant costs is desirable for at least two reasons.

First, only rarely will enough information be available to prepare a detailed income statement for both alternatives. Assume, for example, that you are called on to make a decision relating to a portion of a *single business process* in a multidepartmental, multi-product company. Under these circumstances, it would be virtually impossible to prepare an income statement of any type. You would have to rely on your ability to recognize which costs are relevant and which are not in order to assemble the data necessary to make a decision.

Second, mingling irrelevant costs with relevant costs may cause confusion and distract attention from the information that is really critical. Furthermore, the danger always exists that an irrelevant piece of data may be used improperly, resulting in an incorrect decision. The best approach is to ignore irrelevant data and base the decision entirely on relevant data.

Relevant cost analysis, combined with the contribution approach to the income statement, provides a powerful tool for making decisions. We will investigate various uses of this tool in the remaining sections of this chapter.

IN BUSINESS   Environmental Costs Add Up

A decision analysis can be flawed by incorrectly including irrelevant costs such as sunk costs and future costs that do not differ between alternatives. It can also be flawed by omitting future costs that *do* differ between alternatives. This is particularly a problem with environmental costs because they have dramatically increased in recent years and are often overlooked by managers.

Consider the environmental complications posed by a decision of whether to install a solvent-based or powder-based system for spray-painting parts. In a solvent painting system, parts are sprayed as they move along a conveyor. The paint that misses the part is swept away by a wall of water, called a water curtain. The excess paint accumulates in a pit as sludge that must be removed each month. Environmental regulations classify this sludge as hazardous waste. As a result, the company must obtain a permit to produce the waste and must maintain meticulous records of how the waste is transported, stored, and disposed of. The annual costs of complying with these regulations can easily exceed $140,000 in total for a painting facility that initially costs only $400,000 to build. The costs of complying with environmental regulations include the following:

- The waste sludge must be hauled to a special disposal site. The typical disposal fee is about $300 per barrel, or $55,000 per year for a modest solvent-based painting system.
- Workers must be specially trained to handle the paint sludge.
- The company must carry special insurance.
- The company must pay substantial fees to the state for releasing pollutants (i.e., the solvent) into the air.
- The water in the water curtain must be specially treated to remove contaminants. This can cost tens of thousands of dollars per year.

In contrast, a powder-based painting system avoids almost all of these environmental costs. Excess powder used in the painting process can be recovered and reused without creating a hazardous waste. Additionally, the powder-based system does not release contaminants into the atmosphere. Therefore, even though the cost of building a powder-based system may be higher than the cost of building a solvent-based system, over the long run the costs of the powder-based system may be far lower due to the high environmental costs of a solvent-based system. Managers need to be aware of such environmental costs and take them fully into account when making decisions.

Source: Germain Böer, Margaret Curtin, and Louis Hoyt, "Environmental Cost Management," *Management Accounting*, September 1998, pp. 28–38.

1. Which of the following statements is false? (You may select more than one answer.)
   a. Under some circumstances, a sunk cost may be a relevant cost.
   b. Future costs that do not differ between alternatives are irrelevant.
   c. The same cost may be relevant or irrelevant depending on the decision context.
   d. Only variable costs are relevant costs. Fixed costs cannot be relevant costs.

2. Assume that in October you bought a $450 nonrefundable airline ticket to Telluride, Colorado, for a 5-day/4-night winter ski vacation. You now have an opportunity to buy an airline ticket for a 5-day/4-night winter ski vacation in Stowe, Vermont, for $400 that includes a free ski lift ticket. The price of your lift ticket for the Telluride vacation would be $300. The price of a hotel room in Telluride is $180 per night. The price of a hotel room in Stowe is $150 per night. Which of the following costs is not relevant in a decision of whether to proceed with the planned trip to Telluride or to change to a trip to Stowe?
   a. The $450 airline ticket to Telluride.
   b. The $400 airline ticket to Stowe.
   c. The $300 lift ticket for the Telluride vacation.
   d. The $180 per night hotel room in Telluride.

3. Based on the facts in question 2 above, does a differential cost analysis favor Telluride or Stowe, and by how much?
   a. Stowe by $470.
   b. Stowe by $20.
   c. Telluride by $70.
   d. Telluride $20

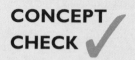

CONCEPT CHECK ✔

ADDING AND DROPPING PRODUCT LINES AND OTHER SEGMENTS

Decisions relating to whether product lines or other segments of a company should be dropped and new ones added are among the most difficult that a manager has to make. In such decisions, many qualitative and quantitative factors must be considered. Ultimately, however, any final decision to drop a business segment or to add a new one is going to hinge primarily on the impact the decision will have on net operating income. To assess this impact, costs must be carefully analyzed.

An Illustration of Cost Analysis

Exhibit 11–2 provides sales and cost information for the preceding month for the Discount Drug Company and its three major product lines—drugs, cosmetics, and housewares. A quick review of this exhibit suggests that dropping the housewares segment would increase the company's overall net operating income by $8,000. However, this would be a flawed conclusion because the data in Exhibit 11–2 do not distinguish between fixed expenses that can be avoided if a product line is dropped and common fixed expenses that cannot be avoided by dropping any particular product line.

In this scenario, the two alternatives under consideration are keeping the housewares product line and dropping the housewares product line. Therefore, only those costs that differ between these two alternatives (i.e., that can be avoided by dropping the housewares product line) are relevant. In deciding whether to drop housewares, it is crucial to identify which costs can be avoided, and hence are relevant to the decision, and which costs cannot be avoided, and hence are irrelevant. The decision should be analyzed as follows:

If the housewares line is dropped, then the company will lose $20,000 per month in contribution margin, but by dropping the line it may be possible to avoid some fixed costs

Topic Tackler

PLUS

Concept 11–1   Video 11–1

EXHIBIT 11–2
Discount Drug Company Product
Lines

	Product Line			
	Drugs	**Cosmetics**	**Housewares**	**Total**
Sales	$125,000	$75,000	$ 50,000	$250,000
Variable expenses	50,000	25,000	30,000	105,000
Contribution margin	75,000	50,000	20,000	145,000
Fixed expenses:				
Salaries	29,500	12,500	8,000	50,000
Advertising	1,000	7,500	6,500	15,000
Utilities	500	500	1,000	2,000
Depreciation—fixtures	1,000	2,000	2,000	5,000
Rent	10,000	6,000	4,000	20,000
Insurance	2,000	500	500	3,000
General administrative	15,000	9,000	6,000	30,000
Total fixed expenses...........	59,000	38,000	28,000	125,000
Net operating income (loss).....	$ 16,000	$12,000	$ (8,000)	$ 20,000

such as salaries or advertising costs. If dropping the housewares line enables the company to avoid more in fixed costs than it loses in contribution margin, then its overall net operating income will improve by eliminating the product line. On the other hand, if the company is not able to avoid as much in fixed costs as it loses in contribution margin, then the housewares line should be kept. In short, the manager should ask, "What costs can I avoid if I drop this product line?"

As we have seen from our earlier discussion, not all costs are avoidable. For example, some of the costs associated with a product line may be sunk costs. Other costs may be allocated fixed costs that will not differ in total regardless of whether the product line is dropped or retained.

To show how to proceed in a product-line analysis, suppose that the management of the Discount Drug Company has analyzed the fixed costs being charged to the three product lines and determined the following:

1. The salaries expense represents salaries paid to employees working directly on the product. All of the employees working in housewares would be discharged if the product line is dropped.
2. The advertising expense represents advertisements that are specific to each product line and are avoidable if the line is dropped.
3. The utilities expense represents utilities costs for the entire company. The amount charged to each product line is an allocation based on space occupied and is not avoidable if the product line is dropped.
4. The depreciation expense represents depreciation on fixtures used to display the various product lines. Although the fixtures are nearly new, they are custom-built and will have no resale value if the housewares line is dropped.
5. The rent expense represents rent on the entire building housing the company; it is allocated to the product lines on the basis of sales dollars. The monthly rent of $20,000 is fixed under a long-term lease agreement.
6. The insurance expense is for insurance carried on inventories in each of the three product lines. If housewares is dropped, the related inventories will be eliminated and the insurance premiums will decrease accordingly.
7. The general administrative expense represents the costs of accounting, purchasing, and general management, which are allocated to the product lines on the basis of sales dollars. These costs will not change if the housewares line is dropped.

With this information, management can determine that $15,000 of the fixed expenses assigned to housewares are avoidable and $13,000 are not.

Fixed Expenses	Total Cost Assigned to Housewares	Not Avoidable*	Avoidable
Salaries	$ 8,000		$ 8,000
Advertising	6,500		6,500
Utilities	1,000	$ 1,000	
Depreciation—fixtures	2,000	2,000	
Rent	4,000	4,000	
Insurance	500		500
General administrative	6,000	6,000	
Total	$28,000	$13,000	$15,000

*These fixed costs represent either sunk costs or future costs that will not change whether the housewares line is retained or discontinued.

As stated earlier, if the housewares product line were dropped, the company would lose the product's contribution margin of $20,000, but would save its associated avoidable fixed expenses. We now know that those avoidable fixed expenses total $15,000. Therefore, dropping the housewares product line would result in a $5,000 *reduction* in net operating income as shown below:

Contribution margin lost if the housewares line is discontinued (see Exhibit 11–2)	$(20,000)
Less fixed costs that can be avoided if the housewares line is discontinued (see above)	15,000
Decrease in overall company net operating income	$ (5,000)

In this case, the fixed costs that can be avoided by dropping the housewares product line ($15,000) are less than the contribution margin that will be lost ($20,000). Therefore, on the basis of the data given, the housewares line should not be discontinued unless a more profitable use can be found for the floor and counter space that it is occupying.

A Comparative Format

This decision can also be approached by preparing comparative income statements showing the effects of either keeping or dropping the product line. Exhibit 11–3 contains such an analysis for the Discount Drug Company. As shown in the last column of the exhibit, if the housewares line is dropped, then overall company net operating income will decrease by $5,000 each period. This is the same answer, of course, as we obtained when we focused just on the lost contribution margin and avoidable fixed costs.

Beware of Allocated Fixed Costs

Go back to Exhibit 11–2. Does this exhibit suggest that the housewares product line should be kept—as we have just concluded? No, it does not. Exhibit 11–2 suggests that the housewares product line is losing money. Why keep a product line that is showing a loss? The explanation for this apparent inconsistency lies in part with the common fixed costs that are being allocated to the product lines. As we observed in Chapter 10, one of the great dangers in allocating common fixed costs is that such allocations can make a product line (or other segment of a business) look less profitable than it really is. In this instance, allocating the common fixed costs among all product lines makes the housewares

EXHIBIT 11–3
A Comparative Format for
Product-Line Analysis

	Keep Housewares	Drop Housewares	Difference: Net Operating Income Increase (or Decrease)
Sales	$50,000	$ 0	$(50,000)
Variable expenses	30,000	0	30,000
Contribution margin	20,000	0	(20,000)
Fixed expenses:			
Salaries	8,000	0	8,000
Advertising	6,500	0	6,500
Utilities	1,000	1,000	0
Depreciation—fixtures	2,000	2,000	0
Rent	4,000	4,000	0
Insurance	500	0	500
General administrative	6,000	6,000	0
Total fixed expenses.	28,000	13,000	15,000
Net operating income (loss)	$ (8,000)	$(13,000)	$ (5,000)

product line appear to be unprofitable. However, as we have shown above, dropping the
product line would result in a decrease in the company's overall net operating income.
This point can be seen clearly if we redo Exhibit 11–2 by eliminating the allocation of the
common fixed costs. Exhibit 11–4 uses the segmented approach from Chapter 10 to estimate the profitability of the product lines.

	Product Line			Total
	Drugs	Cosmetics	Housewares	
Sales.	$125,000	$75,000	$50,000	$250,000
Variable expenses.	50,000	25,000	30,000	105,000
Contribution margin.	75,000	50,000	20,000	145,000
Traceable fixed expenses:				
Salaries	29,500	12,500	8,000	50,000
Advertising.	1,000	7,500	6,500	15,000
Depreciation—fixtures	1,000	2,000	2,000	5,000
Insurance.	2,000	500	500	3,000
Total traceable fixed expenses . .	33,500	22,500	17,000	73,000
Product-line segment margin. . .	$ 41,500	$27,500	$ 3,000*	72,000
Common fixed expenses:				
Utilities.				2,000
Rent.				20,000
General administrative.				30,000
Total common fixed expenses . .				52,000
Net operating income				$ 20,000

*If the housewares line is dropped, this $3,000 in segment margin will be lost to the company.
In addition, the $2,000 depreciation on the fixtures is a sunk cost that cannot be avoided. The
sum of these two figures ($3,000 + $2,000 = $5,000) would be the decrease in the
company's overall profits if the housewares line were discontinued. Of course, the company
may later choose to drop the product if circumstances change—such as a pending decision
to replace the fixtures.

Notice that the common fixed expenses have not been allocated to the product lines in Exhibit 11–4. Only the fixed expenses that are traceable to the product lines and that could be avoided by dropping the product lines are assigned to them. For example, the fixed expenses of advertising the housewares product line can be traced to that product line and can be eliminated if that product line is dropped. However, the general administrative expenses, such as the CEO's salary, cannot be traced to the individual product lines and would not be eliminated if any one product line were dropped. Consequently, these common fixed expenses are not allocated to the product lines in Exhibit 11–4 as they were in Exhibit 11–2. The allocations in Exhibit 11–2 provide a misleading picture that suggests that portions of the fixed common expenses can be eliminated by dropping individual product lines—which is not the case.

Exhibit 11–4 gives us a much different perspective of the housewares line than does Exhibit 11–2. As shown in Exhibit 11–4, the housewares line is covering all of its own traceable fixed costs and is generating a $3,000 *segment margin* toward covering the common fixed costs of the company. The **segment margin** is the difference between the revenue generated by a segment and its own traceable costs. However, the segment margin must be adjusted before making a decision such as dropping a product line. The segment margin may include costs and benefits that, while traceable to the segment, are not avoidable in the specific decision at hand. For example, the traceable fixed expenses of the housewares product line include $2,000 of fixtures depreciation. These costs can be traced to the housewares segment, but they are sunk costs and therefore should be ignored when deciding whether to drop the product line. Adding back this $2,000 of sunk costs to the segment margin of $3,000 yields the $5,000 in net operating income that would be forgone if the housewares product line were dropped.

Additionally, managers may rationally choose to retain an unprofitable product—particularly if selling such a product helps the company sell other products. For example, a company like Hewlett Packard or Lexmark may choose to sell printers for personal computers at a loss in order to sell more of its highly profitable proprietary ink cartridges.

The Trap Laid by Fully Allocated Costs

IN BUSINESS

A bakery distributed its products through route salespersons, each of whom loaded a truck with an assortment of products in the morning and spent the day calling on customers in an assigned territory. Believing that some items were more profitable than others, management asked for an analysis of product costs and sales. The accountants to whom the task was assigned allocated all manufacturing and marketing costs to products to obtain a net profit for each product. The resulting figures indicated that some of the products were being sold at a loss, and management discontinued these products. However, when this change was put into effect, the company's overall profit declined. It was then seen that by dropping some products, sales revenues had been reduced without commensurate reduction in costs because the common manufacturing costs and route sales costs had to be continued in order to make and sell the remaining products.

THE MAKE OR BUY DECISION

A decision whether to produce a part internally or to buy the part externally from a supplier is called a **make or buy decision.** To provide an illustration of a make or buy decision, consider Mountain Goat Cycles. The company is now producing the heavy-duty gear shifters used in its most popular line of mountain bikes. The company's

LEARNING OBJECTIVE 3

Prepare a make or buy analysis.

Topic Tackler

PLUS

Concept 11-2

Accounting Department reports the following annual costs of producing 8,000 units of the shifter internally:

	Per Unit	8,000 Units
Direct materials	$ 6	$ 48,000
Direct labor.	4	32,000
Variable overhead	1	8,000
Supervisor's salary.	3	24,000
Depreciation of special equipment.	2	16,000
Allocated general overhead	5	40,000
Total cost	$21	$168,000

An outside supplier has offered to sell 8,000 shifters a year to Mountain Goat Cycles at a price of only $19 each. Should the company stop producing the shifters internally and buy them from the outside supplier? As always, the focus should be on the relevant costs—those that differ between the alternatives. And the costs that differ between the alternatives consist of the costs that could be avoided by purchasing the shifters from the outside supplier. If the costs that can be avoided by purchasing the shifters from the outside supplier total less than $19, then the company should continue to manufacture its own shifters and reject the outside supplier's offer. On the other hand, if the costs that can be avoided by purchasing the shifters from the outside supplier total more than $19, the outside supplier's offer should be accepted.

Note that depreciation of special equipment is listed as one of the costs of producing the shifters internally. Since the equipment has already been purchased, this depreciation is a sunk cost and is therefore irrelevant. If the equipment could be sold, its salvage value would be relevant. Or if the machine could be used to make other products, this could be relevant as well. However, we will assume that the equipment has no salvage value and that it has no other use except making the heavy-duty gear shifters.

Also note that the company is allocating a portion of its general overhead costs to the shifters. Any portion of this general overhead cost that would actually be eliminated if the gear shifters were purchased rather than made would be relevant in the analysis. However, it is likely that the general overhead costs allocated to the gear shifters are in fact common to all items produced in the factory and would continue unchanged even if the shifters are purchased from the outside. Such allocated common costs are not relevant costs (since they do not differ between the make or buy alternatives) and should be eliminated from the analysis along with the sunk costs.

The variable costs of producing the shifters can be avoided by buying the shifters from the outside supplier, so they are relevant costs. We will assume in this case that the variable costs include direct materials, direct labor, and variable overhead. The supervisor's salary is also relevant if it could be avoided by buying the shifters. Exhibit 11–5 contains the relevant cost analysis of the make or buy decision assuming that the supervisor's salary can indeed be avoided.

EXHIBIT 11–5
Mountain Goat Cycles Make or Buy Analysis

	Total Relevant Costs—8,000 units	
	Make	Buy
Direct materials (8,000 units at $6 per unit)	$ 48,000	
Direct labor (8,000 units at $4 per unit).	32,000	
Variable overhead (8,000 units at $1 per unit)	8,000	
Supervisor's salary	24,000	
Depreciation of special equipment (not relevant)	—	
Allocated general overhead (not relevant).	—	
Outside purchase price.		$152,000
Total cost.	$112,000	$152,000
Difference in favor of continuing to make	$40,000	

Since it costs $40,000 less to make the shifters internally than to buy them from the outside supplier, Mountain Goat Cycles should reject the outside supplier's offer. However, management may wish to consider one additional factor before coming to a final decision—the opportunity cost of the space now being used to produce the shifters.

Outsourcing R&D

A few years ago many experts felt that U.S. companies were unlikely to outsource their research and development (R&D) activities to lower labor cost Asian countries. However, these experts were wrong. Companies such as Procter & Gamble, Boeing, Dell, Eli Lilly, and Motorola are increasingly relying on Asian business partners to meet their R&D needs. In fact, research shows that U.S. technology companies outsource 70% of their personal digital assistant (PDA) designs, 65% of their notebook personal computer designs, and 30% of their digital camera designs.

Allen J. Delattre, head of Accenture's high-tech consulting practice, says "R&D is the single remaining controllable expense to work on. Companies either will have to cut costs or increase R&D productivity." In light of this stark reality, most Western companies are creating a global model of innovation that leverages the skills of Indian software developers, Taiwanese engineers, and Chinese factories. The lower labor rates available in these countries coupled with their strong technology orientation makes "buying" R&D capability from overseas more attractive to U.S. companies than relying solely on their domestic workforce to "make" R&D breakthroughs.

Source: Pete Engardio and Bruce Einhorn, "Outsourcing Innovation," *BusinessWeek,* March 21, 2005, pp. 82–94.

Employee Health Benefits—Make or Buy?

With health care insurance premiums rising by over 10% per year, companies have been searching for ways to reduce the costs of providing health care to their employees. Some companies have adopted the unconventional approach of providing health care services in-house. Quad/Graphics, a printing company with 14,000 employees, hired its own doctors and nurses to provide primary health care on-site. By "making" its own health care for employees rather than "buying" it through the purchase of insurance, the company claims that its health care costs have risen just 6% annually and that their spending on health care is now 17% less than the industry average.

Source: Kimberly Weisul, "There's a Doctor in the House," *BusinessWeek,* December 16, 2002, p. 8.

OPPORTUNITY COST

If the space now being used to produce the shifters *would otherwise be idle,* then Mountain Goat Cycles should continue to produce its own shifters and the supplier's offer should be rejected, as stated above. Idle space that has no alternative use has an opportunity cost of zero.

But what if the space now being used to produce shifters could be used for some other purpose? In that case, the space would have an opportunity cost equal to the segment margin that could be derived from the best alternative use of the space.

To illustrate, assume that the space now being used to produce shifters could be used to produce a new cross-country bike that would generate a segment margin of $60,000 per year. Under these conditions, Mountain Goat Cycles should accept the supplier's offer and use the available space to produce the new product line:

	Make	Buy
Total annual cost (see Exhibit 11–5)	$112,000	$152,000
Opportunity cost—segment margin forgone on a potential new product line	60,000	
Total cost	$172,000	$152,000
Difference in favor of purchasing from the outside supplier	20,000	

Opportunity costs are not recorded in an organization's general ledger because they do not represent actual dollar outlays. Rather, they represent economic benefits that are *forgone* as a result of pursuing some course of action. The opportunity cost for Mountain Goat Cycles is sufficiently large in this case to change the decision.

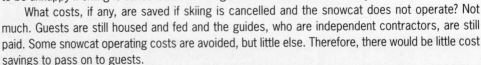

IN BUSINESS

Tough Choices

Brad and Carole Karafil own and operate White Grizzly Adventures, a snowcat skiing and snowboarding company in Meadow Creek, British Columbia. While rare, it does sometimes happen that the company is unable to operate due to bad weather. Guests are housed and fed, but no one can ski. The contract signed by each guest stipulates that no refund is given in the case of an unavoidable cancellation that is beyond the control of the operators. So technically, Brad and Carole are not obligated to provide any refund if they must cancel operations due to bad weather. However, 70% of their guests are repeat customers and a guest who has paid roughly $300 a day to ski is likely to be unhappy if skiing is cancelled even though it is no fault of White Grizzly.

What costs, if any, are saved if skiing is cancelled and the snowcat does not operate? Not much. Guests are still housed and fed and the guides, who are independent contractors, are still paid. Some snowcat operating costs are avoided, but little else. Therefore, there would be little cost savings to pass on to guests.

Brad and Carole could issue a credit to be used for one day of skiing at another time. If a customer with such a credit occupied a seat on a snowcat that would otherwise be empty, the only significant cost to Brad and Carole would be the cost of feeding the customer. However, an empty seat basically doesn't exist—the demand for seats far exceeds the supply and the schedule is generally fully booked far in advance of the ski season. Consequently, the real cost of issuing a credit for one day of skiing is high. Brad and Carole would be giving up $300 from a paying customer for every guest they issue a credit voucher to. Issuing a credit voucher involves an opportunity cost of $300 in forgone sales revenues.

What would you do if you had to cancel skiing due to bad weather? Would you issue a refund or a credit voucher, losing money in the process, or would you risk losing customers? It's a tough choice.

Source: Brad and Carole Karafil, owners and operators of White Grizzly Adventures, www.whitegrizzly.com.

DECISION MAKER

Vice President of Production

You are faced with a make or buy decision. The company currently makes a component for one of its products but is considering whether it should instead purchase the component. If the offer from an outside supplier were accepted, the company would no longer need to rent the machinery currently being used to manufacture the component. You realize that the annual rental cost is a fixed cost, but recall some sort of warning about fixed costs. Is the annual rental cost relevant to this make or buy decision?

SPECIAL ORDERS

Managers must often evaluate whether a *special order* should be accepted, and if the order is accepted, the price that should be charged. A **special order** is a one-time order that is not considered part of the company's normal ongoing business. To illustrate, Mountain Goat Cycles has just received a request from the Seattle Police Department to produce 100 specially modified mountain bikes at a price of $279 each. The bikes would be used to patrol some of the more densely populated residential sections of the city. Mountain Goat Cycles can easily modify its City Cruiser model to fit the specifications of the Seattle Police. The normal selling price of the City Cruiser bike is $349, and its unit product cost is $282 as shown below:

Direct materials	$186
Direct labor	45
Manufacturing overhead	51
Unit product cost	$282

The variable portion of the above manufacturing overhead is $6 per unit. The order would have no effect on the company's total fixed manufacturing overhead costs.

The modifications requested by the Seattle Police Department consist of welded brackets to hold radios, nightsticks, and other gear. These modifications would require $17 in incremental variable costs. In addition, the company would have to pay a graphics design studio $1,200 to design and cut stencils that would be used for spray-painting the Seattle Police Department's logo and other identifying marks on the bikes.

This order should have no effect on the company's other sales. The production manager says that she can handle the special order without disrupting any of the company's regular scheduled production.

What effect would accepting this order have on the company's net operating income?

Only the incremental costs and benefits are relevant. Since the existing fixed manufacturing overhead costs would not be affected by the order, they are not relevant. The incremental net operating income can be computed as follows:

	Per Unit	Total 100 Bikes
Incremental revenue	$279	$27,900
Incremental costs:		
Variable costs:		
Direct materials	186	18,600
Direct labor	45	4,500
Variable manufacturing overhead	6	600
Special modifications	17	1,700
Total variable cost..................	$254	25,400
Fixed cost:		
Purchase of stencils		1,200
Total incremental cost		26,600
Incremental net operating income		$ 1,300

Therefore, even though the $279 price on the special order is below the normal $282 unit product cost and the order would require additional costs, the order would increase net operating income. In general, a special order is profitable if the incremental revenue

LEARNING OBJECTIVE 4

Prepare an analysis showing whether a special order should be accepted.

from the special order exceeds the incremental costs of the order. However, it is important to make sure that there is indeed idle capacity and that the special order does not cut into normal unit sales or undercut prices on normal sales. If the company was operating at capacity, opportunity costs would have to be taken into account as well as the incremental costs that have already been detailed on the previous page.

IN BUSINESS | **Flying the Friendly Aisles**

Shoppers at Safeway can now earn United Airlines frequent flier miles when they buy their groceries. Airlines charge marketing partners such as Safeway about 2¢ per mile. Since airlines typically require 25,000 frequent flier miles for a domestic round-trip ticket, United is earning about $500 per frequent flier ticket issued to Safeway customers. This income to United is higher than many discounted fares. Moreover, United carefully manages its frequent flier program so that few frequent flier passengers displace regular fare-paying customers. The only incremental costs of adding a frequent flier passenger to a flight may be food, a little extra fuel, and some administrative costs. All of the other costs of the flight would be incurred anyway. Thus, the miles that United sells to Safeway are almost pure profit.

Source: Wendy Zellner, *BusinessWeek*, March 6, 2000, pp. 152–154.

PRICING NEW PRODUCTS

When offering a new product or service for the first time, a company must decide on its selling price. A cost-based approach is often followed in practice. In this approach, the product is first designed and produced, then its cost is determined and its price is computed by adding a markup to the cost. This *cost-plus* approach to pricing suffers from a number of drawbacks—the most obvious being that customers may not be willing to pay the price set by the company. If the price is too high, customers may decide to purchase a similar product from a competitor or, if no similar competing product exists, they may decide not to buy the product at all.

Target costing provides an alternative, market-based approach to pricing new products. In the **target costing** approach, management estimates how much the market will be willing to pay for the new product even before the new product has been designed. The company's required profit margin is subtracted from the estimated selling price to determine the target cost for the new product. A cross-functional team consisting of designers, engineers, cost accountants, marketing personnel, and production personnel is charged with the responsibility of ensuring that the cost of the product is ultimately less than the target cost. If at some point in the product development process it becomes clear that the target cost is unattainable, the new product is abandoned.

The target costing approach to pricing has a number of advantages over the cost-plus approach. First, the target costing approach is focused on the market and the customer. A product is not made unless the company is reasonably confident that customers will buy the product at a price that provides the company with an adequate profit. Second, the target costing approach instills a much higher level of cost-consciousness than the cost-plus approach and probably results in less expensive products that are more attractive to customers. In essence, target costing holds managers accountable for ensuring that actual product costs do not exceed a preestablished ceiling. In the cost-plus approach, there is no preestablished ceiling—higher costs simply result in higher prices. This lack of cost accountability allows designers and engineers to create products with expensive features without considering whether the added costs of these features would result in a selling price that exceeds what customers would be willing to pay. Not surprisingly, some companies are abandoning the cost-plus approach to new product pricing in favor of target costing.

Target Costing

Step 1: What will customers pay for this product?	Step 2: What is our target cost?	Step 3: How can we design the product to meet the target cost?	Step 4: Let's manufacture the product!

Market Research Department	Finance Department	Project Engineering Department	Operations Management Department

Tutor

Your financial accounting instructor has suggested that you should consider working with selected students in her class as a tutor. Should you adopt a cost-plus or target costing approach to setting your hourly fee?

UTILIZATION OF A CONSTRAINED RESOURCE

Managers routinely face the problem of deciding how constrained resources are going to be used. A department store, for example, has a limited amount of floor space and therefore cannot stock every product that may be available. A manufacturer has a limited number of machine-hours and a limited number of direct labor-hours at its disposal. When a limited resource of some type restricts the company's ability to satisfy demand, the company has a **constraint.** Since the company cannot fully satisfy demand, managers must decide which products or services should be cut back. In other words, managers must decide which products or services make the best use of the constrained resource. Fixed costs are usually unaffected by such choices, so the course of action that maximizes the company's total contribution margin should ordinarily be selected.

> **LEARNING OBJECTIVE 5**
>
> Determine the most profitable use of a constrained resource and the value of obtaining more of the constrained resource.

Contribution Margin per Unit of the Constrained Resource

If some products must be cut back because of a constraint, the key to maximizing the total contribution margin may seem obvious—favor the products with the highest unit contribution margins. Unfortunately, that is not quite correct. Rather, the correct solution is to favor the products that provide the highest *contribution margin per unit of the constrained resource.* To illustrate, in addition to its other products, Mountain Goat

Cycles makes saddlebags for bicycles called paniers. These paniers come in two models—a touring model and a mountain model. Cost and revenue data for the two models of paniers follow:

	Mountain Panier	Touring Panier
Selling price per unit.	$25	$30
Variable cost per unit	10	18
Contribution margin per unit.	$15	$12
Contribution margin (CM) ratio.	60%	40%

The mountain panier appears to be much more profitable than the touring panier. It has a $15 per unit contribution margin as compared to only $12 per unit for the touring model, and it has a 60% CM ratio as compared to only 40% for the touring model.

But now let's add one more piece of information—the plant that makes the paniers is operating at capacity. This does not mean that every machine and every person in the plant is working at the maximum possible rate. Because machines have different capacities, some machines will be operating at less than 100% of capacity. However, if the plant as a whole cannot produce any more units, some machine or process must be operating at capacity. The machine or process that is limiting overall output is called the **bottleneck**—it is the constraint.

At Mountain Goat Cycles, the bottleneck (i.e., constraint) is a stitching machine. The mountain panier requires 2 minutes of stitching time per unit, and the touring panier requires 1 minute of stitching time per unit. By definition, since the stitching machine is a bottleneck, the stitching machine does not have enough capacity to satisfy the existing demand for mountain paniers and touring paniers. Therefore, some orders for the products will have to be turned down. Naturally, managers will want to know which product is less profitable. To answer this question, they should focus on the contribution margin per unit of the constrained resource. This figure is computed by dividing a product's contribution margin per unit by the amount of the constrained resource required to make a unit of that product. These calculations are carried out below for the mountain and touring paniers:

	Mountain Panier	Touring Panier
Contribution margin per unit (above) (a)	$15.00	$12.00
Stitching machine time required to produce one unit (b)	2 minutes	1 minute
Contribution margin per unit of the constrained resource, (a) ÷ (b)	$7.50 per minute	$12.00 per minute

It is now easy to decide which product is less profitable and should be deemphasized. Each minute on the stitching machine that is devoted to the touring panier results in an increase of $12.00 in contribution margin and profits. The comparable figure for the mountain panier is only $7.50 per minute. Therefore, the touring model should be emphasized. Even though the mountain model has the larger contribution margin per unit and the larger CM ratio, the touring model provides the larger contribution margin in relation to the constrained resource.

To verify that the touring model is indeed the more profitable product, suppose an hour of additional stitching time is available and that unfilled orders exist for both products. The additional hour on the stitching machine could be used to make either 30 mountain paniers

(60 minutes ÷ 2 minutes per mountain panier) or 60 touring paniers (60 minutes ÷ 1 minute per touring panier), with the following profit implications:

	Mountain Panier	Touring Panier
Contribution margin per unit (above)	$ 15	$ 12
Additional units that can be processed in one hour	× 30	× 60
Additional contribution margin	$450	$720

Since the additional contribution margin would be $720 for the touring paniers and only $450 for the mountain paniers, the touring paniers make the most profitable use of the company's constrained resource—the stitching machine.

This example clearly shows that looking at unit contribution margins alone is not enough; the contribution margin must be viewed in relation to the amount of the constrained resource each product requires.

Theory of Constraints Software   IN BUSINESS

Indalex Aluminum Solutions Group is the largest producer of soft alloy extrusions in North America. The company has installed a new generation of business intelligence software created by pVelocity, Inc., of Toronto, Canada. The software "provides decision makers across our entire manufacturing enterprise with time-based financial metrics using TOC concepts to identify bottlenecks." And, it "shifts the focus of a manufacturing company from traditional cost accounting measurements to measuring the generation of dollars per unit of time." For example, instead of emphasizing products with the largest gross margins or contribution margins, the software helps managers to identify and emphasize the products that maximize the contribution margin per unit of the constrained resource.

Source: Mike Alger, "Managing a Business as a Portfolio of Customers," *Strategic Finance*, June 2003, pp. 54–57.

Managing Constraints

Effectively managing an organization's constraints is a key to increased profits. Effective management of a bottleneck constraint involves selecting the most profitable product mix and finding ways to increase the capacity of the bottleneck operation. As discussed above, if the constraint is a bottleneck in the production process, the most profitable product mix consists of the products with the highest contribution margin per unit of the constrained resource. In addition, as discussed below, increasing the capacity of the bottleneck operation should lead to increased production and sales. Such efforts will often pay off in an almost immediate increase in profits.

It is often possible for a manager to increase the capacity of the bottleneck, which is called **relaxing (or elevating) the constraint.** For example, the stitching machine operator could be asked to work overtime. This would result in more available stitching time and hence the production of more finished goods that can be sold. The benefits from relaxing the constraint in such a manner are often enormous and can be easily quantified. The manager should first ask, "What would I do with additional capacity at the bottleneck if it were available?" In our example, if unfilled orders exist for both the touring and mountain paniers, the additional capacity would be used to process more touring paniers, since they earn a contribution margin of $12 per minute, or $720 per hour. Since overtime pay for the operator is likely to be much less than $720 per hour, running the stitching machine on overtime would be an excellent way to increase the company's profits while at the same time satisfying customers.

To reinforce this concept, suppose that there are only unfilled orders for the mountain panier. How much would it be worth to the company to run the stitching machine overtime in this situation? Since the additional capacity would be used to make the mountain panier, the value of that additional capacity would drop to $7.50 per minute or $450 per hour. Nevertheless, the value of relaxing the constraint would still be quite high.

These calculations indicate that managers should pay great attention to the bottleneck operation. If a bottleneck machine breaks down or is ineffectively utilized, the losses to the company can be quite large. In our example, for every minute the stitching machine is down due to breakdowns or setups, the company loses between $7.50 and $12.00.[2] The losses on an hourly basis are between $450 and $720! In contrast, there is no such loss of contribution margin if time is lost on a machine that is not a bottleneck—such machines have excess capacity anyway.

The implications are clear. Managers should focus much of their attention on managing the bottleneck. As we have discussed, managers should emphasize products that most profitably utilize the constrained resource. They should also make sure that products are processed smoothly through the bottleneck, with minimal lost time due to breakdowns and setups. And they should try to find ways to increase the capacity at the bottleneck.

The capacity of a bottleneck can be effectively increased in a number of ways, including:

- Working overtime on the bottleneck.
- Subcontracting some of the processing that would be done at the bottleneck.
- Investing in additional machines at the bottleneck.
- Shifting workers from processes that are not the bottleneck to the process that is the bottleneck.
- Focusing business process improvement efforts such as Six Sigma on the bottleneck.
- Reducing defective units. Each defective unit that is processed through the bottleneck and subsequently scrapped takes the place of a good unit that could have been sold.

The last three methods of increasing the capacity of the bottleneck are particularly attractive because they are essentially free and may even yield additional cost savings.

The methods and ideas discussed in this section are all part of the Theory of Constraints, which was introduced in the Prologue. A number of organizations have successfully used the Theory of Constraints to improve their performance, including Avery Dennison, Bethlehem Steel, Binney & Smith, Boeing, Champion International, Ford Motor Company, General Motors, ITT, National Semiconductor, Pratt and Whitney Canada, Pretoria Academic Hospital, Procter & Gamble, Texas Instruments, United Airlines, United Electrical Controls, the United States Air Force Logistics Command, and the United States Navy Transportation Corps.

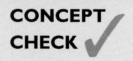

CONCEPT CHECK ✔

4. A company has received a special order from a customer to make 5,000 units of a customized product. The direct materials cost per unit of the customized product is $15, the direct labor cost per unit is $5, and the manufacturing overhead per unit is $18, including $6 of variable manufacturing overhead. If the company has sufficient available manufacturing capacity, what is the minimum price that can be accepted for the special order?
   a. $24   c. $32
   b. $26   d. $38

---

[2]Setups are required when production switches from one product to another. For example, consider a company that makes automobile side panels. The panels are painted before shipping them to an automobile manufacturer for final assembly. The customer might require 100 blue panels, 50 black panels, and 20 yellow panels. Each time the color is changed, the painting equipment must be purged of the old paint color, cleaned with solvents, and refilled with the new paint color. This takes time. In fact, some equipment may require such lengthy and frequent setups that it is unavailable for actual production more often than not.

5. Refer to the facts from question 4; however, in answering this question assume that the company is operating at 100% of its capacity without the special order. If the company normally manufactures only one product that has a contribution margin of $20 per unit and that consumes 2 minutes of the constrained resource per unit, what is the opportunity cost (stated in terms of forgone contribution margin) of taking the special order? Assume the special order would require 1.5 minutes of the constrained resource per unit.
   a. $25,000   c. $75,000
   b. $50,000   d. $100,000

CONCEPT CHECK ✓

(continued)

Elevating a Constraint   IN BUSINESS

The Odessa, Texas, Police Department was having trouble hiring new employees. Its eight-step hiring process was taking 117 days to complete; therefore, the best qualified job applicants were accepting other employment offers before the Odessa Police Department could finish evaluating their candidacy. The Theory of Constraints revealed that the constraint in the eight-step hiring process was the background investigation—which took an average of 104 days. The other seven steps—filling out an application and completing a written exam, an oral interview, a polygraph exam, a medical exam, a psychological exam and a drug screen—took a combined total of 13 days. The Odessa Police Department elevated its constraint by hiring additional background checkers. This resulted in slashing its application processing time from 117 days to 16 days.

Source: Lloyd J. Taylor III, Brian J. Moersch, and Geralyn McClure Franklin, "Applying the Theory of Constraints to a Public Safety Hiring Process," *Public Personnel Management*, Fall 2003, pp. 367–382.

SUMMARY

LO1   Identify relevant and irrelevant costs and benefits in a decision.
Every decision involves a choice from among at least two alternatives. Only those costs and benefits that differ in total between the alternatives are relevant; costs and benefits that are the same for all alternatives are not affected by the decision and can be ignored. Only future costs that differ between alternatives are relevant. Sunk costs are always irrelevant.

LO2   Prepare an analysis showing whether a product line or other business segment should be dropped or retained.
A decision of whether a product line or other segment should be dropped should focus on the differences in the costs and benefits between dropping or retaining the product line or segment. Caution should be exercised when using reports in which common fixed costs have been allocated among segments. If these common fixed costs are unaffected by the decision of whether to drop or retain the segment, they are irrelevant and should be removed before determining the real profitability of a segment.

LO3   Prepare a make or buy analysis.
When deciding whether to make or buy a component, focus on the costs and benefits that differ between those two alternatives. As in other decisions, sunk costs—such as the depreciation on old equipment—should be ignored. Future costs that do not differ between alternatives—such as allocations of common fixed costs like general overhead—should be ignored.

2. If management wants a clearer picture of the profitability of the segments, the general factory over-head should not be allocated. It is a common fixed cost and therefore should be deducted from the total product-line segment margin, as shown in Exhibit 11–4. A more useful income statement format would be as follows:

| | Trampoline | | | |
	Round	Rectangular	Octagonal	Total
Sales.	$140,000	$500,000	$360,000	$1,000,000
Variable expenses	60,000	200,000	150,000	410,000
Contribution margin	80,000	300,000	210,000	590,000
Traceable fixed expenses:				
Advertising—traceable	41,000	110,000	65,000	216,000
Depreciation of special equipment .	20,000	40,000	35,000	95,000
Line supervisors' salaries	6,000	7,000	6,000	19,000
Total traceable fixed expenses	67,000	157,000	106,000	330,000
Product-line segment margin	$ 13,000	$143,000	$104,000	260,000
Common fixed expenses				200,000
Net operating income (loss)				$ 60,000

GLOSSARY

Avoidable cost   A cost that can be eliminated (in whole or in part) by choosing one alternative over another in a decision. This term is synonymous with *relevant cost* and *differential cost.* (p. 452)

Bottleneck   A machine or some other part of a process that limits the output of the entire process. (p. 470)

Constraint   A limitation under which a company must operate, such as limited available machine time or limited available raw materials that restricts the company's ability to satisfy demand. (p. 469)

Differential cost   Any cost that differs between alternatives in a decision. This term is synonymous with *avoidable cost* and *relevant cost.* (p. 453)

Make or buy decision   A decision concerning whether an item should be produced internally or purchased from an outside supplier. (p. 463)

Relaxing (or elevating) the constraint   An action that increases the amount of a constrained resource. Equivalently, an action that increases the capacity of the bottleneck. (p. 471)

Relevant cost   A cost that differs between alternatives in a decision. This term is synonymous with *avoidable cost* and *differential cost.* (p. 452)

Segment margin   The difference between the revenue generated by a segment and its own traceable cost. (p. 463)

Special order   A one-time order that is not considered part of the company's normal ongoing business. (p. 467)

Sunk cost   Any cost that has already been incurred and that cannot be changed by any decision made now or in the future. (p. 452)

Target costing   Before launching a new product, management estimates how much the market will be willing to pay for the product and then takes steps to ensure that the cost of the product will be low enough to provide an adequate profit margin. (p. 468)

Quiz 11   Multiple-choice questions are provided on the text website at www.mhhe.com/brewer4e.

QUESTIONS

11–1   What is a *relevant cost*?
11–2   Define the following terms: *incremental cost, opportunity cost,* and *sunk cost.*
11–3   Are variable costs always relevant costs? Explain.
11–4   Why is the original cost of a machine the company already owns irrelevant in decisions?

11–5 "Sunk costs are easy to spot—they're simply the fixed costs associated with a decision." Do you agree? Explain.

11–6 "Variable costs and differential costs mean the same thing." Do you agree? Explain.

11–7 "All future costs are relevant in decision making." Do you agree? Why?

11–8 Prentice Company is considering dropping one of its product lines. What costs of the product line would be relevant to this decision? Irrelevant?

11–9 "If a product line is generating a loss, then that's pretty good evidence that the product line should be discontinued." Do you agree? Explain.

11–10 What is the danger in allocating common fixed costs among product lines or other segments of an organization?

11–11 How does opportunity cost enter into the make or buy decision?

11–12 Give four examples of possible constraints.

11–13 How does relating product contribution margins to the amount of the constrained resource the products require help a company ensure that profits are maximized?

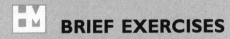 **BRIEF EXERCISES**

BRIEF EXERCISE 11–1 Identifying Relevant Costs (LO1)

A number of costs are listed below that may be relevant in decisions faced by the management of Poulsen & Sonner A/S, a Danish furniture manufacturer:

	Case 1		Case 2	
Item	**Relevant**	**Not Relevant**	**Relevant**	**Not Relevant**
a. Sales revenue				
b. Direct materials				
c. Direct labor				
d. Variable manufacturing overhead				
e. Book value—Model A3000 machine				
f. Disposal value—Model A3000 machine				
g. Depreciation—Model A3000 machine				
h. Market value—Model B3800 machine (cost)				
i. Fixed manufacturing overhead (general)				
j. Variable selling expense				
k. Fixed selling expense				
l. General administrative overhead				

Required

Copy the information above onto your answer sheet and place an X in the appropriate column to indicate whether each item is relevant or not relevant in the following situations. Requirement 1 relates to Case 1 above, and requirement 2 relates to Case 2. Consider the two cases independently.

1. The company chronically runs at capacity and the old Model A3000 machine is the company's constraint. Management is considering purchasing a new Model B3800 machine to use in addition to the company's present Model A3000 machine. The old Model A3000 machine will continue to be used to capacity as before, with the new Model B3800 being used to expand production. This will increase the company's production and sales. The increase in volume will be large enough to require increases in fixed selling expenses and in general administrative overhead, but not in the fixed manufacturing overhead.

2. The old Model A3000 machine is not the company's constraint, but management is considering replacing it with a new Model B3800 machine because of the potential savings in direct materials cost with the new machine. The Model A3000 machine would be sold. This change will have no effect on production or sales, other than some savings in direct materials costs due to less waste.

BRIEF EXERCISE 11–2   Dropping or Retaining a Segment (LO2)

Boyle's Home Center has two departments, Bath and Kitchen. The most recent contribution format income statement for the company follows:

	Department		
	Bath	**Kitchen**	**Total**
Sales............................	$1,000,000	$4,000,000	$5,000,000
Variable expenses....................	300,000	1,600,000	1,900,000
Contribution margin.................	700,000	2,400,000	3,100,000
Fixed expenses.....................	900,000	1,800,000	2,700,000
Net operating income (loss)	$ (200,000)	$ 600,000	$ 400,000

A study indicates that $370,000 of the fixed expenses being charged to the Bath Department are sunk costs or allocated costs that will continue even if the Bath Department is dropped. In addition, the elimination of the Bath Department will result in a 10% decrease in the sales of the Kitchen Department.

Required

If the Bath Department is dropped, what will be the effect on the net operating income of the company as a whole?

BRIEF EXERCISE 11–3   Make or Buy a Component (LO3)

For many years, Diehl Company has produced a small electrical part that it uses in the production of its standard line of diesel tractors. The company's unit product cost, based on a production level of 60,000 parts per year, is as follows:

	Per Unit	**Total**
Direct materials.........................	$ 4.00	
Direct labor...........................	2.75	
Variable manufacturing overhead...........	0.50	
Fixed manufacturing overhead, traceable.....	3.00	$180,000
Fixed manufacturing overhead, common (allocated based on direct labor-hours)	2.25	$135,000
Unit product cost......................	$12.50	

An outside supplier has offered to supply the electrical parts to the Diehl Company for only $10.00 per part. One-third of the traceable fixed manufacturing costs represent supervisory salaries and other costs that can be eliminated if the parts are purchased. The other two-thirds of the traceable fixed manufacturing costs consist of depreciation of special equipment that has no resale value. Economic depreciation on this equipment is due to obsolescence rather than wear and tear. The decision would have no effect on the common fixed costs of the company, and the space being used to produce the parts would otherwise be idle.

Required

Calculate the amount profits would increase or decrease by purchasing the parts from the outside supplier rather than making them inside the company.

BRIEF EXERCISE 11–4   Special Order (LO4)

Glade Company produces a single product. The cost of producing and selling a single unit of this product at the company's normal activity level of 8,000 units per month is:

Direct materials....................................	$2.50
Direct labor.......................................	$3.00
Variable manufacturing overhead....................	$0.50
Fixed manufacturing overhead.......................	$4.25
Variable selling and administrative expense............	$1.50
Fixed selling and administrative expense..............	$2.00

The normal selling price is $15.00 per unit. The company's capacity is 10,000 units per month. An order has been received from an overseas source for 2,000 units at the special price of $12.00 per unit. This order would not affect regular sales.

Required

1. If the order is accepted, how much will monthly profits increase or decrease? (The order will not change the company's total fixed costs.)
2. Assume the company has 500 units of this product left over from last year that are vastly inferior to the current model. The units must be sold through regular channels at reduced prices. What unit cost is relevant for establishing a minimum selling price for these units? Explain.

BRIEF EXERCISE 11–5   Utilization of a Constrained Resource (LO5)

Shelby Company produces three products, X, Y, and Z. Data concerning the three products follow (per unit):

	Product		
	X	Y	Z
Selling price	$80	$56	$70
Less variable expenses:			
Direct materials	24	15	9
Other variable expenses	24	27	40
Total variable expenses	48	42	49
Contribution margin	$32	$14	$21
Contribution margin ratio	40%	25%	30%

Demand for the company's products is very strong, with far more orders each month than the company can produce with the available raw materials. The same material is used in each product. The material costs $3 per pound, with a maximum of 5,000 pounds available each month.

Requried

Which orders would you advise the company to accept first, those for X, for Y, or for Z? Which orders second? Third?

EXERCISES

EXERCISE 11–6   Identification of Relevant Costs (LO1)

Samantha Ringer purchased a used automobile for $10,000 at the beginning of last year and incurred the following operating costs:

Depreciation ($10,000 ÷ 5 years)	$2,000
Insurance	$960
Garage rent	$480
Automobile tax and license	$60
Variable operating cost	8¢ per mile

The variable operating costs consist of gasoline, oil, tires, maintenance, and repairs. Samantha estimates that at her current rate of usage, the car will have zero resale value in five years, so the annual straight-line depreciation is $2,000. The car is kept in a garage for a monthly fee.

Required

1. Samantha drove the car 10,000 miles last year. Compute the average cost per mile of owning and operating the car.
2. Samantha is unsure about whether she should use her own car or rent a car to go on an extended cross-country trip for two weeks during spring break. What costs above are relevant in this decision? Explain.

3. Samantha is thinking about buying an expensive sports car to replace the car she bought last year. She would drive the same number of miles irrespective of which car she owns and would rent the same parking space. The sports car's variable operating costs would be roughly the same as the variable operating costs of her old car. However, her insurance and automobile tax and license costs would go up. What costs are relevant in estimating the incremental cost of owning the more expensive car? Explain.

EXERCISE 11–7   Make or Buy a Component (LO3)

Royal Company manufactures 20,000 units of part R-3 each year for use on its production line. At this level of activity, the cost per unit for part R-3 is as follows:

Direct materials.	$ 4.80
Direct labor.	7.00
Variable manufacturing overhead.	3.20
Fixed manufacturing overhead.	10.00
Total cost per part.	$25.00

An outside supplier has offered to sell 20,000 units of part R-3 each year to Royal Company for $23.50 per part. If Royal Company accepts this offer, the facilities now being used to manufacture part R-3 could be rented to another company at an annual rental of $150,000. However, Royal Company has determined that $6 of the fixed manufacturing overhead being applied to part R-3 would continue even if part R-3 were purchased from the outside supplier.

Required

Prepare computations showing how much profits will increase or decrease if the outside supplier's offer is accepted.

EXERCISE 11–8   Utilization of a Constrained Resource (LO5)

Banner Company produces three products: A, B, and C. The selling price, variable costs, and contribution margin for one unit of each product follow:

	Product		
	A	**B**	**C**
Selling price	$60	$90	$80
Variable expenses:			
Direct materials.	27	14	40
Direct labor.	12	32	16
Variable manufacturing overhead.	3	8	4
Total variable expense.	42	54	60
Contribution margin.	$18	$36	$20
Contribution margin ratio.	30%	40%	25%

Due to a strike in the plant of one of its competitors, demand for the company's products far exceeds its capacity to produce. Management is trying to determine which product(s) to concentrate on next week in filling its backlog of orders. The direct labor rate is $8 per hour, and only 3,000 hours of labor time are available each week.

Required

1. Compute the amount of contribution margin that will be earned per hour of labor time spent on each product.
2. Which orders would you recommend that the company work on next week—the orders for product A, product B, or product C? Show computations.
3. By payment of overtime wages, more than 3,000 hours of direct labor time can be made available next week. Up to how much should the company be willing to pay per hour in overtime wages as long as there is unfilled demand for the three products? Explain.

EXERCISE 11–9 Identification of Relevant Costs (LO1)

Steve has just returned from salmon fishing. He was lucky on this trip and brought home two salmon. Steve's wife, Wendy, disapproves of fishing, and to discourage Steve from further fishing trips, she has presented him with the following cost data. The cost per fishing trip is based on an average of 10 fishing trips per year.

Cost per fishing trip:	
Depreciation on fishing boat* (annual depreciation of $1,500 ÷ 10 trips)..	$150
Boat moorage fees (annual rental of $1,200 ÷ 10 trips)	120
Expenditures on fishing gear, except for snagged lures (annual expenditures of $200 ÷ 10 trips).....................	20
Snagged fishing lures	7
Fishing license (yearly license of $40 ÷ 10 trips).................	4
Fuel and upkeep on boat per trip...........................	25
Junk food consumed during trip	8
Total cost per fishing trip	$334
Cost per salmon ($334 ÷ 2 salmon)	$167

*The original cost of the boat was $15,000. It has an estimated useful life of 10 years, after which it will have no resale value. The boat does not wear out through use, but it does become less desirable for resale as it becomes older.

Required

1. Assuming that the salmon fishing trip Steve has just completed is typical, what costs are relevant to a decision as to whether he should go on another trip this year?
2. Suppose that on Steve's next fishing trip he gets lucky and catches three salmon in the amount of time it took him to catch two salmon on his last trip. How much would the third salmon have cost him to catch? Explain.
3. Discuss the costs that are relevant in a decision of whether Steve should give up fishing.

EXERCISE 11–10 Dropping or Retaining a Segment (LO2)

Dexter Products, Inc., manufactures and sells a number of items, including an overnight case. The company has been experiencing losses on the overnight case for some time, as shown on the following contribution format income statement:

Dexter Products, Inc.
Income Statement—Overnight Cases
For the Quarter Ended June 30

Sales		$450,000
Variable expenses:		
Variable manufacturing expenses	$130,000	
Sales commissions	48,000	
Shipping..	12,000	
Total variable expenses..................................		190,000
Contribution margin......................................		260,000
Fixed expenses:		
Salary of product line manager	21,000	
General factory overhead..........................	104,000*	
Depreciation of equipment (no resale value)...............	36,000	
Advertising—traceable............................	110,000	
Insurance on inventories	9,000	
Purchasing department	50,000†	
Total fixed expenses		330,000
Net operating loss		$ (70,000)

* Common costs allocated on the basis of machine-hours.
† Common costs allocated on the basis of sales dollars.

Discontinuing the overnight cases would not affect sales of other product lines and would have no effect on the company's total general factory overhead or total Purchasing Department expenses.

Required

Would you recommend that the company discontinue making and selling overnight cases? Support your answer with appropriate computations.

EXERCISE 11–11 Evaluating a Special Order (LO4)

Miyamoto Jewelers is considering a special order for 10 handcrafted gold bracelets to be given as gifts to members of a wedding party. The normal selling price of a gold bracelet is $389.95 and its unit product cost is $264.00 as shown below:

Direct materials.	$143.00
Direct labor.	86.00
Manufacturing overhead.	35.00
Unit product cost.	$264.00

Most of the manufacturing overhead is fixed and unaffected by variations in how much jewelry is produced in any given period. However, $7.00 of the overhead is variable with respect to the number of bracelets produced. The customer who is interested in the special bracelet order would like special filigree applied to the bracelets. This filigree would require additional materials costing $6.00 per bracelet and would also require acquisition of a special tool costing $465 that would have no other use once the special order is completed. This order would have no effect on the company's regular sales and the order could be fulfilled using the company's existing capacity without affecting any other order.

Required

What effect would accepting this order have on the company's net operating income if a special price of $349.95 per bracelet is offered for this order? Should the special order be accepted at this price?

PROBLEMS

CHECK FIGURE
(1) Decrease in net operating income if the flight is dropped: $9,300

PROBLEM 11–12A Dropping or Retaining a Flight (LO2)

Profits have been decreasing for several years at Wright Airlines. In an effort to improve the company's performance, consideration is being given to dropping several flights that appear to be unprofitable.

A typical income statement for one such flight (Flight 581) is given below (per flight):

Ticket revenue (150 passengers × 40% occupancy × $400 per passenger).	$ 24,000
Variable expenses (150 passengers × 40% occupancy × $10 per passenger).	600
Contribution margin	23,400
Flight expenses:	
Salaries, flight crew.	1,400
Flight promotion	2,000
Depreciation of aircraft	5,000
Fuel for aircraft	8,000
Liability insurance	6,000
Salaries, flight assistants	1,200
Baggage loading and flight preparation	800
Overnight costs for flight crew and assistants at destination	900
Total flight expenses.	25,300
Net operating loss.	$ (1,900)

The following additional information is available about Flight 581:

a. Members of the flight crew are paid fixed annual salaries, whereas the flight assistants are paid by the flight.

b. One-third of the liability insurance is a special charge assessed against Flight 581 because in the opinion of the insurance company, the destination of the flight is in a "high-risk" area. The remaining two-thirds would be unaffected by a decision to drop Flight 581.

c. The baggage loading and flight preparation expense is an allocation of ground crews' salaries and depreciation of ground equipment. Dropping Flight 581 would have no effect on the company's total baggage loading and flight preparation expenses.

d. If Flight 581 is dropped, Wright Airlines has no authorization at present to replace it with another flight.

e. Aircraft depreciation is due entirely to obsolescence. Depreciation due to wear and tear is negligible.

f. Dropping Flight 581 would not allow Wright Airlines to reduce the number of aircraft in its fleet or the number of flight crew on its payroll.

Required

1. Prepare an analysis showing what impact dropping Flight 581 would have on the airline's profits.
2. The airline's scheduling officer has been criticized because only about 50% of the seats on Wright Airlines flights are being filled compared to an industry average of 60%. The scheduling officer has explained that Wright Airlines' average seat occupancy could be improved considerably by eliminating about 10% of its flights, but that doing so would reduce profits. Explain how this could happen.

PROBLEM 11–13A   Make or Buy a Component (LO3)

Strausser Automotive manufactures a variety of engines for use in heavy equipment. The company has always produced most of the parts for its engines, including all of the pistons. An outside supplier has offered to sell one type of piston to Strausser Automotive at a price of $41 per unit. To evaluate this offer, Strausser Automotive has gathered the following information relating to its own cost of producing the piston internally:

CHECK FIGURE
(1) The part can be made inside the company for $7 less per unit.

	Per Unit	45,000 Units per Year
Direct materials	$13	$ 585,000
Direct labor	16	720,000
Variable manufacturing overhead	4	180,000
Fixed manufacturing overhead, traceable*	3	135,000
Fixed manufacturing overhead, allocated	10	450,000
Total cost	$46	$2,070,000

*One-third supervisory salaries; two-thirds depreciation of special equipment (no resale value).

Required

1. Assuming that the company has no alternative use for the facilities that are now being used to produce the pistons, should the outside supplier's offer be accepted? Show all computations.
2. Suppose that if the pistons were purchased, Strausser Automotive could use the freed capacity to launch a new product. The segment margin of the new product would be $400,000 per year. Should Strausser Automotive accept the offer to buy the pistons for $41 per unit? Show all computations.

CHECK FIGURE
(1) Discontinuing the
bicycling shoes would
decrease net operating
income by $57,000

PROBLEM 11–14A   Dropping or Retaining a Product (LO2)

The Montlake Shoe Company manufactures three types of shoes—hiking shoes, running shoes, and bicycling shoes. Sales and expenses data for the past quarter follow:

	Hiking Shoes	Running Shoes	Bicycling Shoes	Total
Sales	$220,000	$300,000	$280,000	$800,000
Variable expenses	95,000	180,000	175,000	450,000
Contribution margin	125,000	120,000	105,000	350,000
Fixed expenses:				
Advertising, traceable	26,000	32,000	30,000	88,000
Depreciation of special equipment	18,000	20,000	26,000	64,000
Salaries of product-line managers	14,000	17,000	18,000	49,000
Allocated common fixed expenses*	27,500	37,500	35,000	100,000
Total fixed expenses	85,500	106,500	109,000	301,000
Net operating income (loss)	$ 39,500	$ 13,500	$ (4,000)	$ 49,000

*Allocated on the basis of sales dollars.

Management is concerned about the continued losses shown by the bicycling shoes and wants a recommendation as to whether or not the line should be discontinued. The special equipment used to produce bicycling shoes has no resale value and does not wear out.

Required

1. Should production and sale of the bicycling shoes be discontinued? Show computations to support your answer.
2. Recast the above data in a format that would be more usable to management in assessing the long-run profitability of the various product lines.

CHECK FIGURE
(1) Dropping housekeeping
would decrease overall
net operating income by
$10,000.

PROBLEM 11–15A   Dropping or Retaining a Segment (LO2)

Adams County Senior Services is a nonprofit organization devoted to providing essential services to seniors who live in their own homes within the Adams County area. Three services are provided for seniors—home nursing, meals on wheels, and housekeeping. In the home nursing program, nurses visit seniors on a regular basis to check on their general health and to perform tests ordered by their physicians. The meals on wheels program delivers a hot meal once a day to each senior enrolled in the program. The housekeeping service provides weekly housecleaning and maintenance services. Sales and expenses data for the past year follow:

	Home Nursing	Meals on Wheels	House-keeping	Total
Sales	$310,000	$380,000	$210,000	$900,000
Variable expenses	130,000	220,000	150,000	500,000
Contribution margin	180,000	160,000	60,000	400,000
Fixed expenses:				
Depreciation	9,000	18,000	15,000	42,000
Liability insurance	22,000	9,000	12,000	43,000
Program administrators' salaries	42,000	43,000	38,000	123,000
General administrative overhead*	62,000	76,000	42,000	180,000
Total fixed expenses	135,000	146,000	107,000	388,000
Net operating income (loss)	$ 45,000	$ 14,000	$ (47,000)	$ 12,000

*Allocated on the basis of program revenues.

The head administrator of Adams County Senior Services, Mariam Santoya, is concerned about the organization's finances and considers the net operating income of $12,000 last year to be razor thin. (Last year's results were very similar to the results for previous years and are representative of what would be expected in the future.) She feels that the organization should be building its financial reserves at a more rapid rate in order to prepare for the next inevitable recession. After seeing the above report, Ms. Santoya asked for more information about the financial advisability of perhaps discontinuing the housekeeping program.

The depreciation in housekeeping is for a small van that is used to carry the housekeepers and their equipment from job to job. If the program were discontinued, the van would be donated to a charitable organization. None of the general administrative overhead would be avoided if the housekeeping program were dropped, but the liability insurance and the salary of the program administrator would be avoided.

Required

1. Should the housekeeping program be discontinued? Explain. Show computations to support your answer.
2. Recast the above data in a format that would be more useful to management in assessing the long-run financial viability of the various services.

PROBLEM 11–16A   Utilization of a Constrained Resource (LO5)
The Brandilyn Evans Toy Company manufactures a line of dolls and a doll dress sewing kit. Demand for the dolls is increasing, and management requests your assistance in determining an economical sales and production mix for the coming year. The company has provided the following information:

CHECK FIGURE
(2) Hours required:
    161,900 DLHs

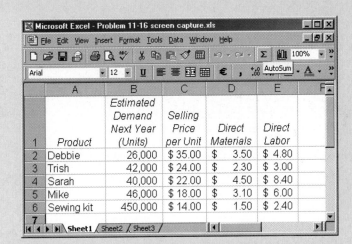

The following additional information is available:

a.   The company's plant has a capacity of 150,000 direct labor-hours per year on a single-shift basis. The company's present employees and equipment can produce all five products.
b.   The direct labor rate of $12.00 per hour is expected to remain unchanged during the coming year.
c.   Fixed costs total $356,000 per year. Variable overhead costs are $4.00 per direct labor-hour.
d.   All of the company's nonmanufacturing costs are fixed.
e.   The company's finished goods inventory is negligible and can be ignored.

Required

1. Determine the contribution margin per direct labor-hour expended on each product.
2. Prepare a schedule showing the total direct labor-hours that will be required to produce the units estimated to be sold during the coming year.
3. Examine the data you have computed in (1) and (2) above. How would you allocate the 150,000 direct labor-hours of capacity to the company's various products?
4. What is the highest price, in terms of a rate per hour, that Brandilyn Evans Toy Company should be willing to pay for additional capacity (that is, for additional direct labor-hours)?
5. Assume again that the company does not want to reduce sales of any product. Identify ways in which the company may be able to obtain the additional output.

(CPA, adapted)

CHECK FIGURE
(1) $11,800 disadvantage
    to close

PROBLEM 11–17A   Shutting Down or Continuing to Operate a Plant (LO2)
(Note: This type of decision is similar to dropping a product line.)

Pritker Devices normally produces and sells 40,000 units of RG-6 each month. RG-6 is a small electrical relay used as a component part in the automotive industry. The selling price is $26 per unit, variable costs are $22 per unit, fixed manufacturing overhead costs total $300,000 per month, and fixed selling costs total $66,000 per month.

Strikes in the companies that purchase the bulk of the RG-6 units have caused Pritker Devices' sales to temporarily drop to only 18,000 units per month. Pritker Devices estimates that the strikes will last for two months, after which sales of RG-6 should return to normal. Due to the current low level of sales, Pritker Devices is thinking about closing down its own plant during the strike, which would reduce fixed manufacturing overhead costs by $60,000 per month and its fixed selling costs by 10%. Start-up costs at the end of the shutdown period would total $1,000. Since Pritker Devices uses Lean Production production methods, no inventories are on hand.

Required

1. Assuming that the strikes continue for two months, would you recommend that Pritker Devices close its own plant? Show computations.
2. At what level of sales (in units) for the two-month period should Pritker Devices be indifferent between closing the plant or keeping it open? Show computations. (*Hint:* This is a type of break-even analysis, except that the fixed cost portion of your break-even computation should include only those fixed costs that are relevant [i.e., avoidable] over the two-month period.)

CHECK FIGURE
(1) Net increase in profits:
     $39,000

PROBLEM 11–18A   Accept or Reject a Special Order (LO4)

Arther & Smith Corporation manufactures and sells a single product called a ret. Operating at capacity, the company can produce and sell 20,000 rets per year. Costs associated with this level of production and sales are given below:

	Unit	Total
Direct materials	$12.00	$240,000
Direct labor	10.00	200,000
Variable manufacturing overhead	2.00	40,000
Fixed manufacturing overhead	4.00	80,000
Variable selling expense	6.00	120,000
Fixed selling expense	4.00	80,000
Total cost	$38.00	$760,000

The rets normally sell for $45.00 each. Fixed manufacturing overhead is constant at $80,000 per year within the range of 15,000 to 20,000 rets per year.

Required

1. Assume that due to a recession, Arther & Smith Corporation expects to sell only 15,000 rets through regular channels next year. A large retail chain has offered to purchase 5,000 rets if Arther & Smith Corporation is willing to accept a 20% discount off the regular price. There would be no sales commissions on this order; thus, variable selling expenses would be slashed by 70%. However, Arther & Smith Corporation would have to purchase a special machine to engrave the retail chain's name on the 5,000 units. This machine would cost $12,000. This would be a one-time order that would have no effect on regular sales. Determine the impact on profits next year if this special order is accepted.
2. Refer to the original data. Assume again that Arther & Smith Corporation expects to sell only 15,000 rets through regular channels next year. The U.S. Army would like to make a one-time-only purchase of 5,000 rets. The Army would pay a fixed fee of $6.00 per ret, and in addition it would

reimburse Arther & Smith Corporation for all costs of production (variable and fixed) associated with the units. There would be no variable selling expenses associated with this order. If Arther & Smith Corporation accepts the order, by how much will profits increase or decrease for the year?

3. Assume the same situation as that described in (2) above, except that the company expects to sell 20,000 rets through regular channels next year. Thus, accepting the U.S. Army's order would require giving up regular sales of 5,000 rets. If the Army's order is accepted, by how much will profits increase or decrease from what they would be if the 5,000 rets were sold through regular channels?

PROBLEM 11–19A   Relevant Cost Analysis in a Variety of Situations (LO2, LO3, LO4)

Lucy 'N Pals Corporation has a single product called Pups. The company normally produces and sells 54,000 Pups each year at a selling price of $20.00 per unit. The company's unit costs at this level of activity are given below:

CHECK FIGURE
(1) $19,400 incremental net operating income
(2) $17.90 break-even price

Direct materials.	$ 8.00	
Direct labor	3.50	
Variable manufacturing overhead	1.80	
Fixed manufacturing overhead	2.50	($135,000 total)
Variable selling expenses	1.20	
Fixed selling expenses	2.00	($108,000 total)
Total cost per unit	$19.00	

A number of questions relating to the production and sale of Pups follow. Each question is independent.

Required

1. Assume that Lucy 'N Pals Corporation has sufficient capacity to produce 70,000 Pups each year without any increase in fixed manufacturing overhead costs. The company could increase its sales by 20% above the present 54,000 units each year if it were willing to increase the fixed selling expenses by $40,000. Would the increase fixed selling expenses be justified?

2. Assume again that Lucy 'N Pals Corporation has sufficient capacity to produce 70,000 Pups each year. A customer in a foreign market wants to purchase 10,000 Pups. Import duties on the Pups would be $1.50 per unit, and costs for permits and licenses would be $5,000. The only selling costs that would be associated with the order would be $2.60 per unit shipping cost. Compute the per unit break-even price on this order.

3. The company has 2,000 Pups on hand that have some irregularities and are therefore considered to be "seconds." Due to the irregularities, it will be impossible to sell these units at the normal price through regular distribution channels. What unit cost figure is relevant for setting a minimum selling price? Explain.

4. Due to a strike in its supplier's plant, Lucy 'N Pals Corporation is unable to purchase more material for the production of Pups. The strike is expected to last for two months. Lucy 'N Pals Corporation has enough material on hand to continue to operate at 40% of normal levels for the two-month period. As an alternative, Lucy 'N Pals Corporation could close its plant down entirely for the two months. If the plant were closed, fixed manufacturing overhead expenses would continue at 60% of their normal level during the two-month period and the fixed selling expenses would be reduced by 30%. What would be the impact on profits of closing the plant for the two-month period?

5. An outside manufacturer has offered to produce Pups for Lucy 'N Pals Corporation and to ship them directly to Lucy 'N Pals Corporation customers. If Lucy 'N Pals Corporation accepts this offer, the facilities that it uses to produce Pups would be idle; however, fixed manufacturing overhead expenses would be reduced by 70%. Because the outside manufacturer would pay for all shipping costs, the variable selling expenses would be only two-thirds of their present amount. Compute the unit cost that is relevant for comparison to the price quoted by the outside manufacturer.

PROBLEM 11–20A   Make or Buy Analysis (LO3)

"That old equipment for producing subassemblies is worn out," said Kari Warner, president of Harleq Corporation. "We need to make a decision quickly." The company is trying to decide whether it should rent new equipment and continue to make its subassemblies internally or whether it should discontinue production of its subassemblies and purchase them from an outside supplier. The alternatives follow:

Alternative 1. New equipment for producing the subassemblies can be rented for $63,000 per year.

Alternative 2. The subassemblies can be purchased from an outside supplier who has offered to provide them for $5.31 each under a five-year contract.

Harleq Corporation's present costs per unit for producing the subassemblies internally (with the old equipment) are given below. These costs are based on a current activity level of 50,000 subassemblies per year:

Direct materials.	$2.30
Direct labor	1.90
Variable overhead.	0.40
Fixed overhead ($0.42 supervision, $0.90 depreciation, and $1.75 general company overhead)	3.07
Total cost per unit	$7.67

The new equipment would be more efficient than the equipment Harleq Corporation has been using and, according to the manufacturer, would reduce direct labor costs and variable overhead costs by 30%. The old equipment has no resale value. Supervision cost ($21,000 per year) and direct materials cost per unit would not be affected by the new equipment. The new equipment's capacity would be 70,000 subassemblies per year.

The company's total general company overhead would be unaffected by this decision.

Required

1. To assist the president in making a decision, prepare an analysis showing the total cost and the cost per drum for each of the two alternatives given above. Assume that 50,000 subassemblies are needed each year. Which course of action would you recommend to the president?
2. Would your recommendation in (1) above be the same if the company's needs were (a) 60,000 subassemblies per year or (b) 70,000 subassemblies per year? Show computations to support your answer, with costs presented on both a total and per unit basis.
3. What other factors would you recommend that the company consider before making a decision?

BUILDING YOUR SKILLS

ETHICS CHALLENGE CASE (LO2)

Marvin Braun had just been appointed vice president of the Great Basin Region of the Financial Services Corporation (FSC). The company provides check processing services for small banks. The banks send checks presented for deposit or payment to FSC, which records the data on each check in a computerized database. FSC then sends the data electronically to the nearest Federal Reserve Bank check-clearing center where the appropriate transfers of funds are made between banks. The Great Basin Region has three check processing centers in Eastern Idaho—Pocatello, Idaho Falls, and Ashton. Prior to his promotion to vice president, Mr. Braun had been manager of a check processing center in Indiana.

Immediately upon assuming his new position, Mr. Braun requested a complete financial report for the just-ended fiscal year from the region's controller, Lance Whiting. Mr. Braun specified that the financial report should follow the standardized format required by corporate headquarters for all regional performance reports. That report appears below:

	Check Processing Centers			
Great Basin Region **Financial Performance**	**Pocatello**	**Idaho Falls**	**Ashton**	**Total**
Sales.	$7,000,000	$8,000,000	$5,000,000	$20,000,000
Operating expenses:				
Direct labor	4,400,000	4,700,000	3,100,000	12,200,000
Variable overhead	150,000	160,000	90,000	400,000
Equipment depreciation	700,000	800,000	600,000	2,100,000
Facility expense	600,000	500,000	900,000	2,000,000
Local administrative expense*	150,000	180,000	120,000	450,000
Regional administrative expense†	140,000	160,000	100,000	400,000
Corporate administrative expense‡	560,000	640,000	400,000	1,600,000
Total operating expense	6,700,000	7,140,000	5,310,000	19,150,000
Net operating income	$ 300,000	$ 860,000	$ (310,000)	$ 850,000

*Local administrative expenses are the administrative expenses incurred at the check processing centers.
†Regional administrative expenses are allocated to the check processing centers based on sales.
‡Corporate administrative expenses are a standard 8% charge against sales.

Upon seeing this report, Mr. Braun summoned Lance Whiting for an explanation.

Braun: What's the story on Ashton? It didn't have a loss the previous year, did it?

Whiting: No, the Ashton facility has had a nice profit every year since it was opened six years ago, but Ashton lost a big contract this year.

Braun: Why?

Whiting: One of our national competitors entered the local market and bid very aggressively on the contract. We couldn't afford to meet the bid. Ashton's costs—particularly their facility expenses—are just too high. When Ashton lost the contract, we had to lay off a lot of employees, but we could not reduce the fixed costs of the Ashton facility.

Braun: Why is Ashton's facility expense so high? It's a smaller facility than either Pocatello or Idaho Falls and yet its facility expense is higher.

Whiting: The problem is that we are able to rent suitable facilities very cheaply at Pocatello and Idaho Falls. No such facilities were available at Ashton, so we had them built. Unfortunately, there were big cost overruns. The contractor we hired was inexperienced at this kind of work and in fact went bankrupt before the project was completed. After hiring another contractor to finish the work, we were way over budget. The large depreciation charges on the facility didn't matter at first because we didn't have much competition at the time and could charge premium prices.

Braun: Well, we can't do that anymore. The Ashton facility will obviously have to be shut down. Its business can be shifted to the other two check processing centers in the region.

Whiting: I would advise against that. The $900,000 in depreciation at the Ashton facility is misleading. That facility should last indefinitely with proper maintenance. And it has no resale value; there is no other commercial activity around Ashton.

Braun: What about the other costs at Ashton?

Whiting: If we shifted Ashton's business over to the other two processing centers in the region, we wouldn't save anything on direct labor or variable overhead costs. We might save $60,000 or so in local administrative expenses, but we would not save any regional administrative expense and corporate headquarters would still charge us 8% of our sales as corporate administrative expense.

In addition, we would have to rent more space in Pocatello and Idaho Falls in order to handle the work transferred from Ashton; that would probably cost us at least $400,000 a year. And don't forget that it will cost us something to move the equipment from Ashton to Pocatello and Idaho Falls. And the move will disrupt service to customers.

Braun: I understand all of that, but a money-losing processing center on my performance report is completely unacceptable.

Whiting: And if you do shut down Ashton, you are going to throw some loyal employees out of work.

Braun: That's unfortunate, but we have to face hard business realities.

Whiting: And you would have to write off the investment in the facilities at Ashton.

Braun: I can explain a write-off to corporate headquarters; hiring an inexperienced contractor to build the Ashton facility was my predecessor's mistake. But they'll have my head at headquarters if I show operating losses every year at one of my processing centers. Ashton has to go. At the next corporate board meeting, I am going to recommend that the Ashton facility be closed.

Required

1. From the standpoint of the company as a whole, should the Ashton processing center be shut down and its work redistributed to the other processing centers in the region? Explain.
2. Do you think Marvin Braun's decision to shut down the Ashton facility is ethical? Explain.
3. What influence should the depreciation on the facilities at Ashton have on prices charged by Ashton for its services?

CHECK FIGURE
(1) $0.05 savings per box to make

COMMUNICATING IN PRACTICE (LO3)

Bronson Company manufactures a variety of ballpoint pens. The company has just received an offer from an outside supplier to provide the ink cartridge for the company's Zippo pen line, at a price of $0.48 per dozen cartridges. The company is interested in this offer because its own production of cartridges is at capacity.

Bronson Company estimates that if the supplier's offer were accepted, the direct labor and variable overhead costs of the Zippo pen line would be reduced by 10% and the direct materials cost would be reduced by 20%.

Under present operations, Bronson Company manufactures all of its own pens from start to finish. The Zippo pens are sold through wholesalers at $4.00 per box. Each box contains one dozen pens. Fixed overhead costs charged to the Zippo pen line total $50,000 each year. (The same equipment and facilities are used to produce several pen lines.) The present cost of producing one dozen Zippo pens (one box) is given below:

Direct materials.	$1.50
Direct labor	1.00
Manufacturing overhead	0.80*
Total cost	$3.30

*Includes both variable and fixed manufacturing overhead, based on production of 100,000 boxes of pens each year.

Required

Write a memorandum to the president of Bronson Company that answers the following questions. Include computations to support your answer as appropriate.

1. Should Bronson Company accept the outside supplier's offer?
2. What is the maximum price that Bronson Company should be willing to pay the outside supplier per dozen cartridges?
3. Due to the bankruptcy of a competitor, Bronson Company could sell as many as 150,000 boxes of Zippo pens next year. As stated above, the company presently has enough capacity to produce the cartridges for only 100,000 boxes of Zippo pens annually. By incurring $30,000 in added fixed cost each year, the company could expand its production of cartridges to satisfy the anticipated demand for Zippo pens. The variable cost per unit to produce the additional cartridges would be the same as at present. Under these circumstances, how many boxes of cartridges should be purchased from the outside supplier and how many should be made by Bronson?
4. What qualitative factors should Bronson Company consider in this make or buy decision?

(CMA, adapted)

CHECK FIGURE
(2) Minimum sales: £198,000

ANALYTICAL THINKING (LO2)

Mrs. Agatha Spencer-Atwood is managing director of the British company Imperial Reflections, Ltd. The company makes reproductions of antique dressing room mirrors. Mrs. Spencer-Atwood would like advice concerning the merit of eliminating the Kensington line of mirrors. These mirrors have never been among the company's best-selling products, although their sales have been stable for many years.

A condensed absorption costing income statement for the company and for the Kensington product line for the quarter ended June 30 follows:

	Total Company	Kensington Product Line
Sales.	£5,000,000	£ 480,000
Cost of goods sold:		
Direct materials	420,000	32,000
Direct labor.	1,600,000	200,000
Fringe benefits (30% of direct labor)	480,000	60,000
Variable manufacturing overhead.	340,000	30,000
Building rent and maintenance	120,000	15,000
Depreciation.	80,000	10,000
Royalties (5% of sales)	250,000	24,000
Total cost of goods sold.	3,290,000	371,000
Gross margin.	1,710,000	109,000
Selling and administrative expenses:		
Product-line managers' salaries.	75,000	8,000
Sales commissions (10% of sales)	500,000	48,000
Fringe benefits (30% of salaries and commissions)	172,500	16,800
Shipping.	120,000	10,000
Advertising.	350,000	15,000
General administrative expenses.	250,000	24,000
Total selling and administrative expenses	1,467,500	121,800
Net operating income (loss).	£ 242,500	£ (12,800)

The currency in Britain is the pound, denoted by £.

The following additional data have been supplied by the company:

a.   The company pays royalties to the owners of the original pieces of furniture from which the reproductions are copied.
b.   All of the company's products are manufactured in the same facility and use the same equipment. The building rent and maintenance and the depreciation are allocated to products on the basis of direct labor dollars. The equipment does not wear out through use; it eventually becomes obsolete.
c.   Ample capacity exists to fill all orders.
d.   Dropping the Kensington product line would have no effect on sales of other product lines.
e.   All products are made to order, so there are no inventories.
f.   Shipping costs are traced to the product lines.
g.   Advertising costs are for ads to promote specific product lines. These costs have been traced directly to the product lines.
h.   General administrative expenses are allocated to products on the basis of sales dollars. There would be no effect on the total general administrative expenses if the Kensington product line were dropped.

Required

1.   Given the current level of sales, would you recommend that the Kensington product line be dropped? Prepare appropriate computations to support your answer.
2.   What would sales of the Kensington product line have to be, at a minimum, in order to justify retaining the product line? Explain your answer. (*Hint:* Set this up as a break-even problem, but include only the relevant costs.)

TEAMWORK IN ACTION (LO1, LO3, LO5)

Storage Systems, Inc., sells a wide range of drums, bins, boxes, and other containers that are used in the chemical industry. One of the company's products is a very heavy-duty corrosion-resistant metal drum, called the XSX drum, used to store toxic wastes. Production is constrained by the capacity of an automated welding machine that is used to make precision welds. A total of 2,000 hours of welding time are available annually on the machine. Since each drum requires 0.8 hours of welding time, annual production is limited to 2,500 drums. At present, the welding machine is used exclusively to make the XSX drums. The accounting department has provided the following financial data concerning the XSX drums:

	XSX Drums
Selling price per drum	$154.00
Cost per drum:	
Direct materials. $44.50	
Direct labor ($18 per hour) 4.50	
Manufacturing overhead 3.15	
Selling and administrative cost 15.40	67.55
Margin per drum.	$ 86.45

Management believes 3,000 XSX drums could be sold each year if the company had sufficient manufacturing capacity. As an alternative to adding another welding machine, management has looked into the possibility of buying additional drums from an outside supplier. Metal Products, Inc., a supplier of quality products, would be able to provide up to 1,800 XSX-type drums per year at a price of $120 per drum.

Jasmine Morita, Storage Systems' production manager, has suggested that the company could make better use of the welding machine by manufacturing premium mountain bike frames, which would require only 0.2 hours of welding time per frame. Jasmine believes that Storage Systems could sell up to 3,500 mountain bike frames per year to mountain bike manufacturers at a price of $65 per frame. The accounting department has provided the following data concerning the proposed new product:

Mountain Bike Frames	
Selling price per frame	$65.00
Cost per frame:	
Direct materials. $17.50	
Direct labor ($18 per hour) 22.50	
Manufacturing overhead 15.75	
Selling and administrative cost 6.50	62.25
Margin per frame	$ 2.75

The mountain bike frames could be produced with existing equipment and personnel. Manufacturing overhead is allocated to products on the basis of direct labor-hours. Most of the manufacturing overhead consists of fixed common costs such as rent on the factory building, but some of it is variable. The variable manufacturing overhead has been estimated at $1.05 per XSX drum and $0.60 per mountain bike frame. The variable manufacturing overhead cost would not be incurred on drums acquired from the outside supplier.

Selling and administrative costs are allocated to products on the basis of sales dollars. Almost all of the selling and administrative costs are fixed common costs, but it has been estimated that variable selling and administrative costs are $0.85 per XSX drum and $0.40 per mountain bike frame. The variable selling and administrative costs of $0.85 per drum would be incurred when drums acquired from the outside supplier are sold to the company's customers.

All of the company's employees—direct and indirect—are paid for full 40-hour workweeks and the company has a policy of laying off workers only in major recessions.

Required

Your team should discuss and then respond to each of the following questions. All team members should understand the answers and be prepared to report to the class.

1. Given the margins of the two products as indicated in the reports submitted by the accounting department, does it make sense to even consider producing the mountain bike frames? Explain.

2. Compute the contribution margin per unit for:
   a. Purchased XSX drums.
   b. Manufactured XSX drums.
   c. Manufactured mountain bike frames.

3. Determine the number of XSX drums (if any) that should be purchased and the number of XSX drums and/or mountain bike frames (if any) that should be manufactured. What is the increase in net income that would result from this plan over current operations?

As soon as your analysis was shown to the top management team at Storage Systems, several managers got into an argument concerning how direct labor costs should be treated when making this decision. One manager argued that direct labor is always treated as a variable cost in textbooks and in practice and has always been considered a variable cost at Storage Systems. After all, "direct" means you can directly trace the cost to products. If direct labor is not a variable cost, what is? Another manager argued just as strenuously that direct labor should be considered a fixed cost at Storage Systems. No one had been laid off in over a decade, and for all practical purposes, everyone at the plant is on a monthly salary. Everyone classified as direct labor works a regular 40-hour workweek and overtime has not been necessary since the company adopted Lean Production techniques. Whether the welding machine is used to make drums or frames, the total payroll would be exactly the same. There is enough slack, in the form of idle time, to accommodate any increase in total direct labor time that the mountain bike frames would require.

4. Redo requirements (2) and (3) above, making the opposite assumption about direct labor from the one you originally made. In other words, if you treated direct labor as a variable cost, redo the analysis treating it as a fixed cost. If you treated direct labor as a fixed cost, redo the analysis treating it as a variable cost.

5. What do you think is the correct way to treat direct labor in this situation—as a variable cost or as a fixed cost?

12

Capital Budgeting Decisions

<< A LOOK BACK

Chapter 11 used the basic decision-making framework, which focuses on relevant costs and benefits, to analyze a wide variety of situations.

A LOOK AT THIS CHAPTER

Chapter 12 expands coverage of decision making by focusing on decisions about investments in long-term projects. It illustrates a variety of techniques used by managers faced with these decisions.

A LOOK AHEAD >>

Chapter 13 covers the statement of cash flows. It addresses how to classify various types of cash inflows and outflows along with the interpretation of information reported on that financial statement.

CHAPTER OUTLINE

LEARNING OBJECTIVES

LP 12

After studying Chapter 12, you should be able to:

LO1 Evaluate the acceptability of an investment project using the net present value method.

LO2 Rank investment projects in order of preference.

LO3 Determine the payback period for an investment.

LO4 Compute the simple rate of return for an investment.

LO5 (Appendix 12A) Understand present value concepts and the use of present value tables.

Capital Investments: A Key to Profitable Growth

Cintas Corporation, headquartered in Cincinnati, Ohio, has experienced 37 years of uninterrupted growth in sales and profits. The company provides highly specialized services to businesses of all types throughout North America, but the backbone of its success is providing corporate identity uniforms to more than five million North American workers. Cintas has 350 uniform rental facilities, 15 manufacturing plants, and seven distribution centers across North America. While these numbers are certain to grow in the future, the challenge for Cintas is choosing among competing capital expansion opportunities.

At Cintas, each capital investment proposal must be accompanied by a financial analysis that estimates the cash inflows and outflows associated with the project. The job of Paul Carmichael, the Controller of Cintas' Rental Division, is to challenge the validity of the assumptions underlying the financial estimates. Is the cost to build the new facility underestimated? Are future revenue growth rates overly optimistic? Is it necessary to build a new facility, or could an existing facility be refurbished or expanded? Asking these types of constructive questions helps Cintas channel its limited investment funds to the growth opportunities that will create the most long-term value for shareholders.

Source: Author's conversation with Paul Carmichael, Controller, Rental Division, Cintas Corporation.

Managers are often involved in making decisions that involve an investment today in the hope of realizing future profits. For example, Tri-Con Global Restaurants, Inc., makes an investment when it opens a new Pizza Hut restaurant. L. L. Bean makes an investment when it installs a new computer to handle customer billing. General Motors makes an investment when it redesigns a product such as the Cadillac Escalade. Merck & Co. invests in medical research. Amazon.com makes an investment when it redesigns its website. All of these investments require committing funds today with the expectation of earning a return on those funds in the future in the form of additional cash inflows or reduced cash outflows.

The term **capital budgeting** is used to describe how managers plan significant investments in projects that have long-term implications such as the purchase of new equipment or the introduction of new products. Most companies have many more potential projects than can actually be funded. Hence, managers must carefully select those projects that promise the greatest future return. How well managers make these capital budgeting decisions is a critical factor in the long-run profitability of the company.

CAPITAL BUDGETING—PLANNING INVESTMENTS

Typical Capital Budgeting Decisions

Video 12–1

Any decision that involves an outlay now in order to obtain a future return is a capital budgeting decision. Typical capital budgeting decisions include:

1. Cost reduction decisions: Should new equipment be purchased to reduce costs?
2. Expansion decisions: Should a new plant, warehouse, or other facility be acquired to increase capacity and sales?
3. Equipment selection decisions: Which of several available machines should be purchased?
4. Lease or buy decisions: Should new equipment be leased or purchased?
5. Equipment replacement decisions: Should old equipment be replaced now or later?

IN BUSINESS　　**The Yukon Goes Online**

Canada's Yukon Territory, which is two-thirds the size of Texas, has only 31,000 residents. Two-thirds of those live in Whitehorse, the territory's capital. All are about to get higher-speed Internet access as part of an ambitious Canadian government program to connect the Yukon with the rest of the world. To date, the Yukon's physical isolation has precluded economic growth in the area. The Internet may change all that. In some ways, it already has. A variety of organizations in the Yukon have made significant outlays on Internet projects that will have long-term implications.

For example, after struggling to stay in business with annual sales of only $10,000, Herbie Croteau, the founder of Midnight Sun Plant Food, spent $1,600 to build a website for the company (www.midnightsunplantfood.com). Just two years later, sales are expected to exceed $65,000. Croteau is in the process of spending another $2,000 to redesign the company's website.

The town of Haines Junction is spending $10,000 to redesign its website. The town's chief administrative officer estimates that printing costs for tourist brochures will drop by 75% since tourist information can now be obtained online at www.yukon.com/community/kluane/hi.html.

Source: David H. Freedman, "Cold Comfort," *Forbes ASAP*, May 29, 2000, pp. 174–182.

Capital budgeting decisions fall into two broad categories—*screening decisions* and *preference decisions*. **Screening decisions** relate to whether a proposed project is acceptable—whether it passes a preset hurdle. For example, a company may have a policy of accepting projects only if they promise a return of 20% on the investment. The required rate of return is the minimum rate of return a project must yield to be acceptable. **Preference decisions,** by contrast, relate to selecting from among several acceptable alternatives. To illustrate, a company may be considering several different machines to replace an existing machine on the assembly line. The choice of which machine to purchase is a preference decision. In this chapter, we first discuss screening decisions and then move on to preference decisions toward the end of the chapter.

The Time Value of Money

As stated earlier, capital investments usually earn returns that extend over fairly long periods of time. Therefore, it is important to recognize *the time value of money* when evaluating investment proposals. A dollar today is worth more than a dollar a year from now if for no other reason than that you could put a dollar in a bank today and have more than a dollar a year from now. Therefore, projects that promise earlier returns are preferable to those that promise later returns.

Capital budgeting techniques that recognize the time value of money involve *discounting cash flows.* We will spend most of this chapter showing how to use discounted cash flow methods in making capital budgeting decisions. If you are not already familiar with discounting and the use of present value tables, you should read Appendix 12A, The Concept of Present Value, at the end of this chapter, before proceeding any further.

Several approaches can be used to evaluate investments using discounted cash flows. The easiest method to use is the *net present value method,* which is the subject of the next several sections.

Screening versus Preference Decisions

Screening Decisions

Preference Decisions

| IN BUSINESS | Choosing a Cat |

Sometimes a long-term decision does not have to involve present value calculations or any other sophisticated analytical technique. White Grizzly Adventures of Meadow Creek, British Columbia, needs two snowcats for its powder skiing operations—one for shuttling guests to the top of the mountain and one to be held in reserve in case of mechanical problems with the first. Bombardier of Canada sells new snowcats for $250,000 and used, reconditioned snowcats for $150,000. In either case, the snowcats are good for about 5,000 hours of operation before they need to be reconditioned. From White Grizzly's perspective, the choice is clear. Since both new and reconditioned snowcats last about 5,000 hours, but the reconditioned snowcats cost $100,000 less, the reconditioned snowcats are the obvious choice. They may not have all of the latest bells and whistles, but they get the job done at a price a small operation can afford.

Bombardier snowcats do not have passenger cabs as standard equipment. To save money, White Grizzly builds its own custom-designed passenger cab for about $15,000, using recycled Ford Escort seats and industrial-strength aluminum for the frame and siding. If purchased at retail, a passenger cab would cost about twice as much and would not be as well-suited for snowcat skiing.

Source: Brad & Carole Karafil, owners and operators of White Grizzly Adventures, www.whitegrizzly.com.

THE NET PRESENT VALUE METHOD

LEARNING OBJECTIVE 1

Evaluate the acceptability of an investment project using the net present value method.

Concept 12-1

Video 12-1

Under the net present value method, the present value of a project's cash inflows is compared to the present values of the project's cash outflows. The difference between the present values of these cash flows, called the **net present value,** determines whether or not the project is an acceptable investment. To illustrate, consider the following data:

> **Example A** Harper Company is contemplating the purchase of a machine capable of performing certain operations that are now performed manually. The machine will cost $50,000, and it will last for five years. At the end of the five-year period, the machine will have a zero scrap value. Use of the machine will reduce labor costs by $18,000 per year. Harper Company requires a minimum pretax return of 20% on all investment projects.[1]

Should the machine be purchased? Harper Company must determine whether a cash investment now of $50,000 can be justified if it will result in an $18,000 reduction in cost in each of the next five years. It may appear that the answer is obvious since the total cost savings is $90,000 ($18,000 per year × 5 years). However, the company can earn a 20% return by investing its money elsewhere. It is not enough that the cost reductions cover just the original cost of the machine; they must also yield a return of at least 20% or the company would be better off investing the money elsewhere.

To determine whether the investment is desirable, the stream of annual $18,000 cost savings should be discounted to its present value and then compared to the cost of the new machine. Harper Company's minimum required return of 20% should be used as the *discount rate* in the discounting process. Exhibit 12–1 illustrates the computation of the net present value of this proposed project. The annual cost savings of $18,000 is multiplied by 2.991, the present value factor of a 5-year annuity at the discount rate of 20%, to obtain $53,838.[2] This is the present value of the annual cost

---

[1]For simplicity, we ignore taxes. The impact of income taxes on capital budgeting decisions is discussed in Appendix 14C of Ray Garrison, Eric Noreen, and Peter Brewer, *Managerial Accounting,* 12th edition, McGraw-Hill, 2008.

[2]Unless otherwise stated, for the sake of simplicity we will assume in this chapter that all cash flows other than the initial investment occur at the ends of years.

EXHIBIT 12–1
Net Present Value Analysis of a
Proposed Project

Initial cost	$50,000
Life of the project.	5 years
Annual cost savings	$18,000
Salvage value	$0
Required rate of return	20%

Item	Year(s)	Amount of Cash Flow	20% Factor	Present Value of Cash Flows
Annual cost savings	1–5	$18,000	2.991*	$53,838
Initial investment	Now	$(50,000)	1.000	(50,000)
Net present value				$ 3,838

*From Table 12B–2 in Appendix 12B at the end of this chapter.

savings. The present value of the initial investment is computed by multiplying the investment amount of $50,000 by 1.000, the present value factor for any cash flow that occurs immediately.

According to the analysis, Harper Company should purchase the new machine. The present value of the cost savings is $53,838, whereas the present value of the required investment (cost of the machine) is only $50,000. Deducting the present value of the required investment from the present value of the cost savings yields the *net present value* of $3,838. Whenever the net present value is zero or greater, as in our example, an investment project is acceptable. Whenever the net present value is negative (the present value of the cash outflows exceeds the present value of the cash inflows), an investment project is not acceptable. In sum:

If the Net Present Value Is…	Then the Project Is…
Positive	Acceptable, since it promises a return greater than the required rate of return.
Zero	Acceptable, since it promises a return equal to the required rate of return.
Negative	Not acceptable, since it promises a return less than the required rate of return.

There is another way to interpret the net present value. Harper Company could spend up to $53,838 for the new machine and still obtain the minimum required 20% rate of return. The net present value of $3,838, therefore, shows the amount of "cushion" or "margin of error." One way to look at this is that the company could underestimate the cost of the new machine by up to $3,838, or overestimate the net present value of the future cash savings by up to $3,838, and the project would still be financially attractive.

Emphasis on Cash Flows

Accounting net income is based on accruals that ignore when cash flows occur. However, in capital budgeting, the timing of cash flows is critical. The present value of a cash flow depends on when it occurs. For that reason, cash flows rather than accounting net income is the focus in capital budgeting.[3] Examples of cash outflows and cash inflows that are often relevant to capital investment decisions are described next.

---

[3]Under certain conditions, capital budgeting decisions can be correctly made by discounting appropriately defined accounting net income. However, this approach requires advanced techniques that are beyond the scope of this book.

Typical Cash Outflows Most projects have at least three types of cash outflows. First, they often require an immediate cash outflow in the form of an initial investment in equipment, other assets, and installation costs. Any salvage value realized from the sale of old equipment can be recognized as a reduction in the initial investment or as a cash inflow. Second, some projects require a company to expand its working capital. **Working capital** is current assets (e.g., cash, accounts receivable, and inventory) less current liabilities. When a company takes on a new project, the balances in the current asset accounts often increase. For example, opening a new Nordstrom's department store requires additional cash in sales registers and more inventory. These additional working capital needs are treated as part of the initial investment in a project. Third, many projects require periodic outlays for repairs and maintenance and additional operating costs.

Typical Cash Inflows Most projects also have at least three types of cash inflows. First, a project will normally increase revenues or reduce costs. Either way, the amount involved should be treated as a cash inflow for capital budgeting purposes. Notice that, from the standpoint of cash flows, *a reduction in costs is equivalent to an increase in revenues*. Second cash inflows are also frequently realized from selling equipment for its salvage value when a project ends, although in some cases the company may actually have to pay to dispose of low-value or hazardous items. Third, any working capital that was tied up in the project can be released for use elsewhere at the end of the project and should be treated as a cash inflow. Working capital is released, for example, when a company sells off its inventory or collects its accounts receivable.

In summary, the following types of cash flows are common in business investment projects:

> Cash outflows:
>   Initial investment (including installation costs)
>   Increased working capital needs
>   Repairs and maintenance
>   Incremental operating costs
> Cash inflows:
>   Incremental revenues
>   Reduction in costs
>   Salvage value
>   Release of working capital

IN BUSINESS

Best Buy's Big Gamble

Best Buy is overhauling hundreds of its stores in an effort to tailor merchandise offerings and employee skills to meet the needs of each store's target customers. The cost to revamp one department of one store can easily exceed $600,000 for lighting and fixtures plus additional costs for employee training. While these initial cash outflows are readily quantifiable, the future cash inflows that they will generate are highly uncertain.

The first few dozen stores overhauled by Best Buy recorded sales growth that was three times greater than nonrenovated stores. Best Buy reacted to these initial results by hastily renovating 154 more stores over the next three months. Shortly after completing these expensive renovations, the company had the misfortune of informing Wall Street that the newly revamped stores' growth rates were only slightly higher than nonrenovated stores. This disappointing news apparently caused the market value of Best Buy's common stock to plummet by almost $3 billion in one day. Clearly, Wall Street analysts had serious concerns about the future cash flow generating ability of this capital investment project. Despite the "bump in the road," Best Buy remains committed to its course of action; however, the company has decided to slow down the pace of its implementation.

Source: Matthew Boyle, "Best Buy's Giant Gamble," *Fortune*, April, 3, 2006, pp. 69–75.

Simplifying Assumptions

Two simplifying assumptions are usually made in net present value analysis.

The first assumption is that all cash flows other than the initial investment occur at the end of periods. This is somewhat unrealistic in that cash flows typically occur *throughout* a period rather than just at its end. The purpose of this assumption is to simplify computations. The second assumption is that all cash flows generated by an investment project are immediately reinvested at a rate of return equal to the discount rate. Unless these conditions are met, the net present value computed for the project will not be accurate.

A Return on Investment of 100%

IN BUSINESS

During negotiations to build a replacement for the old Fenway Park in Boston, the Red Sox offered the city approximately $2 million per year over 30 years in exchange for an investment of $150 million by the city for land acquisition and cleanup. In May 2000, after denying his lack of support for the project, Boston Mayor Thomas M. Menino stated that his goal is a 100% rate of return on any investment that is made by the city. Some doubt that the Red Sox would be able to pay players' salaries if the team were required to meet the mayor's goal. The mayor has countered with a list of suggestions for raising private funds (such as selling shares to the public, as the city's pro basketball team the Celtics did in 1986). Private funds would reduce the investment that would need to be made by the city and, as a result, reduce the future payments made to the city by the Red Sox.

Source: Meg Vaillancourt, "Boston Mayor Wants High Return on Investment in New Ballpark," *Knight-Ridder/ Tribune Business News*, May 11, 2000, pITEM00133018.

Choosing a Discount Rate

A positive net present value indicates that the project's return exceeds the discount rate. A negative net present value indicates that the project's return is less than the discount rate. Therefore, if the company's minimum required rate of return is used as the discount rate, a project with a positive net present value has a return that exceeds the minimum required rate of return and is acceptable. Contrarily, a project with a negative net present value has a return that is less than the minimum required rate of return and is unacceptable.

What is a company's minimum required rate of return? The company's *cost of capital* is usually regarded as the minimum required rate of return. The **cost of capital** is the average rate of return the company must pay to its long-term creditors and its shareholders for the use of their funds. If a project's rate of return is less than the cost of capital, the company does not earn enough to compensate its creditors and shareholders. Therefore, any project with a rate of return less than the cost of capital should be rejected.

The cost of capital serves as a *screening device*. When the cost of capital is used as the discount rate in net present value analysis, any project with a negative net present value does not cover the company's cost of capital and should be discarded as unacceptable.

Negotiator for the Red Sox

DECISION MAKER

As stated in the In Business above, Boston Mayor Thomas M. Menino's goal is a 100% rate of return on any investment that is made by the city to build a new park for the Red Sox. How would you respond to the mayor?

An Extended Example of the Net Present Value Method

Example B presents an extended example of how the net present value method is used to analyze a proposed project. This example helps to tie together (and reinforce) many of the ideas developed thus far.

Example B   Under a special licensing arrangement, Swinyard Company has an opportunity to market a new product for a five-year period. The product would be purchased from the manufacturer, with Swinyard Company responsible for promotion and distribution costs. The licensing arrangement could be renewed at the end of the five-year period. After careful study, Swinyard Company estimated the following costs and revenues for the new product:

Cost of equipment needed	$60,000
Working capital needed	$100,000
Overhaul of the equipment in four years	$5,000
Salvage value of the equipment in five years	$10,000
Annual revenues and costs:	
Sales revenues	$200,000
Cost of goods sold	$125,000
Out-of-pocket operating costs (for salaries,	
advertising, and other direct costs)	$35,000

At the end of the five-year period, if Swinyard decides not to renew the licensing arrangement, the working capital would be released for investment elsewhere. Swinyard Company uses a 14% discount rate. Would you recommend that the new product be introduced?

This example involves a variety of cash inflows and cash outflows. The solution is given in Exhibit 12–2.

EXHIBIT 12–2   The Net Present Value Method—An Extended Example

Sales revenues		$200,000
Less cost of goods sold		125,000
Less out-of-pocket costs for		
salaries, advertising, etc.		35,000
Annual net cash inflows		$ 40,000

Item	Year(s)	Amount of Cash Flows	14% Factor	Present Value of Cash Flows
Purchase of equipment	Now	$(60,000)	1.000	$ (60,000)
Working capital needed	Now	$(100,000)	1.000	(100,000)
Overhaul of equipment	4	$(5,000)	0.592*	(2,960)
Annual net cash inflows from sales				
of the product line	1–5	$40,000	3.433†	137,320
Salvage value of the equipment	5	$10,000	0.519*	5,190
Working capital released	5	$100,000	0.519*	51,900
Net present value				$ 31,450

*From Table 12B–1 in Appendix 12B.
†From Table 12B–2 in Appendix 12B.

Notice how the working capital is handled in this exhibit. It is counted as a cash outflow at the beginning of the project and as a cash inflow when it is released at the end of the project. Also notice how the sales revenues, cost of goods sold, and out-of-pocket costs are handled. **Out-of-pocket costs** are actual cash outlays for salaries, advertising, and other operating expenses.

Since the net present value of the proposal is positive, the new product is acceptable.

EXPANDING THE NET PRESENT VALUE METHOD

So far, all of our examples have involved an evaluation of a single investment project. In the following section we expand the discussion of the net present value method to include evaluation of two alternative projects. In addition, we integrate relevant cost concepts into the discounted cash flow analysis. We use two approaches to compare competing investment projects—the *total-cost approach* and the *incremental-cost approach*. Each approach is illustrated in the next few pages.

The Total-Cost Approach

The total-cost approach is the most flexible method for comparing projects. To illustrate the mechanics of the approach, consider the following data:

Example C   Harper Ferry Company operates a high-speed passenger ferry service across the Mississippi River. One of its small ferryboats is in poor condition. This ferry can be renovated at an immediate cost of $200,000. Further repairs and an overhaul of the motor will be needed five years from now at a cost of $80,000. In all, the ferry will be usable for 10 years if this work is done. At the end of 10 years, the ferry will have to be scrapped at a salvage value of $60,000. The scrap value of the ferry right now is $70,000. It will cost $300,000 each year to operate the ferry, and revenues will total $400,000 annually.

As an alternative, Harper Ferry Company can purchase a new ferryboat at a cost of $360,000. The new ferry will have a life of 10 years, but it will require some repairs costing $30,000 at the end of 5 years. At the end of 10 years, the ferry will have a scrap value of $60,000. It will cost $210,000 each year to operate the ferry, and revenues will total $400,000 annually.

Harper Ferry Company requires a return of at least 14% before taxes on all investment projects.

Should the company purchase the new ferry or renovate the old ferry? Exhibit 12–3 shows the solution using the total-cost approach.

Two points should be noted from the exhibit. First, *all* cash inflows and *all* cash outflows are included in the solution under each alternative. No effort has been made to isolate those cash flows that are relevant to the decision and those that are not relevant. The inclusion of all cash flows associated with each alternative gives the approach its name—the *total-cost* approach.

Second, notice that the net present value is computed for each alternative. This is a distinct advantage of the total-cost approach because an unlimited number of alternatives can be compared side by side to determine the best option. For example, another alternative for Harper Ferry Company would be to get out of the ferry business entirely. If management desired, the net present value of this alternative could be computed to compare with the alternatives shown in Exhibit 12–3. Still other alternatives might be open to the company. In the case at hand, given only two alternatives, the best alternative is to purchase the new ferry.[4]

---

[4]The alternative with the highest net present value is not always the best choice, although it is the best choice in this case. For further discussion, see the section Preference Decisions—The Ranking of Investment Projects.

EXHIBIT 12–3 The Total-Cost Approach to Project Selection

	New Ferry	Old Ferry
Annual revenues............................	$400,000	$400,000
Annual cash operating costs............	210,000	300,000
Net annual cash inflows	$190,000	$100,000

Item	Year(s)	Amount of Cash Flows	14% Factor*	Present Value of Cash Flows
Buy the new ferry:				
Initial investment...............................	Now	$(360,000)	1.000	$(360,000)
Salvage value of the old ferry....................	Now	$70,000	1.000	70,000
Repairs in five years............................	5	$(30,000)	0.519	(15,570)
Net annual cash inflows	1–10	$190,000	5.216	991,040
Salvage value of the new ferry	10	$60,000	0.270	16,200
Net present value				701,670
Keep the old ferry:				
Renovation	Now	$(200,000)	1.000	(200,000)
Repairs in five years............................	5	$(80,000)	0.519	(41,520)
Net annual cash inflows	1–10	$100,000	5.216	521,600
Salvage value of the old ferry	10	$60,000	0.270	16,200
Net present value				296,280
Net present value in favor of buying the new ferry.....................................				$ 405,390

*All present value factors are from Tables 12B–1 and 12B–2 in Appendix 12B.

The Incremental-Cost Approach

When only two alternatives are being considered, the incremental-cost approach offers a simpler and more direct route to a decision. In the incremental-cost approach, only those costs and revenues that *differ* between the two alternatives are included in the analysis. To

EXHIBIT 12–4 The Incremental-Cost Approach to Project Selection

Item	Year(s)	Amount of Cash Flows	14% Factor*	Present Value of Cash Flows
Incremental investment to buy the new ferry	Now	$(160,000)	1.000	$(160,000)
Salvage value of the old ferry now	Now	$70,000	1.000	70,000
Difference in repairs in five years	5	$50,000	0.519	25,950
Increase in net annual cash inflows	1–10	$90,000	5.216	469,440
Difference in salvage value in 10 years	10	$0	0.270	0
Net present value in favor of buying the new ferry				$ 405,390

*All present value factors are from Tables 12B–1 and 12B–2 in Appendix 12B.

illustrate, refer again to the data in Example C relating to Harper Ferry Company. The solution using only differential costs is presented in Exhibit 12–4.[5]

Two things should be noted from the data in this exhibit. First, the net present value in favor of buying the new ferry of $405,390 shown in Exhibit 12–4 agrees with the net present value shown under the total-cost approach in Exhibit 12–3. The two approaches are just different roads to the same destination.

Second, the costs used in Exhibit 12–4 are just the differences between the costs shown for the two alternatives in the prior exhibit. For example, the $160,000 incremental investment required to purchase the new ferry in Exhibit 12–4 is the difference between the $360,000 cost of the new ferry and the $200,000 cost required to renovate the old ferry from Exhibit 12–3. The other figures in Exhibit 12–4 have been computed in the same way.

Least-Cost Decisions

Some decisions do not involve any revenues. For example, a company may be trying to decide whether to buy or lease an executive jet. The choice would be made on the basis of which alternative—buying or leasing—would be least costly. In situations such as these, where no revenues are involved, the most desirable alternative is the one with the *least total cost* from a present value perspective. Hence, these are known as least-cost decisions. To illustrate a least-cost decision, consider the following data:

Example D   Val-Tek Company is considering replacing an old threading machine. A new threading machine is available that would substantially reduce annual operating costs. Selected data relating to the old and new machines are presented below:

	Old Machine	New Machine
Purchase cost when new	$200,000	$250,000
Salvage value now	$30,000	—
Annual cash operating costs	$150,000	$90,000
Overhaul needed immediately	$40,000	—
Salvage value in six years	$0	$50,000
Remaining life	6 years	6 years

Val-Tek Company uses a 10% discount rate.

---

[5]Technically, the incremental-cost approach is misnamed, since it focuses on differential costs (that is, on both cost increases and decreases) rather than just on incremental costs. As used here, the term *incremental costs* should be interpreted broadly to include both cost increases and cost decreases.

EXHIBIT 12–5   The Total-Cost Approach (Least-Cost Decision)

Item	Year(s)	Amount of Cash Flows	10% Factor*	Present Value of Cash Flows
Buy the new machine:				
Initial investment....................................	Now	$(250,000)	1.000	$(250,000)†
Salvage value of the old machine........................	Now	$30,000	1.000	30,000†
Annual cash operating costs	1–6	$(90,000)	4.355	(391,950)
Salvage value of the new machine......................	6	$50,000	0.564	28,200
Present value of net cash outflows......................				(583,750)
Keep the old machine:				
Overhaul needed now	Now	$(40,000)	1.000	(40,000)
Annual cash operating costs	1–6	$(150,000)	4.355	(653,250)
Present value of net cash outflows......................				(693,250)
Net present value in favor of buying the new machine...........................				$ 109,500

*All factors are from Tables 12B–1 and 12B–2 in Appendix 12B.
†These two items could be netted into a single $220,000 incremental-cost figure ($250,000 − $30,000 = $220,000).

Exhibit 12–5 analyzes the alternatives using the total-cost approach. Because this is a least-cost decision, the present values are negative for both alternatives. However, the present value of the alternative of buying the new machine is $109,500 higher than the other alternative. Therefore, buying the new machine is the less costly alternative.

Exhibit 12–6 presents an analysis of the same alternatives using the incremental-cost approach. Once again, the total-cost and incremental-cost approaches arrive at the same answer.

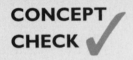

CONCEPT CHECK

1. Which of the following statements is false? (You may select more than one answer.)
   a. The total-cost and incremental-cost approaches to net present value analysis can occasionally lead to conflicting results.
   b. The cost of capital is a screening mechanism for net present value analysis.
   c. The present value of a dollar increases as the time of receipt extends further into the future.
   d. The higher the cost of capital, the lower the present value of a dollar received in the future.

EXHIBIT 12–6   The Incremental-Cost Approach (Least-Cost Decision)

Item	Year(s)	Amount of Cash Flows	10% Factor*	Present Value of Cash Flows
Incremental investment required to purchase the new machine............................	Now	$(210,000)	1.000	$(210,000)†
Salvage value of the old machine	Now	$30,000	1.000	30,000†
Savings in annual cash operating costs....................	1–6	$60,000	4.355	261,300
Difference in salvage value in six years....................	6	$50,000	0.564	28,200
Net present value in favor of buying the new machine				$ 109,500

*All factors are from Tables 12B–1 and 12B–2 in Appendix 12B.
†These two items could be netted into a single $180,000 incremental-cost figure ($210,000 − $30,000 = $180,000).

Trading In That Old Car?

Consumer Reports magazine provides the following data concerning the alternatives of keeping a four-year-old Ford Taurus for three years or buying a similar new car to replace it. The illustration assumes the car would be purchased and used in suburban Chicago.

	Keep the Old Taurus	Buy a New Taurus
Annual maintenance	$1,180	$650
Annual insurance	$370	$830
Annual license	$15	$100
Trade-in value in three years	$605	$7,763
Purchase price, including sales tax		$17,150

Consumer Reports is ordinarily extremely careful in its analysis, but it has omitted in this instance one financial item that differs substantially between the alternatives. What is it? To check your answer, go to the textbook website at www.mhhe.com/brewer4e. After accessing the site, click on the link to this chapter and then the link to the Internet Exercises.

Source: "When to Give Up on Your Clunker," *Consumer Reports*, August 2000, pp. 12–16.

Financing the Sports Car

Assume you would like to buy a new sports car that can be purchased for $21,495 in cash or acquired from the dealer via a leasing arrangement. Under the terms of the lease, you would have to make a payment of $2,078 when the lease is signed and then monthly payments of $300 for 24 months. At the end of the 24-month lease, you can choose to buy the car you have leased for an additional payment of $13,776. If you do not make that final payment, the car reverts to the dealer.

You have enough cash to make the initial payment on the lease, but not enough to buy the car for cash. However, you could borrow the additional cash from a credit union for 1% per month. Do you think you should borrow money from a credit union to purchase the car or should you sign a lease with the dealer?

Hints: The net present value of the cash purchase option, including any payments to the credit union, is $21,495 using 1% per month as the discount rate. (Accept this statement as true; don't try to do the computations to verify it.) Determine the net present value of the lease, using 1% per month as the discount rate. The present value of an annuity of $1 for 24 periods at 1% per period is 21.243 and the present value of a single payment of $1 at the end of 24 periods at 1% per period is 0.788.

PREFERENCE DECISIONS—THE RANKING OF INVESTMENT PROJECTS

Recall that when considering investment opportunities, managers must make two types of decisions—screening decisions and preference decisions. Screening decisions, which come first, pertain to whether or not a proposed investment is acceptable. Preference decisions come *after* screening decisions and attempt to answer the following question: "How do the remaining investment proposals, all of which have been screened and provide an acceptable rate of return, rank in terms of preference? That is, which one(s) would be *best* for the company to accept?"

Sometimes preference decisions are called rationing decisions or ranking decisions because they ration limited investment funds among many competing alternatives. Hence, the alternatives must be ranked.

The net present value of one project cannot be directly compared to the net present value of another project unless the initial investments are equal. For example, assume that a company is considering two competing investments, as shown below:

	Investment	
	A	**B**
Investment required	$(10,000)	$(5,000)
Present value of cash inflows.	11,000	6,000
Net present value.	$ 1,000	$ 1,000

Although each project has a net present value of $1,000, the projects are not equally desirable if the funds available for investment are limited. The project requiring an investment of only $5,000 is much more desirable than the project requiring an investment of $10,000. This fact can be highlighted by dividing the net present value of the project by the investment required. The result, shown below in equation form, is called the **project profitability index.**

$$\text{Project profitability index} = \frac{\text{Net present value of the project}}{\text{Investment required}} \qquad (1)$$

The project profitability indexes for the two investments above would be computed as follows:

	Investment	
	A	**B**
Net present value (a).	$1,000	$1,000
Investment required (b).	$10,000	$5,000
Project profitability index, (a) ÷ (b)	0.10	0.20

When using the project profitability index to rank competing investments projects, the preference rule is: *The higher the project profitability index, the more desirable the project.*[6] Applying this rule to the two investments above, investment B should be chosen over investment A.

The project profitability index is an application of the techniques for utilizing constrained resources discussed in Chapter 11. In this case, the constrained resource is the limited funds available for investment, and the project profitability index is similar to the contribution margin per unit of the constrained resource.

A few details should be clarified with respect to the computation of the project profitability index. The "Investment required" refers to any cash outflows that occur at the beginning of the project, reduced by any salvage value recovered from the sale of old equipment. The "Investment required" also includes any investment in working capital that the project may need.

---

[6]Because of the "lumpiness" of projects, the project profitability index ranking may not be perfect. Nevertheless, it is a good starting point. For further details, see the Profitability Analysis Appendix at the end of Ray Garrison, Eric Noreen, and Peter Brewer, *Managerial Accounting,* 12th edition, McGraw-Hill, 2008.

THE INTERNAL RATE OF RETURN METHOD

The *internal rate of return* method is a popular alternative to the net present value method. The **internal rate of return** is the rate of return promised by an investment over its useful life. It is computed by finding the discount rate at which the net present value of the investment is zero. The internal rate of return can be used either to screen projects or to rank them. Any project whose internal rate of return is less than the cost of capital is rejected and, in general, the higher a project's rate of return, the more desirable it is.

For technical reasons that are discussed in more advanced texts, the net present value method is generally considered to be more reliable than the internal rate of return method for both screening and ranking projects.

Video 12–1

THE NET PRESENT VALUE METHOD AND INCOME TAXES

Our discussion of the net present value method has assumed that there are no income taxes. In most countries—including the United States—income taxes, both on individual income and on business income, are a fact of life.

Income taxes affect net present value analysis in two ways. First, income taxes affect the cost of capital in that the cost of capital should reflect the *after-tax* cost of long-term debt and of equity. Second, net present value analysis should focus on *after-tax cash flows*. The effects of income taxes on both revenues and expenses should be fully reflected in the analysis. This includes taking into account the tax deductibility of depreciation. Whereas depreciation is not itself a cash flow, it reduces taxable income and therefore income taxes, which *are* a cash flow. The techniques for adjusting the cost of capital and cash flows for income taxes are beyond the scope of this book and are covered in more advanced texts.

OTHER APPROACHES TO CAPITAL BUDGETING DECISIONS

The net present value and internal rate of return methods are widely used as decision-making tools. However, some managers also use the payback method and simple rate of return method to make capital budgeting decisions. Each of these methods will be discussed in turn.

Video 12–1

The Payback Method

The payback method focuses on the *payback period*. The **payback period** is the length of time that it takes for a project to cover its initial cost from the net cash inflows that it generates. This period is sometimes referred to as "the time that it takes for an investment to pay for itself." The basic premise of the payback method is that the more quickly the cost of an investment can be recovered, the more desirable is the investment.

The payback period is expressed in years. *When the net annual cash inflow is the same every year,* the following formula can be used to compute the payback period:

$$\text{Payback period} = \frac{\text{Investment required}}{\text{Net annual cash inflow}} \qquad (2)$$

To illustrate the payback method, consider the following data:

Example E   York Company needs a new milling machine. The company is considering two machines: machine A and machine B. Machine A costs $15,000, has a useful life of ten years, and will reduce operating costs by $5,000 per year. Machine B

LEARNING OBJECTIVE 3

Determine the payback period for an investment.

Topic Tackler

PLUS

Concept 12-2

costs only $12,000, will also reduce operating costs by $5,000 per year, but has a useful life of only five years.

Required:

Which machine should be purchased according to the payback method?

$$\text{Machine A payback period} = \frac{\$15,000}{\$5,000} = 3.0 \text{ years}$$

$$\text{Machine B payback period} = \frac{\$12,000}{\$5,000} = 2.4 \text{ years}$$

According to the payback calculations, York Company should purchase machine B because it has a shorter payback period than machine A.

Entrepreneurial Ingenuity at Its Best

Jonathan Pratt owns two Ümani Cafés in Westchester County, New York. He used to pay $200 a month to dispose of the vegetable oil that is used to fry foods in his restaurants. Plus, he bought $700 of gas every month to operate his company's pick-up truck. Then Pratt got an idea. He purchased a diesel-powered Ford F250 on eBay for $11,000 and paid $1,500 to haul the truck from Arizona to New York. Next, he installed an $850 conversion kit on his new truck to enable it to run on vegetable oil. Since he no longer has to pay to dispose of vegetable oil or buy gasoline, Pratt figures that his investment will pay for itself in about 15 months ($13,350 ÷ $900 = 14.83 months). Furthermore, he now has the best smelling car in town—it smells like french fries when he drives down the road.

Source: Jean Chatzky, "Out of the Frying Pan, Into the Ford," *Money*, October, 2004, p. 28.

Evaluation of the Payback Method

The payback method is not a true measure of the profitability of an investment. Rather, it simply tells a manager how many years are required to recover the original investment. Unfortunately, a shorter payback period does not always mean that one investment is more desirable than another.

To illustrate, refer back to Example E above. Machine B has a shorter payback period than machine A, but it has a useful life of only 5 years rather than 10 years for machine A. Machine B would have to be purchased twice—once immediately and then again after the fifth year—to provide the same service as just one machine A. Under these circumstances, machine A would probably be a better investment than machine B, even though machine B has a shorter payback period. Unfortunately, the payback method ignores all cash flows that occur after the payback period.

A further criticism of the payback method is that it does not consider the time value of money. A cash inflow to be received several years in the future is weighed the same as a cash inflow received right now. To illustrate, assume that for an investment of $8,000 you can purchase either of the two following streams of cash inflows:

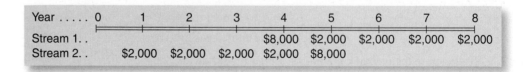

Year	0	1	2	3	4	5	6	7	8
Stream 1..					$8,000	$2,000	$2,000	$2,000	$2,000
Stream 2..		$2,000	$2,000	$2,000	$2,000	$8,000			

Which stream of cash inflows would you prefer to receive in return for your $8,000 investment? Each stream has a payback period of 4.0 years. Therefore, if payback alone is used to make the decision, the streams would be considered equally desirable. However, from a time value of money perspective stream 2 is much more desirable than stream 1.

On the other hand, under certain conditions the payback method can be very useful. For one thing, it can help identify which investment proposals are in the "ballpark." That is, it can be used as a screening tool to help answer the question, "Should I consider this proposal further?" If a proposal doesn't provide a payback within some specified period, it can be dropped without further analysis. In addition, the payback period is often of great importance to new companies that are "cash poor." When a company is cash poor, a project with a short payback period but a low rate of return might be preferred over another project with a high rate of return but a long payback period. The reason is that the company may simply need a faster return of its cash investment. And finally, the payback method is sometimes used in industries where products become obsolete very rapidly—such as consumer electronics. Since products may last only a year or two, the payback period on investments must be very short.

Conservation Is Not Self-Denial

IN BUSINESS

Amory Lovins, the director of the Rocky Mountain Institute in Snowmass, Colorado, is a passionate advocate of energy efficiency as a means of conserving natural resources and reducing pollution. Rather than cutting energy consumption by adopting more austere lifestyles, Lovins believes that energy consumption can be radically cut by using energy more efficiently. This approach has the virtues of combining energy conservation with cash savings and better living standards. He claims that America's annual electric bill of $220 billion could be cut in half by making investments with a payback period of one year or less. To illustrate his point, Lovins designed the institute's headquarters to require no furnace or air conditioning. During the cold winters, daytime solar heat enters the building through a built-in greenhouse, is soaked up by massive stone walls and foundations, and is then released at night. The institute is hardly a chilling, austere structure. Its passive heating system supports a small stand of tropical fruit trees, a mini fish farm, an indoor waterfall, and a hot tub. Lovins claims that the building's efficient design added only $6,000 to its construction costs and the payback period on this investment was only 10 months.

Source: David Stipp, "Can This Man Solve America's Energy Crisis?" *Fortune*, May 13, 2002, pp. 100–110.

An Extended Example of Payback

As shown by formula (2) given earlier, the payback period is computed by dividing the investment in a project by the net annual cash inflows that the project will generate. If new equipment is replacing old equipment, then any salvage value to be received when disposing of the old equipment should be deducted from the cost of the new equipment, and only the *incremental* investment should be used in the payback computation. In addition, any depreciation deducted in arriving at the project's net operating income must be added back to obtain the project's expected net annual cash inflow. To illustrate, consider the following data:

Example F   Goodtime Fun Centers, Inc., operates amusement parks. Some of the vending machines in one of its parks provide very little revenue, so the company is considering removing the machines and installing equipment to dispense soft ice cream. The equipment would cost $80,000 and have an eight-year useful life with no salvage value. Incremental annual revenues and costs associated with the sale of ice cream would be as follows:

Sales	$150,000
Variable expenses	90,000
Contribution margin	60,000
Fixed expenses:	
Salaries	27,000
Maintenance	3,000
Depreciation	10,000
Total fixed expenses	40,000
Net operating income	$ 20,000

The vending machines can be sold for a $5,000 scrap value. The company will not purchase equipment unless it has a payback period of three years or less. Does the ice cream dispenser pass this hurdle?

Exhibit 12–7 computes the payback period of the ice cream dispenser. Several things should be noted from this exhibit. First, depreciation is added back to net operating income to obtain the net annual cash inflow from the new equipment. Depreciation is not a cash outlay; thus, it must be added back to adjust net operating income to a cash basis. Second, the payback computation deducts the salvage value of the old machines from the cost of the new equipment so that only the incremental investment is used in computing the payback period.

Since the proposed equipment has a payback period of less than three years, the company's payback requirement has been met.

EXHIBIT 12–7
Computation of the Payback Period

Step 1: *Compute the net annual cash inflow.* Since the net annual cash inflow is not given, it must be computed before the payback period can be determined:

Net operating income (given above)	$20,000
Add: Noncash deduction for depreciation	10,000
Net annual cash inflow	$30,000

Step 2: *Compute the payback period.* Using the net annual cash inflow figure from above, the payback period can be determined as follows:

Cost of the new equipment	$80,000
Less salvage value of old equipment	5,000
Investment required	$75,000

$$\text{Payback period} = \frac{\text{Investment required}}{\text{Net annual cash inflow}}$$

$$= \frac{\$75,000}{\$30,000} = 2.5 \text{ years}$$

Payback and Uneven Cash Flows

When the cash flows associated with an investment project change from year to year, the simple payback formula that we outlined earlier cannot be used. Consider the following data:

Year	Investment	Cash Inflow
1	$4,000	$1,000
2		$0
3		$2,000
4	$2,000	$1,000
5		$500
6		$3,000
7		$2,000

EXHIBIT 12–8
Payback and Uneven Cash Flows

Year	Investment	Cash Inflow	Unrecovered Investment*
1.................................	$4,000	$1,000	$3,000
2.................................		$0	$3,000
3.................................		$2,000	$1,000
4.................................	$2,000	$1,000	$2,000
5.................................		$500	$1,500
6.................................		$3,000	$0
7.................................		$2,000	$0

*Year X unrecovered investment = Year X − 1 unrecovered investment + Year X investment − Year X cash inflow

What is the payback period on this investment? The answer is 5.5 years, but to obtain this figure it is necessary to track the unrecovered investment year by year. The steps involved in this process are shown in Exhibit 12–8. By the middle of the sixth year, sufficient cash inflows will be realized to recover the entire investment of $6,000 ($4,000 + $2,000).

The Simple Rate of Return Method

The **simple rate of return** method is another capital budgeting technique that does not involve discounting cash flows. The simple rate of return is also known as the accounting rate of return or the unadjusted rate of return.

Unlike the other capital budgeting methods that we have discussed, the simple rate of return method focuses on accounting net operating income rather than cash flows. To obtain the simple rate of return, the annual incremental net operating income from a project is divided by the initial investment in the project as shown below.

LEARNING OBJECTIVE 4
Compute the simple rate of return for an investment.

$$\text{Simple rate of return} = \frac{\text{Annual incremental net operating income}}{\text{Initial investment}} \quad (3)$$

Two additional points should be made. First, depreciation charges that result from making the investment should be deducted when determining the annual incremental net operating income. Second, the initial investment should be reduced by any salvage value realized from the sale of old equipment.

Example G Brigham Tea, Inc., is a processor of low-acid tea. The company is contemplating purchasing equipment for an additional processing line that would increase revenues by $90,000 per year. Incremental cash operating expenses would be $40,000 per year. The equipment would cost $180,000 and have a nine-year life with no salvage value.

Required:
Compute the simple rate of return.

To apply the formula for the simple rate of return, we must first determine the annual incremental net operating income from the project:

Annual incremental revenues.....................		$90,000
Annual incremental cash operating expenses........	$40,000	
Annual depreciation ($180,000 − $0)/9.............	20,000	
Annual incremental expenses		60,000
Annual incremental net operating income		$30,000

Given that the annual incremental net operating income from the project is $30,000 and the initial investment is $180,000, the simple rate of return is 16.7% as shown below:

$$\text{Simple rate of return} = \frac{\text{Annual incremental net operating income}}{\text{Initial investment}}$$

$$= \frac{\$30,000}{\$180,000}$$

$$= 16.7\%$$

Example H   Midwest Farms, Inc., hires people on a part-time basis to sort eggs. The cost of this hand-sorting process is $30,000 per year. The company is investigating an egg-sorting machine that would cost $90,000 and have a 15-year useful life. The machine would have negligible salvage value, and it would cost $10,000 per year to operate and maintain. The egg-sorting equipment currently being used could be sold now for a scrap value of $2,500.

Required:
Compute the simple rate of return on the new egg-sorting machine.

Solution:
This project is slightly different from the preceding project because it involves cost reductions with no additional revenues. Nevertheless, the annual incremental net operating income can be computed by treating the annual cost savings as if it were incremental revenues as follows:

Annual incremental cost savings		$30,000
Annual incremental cash operating expenses	$10,000	
Annual depreciation ($90,000 − $0)/15	6,000	
Annual incremental expenses		16,000
Annual incremental net operating income		$14,000

Thus, even though the new equipment would not generate any additional revenues, it would reduce costs by $14,000 a year, which would increase net operating income by $14,000 a year.

Finally, the salvage value of the old equipment offsets the initial cost of the new equipment as follows:

Cost of the new equipment	$90,000
Less: Salvage value of the old equipment	2,500
Initial investment	$87,500

Given the annual incremental net operating income of $14,000 and the initial investment of $87,500, the simple rate of return is 16.0% computed as follows:

$$\text{Simple rate of return} = \frac{\text{Annual incremental net operating income}}{\text{Initial investment}}$$

$$= \frac{\$14,000}{\$87,500}$$

$$= 16.0\%$$

IN BUSINESS

An Amazing Return

Ipswitch, Inc., a software developer and seller, has moved much of its business to the Web. Potential customers can download free trial copies of the company's software at www.ipswitch.com. After the trial period, a customer must return to the website to purchase and download a permanent copy of the software. The initial investment in setting up a website was modest—roughly $190,000. The cost of keeping the website up and running and updated with the latest product information is about $1.3 million a year—mainly in the form of salaries and benefits for eight employees. The company estimates that additional revenues brought in by the Web amount to about $13 million per year and that the company saves about $585,000 per year in direct mail advertising costs by using the Web for much of its advertising instead. Assuming that the cost of sales is almost zero for downloaded software, the accounting rate of return on the initial investment in the website is 6,466% ([$13,000,000 − $1,300,000 + $585,000] ÷ $190,000)!

Source: Karen N. Kroll, "Many Happy Returns," *Inc.* magazine, November 30, 2001, pp. 150–152.

Criticisms of the Simple Rate of Return

The simple rate of return method ignores the time value of money. It considers a dollar received 10 years from now to be as valuable as a dollar received today. Thus, the simple rate of return method can be misleading if the alternatives have different cash flow patterns. Additionally, many projects do not have constant incremental revenues and expenses over their useful lives. As a result, the simple rate of return will fluctuate from year to year, with the possibility that a project may appear to be desirable in some years and undesirable in others. In contrast, the net present value method provides a single number that summarizes all of the cash flows over the entire useful life of the project.

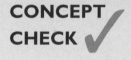

CONCEPT CHECK ✓

2. If a $300,000 investment has a project profitability index of 0.25, what is the net present value of the project?
   a. $75,000
   b. $225,000
   c. $25,000
   d. $275,000
3. Which of the following statements is false? (You may select more than one answer.)
   a. The payback period increases as the cost of capital decreases.
   b. The simple rate of return will be the same for two alternatives that have identical cash flow patterns even if the pattern of accounting net operating income differs between the alternatives.
   c. The internal rate of return will be higher than the cost of capital for projects that have positive net present values.
   d. If two alternatives have the same present value of cash inflows, the alternative that requires the higher investment will have the higher project profitability index.

POSTAUDIT OF INVESTMENT PROJECTS

After an investment project has been approved and implemented, a *postaudit* should be conducted. A **postaudit** involves checking whether or not expected results are actually realized. This is a key part of the capital budgeting process because it helps keep managers honest in their investment proposals. Any tendency to inflate the benefits or downplay the costs in a proposal should become evident after a few postaudits have been conducted. The postaudit also provides an opportunity to reinforce and possibly expand successful projects and to cut losses on floundering projects.

The same capital budgeting method should be used in the postaudit as was used in the original approval process. That is, if a project was approved on the basis of a net present value analysis, then the same procedure should be used in performing the postaudit. However, the data used in the postaudit analysis should be *actual observed data* rather than estimated data. This gives management an opportunity to make a side-by-side comparison to see how well the project has succeeded. It also helps ensure that estimated data received on future proposals is carefully prepared, since the persons submitting the data know that their estimates will be compared to actual results in the postaudit process. Actual results that are far out of line with original estimates should be carefully reviewed.

IN BUSINESS   Counting the Environmental Costs

Companies often grossly underestimate how much they are spending on environmental costs. Many of these costs are buried in broad cost categories such as manufacturing overhead. Kestrel Management Services, LLC, a management consulting firm specializing in environmental matters, found that one chemical facility was spending five times as much on environmental expenses as its cost system reported. At another site, a small manufacturer with $840,000 in pretax profits thought that its annual safety and environmental compliance expenses were about $50,000 but, after digging into the accounts, found that the total was closer to $300,000. Alerted to this high cost, management of the company invested about $125,000 in environmental improvements, anticipating a three- to six-month payback period. By taking steps such as more efficient dust collection, the company improved its product quality, reduced scrap rates, decreased its consumption of city water for cooling, and reduced the expense of discharging wastewater into the city's sewer system. Further analysis revealed that spending $50,000 to improve energy efficiency would reduce annual energy costs by about $45,000. Few of these costs were visible in the company's traditional cost accounting system.

Source: Thomas P. Kunes, "A Green and *Lean* Workplace?" *Strategic Finance*, February 2001, pp. 71–73, 83.

IN BUSINESS   Capital Budgeting in Practice

A survey of Fortune 1000 companies—the largest companies in the United States—asked CFOs how often various capital budgeting methods are used in their companies. Some of the results of that survey are displayed below:

Capital Budgeting Tool	Frequency of Use				
	Always	Often	Sometimes	Rarely	Never
Net present value	50%	35%	11%	3%	1%
Internal rate of return	45%	32%	15%	6%	2%
Payback	19%	33%	22%	17%	9%
Accounting rate of return	5%	9%	19%	16%	50%

Many companies use more than one method—for example, they may use both the net present value and the internal rate of return methods to evaluate capital budgeting projects. Note that the two discounted cash flow methods—net present value and internal rate of return—are by far the most commonly used in practice.

(continued)

A similar survey of companies in the United Kingdom yielded the following results:

Capital Budgeting Tool	Frequency of Use			
	Always	**Mostly**	**Often**	**Rarely**
Net present value..................	43%	20%	14%	7%
Internal rate of return..............	48%	20%	10%	5%
Payback........................	30%	16%	17%	14%
Accounting rate of return	26%	15%	18%	7%

Note that while the results were quite similar for the U.S. and U.K. companies, the U.K. companies were more likely to use the payback and accounting rate of return methods than the U.S. companies.

Sources: Patricia A. Ryan and Glenn P. Ryan, "Capital Budgeting Practices of the Fortune 1000: How Have Things Changed?" *Journal of Business and Management,* Fall 2002, pp. 355–364; and Glen C. Arnold and Panos D. Hatzopoulus, "The Theory-Practice Gap in Capital Budgeting: Evidence from the United Kingdom," *Journal of Business Finance & Accounting* 27(5) & 27(6), June/July 2000, pp. 603–626.

SUMMARY

LOI Evaluate the acceptability of an investment project using the net present value method.
Investment decisions should take into account the time value of money because a dollar today is more valuable than a dollar received in the future. In the net present value method, future cash flows are discounted to their present value so that they can be compared with current cash outlays. The difference between the present value of the cash inflows and the present value of the cash outflows is called the project's net present value. If the net present value of the project is negative, the project is rejected. The company's cost of capital is often used as the discount rate in the net present value method.

LO2 Rank investment projects in order of preference.
After screening out projects whose net present values are negative, the company may still have more projects than can be supported with available funds. The remaining projects can be ranked using the project profitability index, which is computed by dividing the net present value of the project by the required initial investment.

LO3 Determine the payback period for an investment.
The payback period is the number of periods that are required to recover the investment in a project from the project's net cash inflows. The payback period is most useful for projects whose useful lives are short and uncertain. Generally speaking it is not a reliable method for evaluating investment opportunities because it ignores the time value of money and all cash flows that occur after the investment has been recovered.

LO4 Compute the simple rate of return for an investment.
The simple rate of return is determined by dividing a project's accounting net operating income by the initial investment in the project. The simple rate of return is not a reliable guide for evaluating potential projects because it ignores the time value of money.

GUIDANCE ANSWERS TO *DECISION MAKER* AND *YOU DECIDE*

Negotiator for the Red Sox (p. 501)
Apparently, the mayor is suggesting that 100% is the minimum required rate of return. Because the City of Boston does not have shareholders, its cost of capital might be considered the average rate of return that must be paid to its long-term creditors. It is highly unlikely that the city pays interest of 100% on its long-term debt.

Note that it is very possible that the term *return on investment* is being misused either by the mayor, the media, or both. The mayor's goal might actually be a 100% recovery of the city's investment from the Red Sox. Rather than expecting a 100% return *on* investment, the mayor may simply want a 100% return *of* investment. Taking the time to clarify the mayor's intent might change the course of negotiations.

Financing the Sports Car (p. 507)

The formal analysis, using the least-cost approach, appears below:

Item	Month(s)	Amount of Cash Flows	1% Factor	Present Value of Cash Flows
Pay cash for the car:				
Cash payment	Now	$(21,495)	1.000	$(21,495)
Net present value				$(21,495)
Lease the car:				
Cash payment on lease signing	Now	$(2,078)	1.000	$ (2,078)
Monthly lease payment................	1–24	$(300)	21.243	(6,373)
Final payment......................	24	$(13,776)	0.788	(10,855)
Net present value				$(19,306)
Net present value in favor of leasing				$ 2,189

The leasing alternative is $2,189 less costly, in terms of net present value, than the cash purchase alterna-
tive. In addition, the leasing alternative has the advantage that you can choose to not make the final payment of $13,776 at the end of 24 months if for some reason you decide you do not want to keep the car. For
example, if the resale value of the car at that point is far less than $13,776, you may choose to return the
car to the dealer and save the $13,776. If, however, you had purchased the car outright, you would not have
this option—you could only realize the resale value. Because of this "real option," the leasing alternative is
even more valuable than the net present value calculations indicate. Therefore, you should lease the car
rather than pay cash (and borrow from the credit union).

GUIDANCE ANSWERS TO CONCEPT CHECKS

1. **Choices a and c.** The total-cost and incremental-cost approaches always provide identical results.
    The present value of a dollar decreases as the time of receipt extends further into the future.
2. **Choice a.** The net present value of the project is $300,000 × 0.25 = $75,000.
3. **Choices a, b, and d.** The payback period does not consider the time value of money; the cost of cap-
    ital is ignored. The simple rate of return is based on accounting net operating income, not cash flows.
    If two alternatives have the same present value of cash inflows, the alternative that requires the lower
    investment, as opposed to the higher investment, will have the higher project profitability index.

REVIEW PROBLEM: COMPARISON OF CAPITAL BUDGETING METHODS

Lamar Company is considering a project that would have an eight-year life and require a $2,400,000
investment in equipment. At the end of eight years, the project would terminate and the equipment would
have no salvage value. The project would provide net operating income each year as follows:

Sales		$3,000,000
Variable expenses		1,800,000
Contribution margin		1,200,000
Fixed expenses:		
Advertising, salaries, and other		
fixed out-of-pocket costs	$700,000	
Depreciation	300,000	
Total fixed expenses.................		1,000,000
Net operating income................		$ 200,000

The company's discount rate is 12%

Required:
1. Compute the net annual cash inflow from the project.
2. Compute the project's net present value. Is the project acceptable?
3. Compute the project's payback period.
4. Compute the project's simple rate of return.

Solution to Review Problem
1. The net annual cash inflow can be computed by deducting the cash expenses from sales:

Sales	$3,000,000
Variable expenses	1,800,000
Contribution margin	1,200,000
Advertising, salaries, and	
other fixed out-of-pocket costs	700,000
Net annual cash inflow.	$ 500,000

Or the incremental net annual cash inflow can be computed by adding depreciation back to net operating income:

Net operating income.	$200,000
Add: Noncash deduction	
for depreciation.	300,000
Net annual cash inflow.	$500,000

2. The net present value is computed as follows:

Item	Year(s)	Amount of Cash Flows	12% Factor	Present Value of Cash Flows
Cost of new equipment	Now	$(2,400,000)	1.000	$(2,400,000)
Net annual cash inflow.	1–8	$500,000	4.968	2,484,000
Net present value.				$ 84,000

Yes, the project is acceptable because it has a positive net present value.

3. The formula for the payback period is:

$$\text{Payback period} = \frac{\text{Investment required}}{\text{Net annual cash inflow}}$$

$$= \frac{\$2,400,00}{\$500,000}$$

$$= 4.8 \text{ years}$$

4. The formula for the simple rate of return is:

$$\text{Simple rate of return} = \frac{\text{Annual incremental net operating income}}{\text{Initial investment}}$$

$$= \frac{\$200,000}{\$2,400,000}$$

$$= 8.3\%$$

GLOSSARY

Capital budgeting   The process of planning significant investments in projects that have long-term implications such as the purchase of new equipment or the introduction of a new product. (p. 496)

Cost of capital   The average rate of return the company must pay to its long-term creditors and shareholders for the use of their funds. (p. 501)

Internal rate of return   The discount rate at which the net present value of an investment project is zero; the return promised by a project over its useful life. (p. 509)

Net present value   The difference between the present value of an investment project's cash inflows and the present value of its cash outflows. (p. 498)

Out-of-pocket costs   Actual cash outlays for salaries, advertising, repairs, and similar costs. (p. 503)

Payback period   The length of time that it takes for a project to fully recover its initial cost out of the net cash inflows that it generates. (p. 509)

Postaudit   The follow-up after a project has been approved and implemented to determine whether expected results are actually realized. (p. 515)

Preference decision   A decision in which the alternatives must be ranked in order of desirability. (p. 497)

Project profitability index   The ratio of the net present value of a project's cash flows to the investment required. (p. 508)

Screening decision   A decision as to whether a proposed investment project is acceptable. (p. 497)

Simple rate of return   The rate of return computed by dividing a project's annual incremental accounting net operating income by the initial investment required. (p. 513)

Working capital   Current assets less current liabilities. (p. 500)

APPENDIX 12A: THE CONCEPT OF PRESENT VALUE

> **LEARNING OBJECTIVE 5**
>
> Understand present value concepts and the use of present value tables.

A dollar received today is more valuable than a dollar received a year from now for the simple reason that if you have a dollar today, you can put it in the bank and have more than a dollar a year from now. Since dollars today are worth more than dollars in the future, cash flows that are received at different times must be weighted differently.

The Mathematics of Interest

If a bank pays 5% interest, then a deposit of $100 today will be worth $105 one year from now. This can be expressed as follows:

$$F_1 = P(1 + r) \tag{1}$$

where F_1 = the balance at the end of one period, P = the amount invested now, and r = the rate of interest per period.

In the case where $100 is deposited in a savings account that earns 5% interest, $P = \$100$ and $r = 0.05$. Under these conditions, $F_1 = \$105$.

The $100 present outlay is called the **present value** of the $105 amount to be received in one year. It is also known as the *discounted value* of the future $105 receipt. The $100 represents the value in present terms of $105 to be received a year from now when the interest rate is 5%.

Compound Interest   What if the $105 is left in the bank for a second year? In that case, by the end of the second year the original $100 deposit will have grown to $110.25:

Original deposit	$100.00
Interest for the first year: $100 × 0.05	5.00
Balance at the end of the first year	105.00
Interest for the second year: $105 × 0.05	5.25
Balance at the end of the second year	$110.25

Notice that the interest for the second year is $5.25, as compared to only $5.00 for the first year. This difference arises because interest is being paid on interest during the second year. That is, the $5.00 interest earned during the first year has been left in the account and has been added to the original $100 deposit when computing interest for the second year. This is known as **compound interest.** In this case, the compounding is annual. Interest can be compounded on a semiannual, quarterly, monthly, or even more frequent basis. The more frequently compounding is done, the more rapidly the balance will grow.

We can determine the balance in an account after n periods of compounding using the following equation:

$$F_n = P(1 + r)^n \qquad\qquad (2)$$

where n = the number of periods of compounding.

If $n = 2$ years and the interest rate is 5% per year, then the balance in two years will be computed as follows:

$$F_2 = \$100(1 + 0.05)^2$$

$$F_2 = \$110.25$$

Present Value and Future Value   Exhibit 12A–1 shows the relationship between present value and future value. As shown in the exhibit, if $100 is deposited in a bank at 5% interest compounded annually, it will grow to $127.63 by the end of five years.

Computation of Present Value

An investment can be viewed in two ways—either in terms of its future value or in terms of its present value. We have seen from our computations above that if we know the present value of a sum (such as our $100 deposit), the future value in n years can be computed by using equation (1). But what if the situation is reversed and we know the *future* value of some amount but we do not know its present value?

For example, assume that you are to receive $200 two years from now. You know that the future value of this sum is $200 because this is the amount that you will be receiving in two years. But what is the sum's present value—what is it worth *right now*? The present value of any sum to be received in the future can be computed by turning equation (2)

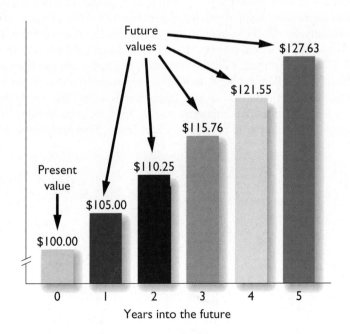

EXHIBIT 12A–1
The Relationship between Present Value and Future Value

around and solving for P:

$$P = \frac{F_n}{(1 + r)^n} \qquad (3)$$

In our example, $F_n = \$200$ (the amount to be received in the future), $r = 0.05$ (the annual rate of interest), and $n = 2$ (the number of years in the future that the amount will be received).

$$P = \frac{\$200}{(1 + 0.05)^2}$$

$$P = \frac{\$200}{(1.1025)}$$

$$P = \$181.40$$

As shown by the computation above, the present value of a $200 amount to be received two years from now is $181.40 if the interest rate is 5%. In effect, $181.40 received *right now* is equivalent to $200 received two years from now.

The process of finding the present value of a future cash flow, which we have just completed, is called **discounting.** We have *discounted* the $200 to its present value of $181.40. The 5% interest that we used to find this present value is called the **discount rate.** Discounting a future sum to its present value is a common practice in business, particularly in capital budgeting decisions.

If you have a power key (y^x) on your calculator, the above calculations are fairly easy. However, some of the present value formulas we will be using are more complex. Fortunately, tables are available in which many of the calculations have already been done for you. For example, Exhibit 12B–1 in Appendix 12B shows the discounted present value of $1 to be received at various periods in the future at various interest rates. The table indicates that the present value of $1 to be received two periods from now at 5% is 0.907. In our example, we want to know the present value of $200 rather than just $1; therefore, we need to multiply the factor in the table by $200:

$$\$200 \times 0.907 = \$181.40$$

This answer is the same as we obtained earlier using the formula in equation (3).

Present Value of a Series of Cash Flows

Although some investments involve a single sum to be received (or paid) at a single point in the future, other investments involve a *series* of cash flows. A series of identical cash flows is known as an **annuity.** For example, assume that a company has just purchased some government bonds. The bonds will yield interest of $15,000 at the end of each year and will be held for five years. What is the present value of the stream of interest receipts from the bonds? As shown in Exhibit 12A–2, if the discount rate is 12%, the present value of this stream is $54,075. The discount factors used in this exhibit were taken from Exhibit 12B–1 in Appendix 12B.

Exhibit 12A–2 illustrates two important points. First, the present value of the $15,000 interest declines the further it is received in the future. The present value of $15,000

EXHIBIT 12A–2
Present Value of a Series of Cash Receipts

Year	Factor at 12% (Table 12B–1) (a)	Interest Received (b)	Present Value (a) × (b)
1	0.893	$15,000	$13,395
2	0.797	$15,000	11,955
3	0.712	$15,000	10,680
4	0.636	$15,000	9,540
5	0.567	$15,000	8,505
			$54,075

received a year from now is $13,395, as compared to only $8,505 if received five years from now. This point simply underscores the time value of money.

The second point is that the computations in Exhibit 12A–2 involved unnecessary work. The same present value of $54,075 could have been obtained more easily by referring to Exhibit 12B–2 in Appendix 12B. Exhibit 12B–2 contains the present value of $1 to be received each year over a *series* of years at various interest rates. Exhibit 12B–2 has been derived by simply adding together the factors from Exhibit 12B–1, as follows:

Year	Exhibit 12B–1 Factors at 12%
1	0.893
2	0.797
3	0.712
4	0.636
5	0.567
	3.605

The sum of the five factors above is 3.605. Notice from Exhibit 12B–2 that the factor for $1 to be received at the end of each year for five years at 12% is also 3.605. If we use this factor and multiply it by the $15,000 annual cash inflow, then we get the same $54,075 present value that we obtained earlier in Exhibit 12A–2:

$$\$15,000 \times 3.605 = \$54,075$$

Therefore, when computing the present value of a series of equal cash flows that begins at the end of period 1, Exhibit 12B–2 should be used.

To summarize, the present value tables in Appendix 12B should be used as follows:

Exhibit 12B–1: This table should be used to find the present value of a single cash flow (such as a single payment or receipt) occurring at the end of a specified number of periods.

Exhibit 12B–2: This table should be used to find the present value of a series of identical cash flows beginning at the end of the current period and continuing at the end of each subsequent period until a specified period.

The use of both of these tables is illustrated in various exhibits in the main body of the chapter. *When a present value factor appears in an exhibit, you should take the time to trace it back into either Exhibit 12B–1 or Exhibit 12B–2 to get acquainted with the tables and how they work.*

SUMMARY OF APPENDIX 12A

LO5   (Appendix 12A) Understand present value concepts and the use of present value tables.
A dollar received today is more valuable than a dollar received a year from now because the dollar received today can be put in the bank to earn interest; therefore, it will be worth more than a dollar a year from now.

The tables shown in Appendix 12B simplify the process of computing the present and future value of cash flows. They summarize the factors used to discount a single sum or annuity received in the future to its present value and the factors used to translate a single sum or annuity to its future value.

GLOSSARY (APPENDIX 12A)

Annuity   A series of identical cash flows. (p. 522)
Compound interest   The process of paying interest on interest in an investment. (p. 521)
Discount rate   The rate of return that is used to find the present value of a future cash flow. (p. 522)
Discounting   The process of finding the present value of a future cash flow. (p. 522)
Present value   The value now of an amount that will be received in some future period. (p. 520)

EXHIBIT 12B-1 Present Value of $1. $P_n = \dfrac{1}{(1+r)^n}$

Periods	4%	5%	6%	7%	8%	9%	10%	11%	12%	13%	14%	15%	16%	17%	18%	19%	20%	21%	22%	23%	24%	25%
1	0.962	0.952	0.943	0.935	0.926	0.917	0.909	0.901	0.893	0.885	0.877	0.870	0.862	0.855	0.847	0.840	0.833	0.826	0.820	0.813	0.806	0.800
2	0.925	0.907	0.890	0.873	0.857	0.842	0.826	0.812	0.797	0.783	0.769	0.756	0.743	0.731	0.718	0.706	0.694	0.683	0.672	0.661	0.650	0.640
3	0.889	0.864	0.840	0.816	0.794	0.772	0.751	0.731	0.712	0.693	0.675	0.658	0.641	0.624	0.609	0.593	0.579	0.564	0.551	0.537	0.524	0.512
4	0.855	0.823	0.792	0.763	0.735	0.708	0.683	0.659	0.636	0.613	0.592	0.572	0.552	0.534	0.516	0.499	0.482	0.467	0.451	0.437	0.423	0.410
5	0.822	0.784	0.747	0.713	0.681	0.650	0.621	0.593	0.567	0.543	0.519	0.497	0.476	0.456	0.437	0.419	0.402	0.386	0.370	0.355	0.341	0.328
6	0.790	0.746	0.705	0.666	0.630	0.596	0.564	0.535	0.507	0.480	0.456	0.432	0.410	0.390	0.370	0.352	0.335	0.319	0.303	0.289	0.275	0.262
7	0.760	0.711	0.665	0.623	0.583	0.547	0.513	0.482	0.452	0.425	0.400	0.376	0.354	0.333	0.314	0.296	0.279	0.263	0.249	0.235	0.222	0.210
8	0.731	0.677	0.627	0.582	0.540	0.502	0.467	0.434	0.404	0.376	0.351	0.327	0.305	0.285	0.266	0.249	0.233	0.218	0.204	0.191	0.179	0.168
9	0.703	0.645	0.592	0.544	0.500	0.460	0.424	0.391	0.361	0.333	0.308	0.284	0.263	0.243	0.225	0.209	0.194	0.180	0.167	0.155	0.144	0.134
10	0.676	0.614	0.558	0.508	0.463	0.422	0.386	0.352	0.322	0.295	0.270	0.247	0.227	0.208	0.191	0.176	0.162	0.149	0.137	0.126	0.116	0.107
11	0.650	0.585	0.527	0.475	0.429	0.388	0.350	0.317	0.287	0.261	0.237	0.215	0.195	0.178	0.162	0.148	0.135	0.123	0.112	0.103	0.094	0.086
12	0.625	0.557	0.497	0.444	0.397	0.356	0.319	0.286	0.257	0.231	0.208	0.187	0.168	0.152	0.137	0.124	0.112	0.102	0.092	0.083	0.076	0.069
13	0.601	0.530	0.469	0.415	0.368	0.326	0.290	0.258	0.229	0.204	0.182	0.163	0.145	0.130	0.116	0.104	0.093	0.084	0.075	0.068	0.061	0.055
14	0.577	0.505	0.442	0.388	0.340	0.299	0.263	0.232	0.205	0.181	0.160	0.141	0.125	0.111	0.099	0.088	0.078	0.069	0.062	0.055	0.049	0.044
15	0.555	0.481	0.417	0.362	0.315	0.275	0.239	0.209	0.183	0.160	0.140	0.123	0.108	0.095	0.084	0.074	0.065	0.057	0.051	0.045	0.040	0.035
16	0.534	0.458	0.394	0.339	0.292	0.252	0.218	0.188	0.163	0.141	0.123	0.107	0.093	0.081	0.071	0.062	0.054	0.047	0.042	0.036	0.032	0.028
17	0.513	0.436	0.371	0.317	0.270	0.231	0.198	0.170	0.146	0.125	0.108	0.093	0.080	0.069	0.060	0.052	0.045	0.039	0.034	0.030	0.026	0.023
18	0.494	0.416	0.350	0.296	0.250	0.212	0.180	0.153	0.130	0.111	0.095	0.081	0.069	0.059	0.051	0.044	0.038	0.032	0.028	0.024	0.021	0.018
19	0.475	0.396	0.331	0.277	0.232	0.194	0.164	0.138	0.116	0.098	0.083	0.070	0.060	0.051	0.043	0.037	0.031	0.027	0.023	0.020	0.017	0.014
20	0.456	0.377	0.312	0.258	0.215	0.178	0.149	0.124	0.104	0.087	0.073	0.061	0.051	0.043	0.037	0.031	0.026	0.022	0.019	0.016	0.014	0.012
21	0.439	0.359	0.294	0.242	0.199	0.164	0.135	0.112	0.093	0.077	0.064	0.053	0.044	0.037	0.031	0.026	0.022	0.018	0.015	0.013	0.011	0.009
22	0.422	0.342	0.278	0.226	0.184	0.150	0.123	0.101	0.083	0.068	0.056	0.046	0.038	0.032	0.026	0.022	0.018	0.015	0.013	0.011	0.009	0.007
23	0.406	0.326	0.262	0.211	0.170	0.138	0.112	0.091	0.074	0.060	0.049	0.040	0.033	0.027	0.022	0.018	0.015	0.012	0.010	0.009	0.007	0.006
24	0.390	0.310	0.247	0.197	0.158	0.126	0.102	0.082	0.066	0.053	0.043	0.035	0.028	0.023	0.019	0.015	0.013	0.010	0.008	0.007	0.006	0.005
25	0.375	0.295	0.233	0.184	0.146	0.116	0.092	0.074	0.059	0.047	0.038	0.030	0.024	0.020	0.016	0.013	0.010	0.009	0.007	0.006	0.005	0.004
26	0.361	0.281	0.220	0.172	0.135	0.106	0.084	0.066	0.053	0.042	0.033	0.026	0.021	0.017	0.014	0.011	0.009	0.007	0.006	0.005	0.004	0.003
27	0.347	0.268	0.207	0.161	0.125	0.098	0.076	0.060	0.047	0.037	0.029	0.023	0.018	0.014	0.011	0.009	0.007	0.006	0.005	0.004	0.003	0.002
28	0.333	0.255	0.196	0.150	0.116	0.090	0.069	0.054	0.042	0.033	0.026	0.020	0.016	0.012	0.010	0.008	0.006	0.005	0.004	0.003	0.002	0.002
29	0.321	0.243	0.185	0.141	0.107	0.082	0.063	0.048	0.037	0.029	0.022	0.017	0.014	0.011	0.008	0.006	0.005	0.004	0.003	0.002	0.002	0.002
30	0.308	0.231	0.174	0.131	0.099	0.075	0.057	0.044	0.033	0.026	0.020	0.015	0.012	0.009	0.007	0.005	0.004	0.003	0.003	0.002	0.002	0.001
40	0.208	0.142	0.097	0.067	0.046	0.032	0.022	0.015	0.011	0.008	0.005	0.004	0.003	0.002	0.001	0.001	0.001	0.000	0.000	0.000	0.000	0.000

EXHIBIT 12B-2 Present Value of an Annuity of $1 in Arrears. $P_n = \dfrac{1}{r}\left[1 - \dfrac{1}{(1+r)^n}\right]$

Periods	4%	5%	6%	7%	8%	9%	10%	11%	12%	13%	14%	15%	16%	17%	18%	19%	20%	21%	22%	23%	24%	25%
1	0.962	0.952	0.943	0.935	0.926	0.917	0.909	0.901	0.893	0.885	0.877	0.870	0.862	0.855	0.847	0.840	0.833	0.826	0.820	0.813	0.806	0.800
2	1.886	1.859	1.833	1.808	1.783	1.759	1.736	1.713	1.690	1.668	1.647	1.626	1.605	1.585	1.566	1.547	1.528	1.509	1.492	1.474	1.457	1.440
3	2.775	2.723	2.673	2.624	2.577	2.531	2.487	2.444	2.402	2.361	2.322	2.283	2.246	2.210	2.174	2.140	2.106	2.074	2.042	2.011	1.981	1.952
4	3.630	3.546	3.465	3.387	3.312	3.240	3.170	3.102	3.037	2.974	2.914	2.855	2.798	2.743	2.690	2.639	2.589	2.540	2.494	2.448	2.404	2.362
5	4.452	4.329	4.212	4.100	3.993	3.890	3.791	3.696	3.605	3.517	3.433	3.352	3.274	3.199	3.127	3.058	2.991	2.926	2.864	2.803	2.745	2.689
6	5.242	5.076	4.917	4.767	4.623	4.486	4.355	4.231	4.111	3.998	3.889	3.784	3.685	3.589	3.498	3.410	3.326	3.245	3.167	3.092	3.020	2.951
7	6.002	5.786	5.582	5.389	5.206	5.033	4.868	4.712	4.564	4.423	4.288	4.160	4.039	3.922	3.812	3.706	3.605	3.508	3.416	3.327	3.242	3.161
8	6.733	6.463	6.210	5.971	5.747	5.535	5.335	5.146	4.968	4.799	4.639	4.487	4.344	4.207	4.078	3.954	3.837	3.726	3.619	3.518	3.421	3.329
9	7.435	7.108	6.802	6.515	6.247	5.995	5.759	5.537	5.328	5.132	4.946	4.772	4.607	4.451	4.303	4.163	4.031	3.905	3.786	3.673	3.566	3.463
10	8.111	7.722	7.360	7.024	6.710	6.418	6.145	5.889	5.650	5.426	5.216	5.019	4.833	4.659	4.494	4.339	4.192	4.054	3.923	3.799	3.682	3.571
11	8.760	8.306	7.887	7.499	7.139	6.805	6.495	6.207	5.938	5.687	5.453	5.234	5.029	4.836	4.656	4.486	4.327	4.177	4.035	3.902	3.776	3.656
12	9.385	8.863	8.384	7.943	7.536	7.161	6.814	6.492	6.194	5.918	5.660	5.421	5.197	4.988	4.793	4.611	4.439	4.278	4.127	3.985	3.851	3.725
13	9.986	9.394	8.853	8.358	7.904	7.487	7.103	6.750	6.424	6.122	5.842	5.583	5.342	5.118	4.910	4.715	4.533	4.362	4.203	4.053	3.912	3.780
14	10.563	9.899	9.295	8.745	8.244	7.786	7.367	6.982	6.628	6.302	6.002	5.724	5.468	5.229	5.008	4.802	4.611	4.432	4.265	4.108	3.962	3.824
15	11.118	10.380	9.712	9.108	8.559	8.061	7.606	7.191	6.811	6.462	6.142	5.847	5.575	5.324	5.092	4.876	4.675	4.489	4.315	4.153	4.001	3.859
16	11.652	10.838	10.106	9.447	8.851	8.313	7.824	7.379	6.974	6.604	6.265	5.954	5.668	5.405	5.162	4.938	4.730	4.536	4.357	4.189	4.033	3.887
17	12.166	11.274	10.477	9.763	9.122	8.544	8.022	7.549	7.120	6.729	6.373	6.047	5.749	5.475	5.222	4.990	4.775	4.576	4.391	4.219	4.059	3.910
18	12.659	11.690	10.828	10.059	9.372	8.756	8.201	7.702	7.250	6.840	6.467	6.128	5.818	5.534	5.273	5.033	4.812	4.608	4.419	4.243	4.080	3.928
19	13.134	12.085	11.158	10.336	9.604	8.950	8.365	7.839	7.366	6.938	6.550	6.198	5.877	5.584	5.316	5.070	4.843	4.635	4.442	4.263	4.097	3.942
20	13.590	12.462	11.470	10.594	9.818	9.129	8.514	7.963	7.469	7.025	6.623	6.259	5.929	5.628	5.353	5.101	4.870	4.657	4.460	4.279	4.110	3.954
21	14.029	12.821	11.764	10.836	10.017	9.292	8.649	8.075	7.562	7.102	6.687	6.312	5.973	5.665	5.384	5.127	4.891	4.675	4.476	4.292	4.121	3.963
22	14.451	13.163	12.042	11.061	10.201	9.442	8.772	8.176	7.645	7.170	6.743	6.359	6.011	5.696	5.410	5.149	4.909	4.690	4.488	4.302	4.130	3.970
23	14.857	13.489	12.303	11.272	10.371	9.580	8.883	8.266	7.718	7.230	6.792	6.399	6.044	5.723	5.432	5.167	4.925	4.703	4.499	4.311	4.137	3.976
24	15.247	13.799	12.550	11.469	10.529	9.707	8.985	8.348	7.784	7.283	6.835	6.434	6.073	5.746	5.451	5.182	4.937	4.713	4.507	4.318	4.143	3.981
25	15.622	14.094	12.783	11.654	10.675	9.823	9.077	8.422	7.843	7.330	6.873	6.464	6.097	5.766	5.467	5.195	4.948	4.721	4.514	4.323	4.147	3.985
26	15.983	14.375	13.003	11.826	10.810	9.929	9.161	8.488	7.896	7.372	6.906	6.491	6.118	5.783	5.480	5.206	4.956	4.728	4.520	4.328	4.151	3.988
27	16.330	14.643	13.211	11.987	10.935	10.027	9.237	8.548	7.943	7.409	6.935	6.514	6.136	5.798	5.492	5.215	4.964	4.734	4.524	4.332	4.154	3.990
28	16.663	14.898	13.406	12.137	11.051	10.116	9.307	8.602	7.984	7.441	6.961	6.534	6.152	5.810	5.502	5.223	4.970	4.739	4.528	4.335	4.157	3.992
29	16.984	15.141	13.591	12.278	11.158	10.198	9.370	8.650	8.022	7.470	6.983	6.551	6.166	5.820	5.510	5.229	4.975	4.743	4.531	4.337	4.159	3.994
30	17.292	15.372	13.765	12.409	11.258	10.274	9.427	8.694	8.055	7.496	7.003	6.566	6.177	5.829	5.517	5.235	4.979	4.746	4.534	4.339	4.160	3.995
40	19.793	17.159	15.046	13.332	11.925	10.757	9.779	8.951	8.244	7.634	7.105	6.642	6.233	5.871	5.548	5.258	4.997	4.760	4.544	4.347	4.166	3.999

QUESTIONS

12–1   What is the difference between capital budgeting screening decisions and capital budgeting preference decisions?

12–2   What is meant by the term *time value of money*?

12–3   What is meant by the term *discounting*?

12–4   Why is the net present value method of making capital budgeting decisions superior to other methods such as the payback and simple rate of return methods?

12–5   What is net present value? Can it ever be negative? Explain.

12–6   If a company has to pay interest of 14% on long-term debt, then its cost of capital is 14%. Do you agree? Explain.

12–7   What is meant by an investment project's internal rate of return? How is the internal rate of return computed?

12–8   Explain how the cost of capital serves as a screening tool when dealing with the net present value method.

12–9   As the discount rate increases, the present value of a given future cash flow also increases. Do you agree? Explain.

12–10 Refer to Exhibit 12–2. Is the return on this investment proposal exactly 14%, more than 14%, or less than 14%? Explain.

12–11 Why are preference decisions sometimes called *rationing* decisions?

12–12 How is the project profitability index computed, and what does it measure?

12–13 What is meant by the term *payback period*? How is the payback period determined?

12–14 How can the payback method be useful to managers?

12–15 What is the major criticism of the payback and simple rate of return methods of making capital budgeting decisions?

Quiz 12   Multiple-choice questions are provided on the text website at www.mhhe.com/brewer4e.

BRIEF EXERCISES

BRIEF EXERCISE 12–1   Net Present Value Method (LO1)

The management of Opry Company, a wholesale distributor of suntan products, is considering the purchase of a $25,000 machine that would reduce operating costs by $4,000 per year. At the end of the machine's 10-year useful life, it will have zero salvage value. The company's required rate of return is 14% on all investment projects.

Required:

1. Determine the net present value of the investment in the machine.
2. What is the difference between the total, undiscounted, cash inflows and cash outflows over the entire life of the machine?

BRIEF EXERCISE 12–2   Net Present Value Analysis of Competing Projects (LO2)

Service Temps, a company that supplies temporary workers for restaurants and other service industries, has $15,000 to invest. Management is trying to decide between two alternative uses for the funds as follows:

	Invest in Project A	Invest in Project B
Investment required	$15,000	$15,000
Annual cash inflows	$4,000	$0
Single cash inflow at the end of 10 years.	—	$60,000
Life of the project	10 years	10 years

The company's discount rate is 16%.

Required:

Which alternative would you recommend that the company accept? Show all computations using the net present value approach. Prepare a separate computation for each project.

BRIEF EXERCISE 12–3 Project Profitability Index (LO2)

Information on four investment proposals at El Torrito, a chain of Mexican restaurants, is given below:

	Investment Proposal			
	A	B	C	D
Investment required.	$(85,000)	$(200,000)	$(90,000)	$(170,000)
Present value of cash inflows	119,000	250,000	135,000	221,000
Net present value	$ 34,000	$ 50,000	$ 45,000	$ 51,000
Life of the project.	5 years	7 years	6 years	6 years

Required:
1. Compute the project profitability index for each investment proposal.
2. Rank the proposals in terms of preference.

BRIEF EXERCISE 12–4 Payback Method (LO3)

The management of Weimar Inc., a civil engineering design company, is considering an investment in a high-quality blueprint printer with the following cash flows:

Year	Investment	Cash Inflow
1.	$38,000	$2,000
2.	$6,000	$4,000
3.		$8,000
4.		$9,000
5.		$12,000
6.		$10,000
7.		$8,000
8.		$6,000
9.		$5,000
10.		$5,000

Required:
1. Determine the payback period of the investment.
2. Would the payback period be affected if the cash inflow in the last year were several times as large? Explain.

BRIEF EXERCISE 12–5 Simple Rate of Return Method (LO4)

The management of Wallingford MicroBrew is considering the purchase of an automated bottling machine for $80,000. The machine would replace an old piece of equipment that costs $33,000 per year to operate. The new machine would cost $10,000 per year to operate. The old machine currently in use could be sold now for a salvage value of $5,000. The new machine would have a useful life of 10 years with no salvage value.

Required:
Compute the simple rate of return on the new automated bottling machine.

BRIEF EXERCISE 12–6 (Appendix 12A) Basic Present Value Concepts (LO5)

Solve each of the following parts independently.

1. Largo Freightlines plans to build a new garage in three years to have more space for repairing its trucks. The garage will cost $400,000. What lump-sum amount should the company invest now to have the $400,000 available at the end of the three-year period? Assume that the company can invest money at:
   a. Eight percent.
   b. Twelve percent.
2. Martell Products, Inc., can purchase a new copier that will save $5,000 per year in copying costs. The copier will last for six years and have no salvage value. Up to how much should Martell Products be willing to pay for the copier if the company's required rate of return is:
   a. Ten percent.
   b. Sixteen percent.

3. Sally has just won the million-dollar Big Slam jackpot at a gambling casino. The casino will pay her $50,000 per year for 20 years as the payoff. If Sally can invest money at a 10% rate of return, what is the present value of her winnings? Did she really win a million dollars? Explain.

EXERCISES

EXERCISE 12–7   Basic Net Present Value Analysis (LO1)

On January 2, Fred Critchfield paid $18,000 for 900 shares of the common stock of Acme Company. Mr. Critchfield received an $0.80 per share dividend on the stock at the end of each year for four years. At the end of four years, he sold the stock for $22,500. Mr. Critchfield has a goal of earning a minimum return of 12% on all of his investments.

Required:

Did Mr. Critchfield earn a 12% return on the stock? Use the net present value method. (Round all computations to the nearest whole dollar.)

EXERCISE 12–8   Project Profitability Index (LO2)

Lake Union Yacht Brokers is investigating four different investment opportunities. Information on the four projects under study follows:

	Project Number			
	1	2	3	4
Investment required	$(480,000)	$(360,000)	$(270,000)	$(450,000)
Present value of cash inflows at a 10% discount rate.	567,270	433,400	336,140	522,970
Net present value.	$ 87,270	$ 73,400	$ 66,140	$ 72,970
Life of the project	6 years	12 years	6 years	3 years

The company's required rate of return is 10%; thus, a 10% discount rate has been used in the present value computations above. Limited funds are available for investment, so the company can't accept all of the available projects.

Required:

1. Compute the project profitability index for each investment project.
2. Rank the four projects according to preference, in terms of:
   a.   Net present value.
   b.   Project profitability index.
3. Which ranking do you prefer? Why?

EXERCISE 12–9   Payback and Simple Rate of Return Methods (LO3, LO4)

Martin Landscaping Company is considering the purchase of a new piece of equipment for laying sprinkler systems. Relevant information concerning the equipment follows:

Purchase cost of the equipment	$180,000
Annual cost savings that will be provided by the equipment	$37,500
Life of the equipment	12 years

Required:

1. Compute the payback period for the equipment. If the company requires a payback period of four years or less, would the equipment be purchased?
2. Compute the simple rate of return on the equipment. Use straight-line depreciation based on the equipment's useful life. Would the equipment be purchased if the company's required rate of return is 14%?

EXERCISE 12–10 Basic Net Present Value Analysis (LO1)

Renfree Mines, Inc., owns the mining rights to a large tract of land in a mountainous area. The tract contains a mineral deposit that the company believes might be commercially attractive to mine and sell. An engineering and cost analysis has been completed, and it indicates that the following cash flows would be associated with opening and operating a mine in the area:

Cost of new equipment	$850,000
Net annual cash receipts	$230,000*
Working capital required	$100,000
Cost of road repairs in three years...............	$60,000
Salvage value of equipment in five years...........	$200,000

*Receipts from sales of ore, less out-of-pocket costs for salaries, utilities, insurance, and so forth.

It is estimated that the mineral deposit would be exhausted after five years of mining. At that point, the working capital would be released for reinvestment elsewhere. The company's required rate of return is 14%.

Required:

Determine the net present value of the proposed mining project. Should the project be accepted? Explain.

EXERCISE 12–11 Net Present Value Analysis of Competing Projects (LO2)

Wriston Legacies, a retailer of fine estate jewelry, has $300,000 to invest. The company is trying to decide between two alternative uses of the funds. The alternatives are:

	Project A	Project B
Cost of equipment required	$300,000	$0
Working capital investment required	$0	$300,000
Annual cash inflows	$80,000	$60,000
Salvage value of equipment in seven years......	$20,000	$0
Life of the project	7 years	7 years

The working capital needed for project B will be released for investment elsewhere at the end of seven years. Wriston Legacies uses a 20% discount rate.

Required:

Which investment alternative (if either) would you recommend that the company accept? Show all computations using the net present value method. Prepare separate computations for each project.

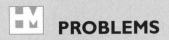 **PROBLEMS**

PROBLEM 12–12A Basic Net Present Value Analysis (LO1)

The Confectioner's Corner Inc. would like to buy a new machine that automatically dips chocolates. The dipping operation is currently done largely by hand. The machine the company is considering costs $100,000. The machine would be usable for 10 years but would require the replacement of several key parts at the end of the fifth year. These parts would cost $7,000, including installation. After 10 years, the machine could be sold for $6,000.

CHECK FIGURE
(2) $28,638 net present value

The company estimates that the cost to operate the machine will be $6,500 per year. The present method of dipping chocolates costs $24,000 per year. In addition to reducing costs, the new machine will increase production by 5,500 boxes of chocolates per year. The company realizes a contribution margin of $2.10 per box. An 18% rate of return is required on all investments.

Required:

1. What are the net annual cash inflows that will be provided by the new dipping machine?
2. Compute the new machine's net present value. Use the incremental cost approach and round all dollar amounts to the nearest whole dollar.

PROBLEM 12–13A   Ranking of Projects (LO2)

Oxford Company has limited funds available for investment and must ration the funds among four competing projects. Selected information on the four projects follows:

Project	Investment Required	Net Present Value	Life of the Project (years)
A......................	$140,000	$42,000	8
B......................	$190,000	$49,400	14
C......................	$175,000	$49,000	9
D......................	$138,000	$31,740	3

The company wants your assistance in ranking the desirability of the projects.

Required:

1. Compute the project profitability index for each project.
2. In order of preference, rank the four projects in terms of:
   a.   Net present value
   b.   Project profitability index
3. Which ranking do you prefer? Why?

PROBLEM 12–14A   Net Present Value; Total and Incremental Approaches (LO1)

San Jose Flights, S.A., of Panama, has a small truck that it uses for intracity deliveries. The truck is worn
out and must be either overhauled or replaced with a new truck. The company has assembled the following
information (Panama uses the U.S. dollar as its currency):

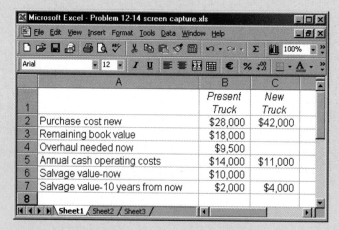

	Present Truck	New Truck
2 Purchase cost new	$28,000	$42,000
3 Remaining book value	$18,000	
4 Overhaul needed now	$9,500	
5 Annual cash operating costs	$14,000	$11,000
6 Salvage value-now	$10,000	
7 Salvage value-10 years from now	$2,000	$4,000

If the company keeps and overhauls its present delivery truck, then the truck will be usable for 10
more years. If a new truck is purchased, it will be used for 10 years, after which it will be traded in on
another truck. The new truck would be diesel operated, resulting in a substantial reduction in annual operating costs, as shown above.

The company computes depreciation on a straight-line basis. All investment projects are evaluated
using a 16% discount rate.

Required:

1. Should San Jose Flights, S.A., keep the old truck or purchase the new one? Use the total-cost
   approach to net present value in making your decision. Round to the nearest whole dollar.
2. Redo (1) above, this time using the incremental-cost approach.

PROBLEM 12–15A   Net Present Value Analysis (LO1)

In 10 years, Jerry Cantrell will retire. He is exploring the possibility of opening a self-service car wash.
The car wash could be managed in the free time he has available from his regular occupation, and it could
be closed easily when he retires. After careful study, Jerry has determined the following:

a.   A building in which a car wash could be installed is available under a 10-year lease at a cost of
     $1,200 per month.
b.   Purchase and installation costs of equipment would total $110,000. In 10 years the equipment could
     be sold for 10% of its original cost.

c. An investment of an additional $1,800 would be required to cover working capital needs for cleaning supplies, change funds, and so forth. After 10 years, this working capital would be released for investment elsewhere.

d. Both an auto wash and a vacuum service would be offered with a wash costing customers $1.50 and the vacuum costing them $0.25 per use.

e. The only variable costs associated with the operation would be $0.23 per wash for water and $0.10 per use of the vacuum for electricity.

f. In addition to rent, monthly costs of operation would be: cleaning, $780; insurance, $60; and maintenance, $510.

g. Gross receipts from the auto wash would be about $1,110 per week. According to the experience of other self-service car washes, 70% of the customers using the wash would also use the vacuum.

Jerry will not open the car wash unless it provides at least a 12% return.

Required:
1. Assuming that the car wash will be open 52 weeks a year, compute the expected annual net cash flow (gross cash receipts less cash disbursements) from its operation. (Do not include the cost of the equipment, the working capital, or the salvage value in these computations.)
2. Would you advise Jerry to open the car wash? Show computations using the net present value method. Round all dollar figures to the nearest whole dollar.

PROBLEM 12–16A Simple Rate of Return and Payback Methods (LO3, LO4)

Otthar's Amusement Center contains a number of electronic games as well as a miniature golf course and various rides located outside the building. Otthar Luvinson, the owner, would like to construct a water slide on one portion of his property. Otthar has gathered the following information about the slide:

a. Water slide equipment could be purchased and installed at a cost of $500,000. The slide would be usable for 10 years, after which it would have no salvage value.

b. Otthar would use straight-line depreciation on the slide equipment.

c. To make room for the water slide, several rides would be dismantled and sold. These rides are fully depreciated, but they could be sold for $40,000 to an amusement park in a nearby city.

d. Otthar has concluded that water slides would increase ticket sales by $320,000 per year.

e. On the basis of experience at other water slides, Otthar estimates that annual incremental operating expenses for the slide would be: salaries, $115,000; insurance, $28,200; utilities, $12,000; and maintenance, $32,000.

Required:
1. Prepare an income statement showing the expected net operating income each year from the water slide.
2. Compute the simple rate of return expected from the water slide. On the basis of this computation, would the water slide be constructed if Otthar requires a simple rate of return of at least 15% on all investments?
3. Compute the payback period for the water slide. If Otthar accepts any project with a payback period of 5 years or less, would the water slide be constructed?

PROBLEM 12–17A Keep or Sell Property (LO1)

Ben Ryatt, professor of languages at Southern University, owns a small office building adjacent to the university campus. He acquired the property 12 years ago at a total cost of $560,000—$52,000 for the land and $508,000 for the building. He has just received an offer from a realty company that wants to purchase the property; however, the property has been a good source of income over the years, so Professor Ryatt is unsure whether he should keep it or sell it. His alternatives are:

1. **Keep the property.** Professor Ryatt's accountant has kept careful records of the income realized from the property over the past 10 years. These records indicate the following annual revenues and expenses:

Rental receipts		$150,000
Less building expenses:		
Utilities	$28,600	
Depreciation of building	17,800	
Property taxes and insurance	19,500	
Repairs and maintenance	10,500	
Custodial help and supplies	43,500	119,900
Net operating income		$ 30,100

CHECK FIGURE
(2) 18.0% simple rate of return

CHECK FIGURE
PV of cash flows for the alternative of keeping the property: $251,543

Professor Ryatt makes a $12,600 mortgage payment each year on the property. The mortgage will be paid off in 10 more years. He has been depreciating the building by the straight-line method, assuming a salvage value of $9,600 for the building, which he still thinks is an appropriate figure. He feels sure that the building can be rented for another 16 years. He also feels sure that 16 years from now the land will be worth 2.5 times what he paid for it.

2. **Sell the property.** A realty company has offered to purchase the property by paying $150,000 immediately and $23,000 per year for the next 16 years. Control of the property would go to the realty company immediately. To sell the property, Professor Ryatt would need to pay the mortgage off, which could be done by making a lump-sum payment of $71,000.

Required:

Professor Ryatt requires a 14% rate of return. Would you recommend he keep or sell the property? Show computations using the total-cost approach to net present value.

CHECK FIGURE
(1) $6,760 NPV of
common stock

PROBLEM 12–18A   Net Present Value Analysis of Securities (LO1)

Anita Vasquez received $160,000 from her mother's estate. She placed the funds into the hands of a broker, who purchased the following securities on Anita's behalf:

a.   Common stock was purchased at a cost of $80,000. The stock paid no dividends, but it was sold for $180,000 at the end of 4 years.

b.   Preferred stock was purchased at its par value of $30,000. The stock paid a 6% dividend (based on par value) each year for 4 years. At the end of 4 years, the stock was sold for $24,000.

c.   Bonds were purchased at a cost of $50,000. The bonds paid $3,000 in interest every six months. After 4 years, the bonds were sold for $58,500. (Note: In discounting a cash flow that occurs semi-annually, the procedure is to halve the discount rate and double the number of periods. Use the same procedure in discounting the proceeds from the sale.)

The securities were all sold at the end of four years so that Anita would have funds available to start a new business venture. The broker stated that the investments had earned more than a 20% return, and he gave Anita the following computation to support his statement:

Common stock:	
Gain on sale ($180,000 − $80,000)...........	$100,000
Preferred stock:	
Dividends paid (6% × $30,000 × 4 years)......	7,200
Loss on sale ($24,000 − $30,000)............	(6,000)
Bonds:	
Interest paid ($3,000 × 8 periods)............	24,000
Gain on sale ($58,500 − $50,000)............	8,500
Net gain on all investments	$133,700

$$\frac{\$133,700 \div 4 \text{ years}}{\$160,000} = 20.9\%$$

Required:

1.   Using a 20% discount rate, compute the net present value of each of the three investments. On which investment(s) did Anita earn a 20% rate of return? (Round computations to the nearest whole dollar.)
2.   Considering all three investments together, did Anita earn a 20% rate of return? Explain.
3.   Anita wants to use the $262,500 proceeds ($180,000 + $24,000 + $58,500 = $262,500) from sale of the securities to open a fast-food franchise under a 10-year contract. What net annual cash inflow must the store generate for Anita to earn a 16% return over the 10-year period? Anita will not receive back her original investment at the end of the contract. (Round computations to the nearest whole dollar.)

CHECK FIGURE
(1b) 9.2% simple rate of
return

PROBLEM 12–19A   Simple Rate of Return and Payback Analysis of Two Machines (LO3, LO4)

Blue Ridge Furniture is considering the purchase of two different items of equipment, as described below:

1.   **Machine A.** A compacting machine has just come onto the market that would permit Blue Ridge Furniture to compress sawdust into various shelving products. At present the sawdust is disposed of as a waste product. The following information is available about the machine:

a.   The machine would cost $780,000 and would have a 25% salvage value at the end of its 10-year useful life. The company uses straight-line depreciation and considers salvage value in computing depreciation deductions.

b. The shelving products manufactured from use of the machine would generate revenues of $350,000 per year. Variable manufacturing costs would be 20% of sales.

c. Fixed expenses associated with the new shelving products would be (per year): advertising, $42,000; salaries, $86,000; utilities, $9,000; and insurance, $13,000.

2. **Machine B.** A second machine has come onto the market that would allow Blue Ridge Furniture to automate a sanding process that is now done largely by hand. The following information is available:

a. The new sanding machine would cost $220,000 and would have no salvage value at the end of its 10-year useful life. The company would use straight-line depreciation on the new machine.

b. Several old pieces of sanding equipment that are fully depreciated would be disposed of at a salvage value of $7,200.

c. The new sanding machine would provide substantial annual savings in cash operating costs. It would require an operator at an annual salary of $26,000 and $3,000 in annual maintenance costs. The current, hand-operated sanding procedure costs the company $85,000 per year in total.

Blue Ridge Furniture requires a simple rate of return of 16% on all equipment purchases. Also, the company will not purchase equipment unless the equipment has a payback period of 4 years or less.

Required:

1. For machine A:
    a. Prepare a contribution format income statement showing the expected net operating income each year from the new shelving products.
    b. Compute the simple rate of return.
    c. Compute the payback period.

2. For machine B:
    a. Compute the simple rate of return.
    b. Compute the payback period

3. According to the company's criteria, which machine, if either, should the company purchase?

BUILDING YOUR SKILLS

COMMUNICATING IN PRACTICE   (LO1, LO3, LO4)

Use an online yellow pages directory to find a manufacturer in your area that has a website. Make an appointment with the controller or chief financial officer of the company. Before your meeting, find out as much as you can about the organization's operations from its website.

Required:

After asking the following questions about a capital budgeting decision that was made by the management of the company, write a brief memorandum to your instructor that summarizes the information obtained from the company's website and addresses what you found out during your interview.

1. What was the nature of the capital project?
2. What was the total cost of the capital project?
3. Did the project costs stay within budget (or estimate)?
4. What financial criteria were used to evaluate the project?

TEAMWORK IN ACTION   (LO1)

Woolrich Company's market research division has projected a substantial increase in demand over the next several years for one of the company's products. To meet this demand, the company will need to produce units as follows:

CHECK FIGURE
(1) $24,640 NPV in favor of the model 5200 machine

Year	Production in Units
1	20,000
2	30,000
3	40,000
4–10	45,000

At present, the company is using a single model 2600 machine to manufacture this product. To increase its productive capacity, the company is considering two alternatives:

Alternative 1. The company could purchase another model 2600 machine that would operate along with the one it now owns. The following information is available on this alternative:

a. The model 2600 machine now in use was purchased for $165,000 four years ago. Its present book value is $99,000, and its present market value is $90,000.

b. A new model 2600 machine costs $180,000 now. The old model 2600 machine will have to be replaced in six years at a cost of $200,000. The replacement machine will have a market value of about $100,000 when it is four years old.

c. The variable cost required to produce one unit of product using the model 2600 machine is given under the "general information" below.

d. Repairs and maintenance costs each year on a single model 2600 machine total $3,000.

Alternative 2. The company could purchase a model 5200 machine and use the old model 2600 machine as standby equipment. The model 5200 machine is a high-speed unit with double the capacity of the model 2600 machine. The following information is available on this alternative:

a. The cost of a new model 5200 machine is $250,000.

b. The variable cost required to produce one unit of product using the model 5200 machine is given under the "general information" below.

c. The model 5200 machine is more costly to maintain than the model 2600 machine. Repairs and maintenance on a model 5200 machine and on a model 2600 machine used as standby would total $4,600 per year.

The following general information is available on the two alternatives:

a. Both the model 2600 machine and the model 5200 machine have a 10-year life from the time they are first used in production. The salvage value of both machines is negligible and can be ignored. Straight-line depreciation is used by the company.

b. The two machine models are not equally efficient. Comparative variable costs per unit of product are as follows:

	Model 2600	Model 5200
Direct materials per unit.	$0.36	$0.40
Direct labor per unit	0.50	0.22
Supplies and lubricants per unit.	0.04	0.08
Total variable cost per unit	$0.90	$0.70

c. No other costs would change as a result of the decision between the two machines.

d. Woolrich Company uses an 18% discount rate.

Required:

Your team should discuss and then respond to the following questions. All team members should agree with and understand the answers and be prepared to present them in class.

1. Which alternative should the company choose? Use the net present value approach.
2. Suppose that the cost of direct materials increases by 50%. Would this make the model 5200 machine more or less desirable? Explain. No computations are needed.
3. Suppose that the cost of direct labor increases by 25%. Would this make the model 5200 machine more or less desirable? Explain. No computations are needed.

CHECK FIGURE
(1) $3,949,950 NPV in favor of leasing

ANALYTICAL THINKING (LO1)

Wyndham Stores operates a regional chain of upscale department stores. The company is going to open another store soon in a prosperous and growing suburban area. In discussing how the company can acquire the desired building and other facilities needed to open the new store, Harry Wilson, the company's marketing vice president, stated, "I know most of our competitors are starting to lease facilities, rather than buy, but I just can't see the economics of it. Our development people tell me that we can buy the building site, put a building on it, and get all the store fixtures we need for $14 million. They also say that property taxes, insurance, maintenance, and repairs would run $200,000 a year. When you figure that we plan to keep a site for 20 years, that's a total cost of $18 million. But then when you realize that the building and property will be worth at least $5 million in 20 years, that's a net cost to us of only $13 million. Leasing costs a lot more than that."

"I'm not so sure," replied Erin Reilley, the company's executive vice president. "Guardian Insurance Company is willing to purchase the building site, construct a building and install fixtures to our specifications, and then lease the facility to us for 20 years for an annual lease payment of only $1 million."

"That's just my point," said Harry. "At $1 million a year, it would cost us $20 million over the 20 years instead of just $13 million. And what would we have left at the end? Nothing! The building would belong to the insurance company! I'll bet they would even want the first lease payment in advance."

"That's right," replied Erin. "We would have to make the first payment immediately and then one payment at the beginning of each of the following 19 years. However, you're overlooking a few things. For one thing, we would have to tie up a lot of our funds for 20 years under the purchase alternative. We would have to put $6 million down immediately if we buy the property, and then we would have to pay the other $8 million off over four years at $2 million a year."

"But that cost is nothing compared to $20 million for leasing," said Harry. "Also, if we lease, I understand we would have to put up a $400,000 security deposit that we wouldn't get back until the end. And besides that, we would still have to pay all the repair and maintenance costs just like we owned the property. No wonder those insurance companies are so rich if they can swing deals like this."

"Well, I'll admit that I don't have all the figures sorted out yet," replied Erin. "But I do have the operating cost breakdown for the building, which includes $90,000 annually for property taxes, $60,000 for insurance, and $50,000 for repairs and maintenance. If we lease, Guardian will handle its own insurance costs and will pay the property taxes, but we'll have to pay for the repairs and maintenance. I need to put all this together and see if leasing makes any sense with our 12% before-tax required rate of return. The president wants a presentation and recommendation in the executive committee meeting tomorrow."

Required:
1. Using the net present value approach, determine whether Wyndham Stores should lease or buy the new store.
2. How will you reply in the meeting if Harry Wilson brings up the issue of the building's future sales value?

13 "How Well Am I Doing?" Statement of Cash Flows

<< A LOOK BACK

Capital budgeting decisions involve significant investments in long-term projects. Chapter 12 covered various techniques used for capital budgeting decisions.

A LOOK AT THIS CHAPTER

The statement of cash flows provides invaluable information. After addressing the classification of various types of cash inflows and outflows, we illustrate techniques for preparing the statement of cash flows and discuss the interpretation of the information reported on this financial statement.

A LOOK AHEAD >>

Chapter 14 covers the use of financial statements to assess the financial health of a company. The focus in that chapter is on analysis of trends and on the use of financial ratios.

CHAPTER OUTLINE

Learning Objectives

LP 13

After studying Chapter 13, you should be able to:

LO1 Classify changes in noncash balance sheet accounts as sources or uses of cash.

LO2 Classify transactions as operating activities, investing activities, or financing activities.

LO3 Prepare a statement of cash flows using the indirect method to determine the net cash provided by operating activities.

LO4 (Appendix 13A) Use the direct method to determine the net cash provided by operating activities.

LO5 (Appendix 13B) Prepare a statement of cash flows using the T-account approach

DECISION FEATURE

Is the Party Over?

There was a time when many thought that e-tailers (e-retailers) might wipe out traditional retailers. Now investors wonder if any e-tailers will be able to survive. It all boils down to cash flows. Unable to generate the cash needed to support their ongoing operations, the dot.coms are having a hard time raising money. The traditional sources of funds are venture capitalists, Wall Street investors, and banks. Venture capitalists, who often made the initial cash investments required to finance the start-up operations of many e-tailers, are unwilling to invest additional cash. After snatching up the initial public offering of almost any dot.com during the late 1990s, Wall Street investors are now guarded. Banks, quite willing to provide financing to established companies with histories of profitability, are reluctant to loan money to e-tailers because the risk of default is high.

Typically, a potential investor would start with a company's financial statements. The balance sheet provides information about the company's financial condition, and the income statement indicates whether or not a company is profitable, but neither helps to predict whether a company will generate cash. Users of financial statements look to the statement of cash flows for that information.

Market Guide, a Wall Street research firm, analyzes the statements of cash flows of selected e-tailers. Market Guide estimates how long it will take for a given company to burn through its available cash. In April 2000 Matt Krantz, a *USA Today* reporter, warned that 5 of the 15 companies included in the *USA Today* "Internet 100" could run out of cash by mid-2001. The five companies cited were Drugstore.com, Egghead.com, EMusic, eToys, and Travelocity. Krantz was on target. Shortly thereafter, Egghead.com and eToys went bankrupt and EMusic laid off more than one-third of its staff.

Sources: Matt Krantz, "Dot-Coms Could Run Out of Cash," *USA Today,* August 18, 2000, 1B; Matt Krantz, "E-Retailers Run Low on Fuel," *USA Today,* April 26, 2000, 1B; News.com website; and ecommercetimes website.

Three major financial statements are ordinarily required for external reports—an income statement, a balance sheet, and a statement of cash flows. The **statement of cash flows** highlights the major activities that directly and indirectly impact cash flows and hence affect the overall cash balance. Managers focus on cash for a very good reason—without sufficient cash at the right times, a company may miss golden investment opportunities or may even go bankrupt.

The statement of cash flows answers questions that cannot be easily answered by looking at the income statement and balance sheet. Where did Delta Airlines get the cash to pay a dividend of nearly $140 million in a year in which, according to its income statement, it lost more than $1 billion? How was The Walt Disney Company able to invest nearly $800 million to expand and renovate its theme parks despite a loss of more than $500 million on its investment in EuroDisney? Where did Wendy's International, Inc., get $125 million to expand its chain of fast-food restaurants in a year when its net income was only $79 million? The answers to such questions can be found on the statement of cash flows.

The statement of cash flows is a valuable analytical tool for managers as well as for investors and creditors, although managers tend to be more concerned with forecasted statements of cash flows that are prepared as part of the budgeting process. The statement of cash flows can be used to answer crucial questions such as:

1. Is the company generating sufficient positive cash flows from its ongoing operations to remain viable?
2. Will the company be able to repay its debts?
3. Will the company be able to pay its usual dividend?
4. Why do net income and net cash flow differ?
5. To what extent will the company have to borrow money in order to make needed investments?

This chapter focuses on how to prepare the statement of cash flows and on how to use it to help assess a company's finances.

IN BUSINESS

Predicting Corporate Failures with Cash Flow Information

Divesh Sharma and Errol Iselin conducted an experiment using 60 bankers from Queensland, Australia, with an average of more than 11 years of lending experience. The researchers gathered accrual accounting and cash flow data concerning 14 Australian companies, of which seven had failed (i.e., become insolvent) and seven had not failed. Without identifying the names of the companies, half of the bankers were presented with accrual accounting information concerning the companies and the other half were presented with cash flow information. Each of the bankers was asked to identify which of the companies had failed and which had not.

Twenty-four of the 30 bankers who were provided cash flow information accurately categorized at least 11 out of 14 companies as failures or nonfailures. Conversely, only 10 of the 30 bankers who were provided accrual accounting information properly categorized at least 11 out of 14 companies. The mean judgment accuracy for the bankers relying on cash flow data was 11.47 out of 14, while the average for the bankers using accrual information was 9.97 out of 14. The authors suggest that the results of their experiment provide "strong and powerful evidence that cash flow information has greater decision usefulness than accrual information for assessing corporate solvency."

Source: Divesh S. Sharma and Errol R. Iselin, "The Decision Usefulness of Reported Cash Flow and Accrual Information in a Behavioural Field Experiment," *Accounting and Business Research* 33, no. 2, 2003, pp. 123–135.

THE BASIC APPROACH TO A STATEMENT OF CASH FLOWS

For the statement of cash flows to be useful to managers and others, it is important that companies use the same definition of cash and follow consistent guidelines for identifying activities that are *sources* of cash and *uses* of cash.

LEARNING OBJECTIVE 1

Classify changes in noncash balance sheet accounts as sources or uses of cash.

Definition of Cash

In a statement of cash flows, *cash* is broadly defined to include both cash and cash equivalents. **Cash equivalents** consist of short-term, highly liquid investments such as Treasury bills, commercial paper, and money market funds that are made solely for the purpose of generating a return on temporarily idle funds. Instead of simply holding cash, most companies invest their excess cash reserves in these types of interest-bearing assets that can be easily converted into cash. Since such assets are equivalent to cash, they are included with cash in a statement of cash flows.

Constructing the Statement of Cash Flows Using Changes in Noncash Balance Sheet Accounts

A type of statement of cash flows could be constructed by simply summarizing all of the debits and credits to the Cash and Cash Equivalents accounts during a period. However, this approach would overlook all of the transactions that involve an implicit exchange of cash. For example, when a company purchases inventory on credit, cash is implicitly exchanged. In essence, the supplier loans the company cash, which the company then uses to acquire inventory from the supplier. Rather than just looking at the transactions that explicitly involve cash, financial statement users are interested in all of the transactions that implicitly or explicitly involve cash. When inventory is purchased on credit, the Inventory account increases, which is an implicit *use* of cash. At the same time, Accounts Payable increases, which is an implicit *source* of cash. In general, increases in the Inventory account are classified as uses of cash and increases in the Accounts Payable account are classified as sources of cash. This suggests that analyzing changes in balance sheet accounts, such as Inventory and Accounts Payable, will uncover both the explicit and implicit sources and uses of cash. And this is indeed the basic approach taken in the statement of cash flows. The logic underlying this approach is demonstrated in Exhibit 13–1.

Exhibit 13–1 shows how net cash flow can be explained in terms of net income, dividends, and changes in balance sheet accounts. The first line in the exhibit is the balance sheet equation: Assets = Liabilities + Stockholders' Equity. Assets can be broken down into cash and noncash assets, which is shown in the second line of the exhibit. The third line in the exhibit recognizes that if the account balances are always equal, then *changes* in the account balances must be equal too. The fourth line in the exhibit recognizes that the change in cash is by definition the company's net cash flow. The fifth line involves

EXHIBIT 13-1   Explaining Net Cash Flow by Analysis of the Noncash Balance Sheet Accounts

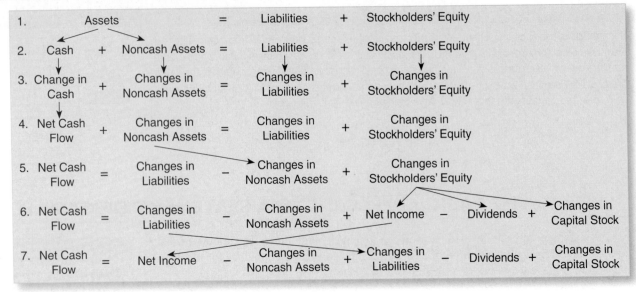

nothing more than moving Changes in Noncash Assets from the left-hand side of the equation to the right-hand side. This is done because we are attempting to explain net cash flow, so it should be isolated on the left-hand side of the equation. The sixth line breaks down the Changes in Stockholders' Equity into three components—Net Income, Dividends, and Changes in Capital Stock. Net income increases stockholders' equity, while dividends reduce stockholders' equity. The seventh line simply rearranges two terms on the right-hand side of the equation.

According to the equation derived in step 7 in Exhibit 13–1, the net cash flow for a period can be determined by starting with net income, then deducting changes in noncash assets, adding changes in liabilities, deducting dividends paid to stockholders, and finally adding changes in capital stock. It is important to realize that changes in accounts can be either increases (positive) or decreases (negative), and this affects how we should interpret the equation shown in step 7 in Exhibit 13–1. For example, increases in liabilities are added back to net income, whereas decreases in liabilities are deducted from net income to arrive at the net cash flow. On the other hand, increases in noncash assets are deducted from net income while decreases in noncash assets are added back to net income. Exhibit 13–2 summarizes the appropriate classifications—in terms of sources and uses—of net income, dividends, and changes in the noncash balance sheet accounts.

EXHIBIT 13-2

Classifications of Sources and Uses of Cash

	Sources	Uses
Net income	Always	
Net loss		Always
Changes in noncash assets	Decreases	Increases
Changes in liabilities*	Increases	Decreases
Changes in capital stock accounts	Increases	Decreases
Dividends paid to stockholders		Always
	Total sources −	Total uses = Net cash flow

*Contra asset accounts, such as the Accumulated Depreciation and Amortization account, follow the rules for liabilities.

The classifications in Exhibit 13–2 are intuitive. Positive net income generates cash, whereas a net loss consumes cash. Decreases in noncash assets, such as the sale of inventories or property, are a source of cash. Increases in noncash assets, such as the purchase of inventories or property, are a use of cash. Increases in liabilities, such as taking out a loan, are a source of cash. Decreases in liabilities, such as paying off a loan, are a use of cash. Increases in capital stock accounts, such as the sale of common stock, are a source of cash. And payments of dividends to stockholders use cash.

Constructing a simple statement of cash flows is a straightforward process. Begin with net income (or net loss) and then add to it everything listed as sources in Exhibit 13–2 and subtract from it everything listed as uses. This will be illustrated with an example in the next section.

What's Up at Amazon?

IN BUSINESS

Amazon.com, the online retailer of books and other merchandise, may have the best chance of eventually succeeding of any Internet retailer. Even so, "[I]t's no news that Amazon has had troubles, but the numbers are worse than many on Wall Street have admitted." Robert Tracy, a CPA and an analyst on the staff of grantsinvestor.com, took a close look at Amazon's financial statements and found that the company was holding its bills longer than it used to, especially at year-end. The cash flow from this increase in accounts payable exceeded the cash flow from all other operating sources combined. "Bulls [i.e., those who are positive about Amazon.com stock] will commend the company on imaginative cash management. Bears [i.e., those who are skeptical about the stock] will accuse it of financial engineering. What is not debatable is that, by stretching out payments into the new year, Amazon has presented a more liquid face to the world than it could otherwise have done."

Source: James Grant, "Diving into Amazon," *Forbes*, January 22, 2001, p. 153.

AN EXAMPLE OF A SIMPLIFIED STATEMENT OF CASH FLOWS

To illustrate the ideas introduced in the preceding section, we will now construct a *simplified* statement of cash flows for Nordstrom, Inc., one of the leading fashion retailers in the United States. This simplified statement does not follow the format required by the Financial Accounting Standards Board (FASB) for external financial reports, but it is a useful learning aid because it shows where the numbers come from in a statement of cash flows and how they fit together. In later sections, we will show how the same basic data can be used to construct a full-fledged statement of cash flows that would be acceptable for external reports.

Constructing a Simplified Statement of Cash Flows

According to Exhibit 13–2, to construct a statement of cash flows we need the company's net income or loss, the changes in each of its balance sheet accounts, and the dividends paid to stockholders for the year. We can obtain this information from the Nordstrom financial statements that appear in Exhibits 13–3, 13–4, and 13–5. In a few instances, the actual statements have been simplified.

Note that changes between the beginning and ending balances have been computed for each of the balance sheet accounts in Exhibit 13–4, and each change has been classified as a source or use of cash. For example, the $17 million decrease in accounts receivable has been classified as a source of cash. This is because, as shown in Exhibit 13–2, decreases in noncash assets, such as accounts receivable, are classified as sources of cash.

EXHIBIT 13–3

Nordstrom, Inc.*
Income Statement
(dollars in millions)

Net sales........	$3,638
Cost of goods sold	2,469
Gross margin	1,169
Selling and administrative expenses.....	941
Net operating income	228
Nonoperating items:	
Gain on sale of store........	3
Income before taxes	231
Income taxes.....	91
Net income	$ 140

*This statement is loosely based on an actual income statement published by Nordstrom. Among other differences, there was no "Gain on sale of store" in the original statement. This "gain" has been included here to illustrate how to handle gains and losses on a statement of cash flows.

EXHIBIT 13–4

Nordstrom, Inc.*
Comparative Balance Sheet
(dollars in millions)

	Ending Balance	Beginning Balance	Change	Source or Use?
Assets				
Current assets:				
Cash and cash equivalents	$ 91	$ 29	+62	
Accounts receivable........	637	654	−17	Source
Merchandise inventory	586	537	+49	Use
Total current assets.........	1,314	1,220		
Property, buildings, and equipment......	1,517	1,394	+123	Use
Less accumulated depreciation				
and amortization	654	561	+93	Source
Net property, buildings, and				
equipment	863	833		
Total assets......	$2,177	$2,053		
Liabilities and Stockholders' Equity				
Current liabilities:				
Accounts payable	$ 264	$ 220	+44	Source
Accrued wages and salaries				
payable......	193	190	+3	Source
Accrued income taxes payable	28	22	+6	Source
Notes payable	40	38	+2	Source
Total current liabilities	525	470		
Long-term debt	439	482	−43	Use
Deferred income taxes	47	49	−2	Use
Total liabilities	1,011	1,001		
Stockholders' equity:				
Common stock.....	157	155	+2	Source
Retained earnings......	1,009	897	+112	†
Total stockholders' equity	1,166	1,052		
Total liabilities and stockholders'				
equity......	$2,177	$2,053		

*This statement differs from the actual statement published by Nordstrom.

†The change in retained earnings of $112 million equals the net income of $140 million less the cash dividends paid to stockholders of $28 million. Net income is classified as a source and dividends as a use.

EXHIBIT 13-5

Nordstrom, Inc.*
Statement of Retained Earnings
(dollars in millions)

Retained earnings, beginning balance	$ 897
Add: Net income	140
	1,037
Deduct: Dividends paid...	28
Retained earnings, ending balance	$1,009

*This statement differs in a few details from the actual statement published by Nordstrom.

A *simplified* statement of cash flows appears in Exhibit 13–6. This statement was constructed by gathering together all of the entries listed as sources in Exhibit 13–4 and all of the entries listed as uses. The sources exceeded the uses by $62 million. This is the net cash flow for the year and is also, by definition, the change in cash and cash equivalents for the year. (Trace this $62 million back to Exhibit 13–4.)

The Need for a More Detailed Statement

While the simplified statement of cash flows in Exhibit 13–6 is not difficult to construct, it is not acceptable for external financial reports. The FASB requires that the statement of cash flows follow a different format and that a few of the entries be modified. Nevertheless, almost all of the entries on a full-fledged statement of cash flows are the same as the entries on the simplified statement of cash flows—they are just in a different order.

EXHIBIT 13-6

Nordstrom, Inc.
***Simplified* Statement of Cash Flows**
(dollars in millions)

Note: This simplified statement is for illustration purposes only. It should *not* be used to complete end-of-chapter homework assignments or for preparing an actual statement of cash flows. See Exhibit 13–11 for the proper format for a statement of cash flows.

Sources

Net income..	$140	
Decreases in noncash assets:		
Decrease in accounts receivable	17	
Increases in liabilities (and contra asset accounts):		
Increase in accumulated depreciation and amortization	93	
Increase in accounts payable	44	
Increase in accrued wages and salaries	3	
Increase in accrued income taxes	6	
Increase in notes payable............................	2	
Increases in capital stock accounts:		
Increase in common stock	2	
Total sources		$307

Uses

Increases in noncash assets:		
Increase in merchandise inventory	49	
Increase in property, buildings, and equipment	123	
Decreases in liabilities:		
Decrease in long-term debt	43	
Decrease in deferred income taxes	2	
Dividends.......................................	28	
Total uses......................................		245
Net cash flow		$ 62

In the following sections, we will discuss the modifications to the simplified statement of cash flows that are necessary to conform to external reporting requirements.

CONCEPT CHECK ✓

1. Which of the following is considered a source of cash on the statement of cash flows? (You may select more than one answer.)
   a. A decrease in the accounts payable account.
   b. An increase in the inventory account.
   c. A decrease in the accounts receivable account.
   d. An increase in the property, plant, and equipment account.

IN BUSINESS

Plugging the Cash Flow Leak

Modern synthetic fabrics such as polyester fleece and Gore-Tex have almost completely replaced wool in ski clothing. John Fernsell started Ibex Outdoor Clothing in Woodstock, Vermont, to buck this trend. Fernsell's five-person company designs and sells jackets made of high-grade wool from Europe.

Fernsell quickly discovered an unfortunate fact of life about the wool clothing business—he faces a potentially ruinous cash crunch every year. Ibex orders wool from Europe in February but does not pay the mills until June when they ship fabric to the garment makers in California. The garment factories send finished goods to Ibex in July and August, and Ibex pays for them on receipt. Ibex ships to retailers in September and October, but doesn't get paid until November, December, or even January. That means from June to December the company spends like crazy—and takes in virtually nothing. Fernsell tried to get by with a line of credit, but it was insufficient. To survive, he had to ask his suppliers to let him pay late, which was not a long-term solution. To reduce this cash flow problem, Fernsell is introducing a line of wool *summer* clothing so that some cash will be flowing in from May through July, when he must pay his suppliers for the winter clothing.

Source: Daniel Lyons, "Wool Gatherer," *Forbes*, April 16, 2001, p. 310.

ORGANIZATION OF THE FULL-FLEDGED STATEMENT OF CASH FLOWS

LEARNING OBJECTIVE 2

Classify transactions as operating activities, investing activities, or financing activities.

Topic Tackler

PLUS

Concept 13-1

To make it easier to compare statements of cash flows from different companies, the Financial Accounting Standards Board (FASB) requires that companies follow prescribed rules for preparing the statement of cash flows. The FASB requires that the statement be divided into three sections: *operating activities, investing activities,* and *financing activities.* The guidelines for applying these classifications are summarized in Exhibit 13–7 and are discussed below.

Operating Activities

Generally, **operating activities** are activities that affect current assets, current liabilities, or net income. Technically, however, the FASB defines operating activities as all transactions that are not classified as investing or financing activities. Generally speaking, this includes all transactions affecting current assets and all transactions affecting current liabilities except for issuing and repaying a note payable. Operating activities also include changes in noncurrent balance sheet accounts that directly affect net income such as Accumulated Depreciation and Amortization.

Operating Activities:
- Net income
- Changes in current assets
- Changes in noncurrent assets that affect net income (e.g., depreciation)
- Changes in current liabilities (except for debts to lenders and dividends payable)
- Changes in noncurrent liabilities that affect net income

Investing Activities:
- Changes in noncurrent assets that are not included in net income

Financing Activities:
- Changes in current liabilities that are debts to lenders rather than obligations to suppliers, employees, or the government
- Changes in noncurrent liabilities that are not included in net income
- Changes in capital stock accounts
- Dividends

EXHIBIT 13–7

Guidelines for Classifying Transactions as Operating, Investing, and Financing Activities

Investing Activities

Generally speaking, **investing activities** include transactions that involve acquiring or disposing of noncurrent assets such as acquiring or selling property, plant, and equipment; acquiring or selling securities held for long-term investment, such as bonds and stocks of other companies; and lending money to another entity (such as a subsidiary) and the subsequent collection of the loan. However, as previously discussed, changes in noncurrent assets that directly affect net income such as depreciation and amortization charges are classified as operating activities.

Financing Activities

As a general rule, borrowing from creditors or repaying creditors and transactions with the company's owners are classified as **financing activities.** For example, when a company borrows money by issuing a bond, the transaction is classified as a financing activity. However, transactions with creditors that affect net income are classified as operating activities. For example, interest on the company's debt is included in operating activities rather than financing activities because interest is deducted as an expense in computing net income. In contrast, a dividend payment to owners does not affect net income and therefore is classified as a financing activity rather than as an operating activity.

Most changes in current liabilities are treated as operating activities unless the transaction involves borrowing money directly from a lender, as with a note payable, or repaying such a debt. Transactions involving accounts payable, wages payable, and taxes payable are included in operating activities rather than financing activities, because these transactions occur on a routine basis and involve the company's suppliers, employees, and the government rather than lenders.

Operating, Investing, and Financing Activities

Operating Activities

Investing Activities

Financing Activities

| IN BUSINESS | Warning Signs on the Statement of Cash Flows |

Herb Greenberg, a columnist for *Fortune* magazine, emphasizes the importance of monitoring a company's cash flows:

> [S]tick with two basic indicators: cash flow from operations (how much money the company's core business generates day to day) and total cash flow (which includes the core business, financing, and any investments). Are these two numbers going up or down? Up, it almost goes without saying, is better than down. A slide in both suggested to Bill Fleckenstein of Fleckenstein Capital that Gateway was headed for earnings trouble back in June. Sure enough, in November the company warned of a profit shortfall. "If earnings are growing and the company is consuming cash, that's one of the largest red lights on the balance sheet decoder ring," Fleckenstein says.

Source: Herb Greenberg, "Minding Your K's and Q's," *Fortune*, January 8, 2001, p. 180.

| IN BUSINESS | Manipulative Cash Flow Reporting |

Professor O. Whitfield Broome from the University of Virginia found a common thread that ties together the fraudulent financial reporting at Tyco International, Dynergy, Qwest Communications International, Adelphia Communications Corporation, and WorldCom. Each company misclassified cash flows among the three sections of the statements of cash flows in an effort to inflate their net cash provided by operating activities. For example, Tyco paid more than $800 million to purchase customer contracts from dealers. The cash paid for these contracts was reported in the investing activities section of the statement of cash flows. However, when customers made payments to Tyco under these contracts, all of the cash received was reported in the operating activities section of the statement of cash flows. As another example, WorldCom recorded a substantial amount of its operating expenses as capital investments. Besides inflating net operating income, this manipulation enabled WorldCom to shift cash outflows from the operating activities section of the statement of cash flows to the investing activities section.

Source: O. Whitfield Broome, "Statement of Cash Flows: Time for Change!" *Financial Analysts Journal*, March/April 2004, pp. 16–22.

OTHER ISSUES IN PREPARING THE STATEMENT OF CASH FLOWS

We must consider two additional issues: (1) whether amounts on the statement of cash flows should be presented gross or net; and (2) whether operating activities should be presented using the direct or indirect method.[1]

Cash Flows: Gross or Net?

Both financing and investing activities should be presented in gross amounts rather than in net amounts. To illustrate, suppose that Macy's Department Stores purchases $50 million in property during the year and sells other property for $30 million. Instead of showing the net change of $20 million, the company must show the gross amounts of both the purchases and the sales. The purchases would be recorded as a use of cash, and the sales would be

---

[1]A third complication is direct exchange transactions in which noncurrent balance sheet items are swapped. For example, a company might issue common stock in a direct exchange for property. Or creditors might swap their long-term debt for common stock of the company. Direct exchange transactions are not reported on the statement of cash flows; however, they are disclosed in a separate schedule that accompanies the statement. More advanced accounting courses cover this topic in greater detail.

recorded as a source of cash. Similarly, if Alcoa receives $80 million from the issue of long-term bonds and then pays out $30 million to retire other bonds, the two transactions must be reported separately on the statement of cash flows rather than being netted against each other.

The gross method of reporting does *not* extend to operating activities, where debits and credits to an account are netted against each other on the statement of cash flows. For example, if Sears adds $600 million to its accounts receivable as a result of sales during the year and $520 million of accounts receivable are collected, only the net increase of $80 million would be reported on the statement of cash flows.

Operating Activities: Direct or Indirect Method?

Topic Tackler

PLUS

Concept 13-2

The net amount of the cash inflows and outflows resulting from operating activities, which is known formally as the **net cash provided by operating activities,** can be computed by either the direct or the indirect method.

Under the **direct method,** the income statement is reconstructed on a cash basis from top to bottom. For example, cash collected from customers is listed instead of sales, and payments to suppliers is listed instead of cost of goods sold. In essence, cash receipts are counted as sales and cash disbursements are counted as expenses. The difference between the cash receipts and cash disbursements is the net cash provided by operating activities for the period.

Under the **indirect method,** net income is adjusted to a cash basis. That is, rather than directly computing cash sales, cash expenses, and so forth, these amounts are arrived at *indirectly* by removing from net income any items that do not affect cash flows. The indirect method has an advantage over the direct method because it shows the reasons for any differences between net income and the net cash provided by operating activities. The indirect method is also known as the **reconciliation method.**

Although both the direct and indirect methods will result in exactly the same amount of net cash provided by operating activities, the FASB *recommends* and *encourages* the use of the direct method for external reports. But there is a catch. If the direct method is used, the company must provide a supplementary reconciliation of net income with operating cash flows. In essence, if a company chooses to use the direct method, it must also construct a statement that uses a form of the indirect method. However, if a company chooses to use the indirect method, there is no requirement that it also report the results using the direct method.

The Popularity of the Indirect Method

IN BUSINESS

A survey of 600 companies revealed that only 7, or 1.2%, use the direct method to construct the statement of cash flows for external reports. The remaining 98.8% probably use the indirect method because it is simply less work.

Source: American Institute of Certified Public Accountants, *Accounting Trends and Techniques: 2004,* Jersey City, NJ, 2004, p. 549

While there are some good reasons for using the direct method, we use the indirect method in this chapter because it is by far the most popular method. The direct method is discussed and illustrated in Appendix 13A at the end of the chapter.

---

2. Which of the following statements is false? (You may select more than one answer.)
   a. Purchasing a new manufacturing plant is classified as an investing activity.
   b. Paying off accounts payable balances is classified as a financing activity.
   c. Dividend payments are classified as a financing activity.
   d. Either the direct or the indirect method can be used to calculate the net cash provided by financing activities.

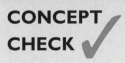

CONCEPT CHECK ✓

AN EXAMPLE OF A FULL-FLEDGED STATEMENT OF CASH FLOWS

In this section, we apply the FASB rules to construct a statement of cash flows for Nordstrom that would be acceptable for external reporting. The approach we take is based on an analysis of changes in balance sheet accounts, as in our earlier discussion of the simplified statement of cash flows. Indeed, as you will see, the full-fledged statement of cash flows is for the most part just a reorganized form of the simplified statement that appears in Exhibit 13–6.

The format for the operating activities section of the statement of cash flows is shown in Exhibit 13–8. Notice that net income is adjusted to net cash provided by operating activities by adding sources of cash and deducting uses of cash. For example, consider the effect of an increase in the Accounts Receivable account on the net cash provided by operating activities. Since the Accounts Receivable account is a noncash asset, we know from Exhibit 13–2 that increases in this account are treated as *uses* of cash. In other words, increases in Accounts Receivable are deducted when determining net cash flows.

Eight Basic Steps to Preparing the Statement of Cash Flows

A number of techniques have been developed to help prepare the statement of cash flows. Preparing a statement of cash flows can be confusing, and important details can be easily overlooked without such aids. We recommend that you use a worksheet, such as the one in Exhibit 13–9, to prepare a statement of cash flows. Another technique relies on the use of T-accounts, which is discussed in Appendix 13B at the end of the chapter.

EXHIBIT 13–8
General Model: Indirect Method of Determining the "Net Cash Provided by Operating Activities"

	Add (+) or Deduct (−) to Adjust Net Income
Net income.	$XXX
Adjustments needed to convert net income to a cash basis:	
Depreciation, depletion, and amortization charges	+
Add (deduct) changes in current asset accounts affecting revenue or expense:*	
Increase in the account	−
Decrease in the account	+
Add (deduct) changes in current liability accounts affecting revenue or expense:†	
Increase in the account.	+
Decrease in the account.	−
Add (deduct) gains or losses on sales of assets:	
Gain on sales of assets.	−
Loss on sales of assets.	+
Add (deduct) changes in the Deferred Income Taxes account:	
Increase if a liability; decrease if an asset.	+
Decrease if a liability; increase if an asset	−
Net cash provided by operating activities.	$XXX

*Examples include accounts receivable, accrued receivables, inventory, and prepaid expenses.
†Examples include accounts payable, accrued liabilities, and taxes payable.

EXHIBIT 13-9

Nordstrom, Inc.
Statement of Cash Flows Worksheet
(dollars in millions)

	(1) Change	(2) Source or Use?	(3) Cash Flow Effect	(4) Adjust-ments	(5) Adjusted Effect (3) + (4)	(6) Classi-fication*
Assets (except cash and cash equivalents)						
Current assets:						
Accounts receivable	−17	Source	$+17		$+17	Operating
Merchandise inventory	+49	Use	−49		−49	Operating
Noncurrent assets:						
Property, buildings, and equipment	+123	Use	−123	$−15	−138	Investing
Contra Assets, Liabilities, and Stockholders' Equity						
Contra assets:						
Accumulated depreciation and amortization	+93	Source	+93	+10	+103	Operating
Current liabilities:						
Accounts payable	+44	Source	+44		+44	Operating
Accrued wages and salaries payable	+3	Source	+3		+3	Operating
Accrued income taxes payable	+6	Source	+6		+6	Operating
Notes payable	+2	Source	+2		+2	Financing
Noncurrent liabilities:						
Long-term debt	−43	Use	−43		−43	Financing
Deferred income taxes	−2	Use	−2		−2	Operating
Stockholders' equity:						
Common stock	+2	Source	+2		+2	Financing
Retained earnings:						
Net income	+140	Source	+140		+140	Operating
Dividends	−28	Use	−28		−28	Financing
Additional Entries						
Proceeds from sale of store				+8	+8	Investing
Gain on sale of store				−3	−3	Operating
Total (net cash flow)			$+62	$ 0	$+62	

*See Exhibit 13–10 (page 552) for the reasons for these classifications.

The worksheet in Exhibit 13–9 can be prepared using the eight steps that follow. This brief summary of the steps will be followed by more detailed explanations later.

1. Copy the title of each account appearing on the comparative balance sheet onto the worksheet except for cash and cash equivalents and retained earnings. Contra asset accounts such as the Accumulated Depreciation and Amortization account should be listed with the liabilities because they are treated like liabilities on the statement of cash flows.
2. Compute the change from the beginning balance to the ending balance in each balance sheet account. Break down the change in retained earnings into net income and dividends paid to stockholders.
3. Using Exhibit 13–2 as a guide, code each entry on the worksheet as a source or a use of cash.
4. Under the Cash Flow Effect column, write sources as positive numbers and uses as negative numbers.
5. Make any necessary adjustments to reflect gross, rather than net, amounts involved in transactions—including adjustments for gains and losses. Some of these adjustments may require adding new entries to the bottom of the worksheet. The net effect of all such adjusting entries must be zero.

6. Classify each entry on the worksheet as an operating, investing, or financing activity according to the FASB's criteria, as given in Exhibit 13–7.

7. Copy the data from the worksheet to the statement of cash flows section by section, starting with the operating activities section.

8. At the bottom of the statement of cash flows prepare a reconciliation of the beginning and ending balances of cash and cash equivalents. The net change in cash and cash equivalents shown at the bottom of this statement should equal the change in the Cash and Cash Equivalents accounts during the year.

On the following pages we will apply these eight steps to the data contained in the comparative balance sheet for Nordstrom, Inc., found in Exhibit 13–4. *As we discuss each step, refer to Exhibit 13–4 and trace the data from this exhibit into the worksheet in Exhibit 13–9.*

Setting Up the Worksheet (Steps 1–4)

As indicated above, step 1 in preparing the worksheet is to list all of the relevant account titles from the company's balance sheet. Note that we have done this for Nordstrom, Inc., on the worksheet in Exhibit 13–9. (The titles of Nordstrom's accounts have been taken from the company's comparative balance sheet, which is found in Exhibit 13–4.) The only significant differences between Nordstrom's balance sheet accounts and the worksheet listing are that (1) the Accumulated Depreciation and Amortization account has been moved down with the liabilities on the worksheet, (2) the Cash and Cash Equivalents accounts have been omitted, and (3) the change in retained earnings has been broken down into net income and dividends.

As stated in step 2, the change in each account's balance during the year is listed in the first column of the worksheet. We have entered these changes for Nordstrom's accounts onto the worksheet in Exhibit 13–9. (Refer to Nordstrom's comparative balance sheet in Exhibit 13–4 to see how these changes were computed.)

Then, as indicated in step 3, each change on the worksheet is classified as either a source or a use of cash. Whether a change is a source or a use can be determined by referring back to Exhibit 13–2, where we first discussed these classifications. For example, Nordstrom's Merchandise Inventory account increased by $49 million during the year. According to Exhibit 13–2, increases in noncash asset accounts are classified as uses of cash, so an entry has been made to that effect in the second column of the worksheet for the Merchandise Inventory account.

So far, nothing is new. All of this was done in Exhibit 13–4 when we constructed the simplified statement of cash flows. Step 4 is mechanical, but it helps prevent careless errors. Sources are coded as positive changes and uses as negative changes in the Cash Flow Effect column on the worksheet.

Adjustments to Reflect Gross, Rather than Net, Amounts (Step 5)

As discussed earlier, the FASB requires that gross, rather than net, amounts be disclosed in the investing and financing sections. This rule requires special treatment of gains and losses. To illustrate, suppose that Nordstrom decided to sell an old store and move its retail operations to a new location. Assume that the original cost of the old store was $15 million, its accumulated depreciation was $10 million, and that it was sold for $8 million in cash. The journal entry to record this transaction (in millions) appears below:

Cash Proceeds.	8	
Accumulated Depreciation and Amortization	10	
Property, Buildings, and Equipment		15
Gain on Sale		3

The $3 million gain is reflected in the income statement in Exhibit 13–3.

We can reconstruct the gross additions to the Property, Buildings, and Equipment account and the gross charges to the Accumulated Depreciation and Amortization account with the help of T-accounts:

Property, Buildings, and Equipment						Accumulated Depreciation and Amortization		
Balance	1,394						561	Balance
Additions (plug*)	138	15	Disposal of store	Disposal of store	10	103		Depreciation charges (plug*)
Balance	1,517						654	Balance

*By *plug* we mean the balancing figure in the account.

According to the FASB rules, the gross additions of $138 million to the Property, Buildings, and Equipment account should be disclosed on the statement of cash flows rather than the net change in the account of $123 million ($1,517 million − $1,394 million = $123 million). Likewise, the gross depreciation charges of $103 million should be disclosed rather than the net change in the Accumulated Depreciation and Amortization account of $93 million ($654 million − $561 million = $93 million). And the cash proceeds of $8 million from sale of the building should also be disclosed on the statement of cash flows. All of this is accomplished, while preserving the correct overall net cash flows on the statement, by using the above journal entry to make adjusting entries on the worksheet. The debits are recorded as positive adjustments, and the credits are recorded as negative adjustments. These adjusting entries are recorded under Adjustments in column (4) in Exhibit 13–9.

It may not be clear why the gain on the sale is *deducted* in the operating activities section of the statement of cash flows. The company's $140 million net income, which is part of the operating activities section, includes the $3 million gain on the sale of the store. But this $3 million gain must be reported in the *investing* activities section of the statement of cash flows as part of the $8 million proceeds from the sale transaction. Therefore, to avoid double counting, the $3 million gain is deducted from net income in the operating activities section of the statement. The adjustments we have made on the worksheet accomplish this. The $3 million gain will be deducted in the operating activities section, and all $8 million of the sale proceeds will be shown as an investing item. As a result, all of the gain will be included in the investing section of the statement of cash flows and none of it will be included in the operating activities section. There will be no double counting of the gain.

In the case of a loss on the sale of an asset, we do the opposite. The loss is added back to net income in the operating activities section of the statement of cash flows. Whatever cash proceeds are received from the sale of the asset are reported in the investing activities section.

Before turning to step 6 in the process of building the statement of cash flows, one small step is required. Add the Adjustments in column (4) to the Cash Flow Effect in column (3) to arrive at the Adjusted Effect in column (5).

Classifying Entries as Operating, Investing, or Financing Activities (Step 6)

In step 6, each entry on the worksheet is classified as an operating, investing, or financing activity using the guidelines in Exhibit 13–7. These classifications are entered directly on the worksheet in Exhibit 13–9 and are explained in Exhibit 13–10. Most of these classifications are straightforward, but the classification of the change in the Deferred Income Taxes account may require some additional explanation. Because of the way income tax expense is determined for financial reporting purposes, the expense that appears on the income statement often differs from the taxes that are actually owed to the government.

EXHIBIT 13–10   Classifications of Entries on Nordstrom's Statement of Cash Flows

Entry	Classification	Reason
• Changes in Accounts Receivable and Merchandise Inventory	Operating activity	Changes in current assets are included in operating activities.
• Change in Property, Buildings, and Equipment	Investing activity	Changes in noncurrent assets that do not directly affect net income are included in investing activities.
• Change in Accumulated Depreciation and Amortization	Operating activity	Depreciation and amortization directly affect net income and are therefore included in operating activities.
• Changes in Accounts Payable, Accrued Wages and Salaries Payable, and Accrued Income Taxes Payable	Operating activity	Changes in current liabilities (except for notes payable) are included in operating activities.
• Change in Notes Payable	Financing activity	Issuing or repaying notes payable is classified as a financing activity.
• Change in Long-Term Debt	Financing activity	Changes in noncurrent liabilities that do not directly affect net income are included in financing activities.
• Change in Deferred Income Taxes	Operating activity	Deferred income taxes result from income tax expense that directly affects net income. Therefore, this entry is included in operating activities.
• Change in Common Stock	Financing activity	Changes in capital stock accounts are always included in financing activities.
• Net Income	Operating activity	Net income is always included in operating activities.
• Dividends	Financing activity	Dividends paid to stockholders are always included in financing activities.
• Proceeds from sale of store	Investing activity	The gross amounts received on disposal of noncurrent assets are included in investing activities.
• Gains from sale of store	Operating activity	Gains and losses directly affect net income and are therefore included in operating activities.

Usually, Income Tax Expense overstates the company's actual income tax liability for the year. When this happens, the journal entry to record income taxes includes a credit to Deferred Income Taxes:

Income Tax Expense	XXX	
Income Taxes Payable		XXX
Deferred Income Taxes (plug).		XXX

Since deferred income taxes arise directly from the computation of an expense, the change in the Deferred Income Taxes account is included in the operating activities section of the statement of cash flows.

In the case of Nordstrom , the Deferred Income Taxes account decreased during the year. Deferred Income Taxes is a liability account for Nordstrom. Since this liability

---

DECISION MAKER   Owner

You are the owner of a small manufacturing company. The company started selling its products internationally this year, which has resulted in a very significant increase in sales revenue and net income during the last two months of the year. The operating activities section of the company's statement of cash flows shows a negative number (that is, cash was *used* rather than *provided* by operations). Would you be concerned?

SEC Requires Caterpillar to Restate Cash Flows

The Securities and Exchange Commission (SEC) required Caterpillar to restate its cash flows for 2002 and 2003 as follows (amounts are in millions):

	2002	2003
Cash flows as originally reported by Caterpillar:		
Net cash provided by operating activities	$2,366	$2,066
Net cash used for investing activities	(2,708)	(2,793)
Total	($ 342)	($ 727)
Caterpillar's restated cash flows:		
Net cash used for operating activities	($3,962)	($5,611)
Net cash provided by investing activities	3,620	4,884
Total	($ 342)	($ 727)

The restatement resulted in a dramatic drop in Caterpillar's net cash provided by operating activities in both 2002 and 2003, although the change in the company's cash and short-term investments remained the same after the restatement. Why do you think the SEC required Caterpillar to report the reclassifications summarized above?

Source: Ghostwriter, "SEC Acts to Curb Cash Flow Shenanigans," *Inc.* magazine, June 2005, p. 26, and Caterpillar's 10-Ks for 2002, 2003, and 2004.

account decreased during the year, the change is counted as a use of cash and is deducted in determining net cash flow for the year.

The Completed Statement of Cash Flows (Steps 7 and 8)

Once the worksheet is completed, the actual statement of cash flows is easy to complete. Nordstrom's statement of cash flows appears in Exhibit 13–11. Trace each item from the worksheet into this statement.

The operating activities section of the statement follows the format laid out in Exhibit 13–8, beginning with net income. The other entries in the operating activities section are adjustments required to convert net income to a cash basis. The sum of all of the entries under the operating activities section is called the "net cash provided by operating activities."

The investing activities section comes next on the statement of cash flows. The worksheet entries that have been classified as investing activities are listed in this section. The sum of all the entries in this section is called the "net cash used for investing activities."

The financing activities section of the statement follows the investing activities section. The worksheet entries that have been classified as financing activities are listed in this section. The sum of all of the entries in this section is called the "net cash used in financing activities."

Finally, for step 8, the bottom of the statement of cash flows contains a reconciliation of the beginning and ending balances of cash and cash equivalents.

Interpretation of the Statement of Cash Flows

The completed statement of cash flows in Exhibit 13–11 provides a very favorable picture of Nordstrom's cash flows. The net cash provided by operating activities is a healthy $259 million. This positive cash flow permitted the company to make substantial additions to its property, buildings, and equipment and to pay off a substantial portion of its long-term debt. If similar conditions prevail in the future, the company can continue to finance substantial growth from its own cash flows without the necessity of raising debt or selling stock.

EXHIBIT 13–11

Nordstrom, Inc.* Statement of Cash Flows—Indirect Method (dollars in millions)	
Operating Activities	
Net income	$140
Adjustments to convert net income to a cash basis:	
Depreciation and amortization charges	103
Decrease in accounts receivable	17
Increase in merchandise inventory	(49)
Increase in accounts payable	44
Increase in accrued wages and salaries payable	3
Increase in accrued income taxes payable	6
Decrease in deferred income taxes	(2)
Gain on sale of store	(3)
Net cash provided by operating activities	259
Investing Activities	
Additions to property, buildings, and equipment	(138)
Proceeds from sale of store	8
Net cash used in investing activities	(130)
Financing Activities	
Increase in notes payable	2
Decrease in long-term debt	(43)
Increase in common stock	2
Cash dividends paid	(28)
Net cash used in financing activities	(67)
Net increase in cash and cash equivalents	62
Cash and cash equivalents at beginning of year	29
Cash and cash equivalents at end of year	$ 91

Reconciliation of the beginning and ending cash balances →

*This statement differs from the actual statement published by Nordstrom.

When interpreting a statement of cash flows, it is particularly important to examine the net cash provided by operating activities. This figure indicates how successful the company is in generating cash on a continuing basis. A negative cash flow from operations may be a sign of fundamental difficulties. A positive cash flow from operations is necessary to avoid liquidating assets or borrowing money just to sustain day-to-day operations.

IN BUSINESS

What's Wrong with This Picture?

Getty Images is the world's biggest stock photo company—owning the rights to over 70 million images and 30,000 hours of film. The company gets its revenues from licensing the use of these images. The stock market is impressed with the potential in this market—despite losses of $63 million in the first six months of the year, the company's stock was worth $1.8 billion. "What is there for a growth company to talk about if earnings are so rotten? Anything but earnings . . . Getty Images declared victory in its cash from operations, which it said had swelled to a robust $17.1 million in the second quarter, up from a deficit of $2.6 million in the first. Does that mean Getty collected its bills and whittled down its inventory? Nope. Both receivables and inventory are rising. The cash flow from operations, rather, comes from not paying bills."

Source: Elizabeth MacDonald, "Image Problem," *Forbes*, October 16, 2000, pp. 104–106.

Free Cash Flow: Do the Math

In 1999, Jim Huguet, the manager of IDEX Great Companies mutual fund, was contemplating investing in an energy company with soaring profits. However, something bothered him about this company. Its profits were growing 27% a year, yet its free cash flow was plummeting. How could such a profitable company be bleeding cash? This unsettling contradiction caused Huguet to bypass investing in the highflying energy company Enron. In light of Enron's stunning financial collapse two years later, it turns out that Huguet's decision to focus on cash flow rather than on artificial accounting gimmicks saved his investors a bundle of money.

Free cash flow is a measure of the money that a company has left over after paying its bills. Investors often overlook this number because it is not directly reported in a set of financial statements; nonetheless, it is worth investing the time to do the math. To compute a company's free cash flow, begin with its net operating income, then add back its depreciation and amortization, and deduct its capital expenditures and dividends paid.

Source: Russell Pearlman, "Go with the Cash Flow," *Smart Money*, October 2004, pp. 86–91.

Depreciation, Depletion, and Amortization

A few pitfalls can trap the unwary when reading a statement of cash flows. Perhaps the most common pitfall is to misinterpret the nature of the depreciation charges on the statement of cash flows. Since depreciation is added back to net income, you might think that you can increase net cash flow by increasing depreciation charges. This is false. In a merchandising company like Nordstrom, increasing the depreciation charge by X dollars would decrease net income by X dollars because of the added expense. Adding back the depreciation charge to net income on the statement of cash flows simply cancels out the reduction in net income caused by the depreciation charge. To refer back to Exhibit 13–2, depreciation, depletion, and amortization charges are added back to net income on the statement of cash flows because they are a decrease in an asset (or, an increase in a contra asset)—not because they generate cash.

Portfolio Manager

Assume that you work for a mutual fund and have the responsibility of selecting stocks to include in the fund's investment portfolio. You have been analyzing the financial statements of a chain of retail clothing stores and noticed that the company's cash flow from operations for the quarter ending on December 31 was negative even though the company had a small positive net operating income for the quarter. Further analysis indicated that most of the negative cash flow was due to a large increase in inventories. Should you be concerned?

SUMMARY

LO1   Classify changes in noncash balance sheet accounts as sources or uses of cash.

The statement of cash flows is one of the three major financial statements. It explains how cash was generated and how it was used during the period. In general, sources of cash include net income, decreases in assets, increases in liabilities, and increases in stockholders' capital accounts. Uses of cash include increases in assets, decreases in liabilities, decreases in stockholders' capital accounts, and dividends. A simplified form of the statement of cash flows can be easily constructed using just these definitions and a comparative balance sheet.

LO2   Classify transactions as operating activities, investing activities, or financing activities.

For external reporting purposes, the statement of cash flows must be organized in terms of operating, investing, and financing activities. While there are some exceptions, operating activities include net income and changes in current assets and current liabilities. And, with a few exceptions, changes in noncurrent assets are generally included in investing activities and changes in noncurrent liabilities are generally included in financing activities.

LO3   Prepare a statement of cash flows using the indirect method to determine the net cash provided by operating activities.

The operating activities section of the statement of cash flows can be constructed using the indirect method (discussed in the main body of the chapter) or the direct method (discussed in Appendix 13A). Although the FASB prefers the use of the direct method, most companies use the indirect method. Both methods report the same amount of net cash provided by operating activities.

When the indirect method is used, the operating activities section of the statement of cash flows starts with net income and shows the adjustments required to adjust net income to a cash basis. A worksheet can be used to construct the statement of cash flows. After determining the change in each balance sheet account, adjustments are made to reflect gross, rather than net, amounts involved in selected transactions, and each entry on the worksheet is labeled as an operating, investing, or financing activity. The data from the worksheet are then used to prepare each section of the statement of cash flows, beginning with the operating activities section.

GUIDANCE ANSWERS TO *DECISION MAKER* AND *YOU DECIDE*

Owner (p. 552)

Even though the company reported positive net income, the net effect of the company's operations was to *consume* rather than *generate* cash during the year. Cash disbursements relating to the company's operations exceeded the amount of cash receipts from operations. If the company generated a significant amount of sales just before the end of the year, it is quite possible that cash has not yet been received from the customers. In fact, given that the additional sales were international, a longer collection period would be expected. Nevertheless, as owner, you probably would want to ensure that the company's credit-granting policies and procedures were adhered to when these sales were made, and you should also monitor the length of time it takes to collect accounts receivable.

Portfolio Manager (p. 555)

The low profit (i.e., net operating income) and negative cash flow for the quarter ending December 31 should definitely be of concern for a clothing retailer. Due to the Christmas and Hanukkah holidays, this is traditionally the best quarter of the year for retailers. Furthermore, the increase in inventories is very troubling. This may indicate that sales fell below expectations and that the goods in inventory may have to be deeply discounted in the new year to clear the shelves for new merchandise. At minimum, some very hard questions should be directed to the executives of the clothing chain before buying its stock.

GUIDANCE ANSWERS TO CONCEPT CHECKS

1. **Choice c.** A decrease in a noncash asset, such as accounts receivable, is a source of cash.
2. **Choices b and d.** Paying suppliers is an operating activity. The direct and indirect methods are used to calculate cash from operating activities, not financing activities.

REVIEW PROBLEM

Rockford Company's comparative balance sheet and income statement for the year 2008 follow:

Rockford Company
Comparative Balance Sheet
December 31, 2008, and 2007
(dollars in millions)

	2008	2007
Assets		
Cash	$ 26	$ 10
Accounts receivable	180	270
Inventory	205	160
Prepaid expenses	17	20
Plant and equipment	430	309
Less accumulated depreciation	(218)	(194)
Long-term investments	60	75
Total assets	$700	$650
Liabilities and Stockholders' Equity		
Accounts payable	$230	$310
Accrued liabilities	70	60
Bonds payable	135	40
Deferred income taxes	15	8
Common stock	140	140
Retained earnings	110	92
Total liabilities and stockholders' equity	$700	$650

Rockford Company
Income Statement
For the Year Ended December 31, 2008
(dollars in millions)

Sales	$1,000
Cost of goods sold	530
Gross margin	470
Selling and administrative expenses	352
Net operating income	118
Nonoperating items:	
Loss on sale of equipment	(4)
Income before taxes	114
Less income taxes	48
Net income	$ 66

Notes: Dividends of $48 million were paid in 2008. The loss on sale of equipment of $4 million reflects a transaction in which equipment with an original cost of $12 million and accumulated depreciation of $5 million was sold for $3 million in cash.

Required
Using the indirect method, determine the net cash provided by operating activities for 2008 and construct a statement of cash flows for the year.

Solution to Review Problem
A worksheet for Rockford Company follows. With use of the worksheet, it is easy to construct the statement of cash flows, including the net cash provided by operating activities.

Rockford Company
Statement of Cash Flows Worksheet
For the Year Ended December 31, 2008
(dollars in millions)

	(1) Change	(2) Source or Use?	(3) Cash Flow Effect	(4) Adjust- ments	(5) Adjusted Effect (3) + (4)	(6) Classi- fication
Assets (except cash and cash equivalents)						
Current assets:						
Accounts receivable	−90	Source	$+90		$+90	Operating
Inventory.	+45	Use	−45		−45	Operating
Prepaid expenses	−3	Source	+3		+3	Operating
Noncurrent assets:						
Property, buildings, and equipment	+121	Use	−121	$−12	−133	Investing
Long-term investments	−15	Source	+15		+15	Investing
Contra Assets, Liabilities, and						
Stockholders' Equity						
Contra assets:						
Accumulated depreciation	+24	Source	+24	+ 5	+29	Operating
Current liabilities:						
Accounts payable	−80	Use	−80		−80	Operating
Accrued liabilities	+10	Source	+10		+10	Operating
Noncurrent liabilities:						
Bonds payable	+95	Source	+95		+95	Financing
Deferred income taxes	+7	Source	+7		+7	Operating
Stockholders' equity:						
Common stock	+0	−	+0		+0	Financing
Retained earnings:						
Net income	+66	Source	+66		+66	Operating
Dividends.	−48	Use	−48		−48	Financing
Additional Entries						
Proceeds from sale of equipment				+3	+3	Investing
Loss on sale of equipment				+4	+4	Operating
Total (net cash flow)			$+16	$ 0	$+16	

Rockford Company
Statement of Cash Flows—Indirect Method
For the Year Ended December 31, 2008
(dollars in millions)

Operating Activities

Net income	$ 66
Adjustments to convert net income to a cash basis:	
Depreciation and amortization charges	29
Decrease in accounts receivable	90
Increase in inventory.	(45)
Decrease in prepaid expenses	3
Decrease in accounts payable	(80)
Increase in accrued liabilities	10
Increase in deferred income taxes	7
Loss on sale of equipment	4
Net cash provided by operating activities	84

(continued)

(concluded)

Rockford Company
Statement of Cash Flows—Indirect Method
For the Year Ended December 31, 2008
(dollars in millions)

Investing Activities

Additions to property, buildings, and equipment.	(133)
Decrease in long-term investments	15
Proceeds from sale of equipment.	3
Net cash used in investing activities.	(115)

Financing Activities

Increase in bonds payable	95
Cash dividends paid.	(48)
Net cash provided by financing activities	47
Net increase in cash and cash equivalents	16
Cash and cash equivalents at beginning of year	10
Cash and cash equivalents at end of year	$ 26

Note that the $16 million increase in cash and cash equivalents agrees with the $16 million increase in the company's Cash account shown in the balance sheet, and it agrees with the total in column (5) in the worksheet on the previous page.

GLOSSARY

Cash equivalents   Short-term, highly liquid investments such as Treasury bills, commercial paper, and money market funds that are made solely for the purpose of generating a return on temporarily idle funds. (p. 539)

Direct method   A method of computing the net cash provided by operating activities in which the income statement is reconstructed on a cash basis from top to bottom. (p. 547)

Financing activities   All transactions (other than payment of interest) involving borrowing from creditors or repaying creditors as well as transactions with the company's owners. (p. 545)

Indirect method   A method of computing the net cash provided by operating activities that starts with net income and adjusts it to a cash basis. It is also known as the *reconciliation method.* (p. 547)

Investing activities   Transactions that involve acquiring or disposing of noncurrent assets. (p. 545)

Net cash provided by operating activities   The net result of the cash inflows and outflows arising from day-to-day operations. (p. 547)

Operating activities   Generally speaking, activities that affect current assets, cuurent liabilities, or net income. (p. 544)

Reconciliation method   See *Indirect method.* (p. 547)

Statement of cash flows   A financial statement that highlights the major activities that directly and indirectly impact cash flows and hence affect the overall cash balance. (p. 528)

APPENDIX 13A: THE DIRECT METHOD OF DETERMINING THE NET CASH PROVIDED BY OPERATING ACTIVITIES

To compute the net cash provided by operating activities under the direct method, we must reconstruct the income statement on a cash basis from top to bottom. Exhibit 13A–1 shows the adjustments that must be made to adjust sales, expenses, and so forth, to a cash basis. To illustrate, we have included in the exhibit the Nordstrom data from the chapter.

Note that the "net cash provided by operating activities" ($259 million) agrees with the amount computed in the chapter by the indirect method. The two amounts agree

LEARNING OBJECTIVE 4

Use the direct method to determine the net cash provided by operating actvities.

because the direct and indirect methods are just different roads to the same destination. The investing and financing activities sections of the statement will be exactly the same as shown for the indirect method in Exhibit 13–11. The only difference between the indirect and direct methods is in the operating activities section.

Similarities and Differences in the Handling of Data

Although we arrive at the same destination under either the direct or the indirect method, not all data are handled in the same way in the adjustment process. Stop for a moment, flip back to the general model for the indirect method in Exhibit 13–8, and compare the adjustments made in that exhibit to the adjustments made for the direct method in Exhibit 13A–1. The adjustments for accounts that affect sales are the same in the two methods. In either case, increases in the accounts are deducted and decreases in the accounts are added. The adjustments for accounts that affect expenses, however, are handled in *opposite* ways in the indirect and direct methods. This is because under the indirect method the adjustments are made to *net income,* whereas under the direct method the adjustments are made to the *expense accounts* themselves.

To illustrate this difference, note the handling of prepaid expenses and depreciation in the indirect and direct methods. Under the indirect method (Exhibit 13–8), an increase in the Prepaid Expenses account is *deducted* from net income in computing the amount of

EXHIBIT 13A–1

General Model: Direct Method of Determining the "Net Cash Provided by Operating Activities"

Revenue or Expense Item	Add (+) or Deduct (−) to Adjust to a Cash Basis	Illustration— Nordstrom (in millions)	
Sales (as reported)		$3,638	
Adjustments to a cash basis:			
Increase in accounts receivable	−		
Decrease in accounts receivable	+	+17	
Total			$3,655
Cost of goods sold (as reported)		2,469	
Adjustments to a cash basis:			
Increase in merchandise inventory	+	+49	
Decrease in merchandise inventory	−		
Increase in accounts payable	−	−44	
Decrease in accounts payable	+		
Total			2,474
Selling and administrative expenses (as reported)		941	
Adjustments to a cash basis:			
Increase in prepaid expenses	+		
Decrease in prepaid expenses	−		
Increase in accrued liabilities	−	−3	
Decrease in accrued liabilities	+		
Period's depreciation, depletion, and amortization charges	−	−103	
Total			835
Income tax expense (as reported)		91	
Adjustments to a cash basis:			
Increase in accrued taxes payable	−	−6	
Decrease in accrued taxes payable	+		
Increase in deferred income taxes	−		
Decrease in deferred income taxes	+	+2	
Total			87
Net cash provided by operating activities			$ 259

net cash provided by operating activities. Under the direct method (Exhibit 13A–1), an increase in Prepaid Expenses is *added* to operating expenses. The reason for the difference can be explained as follows: An increase in Prepaid Expenses means that more cash has been paid out for items such as insurance than has been included as an expense for the period. Therefore, to adjust net income to a cash basis, either we must deduct this increase from net income (indirect method) or we must add this increase to operating expenses (direct method). Either way, we will end up with the same figure for net cash provided by operating activities. Similarly, depreciation is added to net income under the indirect method to cancel out its effect (Exhibit 13–8), whereas it is deducted from operating expenses under the direct method to cancel out its effect (Exhibit 13A–1). These differences in the handling of data are true for all other expense items in the two methods.

In the matter of gains and losses on sales of assets, no adjustments are needed under the direct method. These gains and losses are simply ignored because they are not part of sales, cost of goods sold, operating expenses, or income taxes. Observe that in Exhibit 13A–1, Nordstrom's $3 million gain on the sale of the store is not listed as an adjustment in the operating activities section.

Special Rules—Direct and Indirect Methods

As stated earlier, when the direct method is used, the FASB requires a reconciliation between net income and the net cash provided by operating activities, as determined by the indirect method. Thus, *when a company elects to use the direct method, it must also present the indirect method* in a separate schedule accompanying the statement of cash flows.

On the other hand, if a company elects to use the indirect method to compute the net cash provided by operating activities, then it must also provide a special breakdown of data. The company must provide a separate disclosure of the amount of interest and the amount of income taxes paid during the year. The FASB requires this separate disclosure so that users can take the data provided by the indirect method and make estimates of what the amounts for sales, income taxes, and so forth, would have been if the direct method had been used instead.

SUMMARY OF APPENDIX 13A

LO4   (Appendix 13A) Use the direct method to determine the net cash provided by operating activities.

When the direct method is used to determine the net cash provided by operating activities, the income statement is reconstructed on a cash basis. A worksheet, which starts with the major components of the company's income statement (such as sales, cost of goods sold, selling and administrative expenses, and income tax expense), can be used to organize the data. Each of the income statement components is adjusted to a cash basis by referring to the changes in the related balance sheet account. (For example, the amount of sales reported on the income statement is converted to the amount of cash received from customers by subtracting the increase, or adding the decrease, in accounts receivable during the period.) Special disclosure rules apply when a company uses the direct method.

APPENDIX 13B: THE T-ACCOUNT APPROACH TO PREPARING THE STATEMENT OF CASH FLOWS

A worksheet approach was used to prepare the statement of cash flows in the chapter. The T-account approach is an alternative technique that is sometimes used to prepare the statement of cash flows. To illustrate the T-account approach, we will again use the data for Nordstrom, Inc., from the chapter.

LEARNING OBJECTIVE 5

Prepare a statement of cash flows using the T-account approach.

The T-Account Approach

Note from Nordstrom's comparative balance sheet in Exhibit 13–4 that cash and cash equivalents increased from $29 million to $91 million, an increase of $62 million during the year. To determine the reasons for this change we will again prepare a statement of cash flows. As before, our basic approach will be to analyze the changes in the various balance sheet accounts. However, in this appendix we will use T-accounts rather than a worksheet.

Exhibit 13B–1 contains a T-account, titled "Cash," which we will use to accumulate the cash "Provided" and the cash "Used." The exhibit also includes T-accounts with the beginning and ending balances for each of the other accounts on Nordstrom's balance sheet. *Before proceeding, refer to Nordstrom's comparative balance sheet in Exhibit 13–4 in the main body of the chapter, and trace the data from this exhibit to the T-accounts in Exhibit 13B–1.*

As we analyze each balance sheet account, we will post the related entry(ies) directly to the T-accounts. To the extent that these changes have affected cash, we will also post an appropriate entry to the T-account representing Cash. *As you progress through this appendix, trace each entry to the T-accounts in Exhibit 13B–2. Pay special attention to the placement and description of the entries affecting the T-account representing Cash.*

Observe that in the Cash T-account in Exhibit 13B–2, all operating items are near the top of the Cash T-account, below the net income figure. Also note that the T-account includes a subtotal titled "Net cash provided by operating activities." If the amounts in the "Used" column exceeded the amounts in the "Provided" column, the subtotal would be on the credit side of the T-account and would be labeled "Net cash *used* in operating activities." Also note that all investing and financing items have been placed below the subtotal in the lower portion of the Cash T-account. At the bottom of the T-account is a total titled "Net increase in cash and cash equivalents." If the amounts in the "Used" column exceeded the amounts in the "Provided" column, this total would be on the credit side of the T-account and would be labeled "Net *decrease* in cash and cash equivalents." The entries in the Cash T-account contain all of the entries needed for the statement of cash flows.

EXHIBIT 13B–1   T-Accounts Showing Changes in Account Balances—Nordstrom, Inc. (in millions)

Cash		
	Provided	Used
Net cash provided by operating activities		
Net increase in cash and cash equivalents		

Accounts Receivable			Merchandise Inventory			Property, Buildings, and Equipment			Accumulated Depreciation	
Bal.	654		Bal.	537		Bal.	1,394		561	Bal.
Bal.	637		Bal.	586		Bal.	1,517		654	Bal.

Accounts Payable			Accrued Wages and Salaries Payable			Accrued Income Taxes Payable			Notes Payable	
	220	Bal.		190	Bal.		22	Bal.	38	Bal.
	264	Bal.		193	Bal.		28	Bal.	40	Bal.

Long-Term Debt			Deferred Income Taxes			Common Stock			Retained Earnings	
	482	Bal.		49	Bal.		155	Bal.	897	Bal.
	439	Bal.		47	Bal.		157	Bal.	1,009	Bal.

EXHIBIT 13B–2 T-Accounts after Posting of Account Changes—Nordstrom, Inc. (in millions)

Cash

	Provided		Used		
Net income	(1) 140		49	(4)	Increase in merchandise inventory
Decrease in accounts receivable	(3) 17		3	(5)	Gain on sale of store
Depreciation and amortization charges	(7) 103		2	(13)	Decrease in deferred income taxes
Increase in accounts payable	(8) 44				
Increase in accrued wages and salaries payable	(9) 3				
Increase in accrued income taxes payable	(10) 6				
Net cash provided by operating activities	259				
Proceeds from sale of store	(5) 8		28	(2)	Cash dividends paid
Increase in notes payable	(11) 2		138	(6)	Additions to property, buildings, and equipment
Increase in common stock	(14) 2		43	(12)	Decrease in long-term debt
Net increase in cash and cash equivalents	62				

Accounts Receivable				Merchandise Inventory			Property, Buildings, and Equipment					Accumulated Depreciation		
Bal.	654			Bal.	537		Bal.	1,394					561	Bal.
		17	(3)	(4)	49		(6)	138	15	(5)	(5)	10	103	(7)
Bal.	637			Bal.	586		Bal.	1,517					654	Bal.

Accounts Payable			Accrued Wages and Salaries Payable			Accrued Income Taxes Payable			Notes Payable		
	220	Bal.		190	Bal.		22	Bal.		38	Bal.
	44	(8)		3	(9)		6	(10)		2	(11)
	264	Bal.		193	Bal.		28	Bal.		40	Bal.

Long-Term Debt				Deferred Income Taxes			Common Stock			Retained Earnings		
		482	Bal.		49	Bal.		155	Bal.		897	Bal.
(12)	43			(13) 2				2	(14)	(2) 28	140	(1)
		439	Bal.		47	Bal.		157	Bal.		1,009	Bal.

Retained Earnings The Retained Earnings account is generally the most useful starting point when developing a statement of cash flows. Details of the change in Nordstrom's Retained Earnings account are presented in Exhibit 13–5. Note from the exhibit that net income was $140 million and dividends were $28 million. The entries to record these changes and their effects on Cash are shown below. (The dollar amounts are in millions.)

The entry to record net income and the effect on Cash would be:

(1)

Cash—Provided	140	
Retained Earnings—Net Income		140

Recall that net income is converted to a cash basis when the indirect method is used to prepare the operating activities section of the statement of cash flows. Since net income is the starting point, the cash effect is included at the top of the Cash T-account.

The entry to record the dividends paid and the effect on Cash would be:

(2)

Retained Earnings—Dividends	28	
Cash—Used		28

Since the payment of cash dividends is classified as an investing activity, the cash effect is included in the lower portion of the Cash T-account along with the other investing and financing items.

Once posted to the Retained Earnings T-account in Exhibit 13B–2, these two entries fully explain the change that took place in the Retained Earnings account during the year. We can now proceed through the remainder of the balance sheet accounts in Exhibit 13B–1, analyzing the change between the beginning and ending balances in each account, and recording the appropriate entries in the T-accounts.

Current Asset Accounts   Each of the current asset accounts is examined to determine the change that occurred during the year. The change is then recorded as a debit if the account balance increased or as a credit if the account balance decreased. The offsetting entry in the case of an increase in the account balance is "Cash—Used"; the offsetting entry in the case of a decrease in the account balance is "Cash—Provided."

To demonstrate, note that Nordstrom's Accounts Receivable decreased by $17 million during the year. The entry to record this change and its effect on Cash would be:

(3)

Cash—Provided.	17	
Accounts Receivable.		17

The merchandise inventory account increased by $49 million during the year. The entry to record this change and its effect on Cash would be:

(4)

Merchandise Inventory.	49	
Cash—Used		49

Note that these two entries result in the correct adjusting entries in the current asset T-accounts so as to reconcile the beginning and ending balances. Also note that the changes in these two current asset accounts are included in the upper portion of the Cash T-account. This is because changes in current assets are considered part of operations and therefore are used to convert net income to a cash basis in the operating activities section of the statement of cash flows.

Property, Buildings, and Equipment and Accumulated Depreciation   The activity in the Property, Buildings, and Equipment account and the Accumulated Depreciation account is analyzed in the chapter beginning on page 551. *Reread the analysis of these accounts before proceeding.* Nordstrom sold a store; purchased property, buildings, and equipment; and recorded depreciation expense during the year. The entries in this case for the T-account analysis are more complex than for current assets. These entries are presented below. You should carefully trace each of these entries to the T-accounts in Exhibit 13B–2.

The entry to record the sale of the store and its effect on Cash would be:

(5)

Cash—Provided.	8	
Accumulated Depreciation	10	
Property, Buildings, and Equipment		15
Gain on Sale.		3

Since the sale of property, buildings, and equipment is classified as an investing activity, the cash effect is included in the lower portion of the Cash T-account along with the other investing and financing items. The proceeds from the sale, which will be reported in the investing activities section of the statement of cash flows, include the gain that was recognized on the sale of the store. However, this gain was reported on Nordstrom's income statement in Exhibit 13–3 as part of net income, which is the starting point for the operating activities section. As a result, to avoid double counting, the gain must be subtracted (or removed) from net income in the operating activities section of the statement of cash flows. Accordingly, the gain is recorded in the "Used" column in the upper portion of the Cash T-account along with the other operating items.

The entry to record the purchase of property, buildings, and equipment and its effect on Cash would be:

(6)

Property, Buildings, and Equipment.	138	
Cash—Used		138

Since the purchase of property, buildings, and equipment is classified as an investing activity, the cash effect is included in the lower portion of the Cash T-account along with the other investing and financing items. Entry (6), along with entry (5) above, explains the change in the Property, Buildings, and Equipment account during the year.

The entry to record depreciation and amortization expense for the year would be:

(7)

Cash—Provided	103
Accumulated Depreciation	103

Note that depreciation and amortization expense does not involve an actual cash outflow. Consequently, depreciation and amortization expense must be added to net income to convert it to a cash basis in the operating activities section of the statement of cash flows. Note that the depreciation and amortization expense is recorded in the "Provided" column in the upper portion of the Cash T-account along with the other operating items. Entry (7), along with entry (5) above, explains the change in the Accumulated Depreciation account during the year.

Current Liabilities   The T-accounts in Exhibit 13B–1 show that Nordstrom has four current liability accounts. Three of the four current liability accounts (Accounts Payable, Accrued Wages and Salaries Payable, and Accrued Income Taxes Payable) relate to the company's operating activities. In the entries that follow, increases in current liabilities are recorded as credits, with the offsetting entry being "Cash—Provided." Decreases in current liabilities are recorded as debits, with the offsetting entry being "Cash—Used."

Accounts Payable increased by $44 million during the year. The entry to record this change and its effect on Cash would be:

(8)

Cash—Provided	44
Accounts Payable	44

The Accrued Wages and Salaries Payable account increased by $3 million during the year. The entry to record this change and its effect on Cash would be:

(9)

Cash—Provided	3
Accrued Wages and Salaries Payable	3

The Accrued Income Taxes Payable account increased by $6 million during the year. The entry to record this change and its effect on Cash would be:

(10)

Cash—Provided	6
Accrued Income Taxes Payable	6

Since the changes in these three current liability accounts are considered to be part of operations, their cash effects are included in the upper portion of the Cash T-account along with the other operating items.

The Notes Payable account increased by $2 million during the year. The entry to record this would be:

(11)

Cash—Provided	2
Notes Payable	2

Since transactions involving notes payable are classified as financing activities, their cash effects are included in the lower portion of the Cash T-account along with the other investing and financing items.

Long-Term Debt   Nordstrom's Long-Term Debt account decreased by $43 million during the year. The entry to record this would be:

(12)

Long-Term Debt	43
Cash—Used	43

COMMUNICATING IN PRACTICE (LO3, LO4)

Use an online yellow pages directory to find a company in your area that has a website on which it has an annual report, including a statement of cash flows. Make an appointment with the controller or chief financial officer of the company. Before your meeting, find out as much as you can about the organization's operations from its website.

Required

After asking the following questions, write a brief memorandum to your instructor that summarizes the information obtained from the company's website and addresses what you found out during your interview.

1. Does the company use the direct method or the indirect method to determine the net cash provided by operating activities when preparing its statement of cash flows? Why?
2. How is the information reported on the statement of cash flows used for decision-making purposes?

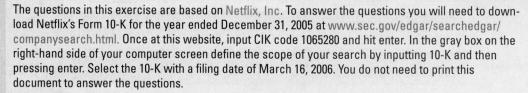

RESEARCH AND APPLICATION   [LO1]

The questions in this exercise are based on Netflix, Inc. To answer the questions you will need to download Netflix's Form 10-K for the year ended December 31, 2005 at www.sec.gov/edgar/searchedgar/companysearch.html. Once at this website, input CIK code 1065280 and hit enter. In the gray box on the right-hand side of your computer screen define the scope of your search by inputting 10-K and then pressing enter. Select the 10-K with a filing date of March 16, 2006. You do not need to print this document to answer the questions.

REQUIRED:

1. What is Netflix's strategy for success in the marketplace? Does the company rely primarily on a customer intimacy, operational excellence, or product leadership customer value proposition? What evidence supports your conclusion?
2. What business risks does Netflix face that may threaten the company's ability to satisfy stockholder expectations? Of the risks that you have identified, which ones are controllable and which ones are largely uncontrollable? (*Hint:* Focus on pages 8–20 of the 10-K.)
3. Prepare a comparative balance sheet similar to the one shown in Exhibit 13–4 (use Netflix's data from 2004 and 2005). For each account shown on Netflix's balance sheet, calculate the change in the balance and whether the change represents a source or a use of cash.
4. Explain how each change shown in your comparative balance sheet is accounted for in Netflix's 2005 statement of cash flows.
5. Refer to the In Business box titled "Free Cash Flow: Do the Math" shown on page 555 of the textbook. Compute Netflix's free cash flow for 2005. What insights are revealed by your calculation?

14 "How Well Am I Doing?" Financial Statement Analysis

<< **A LOOK BACK**

In Chapter 13 we showed how to construct the statement of cash flows and discussed the interpretation of the data found on that statement.

A LOOK AT THIS CHAPTER

In Chapter 14 we focus on the analysis of financial statements to help forecast the financial health of a company. We discuss the use of trend data, comparisons with other organizations, and financial ratios.

CHAPTER OUTLINE

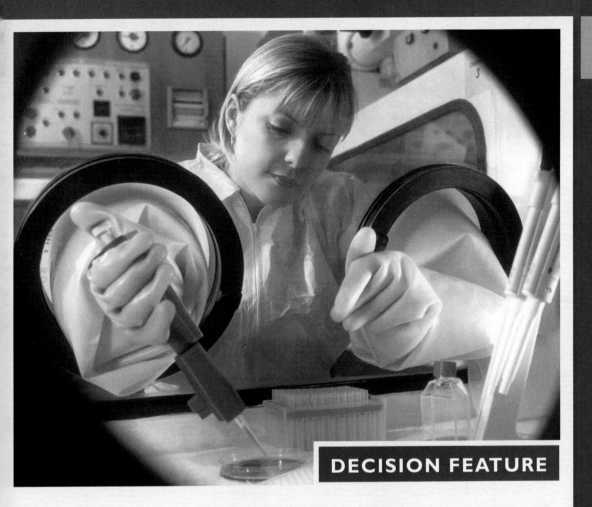

LEARNING OBJECTIVES

LP 14

After studying Chapter 14, you should be able to:

LO1 Prepare and interpret financial statements in comparative and common-size form.

LO2 Compute and interpret financial ratios that would be useful to a common stockholder.

LO3 Compute and interpret financial ratios that would be useful to a short-term creditor.

LO4 Compute and interpret financial ratios that would be useful to a long-term creditor.

DECISION FEATURE

Biotech Companies Go Out of Favor

A venture capitalist invests in a start-up company with the hope of recognizing a significant profit when the start-up company goes public by selling shares of its stock on the open market. During the 1980s and early 1990s, investments by venture capitalists in biotechnology companies helped fund the development of drugs used to treat a variety of diseases that were previously considered untreatable (e.g., cancer, kidney failure, heart attacks, arthritis, and the AIDS virus, among others). However, in 1997, a reallocation of funds took place in the venture capital market. Software vendors, health care service providers, and Internet-based businesses came into favor, and biotech companies went out of fashion. Instead of waiting for returns on biotech investments that took years to realize because of the length of time required to get drugs to market, venture capitalists opted for the quicker payoffs in other industries. Payoffs were especially rapid on investments in dot.com companies, which were managing to go public long before they reached profitability. By 1999, even biotech companies with experienced management teams and well-conceived development plans for a multitude of drugs were finding it difficult, if not impossible, to raise money.

Cynthia Robbins-Roth, the founding partner of BioVenture Consultants, believes that the venture capitalists' decision-making model was flawed. Part of the problem is the tendency for investors to jump on board when a hot new fad (such as the dot.com one) surfaces. She emphasizes the need to separately analyze each company, rather than analyzing just one and then investing in similar companies. Robbins-Roth is also critical of the technical expertise of the analysts that were working for venture capital firms. She highlights the mounting need for new drugs as the population ages and the opportunities provided by recent leaps in biotechnology that will make possible the development of those drugs.

Source: Cynthia Robbins-Roth, "Seduced & Abandoned," *Forbes ASAP,* May 29, 2000, pp. 153–154.

All financial statements are historical documents. They summarize what *has happened* during a particular period. However, most users of financial statements are concerned with what *will happen* in the future. For example, stockholders are concerned with future earnings and dividends and creditors are concerned with the company's future ability to repay its debts. While financial statements are historical in nature, they can still provide users with valuable insights. These users rely on *financial statement analysis,* which involves examining trends in key financial data, comparing financial data across companies, and analyzing financial ratios to assess the financial health and future prospects of a company. In this chapter, we focus our attention on the most important ratios and other analytical tools that financial analysts use.

In addition to stockholders and creditors, managers are also vitally concerned with the financial ratios discussed in this chapter. First, the ratios provide indicators of how well the company and its business units are performing. Some of these ratios might be used in a balanced scorecard approach as discussed in Chapter 8. The specific ratios selected depend on the company's strategy. For example, a company that wants to emphasize responsiveness to customers may closely monitor the inventory turnover ratio discussed later in this chapter. Second, since managers must report to stockholders and may want to raise funds from external sources, managers must pay attention to the financial ratios used by external investors.

LIMITATIONS OF FINANCIAL STATEMENT ANALYSIS

Although financial statement analysis is a useful tool, it has two limitations that should be mentioned before proceeding any further. These two limitations involve the comparability of financial data between companies and the need to look beyond ratios.

Comparison of Financial Data

Comparisons of one company with another can provide valuable clues about the financial health of an organization. Unfortunately, differences in accounting methods between companies sometimes make it difficult to compare their financial data. For example, if one company values its inventories by the LIFO method and another company by the average cost method, then direct comparisons of their financial data such as inventory valuations and cost of goods sold may be misleading. Sometimes enough data are presented in footnotes to the financial statements to restate data to a comparable basis. Otherwise, the analyst should keep in mind any lack of comparability. Even with this limitation in mind, comparisons of key ratios with other companies and with industry averages often suggest avenues for further investigation.

The Need to Look beyond Ratios

Ratios should not be viewed as an end, but rather as a *starting point*. They raise many questions and point to opportunities for further analysis, but they rarely answer any questions by themselves. In addition to ratios, the analyst should evaluate industry trends, technological changes, changes in consumer tastes, changes in broad economic factors, and changes within the company itself.

Pro Forma Earnings—The Feds Crack Down

IN BUSINESS

In the 1990s, many companies got into the practice of reporting "pro forma" earnings to investors and analysts instead of GAAP earnings. While there were no rules for pro forma earnings, companies typically excluded items such as depreciation, goodwill amortization, restructuring charges, unusual gains and losses, and stock-option-related compensation expenses that depress earnings. In a period in which the 100 companies in the Nasdaq 100 index reported a GAAP loss of $82.3 billion, the same companies reported pro forma profits of $19.1 billion! If you want to report a profit instead of a loss, excluding inconvenient expenses like depreciation surely helps. Because of the perception that pro forma earnings were deliberately concocted to mislead investors, Congress acted. The Sarbanes-Oxley Act of 2002 directed the SEC to issue rules that would bar companies from issuing misleading pro forma earnings reports and that would require a reconciliation between GAAP and pro forma earnings. Detailed rules were subsequently issued by the SEC that prohibited companies from (1) giving prominence to pro forma earnings over GAAP earnings; (2) excluding from pro forma earnings any charges or liabilities that would require cash settlement; (3) excluding unusual or nonrecurring items if in fact there had been a similar unusual or nonrecurring item within the prior two years; (4) inserting pro forma earnings into GAAP financial statements; and (5) using titles in a pro forma news release that are the same as or similar to GAAP titles.

Sources: "Why Honesty Is the Best Policy," *The Economist*, March 9, 2002, pp. 9–13; and Mark P. Holtzman, Robert Fonfeder, and J. K. Yun, "Goodbye 'Pro Forma' Earnings," *Strategic Finance*, November 2003, pp. 33–35.

STATEMENTS IN COMPARATIVE AND COMMON-SIZE FORM

An item on a balance sheet or income statement has little meaning by itself. Suppose a company's sales for a year were $250 million. In isolation, that is not particularly useful information. How does that stack up against last year's sales? How do the sales relate to the cost of goods sold? In making these kinds of comparisons, three analytical techniques are widely used:

LEARNING OBJECTIVE 1

Prepare and interpret financial statements in comparative and common-size form.

1. Dollar and percentage changes on statements (*horizontal analysis*).
2. Common-size statements (*vertical analysis*).
3. Ratios.

Topic Tackler

PLUS

Concept 14-1

The first and second techniques are discussed in this section; the third technique is discussed in the remainder of the chapter. Throughout the chapter, we will illustrate these analytical techniques using the financial statements of Brickey Electronics, a producer of specialized electronic components.

Dollar and Percentage Changes on Statements

Horizontal analysis (also known as **trend analysis**) involves analyzing financial data over time. This can involve nothing more complicated than showing year-to-year changes in each financial statement item in both dollar and percentage terms. Exhibits 14–1 and 14–2 show Brickey Electronics' financial statements in this *comparative form*. The dollar

EXHIBIT 14–1

Brickey Electronics
Comparative Balance Sheet
December 31, 2008 and 2007
(dollars in thousands)

	2008	2007	Increase (Decrease) Amount	Increase (Decrease) Percent
Assets				
Current assets:				
Cash...........................	$ 1,200	$ 2,350	$(1,150)	(48.9)%*
Accounts receivable, net............	6,000	4,000	2,000	50.0%
Inventory.......................	8,000	10,000	(2,000)	(20.0)%
Prepaid expenses.................	300	120	180	150.0%
Total current assets.................	15,500	16,470	(970)	(5.9)%
Property and equipment:				
Land...........................	4,000	4,000	0	0%
Buildings and equipment, net........	12,000	8,500	3,500	41.2%
Total property and equipment.........	16,000	12,500	3,500	28.0%
Total assets	$31,500	$28,970	$ 2,530	8.7%
Liabilities and Stockholders' Equity				
Current liabilities:				
Accounts payable.................	$ 5,800	$ 4,000	$ 1,800	45.0%
Accrued payables.................	900	400	500	125.0%
Notes payable, short term	300	600	(300)	(50.0)%
Total current liabilities..............	7,000	5,000	2,000	40.0%
Long-term liabilities:				
Bonds payable, 8%...............	7,500	8,000	(500)	(6.3)%
Total liabilities...................	14,500	13,000	1,500	11.5%
Stockholders' equity:				
Preferred stock, $100 par, 6%	2,000	2,000	0	0%
Common stock, $12 par............	6,000	6,000	0	0%
Additional paid-in capital............	1,000	1,000	0	0%
Total paid-in capital................	9,000	9,000	0	0%
Retained earnings.................	8,000	6,970	1,030	14.8%
Total stockholders' equity	17,000	15,970	1,030	6.4%
Total liabilities and stockholders' equity................	$31,500	$28,970	$ 2,530	8.7%

*The changes between 2007 and 2008 are expressed as a percentage of the dollar amount for 2007. For example, Cash decreased by $1,150 between 2007 and 2008. This decrease expressed in percentage form is computed as follows: $1,150 ÷ $2,350 = 48.9%. Other percentage figures in this exhibit and Exhibit 14–2 are computed in the same way.

EXHIBIT 14-2

Brickey Electronics
Comparative Income Statement and Reconciliation of Retained Earnings
For the Years Ended December 31, 2008 and 2007
(dollars in thousands)

	2008	2007	Increase (Decrease) Amount	Percent
Sales.	$52,000	$48,000	$4,000	8.3%
Cost of goods sold	36,000	31,500	4,500	14.3%
Gross margin.	16,000	16,500	(500)	(3.0)%
Selling and administrative expenses:				
Selling expenses	7,000	6,500	500	7.7%
Administrative expenses	5,860	6,100	(240)	(3.9)%
Total selling and administrative expenses. .	12,860	12,600	260	2.1%
Net operating income	3,140	3,900	(760)	(19.5)%
Interest expense	640	700	(60)	(8.6)%
Net income before taxes	2,500	3,200	(700)	(21.9)%
Income taxes (30%)	750	960	(210)	(21.9)%
Net income	1,750	2,240	$ (490)	(21.9)%
Dividends to preferred stockholders,				
$6 per share (see Exhibit 14–1)	120	120		
Net income remaining for common				
stockholders	1,630	2,120		
Dividends to common stockholders,				
$1.20 per share	600	600		
Net income added to retained				
earnings.	1,030	1,520		
Retained earnings, beginning				
of year	6,970	5,450		
Retained earnings, end of year.	$ 8,000	$ 6,970		

changes highlight the changes that are the most important economically; the percentage changes highlight the changes that are the most unusual.

Horizontal analysis can be even more useful when data from a number of years are used to compute *trend percentages*. To compute **trend percentages,** a base year is selected and the data for all years are stated as a percentage of that base year. To illustrate, consider the sales and net income of McDonald's Corporation, the world's largest food service retailer, with more than 31,000 restaurants worldwide:

	2004	2003	2002	2001	2000	1999	1998	1997	1996	1995
Sales (millions).	$19,065	$17,140	$15,406	$14,870	$14,243	$13,259	$12,421	$11,409	$10,687	$9,795
Net income (millions)	$2,279	$1,471	$893	$1,637	$1,977	$1,948	$1,550	$1,642	$1,573	$1,427

Be careful to note that the above data have been arranged with the most recent year on the left. This may be the opposite of what you are used to, but it is the way financial data are commonly displayed in annual reports and other sources. By simply looking at these data, you can see that sales increased every year, but the net income has not. However, recasting these data into trend percentages aids interpretation:

	2004	2003	2002	2001	2000	1999	1998	1997	1996	1995
Sales	195%	175%	157%	152%	145%	135%	127%	116%	109%	100%
Net income.	160%	103%	63%	115%	139%	137%	109%	115%	110%	100%

In the above table, both sales and net income have been restated as a percentage of the 1995 sales and net income. For example, the 2004 sales of $19,065 are 195% of the 1995 sales of $9,795. This trend analysis is particularly striking when the data are plotted as in Exhibit 14–3. McDonald's sales growth was impressive throughout the entire 10-year period and was closely tracked by net income for the first part of this period, but net income faltered in 1998 and then plummeted in 2001 and 2002, finally recovering dramatically in 2003 and 2004.

Common-Size Statements

Horizontal analysis, which was discussed in the previous section, examines changes in a financial statement item over time. **Vertical analysis** focuses on the relations among financial statement items at a given point in time. A **common-size financial statement** is a vertical analysis in which each financial statement item is expressed as a percentage. In income statements, all items are usually expressed as a percentage of sales. In balance sheets, all items are usually expressed as a percentage of total assets. Exhibit 14–4 contains a common-size balance sheet for Brickey Electronics and Exhibit 14–5 contains a common-size income statement for the company.

Notice from Exhibit 14–4 that placing all assets in common-size form clearly shows the relative importance of the current assets as compared to the noncurrent assets. It also shows that significant changes have taken place in the composition of the current assets over the last year. For example, accounts receivable have increased in relative importance and both cash and inventory have declined in relative importance. Judging from the sharp increase in accounts receivable, the deterioration in the cash balance may be a result of an inability to collect from customers.

To shift now to the income statement, in Exhibit 14–5 the cost of goods sold as a percentage of sales increased from 65.6% in 2007 to 69.2% in 2008. Or looking at this

EXHIBIT 14–3
McDonald's Corporation:
Trend Analysis of Sales
and Net Income

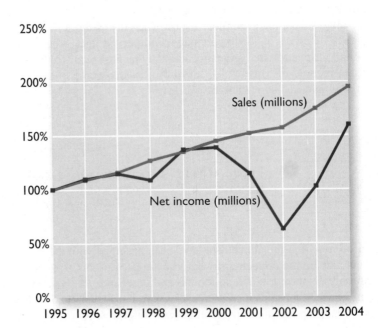

EXHIBIT 14–4

Brickey Electronics
Common-Size Comparative Balance Sheet
December 31, 2008 and 2007
(dollars in thousands)

	2008	2007	Common-Size Percentages 2008	2007
Assets				
Current assets:				
Cash..........................	$ 1,200	$ 2,350	3.8%*	8.1%
Accounts receivable, net...........	6,000	4,000	19.0%	13.8%
Inventory.......................	8,000	10,000	25.4%	34.5%
Prepaid expenses................	300	120	1.0%	0.4%
Total current assets	15,500	16,470	49.2%	56.9%
Property and equipment:				
Land.........................	4,000	4,000	12.7%	13.8%
Buildings and equipment, net........	12,000	8,500	38.1%	29.3%
Total property and equipment	16,000	12,500	50.8%	43.1%
Total assets	$31,500	$28,970	100.0%	100.0%
Liabilities and Stockholders' Equity				
Current liabilities:				
Accounts payable	$ 5,800	$ 4,000	18.4%	13.8%
Accrued payables................	900	400	2.9%	1.4%
Notes payable, short term	300	600	1.0%	2.1%
Total current liabilities.............	7,000	5,000	22.2%	17.3%
Long-term liabilities:				
Bonds payable, 8%...............	7,500	8,000	23.8%	27.6%
Total liabilities...................	14,500	13,000	46.0%	44.9%
Stockholders' equity:				
Preferred stock, $100, 6%	2,000	2,000	6.3%	6.9%
Common stock, $12 par	6,000	6,000	19.0%	20.7%
Additional paid-in capital...........	1,000	1,000	3.2%	3.5%
Total paid-in capital................	9,000	9,000	28.6%	31.1%
Retained earnings	8,000	6,970	25.4%	24.1%
Total stockholders' equity...........	17,000	15,970	54.0%	55.1%
Total liabilities and stockholders' equity	$31,500	$28,970	100.0%	100.0%

*Each asset account on a common-size statement is expressed as a percentage of total assets, and each liability and equity account is expressed as a percentage of total liabilities and stockholders' equity. For example, the percentage figure above for Cash in 2008 is computed as follows: $1,200 ÷ $31,500 = 3.8%.

from a different viewpoint, the *gross margin percentage* declined from 34.4% in 2007 to 30.8% in 2008. Managers and investment analysts often pay close attention to this measure of profitability. The **gross margin percentage** is computed as follows:

$$\text{Gross margin percentage} = \frac{\text{Gross margin}}{\text{Sales}}$$

The gross margin percentage should be more stable for retailing companies than for other companies because the cost of goods sold in retailing excludes fixed costs. When fixed costs are included in the cost of goods sold, the gross margin percentage should

EXHIBIT 14–5

Brickey Electronics Common-Size Comparative Income Statement For the Years Ended December 31, 2008 and 2007 (dollars in thousands)			Common-Size Percentages	
	2008	**2007**	**2008**	**2007**
Sales	$52,000	$48,000	100.0%	100.0%
Cost of goods sold	36,000	31,500	69.2%	65.6%
Gross margin	16,000	16,500	30.8%	34.4%
Selling and administrative expenses:				
Selling expenses	7,000	6,500	13.5%	13.5%
Administrative expenses...........	5,860	6,100	11.3%	12.7%
Total selling and administrative				
expenses	12,860	12,600	24.7%	26.3%
Net operating income.............	3,140	3,900	6.0%	8.1%
Interest expense.................	640	700	1.2%	1.5%
Net income before taxes	2,500	3,200	4.8%	6.7%
Income taxes (30%)	750	960	1.4%	2.0%
Net income......................	$ 1,750	$ 2,240	3.4%	4.7%

*Note that the percentage figures for each year are expressed as a percentage of total sales for the year. For example, the percentage figure for cost of goods sold in 2008 is computed as follows: $36,000 ÷ $52,000 = 69.2%

increase and decrease with sales volume. With increases in sales volume, fixed costs are spread across more units and the gross margin percentage should improve.

Common-size statements are particularly useful when comparing data from different companies. For example, in 2002, Wendy's net income was $219 million, whereas McDonald's was $894 million. This comparison is somewhat misleading because of the dramatically different sizes of the two companies. To put this in better perspective, net income can be expressed as a percentage of the sales of each company. Since Wendy's sales were $2,730 million and McDonald's were $15,406 million, Wendy's net income as a percentage of sales was about 8.0% and McDonald's was about 5.8%. In this light, McDonald's performance did not compare favorably with Wendy's performance.

RATIO ANALYSIS—THE COMMON STOCKHOLDER

LEARNING OBJECTIVE 2

Compute and interpret financial ratios that would be useful to a common stockholder.

Topic Tackler

PLUS

Concept 14-2

A number of financial ratios are used to assess how well a company is doing from the standpoint of its stockholders. These ratios focus on net income, dividends, and stockholders' equity.

Earnings Per Share

An investor buys a stock in the hope of realizing a return in the form of either dividends or future increases in the value of the stock. Since earnings form the basis for dividend payments and future increases in the value of shares, investors are interested in a company's *earnings per share.*

Earnings per share is computed by dividing net income available for common stockholders by the average number of common shares outstanding during the year. "Net income available for common stockholders" is net income minus dividends paid to the owners of the company's preferred stock.[1]

$$\text{Earnings per share} = \frac{\text{Net income} - \text{Preferred dividends}}{\text{Average number of common shares outstanding}}$$

Using the data in Exhibits 14–1 and 14–2, we see that the earnings per share for Brickey Electronics for 2008 is computed as follows:

$$\frac{\text{Earnings}}{\text{per share}} = \frac{\$1,750,000 - \$120,000}{(500,000 \text{ shares}^* + 500,000 \text{ shares})/2} = \$3.26$$

*$6,000,000 total par value ÷ $12 par value per share = 500,000 shares.

Pennies Matter!

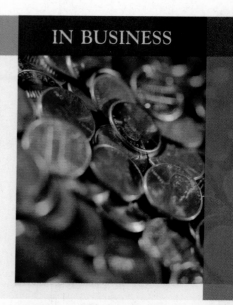

In January 2005, online auctioneer eBay announced that its fourth-quarter earnings for 2004 rose 44% compared with the same quarter of the prior year. While eBay's fourth quarter earnings of 30 cents per share matched the company's own forecast, it came up short of Wall Street analysts' forecasts by an average of four cents per share. Consequently, eBay's stock price tumbled $15.36 in less than 24 hours. Given that eBay had about 662 million shares of common stock outstanding at the time, the company's stockholders saw more than $10 billion of wealth evaporate in one day.

eBay's experience clearly illustrates how Wall Street investors exert pressure on publicly traded companies to deliver quarterly earnings that meet expectations. While it may be easy from a theoretical standpoint to advocate the value of taking a long-run point of view when making decisions, managers face the cold, hard reality that if their companies fail to meet Wall Street investors' quarterly earnings forecasts, their stock prices will probably take a beating.

Source: Mylene Mangalindan, "EBay Posts 44% Jump in Profit; Forecast Is Tepid," *The Wall Street Journal*, January 20, 2005, p. A3.

The Earnings Per Share Game

Over the last several decades, a subtle, but very important, change occurred in how managers viewed earnings per share. Instead of honestly reporting the company's earnings per share and letting the stock market sort out the implications, top executives too often decided to manage the earnings numbers themselves. The goal was steadily growing earnings per share and beating investment analysts' earnings forecasts quarter after quarter. Cisco, for example, regularly "beat" investment analysts' earnings per share forecasts by 1 penny, quarter after quarter. The legendary investor Warren Buffet warns that if you tell Wall Street that your earnings per share will grow 17%—just as it did last year and the year before that—then your earnings had better grow by 17% or the stock market will pummel your stock. To Buffet, the expectations of continuous growth and beating analysts' estimates almost requires cheating with the accounting numbers. "No large company can grow earnings 15% quarter after quarter like that. . . . It isn't the way business works."

Source: Andy Serwer, Janice Revell, and John Boorstin, "Dirty Rotten Numbers," *Fortune*, February 18, 2002, pp. 74–84.

---

[1]A complication can arise when a company has issued securities such as executive stock options or warrants that can be converted into shares of common stock. If these conversions were to take place, the same earnings would have to be distributed among a greater number of common shares. Therefore, a supplemental earnings per share figure, called diluted earnings per share, may have to be computed. Refer to an intermediate financial accounting text for details.

Price-Earnings Ratio

The relationship between the market price of a share of stock and the stock's current earnings per share is often stated in terms of a **price-earnings ratio.** If we assume that the current market price for Brickey Electronics' stock is $40 per share, the company's price-earnings ratio is computed as follows:

$$\text{Price-earnings ratio} = \frac{\text{Market price per share}}{\text{Earnings per share}}$$

$$\frac{\$40 \text{ per share}}{\$3.26 \text{ per share}} = 12.3$$

The price-earnings ratio is 12.3; that is, the stock is selling for about 12.3 times its current earnings per share.

The price-earnings ratio is widely used by investors. A high price-earnings ratio means that investors are willing to pay a premium for the company's stock—presumably because the company is expected to have higher than average future earnings growth. Conversely, if investors believe a company's future earnings growth prospects are limited, the company's price-earnings ratio will be relatively low. For example, not long ago, the stock prices of some dot.com companies—particularly those with little or no earnings—were selling at levels that resulted in huge and nearly unprecedented price-earnings ratios. However, these price-earnings ratios were unsustainable in the long run and the companies' stock prices eventually fell.

Dividend Payout and Yield Ratios

Investors in a company's stock make money in two ways—increases in the market value of the stock and dividends. In general, earnings should be retained in a company and not paid out in dividends as long as the rate of return on funds invested inside the company exceeds the rate of return that stockholders could earn on alternative investments outside the company. Therefore, companies with excellent prospects of profitable growth often pay little or no dividend. Companies with little opportunity for profitable growth, but with steady, dependable earnings, tend to pay out a higher percentage of their cash flow from operations as dividends.

The Dividend Payout Ratio The **dividend payout ratio** gauges the portion of current earnings being paid out in dividends. This ratio is computed by dividing the dividends per share by the earnings per share for common stock:

$$\text{Dividend payout ratio} = \frac{\text{Dividends per share}}{\text{Earnings per share}}$$

For Brickey Electronics, the dividend payout ratio for 2008 is computed as follows:

$$\text{Dividend payout ratio} = \frac{\$1.20 \text{ per share (see Exhibit 14–2)}}{\$3.26 \text{ per share}} = 36.8\%$$

There is no such thing as a "right" dividend payout ratio, although the ratio tends to be similar for companies within the same industry. As noted above, companies with ample growth opportunities at high rates of return tend to have low payout ratios, whereas companies with limited reinvestment opportunities tend to have higher payout ratios.

The Dividend Yield Ratio The **dividend yield ratio** is computed by dividing the current dividends per share by the current market price per share:

$$\text{Dividend yield ratio} = \frac{\text{Dividends per share}}{\text{Market price per share}}$$

The market price for Brickey Electronics' stock is $40 per share, so the dividend yield is computed as follows:

$$\text{Dividend yield ratio} = \frac{\$1.20 \text{ per share}}{\$40 \text{ per share}} = 3.0\%$$

The dividend yield ratio measures the rate of return (in the form of cash dividends only) that would be earned by an investor who buys common stock at the current market price. A low dividend yield ratio is neither bad nor good by itself.

Return on Total Assets

The **return on total assets** is a measure of operating performance. It is defined as follows:

$$\text{Return on total assets} = \frac{\text{Net income} + [\text{Interest expense} \times (1 - \text{Tax rate})]}{\text{Average total assets}}$$

Interest expense is added back to net income to show what earnings would have been if the company had no debt. With this adjustment, the return on total assets can be compared for companies with differing amounts of debt or for a single company that has changed its mix of debt and equity over time. Notice that the interest expense is placed on an after-tax basis by multiplying it by the factor $(1 - \text{Tax rate})$.

The return on total assets for Brickey Electronics for 2008 is computed as follows (from Exhibits 14–1 and 14–2):

$$\text{Return on total assets} = \frac{\$1,750,000 + [\$640,000 \times (1 - 0.30)]}{(\$31,500,000 + \$28,970,000)/2} = 7.3\%$$

Brickey Electronics has earned a return of 7.3% on average total assets employed over the last year.

Return on Common Stockholders' Equity

The **return on common stockholders' equity** is based on the book value of common stockholders' equity. It is computed as follows:

$$\frac{\text{Return on common}}{\text{stockholders' equity}} = \frac{\text{Net income} - \text{Preferred dividends}}{\text{Average common stockholders' equity}}$$

where

$$\frac{\text{Average common}}{\text{stockholders' equity}} = \frac{\text{Average total stockholders' equity}}{- \text{Average preferred stock}}$$

For Brickey Electronics, the return on common stockholders' equity for 2008 is computed as follows:

$$\text{Average total stockholders' equity} = \frac{(\$17,000,000 + \$15,970,000)}{2} = \$16,485,000$$

$$\text{Average preferred stock} = \frac{(\$2,000,000 + \$2,000,000)}{2} = \$2,000,000$$

$$\text{Average common stockholders' equity} = \$16,485,000 - \$2,000,000 = \$14,485,000$$

$$\text{Return on common stockholders' equity} = \frac{\$1,750,000 - \$120,000}{\$14,485,000} = 11.3\%$$

Compare the return on common stockholders' equity above (11.3%) with the return on total assets computed in the preceding section (7.3%). Why is the return on common stockholders' equity so much higher? The answer lies in *financial leverage.*

Financial Leverage

Financial leverage results from the difference between the rate of return the company earns on investments in its own assets and the rate of return that the company must pay its creditors. If the company's rate of return on total assets exceeds the rate of return the company pays its creditors, *financial leverage is positive*. If the rate of return on total assets is less than the rate of return the company pays its creditors, *financial leverage is negative*.

Financial Leverage

| Creditors/Preferred Stockholders | | Common Stockholders | Creditors/Preferred Stockholders | | Common Stockholders |

Positive Financial Leverage   **Negative Financial Leverage**

We can see financial leverage in operation in the case of Brickey Electronics. Notice from Exhibit 14–1 that the company pays 8% interest on its bonds payable. The after-tax interest cost of these bonds is only 5.6% [8% interest rate $\times$ (1 − 0.30) = 5.6%]. As shown earlier, the company's after-tax return on total assets is 7.3%. Since the return on total assets of 7.3% is greater than the 5.6% after-tax interest cost of the bonds, leverage is positive, and the difference goes to the common stockholders. This explains in part why the return on common stockholders' equity of 11.3% is greater than the return on total assets of 7.3%. If financial leverage is positive, having some debt in the capital structure can substantially benefit common stockholders. For this reason, companies often try to maintain a level of debt that is considered to be normal within their industry.

Unfortunately, leverage is a two-edged sword. If assets do not earn a high enough return to cover the interest costs of debt and preferred stock dividends, then the common stockholder suffers. In that case, financial leverage is negative.

IN BUSINESS   ## Looking at McDonald's Financials

McDonald's Corporation provides an interesting illustration of the use of financial ratios. The data below relate to the year ended December 31, 2004. (Averages were computed by adding together the beginning and end of year amounts reported on the balance sheet, and dividing the total by two.)

Net income	$2,279 million
Interest expense	$359 million
Tax rate	28.9%
Average total assets	$26,838 million
Preferred stock dividends	$0 million
Average common stockholders' equity	$13,092 million
Common stock dividends per share	$0.55
Earnings per share	1.81
Market price per share—end of year	$32.06
Book value per share—end of year	$7.88

Some key financial ratios from the standpoint of the common stockholder are computed below:

$$\text{Return on total assets} = \frac{\$2,279 + [\$359 \times (1 - 0.289)]}{\$26,838} = 9.4\%$$

$$\text{Return on common stockholders' equity} = \frac{\$2,279 - \$0}{\$13,092} = 17.4\%$$

$$\text{Dividend payout ratio} = \frac{\$0.55}{\$1.81} = 30.4\%$$

$$\text{Dividend yield ratio} = \frac{\$0.55}{\$32.06} = 1.7\%$$

The return on common stockholders' equity of 17.4% is higher than the return on total assets of 9.4% and, therefore, the company has positive financial leverage. Creditors provide about half of the company's financing; stockholders provide the remainder. (In contrast, the company's return on common stockholders' equity was 9.0% and its return on total assets was 4.8% in 2002.) Note that the market value per share is more than four times as large as the book value per share. (In contrast, the market value per share was two times as large as the book value per share in 2002.)

Source: McDonald's Corporation Annual Report for the year 2004.

Book Value per Share

Book value per share measures the amount that would be distributed to holders of each share of common stock if all assets were sold at their balance sheet carrying amounts (i.e., book values) and if all creditors were paid off. Book value per share is based entirely on historical costs. The formula for computing it is:

$$\text{Book value per share} = \frac{\text{Total stockholders' equity} - \text{Preferred stock}}{\text{Number of common shares outstanding}}$$

The book value per share of Brickey Electronics' common stock at the end of 2008 is computed as follows:

$$\text{Book value per share} = \frac{\$17,000,000 - \$2,000,000}{500,000 \text{ shares}} = \$30 \text{ per share}$$

If this book value is compared with the $40 market value of Brickey Electronics' stock, the stock may appear to be overpriced. However, as we discussed earlier, market prices reflect expectations about future earnings and dividends, whereas book value largely reflects the results of events that have occurred in the past. Ordinarily, the market value of a stock exceeds its book value. For example, in one year, Microsoft's common stock traded at over 4 times its book value, and Coca-Cola's market value was over 17 times its book value.

RATIO ANALYSIS—THE SHORT-TERM CREDITOR

Short-term creditors, such as suppliers, want to be repaid on time. Therefore, they focus on the company's cash flows and on its working capital because these are the company's primary short-term sources of cash.

LEARNING OBJECTIVE 3

Compute and interpret financial ratios that would be useful to a short-term creditor.

Working Capital

The excess of current assets over current liabilities is known as **working capital.**

$$\text{Working capital} = \text{Current assets} - \text{Current liabilities}$$

The working capital for Brickey Electronics at the end of 2008 is computed as follows:

$$\text{Working capital} = \$15,500,000 - \$7,000,000 = \$8,500,000$$

Ample working capital provides some assurance to short-term creditors that they will be paid by the company. However, maintaining large amounts of working capital isn't free. Working capital must be financed with long-term debt and equity—both of which are expensive. Therefore, managers often want to minimize working capital.

A large and growing working capital balance may not be a good sign. For example, it could be the result of unwarranted growth in inventories. To put working capital into proper perspective, it should be supplemented with the following four ratios—the current ratio, the acid-test ratio, the accounts receivable turnover, and the inventory turnover—each of which will be discussed in turn.

Current Ratio

The elements involved in the computation of working capital are frequently expressed in ratio form. A company's current assets divided by its current liabilities is known as the **current ratio:**

$$\text{Current ratio} = \frac{\text{Current assets}}{\text{Current liabilities}}$$

For Brickey Electronics, the current ratio at the end of 2008 would be computed as follows:

$$\text{Current ratio} = \frac{\$15,500,000}{\$7,000,000} = 2.21$$

Although widely regarded as a measure of short-term debt-paying ability, the current ratio must be interpreted with great care. A *declining* ratio might be a sign of a deteriorating financial condition, or it might be the result of eliminating obsolete inventories or other stagnant current assets. An *improving* ratio might be the result of stockpiling inventory, or it might indicate an improving financial situation. In short, the current ratio is useful, but tricky to interpret.

The general rule of thumb calls for a current ratio of at least 2. However, many companies successfully operate with a current ratio below 2. The adequacy of a current ratio depends heavily on the *composition* of the assets. For example, as we see in the table below, both Worthington Corporation and Greystone, Inc., have current ratios of 2. However, they are not in comparable financial condition. Greystone is likely to have difficulty meeting its current financial obligations because almost all of its current assets consist of inventory rather than more liquid assets such as cash and accounts receivable.

	Worthington Corporation	Greystone, Inc.
Current assets:		
Cash	$ 25,000	$ 2,000
Accounts receivable, net	60,000	8,000
Inventory	85,000	160,000
Prepaid expenses	5,000	5,000
Total current assets (a)	$175,000	$175,000
Current liabilities (b)	$ 87,500	$ 87,500
Current ratio, (a) ÷ (b).	2	2

Acid-Test (Quick) Ratio

The **acid-test (quick) ratio** is a more rigorous test of a company's ability to meet its short-term debts than the current ratio. Inventories and prepaid expenses are excluded from total current assets, leaving only the more liquid (or "quick") assets to be divided by current liabilities.

$$\text{Acid-test ratio} = \frac{\text{Cash} + \text{Marketable securities} + \text{Accounts receivable} + \text{Short-term notes receivable}}{\text{Current liabilities}}$$

The acid-test ratio is designed to measure how well a company can meet its obligations without having to liquidate or depend too heavily on its inventory. Ideally, each dollar of liabilities should be backed by at least $1 of quick assets. However, acid-test ratios as low as 0.3 are common.

The acid-test ratio for Brickey Electronics at the end of 2008 is computed below:

$$\text{Acid-test ratio} = \frac{\$1,200,000 + \$0 + \$6,000,000 + \$0}{\$7,000,000} = 1.03$$

Although Brickey Electronics' acid-test ratio is within the acceptable range, an analyst might be concerned about several trends revealed in the company's balance sheet. Notice in Exhibit 14–1 that short-term debts are rising, while the cash balance is declining. Perhaps the lower cash balance is a result of the substantial increase in accounts receivable. In short, as with the current ratio, the acid-test ratio should be interpreted with one eye on its basic components.

Too Much Cash?

IN BUSINESS

Microsoft has accumulated an unprecedented hoard of cash and cash equivalents—over $49 billion at the end of fiscal year 2003—and this cash hoard is growing at the rate of about $1 billion per month. This cash hoard is large enough to give every household in the U.S. a check for $471. What does Microsoft need all this money for? Why doesn't it pay more dividends? Microsoft executives say the cash is needed for antitrust lawsuits. Critics of the company's power, including some of its competitors, claim that the cash gives the company a huge competitive advantage. Because of this huge reserve of cash, the company can afford to lose money to enter risky new markets like the Xbox game console.

Sources: Jay Greene, "Microsoft's $49 Billion 'Problem,'" *BusinessWeek*, August 11, 2003, p. 36; and the Microsoft Annual Report for the year 2003.

Accounts Receivable Turnover

The *accounts receivable turnover* and *average collection period* ratios are used to measure how quickly credit sales are converted into cash. The **accounts receivable turnover** is computed by dividing sales on account (i.e., credit sales) by the average accounts receivable balance for the year:

$$\text{Accounts receivable turnover} = \frac{\text{Sales on account}}{\text{Average accounts receivable balance}}$$

Assuming that all of Brickey Electronics' sales were on account, its accounts receivable turnover for 2008 is computed as follows:

$$\text{Accounts receivable turnover} = \frac{\$52,000,000}{(\$6,000,000 + \$4,000,000)/2} = 10.4$$

The accounts receivable turnover can then be divided into 365 days to determine the average number of days required to collect an account (known as the **average collection period**).

$$\text{Average collection period} = \frac{365 \text{ days}}{\text{Accounts receivable turnover}}$$

The average collection period for Brickey Electronics for 2008 is computed as follows:

$$\text{Average collection period} = \frac{365 \text{ days}}{10.4} = 35 \text{ days}$$

This means that on average it takes 35 days to collect a credit sale. Whether this is good or bad depends on the credit terms Brickey Electronics is offering its customers. Many customers will tend to withhold payment for as long as the credit terms allow. If the credit terms are 30 days, then a 35-day average collection period would usually be viewed as very good. On the other hand, if the company's credit terms are 10 days, then a 35-day average collection period is worrisome. A long collection period may result from having too many old uncollectible accounts, failing to bill promptly or follow up on late accounts, lax credit checks, and so on. In practice, average collection periods ranging from 10 days all the way to 180 days are common, depending on the industry.

Inventory Turnover

The **inventory turnover ratio** measures how many times a company's inventory has been sold and replaced during the year. It is computed by dividing the cost of goods sold by the average level of inventory [(Beginning inventory + Ending inventory) ÷ 2]:

$$\text{Inventory turnover} = \frac{\text{Cost of goods sold}}{\text{Average inventory balance}}$$

Brickey's inventory turnover for 2008 is computed as follows:

$$\text{Inventory turnover} = \frac{\$36,000,000}{(8,000,000 + \$10,000,000)/2} = 4$$

The number of days needed on average to sell the entire inventory (called the **average sale period**) can be computed by dividing 365 by the inventory turnover:

$$\text{Average sale period} = \frac{365 \text{ days}}{\text{Inventory turnover}}$$

$$= \frac{365 \text{ days}}{4 \text{ times}} = 91\tfrac{1}{4} \text{ days}$$

The average sale period varies from industry to industry. Grocery stores, with significant perishable stocks, tend to turn their inventory over very quickly. On the other hand, jewelry stores tend to turn their inventory over very slowly. In practice, average sales periods of 10 days to 90 days are common, depending on the industry.

A company whose inventory turnover ratio is much slower than the average for its industry may have too much inventory or the wrong sorts of inventory. Some managers argue that they must buy in large quantities to take advantage of quantity discounts. But these discounts must be compared to the added costs of insurance, taxes, financing, and risks of obsolescence and deterioration that result from carrying added inventories.

Inventory turnover should increase in companies that adopt Lean Production. If properly implemented, Lean Production should result in both a decrease in inventories and an increase in sales due to better customer service.

IN BUSINESS   **Setting the Standard for Inventory Turnover**

Dell, Inc. has earned a reputation as the world's most efficient computer maker—requiring very little inventory to support its sales. To keep its inventories at the lowest possible level, the company only builds computers to order and relentlessly trims the time required to build a machine. As a result, the company's inventory turnover for the fiscal year ending January 31, 2003, was a phenomenal 99.5 times (cost of sales of $29,055 million divided by average inventories of $292 million). This translates into an average sale period of 3.7 days.

Source: Dell Computer Corporation Annual Report for the year 2003.

1. Total sales at a store are $1,000,000 and 80% of those sales are on credit. The beginning and ending accounts receivable balances are $100,000 and $140,000, respectively. What is the accounts receivable turnover?
   a. 3.33
   b. 6.67
   c. 8.33
   d. 10.67

2. A retailer's total sales are $1,000,000 and the gross margin percentage is 60%. The beginning and ending inventory balances are $240,000 and $260,000, respectively. What is the inventory turnover?
   a. 1.60
   b. 2.40
   c. 3.40
   d. 3.60

CONCEPT
CHECK

Portfolio Manager

YOU DECIDE

Assume that you work for a mutual fund and have the responsibility of selecting stocks to include in its investment portfolio. You have been analyzing the financial statements of a chain of retail clothing stores and noticed that the company's current ratio has increased, but its acid-test (quick) ratio has decreased. In addition, the company's accounts receivable turnover has decreased and its inventory turnover ratio has decreased. Finally, the company's price-earnings ratio is at an all-time high. Would you recommend buying stock in this company?

Vice President of Sales

DECISION MAKER

Although its credit terms require payment within 30 days, your company's average collection period is 33 days. A major competitor has an average collection period of 27 days. You have been asked to explain why your company is not doing as well as the competitor. You have investigated your company's credit policies and procedures and have concluded that they are reasonable and adequate under the circumstances. What rationale would you consider to explain why (1) the average collection period of your company exceeds the credit terms, and (2) the average collection period of your company is higher than that of its competitor?

Watch Those Receivables and Inventories!

IN BUSINESS

Herb Greenberg, an investment columnist for *Fortune* magazine, warns investors to look out for two "sure warning signs: receivables and inventory that rise faster than sales . . . A fast rise in receivables could mean that the company is pulling out all the stops to get customers to take its products. That's good, *unless* it means stealing sales from future quarters. As for a rise in inventory: If finished goods are piling up in warehouses—absent some reasonable explanation, like a looming product launch—they must not be selling." To monitor these possibilities, watch the accounts receivable turnover or average collection period for the receivables and the inventory turnover or average sale period for the inventories.

Source: Herb Greenberg, "Minding Your K's and Q's," *Fortune*, January 8, 2001, p. 180.

IN BUSINESS   Warning Signs at Amazon.com

Ravi Suria, a debt analyst at Lehman Brothers, sounded an early warning about Amazon.com's finances. Amazon's inventory turnover plummeted from 8.5 to 2.9 within two years. And in a year in which its sales grew 170%, its inventories skyrocketed by 650%. Suria points out that "When a company manages inventory properly, it should grow along with its sales growth rate." When inventory grows faster than sales, "it means simply that they're not selling as much as they are buying."

Source: Robert Hof, Debra Sparks, Ellen Neuborne, and Wendy Zellner, "Can Amazon Make It?" *BusinessWeek*, July 10, 2000, pp. 38–43.

RATIO ANALYSIS—THE LONG-TERM CREDITOR

LEARNING OBJECTIVE 4

Compute and interpret financial ratios that would be useful to a long-term creditor.

Long-term creditors are concerned with a company's ability to repay its loans over the long run. For example, if a company were to pay out all of its available cash in the form of dividends, then nothing would be left to pay back creditors. Consequently, creditors often seek protection by requiring that borrowers agree to various restrictive covenants, or rules. These restrictive covenants typically include restrictions on payment of dividends as well as rules stating that the company must maintain certain financial ratios at specified levels. Although restrictive covenants are widely used, they do not ensure that creditors will be paid when loans come due. The company still must generate sufficient earnings to cover payments.

Times Interest Earned Ratio

The most common measure of the ability of a company's operations to provide protection to long-term creditors is the **times interest earned ratio.** It is computed by dividing earnings *before* interest expense and income taxes (i.e., net operating income) by interest expense:

$$\text{Times interest earned ratio} = \frac{\text{Earnings before interest expense and income taxes}}{\text{Interest expense}}$$

For Brickey Electronics, the times interest earned ratio for 2008 is computed as follows:

$$\text{Times interest earned ratio} = \frac{\$3,140,000}{\$640,000} = 4.9$$

The times interest earned ratio is based on earnings before interest expense and income taxes because that is the amount of earnings that is available for making interest payments. Interest expenses are deducted *before* income taxes are determined; creditors have first claim on the earnings before taxes are paid.

Clearly, a times interest earned ratio of less than 1 is inadequate because the interest expense exceeds the earnings that are available for paying interest. In contrast, a times interest earned ratio of 2 or more may be considered sufficient to protect long-term creditors.

Debt-to-Equity Ratio

Long-term creditors are also concerned with a company's ability to keep a reasonable balance between its debt and equity. This balance is measured by the **debt-to-equity ratio:**

$$\text{Debt-to-equity ratio} = \frac{\text{Total liabilities}}{\text{Stockholders' equity}}$$

Brickey's debt-to-equity ratio at the end of 2008 is computed as follows:

$$\text{Debt-to-equity ratio} = \frac{\$14,500,000}{\$17,000,000} = 0.85$$

The debt-to-equity ratio indicates the relative proportions of debt and equity on the company's balance sheet. In 2008, creditors of Brickey Electronics were providing 85 cents for each $1 being provided by stockholders.

Creditors and stockholders have different views about the optimal debt-to-equity ratio. Ordinarily, stockholders would like a lot of debt to take advantage of positive financial leverage. On the other hand, because equity represents the excess of total assets over total liabilities and hence a buffer of protection for the creditors, creditors would like to see less debt and more equity.

In practice, debt-to-equity ratios from 0.0 (no debt) to 3.0 are common. Generally speaking, in industries with little financial risk, creditors tolerate high debt-to-equity ratios. In industries with more financial risk, creditors demand lower debt-to-equity ratios.

3. Total assets are $1,500,000 and stockholders' equity is $900,000. What is the debt-to-equity ratio?
   a. 0.33
   b. 0.50
   c. 0.60
   d. 0.67

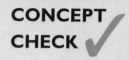

CONCEPT CHECK

SUMMARY OF RATIOS AND SOURCES OF COMPARATIVE RATIO DATA

Exhibit 14–6 contains a summary of the ratios discussed in this chapter. The formula for each ratio and a summary comment on each ratio's significance are included in the exhibit.

Exhibit 14–7 contains a listing of public sources that provide comparative ratio data organized by industry. These sources are used extensively by managers, investors, and analysts. The *EDGAR* database listed in Exhibit 14–7 is a particularly rich source of data. It contains copies of all reports filed by companies with the SEC since about 1995—including annual reports filed as form 10-K.

XBRL: The Next Generation of Financial Reporting   IN BUSINESS

In 2005, the Securities and Exchange Commission (SEC) announced that it would allow companies to submit financial reports using a computer code known as Extensible Business Reporting Language, or XBRL for short. XBRL is a "financial reporting derivation of Extensible Markup Language, or XML—a framework that establishes individual 'tags' for elements in structured documents, allowing specific elements to be immediately accessed and aggregated."

XBRL dramatically improves the financial reporting process in two ways. First, data are tagged in accordance with a generally accepted framework. This simplifies the process of making apples-to-apples comparisons of financial results across companies. For example, "many of the components of a 'property, plant and equipment' listing on a balance sheet . . . may be described differently by different companies, but when tagged in XBRL, a straight comparison becomes much simpler."

Second, XBRL simplifies the exchange of financial data. Without XBRL, a company's financial data are typically stored in a format that is unique to that company's specific financial software application and that cannot be easily read by other financial software. This problem is overcome with XBRL because the tagged data become "independent of the originating application and can readily be shared with any application that recognizes XBRL. This feature of XBRL makes the markup language very attractive for government regulators and financial analysts."

Sources: Glenn Cheney, "U.S. Gets Its XBRL in Gear: SEC, FDIC OK Tagged Data," *Accounting Today*, March 14–April 3, 2005, pp. 26–27; Neal Hannon, "XBRL Fundamentals," *Strategic Finance*, April 2005, pp. 57–58; and Ghostwriter, "From Tags to Riches," *CFO-IT*, Spring 2005, pp. 13–14.

EXHIBIT 14–6 Summary of Ratios

Ratio	Formula	Significance
Gross margin percentage	Gross margin ÷ Sales	A broad measure of profitability
Earnings per share (of common stock)	(Net income − Preferred dividends) ÷ Average number of common shares outstanding	Affects the market price per share, as reflected in the price-earnings ratio
Price-earnings ratio	Market price per share ÷ Earnings per share	An index of whether a stock is relatively cheap or relatively expensive in relation to current earnings
Dividend payout ratio	Dividends per share ÷ Earnings per share	An index showing whether a company pays out most of its earnings in dividends or reinvests the earnings internally
Dividend yield ratio	Dividends per share ÷ Market price per share	Shows the return in terms of cash dividends being provided by a stock
Return on total assets	{Net income + [Interest expense × (1 − Tax rate)]} ÷ Average total assets	Measures how well assets have been employed by management
Return on common stockholders' equity	(Net income − Preferred dividends) ÷ (Average total stockholders' equity − Average preferred stock)	When compared to the return on total assets, measures the extent to which financial leverage is working for or against common stockholders
Book value per share	Common stockholders' equity (Total stockholders' equity − Preferred stock) ÷ Number of common shares outstanding	Measures the amount that would be distributed to common stockholders if all assets were sold at their balance sheet carrying amounts and if all creditors were paid off
Working capital	Current assets − Current liabilities	Measures the company's ability to repay current liabilities using only current assets
Current ratio	Current assets ÷ Current liabilities	Test of short-term debt-paying ability
Acid-test (quick) ratio	(Cash + Marketable securities + Accounts receivable + Short-term notes receivable) ÷ Current liabilities	Test of short-term debt-paying ability without having to rely on inventory
Accounts receivable turnover	Sales on account ÷ Average accounts receivable balance	A rough measure of how many times a company's accounts receivable have been turned into cash during the year
Average collection period	365 days ÷ Accounts receivable turnover	Measures the average number of days taken to collect an account receivable
Inventory turnover ratio	Cost of goods sold ÷ Average inventory balance	Measures how many times a company's inventory has been sold during the year
Average sale period (turnover in days)	365 days ÷ Inventory turnover	Measures the average number of days taken to sell the inventory one time
Times interest earned ratio	Earnings before interest expense and income taxes ÷ Interest expense	Measures the company's ability to make interest payments
Debt-to-equity ratio	Total liabilities ÷ Stockholders' equity	Measures the amount of assets being provided by creditors for each dollar of assets being provided by the stockholders

EXHIBIT 14–7 Sources of Financial Ratios

Source	Content
Almanac of Business and Industrial Financial Ratios, Aspen Publishers; published annually	An exhaustive source that contains common-size income statements and financial ratios by industry and by the size of companies within each industry.
AMA Annual Statement Studies, Risk Management Association; published annually.	A widely used publication that contains common-size statements and financial ratios on individual companies; the companies are arranged by industry.
EDGAR, Securities and Exchange Commission; website that is continually updated www.sec.gov	An exhaustive Internet database that contains reports filed by companies with the SEC; these reports can be downloaded.
FreeEdgar, EDGAR Online, Inc.; website that is continually updated; www.freeedgar.com	A site that allows you to search SEC filings; financial information can be downloaded directly into Excel worksheets.
Hoover's Online, Hoovers, Inc.; website that is continually updated; www.hoovers.com	A site that provides capsule profiles for 10,000 U.S. companies with links to company websites, annual reports, stock charts, news articles, and industry information.
Industry Norms & Key Business Ratios, Dun & Bradstreet; published annually	Fourteen commonly used financial ratios are computed for over 800 major industry groupings.
Mergent Industrial Manual and Mergent Bank and Finance Manual; published annually	An exhaustive source that contains financial ratios on all companies listed on the New York Stock Exchange, the American Stock Exchange, and regional American exchanges.
Standard & Poor's Industry Survey, Standard & Poor's; published annually	Various statistics, including some financial ratios, are given by industry and for leading companies within each industry grouping.

SUMMARY

LO1 Prepare and interpret financial statements in comparative and common-size form.
Raw data from financial statements should be standardized so that the data can be compared over time and across companies. For example, all of the financial data for a company can be expressed as a percentage of the data in some base year. This makes it easier to spot trends over time. To make it easier to compare companies, common-size financial statements are often used in which income statement data are expressed as a percentage of sales and balance sheet data are expressed as a percentage of total assets.

LO2 Compute and interpret financial ratios that would be useful to a common stockholder.
Common stockholders are concerned with the company's earnings per share, price-earnings ratio, dividend payout and yield ratios, return on total assets, book value per share, and return on common stockholders' equity. Generally speaking, the higher these ratios, the better it is for common stockholders.

LO3 Compute and interpret financial ratios that would be useful to a short-term creditor.
Short-term creditors are concerned with the company's ability to repay its debt in the near future. Consequently, these investors focus on the relation between current assets and current liabilities and the company's ability to generate cash. Specifically, short-term creditors monitor working capital, the current ratio, the acid-test (quick) ratio, accounts receivable turnover, and inventory turnover.

LO4 Compute and interpret financial ratios that would be useful to a long-term creditor.
Long-term creditors have many of the same concerns as short-term creditors, but also monitor the times interest earned ratio and the debt-to-equity ratio. These ratios indicate the company's ability to pay interest out of operations and how heavily the company is financially leveraged.

GUIDANCE ANSWERS TO *DECISION MAKER* AND *YOU DECIDE*

Portfolio Manager (p. 597)
All of the ratios—current ratio, acid-test (quick) ratio, accounts receivable turnover, and inventory turnover ratio—indicate deteriorating operations. And yet the company's price-earnings ratio is at an all-time high,

suggesting that the stock market is optimistic about the company's future and its stock price. It would be risky to invest in this company without digging deeper and finding out what has caused the deteriorating operating ratios.

Vice President of Sales (p. 597)

An average collection period of 33 days means that on average it takes 33 days to collect a credit sale. Whether the average of 33 days is acceptable or not depends on the credit terms that your company offers to its customers. In this case, an average collection period of 33 days is good because the credit terms offered by your company are net 30 days. Why might the average collection period exceed the credit terms? Some customers may misjudge the amount of time that it takes mail to reach the company's offices. Certain customers may experience temporary cash shortages and delay payment for short periods of time. Others might be in the process of returning goods and have not paid for the goods that will be returned because they realize that a credit will be posted to their account. Still others may be in the process of resolving disputes regarding the goods that were shipped.

Turning to the competitor's average collection period of 27 days, it is possible that the competitor's credit terms may be shorter than 30 days. Or, the competitor might be offering sales discounts to its customers (e.g., 2/10, n/30) for paying early. Sales discounts are offered as an incentive to customers to motivate them to pay invoices in advance of the due date. If enough customers take advantage of the sales discounts, the average collection period will drop below 30 days.

GUIDANCE ANSWERS TO CONCEPT CHECKS

1. **Choice b.** The accounts receivable turnover is $800,000 of credit sales ÷ $120,000 average accounts receivable balance = 6.67.
2. **Choice a.** First, calculate the cost of goods sold as follows: $1,000,000 × (1 − 0.60) = $400,000. Next, the inventory turnover is calculated as follows: $400,000 of cost of goods sold ÷ $250,000 average inventory = 1.60.
3. **Choice d.** Total assets of $1,500,000 − $900,000 of stockholders' equity = $600,000 of total liabilities. The debt-to-equity ratio is $600,000 ÷ $900,000 = 0.67.

REVIEW PROBLEM: SELECTED RATIOS AND FINANCIAL LEVERAGE

Starbucks Coffee Company is the leading retailer and roaster of specialty coffee in North America selling freshly brewed coffee, pastries, and coffee beans. Data (slightly modified) from its financial statements are given below:

Starbucks Coffee Company
Comparative Balance Sheet
(dollars in millions)

	End of Year	Beginning of Year
Assets		
Current assets:		
Cash	$ 113	$ 71
Marketable securities	107	61
Accounts receivable	90	76
Inventories	221	202
Other current assets	63	48
Total current assets	594	458
Property and equipment, net	1,136	931
Other assets	121	103
Total assets	$1,851	$1,492

(continued)

(continued)

Starbucks Coffee Company
Comparative Balance Sheet
(dollars in millions)

	End of Year	Beginning of Year
Liabilities and Stockholders' Equity		
Current liabilities:		
Accounts payable	$ 128	$74
Short-term bank loans	62	56
Accrued payables	245	174
Other current liabilities	10	8
Total current liabilities	445	312
Long-term liabilities	30	32
Total liabilities	475	344
Stockholders' equity:		
Preferred stock	0	0
Common stock and additional paid-in capital	792	751
Retained earnings	584	397
Total stockholders' equity	1,376	1,148
Total liabilities and stockholders' equity	$1,851	$1,492

Starbucks Coffee Company
Income Statement
(dollars in millions)

	Current Year
Sales	$2,678
Cost of goods sold	1,113
Gross margin	1,565
Selling and administrative expenses:	
Store operating expenses	875
Other operating expenses	93
Depreciation and amortization	164
General and administrative expenses	151
Total selling and administrative expenses	1,283
Net operating income	282
Internet investment losses	(3)
Interest income	11
Interest expense	0
Net income before taxes	290
Income taxes (about 37%)	108
Net income	$ 182

Required:
1. Compute the return on total assets.
2. Compute the return on common stockholders' equity.
3. Is Starbucks' financial leverage positive or negative? Explain.
4. Compute the current ratio.
5. Compute the acid-test (quick) ratio.
6. Compute the inventory turnover.
7. Compute the average sale period.
8. Compute the debt-to-equity ratio.

Solution to Review Problem

1. Return on total assets:

$$\text{Return on total assets} = \frac{\text{Net income} + [\text{Interest expense} \times (1 - \text{Tax rate})]}{\text{Average total assets}}$$

$$= \frac{\$182 + [\$0 \times (1 - 0.37)]}{(\$1,851 + \$1,492)/\,2} = 10.9\% \text{ (rounded)}$$

2. Return on common stockholders' equity:

$$\text{Return on common stockholders' equity} = \frac{\text{Net income} - \text{Preferred dividends}}{\text{Average common stockholders' equity}}$$

$$= \frac{\$182 - \$0}{(\$1,376 + \$1,148)/\,2} = 14.4\% \text{ (rounded)}$$

3. The company has positive financial leverage because the return on common stockholders' equity of 14.4% is greater than the return on total assets of 10.9%. The positive financial leverage was obtained from current and long-term liabilities.

4. Current ratio:

$$\text{Current ratio} = \frac{\text{Current assets}}{\text{Current liabilities}}$$

$$= \frac{\$594}{\$445} = 1.33 \text{ (rounded)}$$

5. Acid-test (quick) ratio:

$$\text{Acid-test ratio} = \frac{\text{Cash} + \text{Marketable securities} + \text{Accounts receivable} + \text{Short-term notes receivable}}{\text{Current liabilities}}$$

$$= \frac{\$113 + \$107 + \$90 + \$0}{\$445} = 0.70 \text{ (rounded)}$$

6. Inventory turnover:

$$\text{Inventory turnover} = \frac{\text{Cost of goods sold}}{\text{Average inventory balance}}$$

$$= \frac{\$1,113}{(\$221 + \$202)/\,2} = 5.26 \text{ (rounded)}$$

7. Average sale period:

$$\text{Average sale period} = \frac{365 \text{ days}}{\text{Inventory turnover}}$$

$$= \frac{365 \text{ days}}{5.26} = 69 \text{ days (rounded)}$$

8. Debt-to-equity ratio:

$$\text{Debt-to-equity ratio} = \frac{\text{Total liabilities}}{\text{Stockholders' equity}}$$

$$= \frac{\$475}{\$1,376} = 0.35 \text{ (rounded)}$$

GLOSSARY

(Note: Definitions and formulas for all financial ratios are shown in Exhibit 14–6. These definitions and formulas are not repeated here.)

Common-size financial statements   A statement that shows the items appearing on it in percentage form as well as in dollar form. On the income statement, the percentages are based on total sales; on the balance sheet, the percentages are based on total assets. (p. 586)

Financial leverage   A difference between the rate of return on assets and the rate paid to creditors. (p. 591)

Horizontal analysis   A side-by-side comparison of two or more years' financial statements. (p. 584)

Trend analysis   See *Horizontal analysis.* (p. 584)

Trend percentages   Several years of financial data expressed as a percentage of performance in a base year. (p. 585)

Vertical analysis   The presentation of a company's financial statements in common-size form. (p. 586)

Multiple-choice questions are provided on the text website at www.mhhe.com/brewer4e.

Quiz 14

QUESTIONS

14–1   Distinguish between horizontal and vertical analysis of financial statement data.

14–2   What is the reason for examining trends in a company's financial ratios and other data? What other kinds of comparisons might an analyst make?

14–3   Assume that two companies in the same industry have equal earnings. Why might these companies have different price-earnings ratios?

14–4   Would you expect a company in a rapidly growing technological industry to have a high or low dividend payout ratio?

14–5   Distinguish between a manager's *financing* and *operating* responsibilities. Which of these responsibilities is the return on total assets ratio designed to measure?

14–6   What is meant by the dividend yield on a common stock investment?

14–7   What is meant by the term *financial leverage*?

14–8   If a stock's market value exceeds its book value, then the stock is overpriced. Do you agree? Explain.

14–9   Weaver Company experiences a great deal of seasonal variation in its business activities. The company's high point in business activity is in June; its low point is in January. During which month would you expect the current ratio to be highest?

14–10 A company seeking a line of credit at a bank was turned down. Among other things, the bank stated that the company's current ratio of 2.0 was not adequate. Give reasons why a current ratio of 2.0 might not be adequate.

 # BRIEF EXERCISES

BRIEF EXERCISE 14–1   Trend Percentages (LO1)

Starkey Office Products' sales, current assets, and current liabilities (all in thousands of dollars) have been reported as follows over the last five years (Year 5 is the most recent year):

	Year 5	Year 4	Year 3	Year 2	Year 1
Sales..........................	$5,625	$5,400	$4,950	$4,725	$4,500
Current assets:					
Cash	$ 64	$ 72	$ 84	$ 88	$ 80
Accounts receivable, net	560	496	432	416	400
Inventory	896	880	816	864	800
Total current assets...............	$1,520	$1,448	$1,332	$1,368	$1,280
Current liabilities	$ 390	$ 318	$ 324	$ 330	$ 300

Required:

1. Express all of the asset, liability, and sales data in trend percentages. (Show percentages for each item.) Use Year 1 as the base year and carry computations to one decimal place.

2. Comment on the results of your analysis.

BRIEF EXERCISE 14–2   Common-Size Income Statement (LO1)

A comparative income statement is given below for Ryder Hardwoods, a retailer of hardwood flooring materials:

Ryder Hardwoods Comparative Income Statement		
	This Year	**Last Year**
Sales.	$5,000,000	$4,000,000
Cost of goods sold	3,160,000	2,400,000
Gross margin.	1,840,000	1,600,000
Selling and administrative expenses:		
Selling expenses	900,000	700,000
Administrative expenses	680,000	584,000
Total selling and administrative expenses.	1,580,000	1,284,000
Net operating income	260,000	316,000
Interest expense	70,000	40,000
Net income before taxes	$ 190,000	$ 276,000

The president is concerned that net income is down this year even though sales have increased during the year. The president is also concerned that administrative expenses have increased because the company made a concerted effort this year to cut "fat" out of the organization.

Required:

1. Express each year's income statement in common-size percentages. Carry computations to one decimal place.
2. Comment briefly on the changes between the two years.

BRIEF EXERCISE 14–3   Financial Ratios for Common Stockholders (LO2)

Comparative financial statements for Heritage Antiquing Services for the fiscal year ending December 31 appear below. The company did not issue any new common or preferred stock during the year. A total of 600 thousand shares of common stock were outstanding. The interest rate on the bond payable was 14%, the income tax rate was 40%, and the dividend per share of common stock was $0.75. The market value of the company's common stock at the end of the year was $26. All of the company's sales are on account.

Heritage Antiquing Services Comparative Balance Sheet (dollars in thousands)		
	This Year	**Last Year**
Assets		
Current assets:		
Cash	$ 1,080	$ 1,210
Accounts receivable, net	9,000	6,500
Inventory	12,000	10,600
Prepaid expenses	600	500
Total current assets.	22,680	18,810
Property and equipment:		
Land.	9,000	9,000
Buildings and equipment, net	36,800	38,000
Total property and equipment	45,800	47,000
Total assets.	$68,480	$65,810

(continued)

(concluded)

Heritage Antiquing Services
Comparative Balance Sheet
(dollars in thousands)

	This Year	Last Year
Liabilities and Stockholders' Equity		
Current liabilities:		
Accounts payable	$18,500	$17,400
Accrued payables	900	700
Notes payable, short term	—	100
Total current liabilities	19,400	18,200
Long-term liabilities:		
Bonds payable	8,000	8,000
Total liabilities	27,400	26,200
Stockholders' equity:		
Preferred stock	1,000	1,000
Common stock	2,000	2,000
Additional paid-in capital	4,000	4,000
Total paid-in capital	7,000	7,000
Retained earnings	34,080	32,610
Total stockholders' equity	41,080	39,610
Total liabilities and stockholders' equity	$68,480	$65,810

Heritage Antiquing Services
Comparative Income Statement and Reconciliation
(dollars in thousands)

	This Year	Last Year
Sales	$66,000	$64,000
Cost of goods sold	43,000	42,000
Gross margin	23,000	22,000
Selling and administrative expenses:		
Selling expenses	11,500	11,000
Administrative expenses	7,400	7,000
Total selling and administrative expenses	18,900	18,000
Net operating income	4,100	4,000
Interest expense	800	800
Net income before taxes	3,300	3,200
Income taxes	1,320	1,280
Net income	1,980	1,920
Dividends to preferred stockholders	60	400
Net income remaining for common stockholders	1,920	1,520
Dividends to common stockholders	450	450
Net income added to retained earnings	1,470	1,070
Retained earnings, beginning of year	32,610	31,540
Retained earnings, end of year	$34,080	$32,610

Required:
Compute the following financial ratios for common stockholders for this year:
1. Gross margin percentage.
2. Earnings per share of common stock.
3. Price-earnings ratio.

4. Dividend payout ratio.
5. Dividend yield ratio.
6. Return on total assets.
7. Return on common stockholders' equity.
8. Book value per share.

BRIEF EXERCISE 14–4   Financial Ratios for Short-Term Creditors (LO3)
Refer to the data in Brief Exercise 14–3 for Heritage Antiquing Services.

Required:
Compute the following financial data for short-term creditors for this year:

1. Working capital.
2. Current ratio.
3. Acid-test ratio.
4. Accounts receivable turnover. (All sales are on account.)
5. Average collection period.
6. Inventory turnover.
7. Average sale period.

BRIEF EXERCISE 14–5   Financial Ratios for Long-Term Creditors (LO4)
Refer to the data in Brief Exercise 14–3 for Heritage Antiquing Services.

Required:
Compute the following financial ratios for long-term creditors for this year:

1. Times interest earned ratio.
2. Debt-to-equity ratio.

EXERCISES

EXERCISE 14–6   Selected Financial Ratios (LO3, LO4)
Recent financial statements for Madison Corporation, a company that sells drilling equipment, are given below:

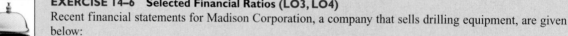

Madison Corporation Balance Sheet June 30		
Assets		
Current assets:		
Cash		$ 21,000
Accounts receivable, net		160,000
Merchandise inventory		300,000
Prepaid expenses		9,000
Total current assets.........................		490,000
Property and equipment, net.................		810,000
Total assets		$1,300,000
Liabilities and Stockholders' Equity		
Liabilities:.		
Current liabilities		$ 200,000
Bonds payable, 10%		300,000
Total liabilities		500,000
Stockholders' equity:.......................		
Common stock, $5 par value..............	$100,000	
Retained earnings.......................	700,000	
Total stockholders' equity		800,000
Total liabilities and stockholders' equity........		$1,300,000

Madison Corporation	
Income Statement	
For the Year Ended June 30	
Sales.	$2,100,000
Cost of goods sold	1,260,000
Gross margin.	840,000
Selling and administrative expenses.	660,000
Net operating income	180,000
Interest expense	30,000
Net income before taxes	150,000
Income taxes (30%)	45,000
Net income	$ 105,000

Account balances at the beginning of the company's fiscal year were: accounts receivable, $140,000; and inventory, $260,000. All sales were on account.

Required:
Compute the following financial ratios:

1. Gross margin percentage.
2. Current ratio.
3. Acid-test (quick) ratio.
4. Average collection period.
5. Average sale period.
6. Debt-to-equity ratio.
7. Times interest earned ratio.
8. Book value per share.

EXERCISE 14–7 Selected Financial Ratios for Common Stockholders (LO2)

Refer to the financial statements for Madison Corporation in Exercise 14–6. In addition to the data in these statements, assume that Madison Corporation paid dividends of $3.15 per share during the year. Also assume that the company's common stock had a market price of $63 per share on June 30 and there was no change in the number of outstanding shares of common stock during the fiscal year.

Required:
Compute the following financial ratios:

1. Earnings per share.
2. Dividend payout ratio.
3. Dividend yield ratio.
4. Price-earnings ratio.

EXERCISE 14–8 Selected Financial Ratios for Common Stockholders (LO2)

Refer to the financial statements for Madison Corporation in Exercise 14–6. Assets at the beginning of the year totaled $1,100,000, and the stockholders' equity totaled $725,000.

Required:
Compute the following financial ratios:

1. Return on total assets.
2. Return on common stockholders' equity.
3. Was financial leverage positive or negative for the year? Explain.

EXERCISE 14–9 Selected Financial Measures for Short-Term Creditors (LO3)

Rightway Gutter Installers had a current ratio of 2.5 on June 30 of the current year. On that date, the company's assets were as follows:

Cash	$ 80,000
Accounts receivable, net	460,000
Inventory	750,000
Prepaid expenses	10,000
Equipment, net	1,900,000
Total assets	$3,200,000

Required:
1. What was the company's working capital on June 30?
2. What was the company's acid-test (quick) ratio on June 30?
3. The company paid an account payable of $100,000 immediately after June 30.
   a.   What effect did this transaction have on working capital? Show computations.
   b.   What effect did this transaction have on the current ratio? Show computations.

EXERCISE 14–10   Selected Financial Ratios for Common Stockholders (LO2)
Selected financial data from the September 30 year-end statements of Kosanka Marine Services Company are given below:

Total assets	$5,000,000
Long-term debt (12% interest rate)	$750,000
Preferred stock, $100 par, 7%	$800,000
Total stockholders' equity	$3,100,000
Interest paid on long-term debt	$90,000
Net income	$470,000

Total assets at the beginning of the year were $4,800,000; total stockholders' equity was $2,900,000. There has been no change in preferred stock during the year. The company's tax rate is 30%.

Required:
1. Compute the return on total assets.
2. Compute the return on common stockholders' equity.
3. Is financial leverage positive or negative? Explain.

PROBLEMS

PROBLEM 14–11A   Interpretation of Financial Ratios (LO1, LO2, LO3)
Shannon Michaels is interested in the stock of Acelicom, a company that sells building materials to the construction industry. Before purchasing the stock, Shannon would like your help in analyzing the following data:

	Year 3	Year 2	Year 1
Sales trend	132	118	108
Current ratio	2.7	2.4	2.3
Acid-test (quick) ratio	0.6	0.8	1.0
Accounts receivable turnover	9.8	10.7	12.8
Inventory turnover	6.4	7.8	8.4
Dividend yield	7.4%	6.8%	5.7%
Dividend payout ratio	42%	52%	62%
Return on total assets	12.8%	11.5%	9.8%
Return on common stockholders' equity	15.1%	10.5%	8.6%
Dividends paid per share*	$1.40	$1.40	$1.40

*There have been no changes in common stock outstanding over the three-year period.

Shannon would like answers to a number of questions about the trend of events in Acelicom over the last three years. His questions are:

a. Is it becoming easier for the company to pay its bills as they come due?
b. Are customers paying their accounts at least as fast now as they were in Year 1?
c. Is the total of accounts receivable increasing, decreasing, or remaining constant?
d. Is the level of inventory increasing, decreasing, or remaining constant?
e. Is the market price of the company's stock going up or down?
f. Are the earnings per share increasing or decreasing?
g. Is the price-earnings ratio going up or down?
h. Is the company employing financial leverage to the advantage of the common stockholders?

Required:
Answer each of Shannon's questions and explain how you arrived at your answer.

PROBLEM 14–12A Common-Size Statements and Financial Ratios for Creditors (LO1, LO3, LO4)
Vicki Newport organized Newport Industry 10 years ago to produce and sell several electronic devices on which she had secured patents. Although the company has been fairly profitable, it is now experiencing a severe cash shortage. For this reason, it is requesting a $500,000 long-term loan from San Juan Bank, $80,000 of which will be used to bolster the Cash account and $420,000 of which will be used to modernize equipment. The company's financial statements for the two most recent years follow:

CHECK FIGURE
(1e) Inventory turnover this year: 5.0
(1g) Times interest earned last year: 6.0

Newport Industry
Comparative Balance Sheet

	This Year	Last Year
Assets		
Current assets:		
Cash	$ 60,000	$ 140,000
Marketable securities	0	30,000
Accounts receivable, net	470,000	290,000
Inventory	940,000	590,000
Prepaid expenses	35,000	40,000
Total current assets	1,505,000	1,090,000
Plant and equipment, net	1,410,000	1,300,000
Total assets	$2,915,000	$2,390,000
Liabilities and Stockholders' Equity		
Liabilities:		
Current liabilities	$ 703,000	$ 371,000
Bonds payable, 12%	500,000	500,000
Total liabilities	1,203,000	871,000
Stockholders' equity:		
Preferred stock, $25 par, 8%	300,000	300,000
Common stock, $10 par	550,000	550,000
Retained earnings	862,000	669,000
Total stockholders' equity	1,712,000	1,519,000
Total liabilities and equity	$2,915,000	$2,390,000

Newport Industry
Comparative Income Statement and Reconciliation

	This Year	Last Year
Sales	$4,960,000	$4,380,000
Cost of goods sold	3,839,000	3,470,000
Gross margin	1,121,000	910,000
Selling and administrative expenses	651,000	550,000

(continued)

(concluded)

Newport Industry
Comparative Income Statement and Reconciliation

	This Year	Last Year
Net operating income	470,000	360,000
Interest expense	60,000	60,000
Net income before taxes	410,000	300,000
Income taxes (30%)	123,000	90,000
Net income	287,000	210,000
Dividends paid:		
Preferred dividends	24,000	24,000
Common dividends	70,000	60,000
Total dividends paid.	94,000	84,000
Net income retained	193,000	126,000
Retained earnings, beginning of year	669,000	543,000
Retained earnings, end of year.	$ 862,000	$ 669,000

During the past year, the company introduced several new product lines and raised the selling prices on a number of old product lines in order to improve its profit margin. The company also hired a new sales manager, who has expanded sales into several new territories. Sales terms are 2/10, n/30. All sales are on account. The following ratios are typical of companies in this industry:

Current ratio	2.5
Acid-test (quick) ratio	1.3
Average collection period	17 days
Average sale period	60 days
Debt-to-equity ratio	0.90
Times interest earned	6.0
Return on total assets	13%
Price-earnings ratio.	12

Required:

1. To assist the San Juan Bank in making a decision about the loan, compute the following ratios for both this year and last year:
   a. The amount of working capital.
   b. The current ratio.
   c. The acid-test (quick) ratio.
   d. The average collection period. (The accounts receivable at the beginning of last year totaled $240,000.)
   e. The average sale period. (The inventory at the beginning of last year totaled $490,000.)
   f. The debt-to-equity ratio.
   g. The times interest earned ratio.
2. For both this year and last year:
   a. Present the balance sheet in common-size format.
   b. Present the income statement in common-size format down through net income.
3. Comment on the results of your analysis in (1) and (2) above and make a recommendation as to whether or not the loan should be approved.

CHECK FIGURE
(1a) Earnings per share this year: $4.78
(1c) Dividend payout ratio last year: 32.2%

PROBLEM 14–13A   Financial Ratios for Common Stockholders (LO2)
Refer to the financial statements and other data in Problem 14–12A. Assume that you are an account executive for a large brokerage house and that one of your clients has asked for a recommendation about the possible purchase of Newport Industry stock. You are not acquainted with the stock and for this reason wish to do some analytical work before making a recommendation.

Required:

1. You decide first to assess the well-being of the common stockholders. For both this year and last year, compute:

   a. The earnings per share. There has been no change in preferred or common stock over the last two years.

   b. The dividend yield ratio for common stock. The company's stock is currently selling for $38 per share; last year it sold for $35 per share.

   c. The dividend payout ratio for common stock.

   d. The price-earnings ratio. How do investors regard Newport Industry as compared to other companies in the industry? Explain.

   e. The book value per share of common stock. Does the difference between market value and book value suggest that the stock is overpriced? Explain.

2. You decide next to assess the company's rate of return. Compute the following for both this year and last year:

   a. The return on total assets. (Total assets at the beginning of last year were $2,230,000.)

   b. The return on common stockholders' equity. (Stockholders' equity at the beginning of last year was $1,418,000.)

   c. Is the company's financial leverage positive or negative? Explain.

3. Would you recommend that your client purchase shares of Newport Industry stock? Explain.

PROBLEM 14–14A   Effects of Transactions on Various Ratios (LO3)

Cribbit Inc. operates a self-storage facility and sells storage supplies. The company's working capital accounts at the beginning of the year are given below:

CHECK FIGURE
(1c) Acid-test ratio: 1.6

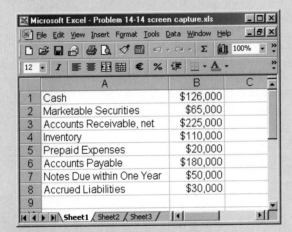

	A	B	C
1	Cash	$126,000	
2	Marketable Securities	$65,000	
3	Accounts Receivable, net	$225,000	
4	Inventory	$110,000	
5	Prepaid Expenses	$20,000	
6	Accounts Payable	$180,000	
7	Notes Due within One Year	$50,000	
8	Accrued Liabilities	$30,000	
9			

During the year, Cribbit completed the following transactions:

x. Paid a cash dividend previously declared, $15,000.
a. Issued additional shares of common stock for cash, $120,000.
b. Sold inventory costing $60,000 for $90,000, on account.
c. Wrote off uncollectible accounts in the amount of $12,000, reducing the accounts receivable balance accordingly.
d. Declared a cash dividend, $18,000.
e. Paid accounts payable, $65,000.
f. Borrowed cash on a short-term note with the bank, $40,000.
g. Sold inventory costing $25,000 for $15,000 cash.
h. Purchased inventory on account, $70,000.
i. Paid off all short-term notes due, $45,000.
j. Purchased equipment for cash, $22,000.
k. Sold marketable securities costing $24,000 for cash, $21,000.
l. Collected cash on accounts receivable, $100,000.

Required:

1. Compute the following amounts and ratios as of the beginning of the year:

   a. Working capital.

   b. Current ratio.

   c. Acid-test (quick) ratio.

2. Indicate the effect of each of the transactions given above on working capital, the current ratio, and the acid-test (quick) ratio. Give the effect in terms of increase, decrease, or none. Item (x) is given below as an example of the format to use:

	The Effect on		
Transaction	Working Capital	Current Ratio	Acid-Test Ratio
(x) Paid a cash dividend previously declared	None	Increase	Increase

CHECK FIGURE
(2a) Earnings per share this year: $8.08
(2b) Dividend yield ratio last year: 5.5%

PROBLEM 14–15A   Comprehensive Ratio Analysis (LO2, LO3, LO4)

You have just been hired as a loan officer at Wamamish Bank. Your supervisor has given you a file containing a request from SafeT Corp., a manufacturer of safety helmets, for a $4,000,000, five-year loan. Financial statement data on the company for the last two years follow:

SafeT Corp.
Comparative Balance Sheet

	This Year	Last Year
Assets		
Current assets:		
Cash	$ 158,000	$ 360,000
Marketable securities....................	0	200,000
Accounts receivable, net	2,590,000	1,950,000
Inventory	4,610,000	3,320,000
Prepaid expenses	340,000	280,000
Total current assets.....................	7,698,000	6,110,000
Plant and equipment, net	9,500,000	8,840,000
Total assets...........................	$17,198,000	$14,950,000
Liabilities and Stockholders' Equity		
Liabilities:		
Current liabilities	$ 3,900,000	$ 2,560,000
Note payable, 10%	4,000,000	3,600,000
Total liabilities	7,900,000	6,160,000
Stockholders' equity:		
Preferred stock, 8%, $100 par value	2,500,000	2,500,000
Common stock, $50 par value...........	5,000,000	5,000,000
Retained earnings.....................	1,798,000	1,290,000
Total stockholders' equity	9,298,000	8,790,000
Total liabilities and stockholders' equity.......	$17,198,000	$14,950,000

Vanna Cho, who just a year ago was appointed president of SafeT Corp., argues that although the company has had a "spotty" record in the past, it has "turned the corner," as evidenced by a 19% jump in sales and by a greatly improved earnings picture between last year and this year. Ms. Cho also points out that investors generally have recognized the improving situation at SafeT Corp., as shown by the increase in market value of the company's common stock, which is currently selling for $63.80 per share (up from $45.80 per share last year). Ms. Cho feels that with her leadership and with the modernized equipment that the $4,000,000 loan will permit the company to buy, profits will be even stronger in the future. Ms. Cho has a reputation in the industry for being a good manager who runs a "tight" ship.

SafeT Corp.
Comparative Income Statement and Reconciliation

	This Year	Last Year
Sales (all on account)	$15,200,000	$12,800,000
Cost of goods sold	9,270,000	7,420,000
Gross margin.	5,930,000	5,380,000
Selling and administrative expenses.	4,090,000	4,060,000
Net operating income	1,840,000	1,320,000
Interest expense	400,000	360,000
Net income before taxes	1,440,000	960,000
Income taxes (30%)	432,000	288,000
Net income	1,008,000	672,000
Dividends paid:		
Preferred dividends	200,000	200,000
Common dividends	300,000	250,000
Total dividends paid.	500,000	450,000
Net income retained	508,000	222,000
Retained earnings, beginning of year	1,290,000	1,068,000
Retained earnings, end of year.	$ 1,798,000	$ 1,290,000

Not wanting to botch your first assignment, you decide to generate all the information that you can about the company. You determine that the following ratios are typical of companies in SafeT Corp.'s industry:

Current ratio	2.3
Acid-test (quick) ratio	1.0
Average collection period	33 days
Average sale period	126 days
Return on assets.	10.7%
Debt-to-equity ratio	0.72
Times interest earned	6.0
Price-earnings ratio.	10.9

Required:

1. You decide first to assess the rate of return that the company is generating. Compute the following for both this year and last year:
   a. The return on total assets. (Total assets at the beginning of last year were $14,384,000.)
   b. The return on common stockholders' equity. (Stockholders' equity at the beginning of last year totaled $8,568,000.) There has been no change in preferred or common stock over the last two years.)
   c. Is the company's financial leverage positive or negative? Explain.

2. You decide next to assess the well-being of the common stockholders. For both this year and last year, compute:
   a. The earnings per share.
   b. The dividend yield ratio for common stock.
   c. The dividend payout ratio for common stock.
   d. The price-earnings ratio. How do investors regard SafeT Corp. as compared to other companies in the industry? Explain.
   e. The book value per share of common stock. Does the difference between market value per share and book value per share suggest that the stock at its current price is a bargain? Explain.
   f. The gross margin percentage.

3. You decide, finally, to assess creditor ratios to determine both short-term and long-term debt-paying ability. For both this year and last year, compute:
   a. Working capital.
   b. The current ratio.

    c.   The acid-test ratio.
    d.   The average collection period. (The accounts receivable at the beginning of last year totaled $1,660,000.)
    e.   The average sale period. (The inventory at the beginning of last year totaled $1,800,000.)
    f.   The debt-to-equity ratio.
    g.   The times interest earned ratio.
  4.   Would you recommend that the loan be granted?

PROBLEM 14–16A   Common-Size Financial Statements (LO1)
Refer to the financial statement data for SafeT Corp. given in Problem 14–15A.

Required:
For both this year and last year:

1.   Present the balance sheet in common-size format.
2.   Present the income statement in common-size format down through net income.
3.   Comment on the results of your analysis.

PROBLEM 14–17A   Effects of Transactions on Various Financial Ratios (LO2, LO3, LO4)
In the right-hand column below, certain financial ratios are listed. To the left of each ratio is a business transaction or event relating to the operating activities of Stuen Inc., an importer of marble and other fine building stones.

Business Transaction or Event	Ratio
1. Declared a cash dividend.	Current ratio
2. Sold inventory on account at cost.	Acid-test (quick) ratio
3. Issued bonds with an interest rate of 12%. The company's return on assets is 16%.	Return on common stockholders' equity
4. Net income decreased by 3% between last year and this year. Long-term debt remained unchanged.	Times interest earned ratio
5. A previously declared cash dividend was paid.	Current ratio
6. The market price of the company's common stock dropped from $27.50 to $21.00. The dividend paid per share remained unchanged.	Dividend payout ratio
7. Obsolete inventory totaling $85,000 was written off as a loss.	Inventory turnover ratio
8. Sold inventory for cash at a profit.	Debt-to-equity ratio
9. Changed customer credit terms from 2/10, n15 to 2/15, n/30 to comply with a change in industry practice.	Accounts receivable turnover ratio
10. Issued a common stock dividend on common stock.	Book value per share
11. The market price of the company's common stock increased from $27.50 to $33.00.	Book value per share
12. Paid $60,000 on accounts payable.	Working capital
13. Issued a stock dividend to common stockholders.	Earnings per share
14. Paid accounts payable.	Debt-to-equity ratio
15. Purchased inventory on credit terms.	Acid-test (quick) ratio
16. An uncollectible account was written off against the Allowance for Bad Debts.	Current ratio
17. The market price of the company's common stock increased from $27.50 to $33.00. Earnings per share remained unchanged.	Price-earnings ratio
18. The market price of the company's common stock increased from $27.50 to $33.00. The dividend paid per share remained unchanged.	Dividend yield ratio

Required:
Indicate the effect that each business transaction or event would have on the ratio listed opposite to it. State the effect in terms of increase, decrease, or no effect on the ratio involved, and give the reason for your answer. In all cases, assume that the current assets exceed the current liabilities both before and after the event or transaction. Use the following format for your answers:

Effect on Ratio	Reason for Increase, Decrease, or No Effect
1.	
Etc. . . .	

BUILDING YOUR SKILLS

COMMUNICATING IN PRACTICE   (LO1, LO2, LO3, LO4)

Typically, the market price of shares of a company's stock takes a beating when the company announces that it has not met analysts' expectations. As a result, many companies are under a lot of pressure to meet analysts' revenue and earnings projections. To manage (that is, to inflate or smooth) earnings, managers sometimes record revenue that has not yet been earned by the company, delay the recognition of expenses that have been incurred, or employ other accounting tricks.

A wave of accounting scandals related to earnings management swept over the capital markets in the wake of the collapse of Enron in 2002. Some earlier examples illustrate how companies have attempted to manage their earnings. On March 20, 2000, MicroStrategy announced that it was forced to restate its 1999 earnings; revenue from multiyear contracts had been recorded in the first year instead of being spread over the lives of the related contracts as required by GAAP. On April 3, 2000, Legato Systems Inc. announced that it had restated its earnings; $7 million of revenue had been improperly recorded because customers had been promised that they could return the products purchased. As further discussed in this chapter, America Online overstated its net income during 1994, 1995, and 1996. In May 2000, upon completing its review of the company's accounting practices, the SEC levied a fine of $3.5 million against AOL. Just prior to the announcement of the fine levied on AOL, Helane Morrison, head of the SEC's San Francisco office, reemphasized that the investigation of misleading financial statements is a top priority for the agency. [Sources: Jeff Shuttleworth, "Investors Beware: Dot.Coms Often Use Accounting Tricks," *Business Journal Serving San Jose & Silicon Valley,* April 14, 2000, p. 16; and David Henry, "AOL Pays $3.5M to Settle SEC Case," *USA Today,* May 16, 2000, p. 3B.]

Required:

Write a memorandum to your instructor that answers the following questions. Use headings to organize the information presented in the memorandum. Include computations to support your answers, when appropriate.

1. Why would companies be tempted to manage earnings?
2. If the earnings that are reported by a company are misstated, how might this impact business decisions made about that company (such as the acquisition of the company by another business)?
3. What ethical issues, if any, arise when a company manages its earnings?
4. How would investors and financial analysts tend to view the financial statements of a company that has been known to manage its earnings in the past?

ETHICS CHALLENGE   (LO3, LO4)

Mountain Aerosport was founded by Jurgen Prinz to produce a ski he had designed for doing aerial tricks. Up to this point, Jurgen has financed the company with his own savings and with cash generated by his business. However, Jurgen now faces a cash crisis. In the year just ended, an acute shortage of a vital tungsten steel alloy developed just as the company was beginning production for the Christmas season. Jurgen had been assured by his suppliers that the steel would be delivered in time to make Christmas shipments, but the suppliers had been unable to fully deliver on this promise. As a consequence, Mountain Aerosport had large stocks of unfinished skis at the end of the year and had been unable to fill all of the orders that had come in from retailers for the Christmas season. Consequently, sales were below expectations for the year, and Jurgen does not have enough cash to pay his creditors.

Well before the accounts payable were due, Jurgen visited a local bank and inquired about obtaining a loan. The loan officer at the bank assured Jurgen that there should not be any problem getting a loan to pay off his accounts payable—providing that on his most recent financial statements the current ratio was above 2.0, the acid-test ratio was above 1.0, and net operating income was at least four times the interest on the proposed loan. Jurgen promised to return later with a copy of his financial statements.

Jurgen would like to apply for a $120 thousand six-month loan bearing an interest rate of 10% per year. The unaudited financial reports of the company appear below.

Mountain Aerosport
Comparative Balance Sheet
As of December 31
(in thousands of dollars)

	This Year	Last Year
Assets		
Current assets:		
Cash	$105	$225
Accounts receivable, net	75	60
Inventory	240	150
Prepaid expenses	15	18
Total current assets	435	453
Property and equipment	405	270
Total assets	$840	$723
Liabilities and Stockholders' Equity		
Current liabilities:		
Accounts payable	$231	$135
Accrued payables	15	15
Total current liabilities	246	150
Long-term liabilities	0	0
Total liabilities	246	150
Stockholders' equity:		
Common stock and additional paid-in capital	150	150
Retained earnings	444	423
Total stockholders' equity	594	573
Total liabilities and stockholders' equity	$840	$723

Mountain Aerosport
Income Statement
For the Year Ended December 31, This Year
(in thousands of dollars)

Sales (all on account)	$630
Cost of goods sold	435
Gross margin	195
Selling and administrative expenses:	
Selling expenses	63
Administrative expenses	102
Total selling and administrative expenses	165
Net operating income	30
Interest expense	0
Net income before taxes	30
Income taxes (30%)	9
Net income	$ 21

Required:

1. On the basis of the above unaudited financial statements and the statement made by the loan officer, would the company qualify for the loan?
2. Last year Jurgen purchased and installed new, more efficient equipment to replace an older heat-treating furnace. Jurgen had originally planned to sell the old equipment but found that it is still needed whenever the heat-treating process is a bottleneck. When Jurgen discussed his cash flow problems with his brother-in-law, he suggested to Jurgen that the old equipment be sold or at least reclassified as inventory on the balance sheet since it could be readily sold. At present, the equipment

is carried in the Property and Equipment account and could be sold for its net book value of $68 thousand. The bank does not require audited financial statements. What advice would you give to Jurgen concerning the machine?

ANALYTICAL THINKING   (LO2, LO3, LO4)

Incomplete financial statements for Tanner Corporation follow:

Tanner Corporation
Income Statement
For the Year Ended December 31

Sales	$2,700,000
Cost of goods sold	?
Gross margin	?
Selling and administrative expenses	?
Net operating income	?
Interest expense	45,000
Net income before taxes	?
Income taxes (40%)	?
Net income	$?

Tanner Corporation
Balance Sheet
December 31

Current assets:	
Cash	$?
Accounts receivable, net	?
Inventory	?
Total current assets	?
Plant and equipment, net	?
Total assets	$?
Liabilities:	
Current liabilities	$250,000
Bonds payable, 10%	?
Total liabilities	?
Stockholders' equity:	
Common stock, $2.50 par value	?
Retained earnings	?
Total stockholders' equity	?
Total liabilities and stockholders' equity	$?

The following additional information is available about the company:

a.   Selected financial ratios computed from the statements above are given below:

Current ratio	2.40
Acid-test (quick) ratio	1.12
Accounts receivable turnover	15.0
Inventory turnover ratio	6.0
Debt-to-equity ratio	0.875
Times interest earned ratio	7.0
Earnings per share	$4.05
Return on total assets	14%

b. All sales during the year were on account.

c. The interest expense on the income statement relates to the bonds payable; the amount of bonds outstanding did not change during the year.

d. There was no change in the number of shares of common stock outstanding during the year.

e. Selected balances at the *beginning* of the current year were:

Accounts receivable	$160,000
Inventory	$280,000
Total assets	$1,200,000

Required:

Compute the missing amounts on the company's financial statements. (*Hint*: You may find it helpful to think about the difference between the current ratio and the acid-test ratio.)

TEAMWORK IN ACTION   (LO1, LO2, LO3, LO4)

Obtain the most recent annual report or SEC filing 10-K of a publicly traded company that interests you. It may be a local company or it may be a company in an industry that you would like to know more about. Using the annual report, compute as many of the financial ratios covered in this chapter as you can for at least the past two years. This may pose some difficulties—particularly because companies often use different terms for many income statement and balance sheet items than were shown in the chapter. Nevertheless, do the best that you can. After you have computed the financial ratios, summarize the company's performance for the current year. Has it improved, gotten worse, or remained about the same? Do the ratios indicate any potential problems or any areas that have shown significant improvement? What recommendations, if any, would you make to a bank about extending short-term credit to this company? What recommendations, if any, would you make to an insurance company about extending long-term credit to this company? What recommendations, if any, would you make to an investor about buying or selling this company's stock?

| RESEARCH AND APPLICATION | [LO1, LO2, LO3, LO4] |

The questions in this exercise are based on Target Corporation. To answer the questions, you will need to download Target's 2004 annual report (the company's fiscal year ended on January 29, 2005) at http://investors.target.com/. You do not need to print the annual report to answer the questions.

REQUIRED

1. Prepare a five-year horizontal analysis of Target's sales and earnings from continuing operations. Use 2000 as your base year and present the trended data in dollar and percentage form. What insights are revealed by the data?
2. Prepare a common-size balance sheet as of the fiscal years ended January 29, 2005, and January 31, 2004. Use the format shown in Exhibit 14–4 within the chapter.
3. When performing a vertical analysis of its profitability does Target use sales ($45,682 for 2004) or total revenues ($46,839 for 2004)? Why? (*Hint:* Look at how Target computes its gross margin rates and selling, general, and administrative expense rates on pages 17 and 18 of the annual report.)
4. Calculate Target's earnings per share, price-earnings ratio, dividend payout ratio, dividend yield ratio, return on total assets, return on common stockholders' equity, and book value per share for the fiscal year ended January 29, 2005. Use earnings from continuing operations for all of your calculations. Assume that Target's market price per share of common stock was $49.49 as of January 29, 2005.
5. Calculate Target's working capital, current ratio, acid-test ratio, inventory turnover ratio, and average sale period for the fiscal year ended January 29, 2005.
6. Calculate Target's times interest earned ratio and debt-to-equity ratio for the fiscal year ended January 29, 2005.
7. Below are selected financial ratios for Wal-Mart Stores, Inc., for its fiscal year ended January 31, 2005. How does Target's performance compare to Wal-Mart's?

Current ratio	0.90
Acid-test ratio	0.17
Average sale period	46.6 days
Times interest earned ratio	17.3
Debt-to-equity ratio	1.43
Return on total assets	9.3%
Price-earnings ratio	21.7

CREDITS

Company Logos

INDEX

Page numbers with n indicate material found in notes.